SPANISH
Here & Now

SPANISH
Here & Now

Gary D. Keller
York College of the City University of New York

Nancy A. Sebastiani
University of Houston

Francisco Jiménez
University of Santa Clara

 Harcourt Brace Jovanovich, Inc.
New York   San Diego   Chicago   San Francisco   Atlanta

COVER La Plaza de Cibeles and La Puerta de Alcalá, Madrid
Photo by Peter Menzel

Excerpt from *Soy animal de fondo* by Juan Ramón Jiménez, courtesy
of Francisco H. Pinzón Jiménez.

ISBN: 0–15–583110–0

Library of Congress Catalog Card Number: 77–83741

Printed in the United States of America

Picture credits appear on page 562.

Preface

Spanish Here and Now has been prepared with three basic goals in mind: to be a source of enjoyment, and therefore of motivation, for beginning students; to provide a flexible, practical, and individualized introduction to Spanish; and to present the Spanish language and Hispanic life in a full, rich, and authentic way.

To achieve these goals, we have introduced a number of special features. In the dialogs and readings we evoke concerns and present situations students can identify with, such as dating, looking for jobs, the status of women, student concern with social justice, travel in Latin America and Spain, and glimpses of Hispanic life and culture in the United States. Moreover, these materials are meant to engage students and enlist their active interest rather than merely to impart information. The vocabulary not only focuses on the practical aspects of language learning but also includes a wealth of terms and idioms reflecting emotional life, definitions of self-identity, kinship, contemporary expression in social situations, and so on. A wide variety of exercises have been incorporated into the text and Student Manual in order to provide students with as rich and varied a language-learning environment as we could devise. The culturally authentic photographs and realia relate to the text, and many of the humorous drawings are used to clarify an ambiguous usage or grammatical structure. A second color is used to highlight important grammatical points and vocabulary.

We have planned *Spanish Here and Now* to free the instructor from the time-consuming task of preparing exercises, readings, and tests and to help students learn the major points of grammar on their own, thus allowing more time in the classroom for the essential activity of practicing the language. Each dialog illustrates the six grammar components of the lesson in a natural context. A supplementary reading enables students to expand their vocabulary and read connected passages of Spanish with ease. The grammar is presented in a logical, graded sequence. The explanations are straightforward and concise but avoid undue simplifications or statements that might cause confusion or make it necessary for students to unlearn false generalizations later. The most important grammatical structures are presented three times—in the lesson itself, in the review lesson, and in the Student Manual. While there are enough exercises for intensive classes of six hours per week or more, no single type of exercise is essential to the effective use of the book. Thus the instructor has maximum freedom to choose the number as well as the type of exercises, in accordance with her or his method of teaching.

Spanish Here and Now is organized in the following way:

A preliminary lesson presents the sound system, pronunciation, and punctuation as well as some observations on the variety of Spanish the students will be learning (Spanish American) and certain characteristics of Spanish, such as formal (*Ud.*) and familiar (*tú*) forms of address. The sections dealing with the Spanish sound system are for reference; practice drills on pronunciation appear in the first half of the textbook, the first half of the workbook, and throughout the tape program. The following twenty-four lessons consist of eighteen expository lessons and six review lessons; the latter appear after every third regular lesson.

The expository lessons begin with a dialog, followed by notes on vocabulary or cultural items that appear in the dialog. Each of the six grammatical structures presented next is immediately followed by a variety of exercises. After the grammar presentations, review exercises reinforce the grammar and vocabulary of the entire lesson and a guided dialog or composition provides writing practice. The pronunciation exercises that follow drill those aspects of spoken Spanish that require particular attention and reinforcement. The lesson ends with Cognates and Contexts, a reading based on the dialog that uses cognates and linguistic contexts to help students read extended passages on their own.

Each review lesson recapitulates the materials covered in the three preceding lessons. They begin with a reading that includes the structures covered in these lessons and provides additional useful vocabulary. A vocabulary study section and accompanying exercises review and expand previously learned vocabulary. The self-test, with a question-answer format, systematically reviews the grammatical structures of the three lessons. The exercises following reinforce these structures and include a guided composition for writing practice. An additional feature is the "Remember!" section, which highlights subtle but important aspects of usage.

Interspersed throughout the lessons, several unique features serve a pedagogical purpose while providing an amusing and visually appealing break. "*¡Cuidado!*" draws attention to predictable pitfalls that students may encounter while learning Spanish. In "Word Play" amusing phrases or anecdotes illustrate a particular grammar point. "*Rompecabezas*" (in the review lessons only) is a scrambled sentence for students to rearrange into an amusing saying that calls attention to a specific structure.

The appendix contains a short lesson on the use of *vosotros* and its related forms, charts of regular and irregular verbs, and a list of words common to United States Spanish. The Spanish-English vocabulary contains all the words used in the textbook; the shorter English-Spanish vocabulary includes the more common English words and idioms that the students might need for translation drills.

The Student Manual has been designed to reinforce the material of the textbook and to afford the students and instructor additional flexibility. The manual consists of dictation exercises based on the dialogs of the textbook; listening and writing practices (first half of the book only); written exercises for all the language structures covered in the corresponding textbook lesson; guided compositions (second half of the book only); programmed reviews of the important grammar structures presented in the corresponding textbook lesson; comprehensive practice tests, with answers provided for the student; and three-lesson comprehensive tests, with answers provided, corresponding to each review lesson in the text.

A tape program is also available. The textbook serves as the laboratory manual, since the recorded exercises are indicated in the text by a tape symbol.

The Instructor's Manual contains suggestions for use of the program and comprehensive tests for the instructor's use on completion of every three expository lessons.

Throughout *Spanish Here and Now* we have sought to present the Spanish language as authentically as possible, avoiding artificial or contrived situations. The dialogs and readings are set in all the major Spanish-speaking regions: Spain, South America, Central America, the Caribbean, and the three principal Spanish-speaking areas of the United States—the Southwest, the Northeast, and Florida. We have used Spanish as it is actually spoken, to the extent that this is possible in a language text. Moreover, since we believe that students in the United States are interested in learning Spanish not only for traditional reasons such as professional advancement and employment, travel, and so on, but also because they are aware that so many American citizens are native speakers of Spanish, we have included the lifestyles and cultural contributions of United States Hispanics.

We would like to express our deep appreciation to William Pullin, Albert Richards, Tina Norum, Patricia Smythe, Marian Griffith, and Robert Karpen of Harcourt Brace Jovanovich for their contributions to the conception, development, editing, and design of the book. We would also like to thank Dwight Bolinger and John Staczek for their helpful review and criticism of the complete manuscript; Karen S. Van Hooft, who made many suggestions for improving the text while coauthoring the Student Manual; and Eugene Long, María Inés Lagos de Pope, and Elliot Glass, who reviewed portions of the manuscript.

Gary D. Keller

Nancy A. Sebastiani

Francisco Jiménez

Contents

x **Contents**

Lección preliminar

Language Varieties

Students often wonder if the Spanish language is spoken uniformly throughout the Hispanic world or if there are varieties of Spanish. And of course, they are interested in relating this to the Spanish that is taught to them.

Spanish, like English and all other languages spoken by large numbers of people, does display varieties. One of these reflects the physical separation of the two main Spanish-speaking regions, Spain and Spanish America. But even within these regions differences can be distinguished. For example, the Spanish spoken in the Caribbean is pronounced somewhat differently from the Spanish of Mexico and the American Southwest. Argentina has its own unique pronunciation features. The pronunciation of Spanish in north central Spain (Castilla) can be distinguished from that of the south (Andalucía). These differences are analogous to the differences among the pronunciations of English in Boston, Atlanta, Los Angeles, London, or Melbourne.

Physical distance also causes variations in vocabulary. In the United States we use *elevator* and *apartment*. In England the same concepts are expressed by *lift* and *flat*. Australia has certain words and phrases peculiar to that country, such as *outback* and *three dog night*. Spanish vocabulary exhibits similar variations. For example, in some Spanish-speaking areas the word **autobús** is used to mean *bus*, in others **camión** is used, and in Cuba and Puerto Rico the word **guagua** is used. The word for *raincoat* can be rendered either **impermeable** or **gabardina** by various speakers of Spanish.

Another way of looking at language variation is from the point of view of social context. There are formal levels of language, such as that used in a public speech or in writing a term paper. There is a semiformal variety of language, often called the standard, which is what we frequently encounter in college and university classrooms, on television news broadcasts, in newspapers, and so on. Finally there is a colloquial register of language. This is the most relaxed and unguarded form of speech in which we may use expressions such as *ain't* or *I don't got no*, which in more vigilant contexts we would consider inappropriate. Spanish also displays differences that are attributable to social context.

What remains virtually the same in every language, despite pronunciation, vocabulary, or contextual variations, is the grammar of that language.

These general features of language variation also apply to the Spanish taught in this textbook. The grammar that is used in *Spanish Here and Now* is the grammar that is used all over the Spanish-speaking world. There are only a few variations from this grammar, and these are noted in the text.[1] The same is true for the vocabulary. For most items there are only standard words in Spanish. When there are variations, in general the most common, widely-used vocabulary term is used. However, occasionally items that are more regional appear, and these are so noted.

[1] The two best-known differences are that in Spain the pronoun **vosotros** is used in addition to **ustedes** and that in parts of Spain **le** is used not only as an indirect object pronoun but also as a direct object pronoun.

The pronunciation features that are underscored in this text are also largely universal in the Spanish-speaking world. When there are variations, Spanish American pronunciation is emphasized, but the differences peculiar to Spain are noted.

From the perspective of social context the level of language in *Spanish Here and Now* is largely the standard language usage of unaffected, educated speakers. Nevertheless, a substantial number of informal, colloquial words and expressions have been included in order to permit you to speak and enjoy Spanish on a more intimate and friendly basis as well. These informal locutions would not be considered grammatically inappropriate in a public context.

Finally, because most of you will be learning Spanish in an American educational context and since Spanish is a major language within the United States itself, *Spanish Here and Now* seeks to aid you in communicating with the native speakers of Spanish with whom you will probably be coming in contact. Vocabulary that is characteristic of United States Spanish has been included when such words and expressions are not variants of more common words used in the other Spanish-speaking regions (for example, **chicano**, **boricua**). In addition, the Appendix provides a list of commonly used vocabulary that is unique to United States Spanish but for which there are more common terms used in the other Spanish-speaking locales.

Language and Physical Reality

One of the benefits of learning a second language is that in a sense we are able to step outside of our unexamined assumptions about the make-up of the world and to begin to realize that much of what we perceive is determined by the structure of the language we speak. The Navaho, for example, do not have separate words for the colors red and orange; they use one word for this whole spectrum of color. When speakers of this language view these two colors, they do not articulate a difference between them. In English we have one verb *to be*, but Spanish perceives gradients of being in such a way that it separates and codifies the concept into two words, **ser** and **estar**. **Ser** relates to permanence, to essences; **estar** to change, to nonessential characteristics, or to location, being in a place. Another example is English, *to know*, a concept that Spanish splits into two verbs, **conocer** and **saber**. **Saber** is a deeper, more profound, thorough sense of knowledge. **Conocer** means *to be acquainted with, to be familiar with*. On the other hand,

Spanish has one verb, **hacer** that combines the two functions that are perceived and separately codified in English as *to do* and *to make*. A similar if less overt case is Spanish **decir**, which is translated by English *to say* and *to tell*.

Language and Culture

Language is an integral part of a specific culture, and one of the reasons we study other languages is to use them as the means of fully understanding the values and traditions of other people. *Spanish Here and Now* attempts to provide you, by means of the Spanish language, a wealth of insights into the way Hispanic people view life in such areas as social and student relationships, child-rearing practices, art, literature, culture, business and commercial procedures, kinship relations, attitudes toward death, the role of women, and many others.

Tú and **usted.**   One cultural aspect of Spanish, because it is so pervasive in the language, deserves special attention here: the relationship between the familiar (**tú**) and the formal (**usted**) forms of address. When addressing another person, every speaker of Spanish has the option of speaking to the other party in either a familiar or a formal form. English is not too different. For example, we can call a person Mr. Smith, or John or even Johnny; we can use *mother* or *mom*. However, in addition to the sort of devices that English uses—titles, nicknames, and the like—Spanish codifies the familiar/formal distinction in its verbal and pronoun system. In general, **usted** is used when addressing elders (except persons of the immediate family such as the mother or father), teachers, employers, and other persons who merit respect or deference. It is also used with strangers, unless they are children. **Tú** is used among siblings, friends, classmates, and peers—in general, persons with whom the speaker is acquainted, unless because of their position they deserve a special show of respect.

Language Borrowing

All languages borrow from each other. As a matter of fact, the basic reason why Spanish and English share an estimated 50,000 cognates (words that are identical or similar in spelling in both languages and have identical or similar meanings) is that both of these languages borrowed some of their vocabulary from Latin. This process of borrowing continues in the present between Spanish and English, so that Spanish has incorporated words such as *sweater* (**suéter**), *baseball* (**béisbol**), and *hamburger* (**hamburguesa**) from English, and English has accepted words such as **vainilla** (*vanilla*), **rancho** (*ranch*), and **cafetería** (*cafeteria*) from Spanish. In learning and, particularly, in reading Spanish, you should trust your intuition. Although there will be exceptions, generally if a Spanish word seems familiar to you, it will be because it is a counterpart of a word that you know in English.

The Sounds of Spanish

This section summarizes the fundamentals that you need to know in order to pronounce and write Spanish. Exercises on many of the points presented here are provided in the Pronunciation section of each of the lessons in the first half of the book.

The Spanish Alphabet

Letter	Name	Letter	Name	Letter	Name
a	a	**j**	jota	**r**	ere
b	be	**k**	ka	**rr**	erre
c	ce	**l**	ele	**s**	ese
ch	che	**ll**	elle	**t**	te
d	de	**m**	eme	**u**	u
e	e	**n**	ene	**v**	ve, uve
f	efe	**ñ**	eñe	**w**	doble ve, doble u
g	ge	**o**	o	**x**	equis
h	hache	**p**	pe	**y**	i griega
i	i	**q**	cu	**z**	zeta

In addition to the letters used in the English alphabet, the Spanish alphabet includes **ch**, **ll**, **ñ**, and **rr**, which represent single sounds and are considered single letters. Words or syllables beginning with **ch**, **ll**, or **ñ** are alphabetized in dictionaries after words or syllables beginning with **c**, **l**, or **n**. On the other hand, **rr** is alphabetized as in English. The letters **k** and **w** occur only in words of foreign derivation.

The Sounds of Spanish

In order to distinguish a sound from the letter or letters that represent it, the sound is designated by a symbol set in slashes / /.

Vowels

Spanish has five basic vowel sounds.

/a/, represented by the letter **a**

/a/ is pronounced like the English exclamation, *Ah!* but the sound is shorter and more clipped: **habla, casa, mamá**.

/e/, represented by the letter **e**

/e/ is pronounced like the *e* in English *set*: **mesa, español, México**.

/i/, represented by the letter **i**, except at the end of the word when it is represented by **y**.[2]

/i/ is pronounced like the *i* in English *machine*: **chile, sí, inglés**.

/o/, represented by the letter **o**

/o/ is pronounced like the *o* in English *go*, but it is shorter and more clipped: **poco, profesor, no**.

/u/, represented by the letter **u**

/u/ is pronounced like the *u* in English *Susan*: **alumna, mucho, un**.

Consonants

The consonants are not presented in alphabetical order but rather in clusters according to their manner of pronunciation.

/p/, represented by the letter **p**

/p/ is similar to English /p/ but it is not aspirated (there is no puff of air) as in English: **palma, para, Pepe**.

/b/, represented by the letters **b** and **v**

In initial position or after **m** or **n**, /b/ is pronounced like the /b/ in English *boy*: **vende, bien, verde, bonito, hombre**.

In other positions, particularly between vowels, the sound is weaker, /b̸/: **Cuba, escribe, ribera**. There is no comparable sound in English.

/t/, represented by the letter **t**

Spanish /t/ is pronounced by placing the tip of the tongue against the back of the upper teeth. The tongue is further forward than it is with English /t/ and there is no aspiration: **tienda, tonto, tiempo**.

---

[2] Also the word **y**, which is pronounced /i/.

/d/, represented by the letter **d**

In initial position and after **l** or **n**, /d/ is pronounced like /d/ in English *dog*, but the tip of the tongue is placed further forward than in English: **donde, día, después**.

In all other positions the sound is weaker, /ḏ/. It is similar to a weak *th* in English *father* and *this*: **verdad, todo, usted**.

/č/, represented by the letter **ch**

/č/ is pronounced like the *ch* in English *chess*: **mucho, chocolate, chico**.

/k/, represented by **k**; by **c** before consonants or **a**, **o**, and **u**; and by **qu**

/k/ is pronounced like the /k/ in English *cat* or *kite*, but it is not aspirated: **kilo, crema, casa, cosa, cubano, que**.

/g/, represented by the letters **g** and **gu**

In initial position or after **n**, /g/ is pronounced like the /g/ in English *go*: **gracias, tengo, grande**.

In other positions, particularly between vowels, the sound is much weaker, /ǥ/: **portugués, luego, salgo**.[3]

/f/, represented by the letter **f**

/f/ is pronounced like English /f/: **fácil, familia, café**.

/s/, represented by the letters **s**, **z**, and **c** when it precedes **e** and **i**[4]

/s/ is pronounced like the /s/ in English *see*: **soy, esta, zapato, perspicaz, cerrar, cínico**.

However, in certain positions, Spanish /s/ is pronounced like the *s* in English *rose*: **desde, mismo**.

/x/, represented by the letter **j** and the letter **g** when it precedes **e** and **i**

/x/ is pronounced like the *h* in *halt*, but in a more exaggerated, guttural fashion: **joven, jefe, mujer, gitano, generalmente, región**.

/m/, represented by the letter **m**, and occasionally by **n**

/m/ is pronounced like English /m/: **mesa, música, amor**.

In certain positions the letter **n** is pronounced /m/: **inmediatamente, un poco**.

/n/, represented by the letter **n**

/n/ is usually pronounced like the English /n/ in *no*: **no, nada, lección**.

In certain positions it is pronounced like the *n* in *bring*: **tango, blanco, pongo**.

---

[3] In Spanish when **g** is followed by **ua** or **uo**, the **u** is pronounced similarly to *w* in English *well*: **agua, lengua, ambiguo**. When the combinations **gue** and **gui** are written with a dieresis (¨), the **u** has the same sound: **bilingüe, vergüenza, lingüística**.

[4] In many parts of Spain **z** and **c** before **e** and **i** are pronounced like the *th* in English *thin*.

/ñ/, represented by the letter **ñ**

It is pronounced like the *ni* in English *onion*: **señorita**, **España**, **mañana**.

/l/, represented by the letter **l**

/l/ is pronounced like English /l/: **loco**, **malo**, **papel**.

/y/, represented by the letters **y** and **ll**

/y/ is pronounced like the *y* in *yet*:[5] **ya, llamar, yo, lluvia, ayudar, millón**.

/r/, represented by the letter **r**

/r/ is pronounced similarly to *dd* in *ladder*: it is pronounced with a single tap of the tip of the tongue against the upper gum ridge. This sound does not occur in initial position or after **l**, **n**, or **s**: **para, pero, cero, palabra, cuatro, amor, hablar**.

/rr/ represented by the letter **rr** and sometimes by **r**

/rr/ consists of a series of three or more rapid taps of the tongue against the upper gum ridge: **parra, perro, cerro**.

Initial **r** and **r** after **n**, **l**, or **s** have precisely the same multiple trill as **rr**: **rápidamente, Rubén, Enrique, Israel**.

Peculiarities of Spanish x, h, k, and w

Spanish **x** has various pronunciations. Before a consonant it is pronounced like /s/: **explorar, extraño**. Between vowels it is pronounced /ks/: **examen, existir, sexo**. In addition, in the Americas the spellings **México, mexicano**, and **Texas** are used instead of peninsular spellings **Méjico, mejicano**, and **Tejas**, and in these words **x** is pronounced /x/ (as in **mujer** and **gitano**).

The letters **k** and **w** occur only in words of foreign origin.

The letter **h** is always silent in Spanish.

Vowel Combinations

In Spanish, two, and occasionally three, vowels may combine. In certain cases they are linked, in others they fuse together, forming diphthongs or triphthongs. Linked words are pronounced without a pause between them but they do not form a single syllable. There can be three types of linked vowels.

1. Combinations of two identical vowels: **cree, lee, mi hijo, va a comer.**

---

[5] In some parts of Spain the letter **ll** is pronounced like English *lli* in *million*.

2. Any combination of the strong vowels, /a, o, e/: **le hablo, teatro, toalla, poema**.

3. Stressed /i/ or /u/ preceding or following a strong vowel: **día, mío, país, Raúl**.

Fused vowels (diphthongs or triphthongs) form one single syllable. Diphthongs occur when unstressed /i/ or /u/ combines with a strong vowel or when they combine with each other. When /i/ begins the diphthong, **i** is pronounced like *y* in *yet*, and when /u/ begins the diphthong, **u** is pronounced like *w* in *wet*: **gracias, adiós, familia, cien, cuando, bueno, ambiguo, fui**. When /i/ or /u/ ends the diphthong, the combination of the two vowels gives the overall effect of a glide in which neither of the vowels lose their identity: **baile, veinte, soy, autor, Europa**.

Triphthongs are the combination of three vowels (a strong vowel between two weak vowels) into one syllable: **Uruguay, buey, continuais**.

Syllabication

Spanish is divided into syllables in the following manner:

1. A single consonant (including **ch**, **ll**, and **rr**) between two vowels forms a syllable with the vowel following it: **a-me-ri-ca-no, mu-cho, pe-rro, mi-lla**.

2. When two consonants occur together, they are usually divided: **es-pa-ñol, lec-ción, us-ted**. However, consonants followed by **l** or **r** generally form a cluster and are pronounced together with the following vowel as one syllable: **li-bro, pre-pa-ro, ma-dre**. Exceptions are the groups **nl**, **rl**, **sl**, **tl**, **nr**, and **sr**. These groups are divided into two syllables: **en-la-ce, per-la, is-la, At-lán-ti-co, En-ri-que, Is-ra-el**.

3. In combinations of three or more consonants only the last consonant or a consonant cluster (consonant followed by **l** or **r**) begins a syllable: **trans-por-te, in-glés, hom-bre, siem-pre**.

4. Two strong vowels (**a, e, o**) that occur together go in separate syllables: **cre-o, le-e, tra-e**.

5. Combinations of a strong vowel and an unstressed weak vowel or two weak vowels form a single syllable (diphthong): **bue-no, fa-mi-lia, ciu-dad, a-diós, cuán-to**.

6. When a strong vowel occurs with a weak vowel that has a written accent mark, the two vowels are separated: **ba-úl, dí-a, ma-íz**.

Stress

The patterns of stress placement in Spanish are as follows:

1. Words that end in a vowel or in **n** or **s** are regularly stressed on the next-to-last syllable. No written accent is used: **habla, cubano, profesora, preparan, buenos**.

2. Words ending in a consonant other than **n** or **s** are regularly stressed on the last syllable. Again, no written accent is used: **hablar, general, profesor, usted, igualdad, dolor**.

3. If the placement of stress does not follow the two preceding rules, a written accent (′) is used to mark the stressed vowel.

   a. These words do not follow rule 1 because although they end in a vowel, **n**, or **s**, the stress is on the last syllable: **café, mamá, José, también, inglés**.

   b. These words do not follow rule 2 because even though they end in a consonant other than **n** or **s**, they are stressed on the next-to-last syllable: **fácil, dólar, César, López**.

   c. These words do not follow either rule 1 or rule 2 because they are stressed two or more syllables from the end: **teléfono, lógico, México, díganmelo**.

In addition to indicating stress, the written accent is also used to distinguish two words that have the same spellings but different meanings.

sí	*yes*	si	*if*
tú	*you*	tu	*your*
él	*he*	el	*the*
dé	*give*	de	*of, from*

Linking

While words are separate when written, in the spoken language they are usually linked together in logical groupings such as phrases, clauses, or sentences. Thus syllabication may actually cross word boundaries. For example, in the sentence **Es el alumno**, the syllable division is the following: **e-se-la-lum-no**.

Linking also explains why certain words are pronounced differently, depending on what immediately precedes or follows them. For example, the **n** of **un** in **un alumno** is pronounced /n/, but in **un poco** it is pronounced /m/.

The general rules of linking are as follows:

1. Linking occurs when one word ends in a consonant and the next begins with a vowel (the consonant forms a syllable with the vowel): **¿Hablan ustedes inglés? Somos italianos.**

2. Linking also occurs when one word ends in a vowel and the following word begins with the same vowel (the two vowels are pronounced as one syllable): **Va a comer. La profesora de español.**

3. Unlike vowels that come together across a word boundary

   a. are linked and pronounced as one syllable (form a diphthong) if one is a strong vowel (**a**, **e**, **o**) and the other is a weak vowel (**i**, **u**), or if both are weak vowels: **¿Habla usted? Casi uno.**

   b. are linked but pronounced as two different syllables if both are strong vowels: **¿Habla o escribe?**

Punctuation and Capitalization

Spanish differs from English in the following ways:

An inverted question mark (**¿**) or exclamation point (**¡**) always precedes a question or exclamation. These punctuation marks need not appear at the beginning of the sentence, but rather where the actual exclamation or question begins.

> ¿Dónde está la tienda de discos?
> Y tú Juan, ¿vas a la reunión?
> ¡Qué interesante!
> Pero José, ¡qué lástima!

A dash is normally used instead of quotations marks to indicate dialog. It appears at the beginning of each speech, but is omitted at the end, unless narrative material follows.

> —Buenos días. ¿Cómo estás?
> —Muy bien, gracias. ¿Y tú? —dijo Pedro.

Spanish does not capitalize as frequently as English. The following are *not* capitalized.

> Languages and adjectives of nationality: **español, inglés, cubano**
> Months and days of the week: **enero, junio, lunes, domingo**
> Titles referring to people: **señor, señora, señorita**

Only the first word of the title of a book, painting, etc., is capitalized:

> *La rebelión de las masas*

Lección primera

UNA CLASE DE ESPAÑOL EN LOS ESTADOS UNIDOS

una *a*

los Estados Unidos *the United States*

PANCHO	¿Quién es la señorita simpática? ¿Es alumna?	¿Quién? (plural ¿quiénes?) *Who?* señorita simpática *nice lady* alumna *student*
PEPITA	¡No, hombre! No es alumna. Es la profesora de español.	hombre *man*
PANCHO	¿Ah, sí?	¿Ah, sí? *Really?*
PEPITA	¡Pues sí!	¡Pues sí! *Sure!*
PANCHO	¡Qué bien!	¡Qué bien! *Great!*
SRTA. AZUELA	Buenos días, jóvenes.	Srta. (abbrev. of señorita) *Miss* buenos días *good morning* jóvenes *young people*
ALUMNOS	Buenos días, Srta. Azuela.	
SRTA. AZUELA	¿Ya hablan Uds. español?	ya *already* hablar *to speak* Uds. (abbrev. of ustedes) *you (plural)*
RAFA	Sí, ya hablamos español un poco.	un poco *a little*
SRTA. AZUELA	Y preparan y practican bien las lecciones, ¿no es verdad?	bien *well* lecciones *lessons* ¿no es verdad? *isn't it true?*
TERE	¡Oh, sí! Hablamos poco pero preparamos y practicamos mucho.	mucho *a lot*
SRTA. AZUELA	¿En qué países hablan español?	¿en qué...? *in what...?* países *countries*
PEPITA	Hablan español en España.	
SRTA. AZUELA	¿En dónde más hablan mucho español?	¿(en) dónde más? *where else?*
RAFA	Hablan español en Hispanoamérica.	
PANCHO	Profesora, ¿de dónde es Ud.? ¿Es Ud. de España o de Hispanoamérica?	¿de dónde es Ud.? *where are you from?* Ud. (abbrev. of usted) *you (singular, formal)*

SRTA. AZUELA	Soy de los Estados Unidos.	
PANCHO	¿De los Estados Unidos? ¿Es Ud. de California?	
SRTA. AZUELA	No, no soy de California. Soy de Nuevo México.	
RAFA	¿Y hablan español en Nuevo México?	
SRTA. AZUELA	Claro que sí. Hablan inglés y español en Nuevo México. ¿En qué otras partes de los Estados Unidos hablan español?	**Claro que sí.** *Of course.* **otras partes de** *other parts of*
TERE	En Nueva York los puertorriqueños y muchos otros hispanos hablan español.	
RAFA	También en la Florida los cubanos hablan español.	**también** *also*
TERE	En el suroeste, en California, Arizona, Texas, Nuevo México y Colorado muchos chicanos hablan español.	**suroeste** *Southwest* **muchos** *many*
PEPITA	En todas partes de los Estados Unidos muchas personas hablan español.	**todas** *all* (**todos** *everybody*)
PANCHO	Profesora, ¿habla Ud. español o inglés en casa?	**en casa** *at home*
SRTA. AZUELA	En casa, entre familia, generalmente hablamos español.	**entre familia** *among the family* **generalmente** *generally*
PANCHO	Entonces, Ud. es chicana, ¿verdad?	**entonces** *then*
SRTA. AZUELA	Exactamente, y Ud. es muy perspicaz.	**muy perspicaz** *very observant, clever*

School teacher, California

NOTES

National Origins

el chicano
la chicana — *the Chicano, the Chicana.* Inhabitant of the United States of Indo-Hispanic-Mexican descent who usually speaks Spanish and identifies with Hispanic culture and values.

el puertorriqueño
la puertorriqueña
(el or **la boricua)** — Both **el puertorriqueño, la puertorriqueña** and **el** or **la boricua** translate as *the Puerto Rican.* **Boricua,** which is used with particular ethnic pride, is a term derived from the original pre-Hispanic name of the Island of Puerto Rico: **Borinquen.**

el hispano
la hispana — A general term referring to any Hispanic person.

Nicknames

Rafa	**Rafael**
Pancho	**Francisco** (**Paco** and **Curro** may also be used as nicknames for **Francisco.**)
Tere	**Teresa**
Pepita	**Josefa**

Conjunctions

y	*and*
pero	*but*
o	*or*

¡Cuidado! Beware!

en casa	*at home*	**en clase**	*in class*
en la casa	*in the house*	**en la clase**	*in the classroom*

LANGUAGE STRUCTURES

1 Subject pronouns

Singular		Plural	
yo	*I*	nosotros	*we*
tú	*you* (familiar)	nosotras	*we* (feminine)
usted (Ud.)	*you* (formal)	ustedes (Uds.)[1]	*you* (plural); *you all*
él	*he*	ellos	*they*
ella	*she*	ellas	*they* (feminine)

Examples:

1. ¿Ya hablan ustedes español?   *Do you speak Spanish already?*
2. Nosotros preparamos y practicamos mucho.   *We prepare and practice a lot.*
3. Yo soy de los Estados Unidos.   *I am from the United States.*
4. Tú eres chicana, ¿verdad?   *You're a Chicana, right?*

▶ Subject pronouns are not always used in Spanish because the verb ending often clearly indicates the subject.[2]

---

[1] In most Spanish-speaking areas **ustedes** is used for the plural *you*, without making a distinction between familiar and formal usage. Another form for the familiar plural *you* exists in Spanish—**vosotros, vosotras** (feminine)—but it is not generally used except in parts of Spain.

[2] However, subject pronouns are expressed when combined with other nouns or pronouns: **Rafa, Tere y yo preparamos la lección.** *Rafa, Tere, and I are preparing the lesson.* **Tú y ella son de Nuevo México.** *You and she are from New Mexico.*

▶ **Yo**, **tú**, and **nosotros** are generally used for emphasis.

> **Yo soy de Nueva York.**   *I am from New York.*

In addition, **él**, **ella**, and **ellos**, **ellas** can be used to clarify the gender of the third person subject.

> **Tere y Pancho hablan español;**   *Tere and Pancho speak Spanish;*
> **él habla mucho pero ella habla poco.**   *he speaks a lot but she speaks a little.*

Usted and **ustedes** are generally used for courtesy, at least the first time someone is addressed in a conversation. Often they are used only intermittently as the conversation progresses.

▶ *It* is not expressed as a subject in Spanish.

> **Es verdad**   *It is true.*

Usted versus **Tú**

¿Cómo está usted?
How are you?

¿Cómo estás?
How are you?

Why does the speaker on the left use **usted** and the speaker on the right use **tú**? (If necessary, review the discussion of **tú** and **usted** on page 5.)

A • Replacement Drill

> MODEL   Francisco y Josefa hablan español.
> STUDENT **Ellos hablan español.**

1. Tere y Curro hablan español.
2. Tere y Pepita hablan español.
3. La señorita Azuela habla español.
4. Paco habla español.
5. Los alumnos hablan español.
6. Las mujeres hablan español.
7. Él y ella hablan español.
8. Él y yo hablamos español.
9. Tú y yo hablamos español.
10. Tú y Pepita hablan español.

2 Present tense forms of **-ar** verbs

▶ Spanish has three types of infinitives, indicated by **-ar**, **-er**, and **-ir** endings. To form the present tense of regular **-ar** verbs, drop the **-ar** from the infinitive and add the appropriate ending (**-o, -as, -a, -amos, -an**) to the stem.

	Stem	Ending		Stem	Ending
hablar *to speak, talk*					
(yo)	habl	-o	(nosotros) (nosotras) Rafa y yo tú y yo	habl	-amos
(tú)	habl	-as			
Ud. (él) (ella) Tere	habl	-a	Uds. (ellos) (ellas) Tere y Pancho	habl	-an[3]

Note that **usted** and **ustedes** utilize third person endings.

▶ The present tense has three possible equivalents in English. The context determines which equivalent is most appropriate.

Hablas español.   *You speak Spanish.*
                  or
                  You are speaking Spanish.

Also
¿Hablas español?   *Do you speak Spanish?*

The three possible translations apply to all the persons:

¿Hablan bien?   *They speak well?*
                 Are they speaking well?
                 Do they speak well?

[3] The present tense **vosotros** forms can be found in the Appendix, section 1.

▶ In order to express English *do* in an affirmative expression, Spanish utilizes **sí**: **Sí hablo español.** *I do speak Spanish.*

Further examples:

1. Practicamos en casa.	*We practice at home. We are practicing at home.*
2. Rosa y Pancho no practican en casa.	*Rosa and Pancho do not practice (are not practicing) at home.*
3. ¿Practica usted en casa?	*Do you practice at home? Are you practicing at home?*
4. Hablamos mucho.	*We talk a lot. We are talking a lot.*
5. Sí preparamos mucho.	*We do prepare a lot.*
6. Ella habla bien.	*She speaks well. She is speaking well.*

A • Substitution Drill

MODEL   Tere habla español.
Nosotros
STUDENT   Nosotros **hablamos** español.

1. Curro habla español.
Yo
Tú
Tú y yo
Tere
Nosotros

2. ¿Qué practica usted?
ella?
él?
él y ella?
ellos?
yo?

3. Nosotros preparamos mucho.
Ustedes
Nosotras
Pepita
Rafa
Yo

4. Todos preparan y practican la lección.
Tú y Josefa
Ellas
Paco
Curro y yo
Tere

B • Query   Patterned Response

MODEL   ¿Quién habla mucho? ¿Tú?
STUDENT   **¡Pues sí! Yo hablo mucho.**

1. ¿Quién practica mucho? ¿Pepita?
2. ¿Quiénes hablan español? ¿Los puertorriqueños?
3. ¿Quién habla español? ¿La señorita Azuela?[4]
4. ¿Quién prepara la lección? ¿Tere?
5. ¿Quién habla inglés? ¿La profesora?

[4] The definite article in Spanish is used with titles (**señorita, profesora,** etc.) except in direct address (see grammar section **4**).

6. ¿Quiénes preparan y practican bien? ¿Los alumnos?
7. ¿Quién habla mucho? ¿Francisco?
8. ¿Quiénes hablan español un poco? ¿Nosotros?
9. ¿Quién habla inglés y español? ¿Tú?
10. ¿Quién habla inglés entre familia? ¿Yo?

C • Query   Patterned Response   Negative → Affirmative

MODEL   Tú no practicas mucho, ¿verdad?
STUDENT   **¿Qué? ¡Hombre! Yo sí practico mucho.**

1. Tú no hablas inglés, ¿verdad?
2. Usted no practica el español, ¿verdad?
3. Ustedes no preparan la lección en casa, ¿verdad?
4. Ustedes no hablan bien, ¿verdad?
5. Nosotros no practicamos en casa, ¿verdad?
6. Tú no hablas español también, ¿verdad?
7. Ella no practica mucho, ¿verdad?
8. Ellos no hablan inglés y español, ¿verdad?
9. Tú no practicas la lección, ¿verdad?
10. En California no hablan español, ¿verdad?

D • Query   Free Response

Answer the questions in Spanish. Throughout the text, exercise items will often be expressed in both the familiar (**tú**) form and the formal (**usted**) form. It is important for you to practice both.

1. ¿Qué habla usted?
2. ¿Qué hablas?
3. ¿Dónde practica usted?
4. ¿Dónde practicas?
5. ¿Qué hablan ellos?

6. ¿Quiénes preparan la lección?
7. ¿Qué hablamos en los Estados Unidos?
8. ¿Dónde practicamos?
9. ¿Qué hablo yo?
10. ¿Quiénes practican?

3 Present indicative of **ser**, *to be*

(yo)	**soy**	*I am*	(nosotros) (nosotras) Rafa y yo tú y yo	**somos**	*we are* *Rafa and I are* *you and I are*
(tú)	**eres**	*you are*			
Ud.		*you are*	Uds.		*you are*
(él)	**es**	*he is*	(ellos)	**son**	*they are*
(ella)		*she is*	(ellas)		*they are*
Pepita		*Pepita is*	Pepita y Curro		*Pepita and Curro are*

Ser is one of the Spanish irregular verbs. Forms of the irregular verbs must be learned separately.

A • Substitution Drill

MODEL   ¿De dónde es usted?
                        tú?

STUDENT   ¿De dónde **eres** tú?

1. ¿De dónde es usted?
   ella?
   tú?
   nosotros?
   yo?
   Pancho?

2. Yo soy de California.
   Tú
   Tú y yo
   Él
   Él y ella
   Ellas

3. Usted es de España, ¿verdad?
   Tú
   Tere
   Paco
   Tere y Paco
   Ellos

4. No, ¡hombre! Ella no es de Colorado.
   Él
   Usted
   Nosotros
   Tú
   Paco y Pepita

B • Query   Patterned Response

MODEL   ¿Qué es Ud.? ¿Alumno?
STUDENT   **Sí, soy alumno (alumna).**

1. ¿Qué es la señorita Azuela? ¿Chicana?
2. ¿Quiénes son ellas? ¿Tere y Pepita?
3. ¿Qué eres? ¿Alumna?
4. ¿De dónde es usted? ¿De Nuevo México?
5. ¿De dónde somos? ¿De los Estados Unidos?
6. ¿De dónde soy? ¿De Colorado?
7. ¿Qué son ellas? ¿Simpáticas?
8. ¿De dónde eres? ¿De los Estados Unidos?
9. ¿Qué es la señorita Azuela? ¿Profesora?
10. ¿De dónde es Pepita? ¿De California?

C • Query   Free Response

Answer in Spanish.

1. ¿De dónde eres?
2. ¿De dónde es usted?
3. ¿Qué es la señorita Azuela?
4. ¿Qué es Tere?

5. ¿Quién es la profesora de español?
6. ¿Quién es la señorita simpática?
7. ¿Qué es usted?
8. ¿Qué eres?

4 Definite articles

▶ The definite article (equivalent to *the*) is **el** before masculine singular nouns and **la** before feminine singular nouns. The corresponding plural forms are **los** and **las**.

	Singular	*Plural*
Masculine	el	los
Feminine	la	las

La señorita prepara la lección. *The young lady prepares the lesson.*
Las alumnas practican el español. *The students (all female) practice Spanish.*

▶ The definite article is used with names of languages in Spanish except when they immediately follow the verb **hablar**.

El chicano habla español. *The Chicano speaks Spanish.*

A • Transformation Drill Singular → Plural

MODEL   el cubano
        cubanos
STUDENT **los** cubanos

Plural → Singular

1. la profesora
   profesoras
2. el alumno
   alumnos
3. la señorita
   señoritas
4. el joven
   jóvenes
5. el puertorriqueño
   puertorriqueños

6. los hispanos
   hispano
7. las lecciones
   lección
8. las casas
   casa
9. las personas
   persona
10. los chicanos
    chicano

B • Query Patterned Response

MODEL   ¿Dónde hablan ustedes? ¿En casa?
STUDENT **Sí, nosotros hablamos en casa.**

1. ¿Dónde hablan español? ¿En casa?
2. ¿Dónde practican el español? ¿En la clase?
3. ¿Qué habla la señorita Azuela? ¿Español?
4. ¿Qué practica Paco? ¿El inglés?
5. ¿Dónde hablamos español? ¿En la clase?

6. ¿Dónde practican el español? ¿En clase?
7. ¿Dónde preparan la lección? ¿En casa?
8. ¿Qué habla Rafael en casa? ¿Inglés?
9. ¿Qué prepara y practica la alumna? ¿El español?
10. ¿En qué país hablan español? ¿En México?

5 Gender and number of nouns

▶ Nouns in Spanish are either masculine or feminine, singular or plural.

	Singular	Plural
Masculine	el alumno	los alumnos
	el profesor	los profesores
	el joven	los jóvenes[5]
	el día	los días
	el español	los españoles
Feminine	la alumna	las alumnas
	la profesora	las profesoras
	la joven	las jóvenes
	la casa	las casas
	la española	las españolas

▶ Most nouns that end in **-o** are masculine, and most that end in **-a** are feminine.[6] There are some exceptions, however, such as **el día**. Since many nouns do not end in **-o** or **-a**, it is useful to learn the definite article associated with each noun.

▶ If the singular of a noun ends in a vowel, the plural is formed by adding **-s**; if the noun ends in a consonant, the plural is formed by adding **-es**. Exceptions are nouns expressing nationality, occupation, etc., which add **-a** for the feminine singular and **-as** for the feminine plural even though the masculine singular may end in a consonant.

| el español | la española | las españolas |
| el profesor | la profesora | las profesoras |

But:

| el joven[7] | la joven | las (los) jóvenes |

---

[5] See page 11 for an explanation of the accent on **jóvenes**.

[6] Also, most nouns ending in **-or** (**profesor, amor, motor**) are masculine, and most nouns ending in **-ión, -ad**, and **-ud** (**nación, universidad, quietud**) are feminine.

[7] Note that **joven** does not refer to nationality or occupation, and does not add **-a** for the feminine singular or **-as** for the feminine plural.

Most nouns referring to nationality, occupation, family relationship, and the like assign masculine gender to male beings and feminine gender to female.

el alumno   *the student (male)*
la alumna   *the student (female)*
el español   *the Spaniard (male)*
la española   *the Spaniard (female)*
el profesor   *the professor (male)*
la profesora   *the professor (female)*

Matched Nouns: Masculine and Feminine

Here are some nouns that have masculine and feminine forms. Can you guess the form that is left blank?

la hermana   *the sister*
_____   *the doctor (female)*
la japonesa   *the Japanese (female)*

_____   *the brother*
el doctor   *the doctor (male)*
_____   *the Japanese (male)*

 The masculine plural of a noun may include both sexes.

los alumnos   male and female *students* or only male *students*, depending on the context

los profesores   men and women *teachers* or only men *teachers*, depending on the context

The same phenomenon occurs with subject pronouns.

ellos   *they*, males and females, or *they*, only males.

▶ Adjectives of nationality are freely used as nouns.[8] When used in this way, they maintain the gender and number of the noun they replace.

Las alumnas españolas son simpáticas.	*The Spanish students (female) are nice.*
Las españolas son simpáticas.	*The Spaniards (female) are nice.*

A • Variable Substitution Drill

MODEL   ¿Quién es el alumno?
                las
STUDENT   **¿Quiénes son las alumnas?**

1. ¿Quién es el profesor?
    los
    la
      español?
      españolas?
    la
      joven?
    el
      jóvenes?
    las
    los

2. ¿Qué habla el alumno?
    los
    las
      chicana?
      chicanas?
    la
    el
      puertorriqueño?
      cubano?
    las
    los

B • Transformation Drill   Singular → Plural

MODEL   La familia practica en casa.
STUDENT   **Las familias practican** en casa.

1. El alumno prepara la lección.
2. La mujer habla inglés.
3. La señorita no habla bien.
4. La alumna practica mucho.
5. El joven practica mucho.
6. La joven es de California.
7. El profesor es boricua.
8. El hispano habla inglés y español.

Plural → Singular

9. Los jóvenes son de los Estados Unidos.
10. Las jóvenes hablan inglés y español.
11. Los profesores preparan la lección también.
12. Las profesoras hablan español en casa.

---

[8] In fact, most adjectives in Spanish can be used as nouns. See grammar section **39**.

13. <u>Los alumnos</u> practican el inglés.
14. <u>Las alumnas</u> preparan la lección.
15. <u>Los chicanos</u> son de los Estados Unidos, ¿verdad?
16. <u>Los hombres</u> son de Colorado.

6 Negative and interrogative sentences

▶ To make a sentence negative in Spanish, simply place **no** immediately before the verb.

    1. No hablo mucho inglés.   *I do not speak much English.*
    2. No somos de la Florida.   *We are not from Florida.*
    3. Rafael no practica en casa.   *Rafael does not practice at home.*

▶ Just as in English, questions in Spanish may be formed simply on the basis of intonation.

    ¿Usted es chicana?

They are also formed by means of intonation plus placing the subject after the verb.

    ¿Es usted chicana?[9]

When Spanish does not use subject pronouns, there is no inversion.

    Hablas español.   *You speak Spanish.*
    ¿Hablas español?   *Do you speak Spanish? You speak Spanish?*

Examples:

    1. ¿Practican ustedes en casa?   *Do you practice at home?*
    2. ¿Preparas la lección?   *Do you prepare the lesson?*
    3. ¿Habla Teresa inglés o español?   *Does Teresa speak English or Spanish?*
    4. ¿No es usted chicano?   *Aren't you Chicano?*

▶ The following are interrogative words or phrases.

¿qué?	*what?*
¿dónde?	*where?*
¿de dónde?	*from where?*
¿quién? (*plural* ¿quiénes?)	*who? whom?*
¿en qué?	*in what?*

[9] If the subject is as long as, or longer than, the object, it is placed at the end of the question: **¿Habla español el profesor de inglés?** *Does the English professor speak Spanish?* If an adverb such as **mucho, bien,** or **(un) poco** is used, the word order is verb, adverb, subject: **¿Hablan mucho las alumnas?** *Do the students speak a lot?*

▶ When an interrogative word or phrase introduces the question, it always has a written accent. This accent distinguishes the word as an interrogative.

1.	¿Qué practicas?	*What are you practicing?*
2.	¿Quién es ella?	*Who is she?*
3.	¿En qué países hablan español?	*In what countries do they speak Spanish?*
4.	¿De dónde es Tere?	*Where is Tere from? (From where . . . ?)*
5.	¿Dónde hablan español?	*Where do they speak Spanish?*

But:

6.	Yo soy de España donde todos hablan español.	*I am from Spain where everybody speaks Spanish.*

A • Transformation Drill   Affirmative → Negative

MODEL   Ella es alumna.
STUDENT   Ella **no** es alumna.

1. Ustedes hablan español.
2. ¿Hablan ustedes español?
3. Soy de Texas.
4. ¿Eres de los Estados Unidos?
5. Paco es muy perspicaz.

6. Preparamos la lección.
7. En casa generalmente hablan español.
8. ¿Practica Tere en casa?
9. La señorita Azuela es alumna.
10. Josefa es profesora.

B • Transformation Drill   Affirmative → Interrogative

MODEL   La alumna habla bien.
STUDENT   **¿Habla bien la alumna?**

1. Los profesores hablan español.
2. La familia practica en casa.
3. Son de Nuevo México.
4. La señorita Azuela es chicana.
5. Practicas mucho.

6. Preparas bien la lección.
7. Yo practico mucho.
8. Tú preparas la lección.
9. Los hispanos hablan español.
10. Hablamos inglés entre familia.

C • Transformation Drill

Using an interrogative word, make questions for the following sentences that will ask for the underlined information.

MODEL   Rafael es <u>de Nuevo México</u>.
STUDENT   **¿De dónde** es Rafael?

1. Tere y Pepita practican <u>la lección</u>.
2. Hablan español <u>en España y México</u>.
3. <u>Los hombres</u> preparan mucho.
4. La señorita Azuela es <u>de California</u>.

5. Tú practicas entre familia.
6. Teresa es una señorita simpática.
7. Los cubanos hablan inglés en la Florida.
8. Los boricuas son de Puerto Rico.

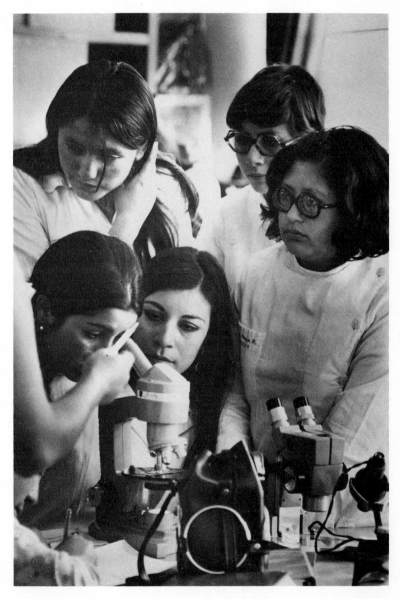

Science class,
Miami, Florida

REVIEW

I   The following questions are related to the dialog. Answer in Spanish.

1. ¿Hablan inglés y español en los Estados Unidos?
2. ¿Qué habla la señorita Azuela?
3. ¿Qué hablan los puertorriqueños?
4. ¿En qué países hablan español?
5. ¿Quién es una señorita simpática?
6. ¿Quiénes preparan y practican bien las lecciones?
7. ¿Quiénes hablan español en el suroeste de los Estados Unidos?
8. ¿Quién es muy perspicaz?

II   Translation.   Translate the following into Spanish.

1. Who is Pancho? What does he speak at home? Who is it? What is it?
2. Where is Miss Azuela from? (From where is Miss Azuela?)
3. Many persons are practicing Spanish in all parts of the United States.
4. Man! I prepare and practice Spanish a lot.
5. Pancho is from Arizona where [not interrogative] everybody speaks Spanish a little.
6. Of course! Generally, at home among (the) family the students speak English.
7. In what countries do they speak Spanish? In Spanish America, Spain, and the United States, too. Really? Sure!
8. Who is she? She is Pepita. She prepares the lesson at home.

III   Write your own dialog.

The students in "Una clase de español en los Estados Unidos" discuss where Spanish is spoken. You are a new student in their class. Ask them three or four questions in Spanish about where Spanish is spoken, and try to write down their probable answers.

PRONUNCIATION

I   **Vowel Contrasts in Stressed Syllables**

Reread "Vowels," page 7. The following words illustrate vowel contrasts in stressed syllables. Repeat the pairs of words after your instructor.

/a/	/e/		/a/	/i/		/a/	/o/		/a/	/u/
palo	pelo		paso	piso		palo	polo		paso	puso
masa	mesa		mal	mil		masa	moza		mala	mula
da	dé		da	di		da	do		dada	duda
rato	reto		rasa	risa		rata	rota		rata	ruta
saca	seca		san	sin		saga	soga		sayo	suyo

/e/	/i/		/e/	/o/		/e/	/u/		/i/	/o/
peso	piso		peso	pozo		peso	puso		piso	pozo
mesa	misa		mesa	moza		mesa	musa		misa	moza
dé	di		dé	do		dedo	dudo		di	do
reza	risa		reto	roto		reta	ruta		rima	Roma
sé	sí		seso	soso		cedo	sudo		sin	son

/i/	/u/		/o/	/u/
piso	puso		pozo	puso
mida	muda		moza	musa
dique	duque		dona	duna
risa	rusa		rota	ruta
cima	suma		sor	sur

II Vowel Contrasts in Unstressed Syllables

The following words illustrate vowel contrasts in unstressed syllables. Repeat the pairs of words after your instructor.

/a/	/e/		/a/	/i/		/a/	/o/
para	pare		pasar	pisar		para	paro
mesas	meses		mamar	mimar		mata	mato
marcado	mercado		matad	mitad		derecha	derecho
preguntas	preguntes		paquete	piquete		roba	robo
sobras	sobres		pañal	piñal		saca	saco

/a/	/u/		/e/	/i/		/e/	/o/
pajar	pujar		pesar	pisar		pare	paro
maleta	muleta		pecar	picar		mate	mato
lagar	lugar		pesada	pisada		doble	doblo
palidez	pulidez		remar	rimar		robe	robo
sabido	subido		rezar	rizar		siente	siento

/e/	/u/		/i/	/o/		/i/	/u/
pechero	puchero		pisada	posada		pintar	puntar
legar	lugar		mirada	morada		mirar	murar
temor	tumor		imito	omito		ligar	lugar
lechar	luchar		mirar	morar		pidiendo	pudiendo
retina	rutina		timó	tomó		birlar	burlar

/o/	/u/
plomero	plumero
morar	murar
bocal	bucal
acosar	acusar
motilar	mutilar

III   Linking

Review "Linking," page 11, and pronounce the following after your instructor.

A. Final consonant joined with initial vowel
    ¿Quién es el profesor?
    ¿Hablan ustedes inglés?
    ¿Hablan español en España.
    ¿Es usted alumno?

B. Two identical vowels together
    La clase de español
    ¿Ya hablan ustedes español?
    ¡No, hombre!
    ¿De dónde es usted?
    La señorita Azuela habla aquí.

C. Unlike vowels together
    No es alumna.
    ¿Habla usted?
    Hable usted.
    Tú hablas.
    Es un hombre inteligente.
    ¿Prepara o practica?
    España y México
    ¿Qué otras partes?

Cognates & Contexts

Moral *Director* RADIO *Adorable*

Rodeo

Animal

COLOR

personal

It is estimated that over 50,000 words in Spanish are cognate with English! The passages below make use of such cognates. Other Spanish words can be understood from the context, particularly when they are antonyms or synonyms of words already known. Pronounce the passages out loud several times. Try to understand each passage in Spanish. The meaning of most of these sentences will be so obvious that you will not need to translate them into English in order to understand them fully. If in doubt as to the meaning of the word, refer to the end vocabulary. Words that are not cognates and cannot be readily derived from the context will be glossed in the margin.

Pepita es una alumna (una *estudiante*) simpática y aplicada; Paco es un alumno (un *estudiante*) *antipático*, pero con mucho talento para los idiomas extranjeros. Paco habla mucho español y Pepita *sólo* habla un poco.

aplicada *diligent*

con *with*

para *for* **idiomas extranjeros** *foreign languages*

En los Estados Unidos hablan inglés y español; en el *Canadá* hablan inglés y *francés*; en *Francia* hablan francés; en Portugal y Brasil hablan *portugués*; y en *Italia* hablan *italiano*. ¿Qué hablan en Inglaterra?

Inglaterra *England*

Los hispanos hablan español. Los chicanos son hispanos; también los boricuas (los puertorriqueños) son hispanos. ¿Quiénes son otros hispanos? Los españoles, los *mexicanos*, los *argentinos*, los *chilenos*, los *bolivianos*, los *peruanos*, los *guatemaltecos*, los *dominicanos* (de la *República Dominicana*), los *hondureños*... y muchos otros. ¡Todos son hispanos!

acción

TIEMPO

Libertad

Europa

modelo *Televisión* *mágica* PRODUCTOS

Record store,
New York City

Lección dos

UNA COMPRA DE DISCOS EN NUEVA YORK

compra *purchase*

discos *records*

RUBÉN	Hola, guapa, ¿cómo estás?
RAQUEL	¡Ay, Rubén! ¿Qué haces tú por aquí?
RUBÉN	Voy a comprar unos discos.
RAQUEL	¿Cuándo, ahora? Hay una tienda de discos cerca de aquí.
RUBÉN	¿Dónde está? ¿Es grande?
RAQUEL	¡Oh, sí! Es muy grande y es nueva. Está en la Avenida de las Américas. Venden toda clase de música y canciones latinoamericanas.
RUBÉN	¿Ah, sí? ¿Cuáles venden?
RAQUEL	Venden tangos de la Argentina, sambas del Brasil, bombas de Puerto Rico, bambas de México y guajiras y chachachás de Cuba. Hasta venden bailes flamencos de los gitanos de España.
RUBÉN	¿Guajiras de Cuba? ¿Qué son?
RAQUEL	¡Tonto! Voy a cantar un ejemplo...
RUBÉN	¿Aprendes a bailar y cantar en la clase de baile?
RAQUEL	Guantanamera,

guapa *good-looking*
¿cómo estás? *how are you?*
¿qué haces? *what are you doing?* por aquí *around here*

voy a comprar *I'm going to buy* unos *some*

ahora *now* hay *there is* tienda *store* cerca (de + obj.) *near*

grande *big, large*

nueva *new*

vender *to sell* toda clase de *all kinds of* canciones *songs*

¿cuáles? *which ones?*

hasta *even*

bailes *dances* gitanos *gypsies*

tonto *silly, stupid* cantar *to sing* ejemplo *example*
aprender *to learn* bailar *to dance*

Guajira guantanamera.
Guantanamera,
Guajira guantanamera.
Yo soy un hombre sincero
de donde crece la palma...

		crece la palma *the palm tree grows*
RUBÉN	¡Ah, sí! Hay un disco donde Pete Seeger canta la canción. Es muy bonita, y además, de admirable tono moral.	**bonita** *pretty* **además** *moreover*
RAQUEL	Rubén, tú escribes canciones y poemas también, ¿verdad?	**escribir** *to write*
RUBÉN	¿Yo? ¡Muchacha! ¿Estás loca?	**muchacha** *girl* **loca** *crazy*
RAQUEL	¿Y en la clase de matemáticas? Siempre escribes y escribes como un loco. Después borras y escribes otra vez. ¡Poeta!	**siempre** *always* **como** *like* **después (de** + obj.) *later, after (*+ obj.) **borrar** *to erase* **otra vez** *again*
RUBÉN	¿Poeta? ¿Yo? Escribo la composición de español en la clase de matemáticas. Es fácil así. Termino la tarea en clase y no en casa, mujer.	**fácil** *easy* **así** *that way* **terminar** *to finish* **tarea** *homework* **mujer** *woman*
RAQUEL	¡Rubén! ¡Mentiroso! ¿Quién es la muchacha? ¿Quién recibe los versos de amor que escribes?	**mentiroso** *liar* **recibir** *to receive* **que** *that*

NOTES

Interrogatives

Three additional interrogatives appear in the dialog.

¿cómo? *how?*
¿cuál? (plural **¿cuáles?**) *which? (which ones?)*
¿cuándo? *when?*

Irregular gender

Two nouns in this dialog are masculine although they end in **-a**.

el poema *the poem*
el poeta *the poet*

Recall from Lección primera: **el día** *the day*, **el idioma** *the language*.

Vocabulary Meanings

¡Ay! ¡Oh! ¡Ah! These are common interjections in Spanish. **¡Ay!** is characteristically used in anguish; **¡Oh!** and **¡Ah!** normally convey positive feelings such as surprise, pleasure, etc.

guapo, guapa *handsome, good-looking.* This adjective has both masculine and feminine forms, but it is normally used only to refer to the opposite sex; for example, a male may refer to a female as **guapa**, but would not normally use **guapo** to refer to a male.

que *that, which, who.* **Que**, when used as a relative pronoun (to connect two clauses), may translate *that, which,* or *who.*

El muchacho que está aquí...   *The boy who is here . . .*
El disco que venden...   *The record that (which) they are selling . . .*

More Matched Nouns

Recall that certain nouns assign masculine gender to male beings and feminine gender to female (grammar section 5). Since this is the case, what are the meanings of the following nouns?

la muchacha	el mentiroso	el gitano
el muchacho	la mentirosa	la gitana

THE GUAJIRA GUANTANAMERA

Guajiro (-a) literally means a Cuban peasant; by extension, the word has come to mean a peasant folk song. **Guantanamera** refers to the region of Guantánamo. Thus, **Guajira guantanamera** means folk song from (and about) Guantánamo. The "Guajira guantanamera," one of the most popular of the *guajiras*, is based on poems in José Martí's *Versos sencillos*. José Martí (1853–1895) was a great Cuban poet, essayist, and patriot. He died in an unsuccessful rebellion against Spanish rule. Two stanzas of the "Guajira guantanamera" follow.

Yo soy un hombre sincero
de donde crece la palma,
y antes de morirme quiero
echar mis versos del alma.

Con los pobres de la tierra
quiero yo mi suerte echar,
el arroyo de la sierra
me complace más que
el mar.

I am a sincere man
from where the palm tree grows,
before I die I want
to give forth these verses from my
*   soul.*

With the poor of this earth
I want to cast my lot,
the stream in the mountain
pleases me more than the sea.

LANGUAGE STRUCTURES

7 Present tense forms of **-er** and **-ir** verbs

▶ There is only one difference between **-er** and **-ir** verbs and it occurs in the present tense. The first person plural of **-er** verbs is **-emos**; that of **-ir** verbs is **-imos**. For all other tenses (past, future, etc.) the forms of regular **-er** and **-ir** verbs are the same.

	aprender *to learn*		**escribir** *to write*	
	Stem	Ending	Stem	Ending
(yo)	aprend	-o	escrib	-o
(tú)	aprend	-es	escrib	-es
Ud. (él) (ella) Raquel	aprend	-e	escrib	-e
(nosotros) (nosotras)	aprend	**-emos**	escrib	**-imos**
Uds. (ellos) (ellas) Raquel y Rubén	aprend	-en	escrib	-en

▶ Recall the possible meanings of the present tense. For example, **aprendes** *you learn, you are learning;* **¿aprendes?** *do you learn? are you learning?;* **escribimos** *we write, we are writing;* **no escribimos** *we do not write, we are not writing.*

A • Substitution Drill

MODEL   Paco vende discos latinoamericanos.
               Nosotros
STUDENT Nosotros **vendemos** discos latinoamericanos.

1. Nosotros aprendemos un baile bonito.
   Tú
   Tú y yo
   Raquel
   Rubén y Raquel
   Yo

2. ¿Escribes tú la tarea en clase?
   Rubén
   Rafa y Rubén
   Pepita y yo
   ustedes
   ellas

3. Paco vende discos latinoamericanos.
Paco y Pepita
Yo
Nosotros
Usted
Él

4. ¿Recibe ella poemas de amor?
ellos
ustedes
él y ella
nosotras
Teresa

B • Query   Patterned Response

MODEL   ¿Dónde hay un hombre sincero? ¿En Nueva York?

STUDENT   **¡Claro! Hay un hombre sincero en Nueva York.**

1. ¿Qué poemas reciben? ¿Poemas de amor?
2. ¿Qué son las canciones? ¿Guajiras?
3. ¿Cuándo aprende Raquel el baile? ¿Ahora?
4. ¿En qué país cantan flamenco? ¿En España?
5. ¿Qué escribes en casa? ¿La composición?
6. ¿Dónde bailan el tango? ¿En la Argentina?
7. ¿Qué música venden? ¿Bombas y bambas?
8. ¿Quién escribe la composición? ¿Rubén?
9. ¿Quién aprende un ejemplo? ¿Raquel?
10. ¿Dónde hay una tienda de discos? ¿En la Avenida de las Américas?

C • Query   Free Response

Answer in Spanish.

1. ¿Qué escribe usted?
2. ¿Qué aprendemos?
3. ¿Qué compra usted?
4. ¿Recibes versos de amor?
5. ¿Qué escribimos en clase?

6. ¿Cantas bien?
7. ¿Dónde aprende usted el español?
8. ¿Terminas la tarea en casa?
9. ¿Venden discos por aquí?
10. ¿Dónde hay una tienda de discos?

8 Present indicative of **estar**, *to be*

(yo)	**estoy**	*I am*	(nosotros)		estamos	*we are*
(tú)	estás	*you are*	(nosotras)			
Ud.		*you are*	Uds.			*you are*
(él)	está	*he, she,*	(ellos)		están	*they, Raquel*
(ella)		*Raquel is*	(ellas)			*and Rubén*
Raquel			Raquel y Rubén			*are*

▶ The two verbs **ser** and **estar** cover most of the meanings of *to be* in English. Spanish makes a distinction between two types of being. **Ser** is inherent, essential, characteristic, much like the = sign in mathematics.

Paco es perspicaz.	*Paco is clever.*
Usted es chicana, ¿verdad?	*You are a Chicana, right?*

Estar refers to location or expresses a condition or state subject to change.

¿Dónde está? Está en la Avenida de las Américas.	*Where is it? It's on the Avenue of the Americas.*
¿Cómo estás? Estoy bien.	*How are you? I'm fine.*

The option of using **ser** or **estar** provides Spanish with a peculiar flexibility and richness. More examples of this option are given in a later lesson.

Es la profesora.
She is the teacher.

La profesora está en la clase.
The teacher is in the classroom.

A • Substitution Drill

MODEL   Hola, guapa.   ¿Dónde está Raquel?
                                          ellas?

STUDENT   Hola, guapa.   ¿Dónde **están** ellas?

1. Hola, guapa. ¿Dónde está Raquel?
          ellas?
          el baile?
          la avenida?
          Rafa y Rubén?
          nosotros?

2. La tienda está cerca de aquí.
   Ellas
   El loco
   Tú
   Ustedes
   Usted

B • Query   Patterned Response

MODEL   ¿Qué es y dónde está?   un disco bonito / en la tienda grande
STUDENT   **Es un disco bonito y está en la tienda grande.**

1. ¿Qué es y dónde está?   una tienda grande / en la Avenida de las Américas
2. ¿Quién es y dónde está?   el profesor latinoamericano / en la clase de matemáticas
3. ¿Quién es y dónde está?   un poeta boricua / en los Estados Unidos
4. ¿Qué es y dónde está?   un poema sincero / en la lección dos
5. ¿Quién es y dónde está?   una persona perspicaz / en la clase de español

C • Completion Drill   ser/estar

MODEL   Yo _____ alumno.
STUDENT   Yo **soy** alumno.

1. La tienda _____ en la Avenida de las Américas.
2. Rubén _____ profesor.
3. La canción _____ muy fácil.
4. Los versos _____ sinceros.
5. Las canciones _____ en los discos.
6. Yo _____ cerca de la tienda.
7. Tú _____ admirable.
8. Pepita y yo _____ donde compran y venden discos.
9. ¿Quién _____ la señorita simpática?
10. Hola, guapo. ¿Dónde _____ Rubén?

9 Present tense of **ir**, *to go*; **ir a** + infinitive

(yo)	**voy**	I go, am going	(nosotros) (nosotras)	**vamos**	we go, are going
(tú)	**vas**	you go, are going			
Ud.		you go, are going	Uds.		you go, are going
(él) (ella) Rubén	**va**	he, she, Rubén goes, is going	(ellos) (ellas) Raquel y Rubén	**van**	they, Raquel and Rubén go, are going

▶ The construction **ir a** + infinitive indicates a future idea, much as the English *to be going* + infinitive. In this construction **a** has no translation into English.

Hay un baile; ¿vas a ir?   *There's a dance. Are you going to go?*
¿Vas a ser profesor?   *Are you going to be a professor?*
¿Quién va a escribir?   *Who is going to write?*

▶ The preposition **a** also follows **ir** and other verbs of motion before a noun object to indicate the movement inherent in the verb.

> **Raquel va a la tienda.**   *Raquel goes to the store.*
> **Nosotros vamos a la clase de matemáticas.**   *We are going to math class.*

▶ The form **¿adónde?** is used with **ir** in a question.

> **¿Adónde van?**   *Where are they going?*

A • Substitution Drill

MODEL   ¡Hola! ¿Adónde vas tú?
                           ellos?
STUDENT   ¡Hola! ¿Adónde **van** ellos?

1. ¡Hola! ¿Adónde vas tú?
          ellos?
          Josefa?
          Pepita y Tere?
          nosotros?
          la señorita Azuela?

2. Rubén va a la clase.
   Tú
   Tú y yo
   Ellas
   Usted
   Rubén y Raquel

B • Substitution Drill

MODEL   ¿Adónde <u>vamos</u>?
STUDENT   **¿Dónde estamos?**

Now in reverse:

1. ¿Adónde <u>vas</u>?
2. ¿Adónde <u>van</u>?
3. ¿Adónde <u>va</u> usted?
4. ¿Adónde <u>van</u> ustedes?
5. ¿Adónde <u>vamos</u>?

6. ¿Dónde <u>estamos</u>?
7. ¿Dónde <u>están</u> Pepita y Tere?
8. ¿Dónde <u>estamos</u> tú y yo?
9. ¿Dónde <u>está</u> usted?
10. ¿Dónde <u>están</u> ellos?

C • Transformation Drill   Present Tense → **ir a+Infinitive**

MODEL   El poeta escribe unos versos.
STUDENT   El poeta **va a escribir** unos versos.

1. Raquel está en el baile.
2. Soy un poeta admirable.
3. Recibimos versos de amor.
4. Ellos practican la lección.
5. El hombre vende pocos discos flamencos.

ir a+Infinitive → Present Tense

6. La alumna va a escribir la tarea.
7. Voy a cantar la canción de amor.

8. Vamos a bailar la bamba.
9. ¿Vas a aprender el español?
10. ¿Van a estar en casa?

D • Query   Patterned Response

MODEL   ¿Qué eres? ¿Un hombre sincero?

STUDENT   **¡Oh, sí! Soy** un hombre sincero.

1. ¿Qué son? ¿Guajiros?
2. ¿Dónde está usted? ¿En Nueva York?
3. ¿Cómo estás? ¿Bien?
4. ¿Qué vas a comprar? ¿Discos?
5. ¿Cuándo va Raquel a la clase de baile? ¿Ahora?
6. ¿Adónde vamos? ¿A la tienda de discos?
7. ¿De dónde son ustedes? ¿De Borinquen?
8. ¿Quién está en la tienda? ¿Rubén?
9. ¿Qué es? ¿Poeta?
10. ¿Quiénes están aquí? ¿Los alumnos?

E • Query   Free Response

Answer in Spanish.

1. ¿Dónde estás?
2. ¿Qué hay cerca de aquí?
3. ¿De dónde son ellos?
4. ¿Cómo está usted?
5. ¿Dónde estamos?
6. ¿Qué practicamos en clase?
7. ¿Adónde vas después de la clase?
8. ¿Adónde van los alumnos a practicar el español?
9. ¿Qué canciones venden en las tiendas de discos?
10. ¿Qué vas a cantar?

10 Agreement of adjectives with nouns

	Singular	Plural
Masculine	latinoamericano	latinoamericanos
	bonito	bonitos
	fácil	fáciles
	grande	grandes
	inglés	ingleses[1]
Feminine	latinoamericana	latinoamericanas
	bonita	bonitas
	fácil	fáciles
	grande	grandes
	inglesa	inglesas

▶ Adjectives agree in number and gender with the nouns they modify.

▶ Most adjectives show agreement by the four endings **-o, -os, -a, -as**.

▶ Adjectives that do not end in **-o** in the masculine singular (**grande, fácil**) are the same in the masculine and feminine. As in the case of nouns, the plurals of these adjectives

---

[1] Words that end in **-és** (**francés, inglés, portugués**) or **-ión** (**nación, lección, canción**) drop the written accent in the plural and in the feminine singular. The stress is still on the same syllable (**franceses, lecciones, inglesa**), but a written accent is no longer required because the next-to-last syllable is normally where Spanish stresses words with these endings (see p. 11).

are formed by adding **-s** if the adjective ends in a vowel or **-es** if the adjective ends in a consonant. However, adjectives of nationality that end in a consonant (**inglés**) add **-a** and **-as** to form the feminine singular and feminine plural.

	Singular	*Plural*
Masculine	1. el disco latinoamericano	1. los discos latinoamericanos
	2. el hombre grande	2. los hombres grandes
	3. el alumno inglés	3. los alumnos ingleses
Feminine	1. la canción bonita	1. las canciones bonitas
	2. la palma grande	2. las palmas grandes
	3. la alumna inglesa	3. las alumnas inglesas

A • Variable Substitution Drill

Complete each sentence, using the preceding one as a model and changing only what is required by the cue.

MODEL   Escribe unos versos bonitos.
                    una composición
STUDENT   Escribe una composición **bonita.**

1. Escribe unos versos bonitos.
       una composición
       un poema
       unos poemas
       unas composiciones
       una canción

2. ¿Es grande la casa? Sí, es grande.
       grandes
       nueva
               las casas?
       bonita
               el día?
               los días?

3. ¿Es chicana la alumna nueva?
   ¿Son
       chicano
               los
                   alumnas
               la
                       nuevas?
       chicanos
               alumno

B • Transformation Drill   Singular → Plural

MODEL   La canción es bonita.
STUDENT   **Las canciones son bonitas.**

1. El hombre es sincero.
2. La palma es bonita.

3. La tienda es grande.
4. ¿Es grande la palma?
5. ¿Vende usted el disco nuevo?
6. Ella aprende la canción latinoamericana.
7. La casa es nueva.
8. ¿Es bonito el disco?
9. Es una joven guapa.
10. Escribe una canción fácil.

11 Hay: meaning and use

▶ **Hay** means either *there is* or *there are*. Since **hay** has no expressed subject, questions are conveyed purely by intonation and not by inverted word order.

1. ¿Hay una tienda de discos cerca de aquí?

   Is there a record shop around here?

2. Sí, claro. Hay una tienda en la Avenida de las Américas.

   Yes, of course. There's a store on the Avenue of the Americas.

3. ¿Hay muchas palmas en Puerto Rico?

   Are there many palm trees in Puerto Rico?

A • Query   Patterned Response

MODEL   ¿Vende usted discos latinoamericanos?
STUDENT   **Pues sí. Hay discos latinoamericanos.**

1. ¿Están muchas personas en la tienda?
2. ¿Escribes versos en la composición?
3. ¿Cantan guajiras en el disco?
4. ¿Aprendemos bailes flamencos en la clase?
5. ¿Venden toda clase de música?
6. ¿Hablan otros idiomas en el Canadá?
7. ¿Bailan chachachás en el baile?
8. ¿Son muchos chicanos de California?

B • Query   Free Response

Answer in Spanish.

1. ¿Hay alumnos en la clase?
2. ¿Hay discos latinoamericanos en los Estados Unidos?
3. ¿Hay personas que escriben mucho en clase?
4. ¿Hay poetas puertorriqueños en Nueva York?
5. ¿Qué hay en la clase?

12   The indefinite article

▶ The indefinite article (equivalent to *a* or *an*) is **un** before a masculine singular noun and **una** before a feminine singular noun. These words also mean *one*.

▶ After **ser**, the indefinite article is not used with an unmodified noun that merely identifies someone as to nationality, profession, religion, political party, etc. (examples 2 and 3).[2]

1. Escribo un poema y una composición.	*I'm writing a (or one) poem and a (or one) composition.*
2. Raquel es alumna.	*Raquel is a student.*
3. Soy hispano.	*I'm a Hispano.*

▶ **Unos, unas,** the plurals of **un** and **una,** are adjectives meaning *some* or *a few*.[3]

Escribo unos versos.   *I am writing some verses.*
Aprendo unas canciones.   *I'm learning a few songs.*

A • Substitution Drill

MODEL   Hay una familia aquí.
                      profesor
STUDENT   Hay **un** profesor aquí.

1. Hay una familia aquí.
   profesor
   tienda
   alumno
   señorita
   cubana
   cubano
   chicana
   chicano

2. Aprendemos unas rumbas en clase.
   bailes
   canciones
   sambas
   versos
   bambas
   poemas
   bombas
   lecciones

[2] In Spanish, the indefinite article *is* used with unmodified nouns that follow **ser**, when the purpose is not merely to identify but to make the person or thing stand out: **Es poeta.** *He is a poet.* versus **¡Es un poeta!** *He is a poet!*

[3] Note that, as in English, the concept of "some" can also be conveyed simply by not using any article before the noun: **Venden tangos, bambas, bombas y guajiras.** *They sell (some) tangos, bambas, bombas, and guajiras.*

B • Transformation Drill   Plural → Singular

MODEL   unos hombres sinceros
STUDENT   **un hombre sincero**

1. unas casas nuevas
2. las canciones bonitas
3. unos días bonitos
4. los bailes fáciles
5. unos tonos admirables
6. las familias hispanas
7. unos mentirosos locos
8. las gitanas españolas
9. unos ejemplos tontos
10. las tiendas grandes

C • Replacement Drill   Definite Article → Indefinite Article

MODEL   ¿Compras la tienda?
STUDENT   ¿Compras **una** tienda?

1. ¿Vendes el disco?
2. Practico las canciones.
3. Reciben el verso de amor.
4. Aprendemos los bailes en casa.
5. ¿Escriben ustedes la composición?

Indefinite Article → Definite Article

6. Rubén aprende unas guajiras.
7. Raquel escribe un verso.
8. ¿No preparan una composición?
9. Tere practica un baile.
10. Es una casa bonita.

REVIEW

I   The following questions are related to the dialog. Answer in Spanish.

1. ¿Bailan el tango o bailan la samba en el Brasil?
2. ¿Aprende Raquel a cantar en la clase de baile?
3. ¿Es una canción bonita la "Guajira guantanamera"?
4. ¿Escribe Rubén poemas en clase o en casa?
5. ¿Dónde hay una tienda de discos?
6. ¿Qué bailes venden?
7. ¿Qué tiene un admirable tono moral?
8. ¿Quién es un mentiroso?

II   Translation.   Translate the following into Spanish.

1. How are you? Who are you? Where are you? Where are you from? Where are you going? When are you going?
2. Where is the record shop? Where is it? It's here. It's near here. It's very large.
3. We are learning all kinds of songs and dances from México and Puerto Rico.
4. Are you crazy? We write the homework at home; we do not write in mathematics class.
5. There are some persons around here who write Spanish.
6. I am going to buy a record in the store where they speak Spanish.
7. Is Rubén selling the record where Pete Seeger sings "Guajira guantanamera"?
8. Teresa is practicing the flamenco dances of the Spanish gypsies.

III   Write your own dialog.

You are going to buy some records. In Spanish you discuss what types of music there are with your friends José and Josefa.

PRONUNCIATION

Spanish Sounds Represented by More than One Spelling

Spellings	Sound	Examples
b, v	/b/	verde, bonito
j,[4] ge, gi	/h/	joven, general
s, z, ce, ci[5]	/s/	Sara, zebra, cera
ll,[6] y	/y/	lluvia, yunta

b and **v**   The written letters *b* and *v* are pronounced exactly alike by most Spanish speakers. In initial position the sound is similar to English *b*; in other places, particularly between vowels, the sound is weaker. Avoid the English *v* sound. Pronounce the following after your instructor.

1. vende	va	verde	Vicente
bien	baila	bonito	buenos días
2. se vende	se va	Rivera	vive
se baila	se bebe	ribera	escribe
3. vaca	boca	vista	banda
la vaca	la boca	la vista	la banda

[4] In America *x* is preferred to *j* in the spelling of the words **México, Nuevo México,** and **mexicano.**
[5] In parts of Spain, *z*, and *c* before *e* and *i*, are pronounced like the *th* in English *thing*.
[6] In parts of Spain, *ll* is pronounced like *lli* in English *million*.

j, ge, gi The written letters *j* and *g* before *e* or *i* are pronounced exactly alike. Pronounce the following words after your instructor.

1. joven   jirafa   ejemplo   guajira
   general   gigante   Argentina   región

2. Remember, *h* is silent.
   jirafa   gimnasio   jalamos   general
   hipopótamo   hispano   hablamos   henchir

s, z, ce, ci These letters are pronounced exactly alike in most Spanish-speaking areas. Pronounce the following after your instructor.

1. Sara   zona   zebra   ciega
   cera   sonata   cebra   siega

2. haces   casas   hacia   pase
   ases   cazas   Asia   pace

ll, y These letters are pronounced exactly alike in almost all Spanish-speaking areas. Pronounce the following after your instructor.

1. llama   lluvia   malla   silla
   yema   yunta   maya   suya

Mexico City

Cognates & Contexts

Pronounce the following passages out loud several times.
Try to understand each passage in Spanish.

MARTA   Hay una tienda grande por aquí donde venden
        discos.

MARÍA   ¿Ah, sí? ¡Qué bien! ¿Y venden discos latino-
        americanos?

MARTA   No muchos.

MARÍA   ¡Ay! ¡Qué lástima!   **¡Qué lástima!** *What a shame!*

MARTA   Pero también hay una tienda pequeña cerca de
        aquí donde especializan en música latinoamericana.

MARÍA   ¡Magnífico!

Yo canto toda clase de canciones. Canto canciones bonitas
y canto canciones feas. Canto canciones tontas, insinceras y
triviales pero también canto canciones tremendas, inteli-
gentes y de admirable tono moral. Canto canciones acerca   **acerca de** *about, concerning*
de la tierra y el mar, la inocencia de los niños y el cinismo de   **tierra** *land, earth*   **niños** *children*
los adultos. En fin, ¡la vida!   **en fin** *in short*   **vida** *life*

¿Qué hay de nuevo, Juan, cómo estás?   **¿Qué hay de nuevo?** *What's new?*
Estoy bien, gracias. ¿Y tú?
Así así, regular.
¿Y tú, Rosa?
Estoy mal, horrible.
¡Oh! ¡Qué lástima!

Student demonstration, Panama

Lección tres

REUNIÓN ESTUDIANTIL EN UNA UNIVERSIDAD LATINOAMERICANA

reunión *meeting*
estudiantil *student* (adj.)

ÁLVARO	¡Compañeros! Aquí viene Carlos Posada, nuestro líder del comité estudiantil.
CARMEN	Carlos, ¿qué ocurre en la oficina del rector?
EUGENIO	Carlos, ¿van a aceptar nuestras demandas?
CARLOS	Vengo con noticias importantes. El rector acepta muchas de nuestras demandas. Por ejemplo, van a abrir la biblioteca los domingos.
	Sin embargo, desea más tiempo para estudiar
	las demandas y consultar con el profesorado y la autoridad sobre otros puntos.
MÓNICA	¿Por qué no consulta más con los estudiantes?
ÁLVARO	¿Qué vamos a hacer?
CARLOS	Mi opinión es dar al rector una oportunidad. Tenemos su palabra de honor. Él desea ayudar pero necesita más tiempo.
EUGENIO	El rector es buena gente. Pero la autoridad

venir *to come*

¿qué ocurre? *what's happening?* **rector** *president (of university)*

noticias *news*

por ejemplo *for example*

abrir *to open* **biblioteca** *library* **los domingos** *on Sundays*
sin embargo *however* **desear** *to want* **para** *in order to* **estudiar** *to study*
profesorado *faculty*

autoridad *the authorities* **sobre otros puntos** *on other points*

hacer *to do*

dar *to give*

tener *to have* **palabra** *word* **ayudar** *to help*

gente *people*

	municipal sencillamente no ayuda. La situación es ambigua. Tenemos que insistir.	**sencillamente** *simply* **tener que** *to have to*
MÓNICA	Tenemos que actuar democráticamente. Hay que votar.	**hay que** *one has to; it is necessary to*
CARMEN	Sí. ¡Tenemos que votar!	
CARLOS	O esperamos unos días o seguimos con nuestra protesta. Hay que decidir.	**o... o** *either ... or* **esperar** *to wait (for)* **seguimos** (from **seguir**) *we continue*
ÁLVARO	Tienen que conceder el dinero para la clínica dental.	**conceder** *to grant* **dinero** *money*
CARMEN	Y si no, continuamos nuestras actividades militantes y cerramos la universidad.	**si** *if* **cerramos** (from **cerrar**) *we close*
MÓNICA	¿Y si todavía no conceden el dinero?	**todavía** *still*
EUGENIO	Entonces... entonces la situación va a ser muy grave.	
CARLOS	¡Tenemos que luchar por la justicia social!	**luchar** *to fight*
TODOS	¡Siempre! ¡Adelante! ¡Libertad y progreso! ¡Venceremos!	**¡Adelante!** *Forward!* **¡Venceremos!** *We shall triumph!*

57

NOTES

The Suffix -mente

The Spanish suffix **-mente** is added to adjectives (in the feminine form if the adjective makes a masculine/feminine distinction) to form adverbs of manner. Thus Spanish **-mente** = English *-ly*.

> If **sencilla** is *simple* and **sencillamente** is *simply*, what are the following?
>
> | | |
> |---|---|
> | realmente | generalmente |
> | totalmente | exactamente |
> | sinceramente | democráticamente[1] |

Plural Versus Singular in English and Spanish

Occasionally a noun that is singular (or plural) in Spanish will not be singular (or plural) in English. In the context above **la autoridad** is translated *the authorities*. Another such example is **las vacaciones** *the vacation*. On the other hand, *the news is* = **las noticias son** in Spanish.

Vocabulary Meanings

buena gente   *decent guy*. Normally **gente** means *people* (it is a collective noun); here it is used idiomatically.

¿Por qué? Porque, A causa de

¿por qué? *why?*

¿Por qué no consulta con los estudiantes?   *Why doesn't he consult with the students?*

porque (+ clause) *because*

Porque necesita más tiempo.   *Because he needs more time.*

a causa de (+ object) *because of*

A causa de la protesta, conceden el dinero.   *Because of the protest, they grant the money.*

---

[1] If the adjective form has a written accent, the adverb form retains the accent.

Library of the National
University of Mexico,
Mexico City

LANGUAGE STRUCTURES

13 Present indicative of **tener**, *to have* and **venir**, *to come*

tener	*venir*
tengo	**vengo**
tienes	**vienes**
tiene	**viene**
tenemos	venimos
tienen	**vienen**

A • Substitution Drill

MODEL   Juana viene mucho a la universidad.
Tú
STUDENT   Tú **vienes** mucho a la universidad.

1. Mónica viene mucho a la universidad.
Tú
Yo
Eugenio
Ellos
Nosotros

2. ¿Tienen ellos su palabra de honor?
nosotros
los estudiantes
ella y él
tú y yo
tú

B • Query   Patterned Response

MODEL   ¿De dónde viene? ¿De Madrid?
STUDENT   **Sí, compañero. Vengo** de Madrid.

1. ¿Qué tengo? ¿Muchas demandas?
2. ¿Qué vamos a hacer? ¿Protestar?
3. ¿Quién viene? ¿El rector?
4. ¿Qué desean los estudiantes? ¿La justicia social?
5. ¿Con qué viene Carlos? ¿Con noticias importantes?
6. ¿Dónde tienen las actividades? ¿En la universidad?
7. ¿Quiénes tienen su palabra de honor? ¿Los estudiantes?
8. ¿Cómo es la situación? ¿Grave?
9. ¿Qué van a abrir? ¿La biblioteca?
10. ¿Dónde está la universidad? ¿En Latinoamérica?

C • Query   Free Response

Answer in Spanish.

1. ¿Viene usted siempre a la clase de español?
2. ¿Qué ocurre en la clase de matemáticas?
3. ¿Tienes los libros?
4. ¿Desea usted ir a Latinoamérica?
5. ¿Son sinceros los estudiantes militantes?
6. ¿Tienen mucho dinero las autoridades?
7. ¿Es buena gente el profesor (la profesora)?
8. ¿Necesita usted más tiempo para estudiar?

14 **Tener que** and **hay que**

▶ The idiomatic expression **tener que** + infinitive indicates necessity and means *to have to*. **Hay que** + infinitive has the same meaning on an impersonal level.

1. Tengo que protestar.   *I have to protest.*
2. Hay que votar.   *We (one, everyone) must vote;*
                                             it is necessary to vote.
3. Tenemos que tener el dinero ahora.   *We have to have money now.*
4. ¿Hay que ir?   *Do we (does one) have to go?*

A • Substitution Drill

MODEL   Carlos tiene que decidir.
           Los estudiantes
STUDENT   Los estudiantes **tienen** que decidir.

1. Ellos tienen que actuar democráticamente.   2. Hay que votar.
   El rector   ir.
   Yo   preparar la tarea.
   Usted   luchar por la causa.
   Ustedes   consultar con el rector.
   Carmen   esperar unos días.

B • Query   Patterned Response

MODEL   ¿Hay que ir?
STUDENT   **Sí,** hay que ir.

MODEL   ¿Tengo que ir?
STUDENT   **Sí, tienes** que ir.

1. ¿Hay que protestar?
2. ¿Tienes que protestar?
3. ¿Hay que luchar por la justicia social?
4. ¿Tienen los chicanos y los boricuas que luchar por la justicia social?
5. ¿Hay que votar?
6. ¿Tiene usted que votar?
7. ¿Hay que conceder el dinero?
8. ¿Tenemos que conceder el dinero?
9. ¿Hay que aceptar las demandas?
10. ¿Tienes que aceptar las demandas?
11. ¿Hay que escribir versos?
12. ¿Tiene que escribir versos Rubén?

15 Verbs that take a preposition before an object. The contraction **al**

▶ Recall that **ir** and other verbs of motion (such as **venir**) take an **a** before an object (infinitive or noun). This **a**, which is not translated when the object is an infinitive, functions to indicate the "forward" direction of the verb. In addition, verbs of teaching, learning, and beginning take **a** before an infinitive.

    1. Van a la reunión.   *They are going to the meeting.*
    2. ¿Vienen a la protesta?   *Are they coming to the protest?*
    3. Aprendo a hablar español.   *I am learning to speak Spanish.*
    4. ¿Vienes a preparar la lección? *Are you coming to prepare the lesson?*

▶ As in English, these verbs can also be followed by other prepositions.

    1. Van de California a Nueva York. *They are going from California to New York.*
    2. Vengo con noticias importantes.   *I come with important news.*
    3. Aprendemos de la profesora.   *We learn from the professor.*

▶ When **a** is followed by the definite article **el**, the two words are pronounced and written as one: **al**. There is no contraction formed with the other definite articles.

    ¿Vienes al baile?   *Are you coming to the dance?*

▶ In subsequent lessons you will encounter other verbs that require a preposition to complete their meaning.

A • Substitution Drill

    MODEL   Voy al baile.
                    casa.
    STUDENT Voy **a la** casa.

Voy al baile.
      universidad.
      aprender.
      cantar.
      comité.
      tiendas.
      biblioteca.
      oficina.
      escribir.

B • Translation Drill

Translate the following into Spanish.

1. They are going to go.
2. They are going to come.
3. Carlos is coming to the dance.
4. Pepita comes to learn.

5. Where are you going?
6. Where are you coming from?
   (From where are you coming?)
7. Is he going with Carmen?
8. They are coming from the store.

16 Possession.   The contraction **del**

▶ To express possession, Spanish does not use the apostrophe as English often does (John's), but instead uses the preposition **de**.

1. El lider del comité.   *The leader of the committee.*
2. La protesta de los estudiantes.   *The students' protest.*
3. El disco de Rubén.   *Rubén's record.*
4. El disco es de Rubén.   *The record is Rubén's.*
5. ¿Dónde está la oficina del rector?   *Where is the president's office?*

▶ When **de** is followed by the definite article **el,** the two words are pronounced and written as one: **del** (examples 1 and 5). **Al** and **del** are the only contractions in standard written Spanish.

A • Substitution Drill

MODEL   El verso es de los muchachos.
                              compañero.
STUDENT   El verso es **del** compañero.

El verso es de los muchachos.
                muchachas.
                rector.
                poetas.
                poeta.
                líder.
                profesora.
                profesor.
                señorita.

B • Translation Drill

Translate the following into Spanish.

1. Tere's house.
2. Paco's record.
3. The students' poem.
4. The boys' family.

5. It's Juan's homework.
6. Where is the student's composition?
7. What is the faculty's decision?
8. We have the authorities' money.

17 Possessive adjectives

Singular (one thing possessed)	*Plural* (more than one thing possessed)	
mi	mis	*my*
tu[2]	tus	*your* (fam.)
su	**sus**[3]	*your* (formal)
		his, her, its
nuestro, nuestra	nuestros, nuestras	*our*
su	**sus**[3]	*your* (plural)
		their

▶ Possessive adjectives agree in number with the noun they modify. Thus they agree with *the thing possessed* and *not* with the possessor. In addition, **nuestro, nuestra** agree in gender. These possessive forms precede the noun.[4]

Singular (one thing possessed)

1. mi disco, mi canción
   my record, my song
2. tu hermano, tu hermana
   your brother, your sister

3. su tienda, su profesor
   his, her, your (singular
   and plural), *its, their*
   store, professor

4. nuestro amor, nuestra composición
   our love, our composition

Plural (more than one thing possessed)

mis discos, mis canciones
   my records, my songs
tus hermanos, tus hermanas
   your brothers or brothers and sisters,
   your sisters

sus tiendas, sus profesores
   his, her, your (singular and plural),
   its, their stores, professors

nuestros amores, nuestras composiciones
   our loves, our compositions

Su dinero.   Su dinero.
Her money.   *Their money.*

---

[2] Be sure not to confuse **tu** (the adjective) with **tú** (the pronoun):
   Tú hablas español.   *You speak Spanish.*
   Tu compañero está aquí.   *Your companion (friend) is here.*

[3] The **vosotros** form of possessive adjectives can be found in the Appendix, section **1**.

[4] See section **64** for the possessive adjectives that follow the noun.

Your money.   *Your money.*

A • Substitution Drill

MODEL   Nuestro líder escribe bien.
        profesora
STUDENT   **Nuestra** profesora escribe bien.

1. Nuestro líder escribe bien.
    rector
    líderes
    alumnas
    alumna
    poeta

2. Mis versos son sinceros.
    Mi
    Sus
    Su
    Tu
    Nuestros

B • Query   Patterned Response

MODEL   ¿Dónde está su casa? ¿La casa de Mónica y Raquel?
STUDENT   **La casa de Mónica y Raquel está aquí.**

1 ¿Dónde está su disco? ¿El disco de Carlos?
2 ¿Dónde están sus discos? ¿Los discos de Rafael?
3. ¿Dónde está su disco? ¿El disco de Juana?
4. ¿Dónde están sus discos? ¿Los discos de Mónica?
5. ¿Dónde está su composición? ¿La composición de Rafa y Pancho?
6. ¿Dónde están sus composiciones? ¿Las composiciones de Eugenio y Álvaro?
7. ¿Dónde están sus composiciones? ¿Las composiciones de Eugenio?
8. ¿Dónde está su composición? ¿La composición de Rafa?
9. ¿Dónde están tus ejemplos? ¿Los ejemplos de música latina?
10. ¿Dónde está tu libro? ¿El libro de versos?

C • Query   Patterned Response

MODEL   ¿Dónde está el comité de los estudiantes?
STUDENT   **Su comité está aquí.**

1. ¿Dónde está la clase de los estudiantes?
2. ¿Dónde está la casa de los profesores?

3. ¿Dónde está la familia de la señorita Azuela?
4. ¿Dónde está la oficina del rector?
5. ¿Dónde están los versos del compañero?
6. ¿Dónde están los versos de los poetas?
7. ¿Dónde está la biblioteca de la universidad?
8. ¿Dónde está la biblioteca de las alumnas?
9. ¿Dónde está la clínica del profesorado?
10. ¿Dónde están las oficinas de las autoridades?

D • Query Patterned Response su/sus → mi/mis

(singular) MODEL   ¿Es perspicaz su profesor?
STUDENT   **Sí, mi profesor es perspicaz.**

(plural)   MODEL   ¿Son sinceros sus profesores?
STUDENT   **Sí, mis profesores son sinceros.**

1. ¿Es chicana su profesora?
2. ¿Habla inglés su familia?
3. ¿Son buenos sus discos?
4. ¿Es grande su universidad?
5. ¿Son sinceros sus amores?
6. ¿Es grave su situación?
7. ¿Son importantes sus demandas?
8. ¿Son militantes sus actividades?
9. ¿Es grande su familia?
10. ¿Es sincera su opinión?

E • Translation Drill

Translate the following into Spanish.

1. his house, her house, its house, your (formal) house
2. their day, your (plural) day
3. my family, my country, my poems
4. your (familiar) homework, your (familiar) lessons
5. our situation, our committees, our compositions, our faculty

18 The usual position of adjectives

▶ Descriptive adjectives, which tell something about the nature of a noun (size, shape, color, nationality, affiliation, etc.), are usually placed after the noun.

▶ Limiting adjectives (definite and indefinite articles, numerals, possessive adjectives, etc.) are usually placed before the noun.

▶ There are significant exceptions to the above. These will be covered in subsequent lessons.

Examples:

1. El comité estudiantil, la justicia social.   *The student committee, social justice.*
2. Nuestras actividades militantes.   *Our militant activities.*
3. Una autoridad municipal.   *A municipal authority.*
4. Muchos otros hispanos.   *Many other Hispanos.*
5. ¿En qué otras partes?   *Where else? (In what other areas?)*
6. Unas canciones bonitas y sinceras.   *Some pretty, sincere songs.*
7. Todos los hombres.   *All men (or All the men).*

▶ More than one limiting adjective may precede a noun (as in examples 4 and 5); usually two descriptive adjectives are placed after a noun and are connected by **y** (example 6). **Todo** precedes the article, as in English (example 7).

A • Variable Substitution Drill

Complete each sentence, using the preceding one as a model and changing only what is required by the cue.

MODEL   Los gitanos practican una canción bonita.
         Un
STUDENT   Un **gitano practica** una canción bonita.

Los gitanos practican una canción bonita.
Unos
     gitano
Muchos
Muchas

                              bonitas.
                              sinceras.
                              sincera.
                 versos
                              simpático.
              baile
Otras
Otros
            muchos

B • Query   Patterned Response

MODEL   ¿Quién es y dónde está?   mi profesor / en la oficina del rector
STUDENT   **Es mi profesor y está en la oficina del rector.**

1. ¿Quién es y dónde está?   nuestro líder estudiantil / con sus compañeros
2. ¿Quién es y dónde está?   la señorita Azuela / en la biblioteca de la universidad

3. ¿Quiénes son y dónde están?   estudiantes militantes / en una universidad latinoamericana
4. ¿Qué es y dónde está?   una clínica dental / en la Avenida de las Américas
5. ¿Qué es y dónde está?   una canción admirable / en el disco de Pete Seeger
6. ¿Qué es y dónde está?   una tienda de discos / en Nueva York
7. ¿Quién es y dónde está?   Carlos Posada / en casa, con su familia
8. ¿Quién es y dónde está?   una muchacha que recibe versos / en la clase de matemáticas
9. ¿Quiénes son y dónde están?   unos estudiantes de español / en la clase de español
10. ¿Qué son y dónde están?   canciones latinoamericanas / en la tienda de discos

REVIEW

I   The following questions are related to the dialog. Answer in Spanish.

1. ¿Quién es Carlos Posada?
2. ¿De dónde viene Carlos Posada?
3. ¿Qué desean los estudiantes?
4. ¿Acepta el rector unas demandas del comité estudiantil?
5. ¿Con quién desea consultar el rector?
6. ¿Cuándo van a abrir la biblioteca?
7. ¿Qué van a hacer los estudiantes?
8. ¿Quiénes tienen que luchar por la justicia social?

II   Translation.   Translate the following into Spanish.

1. What is happening? Who is coming? Where are you going? What do you have?
2. What do you have to do? Where are we going to go?
3. If they don't accept our demands we have to protest. We shall triumph!
4. The president (**rector**) has to have more time. He wants to talk with the leader of our student committee.
5. Mónica's sister goes to the library on Sundays in order to prepare her homework.
6. We have to (one has to) act democratically, but we have to (one has to) fight for social justice.
7. Do I write my composition or do I wait a few days?
8. We have some important news. We have the professor's word of honor.

III   Write your own dialog.

You are participating in a protest concerning the conditions at your school. You and your fellow students are preparing a list of demands for the president and faculty.

Campus of the University of the
Andes, Bogotá, Colombia

PRONUNCIATION

Dividing Words into Syllables

A. In Spanish, when vowels are separated by consonants, usually there are as many syllables as there are vowels. Each consonant forms a syllable with the vowel following it. The word **medicina**, for example, has four vowels (**e, i, i, a**) and therefore four syllables: **me-di-ci-na**.

B. Two strong vowels (**a, e, o**) occurring together form separate syllables: **cre-o, cre-e, tra-e, ba-ca-la-o, pro-a.**

C. The vowels **i** and **u** are called weak vowels. Combinations of a strong and a weak vowel or of two weak vowels normally form single syllables. Such combinations are called diphthongs (see page 10). Examples: **bue-no, fa-mi-lia, ciu-dad, Eu-ro-pa, bai-le.**

D. When a strong and weak vowel occur together, a written accent mark on the weak vowel divides the two vowels into separate syllables (there is no diphthong): **Ra-úl, dí-a, pa-ís.**

An accent on the strong vowel of such combinations does not result in two syllables: **lec-ción, tam-bién.**

E. When two consonants occur together, they are usually divided: **es-pa-ñol, tam-bién, lec-ción.**

Remember that **ch, ll,** and **rr** are considered one consonant: **mu-cho, lla-ma, pe-rro.**

Consonants followed by **l** or **r,** however, generally form a cluster (are pronounced together) and form one syllable with the following vowel: **li-bro, ma-dre, pre-pa-ro.**

Exceptions are the groups **nl, rl, sl, tl, nr,** and **sr: en-la-ce, Car-los, is-la, At-lán-ti-co, En-ri-que, Is-ra-el.**

F. In combinations of three or more consonants only the last consonant or the clusters mentioned above (consonant plus **l** or **r**) begin a syllable: **trans-por-te, in-glés, hom-bre, siem-pre.**

 Exercises

These words follow rule A. Pronounce them and then divide into syllables.

médico	Colorado	cubano	todos
señorita	americanos	recibe	rosa

These words follow rule B. Pronounce them and then divide them into syllables.

caer	caos	león	posta
pasear	océano	leo	lee

These words follow rule C. Pronounce them and then divide them into syllables.

reina	siete	causa	tienda
deuda	guapa	baile	guajira

These words follow rule E. Pronounce them and then divide them into syllables.

canciones	venden	hasta	termino
aprende	padre	practico	perla

Cognates & Contexts

Bullring, Bogotá, Colombia

EUGENIO En nuestra sociedad, en todas las sociedades, siempre hay personas buenas y personas malas. Tiene que ser así.

ÁLVARO Sí, pero el fenómeno es muy relativo. Depende del grupo social. Un acto admirable en una sociedad particular es un acto horrible en otra. Por ejemplo, en nuestra sociedad matar un toro en una corrida de toros es un acto artístico. Pero estimamos el fútbol americano en los Estados Unidos como un deporte bárbaro, cruel. Y vice versa, los norteamericanos estiman que el fútbol americano es un deporte sano y que la corrida de toros es un espectáculo depravado y cruel.

matar *to kill* **toro** *bull*
  corrida de toros *bullfight*

deporte *sport*

sano *healthy*

EUGENIO   No, no, no. Todos los hombres tienen nociones sólidas de la moralidad. Y si aceptan esas nociones son buenos. Y si no, son malos, hipócritas, viciosos, depravados, inhumanos. Tus ejemplos son triviales. Los toros y el fútbol no son ejemplos de la moralidad o de la inmoralidad. Son excepciones históricas, costumbres características de una sociedad.

ÁLVARO   Mmm. ¿Qué eres tú? ¿Filósofo? ¿O sofista?

sofista *sophist, a captious reasoner*

Paseo del Río, San Antonio, Texas

Lección cuatro

Lectura y estudio

CARTA AL HERMANO[1]

San Antonio, Texas, 2 de octubre de 1978

Querido hermano Pablo:

Tu carta acaba de llegar y voy a contestar ahora.

Mis impresiones de esta ciudad y de la gente que vive aquí son muy buenas. Es un poco como estar en casa. Ya ves que San Antonio es un nombre español y muchas calles y avenidas también tienen nombres españoles. Yo vivo con un compañero en la calle Camarón y él ríe mucho cuando digo "Tú vives en 'Shrimp Street'."

También hay muchas comidas similares a las comidas mexicanas. Aquí nuestras tostadas son "corn chips" y son muy populares. Los americanos creen que tienen algo especial con sus "grits" —no saben que comemos toda clase de maíz en México desde tiempos antiguos.

Muchos alumnos en la universidad son chicanos y hablan español pero a veces usan palabras distintas que toman del inglés. Sus padres o sus abuelos llevan

querido *dear*

carta *letter*   **acaba de llegar** *just arrived*   **contestar** *to answer*
esta ciudad *this city*

ver *to see*   **nombre** *name*

calles *streets*

vivir *to live*

ríe (from **reír**) *he laughs*   **digo** (from **decir**) *I say*

comidas *foods; meals*

creer *to believe*   **algo** *something*

saber *to know*   **comer** *to eat*
maíz *corn*
desde tiempos antiguos *since ancient times*

a veces *at times*   **distinto** *different*

tomar *to take*   **padres** *parents*
abuelos *grandparents*

[1] New vocabulary in the Lectura will not be considered active vocabulary until it appears in subsequent lessons.

muchos años aquí y tienen un vocabulario algo diferente del mexicano. Pero el resultado es curioso y muy expresivo.

Mañana voy a ir a un festival en "La Villita", que es un barrio restaurado cerca del río San Antonio. Van a presentar canciones y bailes auténticos de México. La autoridad municipal desea informar a los ciudadanos que no toda nuestra música es de mariachis con pistolas. ¡Qué bien!

En mi próxima carta a mamá voy a incluir detalles del programa bilingüe que tienen en la Universidad de México en San Antonio. Estoy contento de tener la oportunidad de participar en sus proyectos urbanos. Parece que los resultados son muy buenos. Con las facilidades que hay y la libre comunicación en inglés y español, todos vamos a ser bilingües en poco tiempo.

Con un abrazo cariñoso para toda la familia te dice adiós por ahora,

Andrés

llevan muchos años *have spent many years*
algo *somewhat*

mañana *tomorrow*

barrio *neighborhood* **río** *river*

ciudadanos *citizens*

próxima *next* **incluir** *to include*
detalles *details*

estar contento *to be happy*

parece *it seems*

libre *free*

en poco tiempo *in a short time*

un abrazo cariñoso *a warm hug*

por ahora *for now*

NOTES

Letter Writing

The format for writing letters in Spanish varies only slightly from the English. The place and date of writing are usually on one line, separated by a comma. The date is given with the day preceding the month (which is not capitalized). Remember that **de** indicates *of*, so it is the *2 (nd) of October of 1978*. While English might abbreviate October 2, 1978 to 10/2/78, Spanish uses its own word order, the month often expressed in Roman numerals: 2/X/78.

The opening greeting, even to family and close friends, is often more effusive than we see in English.

> **Mi queridísima amiga Adela:**   *My dearest friend Adela,*

is not uncommon. But this greeting is punctuated by a colon, which English associates with more formal letters.

In closing, the writer will frequently refer to himself in the third person, making the signature complete a phrase:

> Recuerdos a todos de   Regards to all from
> Andrés   Andrés

Formal letters will be dealt with in a later lesson.

Restaurant, Oaxaca, Mexico

VOCABULARY STUDY

Some nouns do not have the gender that their endings suggest. Many such words end in **-ma**.

el poeta	el poema
el día	el drama
el problema	el idioma
el tema	

Here are more matched nouns that do not change their endings to indicate gender.

el hipócrita, la hipócrita	el joven, la joven
el sofista, la sofista	el estudiante, la estudiante

Learn the gender of these words.

el deporte	el comité
el suroeste	la gente
el fútbol	la parte
el país (*country*, as in *nation*)	

Accents are important! Be sure you know the difference between these words.

tu	el	si	porque	como
tú	él	sí	¿por qué?	¿cómo?

Srta. = **señorita**   *miss*
 Sra. = **señora**   *Mrs., lady*
 Sr. = **señor**   *Mr., sir, man*

Remember:
   otro = *another;* never say "un otro"
   acerca de = *about, concerning*
   cerca de = *near*

Rompecabezas

Unscramble the following:

¡IS ÚT CRIBESES NEIB DASTO SAL BRASPALA, SERE YUM SPICAZPER!

¡Cuidado!

Here are some words that, although similar to English in spelling, are quite different in meaning. Such words are called *false cognates*.

regular = *so-so,* not *regular* (Do you remember another Spanish expression with this meaning?)

relativo = *relative, as compared to,* not *family.*
What does **relativamente** mean?

pariente = *relative* (family)

sano = *healthy*

cuerdo = *sane*

idioma = *language,* not *idiom*

modismo = *idiom*

viciosos = *addicted to vice, depraved, perverted,* not *vicious*

librería = *bookstore*

biblioteca = *library*

A • Give the antonyms for the underlined words.

1. Mi profesor es muy antipático.
2. Tenemos una idea buena.
3. ¿Tere y Pablo van a comprar unos discos?
4. ¿Ayudas a Paco a cerrar la tienda?
5. Mi país es pequeño y muy hermoso.
6. Hoy vamos a hablar acerca de la moralidad de una corrida de toros.

Give the synonyms for the underlined words.

7. Mónica es una alumna muy perspicaz.
8. Carlos escribe poemas excelentes.
9. ¿Es guapa la señorita Salcedo?

B • Complete each sentence with words from the list. The words are to be used in the form in which they appear.

versos	profesora	practican
preparan	clase	discos
tienda	bailar	poeta

1. La _____ presenta la lección a la _____.
2. Los alumnos _____ y _____ la lección.

3. Juana aprende a _____ la bamba en la clase de baile.
4. Los compañeros compran _____ latinoamericanos en la _____ de discos.
5. El _____ escribe muchos _____.

¿Cómo?	reunión	luchar
palabra	cantar	días
biblioteca	país	rector

6. Hola. Buenos _____. ¿_____ está usted?
7. Hay una _____ estudiantil en la _____.
8. Hay que _____ la canción en español.
9. Tenemos que _____ por la justicia social en nuestro _____.
10. Carlos y Eugenio tienen la _____ de honor del _____.

familia	tonto	problemas
casa	hermano	mentiroso
dinero	esperar	demandas

11. Siempre ocurre cuando necesito terminar la tarea: viene mi _____ pequeño para hablar de sus _____.
12. La autoridad concede el _____ para la clínica dental, pero desea _____ unos días.
13. Nuestro líder es un _____ y también es un _____.
14. Los jóvenes reciben ayuda porque sus _____ son sinceras.
15. ¿Por qué no hablas español en _____, entre _____?

C • Make questions for the following statements, using interrogative words. There may be more than one possible question for each statement.

MODEL   Mi compañera va a la reunión.
STUDENT   **¿Quién va a la reunión?**
or
¿Adónde va su compañera?

1. Tengo muchos discos en casa.
2. La muchacha viene de Cuba.
3. Estudiamos el español porque vamos a España.
4. Vamos a la biblioteca los domingos.
5. El estudiante escribe versos bonitos.
6. Deseo comprar el disco.
7. Mi país es los Estados Unidos.
8. Las autoridades no tienen el dinero.
9. Juana y Mónica van a la universidad por aquí.
10. Tú esperas cerca de tu casa.

GRAMMAR: SELF-TESTING

Cover the right side of the page and try to answer the questions in the left margin.

VERBS

Present Tense

REGULAR VERBS   (*Sections 2, 7*)

The infinitives of all verbs in Spanish end in **-ar**, **-er**, or **-ir**.

What are the infinitive endings in Spanish?

What are the present tense endings for **-ar** *verbs? For* **-er** *verbs? For* **-ir** *verbs?*

To conjugate regular verbs in the present tense, drop the infinitive endings and add the present tense endings.

	habl-ar *to speak*	**aprend-er** *to learn*	**escrib-ir** *to write*
yo	-o	-o	-o
tú	-as	-es	-es
Ud., él, ella	habl -a	aprend -e	escrib -e
nosotros (-as)	-amos	-emos	-imos
Uds., ellos, ellas	-an	-en	-en

IRREGULAR VERBS   (*Sections 3, 8, 9, 13*)

You have learned some irregular verbs in Spanish. How is **estar** *conjugated?* **Ser?** **Ir?**

estar *to be* (location/condition)	**ser** *to be* (inherent characteristic)	**ir** *to go*
estoy	soy	voy
estás	eres	vas
está	es	va
estamos	somos	vamos
están	son	van

How are **tener** *and* **venir** *similar in the present?*

venir *to come*	**tener** *to have*
vengo	tengo
vienes	tienes
viene	tiene
venimos	tenemos
vienen	tienen

NOUNS

What are common masculine endings for nouns? Examples?

What are common feminine endings? Examples?

How is the plural of nouns formed?

What are the feminine forms of **profesor** and **español** (*Spaniard*)? What rule does this illustrate?

GENDER AND NUMBER OF NOUNS (*Section 5*)

All nouns in Spanish are either masculine or feminine, singular or plural.

Most nouns ending in **-o** or **-or** are masculine.

el disco	el color
el hermano	el profesor

Most nouns ending in **-a**, **-ad**, **-ud**, or **-ión** are feminine.

la alumna	la quietud
la universidad	la lección

Singular nouns ending in a vowel add **-s** to form the plural; when they end in a consonant, they add **-es**.

estudiante	estudiantes
autoridad	autoridades

Nouns of nationality or occupation add **-a** to masculine singular consonant endings to form the feminine noun.

español	española
profesor	profesora

ARTICLES

What are the definite articles in Spanish?

In what way do definite articles agree with the nouns they refer to?

Are definite articles used with languages?

What are the indefinite articles in Spanish?

DEFINITE ARTICLES   (*Section 4*)

el, la, los, las

They precede the noun they refer to and agree with it in gender and number.

Definite articles are used with the names of languages except when the languages immediately follow the verb **hablar.**

Hablamos inglés, pero estudiamos el español.

INDEFINITE ARTICLES   (*Section 12*)

Un, una, unos, unas

Do they agree with the noun they refer to?

They precede the noun they refer to and agree with it in gender and number.

When are indefinite articles omitted after **ser**?

They are not used after **ser** with unmodified nouns that are not being emphasized.

> **Ella es profesora.**

How is the idea of "some" conveyed in Spanish?

Unos, **unas** convey the idea of "some."

> **Deseo comprar unos discos.** *I wish to buy some records.*

ADJECTIVES

In what way do adjectives agree with the nouns they modify?

Adjectives agree in gender and in number with the nouns they modify (*Section 10*).

Is there a gender distinction for adjectives ending in **-e**?

Adjectives ending in **-e** do not have separate forms for masculine and feminine (*Section 10*).

> **La alumna inteligente.**
> **El alumno inteligente.**

How are adjectives usually placed in relation to the nouns they modify?

Adjectives that describe normally follow the noun; adjectives that limit precede the noun (*Section 18*).

> **la muchacha bonita**   **dos lecciones**
> **el alumno perspicaz**   **unos discos**

What are the possessive adjectives in Spanish?

Possessive adjectives (*Section 17*):

mi, mis	nuestro, nuestra
	nuestros, nuestras
tu, tus	
su, sus	su, sus

How are possessive adjectives placed in relation to the nouns they modify? Do they agree in number and gender?

Possessive adjectives precede the noun and agree with it in number; **nuestro**, **nuestra** also agree in gender (*Section 17*).

How else does Spanish indicate possession?

Possession is also indicated by **de** + noun (*Section 16*).

> **El disco de Rubén.**   *Rubén's record.*
> **La casa es de Carmen.**   *The house is Carmen's.*

Is an apostrophe used in Spanish?	An apostrophe is not used in Spanish (*Section 16*).

ADVERBS

How are adverbs derived from adjectives in Spanish?	Adverbs are derived by adding **-mente** to the form of the adjective that modifies a feminine noun (see page 60).

sencillamente   generalmente
totalmente   democráticamente

REMEMBER!

- *It* is not expressed as a subject in Spanish (*Section 1*).

    Es interesante.   *It is interesting.*

- **a** + **el** = **al** (*Section 15*)
  de + **el** = **del** (*Section 16*)

- **Hay** = *there is*, *there are* (impersonal) (*Section 11*)

    Hay un problema.   *There is a problem.*
    Hay dos alumnos en la clase.   *There are two students in the class.*

- The masculine plural of nouns or pronouns may include both genders.

    los hermanos   *the brothers* or *the brother(s) and sister(s)*

- **Ir** is followed by **a** before a destination or an infinitive (*Section 15*).

- In questions use **¿adónde?** with **ir** and other verbs of motion when referring to a goal or destination (*Section 9*).

    ¿Adónde vas?   *Where are you going?*

- The present tense of **ir a** + infinitive may be used to express the future, as in the English *to be going* + infinitive (*Section 9*).

    Voy a escribir una composición.   *I'm going to write a composition.*

- In negative sentences (*Section 6*), place **no** before the verb.

    Tere no va a la tienda.   *Tere isn't going to the store.*

- Interrogative sentences (*Section 6*) are formed by
    - (a) inversion of subject-verb order

        ¿Escribe Rafael poemas?   *Does Rafael write poems?*

    - (b) intonation

        ¿Hay clases los domingos?   *Are there classes on Sundays?*

- Question marks surround the actual question.

    Señorita Azuela, ¿cómo está usted?   *Miss Azuela, how are you?*

- Interrogative words are accented.

    ¿quién?   **¿adónde?**
    ¿cómo?   **¿por qué?** etc.

A • Variable Substitution Drill

MODEL   Carlos canta una canción cubana.
                          cantas   bonitas.
STUDENT   **Tú** cantas **unas canciones** bonitas.

1. Tú   escribes   unos   versos   bonitos.
2. Carlos   canciones
3.   canta   tonta.
4. Mónica y yo   española.
5.   aprendemos la
6. Ustedes   fútbol americano.
7.   tienen   discos
8. Juana y Tere   unos   cubanos.
9.   bailan   baile
10. Yo   chachachás.

B • Completion Drill

Complete the sentences with the correct form of the verb indicated in parentheses.

MODEL   (ser)   Yo _____ un militante sincero, no hipócrita.
STUDENT   Yo **soy** un militante sincero, no hipócrita.

1. (ser)   Nosotros _____ un grupo de militantes sinceros, no hipócritas.
2. (desear)   ¿Quién no _____ nuevos ejemplos de justicia social?
3. (recibir)   Los chicanos y otros hispanos no _____ las oportunidades de otros grupos sociales.
4. (decidir)   Nuestro líder _____ tener una reunión.
5. (consultar)   Tú _____ con el comité estudiantil.

Chicano students,
Sacramento, California

6. (venir) Yo _____ a todas las clases para hablar de nuestras actividades.
7. (tener) Nosotros _____ que informar a la gente.
8. (esperar) El profesorado _____ nuestras opiniones sobre la situación del país.
9. (ir) ¿Tú no _____ a luchar también? ¡Claro que sí!
10. (ser/estar) O _____ nosotros compañeros o _____ en malas condiciones.

C • Query   Free Response

Treat exercise B as a paragraph. Imagine yourself as a participant and answer the following questions in Spanish.

1. ¿Quiénes no reciben las oportunidades de otros grupos sociales?
2. ¿Qué decide hacer nuestro líder?
3. ¿Por qué tenemos que venir a todas las clases?
4. ¿Con quién consultas tú?
5. ¿Es tu grupo sincero o hipócrita?

D • Transformation Drill   Affirmative → Interrogative → Negative → Interrogative Word

MODEL   Los estudiantes desean una clínica.
STUDENT 1 **¿Desean los estudiantes** una clínica?
STUDENT 2 Los estudiantes **no** desean una clínica.
STUDENT 3 **¿Qué desean los estudiantes?**

1. Pepe y Carmen van a la biblioteca.
2. El rector estudia la situación.
3. Marta es la estudiante inteligente.
4. La señorita Posada viene de la tienda.
5. Hay que ir ahora.

E • Completion Drill

Fill in the blanks with a definite article wherever one is necessary. Watch for contractions.

1. _____ biblioteca está cerca de _____ universidad.
2. _____ rector necesita ir a _____ reunión.
3. _____ francesas están en _____ clase.
4. _____ estudiantes vienen a _____ baile.
5. Practicamos mucho _____ español, pero hablamos _____ inglés en casa.

Now use the indefinite article wherever necessary.

6. María y Paco son _____ españoles.
7. Voy a comprar _____ discos en _____ tienda cerca de mi casa.
8. Mis compañeras son _____ alumnas malas.
9. Escribimos _____ poema y _____ composición.
10. Tú eres _____ mentiroso; no tienes _____ disco de Pete Seeger, tienes tres.

F • Query   Free Response

Answer in Spanish.

1. ¿Por qué tiene que ir usted a la universidad?
2. Generalmente, ¿habla usted español en casa?
3. ¿Tiene usted hermanos?
4. ¿Vas a escribir tu tarea en clase o en casa?
5. ¿Tus compañeros tienen nociones buenas de la moralidad?
6. ¿Hay una tienda de deportes cerca de tu casa?
7. ¿Es José Martí un poeta sincero o trivial?
8. ¿Quién es tu líder estudiantil?
9. ¿Hay mucha gente en tu comité?
10. ¿Tienes buenas noticias para tu familia?

G • Translation Drill

Translate into Spanish.

1. We learn the Cuban dances.
2. Afterwards, our sisters decide to go to the store.
3. You have to prepare your math homework.
4. The municipal authorities receive the news.
5. There is a new clinic around here.
6. We still have his word of honor.
7. Nevertheless, they don't accept our demands.
8. He is a silly poet!
9 Who is the nice lady near the library?
10. She is not your teacher. What a shame!

H • Guided Composition

Imagine you are studying in a university in Latin America. Write a brief letter in Spanish to a friend describing student activities, your friends, your surroundings.

Cafeteria, University of the Andes, Bogotá, Colombia

Restaurant stall, Guadalajara, Mexico

Lección cinco

VENTA DE ARTÍCULOS, MÉXICO, DISTRITO FEDERAL

venta *sale*

MIGUEL	Ignacio, ¿dónde pongo estas revistas? ¡Ay, pesan por lo menos quince kilos!

poner *to put, place*
revistas *magazines*
pesar *to weigh* **por lo menos** *at least* **quince** *fifteen*
libros *books*

IGNACIO	Ahí, con los libros. ¡Miguel! ¡Oye, compadre! ¿Qué haces por aquí? ¿Qué hay de nuevo?
MIGUEL	Nada de particular. Vengo a ayudar la causa. Traigo libros, traigo revistas y periódicos, y... el plato fundamental, el guacamole retesabroso de mi esposa. ¿Dónde pongo el guacamole?

nada *nothing*
traer *to bring* **periódicos** *newspapers*
plato *dish* **retesabroso** *superdelicious*
esposa *wife*

IGNACIO	Allí, en la mesa.

allí *there* **mesa** *table*

MIGUEL	¿Ésa, allí?
IGNACIO	Sí, la mesa que tiene la comida. Carlota, mira quien está aquí. ¡Miguel!

comida *food* **mirar** *to look (at)*

MIGUEL	Hola, mi Carlita. ¡Huy! ¡Cuánta comida! Enchiladas suizas, tamales yucatecos, queso de Chihuahua. ¿Qué es eso?

¡Huy! *Wow!* **¡cuánta...!** *what a lot of...!*
suizas *Swiss* **queso** *cheese*

CARLOTA	¿Eso? Un lomo de cerdo en chile verde.

lomo de cerdo *loin of pork*
verde *green*

MIGUEL	¡Qué sabroso! ¿A qué hora comemos? Pero primero tomamos una cerveza, ¿no?

sabroso *tasty, delicious* **¿a qué hora?** *at what time?*
comer *to eat*
primero *first* **tomar** *to have (drink)* **cerveza** *beer*

IGNACIO	Sí, hombre, claro. Tú sí eres amigo de verdad. Traes tantas cosas y no tienes hijos en la orquesta infantil.

amigo *friend*
tantas *so many* **cosas** *things* **hijos** *children*

MIGUEL	¡Eso qué importa! Además, estoy aquí por razones egoístas. Vengo exclusivamente a comer. A propósito, ¿cuándo sale la orquesta? Van al norte, ¿verdad?	**¡Eso qué importa!** *What does that matter!* **egoístas** *selfish* **a propósito** *by the way* **salir** *to leave*
IGNACIO	Así es. Bueno, primero tenemos que conseguir el dinero necesario. Necesitamos vender esa bicicleta allí, que ya está usada, aquellos trastes viejos allí, la comida, —en fin, todo. Los viajes exigen muchos billetes.	**Así es.** *That's right.* **conseguir** *to get* **trastes** *contraptions* **viejos** *old* **viajes** *trips* **exigen** (from **exigir**) *require* **billetes** (coll.) *folding money*
MIGUEL	¡Eso sí!	**¡Eso sí!** *That's for sure!*
CARLOTA	Pero si todo va bien, los chamacos salen esta noche.	**chamacos** (*Mexican*) *kids* **esta noche** *tonight*
MIGUEL	¿Ah, sí? ¿A qué hora?	
CARLOTA	A las nueve y media en punto de la noche. Primero van a Baja California. Van a dar la *Sinfonía India* de Carlos Chávez. Es una sinfonía muy bella.	**en punto** *sharp* **noche** *night* **bella** *beautiful*
MIGUEL	¿Y luego qué?	**luego** *then*
CARLOTA	Luego van a Los Ángeles para el concurso internacional.	**concurso** *contest*
MIGUEL	¿Y si ganan?	**ganar** *to win*
CARLOTA	¡Qué premio! ¡Van directamente al Conservatorio de París!	**premio** *prize*

NOTES

Friendship

The term **compadre**, and its feminine counterpart **comadre**, are used between very close adult friends. This relationship carries an implicit commitment to take care of each other's family in times of crisis.

Prefixes and Suffixes

When the colloquial prefix **rete-** is attached to a word, it intensifies its meaning.

> **sabroso**   *tasty* → **retesabroso**   *supertasty, really tasty*

> > Additional examples:
> > **retebueno**   *really good*
> > **retemalo**   *really bad*

Diminutive suffixes **-ito**, **-ita** are used in Spanish to indicate either smallness of size or to express emotion (usually positive).

> size   **una bicicletita**   *a small or tiny bicycle*
> > **un quesito**   *a small cheese*

> emotion or   **Juanito**   equivalent to *Johnny*
> endearment   **Miguelito**   equivalent to *Mickey*
> > **Es simpático pero tontito.**   *He's nice but kind of dumb.*

Carlos Chávez (b. 1899)

Foremost Mexican conductor and composer. The *Sinfonía India*, which he wrote in 1935, combines Mexican and Indian themes.

Mexican Foods

Mexican cuisine includes a number of pre-Columbian dishes, such as **guacamole, enchiladas suizas, tamales yucatecos. Guacamole** is a salad based on mashed avocado laced with chiles. **Tamales** usually feature a meat stuffing inside a corn dough that is then wrapped in corn husks (in central Mexico) or banana leaves (in the Yucatán peninsula). A Mexican **tortilla** (a corn pancake) is wrapped around a filling and sometimes covered with a spicy sauce to make **enchiladas**. If the filling is cheese, they're called **enchiladas suizas. Queso de Chihuahua** is a cheese produced in the northern state of Chihuahua.

Abbreviations

Some common Spanish abbreviations:

la motocicleta → **la moto**   *the motorcycle*
la fotografía → **la foto**   *the photograph*
la bicicleta → **la bici**   *the bicycle*

LANGUAGE STRUCTURES

19   Present indicative of **hacer**, **poner**, **traer**, and **salir**

hacer *to do; to make*	**poner** *to put*
hago	**pongo**
haces	pones
hace	pone
hacemos	ponemos
hacen	ponen

traer *to bring*	**salir** *to leave, go out*
traigo	**salgo**
traes	sales
trae	sale
traemos	salimos
traen	salen

▶ Spanish verbs follow specific patterns even in their irregularities. The above verbs are irregular only in the first person singular of the present indicative and are similar in their irregularities.

▶ **Hacer** translates both *to do* and *to make*.

A • Substitution Drill

MODEL   ¿Qué hace Ud. para la venta?
               sus compadres
STUDENT   ¿Qué **hacen** sus compadres para la venta?

1. ¿Qué hace Ud. para la venta?
   tus amigos
   sus hijos
   tu hija
   yo
   nosotros

2. Rafa no trae la bici.
   Él y yo
   Ellas
   Ella
   El estudiante
   Yo

3. Ignacio pone el guacamole en la mesa.
   Yo
   Tú
   Ellos
   Ignacio y Miguel
   Ud.

4. Tere sale a las cinco en punto de la tarde.
   Los compadres
   Carlota y yo
   Yo
   Tú y yo
   Tú

B • Query   Patterned Response

MODEL   ¿Quién trae las revistas? ¿Miguel?
STUDENT   **Así es. Miguel trae las revistas.**

1. ¿Cuándo sale la orquesta infantil? ¿Esta noche?
2. ¿Quién hace las enchiladas? ¿Carlota?
3. ¿Dónde ponen el traste? ¿Con la bicicleta?
4. ¿Qué traigo? ¿Un lomo de cerdo?
5. ¿Cuándo vienes a la venta? ¿A las nueve de la mañana?
6. ¿Dónde hay que poner las revistas? ¿En la mesa?
7. ¿Cuándo salimos para California? ¿A las siete de la noche?
8. ¿Con quién venimos al concierto? ¿Con nuestro amigo?

C • Query   Free Response

Answer in Spanish.

1. ¿Traes muchos libros a la clase?
2. ¿Come Ud. comida mexicana?
3. ¿Vienes a ayudar la causa estudiantil?
4. ¿Qué haces por aquí?
5. ¿Necesita Ud. mucho dinero?
6. ¿A qué hora sales de casa?
7. ¿Tiene Ud. un amigo de verdad?
8. ¿Va a hacer una venta su familia?
9. ¿Toma Ud. cerveza o tequila?
10. ¿Miran Uds. revistas con fotos?

20 Demonstratives

Demonstrative Adjectives

Singular					
Masculine					
este libro	*this book*	**ese** artículo	*that article* (nearby)	**aquel** viaje	*that trip* (distant)
Feminine					
esta revista	*this magazine*	**esa** cosa	*that thing* (nearby)	**aquella** venta	*that sale* (distant)

			Plural				

Masculine
estos platos   *these dishes*   **esos** quesos   *those cheeses*
(nearby)   **aquellos** días   *those days*
(distant)

Feminine
estas cervezas   *these beers*   **esas** orquestas   *those orchestras*
(nearby)   **aquellas** mesas   *those tables*
(distant)

▶ Demonstrative adjectives come before the noun they modify and agree with it in gender and number.

▶ **Este, -a, -os, -as**, refer to something near the speaker; **ese, -a, -os, -as** refer to something near the person spoken to or not far from either speaker in a conversation; **aquel, aquella, -os, -as**, refer to something that is somewhat (or very) distant from both the speaker and the person spoken to. Apart from the use of the **ese** and **aquel** forms for expressing the closeness or distance of things, **ese** is the general term for *that* with **aquel** used to stress remoteness.

A • Substitution Drill

MODEL   ¿Quién compra este libro?
                              revistas?
STUDENT   ¿Quién compra **estas** revistas?

1. ¿Quién compra este libro?
           libros?
           guacamole?
           cervezas?
           periódicos?
           lomo de cerdo?

2. Aquella mesa allí pesa mucho.
           hombre
           mujer
           revistas
           traste
           cosas

3. Tenemos que vender toda esta comida.   4. ¡Huy! Ese traste ahí es muy viejo.

libros.	trastes
tamales.	bici
bicicletas.	moto
periódicos.	discos
mesas.	cosas

B • Query   Patterned Response   Exchange Pattern: ese, -a, -os, -as → este, -a, -os, -as

MODEL   ¿Es sabroso ese queso?
STUDENT   **Sí, compadre, este queso es sabroso.**

1. ¿Son sabrosas esas enchiladas?
2. ¿Es trivial ese periódico?
3. ¿Es nueva esa bicicleta?
4. ¿Es bueno ese disco?
5. ¿Es sabroso ese lomo de cerdo?

este, -a, -os, -as → ese, -a, -os, -as

6. ¿Es bueno este libro?
7. ¿Son viejos estos trastes?
8. ¿Son sabrosas estas enchiladas?
9. ¿Es grave esta situación?
10. ¿Es pequeña esta biblioteca?

Demonstrative Pronouns

		Singular					
Masculine	**éste**	*this one*	**ése**	*that one* (nearby)	**aquél**	*that one* (distant)
Feminine	**ésta**	*this one*	**ésa**	*that one* (nearby)	**aquélla**	*that one* (distant)

		Plural					
Masculine	**éstos**	*these*	**ésos**	*those* (nearby)	**aquéllos**	*those* (distant)
Feminine	**éstas**	*these*	**ésas**	*those* (nearby)	**aquéllas**	*those* (distant)
Neuter	**esto** **eso** **aquello**		(only in the singular)			

▶ When demonstrative adjectives are used as pronouns, they are written with an accent mark, except the neuter forms: **esto, eso, aquello.**

1. Éstos son mis compañeros.   *These are my classmates.*
2. ¿En qué mesa está la comida?   *What table is the food on?*
   ¿En ésa, allí?   *On that one there?*
3. ¿Dónde pongo estas revistas?   *Where do I put these magazines?*
   ¿Y ésas? ¿Y aquéllas?   *And those? And those over there?*

▶ The three neuter pronouns refer to a general idea, action, or something that has not been identified.

1. ¿Qué es eso?	*What's that?* (the thing is unidentified)
2. ¡Eso sí!	*That's for sure!*
3. Siempre hablan de esto y aquello.	*They're always talking about this and that (stuff).*

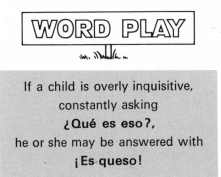

WORD PLAY

If a child is overly inquisitive, constantly asking **¿Qué es eso?**, he or she may be answered with **¡Es queso!**

▶ The demonstrative pronoun **éste, -a, -os, -as**, often translates *the latter* in Spanish and **aquél, aquélla, -os, -as**, often translates *the former*.

Eugenio y Pancho son compadres. Éste pesa ochenta kilos; aquél, solamente setenta y cinco.	*Eugenio and Pancho are compadres. The latter weighs eighty kilos; the former, only seventy-five.*

A · Replacement Drill Demonstrative Adjective → Demonstrative Pronoun

MODEL   Este hombre es mi compadre.
STUDENT **Éste** es mi compadre.

1. Esa mujer es mi comadre.
2. Aquel estudiante es italiano.
3. Este alumno es boricua.
4. Esas señoritas son hispanas.
5. Estas canciones son bonitas.

6. Aquellos trastes son viejos.
7. Esos libros son nuevos.
8. Estos tamales son sabrosos.
9. ¿Dónde pongo estas revistas?
10. ¿Traigo ese periódico a la venta?

B · Query Patterned Response éste, -a, -os, -as → ése, -a, -os, -as

MODEL   ¿Qué libros necesitas? ¿Éstos?
STUDENT **No, no necesito ésos.**

1. ¿Qué revistas necesitas? ¿Éstas?
2. ¿Qué comida come Ud.? ¿Ésta?

3. ¿Qué trastes vendes? ¿Éstos?
4. ¿Qué plato traigo? ¿Éste?

ése, -a, -os, -as → éste, -a, -os, -as

5. ¿Cuáles composiciones preparas? ¿Ésas?
6. ¿Qué periódico miras? ¿Ése?
7. ¿Qué bicicleta compras? ¿Ésa?
8. ¿Qué libros traes? ¿Ésos?

21   Locative adverbs

aquí	*here* (precise)
ahí	*there* (nearby or near the person spoken to)
allí	*there* (somewhat distant from either speaker in a conversation)
allá	*there* (remote or without precise location)

▶ Note the analogy between the demonstratives (**este**, **ese**, **aquel**) and the locative adverbs. **Aquí** refers to something near the speaker; **ahí** refers to something near the person spoken to or not far from either speaker in a conversation; **allí** refers to something distant from either speaker; **allá** indicates even greater remoteness and often an imprecise location.

1. Necesito este libro aquí y ése ahí, cerca de Ud.

   I need this book here and that one there, close to you.

2. Muy bien. ¿También necesita Ud. aquellos libros allí, en la mesa? No, no necesito aquéllos.

   Fine. Do you also need those books over there, on the table? No, I don't need those.

3. ¿Va a ir allá, a California?

   Are you going to go out there, to California?

El más allá

The remoteness of **allá** is indicated by the following noun formed from the adverb: **el más allá** (literally, the *"outer"* *there*), *the other world, life after death.*

A • Query   Patterned Response   Exchange Pattern: este/aquí → ése/ahí

MODEL   ¿Qué son estas cosas aquí? (revistas)

STUDENT   **¿Ésas ahí? Son revistas.**

1. ¿Qué son estos trastes aquí?   (discos)
2. ¿Qué es esta comida aquí?   (queso de Chihuahua)
3. ¿Qué es este plato aquí?   (lomo de cerdo)
4. ¿Quién es este hombre aquí?   (mi compadre)
5. ¿Qué es esta cosa aquí?   (un poema)
6. ¿Quién es esta mujer aquí?   (la esposa de Miguel)
7. ¿Qué es este libro aquí?   (un libro de español)
8. ¿Qué es este periódico aquí?   (un periódico francés)

B • Query   Patterned Response   Exchange Pattern: ese/ahí → éste/aquí

MODEL   ¿Qué son esas cosas ahí? (revistas)

STUDENT   **¿Éstas aquí? Son revistas.**

1. ¿Qué es ese traste ahí?   (una mesa)
2. ¿Qué es esa comida ahí?   (guacamole)
3. ¿Qué es ese plato ahí?   (tamales yucatecos)
4. ¿Quiénes son esos hombres ahí?   (los profesores)
5. ¿Qué es esa cosa ahí?   (un premio)
6. ¿Quién es esa mujer ahí?   (la profesora Azuela)
7. ¿Qué son esos libros ahí?   (libros de inglés)
8. ¿Qué son esos periódicos ahí?   (periódicos portugueses)

C • Query   Patterned Response   Exchange Pattern: aquel → aquél/allí

MODEL   ¿Qué son aquellos trastes?   (bicicletas)

STUDENT   **¿Aquéllos allí? Son bicicletas.**

1. ¿Qué son aquellas cosas?   (revistas)
2. ¿Quiénes son aquellos estudiantes?   (estudiantes militantes)
3. ¿Qué es aquella cosa?   (una mesa)
4. ¿Quién es aquella muchacha?   (Raquel)
5. ¿Quién es aquel hombre?   (mi compadre)
6. ¿Qué es aquel muchacho?   (un mentiroso)
7. ¿Qué es aquella tienda?   (una tienda de discos)
8. ¿Qué es aquel libro?   (un libro de matemáticas)

D • Translation Drill

Translate the following into Spanish.

1. What's this? What's that? What's that over there?
2. That is interesting. That is all. Who needs this?

3. We don't need that (stuff). This boy and that one.
4. That girl and that one over there. That table (near you), and this one here.
5. He's not here. He's out there in Arizona.
6. My newspapers are these here. Are those Carmen's?
7. Those bicycles there are old; this one here is not old.
8. Over there they speak Italian.

22 Confirmation tags

¿no es verdad?	¿eh?
¿verdad?	¿Verdad que...?
¿no?	

▶ **¿No es verdad?** (literally, *Isn't it true?*) or **¿no?** after an affirmative expression and **¿verdad?** after either an affirmative or negative expression correspond to the English confirmation tags, *right? OK? do you? don't you? isn't it? doesn't it? will he? won't he?* etc. **¿Eh?** just like the English *huh?* and *hmm?* may also be used to seek confirmation.

▶ **¿Verdad que...?** is similar to **¿verdad?** except that it precedes the expression (example 5).

1. La comida es muy buena aquí, ¿no es verdad? — *The food is really good here, isn't it?*
2. Van al norte, ¿verdad? — *They're going north, aren't they?*
3. Primero tomamos una cerveza, ¿no? — *First we're going to have a beer, right?*
4. Tú vienes a la venta, ¿eh? — *You're coming to the sale, okay?*
5. ¿Verdad que Ignacio es el compadre de Miguel? — *Isn't it true that Ignacio is Miguel's compadre?*

A • Transformation Drill   ¿Verdad que...? → ¿verdad?

MODEL   ¿Verdad que ése es el profesor?
STUDENT   **Ése es el profesor, ¿verdad?**

1. ¿Verdad que Rafa está aquí?
2. ¿Verdad que la situación es grave?
3. ¿Verdad que las enchiladas son sabrosas?
4. ¿Verdad que eres mi amiga?
5. ¿Verdad que las revistas pesan mucho?

¿verdad? ¿no? ¿eh? → ¿Verdad que...?

6. Salen a las doce, ¿verdad?
7. El rector desea más tiempo, ¿verdad?
8. Ese hombre ya está aquí, ¿no?
9. Tú vienes a la venta, ¿eh?
10. Los viajes exigen muchos billetes, ¿no?

23 Cardinal numerals 0–99

0	cero	
1	uno = number one	*But:* un hombre una mujer

2	dos	
3	tres	
4	cuatro	
5	cinco	
6	seis	
7	siete	
8	ocho	hombres / mujeres
9	nueve	
10	diez	
11	once	
12	doce	
13	trece	
14	catorce	
15	quince	

16	dieciséis	(diez y seis)	
17	diecisiete	(diez y siete)	
18	dieciocho	(diez y ocho)	hombres / mujeres
19	diecinueve	(diez y nueve)	
20	veinte		

21	veintiuno	(veinte y uno) = number twenty-one.	
		But: veintiún hombres	
		veintiuna mujeres	

22	veintidós	(veinte y dos)	
23	veintitrés	(veinte y tres)	
24	veinticuatro	(veinte y cuatro)	
25	veinticinco	(veinte y cinco)	hombres / mujeres
26	veintiséis	(veinte y seis)	
27	veintisiete	(veinte y siete)	
28	veintiocho	(veinte y ocho)	
29	veintinueve	(veinte y nueve)	

Numerals above 29

			uno	*But:* **un** before a masculine noun;	
30	treinta		dos	**una** before a feminine noun	
40	cuarenta		tres		
50	cincuenta		cuatro		
60	sesenta	y	cinco		
70	setenta		seis		
80	ochenta		siete		
90	noventa		ocho		
			nueve		

▶ Alternate, less frequently used spellings of the numerals are given in parenthesis (**diez y siete, veinte y uno,** etc.). However, within the tens from 30 up, the units are added solely with **y**: 33 is **treinta y tres**; 87 is **ochenta y siete**.

▶ Recall that **un** is used directly before a masculine singular noun: **un libro** *a (one) book.* It is also used with an intervening adjective (1 in the following examples). **Uno** is used elsewhere (examples 2 and 3). **Una** is used invariably in the feminine (examples 4, 5, and 6). Both **un** and **una** may be translated by *a* (or *an*) or *one*, depending on the context.

1. un viejo amigo[1]   *an old friend*
2. Voy a enumerar los ejemplos: *I'm going to enumerate the examples:*
   uno, dos, tres...   *one, two, three . . .*
3. Uno de mis libros; uno o dos de   *One of my books; one or two of your*
   tus compañeros.   *pals.*
4. una revista   *a magazine*
5. una vieja amiga[1]   *an old friend*
6. Una de mis revistas; una o dos   *One of my magazines; one or two of*
   de tus comadres.   *your comadres.*

▶ Numerals ending in **-uno** (**veintiuno, treinta y uno,** etc.) drop **-o** before a masculine noun (example 1); **una** is used before a feminine noun (example 2).

1. veintiún quesos, treinta y un días   *twenty-one cheeses; thirty-one days*
2. cuarenta y una cosas, cincuenta y   *forty-one things, fifty-one orchestras*
   una orquestas

▶ Addition, subtraction, multiplication, and division are expressed as follows.

| + | **y** | × | **por** |
| - | **menos** | ÷ | **dividido por** |

¿Cuántos son tres y tres? Tres y   *How much are three and three? Three*
tres son seis.   *and three are six.*
Cinco menos tres son dos.   *Five minus three is two.*

A • Replacement Drill
Read in Spanish.

MODEL   4 días
STUDENT **cuatro días**

1. 5 enchiladas	3. 31 estudiantes	5. 7 viajes	7. 1 compadre
2. 21 canciones	4. 2 causas	6. 3 compadres	8. 1 comadre

[1] In the examples **un viejo amigo, una vieja amiga,** descriptive adjectives are placed before the noun in order to express a special meaning. **Un viejo amigo** refers to a friend of long standing (irrespective of the friend's age) whereas **un amigo viejo** refers to a friend who is elderly. See section **76** for a discussion of the positioning of adjectives for special meanings.

9. 11 hijos	12. 70 revistas	15. 14 periódicos	18. 15 kilos
10. 99 cervezas	13. 51 mesas	16. 1 esposa	19. 8 billetes
11. 60 libros	14. 9 días	17. 1 esposo	20. 19 premios

B • Query   Patterned Response

MODEL ¿Cuántos son 2 y 2?
STUDENT **Dos y dos son cuatro.**

1. ¿Cuántos son 2 y 1?
2. ¿Cuántos son 10 y 10?
3. ¿Cuántos son 5 y 6?
4. ¿Cuántos son 9 y 7?
5. ¿Cuántos son 30 y 30?

6. ¿Cuántos son 30 y 40?
7. ¿Cuántos son 50 y 1?
8. ¿Cuántos son 3 y 4?
9. ¿Cuántos son 10 y 8?
10. ¿Cuántos son 66 y 33?

C • Query   Patterned Response

MODEL ¿Cuántos son 5 menos 5?
STUDENT **Cinco menos cinco son cero.**

1. ¿Cuántos son 15 menos 3?
2. ¿Cuántos son 16 menos 1?
3. ¿Cuántos son 17 menos 1?
4. ¿Cuántos son 30 menos 10?
5. ¿Cuántos son 99 menos 1?

6. ¿Cuántos son 22 menos 2?
7. ¿Cuántos son 28 menos 7?
8. ¿Cuántos son 31 menos 31?
9. ¿Cuántos son 70 menos 60?
10. ¿Cuántos son 99 menos 33?

24   Time of day

Verb (ser)	Hour	Minutes before the next hour	Half-hour	Minutes after the hour	Period of the day
Es	la una	menos cinco		y cinco	de la mañana[2]
		menos cuarto	y media	y cuarto	de la tarde[2]
		menos veinte, etc.		y veinte, etc.	de la noche[2]
Son	las dos				
	las tres				
	las cuatro, etc.				

[2] **Mañana**, *morning*, corresponds to English A.M.; **tarde**, *afternoon*, and **noche**, *evening* or *night*, correspond to P.M.

▶ The word **hora** means *time* in the sense of time of day. In stating the time, **hora(s)** is understood; hence the feminine articles **la** and **las** are used with the cardinal numeral expressing the hour.

¿Qué hora es?	*What time is it?*
Es la una y media.	*It's half-past one (one-thirty).*
Salgo a las cinco de la tarde.	*I leave at 5:00* P.M.

▶ **Es** is used only when followed by **la una** (with or without minutes expressed); in all other cases **son** is used.

¿Es la una y media?	*Is it one-thirty?*
No, son las dos menos cuarto.	*No, it's a quarter to two.*

▶ Spanish uses **y** to indicate minutes added to the hour up to and including the half-hour. **Menos** (*minus*) is used to express the time between the half-hour and the next hour. **Cuarto** is used for a quarter of an hour and **media** for the half-hour. To indicate *sharp* or *on the dot*, Spanish uses **en punto**.

Son las once y veinte.	*It's eleven-twenty.*
Son las once menos dieciséis.	*It's sixteen minutes to eleven.*
Van a la universidad a las nueve y cuarto en punto.	*They go to the university at 9:15 sharp (on the dot).*

▶ When the hour is specified, the period of the day (**mañana**, *morning*; **tarde**, *afternoon*; **noche**, *evening, night*) is introduced by **de**; when no definite hour is given, **por** is used. The division between **tarde** and **noche** is not clear-cut but rather depends on the season of the year, since usually **tarde** corresponds to daylight hours.

Vengo a las ocho de la noche.	*I come at 8:00 at night* (P.M.).
Escribo por la mañana (tarde, noche).	*I write in the morning (afternoon, evening or night).*

▶ In Spanish, *noon* is **mediodía**, *midnight* is **medianoche**, usually preceded by the appropriate article.

Llegan al mediodía (a la medianoche).	*They arrive at noon (midnight).*

A • Query   Patterned Response

MODEL   ¿Qué hora es? La una, ¿verdad?
STUDENT   **Así es. Es la una.**

1. ¿Qué hora es? Las cinco de la tarde, ¿verdad?
2. ¿Qué hora es? La una y media, ¿verdad?
3. ¿Qué hora es? Mediodía, ¿verdad?
4. ¿Qué hora es? Las dos menos cuarto, ¿no?
5. ¿Qué hora es? La una menos cuarto, ¿verdad?

6. ¿Qué hora es? Las diez de la noche, ¿no es verdad?
7. ¿Qué hora es? Las tres de la mañana, ¿no?
8. ¿Qué hora es? Medianoche, ¿verdad?
9. ¿Qué hora es? Las once y cuarto, ¿no es verdad?
10. ¿Qué hora es? Las diez menos veinte, ¿eh?

B • Translation Drill

Translate into Spanish.

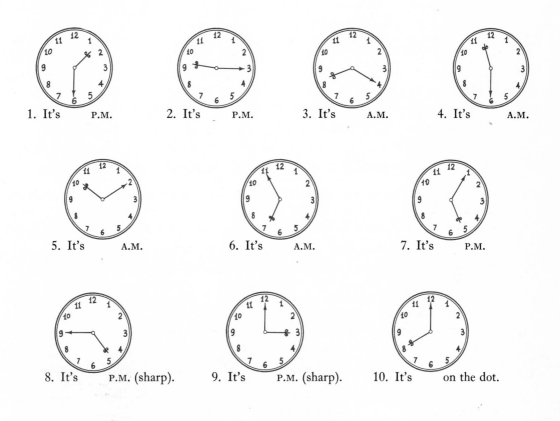

1. It's ____ P.M.   2. It's ____ P.M.   3. It's ____ A.M.   4. It's ____ A.M.

5. It's ____ A.M.   6. It's ____ A.M.   7. It's ____ P.M.

8. It's ____ P.M. (sharp).   9. It's ____ P.M. (sharp).   10. It's ____ on the dot.

C • Query   Free Response

Answer in Spanish.

1. ¿Qué hora es?
2. ¿Cuándo sale Ud. para la escuela?
3. ¿A qué hora comes?
4. ¿Cuándo haces tu tarea?
5. ¿Cuándo va Ud. a la biblioteca?
6. ¿Practicas el español por la mañana?
7. ¿A qué hora hay que ir a la clase?
8. ¿Cuándo hablas en español?

REVIEW

I   The following questions are related to the dialog. Answer in Spanish.

1. ¿Adónde va a ir la orquesta infantil?
2. ¿Qué artículos venden en la venta?
3. ¿Por qué viene Miguel a la venta?
4. ¿Qué trae Miguel a la venta?
5. ¿Hay mucha comida en la mesa?
6. ¿Pesan mucho las revistas?
7. ¿Quién no tiene hijos en la orquesta infantil?
8. ¿A qué hora sale la orquesta infantil?

II   Translation. Translate the following into Spanish.

1. It is going to be five-thirty. We have to go at three o'clock sharp.
2. What are you doing? I am making food for the sale.
3. When are we going to eat? We always eat at two, when Ignacio brings the beer.
4. I don't need those old contraptions over there. But we need the money!
5. They're leaving tonight, right? That's right, *compadre*. And if they win . . . What a prize!
6. By the way, when do you have to leave? In the afternoon?
7. These magazines on the table weigh 80 kilos. Wow! The table only weighs 12 kilos!
8. Why are you here? I'm here to help the cause. I have 99 old books. Man, you are a true friend!

III   Write your own dialog.

You and your friends want to have a sale. Discuss the details of your activity, including such things as what sorts of, and how many, objects you'll be selling.

Young boy transporting
candy, Mexico City

Quiz on nouns

From what you know about matched nouns,
what are the meanings of the following?

el hijo   el esposo
la hija   la esposa
los hijos   los esposos

PRONUNCIATION

Stress and Accent

Review the patterns of stress placement in Spanish (page 11) and read each example aloud several times.

A. Words that end in a vowel or in **n** or **s** are regularly stressed on the next-to-last syllable. Since this is the most common pattern, no written accent is used.

hablamos	España	Arizona
preparan	¡Claro!	chicano
Colorado	Nevada	chicana
puertorriqueño	puertorriqueña	profesora
Estados Unidos	Florida	cubano

B. Words ending in a consonant other than **n** or **s** are regularly stressed on the last syllable. No written accent is used.

español	general	¿verdad?
libertad	fraternidad	igualdad
perspicaz	profesor	preparar
hablar	practicar	motor
hablador	favor	usted

C. If stress is not according to the two preceding rules, then a written accent (´) is used to mark the stressed vowel.

1. These words don't follow Rule A because although they end in a vowel or **n** or **s**, the stress is on the last syllable.

café	papá	mamá
también	inglés	francés
portugués	lección	José

2. These words don't follow Rule B because even though they end in a consonant other than **n** or **s**, they are stressed on the next-to-last syllable.

César Chávez	dólar	Sánchez
Pérez	útil	López
González	fácil	fértil

3. These words or expressions don't follow either Rule A or Rule B because they are stressed two or more syllables from the last.

teléfono	rápido	México
Los Ángeles[3]	lógico	jóvenes
díganselo	cántamela	cómico

Exercises

The following are stress contrasts. Repeat the words after your instructor.

practico (*I practice*)	practicó (*he practiced*)	práctico (*practical*)
termino (*I finish*)	terminó (*he finished*)	término (*term*)
solicito (*I solicit*)	solicitó (*he solicited*)	solícito (*solicitous*)
hablo (*I speak*)	habló (*he spoke*)	
preparo (*I prepare*)	preparó (*he prepared*)	
esta (*this*)	está (*is*)	
hacia (*toward*)	hacía (*he used to do, make*)	
abra (*open*)	habrá (*there will be*)	
jugo (*juice*)	jugó (*he played*)	
libro (*book*)	libró (*he freed*)	
papa (*potato*)	papá (*father*)	

The following English and Spanish cognates exemplify the striking difference between the stress patterns of the two languages. Spanish tends to stress the latter part of a word, English, the earlier part. Repeat the pairs of words after your instructor.

A.
English (´ -)	Spanish (- ´)
rival	rival
actor	actor
collar	collar
error	error
local	local
jaguar	jaguar
moral	moral
vigor	vigor

[3] Often, written accents are omitted from capital letters. This textbook includes them, however.

B. English (´ - -)   Spanish (- - ´)

English	Spanish
hospital	hospital
natural	natural
regular	regular
liberal	liberal
general	general
animal	animal
cultural	cultural
capital	capital

C. Syllable Exercise. Pronounce the following words. Then underline the stressed syllable(s). (Disregard one-syllable words.)

Hernán Cortés	René Marqués	Pedro Juan Soto
Miguel de Cervantes	Francisco (Pancho) Villa	Ponce de León
Cabeza de Vaca	Pedro Calderón de la Barca	La Jolla (la joya)
Escondido	San Francisco	Boca Ratón
Sacramento	El Paso	Roberto Clemente
Beto Ávila	¡Venceremos!	América
sílaba	política	sátira
espectáculo	civilización	represión

Cognates & Contexts

RODOLFO	Bueno, chica, ¿qué hacemos?	
SUSANA	¿Por qué no vamos a escuchar la sinfonía? Van a poner a Villa-Lobos, a de Falla...	**escuchar** *to listen (to)*
RODOLFO	No, esa música es muy aburrida. Yo soy aficionado a la música nueva, al «rock-and-roll».	**aburrida** *boring* **aficionado a** *fond of*
SUSANA	Bueno, yo también soy aficionada a esa música. Pero, ¿qué tiene de nueva? Ya tiene por lo menos quince años de existencia. Además, la música no es buena o mala porque es nueva o vieja. Tú necesitas un poco más de cultura. Debemos ir a la sinfonía.	**años** *years* **deber** *ought to, must, should*
RODOLFO	Está bien. Pero después creo que debemos ir a una discoteca a bailar.	**creer** *to think, believe*

Heitor Villa-Lobos (1887–1959) Brazilian composer inspired by the folklore of his country to write music of all genres, mostly for the piano.

Manuel de Falla (1876–1946) Spanish composer of impressionistic operas, ballets, and other pieces. Best known for his ballet *El sombrero de tres picos* (*The Three-Cornered Hat*), written in 1919.

¡Cuidado!

This section has consistently made use of cognates in order to expand your vocabulary. But there are a small number of so-called false or deceptive cognates. For example

largo = *long*	**Es una avenida larga.**
éxito = *success*	**Voy a tener éxito con el español.**
sopa = *soup* (not *soap,* which is **jabón**)	**¡Mamá! ¡Quiero más sopa!**
firma = *signature*	**Necesito tu firma aquí, por favor.**
periódico = *newspaper*	**Compro el periódico todos los días por la mañana.**

Some deceptive cognates can be real howlers.

estar constipado = *to have a cold*	**¿Estás constipado hoy?**
estar embarazada = *to be pregnant*	**¿Está embarazada Mónica?**

Lección seis

SOÑANDO EN LOS PASILLOS

soñando *dreaming*

pasillos *hallways*

GONZALO   ¡Ánimo, Alfonso! Seguramente algún día la vas a conocer.

¡ánimo! *cheer up!*
seguramente *surely*
algún día *someday*
conocer *to meet; to know*

ALFONSO   ¡Pero ya la quiero!

querer *to love*

GONZALO   ¿Ya? ¿Tan rápidamente? No te creo. ¿Cómo lo sabes? Me dices que no la conoces.

tan *so*

saber *to know*   decir *to tell*

ALFONSO   ¡Bah! ¿Eso qué importa? La conozco de lejos y sé su nombre.

de lejos *from afar*

nombre *name*

GONZALO   De lejos es mejor, ¿no? Uno no ve los granitos.

mejor *better*   ver *to see*
granitos *pimples*

ALFONSO   ¡Cuidado, majadero! ¡Ay! Sé de memoria su rutina. Todos los días la oigo pasar por el pasillo. Por la tarde ella compra una Coca-Cola de la maquinita. Me ve, me da una de esas sonrisitas ambiguas . . .

¡majadero! *pest!*
saber de memoria *to know by heart*
todos los días *every day*
oír *to hear*   pasar por *to pass through*
máquina *machine*
sonrisas *smiles*

GONZALO   ¿Y luego, qué?

ALFONSO   Pues nada. Quiero decirle algo pero no puedo. Las palabras no salen de mi boca. Soy un pobre alucinado.

algo *something*   poder (ue) *to be able to, can*
boca *mouth*   un pobre alucinado *a poor bewitched creature*

GONZALO   ¿Qué piensas hacer?

pensar *to intend, plan*

ALFONSO   Nada.

GONZALO   ¿Sabes qué? Tu problema es que eres uno de esos tíos archirrománticos. Con la Cecilia charlas como un loro. Con la Susana hablas en cantidades industriales. Con ella: nada. ¡Eres imposible! Practicas la timidez como un culto.

charlar *to chat* **loro** *parrot*
cantidades *quantities*
la timidez *shyness*

ALFONSO Ahí viene. ¡Ay, qué linda es! ¿Cómo puedes ser tan cínico? Tú no puedes comprender a una persona de mis finas sensibilidades.

linda *pretty*
comprender *to understand*
finas sensibilidades *refined sensibilities*

GONZALO ¿Ah, sí? (Le da un empujón.)

empujón *shove*

ALFONSO ¡Sinvergüenza! ¡Te mato!

sinvergüenza *creep, scoundrel*

GONZALO ¡Huy! ¡Qué fina sensibilidad! Bueno, tengo algo que hacer a unos quince kilómetros de aquí. Adiosito.

MUCHACHA ¡Cuidado! Casi me tiras al suelo.

casi *almost* **tirar** *to knock over* **suelo** *floor*

ALFONSO Oh, perdón, señorita. ¡Qué torpe soy! Te doy mis disculpas. ¿Puedo convidarte a un refresco?

torpe *clumsy*
disculpas *apologies*
convidar a *to invite*
refresco *soda*

MUCHACHA Bueno. ¿Por qué no? Y tu amigo, ¿no quiere uno también?

ALFONSO Ése no es mi amigo. Además tiene algo que hacer.

MUCHACHA ¡Qué lástima!

ALFONSO ¿Lástima? ¿Por qué?

MUCHACHA Le debo agradecer la idea a tu amigo. Si no, esto continúa indefinidamente. Ya son dos semanas que me esperas venir por el pasillo como un espectro aturdido.

agradecer *to thank for*
indefinidamente *indefinitely*
semanas *weeks*
espectro *ghost, spook* **aturdido** *bewildered*

NOTES

More Prefixes and Suffixes

The diminutives in the dialog primarily communicate smallness of size, but they also express varying degrees of positive (or negative) emotion.

granitos   *pimples*, literally *fine grains* (**-itos** gives a negative connotation to **grano**)

maquinita   **-ita** expresses a positive connotation; Alfonso uses the suffix not so much because the Coke machine is small but because the girl frequents it.

sonrisitas   *vague smiles*, *half-smiles* (**-itas** adds an enigmatic quality to the noun)

adiosito   **-ito** adds a degree of intimacy to the standard **adiós**, *goodbye*. Here, of course, Gonzalo uses it to express sarcasm.

-ón, -ona   is an augmentative, the counterpart of **-ito, -ita**.

empuje = *push*, therefore **empujón** = *shove*. Here are other examples of **-ón**:

hombre → hombrón; depending on context, either *hefty man* or *impressive man*

pregunta = *question*   **preguntón** = *a nosy person, a snooper*

archi-, like **rete-**, is used colloquially as an intensifier, the equivalent of *very* or *really*.

Colloquialisms

sinvergüenza   *rogue, creep*, is derived from two words, **sin**, *without* and **vergüenza**, *shame*. (Recall that ¨ indicates that the **u** is not silent. See page 8)

tío   literally, *uncle*, is used colloquially, particularly in Spain, to mean "*guy*."

la Cecilia, la Susana   The use of the definite article before the first name is common in colloquial speech in contexts where the persons conversing know each other well.

LANGUAGE STRUCTURES

25   Present indicative of **dar**, **decir**, **pensar**, **querer**, **poder**, **ver**, and **oír**

dar *to give*	**decir** *to say*	**pensar** *to think*[1]	**querer** *to want; to love*
doy	digo	pienso	quiero
das	dices	piensas	quieres
da	dice	piensa	quiere
damos	decimos	pensamos	queremos
dan	dicen	piensan	quieren

poder *to be able to, can*	**ver** *to see*	**oír** *to hear*
puedo	veo	oigo
puedes	ves	oyes
puede	ve	oye
podemos	vemos	oímos
pueden	ven	oyen

▶ The irregularities in the above Spanish verbs follow a few basic patterns. **Dar** is irregular in the first person singular: **doy.** Compare with **soy, estoy** and **voy. Decir** changes **e → i**; other verbs of this type will be given in subsequent lessons. The irregular first person **digo** is comparable to **vengo, tengo, hago, pongo, traigo,** and **salgo. Pensar** and **querer** change **e → ie,**[2] and **poder** changes **o → ue** in all forms except the first person plural: **pensamos, queremos, podemos.** These are common irregularities and other such verbs will be given later. **Oír** is irregular in all forms except the first person plural. **Ver** is irregular only in the first person singular where the **e** is retained from the infinitive ending.

A • Substitution Drill

MODEL   Ella me da unas sonrisitas ambiguas.
Ellas
STUDENT   Ellas me **dan** unas sonrisitas ambiguas.

1. Ella te da unas sonrisitas ambiguas.
   Las muchachas
   Yo
   Nosotros
   Susana
   Susana y yo

2. ¿Qué piensa Ud. hacer?
   tú
   ella
   Alfonso
   Alfonso y yo
   él

---

[1] **Pensar** + infinitive has the special meaning of *to intend, plan* (to do something).
  ¿Qué piensas hacer?   *What do you intend to do?*
  Pienso decirle que la amo.   *I intend to tell her (him) that I love her.*

[2] Recall similar stem changes in **venir: vengo, vienes, viene, venimos, vienen** and **tener: tengo, tienes, tiene, tenemos, tienen.**

3. Nosotros te decimos que no puedes ir.
   Yo
   Cecilia
   Cecilia y Gonzalo
   Todos
   El estudiante
5. La muchacha ve al compañero simpático.
   Uds.
   Tú
   Tú y yo
   Yo
   Ellos
7. Alfonso la oye pasar.
   Alfonso y yo
   Alfonso y tú
   Ella
   Nosotras
   Yo

4. Ella no puede convidarnos a un refresco.
   Tú
   Gonzalo
   Susana y Cecilia
   La muchacha
   Uds.
6. Yo quiero pero no puedo.
   Tú
   Nosotras
   Ella
   Ellos
   Ud.

B • Transformation Drill   First Person Plural → First Person Singular

MODEL   Venimos a aprender.
STUDENT **Vengo** a aprender.

1. Venimos de la oficina del rector.
2. Tenemos que estudiar.
3. Salimos a las nueve.
4. Hacemos el guacamole mañana.
5. ¿Dónde ponemos estas revistas?
6. Traemos el dinero para la orquesta.
7. Decimos "buenos días" al profesor de español.
8. Somos alumnos de inglés y de español.
9. Estamos en una universidad de Latinoamérica.
10. Le damos nuestras disculpas a la muchacha.
11. Vamos a hablar con el rector.
12. Vemos a unos estudiantes torpes.
13. Queremos ir al norte.
14. Pensamos hacer esta composición ahora.
15. No podemos conceder el dinero.
16. La oímos pero no la escuchamos.

C • Transformation Drill   First Person Plural → Third Person Singular

Redo Drill B.

MODEL   Venimos a aprender.
STUDENT **Viene** a aprender.

D • Query   Patterned Response

MODEL   ¿Qué puede pedir? ¿Una disculpa?
STUDENT **¡Claro! Puede pedir una disculpa.**

1. ¿Quiénes piensan ir a París? ¿Los esposos?
2. ¿Qué quieres? ¿Conocer a la muchacha?
3. ¿Qué le dan ustedes? ¿Un refresco?
4. ¿Quiénes ven algo en el pasillo? ¿Cecilia y Susana?
5. ¿Quién puede venderlo? ¿Gonzalo?
6. ¿Quién dice que la situación es grave? ¿Alfonso?
7. ¿Qué ves? ¿La máquina de las Coca-Colas?
8. ¿Qué digo? ¿Una palabra nueva?
9. ¿Quién soy? ¿Tu amigo?
10. ¿Qué oyes? ¿Una canción linda?

E • Query   Free Response

Answer in Spanish.

1. ¿Compras refrescos de las máquinas o de las tiendas?
2. ¿Tienes un amigo (una amiga) que charla como un loro?
3. ¿Es Ud. una persona de finas sensibilidades?
4. ¿Eres un cínico (una cínica)?
5. ¿Qué piensas hacer por la tarde?
6. ¿Qué quieres hacer ahora?
7. ¿Espera Ud. a su profesor todos los días?
8. ¿Entiendes muchas palabras en español?

26   The personal **a**

▶ A distinctive feature of Spanish is the use of the preposition **a** before all direct object nouns that refer to definite persons. An exception is the verb **tener**, which does not usually require it.

▶ Do not confuse the personal **a** (which has no counterpart and is untranslated in English) with the word **a** that means *to*. Both words combine with **el** to form the contraction **al**.

1. Alfonso quiere a María.   *Alfonso loves Maria.*
2. ¿Ves al señor allí?   *Do you see the man over there?*
3. ¿A quién mira Susana?   *Who is Susana looking at?*

But

4. Tengo muchos amigos buenos. *I have a lot of good friends.*
5. ¿Ves la máquina en el pasillo? *Do you see the machine in the hallway?*

A • Substitution Drill

MODEL   Todos queremos una Coca-Cola.
                                Marta.
STUDENT   Todos queremos **a** Marta.

1. Todos queremos a Marta.
    el dinero necesario.
    nuestro rector.
    esperar aquí.
    nuestros amigos.
    Susana.

2. ¿No oyes la canción?
    señorita linda?
    máquina?
    Alfonso?
    mi compañero?
    pobre alucinado?

3. Voy a traer la mesa.
    Ignacio.
    el guacamole.
    mis hijos.
    mi esposa.
    la bicicleta.

B • Query   Patterned Response

MODEL   ¿Dónde está el señor?
STUDENT   **No vemos al señor.**

1. ¿Dónde está el libro?
2. ¿Dónde está Susana?
3. ¿Dónde está el pasillo?
4. ¿Dónde está nuestro amigo?
5. ¿Dónde está la máquina de las Coca-Colas?
6. ¿Dónde están mis hijos?
7. ¿Dónde están nuestras revistas?
8. ¿Dónde está la persona que charla como un loro?

27   Direct and indirect object pronouns

	Direct	Direct and Indirect	Indirect	
me		me		*(to, for) me*
you		te		*(to, for) you*
you, him, it (masculine)	lo		le	*(to, for) you, him, her, it*
you, her, it (feminine)	la			
us		nos		*(to, for) us*
you, them (masculine)	los[3]		les[3]	*(to, for) you, them*
you, them (feminine)	las[3]			

▶ Direct object and indirect object pronouns are the same in the **me**, **te**, and **nos** forms and different in the third person **l-** forms.[4]

[3] The **vosotros** form for direct and indirect object pronouns can be found in the Appendix, section 1.

[4] Some Spanish-speaking people, particularly in Spain, use **le** both as an indirect object pronoun and as a direct object pronoun to express *him* or *you* (masculine polite). In this text **le** is used exclusively as an indirect object pronoun.

▶ Direct and indirect object pronouns are distinguished on the basis of context with respect to **me**, **te**, and **nos**, and on the basis of form in the case of the third person **l-** forms.

▶ A direct object directly receives the action of the verb. An indirect object tells to or for whom an action is done; hence, Spanish indirect objects often correspond to English phrases with *to* or *for*. However, in English the word *to* is often omitted if the indirect object precedes a direct object.
Examples:

Abbreviations: DO   direct object   IO   indirect object
               DP   direct object pronoun IP   indirect object pronoun

              DO   IO
1. Susana trae el refresco a Juan.   *Susana brings the soda to Juan.*

      IP   DO
2. Susana le trae el refresco.   *Susana brings the soda to him; or*
                                          Susana brings him the soda.

      DP   IO
3. Susana lo trae a Juan.   *Susana brings it to Juan.*

    IP   DO
4. ¿Me compras una bicicleta?   *Will you buy a bike for me? or*
                                          Will you buy me a bike?

▶ Recall that when the direct object is a person, it is introduced by the personal **a.** However, when the direct object appears as a pronoun, the personal **a** is not used.

Miguel quiere a Raquel; Miguel la quiere.   *Miguel loves Raquel;*
                                                 Miguel loves her.

Mónica le da el
periódico a Rafa.

28 Position of object pronouns

▶ Normally, object pronouns immediately precede the verb. However, they follow and are attached to infinitives (example 1) unless the infinitive completes the meaning of a preceding conjugated verb. In this case the object pronoun may either come before the conjugated verb (example 2) or be attached to the infinitive (example 3).

	IP	DO	DP

1. Le escribo una carta para conocerla mejor.

I'm writing a letter to her (in order) *to know her better.*

	IP	DO

2. Te quiero decir algo muy importante.

I want to say something very important to you; or *I want to tell you something very important.*

	IP DO

3. Quiero decirte algo muy importante.

▶ Spanish regularly uses both the indirect object and the indirect object pronoun together, even though both of them refer to the same person.

	IP	IO

1. ¿No le hablas al profesor?

Don't you speak to the teacher?

	IP	DO	IO

2. Alfonso le da una sonrisa ambigua a Susana.

Alfonso gives an ambiguous smile to Susana (*gives Susana an ambiguous smile*).

A • Replacement Drill   DO → DP

MODEL   No veo a María.
STUDENT   No **la** veo.

1. Ves a Carlos.
2. Alfonso oye a Juana.
3. No traen el dinero.
4. No tengo muchos libros.
5. Ella compra una Coca-Cola.
6. Ignacio y Miguel venden unos trastes.
7. ¿Dónde pongo el guacamole?
8. Mi esposo prepara la comida.
9. ¿Primero tomamos una cerveza?
10. ¿No tenemos su palabra de honor?

B • Query   Patterned Response   DO → DP

MODEL   ¿Conoce Ud. a Juan?
STUDENT   **¿A Juan? ¡Claro que lo conozco!**

1. ¿Conoce Ud. a Susana?
2. ¿Conoce Ud. los poemas?
3. ¿Conoce Ud. al rector?
4. ¿Conoce Ud. el pasillo?

5. ¿Conoce Ud. a las muchachas?
6. ¿Conoce Ud. al muchacho?
7. ¿Conoce Ud. a mi compadre?

8. ¿Conoce Ud. a mi comadre?
9. ¿Conoce Ud. las revistas?
10. ¿Conoce Ud. el libro?

C • Query   Patterned Response   me → te

MODEL   ¿Quién me ayuda? ¿Alfonso?
STUDENT   **No, hombre (mujer). Alfonso no te ayuda.**

te → me

1. ¿Quién me necesita? ¿El profesor?
2. ¿Quién me habla? ¿Susana?
3. ¿Qué me venden? ¿Unos trastes?
4. ¿Qué me dan? ¿Un refresco?
5. ¿Quiénes me quieren? ¿Ellos?

6. ¿Quién te comprende? ¿Gonzalo?
7. ¿Quién te convida a un refresco? ¿La muchacha?
8. ¿Qué te dicen? ¿Una disculpa?
9. ¿Qué te damos? ¿Una sonrisa?
10. ¿Quiénes te ayudan? ¿Los estudiantes?

D • Query   Patterned Response

MODEL   ¿Piensa Ud. hacer la tarea?
STUDENT 1   **No, no pienso hacerla.**
STUDENT 2   **No, no la pienso hacer.**

MODEL   ¿Piensan Uds. hacer la tarea?
STUDENT 1   **No, no pensamos hacerla.**
STUDENT 2   **No, no la pensamos hacer.**

1. ¿Piensa Ud. hacer la composición?
2. ¿Puede Ud. ayudar al muchacho?
3. ¿Quiere Ud. traer esa mesa?
4. ¿Tiene Ud. que hacer esas cosas?
5. ¿Desea Ud. hablar español?

6. ¿Van Uds. a esperar a Carlota?
7. ¿Piensan Uds. hacer algo importante?
8. ¿Pueden Uds. escribir los poemas?
9. ¿Quieren Uds. oír una canción?
10. ¿Piensan Uds. aceptar las demandas?

E • Query   Patterned Response   me → te

MODEL   ¿Puedes convidarme a un refresco?
STUDENT   **Bueno. Te convido a un refresco.**

1. ¿Puedes decirme dónde está la biblioteca?
2. ¿Puedes darme los libros allí?
3. ¿Quieres ayudarme con la tarea de español?
4. ¿Quieres traerme las demandas de los estudiantes?
5. ¿Piensas darme el dinero necesario?
6. ¿Puedes decirme dónde está la Avenida de las Américas?
7. ¿Piensas decirme quién es tu amigo?
8. ¿Puedes darme tus discos latinoamericanos?
9. ¿Quieres darme tus versos de amor?
10. ¿Piensas cantarme una canción?

F • Substitution Drill

MODEL   Cuando María pasa por aquí todos la miran.
                            Alfonso
STUDENT   Cuando Alfonso pasa por aquí todos **lo** miran.

1. Cuando Mónica pasa por aquí todos la miran.

    yo
    tú
    Carlos y Susana
    Carlos y Gonzalo
    él
    nosotros
    Teresa y Susana
    Ud.
    Uds.
    ellos

2. Si Mónica está en casa le voy a dar el dinero.

    tú
    Pancho
    ella
    Pancho y Rafa
    él
    Susana
    Ud.
    Susana y Rafa
    Uds.
    Susana y Josefa

G • Query   Patterned Response   nos → los or les

                                                        DP
(direct object pronoun)   MODEL   ¿Quién nos quiere? ¿Alfonso?

                                                        DP
            STUDENT   **Así es. Alfonso los quiere.**

                                                DO   IP
(indirect object pronoun)   MODEL   ¿Qué nos da la Srta. Azuela? ¿La tarea?

                                                            IP   DO
            STUDENT   **Así es. La Srta. Azuela les da la tarea.**

1. ¿Quién nos quiere? ¿Gonzalo?   6. ¿Quién nos necesita? ¿Nuestra comadre?
2. ¿Qué nos da Juan? ¿Una Coca-Cola?   7. ¿Qué nos da el señor? ¿Nuestro dinero?
3. ¿Qué nos venden? ¿Unas revistas?   8. ¿Adónde nos traen? ¿A nuestra casa?
4. ¿Cuándo nos ayudan? ¿A las cinco?   9. ¿Quiénes nos escriben las noticias? ¿Nuestros hijos?
5. ¿Adónde nos traen? ¿A la clínica?   10. ¿Quién nos dice eso? ¿Nuestra profesora?

H • Variable Substitution Drill

	IP	DO	DP
MODEL	Le escribe una carta para ayudarla.		
	Te		
STUDENT	**Te** escribe una carta para ayudar**te**.		

1. Le escribe una carta para ayudarla.
   Te
                 ayudarme.
   Nos
                 ayudarlo.
   Me
                 ayudarla.
                 ayudarlas.
                 ayudarlos.

2. Cuando me trae siempre me da un café.

DP	IP	DO
los		
	te	
las		
		nos
la		
		me
lo		
		te

I • Translation Drill

Translate the following into Spanish.

1. They need him. They buy it. We sell them.
2. I see it. I hear it. They don't want to do it. I help her.
3. We write to him. We write to her. We write it.
4. She speaks to him. She speaks to her. She speaks to them.
5. I love her! I give the poem to her. She loves him! She gives the poem to him.

29   Verbs that take a direct object without a preposition

buscar   *to look for, seek*   **esperar**   *to wait (for); expect; hope*
escuchar   *to listen (to)*   **mirar**   *to look (at)*

▶ The prepositions *for, at,* and *to,* are included in the meanings of **buscar, escuchar, esperar,** and **mirar.** These verbs take a direct object in Spanish without any preposition, although the personal **a** is used when the direct object noun is a definite person.

1. Buscamos la tienda.   *We are looking for the store.*
2. ¿A quién buscas? Busco a Alfonso.   *Who are you looking for? I'm looking for Alfonso.*
3. Pepita mira la revista.   *Pepita is looking at the magazine.*
4. Escuchan al profesor.   *They are listening to the professor.*
5. Los esperamos.   *We are waiting for them.*

A • Query   Patterned Response

MODEL   ¿Qué busca Ud.? ¿El pasillo?
STUDENT   **Sí. Busco el pasillo.**

1. ¿Qué busca Ud.? ¿El libro?
2. ¿Qué mira Ud.? ¿La venta?
3. ¿A quién escucha Ud.? ¿A Susana?
4. ¿A quién espera Ud.? ¿A la muchacha?
5. ¿A quién mira Ud.? ¿A Francisca?

6. ¿A quién tiene Ud. que esperar? ¿Al rector?
7. ¿A quién va Ud. a escuchar? ¿A su amigo?
8. ¿A quién piensa Ud. esperar? ¿A Mónica y a Gonzalo?
9. ¿A quién puede Ud. buscar? ¿Al estudiante?
10. ¿A quién quiere Ud. escuchar? ¿A su hijo?

B • Translation Drill

Translate the following into Spanish.

1. Who are you looking for? Who are you waiting for?
2. What are you listening to? What are you looking at?
3. We're waiting for her. We're looking at the book.
4. They're listening to the teacher. She's looking for the sale.
5. Can you look for it? Are you going to wait for me?

30   Saber and conocer

saber to know facts, know how to do something, know something thoroughly		conocer to be familiar with or be acquainted with, know a person	
sé		**conozco**[5]	
sabes		conoces	
sabe		conoce	
sabemos		conocemos	
saben		conocen	

▶ The range of meaning covered by "knowing" is divided between **saber** and **conocer**. **Saber** represents knowledge that can be communicated, taught, and learned. **Conocer** represents degrees of awareness from close acquaintance to mere recognition.

[5] Practically all verbs that end in **-ecer** have the same irregularity as **conocer**: **-zco** as the first person singular ending in the present indicative. For example, **agradecer**: **Te agradezco**, I thank (am thankful to) you.

▶ **Saber** means *to know facts* (example 1), *to know how to do something*, or *to know something thoroughly* (examples 2 and 3). **Saber** is not normally followed by **cómo** before an infinitive (example 3).

1. Todos sabemos que la situación es grave.   *We all know that the situation is grave.*

2. Sé los versos de memoria; saben escribir.   *I know the verses by heart; they know how to write.*

3. Sé leer el inglés y el español.   *I know how to read English and Spanish.*

▶ **Conocer** means *to be familiar with* or *to be acquainted with* (examples 1 and 2), or *to know a person* (examples 3 and 4). Often, **conocer** is translated in English by *to meet* (a person for the first time).

1. ¿Conoces esta revista?   *Do you know (are you familiar with) this magazine?*

2. Conozco el poema pero no lo sé de memoria.   *I know (am acquainted with) the poem but I don't know it by heart.*

3. Todos conocemos al hijo de Ignacio.   *We all know (are acquainted with) Ignacio's son.*

4. Quiero conocer a Susana y a Gonzalo.   *I want to meet Susana and Gonzalo.*

A • Query   Patterned Response

MODEL   ¿Conoces a mi esposo?
STUDENT   **Sí, lo conozco.**
MODEL   ¿Sabes quién es?
STUDENT   **No, no sé quién es.**

1. ¿Conoces a Susana?
   ¿Sabes dónde vive?
2. ¿Conoces Barcelona?
   ¿Sabes escribir en español?
3. ¿Conoces la música mexicana?
   ¿Sabes hacer guacamole?
4. ¿Conoces la Avenida de las Américas?
   ¿Sabes dónde está?
5. ¿Conoces la biblioteca?
   ¿Sabes dónde tienen los periódicos latinoamericanos?

B • Query   Free Response

Answer in Spanish.

1. ¿Sabe Ud. qué hora es?
2. ¿Conoce Ud. el estado de California?
3. ¿Sabes hablar ahora un poco de español?
4. ¿Conoces a los muchachos y a las muchachas en la clase?
5. ¿Sabes esta lección de memoria?
6. ¿Sabe Ud. de dónde es el profesor de español?
7. ¿Sabes escribir en español?
8. ¿Quieres conocer a la muchacha linda (al muchacho guapo)?

REVIEW

I The following questions are related to the dialog. Answer in Spanish.

1. ¿Dónde espera Alfonso a la muchacha todos los días?
2. ¿Conoce a la muchacha?
3. ¿La muchacha le da algo a Alfonso?
4. ¿Cuál es el problema de Alfonso?
5. ¿Charla mucho Alfonso con otras muchachas?
6. ¿Quién le da un empujón a Alfonso?
7. ¿Sabe la señorita que Alfonso la quiere?
8. ¿Es Gonzalo un amigo de verdad?

II Translation. Translate the following into Spanish.

1. Cheer up! One day surely you are going to meet him. How do you know that?
2. What do I intend to do? I love her. What can I do?
3. Do you know what? Your problem is that you want to tell her something but you can't.
4. Do you believe him when he says that he waits for you every day in the hallway?
5. Well, why doesn't he talk to me? Why doesn't he buy me a Coca-Cola or something?
6. I don't know. When he sees us in the library he always gives us one of those ambiguous smiles.
7. I know it. What a shame! We ought to give him a shove.
8. I want to tell her that I love her in Spanish. But first I have to write it and practice it.

III Write your own dialog.

You are eavesdropping on a conversation in which a forward boy (girl) is trying to meet and talk with a timid member of the opposite sex. What do they say?

PRONUNCIATION

Spanish r and rr

Spanish **r** and **rr** are not similar to the English *r*. However, the Spanish single **r** between vowels does resemble English *d* (or *dd*) and *t* (or *tt*) in words such as *ladder*, *water*, *Eddie*, *butter*, and so forth, when they are pronounced rapidly. Pronounce the following and note the similarities.

rudder	rara (*rare*)	lotta	Lara (proper name)
putter	pura (*pure*)	pot o' tea	para ti (*for you*)
matter	Mara (proper name)	Eddies	eres (*you are*)

Pronounce the following after your instructor.

eres	hora	señorita
enamorado	ahora	pero
mira	dinero	para

¿La miras pasar por aquí?
Quiero pero no puedo.
La señorita americana mira ahora.

Spanish **r** after a consonant is pronounced just as it is between vowels, and not like the English *r*. Pronounce the following after your instructor.

escribes	palabras	otras
primero	pobre	tres
refresco	agradecer	cuatro
bruto	espectro	pronto

Primero escribo palabras.
El espectro me agradece el refresco.
Aquí hay tres o cuatro brutos.

Spanish **rr** consists of a rapid series of three, four or more taps of the tongue against the upper gum ridge. For Spanish speakers **r** and **rr** are just as different as **p** and **b** or **t** and **d**. Many pairs of words are distinguished solely by this contrast. Pronounce after your instructor.

pero (*but*)	para (*for*)	cero (*zero*)
perro (*dog*)	parra (*grapevine*)	cerro (*hill*)
caro (*expensive*)	foro (*forum*)	moro (*Moor*)
carro (*cart, car*)	forro (*lining*)	morro (*knob*)

Words that begin with **r** and words with **r** after **n, l,** or **s** are not written **rr,** but they have the same multiple trill as written **rr.** The letter **rr** never begins a word in Spanish. If a prefix is put before a word beginning with **r,** it is then written **rr: romántico, archirromántico.** Pronounce after your instructor.

Rubén Ramírez	Enrique
rápidamente	Israel
refresco	enredo
romántico	alrededor

Rubén Ramírez, eres un romántico.

Enrique no es rico, es pobre.

Escribe rápidamente los versos para ti.

Here is a Spanish tongue twister based on **r** and **rr!**

Ere con ere cigarro,	R *with* r: *cigar*
ere con ere barril	r *with* r: *barrel*
rápidamente corren los carros	*rapidly race the cars*
por las vías del ferrocarril.	*along the railroad tracks.*

Cognates & Contexts

MARGARITA	Hola, chica. ¿Qué escribes?	**chica** *girl*
ESTELA	Nada, nada.	
MARGARITA	¿Cómo? Veo que escribes algo.	
ESTELA	No es nada. Sólo un poema.	
MARGARITA	¿Un poema? ¿Qué clase de poema?	
ESTELA	¡Ay! Un poco de paz, ¡por favor! Es un poema de amor.	
MARGARITA	De amor, ¿tú? ¿Por qué?	
ESTELA	Pues, porque estoy enamorada.	
MARGARITA	¿Qué? ¡No te creo!	
ESTELA	Pues, allá tú.	**allá tú** *that's up to you*
MARGARITA	¿Y compones un poema de amor?	**componer** *to compose*
ESTELA	Sí, de amor. También busco mi identidad . . . es decir, en el poema.	
MARGARITA	No lo creo.	
ESTELA	No soy la primera. ¿No conoces los poemas de Gabriela Mistral? ¿O de Alfonsina Storni? ¿O de Julia de Burgos?	
MARGARITA	Bueno... ya no digo más. No quiero meter la pata. ¿Cómo es tu poema?	**meter la pata** *to goof, put one's foot in one's mouth*
ESTELA	Tienes que esperar unos días. Quiero refinarlo. Me da vergüenza recitarlo ahora. Estas cosas son difíciles; es un proceso lento.	**lento** *slow*

MARGARITA   Bueno, la romántica y enigmática Estela, como siempre. Si no me vas a recitar tu misterioso poema, por lo menos me puedes decir en quién piensas cuando dices, tan apasionadamente, "¡estoy enamorada!"

pensar en to think about

ESTELA   ¿No lo sabes ya?

MARGARITA   Hmmm. ¡A poco es Fernando Ramírez! Ese majadero que charla como un loro en la clase y piensa que es un experto sobre la sexualidad en general.

a poco es (coll.) it's probably

ESTELA   Yo, ¿enamorada de ese bruto? Lo odio. Mi amorcito es una persona de finas sensibilidades. Guapo, serio, grave. Tú me tientas. Sé que sabes. ¡Y si no sabes, no te voy a decir nada!

odiar to hate

me tientas you are probing me, tempting me

Gabriela Mistral (1889–1957)   Chilean poet who won the Nobel Prize in Literature in 1945. She was a post-modernist poet whose themes include desolation and death, love, sympathy, and tenderness for children.

Alfonsina Storni (1892–1938)   Argentine poet well-known for her impassioned poetry about her frustrated life, which she ended by leaping into the sea.

Julia de Burgos (1916–1953)   Puerto Rican poet who also lived for many years in New York City. Her works cover both erotic themes and themes of social protest.

16 ENERO 79

Lección siete

DISCUSIONES SOBRE EL PORVENIR

(handwritten: 23 ENERO 79)

(handwritten: as in Clausa)

sobre *about; on; over*

porvenir *future*

LAURA ¡Ay, no sé, chica! En la situación en que estoy, es muy difícil decidir.

CECILIA No tan difícil. Si te aceptan en la facultad de medicina... ¿cómo no vas a ir? ¡Tienes que hacerlo! Estás obligada.

LAURA Roberto cree que cuatro años de trabajo intenso son muchos para esperar. ¿No tiene un poco de chauvinista?

trabajo *work*

CECILIA Roberto piensa ser ingeniero, ¿no? Eso cuesta mucho trabajo. ¿No lo encuentras algo asimétrico?

ingeniero *engineer* **costar (ue)** *to require; to cost*
encontrar (ue) *to find*
algo *somewhat*
asimétrico *asymmetrical, out of balance*

LAURA Bueno, pensándolo bien, es verdad que lo estoy encontrando así. Sin embargo, alguien tiene que permanecer en casa para tener una familia. Por lo menos, así dice Roberto... y también su padre, el señor López.

alguien *someone*

permanecer *to remain*

CECILIA Y tú, ¿qué dices?

LAURA Pues, muy poco. En esas ocasiones siempre estoy de mal humor.

de mal humor *in a bad mood*

CECILIA A propósito. El anillo que llevas puesto es precioso. ¿Es tu anillo de compromiso?

anillo *ring* **llevar puesto** *to have on*
precioso *beautiful* **de compromiso** *engagement (adj.)*

LAURA	Sí. ¿No es magnífico? Sólo que mamá está furiosa porque son ópalos en vez de brillantes y me dice que tengo que devolverlo.	**sólo que** *only (that)* **en vez de** *instead of* **brillantes** *diamonds* **devolver (ue)** *to give back*
CECILIA	Ay, Laura. ¿Cuándo vamos a acabar con esas actitudes anticuadas?	**acabar (con)** *to finish (with)*
LAURA	Bueno. Hoy mismo empiezo, diciéndole al señor López que pienso estudiar medicina.	**hoy mismo** *today (emphatic)* **empezar (ie)** *to begin*
CECILIA	¿Qué? ¿Todavía no lo sabe? ¿El padre de tu novio?	**novio** *boyfriend, fiancé*
LAURA	Pero, Cecilia, ¡si yo no lo sé todavía! ¿Por qué tienen que saberlo los señores López?	
CECILIA	Pero, Laura. Todo el día me tienes encerrada aquí en tu cuarto. Aquí estoy escuchando tus dudas y vacilaciones... Roberto, la medicina la boda, los padres...	**todo el día** *all day* **encerrada** *locked up* **cuarto** *room* **dudas** *doubts* **boda** *wedding*
LAURA	Cecilia, ¿qué te pasa? ¿No puedo confiar en una amiga?	**¿qué te pasa?** *what's the matter with you?* **confiar** *to confide*
CECILIA	¡Sí, mujer! Pero no debes esconder tus pensamientos e intenciones. Tienes que debatir esto y decidirlo en público. Y si te critican, defiendes tu decisión. ¡Vamos, mujer! A salir del cuartito. ¡Adelante!	**esconder** *to hide* **pensamientos** *thoughts* **en público** *openly, publicly* **defender (ie)** *to defend* **¡vamos!** *come on!* **a salir de** *get out of*

NOTES

Vocabulary Meanings

facultad a school or division within a university, not a group of professors.

el chauvinista, la chauvinista the chauvinist. The original meaning of **chauvinismo** (*chauvinism*) is fanatical patriotism. In the last decade it has taken on the additional meaning of undue and excessive favoring of men over women (or vice versa). This latter meaning is used here. Another term that relates to male chauvinism is **machismo** (*male chauvinism, exaltation of masculinity*, from **macho**, *male*). **Macho** has its counterpart in **hembra**, *female*.

la novia, el novio *bride* and *groom*, respectively, or *fiancée* and *fiancé* (as in the context of the dialog), or more commonly, *girlfriend* and *boyfriend*.

Conjunctions y and e, o and u

The conjunction **y** (*and*) is used in all cases except before words beginning with the sound /i/, where **e** is used (examples 1 and 2). Similarly, **o** (*or*) is used in all cases except before the sound /o/, where **u** is used (examples 3 and 4).

1. López e hijos   *López and sons*
2. ¿Cuáles son tus pensamientos   *What are your thoughts and*
   e intenciones?   *intentions?*
3. Necesito siete u ocho.   *I need seven or eight.*
4. ¿Qué son ustedes? ¿Niños u   *What are you? Boys or men?*
   hombres?

LANGUAGE STRUCTURES

31   Stem-changing verbs, Class I: e → ie, o → ue

▶   In certain verbs the last vowel of the stem, *when stressed*, changes **e** → **ie** or **o** → **ue**. These Class I verbs end in **-ar** and **-er**. This stem change cannot be predicted from the infinitive; it has to be learned by practice. Verbs of this type are indicated thus: empezar (ie)   encontrar (ue).

emp**ie**zo	enc**ue**ntro
emp**ie**zas	enc**ue**ntras
emp**ie**za	enc**ue**ntra
empezamos	encontramos
empie**ie**zan	enc**ue**ntran

Here are some examples of Class I stem-changing verbs. The verbs in color are new vocabulary.

cerrar (ie)	*to close*	costar (ue)	*to cost; to require*
encerrar (ie)	*to lock up, shut in*	encontrar (ue)	*to find*
defender (ie)	*to defend*	**mostrar (ue)**	*to show*
empezar (ie)	*to begin*	poder (ue)	*to be able, can*
entender (ie)	*to understand*	volver (ue)	*to return, go back*
pensar (ie)	*to think*	devolver (ue)	*to return, give back*
perder (ie)	*to lose*		
querer (ie)	*to want; to love*		

Also: venir (ie) (but **vengo**)   tener (ie) (but **tengo**)

Volver versus Devolver

Volver means *to return, come back* (the subject does the returning). **Devolver** means *to return* or *to give back a thing* (the object is what is returned).
Fill in the blank:

La Sra. Azuela _____
a su familia.

Álvaro le _____ el libro
a Eugenio.

A • Substitution Drill

MODEL   Nosotros lo encontramos algo asimétrico.
         Yo
STUDENT Yo lo **encuentro** algo asimétrico.

1. Nosotros lo encontramos algo cínico.
   Cecilia
   Cecilia y Laura
   Nosotras
   Yo
   Tú

2. Yo defiendo a mi familia.
   Juan   su
   Tú
   Él
   Nosotros
   Mi novio

3. Ahora mismo ella empieza la canción.
   nosotros
   yo
   Alfonso y yo
   él y ella
   Uds.

4. ¿Cierra Pancho la tienda?
   tú
   Rafa
   Rafa y Margarita
   Ud.
   nosotros

5. Ella entiende mucho español.
   Ellas
   Él
   Él y yo
   Eugenio
   Yo

6. ¿Cuándo vuelve Tere?
   tú?
   nosotros?
   él?
   Paco?
   Rosa y Rubén?

B • Substitution Drill   First Person Plural → First Person Singular

MODEL   Pensamos ser ingenieros.
STUDENT **Pienso** ser ingeniero.

1. Pensamos defender la causa.
2. Queremos decidir qué hacer.
3. Empezamos a hacerlo.
4. Podemos decidirlo.
5. Entendemos cómo hacerlo.

6. Te mostramos cómo hacerlo.
7. Tenemos que ayudarlos.
8. Defendemos la libertad.
9. Venimos a votar.
10. Lo encontramos muy difícil.

C • Substitution Drill   Third Person Plural → First Person Plural

MODEL   Quieren el anillo.
STUDENT **Queremos** el anillo.

1. Quieren ayudar.
2. Devuelven el libro.
3. Vienen a tomar una cerveza.
4. Encuentran la revista.
5. No pueden decidirlo.

6. Tienen que luchar.
7. Piensan ser ingenieros.
8. Defienden a Cecilia.
9. Pierden las oportunidades.
10. Entienden bien.

D • Query   Free Response

Answer in Spanish.

1. ¿Qué piensas hacer?
2. ¿Escondes tus pensamientos o los defiendes?
3. ¿Generalmente estás de buen humor o del mal humor?
4. ¿Tienes un novio (una novia)?
5. ¿Qué piensas de tu profesor (profesora)?
6. ¿Estás obligada (obligado) a estudiar?
7. ¿Quieres encontrar un trabajo este año?
8. ¿Puedes confiar en tus padres?
9. ¿Qué haces cuando pierdes algo?
10. ¿Muestras siempre que eres una persona perspicaz?

32   Formation and uses of the present participle

▶ The present participle, which in English ends in *-ing*, is regularly formed in Spanish by adding **-ando** to the stem of **-ar** verbs and **-iendo** to the stems of **-er** and **-ir** verbs. Most **-er** and **-ir** verbs that have a stem ending in a vowel add **-yendo**.[1] In addition, there are a few irregular present participles, such as those listed below.

Regular verbs	hablar	habl	-ando	hablando	*speaking*
	aprender	aprend	-iendo	aprendiendo	*learning*
	escribir	escrib	-iendo	escribiendo	*writing*
Verbs with a stem ending in a vowel	traer	tra	-yendo	trayendo	*bringing*
	creer	cre	-yendo	creyendo	*believing*
	oír	o	-yendo	oyendo	*hearing*
Some irregular verbs	decir	**dic**	-iendo	diciendo	*saying, telling*
	poder	**pud**	-iendo	pudiendo	*being able*
	ir		-yendo	yendo	*going*

▶ Present participles are used to make the progressive form of the tenses, such as the present progressive. The progressive form regularly uses **estar** as the auxiliary verb (never **ser**)[2] plus the present participle. The present progressive emphasizes that an action is currently in progress.

¿Qué está Ud. escuchando?   *What are you listening to?*
Estoy buscando a Carla.   *I'm looking for Carla.*

---

[1] Exceptions are Class III stem-changing verbs, which will be discussed in Lección quince.
[2] See section **95** for other verbs that may be used as auxiliaries in the progressive.

¡Cuidado!

Unlike English, Spanish never uses the present progressive to refer to future action. However, the simple present *can be* used to express future action in Spanish.[3]

Van a California mañana.   *They are going to California tomorrow.*

Since Spanish does not use the present progressive for future action, the present participle **yendo** is rarely used.

Pero primero vamos a tomar una   *But first we're going to cerveza, ¿ no ?*   *have a beer, right ?*

▶ Present participles are used in Spanish as modifiers (although they always end in **-o**). They indicate the circumstances under which an occurrence takes place. They do not take a preposition before them, although the English equivalent often requires a preposition to translate their meaning.

Estudiando, aprendemos.   *By studying, we learn.*

A • Substitution Drill

MODEL   Rafa está buscando a Carlota.
          Yo

STUDENT   Yo **estoy** buscando a Carlota.

1. Rafa está buscando a Carlota.
   Tú
   Tú y yo
   Roberto y Cecilia
   Los estudiantes
   El novio

2. Mónica está viviendo con sus padres.
   Tú y yo
   Ella y yo
   Andrés y su hermano
   Ustedes
   Yo

B • Query   Patterned Response

MODEL   ¿Qué estás haciendo? ¿Escribiendo una carta?
STUDENT   **Sí, estoy escribiendo una carta.**

1. ¿Qué están haciendo ellos? ¿Criticando a Eugenio?
2. ¿Qué estás haciendo? ¿Defendiendo la causa?
3. ¿Qué están haciendo Uds.? ¿Preparando una venta?

[3] The use of the simple present in this context is limited, usually requiring time designators (**primero, mañana**, etc.). On the other hand, **ir** in the present tense + **a** + infinitive can be used to express future action in most circumstances, see section **9.**

4. ¿Qué estamos haciendo? ¿Devolviendo una foto?
5. ¿Qué están haciendo ellos? ¿Esperando al señor López?
6. ¿Qué están haciendo Uds.? ¿Pensando qué hacer?
7. ¿Qué está haciendo Ud.? ¿Escondiendo un libro?
8. ¿Qué está haciendo ella? ¿Encerrando a Mauricio?
9. ¿Qué está haciendo Laura? ¿Decidiendo qué hacer?
10. ¿Qué estamos haciendo Laura y yo? ¿Estudiando la tarea?

33 Position of object pronouns with the present participle

▶ Object pronouns, just as in the case of infinitives (see section **28**), are attached to present participles unless the present participle completes the meaning of a previously conjugated verb. In this case they either come before the conjugated verb or are attached to the end of the present participle.

1. Pensándolo[4] bien, no voy a ir.   *Thinking it over (well), I'm not going to go.*
2. Hoy empiezo, diciéndole[4] la   *Today I begin, by telling Mr. López the*
  verdad al Sr. López.   *truth.*
3. Así lo estoy encontrando.
         or   *That's how I'm finding it.*
   Así estoy encontrándolo.[4]

A • Variable Substitution Drill

MODEL   Haciéndolo nosotros, ayudamos la causa.
                  tú
STUDENT   Haciéndolo tú, **ayudas** la causa.

1. Mostrándolo nosotros, ayudamos la causa.
             tú
   Haciéndolo
             ella
   Cantándola
             yo
   Hablándote

2. Hoy comienzo, diciéndole al Sr. López mi decisión.
                 les
                   a la señora López
             dándole
                   a los señores López
             mostrándoles

---

[4] When a pronoun is attached to a present participle, the original stressed syllable is not displaced. Therefore, a written accent is necessary on the stressed vowel because an extra syllable has been added (see p. 11).

B • Transformation Drill   Present → Present Progressive

MODEL   Lo encuentro así.
STUDENT 1   **Lo estoy encontrando** así.
STUDENT 2   **Estoy encontrándolo** así.

1. Lo hago bien.
2. No me escucha.
3. ¿Lo buscas por aquí?
4. Te vendemos revistas nuevas.
5. No les digo las razones.

6. Parece que no nos entiende.
7. ¿Por qué me traes tantas cosas?
8. ¿Por qué me escondes tus pensamientos?
9. Lo oigo en casa.
10. La orquesta la empieza hoy.

C • Translation Drill

Translate the following into Spanish, using the present progressive.

1. What are you telling them?
2. They are bringing the sodas here.
3. The wedding is beginning now.

4. Mauricio and Tere are dancing a tango.
5. I am not doing it well.
6. By listening, we learn to speak Spanish.

34   Ser versus estar

▶ **Ser** and **estar** both mean *to be*. However, these two verbs are widely different in their concepts, just as *to do* and *to make* (both **hacer** in Spanish) or *to say* and *to tell* (both **decir** in Spanish) are for English speakers. **Ser** and **estar** cannot be interchanged without a basic change in meaning. In most cases, they cannot be interchanged at all.

▶ **Ser** tells who the subject is or what it is in a fundamental, essential way. **Estar** usually tells where the subject is, or its state or condition. Keep in mind the following nouns: **un ser**, *a being*, *an essence*; **un estado**,[5] *a state*; **un estado de ánimo**, *a state of mind*.

Estar

A.   Location.

1. ¿Está Raquel? ¡Claro que está!
2. Estamos en la Avenida de las Américas.

Is Raquel here? Of course she is!
We are on the Avenue of the Americas.

B.   As the auxiliary verb with a present participle to express the progressive form of the tenses.

1. Están esperándolo.
2. Estamos defendiendo la causa.
3. Estoy escribiendo una composición.

They are waiting for him.
We are defending the cause.
I am writing a composition.

---

[5] This form is also the past participle of **estar**.

C.   With adjectives to express noninherent, accidental, or variable conditions or states.

1. Mi compadre ya está bueno (coll.).	*My compadre is all right now.*
2. Las aceitunas están verdes.	*The olives are green (unripe).*
3. ¿Cómo está Pancho?	*How is Pancho (feeling)?*
4. Ese libro está sucio.	*That book is dirty (dusty).*

Ser

A.   With adjectives to express what something is, inherently, by nature.

1. Mi compadre es muy bueno.	*My compadre is very good (a good guy).*
2. Las aceitunas son verdes.	*Olives are green (their normal color).*
3. ¿Cómo es Pancho?	*What is Pancho like? (What kind of guy is he?)*
4. Ese libro es sucio.	*That book is dirty (obscene).*

B.   Linking the subject with nouns and pronouns.

1. La Srta. Azuela es la profesora.	*Miss Azuela is the teacher.*
2. Soy un pobre alucinado.	*I'm a poor bewitched creature.*
3. ¿Quién es el líder?	*Who is the leader?*

C.   To indicate origin, possession, or material with **de**; destination with **para**.

1. Soy de Borinquen. Somos de México.	*I'm from Borinquen (Puerto Rico). We're from Mexico.*
2. ¿De quién es la moto? La moto es de Rubén.	*Whose motorcycle is it? The motorcycle is Rubén's.*
3. El anillo es de oro.	*The ring is (of) gold.*
4. Los versos son para mi novia.	*The verses are for my girlfriend.*

D.   To tell time of day.

1. ¿Qué hora es?	*What time is it?*
2. Son las cuatro y cuarto.	*It is a quarter after four.*

▶   Only **estar** is used for location and to make the progressive form of the tenses. Only **ser** is used to link the subject with nouns or pronouns; to indicate origin, possession, material or destination; or to tell time of day.

23 ENERO 79
—lo here

▶ As the sections in color indicate, the only sentences in which **ser** and **estar** may be interchanged (with a consequent change in meaning) are those with predicate adjectives. **Ser** is used to express an essential characteristic or quality, what something is by nature. With **estar**, the things linked are thought of as not really "belonging" to the subject. **Estar** expresses the condition or state the subject is *in*.

▶ Sometimes words themselves change in meaning if used with **ser** or **estar**.

    1. Laura está lista.   *Laura is ready.*
      Mónica es lista.   *Mónica is clever.*
    2. Todavía está vivo.   *He is still alive.*
      Fernando es vivo.   *Fernando is lively ("sharp").*

Contrary to what you might expect, the adjectives **muerto**, *dead*, and **vivo**, *alive*, take **estar**, not **ser**. Think of it this way, the state of being alive or dead does not really alter one's basic identity.

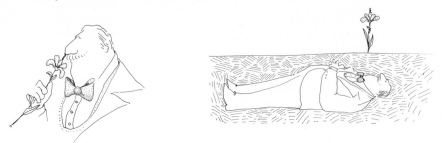

      Está vivo.   Está muerto.

Try to interpret these additional sentences that take predicate adjectives and change their meaning with **ser** versus **estar**.

    1. Las uvas son verdes. Las uvas están verdes.   **uvas** *grapes*
    2. El hombre es malo. El hombre está malo.   **malo** *bad, ill*
    3. El joven es pálido. El joven está pálido.   **pálido** *pale*
    4. El valle es seco, pero ahora no está seco.   **seco** *dry*
    5. Cecilia es bonita. Mónica está bonita con su
      vestido verde.
    6. ¿Cómo es la comida aquí? ¿Cómo está la comida hoy?

Now explain why in the first of the following pairs of sentences **ser** is appropriate and in the second **estar** is appropriate.

    1. El hielo es frío. El café está frío.   **hielo** *ice* **frío** *cold*
    2. ¿De dónde es Alvaro? ¿Dónde está Alvaro?
    3. ¡Mujer! ¡Eres muy linda! ¡Mujer! ¡Estás obligada!

4. El anillo es precioso. Mamá está furiosa.
5. Pienso ser ingeniero. Pienso estar allí.
6. Así es. Está bien.

Very often writers will build upon the grammatical structures that are unique to a language; they will exploit the linguistic potentials of the language for esthetic reasons. This excerpt from a poem written by Nobel Prize-winning poet Juan Ramón Jiménez expresses man's relationship to God on the basis of the **ser/estar** distinction.

Pero tú, Dios...   But you, God . . .
tú estás y eres   you are [within] and are
lo grande y lo pequeño que yo soy   the big and the little of what I am

   (de *Soy animal de fondo*)

A • Query   Patterned Response

Answer with either **ser** or **estar**, whichever is appropriate.

(estar)   MODEL   ¿Laura? ¿Obligada?
          STUDENT   **Sí, Laura está obligada.**

(ser)   MODEL   ¿Laura? ¿Poeta?
          STUDENT   **Sí, Laura es poeta.**

1. ¿Laura? ¿Furiosa?
2. ¿La familia? ¿Aquí?
3. ¿Pancho? ¿Cantando?
4. ¿El anillo? ¿Magnífico?
5. ¿Los brutos? ¿Encerrados?
6. ¿Laura? ¿De buen humor?
7. ¿El joven? ¿Guapo?
8. ¿Los chicanos? ¿De Texas?
9. ¿La tienda? ¿Grande?
10. ¿El poema? ¿De admirable tono moral?

B • Query   Patterned Response

MODEL   ¿Está Tere?
STUDENT   **¿Quién es Tere?**

MODEL   Es mi amiga.
STUDENT   **No, no está aquí.**

1. ¿Está el señor López?
   Es el padre de mi novio.
2. ¿Está mi comadre?
   Es Margarita Ramírez.
3. ¿Está Mauricio Azuela?
   Es un poeta.
4. ¿Está el chauvinista?
   Es Pancho Posada.

5. ¿Está el mentiroso?
   Es Alfonso, el cínico.
6. ¿Está ese estudiante archirromántico?
   Es Gonzalo, el alucinado.

7. ¿Está el líder?
   Es Eugenio, el puertorriqueño.
8. ¿Está el sinvergüenza?
   Es Rafa.

C • Query   Free Response

Answer in Spanish.

1. ¿Estás furiosa (furioso)?
2. ¿Estás de buen humor o de mal humor?
3. ¿Cómo está usted?
4. ¿Cómo es el profesor?

5. ¿Dónde estamos?
6. ¿De dónde eres?
7. ¿Qué hora es?
8. ¿Eres un (una) chauvinista?

D • Translation Drill

Translate the following into Spanish.

1. How is he? What is he like?
2. Where are you? Where are you from?
3. Who are you? Who is here?
4. The girl is lively. The boy is alive.
5. What is your situation? I am in a difficult situation.
6. It is difficult to decide. I am obliged (**a**) to decide.

35   Spanish **de** phrase to modify a noun

▶ While in English one noun can directly modify another, Spanish uses **de** plus the noun. Of course this type of phrase is familiar in English too.

un lomo de cerdo   *a loin of pork* or *a pork loin*

Here are more examples of **de** phrases that we have encountered before.

el anillo de compromiso	*the engagement ring*
la profesora de español[6]	*the Spanish teacher*
la clase de matemáticas	*the mathematics class*
la tienda de discos	*the record shop*

A • Translation Drill

Translate the following into Spanish.

1. This is my engagement ring.
2. There is the Spanish teacher.
3. I want a loin of pork.
4. Where is the record store?
5. Here is the mathematics class.
6. This is Chihuahua cheese.
7. I'm going to the Paris Conservatory.
8. He writes love poems.
9. Are you the Spanish students?
10. Where is the book sale?

[6] Note that **la profesora de español** is a teacher of Spanish (we don't know her nationality because **español** is a noun indicating her area of competence); **una profesora española** is a teacher who is Spanish (we don't know what she teaches because **española** is an adjective indicating her nationality).

36 The definite article with titles and geographical locations

▶ The definite article is used before titles such as **señor, señora, señorita, doctor, profesor**, etc. (examples 1, 2 and 3) or before proper names such as **Avenida, Calle**, etc. (example 4).

1. ¿Dónde están los señores López?	*Where are Mr. and Mrs. Lopez?*
2. ¿Conoces al profesor Ulibarri?	*Do you know (are you acquainted with) Professor Ulibarri?*
3. Yo soy el doctor Aguilar.	*I'm Doctor Aguilar.*
4. Estamos en la Avenida de las Américas. Ahora, ¿dónde está la Calle Seis?	*We're on the Avenue of the Americas. Now, where is Sixth Street?*

▶ The definite article is *not* used when directly addressing a person by his title (example 1) nor before **don** or **doña** (example 2). Remember that **los señores López** means *Mr. and Mrs. Lopez*.

1. ¿Cómo está Ud., señor Méndez?	*How are you, Mr. Méndez?*
Bien, ¿y usted, profesora Quintana?	*Fine, and you, Professor Quintana?*
2. Aquí está don Carlos Cruz.	*Here is Don Carlos Cruz.*

▶ The definite article is frequently used with the following geographical locations.[7]

la Argentina	el Brasil	el Canadá
el Ecuador	los Estados Unidos	la Florida
la Habana	el Paraguay	el Perú
la República Dominicana	el Uruguay	

A • Fill in the blanks with the definite article, if needed.

1. Buenos días, _____ señora.
2. ¿Está aquí _____ señor Ramírez?
3. ¡Ah! Está en su oficina en _____ Avenida Emiliano Zapata y _____ Calle Quince.
4. Quiero ir a _____ Florida para visitar a unos amigos cubanos.
5. ¿Así que vas a visitar a _____ Estados Unidos?
6. Pues sí, _____ doña Carmen.
7. Y, ¿cómo van las cosas con _____ señor López?
8. Pues, _____ doctor Ramírez, no sé realmente.
9. ¡Ah! Allí está _____ doctora Méndez.
10. ¿Conoce Ud. a _____ don Rafael?

[7] In the case of **El Salvador**, the definite article is part of the official name and must be used (without a contraction): **Voy a El Salvador.**

B • Translation Drill

Translate the following into Spanish.

1. Good morning, Mr. and Mrs. Ramírez. Where is Miss Laura?
2. Good afternoon, Doctor Méndez. Where is Don Enrique?
3. Good evening, Professor Sánchez. How is Professor Álvarez?
4. How are you, Don Emiliano? How are Mr. and Mrs. González?

REVIEW

I   The following questions are related to the dialog. Answer in Spanish.

1. ¿Es difícil la situación de Laura?
2. ¿Es Roberto un chauvinista?
3. ¿Por qué tiene que permanecer alguien en casa?
4. ¿Por qué está furiosa la mamá de Laura?
5. ¿Qué hace Cecilia en el cuarto de Laura?
6. ¿Tiene Laura mucho carácter?
7. ¿Es Cecilia una chauvinista?
8. En tu opinión, ¿qué va a hacer Laura?

II   Translation. Translate the following into Spanish.

1. I think that your boyfriend is a tremendous chauvinist!
2. And you . . . who do you think (that) you are? My boyfriend is magnificent! He always defends me.
3. Bah! He has you locked up in your room all day.
4. Is it true that you are not going to study medicine? That you are going to remain at home?
5. Woman! Are you crazy? I'm not going to study medicine because I want to return to El Salvador.
6. Of course I'm going to have a family, but I'm not going to remain at home.
7. What does your boyfriend's father think? Does he know all this yet?
8. By the way, is that your engagement ring? Those are not diamonds; you should return it.

III   Write your own dialog.

Your friend is undecided whether he or she should have a family or study to be an engineer. You are discussing the problem. What do you say?

PRONUNCIATION

Spanish ch, h, j, ge and gi

Ch, which is a separate letter in the Spanish alphabet, is pronounced like English *ch* in *chess*. Repeat the following after your instructor.

chica	chauvinista
chamaco	chicano
charla	chile

El chicano charla con la chica.
El chamaco come chile.

Remember that **h** (do not confuse it with **ch**) is silent in Spanish. (It appears because it was once aspirated in certain words.) Pronounce after your instructor.

habla	hermano	ahora
hace	hermana	ahí
hay	hombre	mi hijo
hoy	honor	mi hija

Su hermano habla con el hombre.
Hola, hombre ¿qué hay ahí?

The letter **j** and the letter **g** when it precedes **e** or **i** are pronounced in a way comparable to English *h*, but the Spanish sound is harsher and more energetic. (Remember that the letter **x** in the words **México** and **mexicano** is pronounced in the same fashion.) Repeat after your instructor.

jabón	México	gente
jóvenes	mexicano	gitano
justicia	majadero	viaje
generalmente	mujer	viejo

Generalmente los gitanos viajan.
Los jóvenes mexicanos trabajan por la justicia.

Cognates & Contexts

¡Abajo el machismo! ¡Arriba el feminismo! ¡Abajo la esclavitud doméstica! ¡Arriba la emancipación de la mujer! Mujeres y hombres, ¡sí! Mujeres y machos, ¡no!

esclavitud *slavery*

¡Necesitamos más mujeres en las escuelas profesionales! Necesitamos más ingenieras, dentistas y profesoras. Necesitamos más mujeres en el gobierno. ¿Quiénes son los embajadores, los gobernadores, los alcaldes? ¡Necesitamos embajadoras, gobernadoras y alcaldesas!

escuelas *schools*

alcaldes, alcaldesas *mayors*

MARIANA Yo creo que el hombre y la mujer deben tener los mismos derechos. Deben tener la oportunidad de hacer el mismo tipo de trabajo en la sociedad. Y cuando regresan a casa, deben compartir los trabajos domésticos.

mismos *same* **derechos** *rights*

regresar *to return* **compartir** *to share*

SERGIO Pero eso es imposible. Tú sabes que la mujer es más débil que el hombre. La mujer no puede resistir los trabajos duros e intensos o difíciles. Necesita trabajos fáciles. Además, tú sabes cómo son algunos hombres en nuestra sociedad. Ven a una mujer sola y tratan de tomar toda clase de ventajas.

débil *weak* **resistir** *to withstand; to resist*

algunos *some*

tratar (de) *to try (to)*

ventajas *advantages*

MARIANA ¡Ajá! ¡Ahora sale la verdad! Es el viejo cuento otra vez del machismo y el código de honor. Tenemos que terminar con esa tradición anticuada de una vez.

cuento *story*

de una vez *once and for all*

Children's parade, Pamplona, Spain

Lección ocho

Lectura y estudio

LA CRIANZA TRADICIONAL DEL NIÑO HISPANO

crianza *upbringing*

El niño hispano es un ser privilegiado durante los primeros años de su vida. Es mimado por toda la familia que, en la mayoría de los casos, es grande y vive cerca, si no junta. Tradicionalmente hay una clara distinción de sexo desde la infancia: el niño sube árboles, juega al soldado, al torero o al futbolista, mientras que la niña, casi siempre bien vestida, juega a ser una señorita, luego una esposa y madre.

durante *during*

ser mimado *to be spoiled*

en la mayoría de los casos *in a majority of cases*
vivir *to live*   junta *together*

árboles *trees*   jugar(ue) a *to play at*   soldado *soldier*   torero *bullfighter*
mientras que *while*   vestida *dressed*

Desde muy pequeños, los niños hispanos aprenden que tienen que tener mucho respeto por las personas mayores que los rodean; el castigo por un descuido de modales es rápido e inequívoco. Cuando le preguntamos a un niño hispano de una pequeña aldea cuál es su nombre, responde con su nombre de pila, su apellido por parte de padre y hasta su apellido por parte de madre, ya que en los países hispanos la costumbre es usar ambos. A veces incluye una frase al final: "para servirle" o "para servirles a Dios y a usted". Así que de estas pequeñas personas oímos,

desde *from*

personas mayores *adults*

rodear *to surround*   castigo *punishment*   descuido *neglect*
modales *manners*   preguntar *to ask*

nombre de pila *first name*

apellido *surname*   por parte de padre *on the father's side*

ambos *both*   a veces *at times*

al final *at the end*

"Me llamo Francisco José Álvarez Rodríguez, para servirles a Dios y a usted."

En España esto puede estar acompañado por una reverencia, pero no en Hispanoamérica.

reverencia *bow, curtsy*

A veces los hijos tratan a sus padres de "usted", aun cuando son mayores y tienen sus propios hijos.

aun *even*

La madre, sobre todo, ocupa un lugar muy especial para sus hijos.

Sin embargo, toda esta educación tradicional está cambiando poco a poco debido al movimiento feminista, a la industrialización y al crecimiento de una clase media urbana con mayor flexibilidad social.

Hay muchas fiestas y ferias que se centran en el niño. No celebran tanto el cumpleaños (en algunos países, como Honduras, es la madre quien recibe flores y regalos los primeros dos o tres años) como el día del santo que tiene el nombre del niño. Todos los Migueles celebran el Día de San Miguel (29 de septiembre), todas las Elenas celebran el Día de Santa Elena, etc.

En el mundo hispano, la Nochebuena es una fiesta familiar con una cena grande en casa, pero las fiestas de Navidad varían un poco de país en país. En Puerto Rico los niños van de casa en casa cantando villancicos y pidiendo el aguinaldo. En México tienen las Posadas: dos niños vestidos de José y María van por las calles pidiendo alojamiento. Los otros niños del pueblo o del vecindario los siguen, cantando una canción tradicional. En todas las casas les niegan la entrada hasta que finalmente hay una donde abren las puertas y hay una gran fiesta dentro. Hay algo

sobre todo *especially, above all*
lugar *place*

cambiar *to change* **poco a poco** *little by little* **debido a** *due to*
crecimiento *growth*

cumpleaños *birthday*

regalos *gifts*

Nochebuena *Christmas Eve*

familiar *family* (adj.) **cena** *dinner*

Navidad *Christmas*

villancicos *Christmas carols*

aguinaldo *Christmas bonus*

alojamiento *lodging*

vecindario *neighborhood*

negar (ie) *to deny*

hasta que *until*

dentro *inside*

similar en el Ecuador: el Paso del Niño, en que todos los niños andan por las calles siguiendo una imagen del niño Jesús y cantando villancicos. Los mayores están a ambos lados de las calles, ya que no pueden participar en el desfile. Durante estos días hay una Feria del Juguete en Barranquilla, Colombia, donde exhiben toda clase de juguetes y antojos para los niños y sus padres. Pero no dan los regalos hasta el Día de Reyes (6 de enero). Los niños ponen yerba en sus zapatos para los camellos de los Reyes y esperan con impaciencia su pasada. El niño desobediente sabe que solamente va a recibir algunas piedras de carbón.

Mimo, disciplina, tradiciones y fiestas, el niño tiene un papel muy importante en la sociedad hispana: el de ser un niño.

andar *to walk*

lados *sides*   **ya que** *since, as*

desfile *parade*

juguete *toy*

antojos *whims, gadgets*

Día de Reyes *Epiphany*   **yerba** *grass*

zapatos *shoes*

pasada *passing through*

mimo *pampering*

papel *role*

A *posada*, Jocotepec, Mexico

NOTES

villancicos   folk songs sung at Christmas.

Posadas   traditional festivities in Mexico celebrated on the days preceding Christmas that commemorate Mary and Joseph's search for an inn (**posada**) on the way to Bethlehem.

pidiendo el aguinaldo   a custom observed during the Christmas holidays. A group of children serenade the community with **villancicos** and are then rewarded with treats or coins.

VOCABULARY STUDY

The following words have additional meanings or forms besides those already given in the dialogs.

brillante   diamond; *brilliant* (adj.)

plato   dish; *plate*

vajilla   (set of) dishes

¿Quieres ver un plato de mi vajilla?   *Do you want to see a plate from my set of dishes?*

enseñar   to show; *to teach*

decir   to tell; *to say*

componer   to compose; *to fix, repair*

ganar   to win; *to earn*

Manuel gana mucho dinero porque trabaja mucho.   *Manuel earns a lot of money because he works a lot.*

pasar   to pass; *to spend* (time)

tirar   to knock over; *to throw*

confiar (en)   to confide (in); *to trust*

Tienes que confiar en mí.   *You have to trust me.*

tomar   to have (drink); *to take*

firma   signature; *firm, company*

algo   somewhat (before an adjective or adverb); something; *anything*

alguien   someone; *somebody, anyone*

precioso   beautiful; *precious*

deber   ought to, must; should; *to owe*

sólo (from solamente)   only
Sólo hay tres alumnos aquí.   *There are only three students here.*

solo (no accent) alone
La señora Posada viene sola.   *Mrs. Posada is coming alone.*

Some verbs will usually be followed by a certain preposition before an object to convey a particular meaning. Verbs of this type are

acabar (**con**)   *to finish* (*with*), *put an end to*
Tenemos que acabar con esas tradiciones.   *We have to put an end to those traditions.*

convidar a   *to invite*
Siempre nos convidan a comer con ellos.   *They always invite us to eat with them.*

enseñar (**a** + infinitive)   *to teach* (+ infinitive)
Los enseño a escribir.   *I teach them to write.*

empezar (**a** + infinitive)   *to begin* (+ infinitive)
Empezamos a entender.   *We begin to understand.*

pensar (**en** + obj.)   *to think* (*about*), *reflect* (*upon*)
Pienso mucho en ella.   *I think about her a lot.*

pensar + infinitive   *to plan, to intend* (to do something)
Pienso escribir a mis padres hoy.   *I plan to write my parents today.*

salir (**de**)   *to leave; to go or come out* (*of*)
¿A qué hora sales de tu casa?   *At what time do you leave your house?*

tratar (**de**)   *to try*
Tratamos de llegar a las ocho.   *We try to arrive at eight.*

tratar de   *to be about, deal with*
El libro trata de un loco.   *The book is about a crazy person.*

volver (**a**)   *to return*

volver a + infinitive   verb + *again*
Te vuelvo a ver mañana.   *I'll see you again tomorrow.*

But

buscar	*to look for*	
escuchar	*to listen to*	include the preposition used in
mirar	*to look at*	the English equivalent
esperar	*to wait for*	

¡Cuidado!

el dentista
la foto (from fotograf*í*a)
la moto (from motocicle*ta*)
cua**rto**   *room*; *quarter* (Do not confuse with cua**tro**, *four*.)
sinvergüenza (Remember the *u* has a dierisis
and is therefore pronounced.)

Querer means *to love* (living beings) as well as *to want*; **amar**, *to love*, is usually encountered in literature, rarely in conversational Spanish.

Remember that Spanish will often use the masculine plural of a family relation or social title to include two or more persons of both genders.

el padre)
la madre ∫   los padres

el hijo)
la hija ∫   los hijos

el hermano)
la hermana ∫   los hermanos

Some of these composite nouns are often not translatable into English.

el tío
la tía   los tíos

¿Vas a visitar a tus tíos?   *Are you going to visit your aunt and uncle?*

el señor
la señora   los señores

¿Conoces a los señores Azuela?   *Do you know Mr. and Mrs. Azuela?*

el esposo
la esposa   los esposos

Los esposos nuevos ya están aquí.   *The new husband and wife are here.*

Rompecabezas

 Ay tamoses pezanemdo a haralb chomu pañoles, ¿dadver?

A • Time Expressions

Match the sentences on the left with a logical completion from the column on the right. Occasionally there may be more than one appropriate answer.

1. _____ tengo que tomar el tren mañana?   a. esta noche
2. Elena está aburrida hoy porque tiene que estudiar _____.   b. por la tarde
3. Generalmente, los periódicos salen _____.   c. ¿A qué hora
4. Ya tengo el dinero; voy a comprar su anillo de compromiso _____.   d. algún día
5. Si tienen tiempo, mis amigos vienen a verme _____.   e. todo el día
6. _____ a las diez hay un programa magnífico en la televisión.   f. hoy mismo
7. No sé hablar español ahora, pero espero hablarlo _____.   g. todos los días

B • Complete each sentence with a suitable word or phrase from the list. The words are to be used in the form in which they appear.

Primero	conocen	pasar
convidan a	charlar	hijos
señores	viajes	En vez de

1. Los _____ Ayala quieren _____ una semana en Colombia.
2. Sus _____, Pedro y Marta, ya _____ Bogotá, pero van también.
3. _____ _____ _____ permanecer con sus padres, van a hacer _____ a otras partes del país.
4. _____ van a Barranquilla donde conocen a unos estudiantes de la Universidad del Atlántico.
5. Éstos les _____ _____ tomar una cerveza y a _____ con ellos.

cosas	trastes	ventas
amigos	tradiciones	aficionada
aburrido	ver	nada

6. Después de unas horas son buenos _____ y deciden todos ir a la Feria del Juguete.
7. Marta no sabe qué va a _____, pero es muy _____ a las _____ de otras gentes.
8. Pedro cree que va a estar _____; sin embargo, no dice _____.
9. Cuando encuentran la Feria, ven _____ magníficas: hay _____ por todas las calles.
10. Marta no sabe qué comprar; hasta los _____ son interesantes.

por lo menos	encerrado	salir de
fotografías	sabrosas	padres
Está constipado	de mal humor	por la noche

11. También hay toda clase de comidas _____.
12. Pedro toma muchas _____ para mostrar a sus _____.
13. Cuando vuelven a Bogotá _____ _____ _____, el señor Ayala está _____ _____ _____ _____.
14. _____ _____ y no puede _____ _____ su cuarto.
15. Va a pasar _____ _____ _____ dos días allí _____ en el hotel. ¡Qué lástima!

Market in Guanajuato, Mexico

C • Query   Free Response

Treat exercise B as a narrative and answer the following questions in Spanish.

1. ¿Van los señores Ayala a Barranquilla?
2. ¿Permanecen Pedro y Marta en Bogotá?
3. ¿Sabe Ud. dónde está Barranquilla? ¿Y Bogotá?
4. ¿A quiénes conocen Pedro y Marta en Barranquilla?
5. ¿Marta está aburrida?
6. ¿Qué tipo de feria visitan los muchachos?
7. ¿Cuándo vuelven a Bogotá?
8. ¿Está de buen humor el señor Ayala?

D • Give the synonyms for the underlined words.

1. Todos los días <u>charlamos</u> durante varias horas.
2. ¿Quieres <u>ver</u> el periódico?
3. Su hermana es muy <u>linda.</u>
4. <u>Comprendo</u> bien la lección.
5. ¿Cuándo <u>termina</u> el concierto?
6. ¿Qué <u>quiere</u> Ud. tomar?

Give the antonyms for the underlined words.

7. El Real Madrid va a <u>ganar</u> el partido.
8. Este examen no es <u>difícil.</u>
9. Los jóvenes bailan todo <u>el día.</u>
10. Miguel siempre <u>esconde</u> mi anillo.
11. Nada es <u>fácil</u> en este mundo.
12. Esas revistas son <u>nuevas.</u>

to here
29 ENERO 79

GRAMMAR: SELF-TESTING

Cover the right side of the page and try to answer the questions in the left margin.

VERBS

What are some examples of verbs that are irregular only in the **yo** form?

I IRREGULAR VERBS

The following verbs are all irregular in the present.

A. Verbs that are irregular only in the first person singular **(yo)** *(Sections 19, 25, 30)*

hacer	hago
poner	pongo
traer	traigo
salir	salgo
dar	doy
saber	sé
conocer	conozco
permanecer	permanezco
agradecer	agradezco

regular in all other persons

In Class I stem-changing verbs, **e** changes to . . .
and o changes to . . .
In what persons do these changes occur?
What are some examples of Class I stem-changing verbs?

B. Stem-changing verbs: Class I **(-ar, -er)** *(Section 31)*
Stem: **e → ie / o → ue**, when stressed
in first, second, third persons singular, third person plural

cerrar	costar
defender	encontrar
empezar	mostrar
entender	poder
pensar	volver
perder	
querer	

Why aren't **tener** and **venir** considered Class I stem-changing verbs?

Tener and **venir** also have **e → ie** stem change, but they are not considered Class I verbs because the first person singular has a further irregularity:

ten**go**   ven**go**

<table>
<tr>
<td>

What is the present tense conjugation of **decir?**

</td>
<td>

C. **Decir** has two irregularities (*Section 25*):
   1. first person singular **digo**
   2. stem change **e** → **i** in stressed syllables

                        dices
                        dice
                           decimos
                        dicen

Other **-ir** verbs of this type will be studied soon.

</td>
</tr>
</table>

What is the present tense conjugation of **oír**?

D. **Oír** is also irregular in four persons oigo
(*Section 25*): oyes
oye
oímos
oyen

How is **ver** irregular in the present?

E. **Ver** is irregular only in the first person singular, since the **e** is retained from the infinitive ending.

II   PRESENT PARTICIPLES   (*Section 32*)

Formation:

How is the present participle of regular verbs formed?

Regular verbs: -ar   habl-   + -ando   hablando
              -er   aprend- ⎫   aprendiendo
              -ir   escrib- ⎬ + -iendo   escribiendo

What is the present participle ending for **-er** and **-ir** verbs when the stem ends in a vowel?

-Er and **-ir** verbs with a stem ending in a vowel add **-yendo** (**oyendo, trayendo**).

What are the present participles of **decir**, **poder**, and **ir**?

Irregular verbs encountered so far

        decir   diciendo
        poder   pudiendo
        ir   yendo

How are present participles used?

Which is used, **ser** or **estar**, to express the progressive forms of tenses?

Use:
   a. with **estar** (never **ser**) to make the progressive forms of tenses, emphasizing that an action is currently in progress.
      ¿Qué están haciendo Uds.?   *What are you doing?*

   b. as a modifier to indicate the circumstances under which an occurrence takes place, often equivalent to the English *by* + present participle construction.
      Estudiando, aprendemos.   *By studying, we learn.*

What are the uses of **estar**?

III SER VERSUS ESTAR *(Section 34)*

Estar is used
a. to express location:
   El libro está sobre la mesa.   *The book is on the table.*
b. with the present participle to convey progressive forms of tenses:
   Estamos escuchando la música.   *We are listening to the music.*
c. with adjectives to describe non-inherent conditions or states:
   El suelo está sucio.   *The floor is dirty.*

What are the uses of **ser**?

Ser is used
a. with adjectives to express an inherent, essential characteristic:
   Mi padre es inteligente.   *My father is intelligent.*
b. to link subjects with nouns or pronouns:
   Juan es alumno.   *Juan is a student.*
c. to indicate origin, possession, or composition with **de**; destination with **para**:
   Susana es de Cuba.   *Susana is from Cuba.*
   El anillo es para Tere.   *The ring is for Tere.*
d. to tell time of day:
   Son las tres.   *It's three o'clock.*

PRONOUNS

DIRECT AND INDIRECT OBJECT PRONOUNS
(Section 27)

What are the direct object pronouns in Spanish?

Direct object pronouns: **me   te   lo, la   nos   los, las**

What are the indirect object pronouns in Spanish?

Indirect object pronouns: **me   te   le   nos   les**

Where are object pronouns placed in relation to the verb?

Position of object pronouns   *(Sections 28, 33)*
Object pronouns
a. precede a conjugated verb.

b. follow and are attached to an infinitive or present participle.

Hay un muchacho nuevo en nuestra clase.

Lo vemos todos los días.

Lo vamos a ver todos los días.
or
Vamos a verlo todos los días.

Lo estamos viendo todos los días.
or
Estamos viéndolo todos los días.

DEMONSTRATIVE PRONOUNS (*Sections 20, 21*)

In what way do demonstrative pronouns differ from demonstrative adjectives?

Taken from demonstrative adjectives, they are indicated by adding an accent to the stressed vowel.

What is the distance from the speaker conveyed by **éste, ése**, and **aquél**?

	DEMONSTRATIVE ADJECTIVE	DEMONSTRATIVE PRONOUN	
this	este periódico	éste	here (near the speaker)
	esta revista	ésta	
these	estos platos	éstos	
	estas orquestas	éstas	
that	ese premio	ése	there (near the listener or somewhat distant from both speaker and listener)
	esa mesa	ésa	
those	esos anillos	ésos	
	esas bicicletas	ésas	
that	aquel señor	aquél	over there (at some distance from both speaker and listener)
	aquella máquina	aquélla	
those	aquellos chamacos	aquéllos	
	aquellas chicas	aquéllas	

What are the neuter demonstrative pronouns? What do they refer to? Are they accented?

esto
eso
aquello

"Neuter" pronouns refer to previously mentioned statements or ideas, or unidentified objects, not to a specific entity. They do not have written accents.

TIME OF DAY (Section 24)

How is time told in Spanish?	In telling time, the article **la** or **las** is used with the cardinal numeral after **ser** or a preposition.

	Es la una.	*It is one o'clock.*
	Son las dos.	*It is two o'clock.*
	Comemos a las tres.	*We eat at three.*

How are minutes past the hour expressed?

Y is used for minutes after the hour up through the half hour.

    Es la una y media.   *It is half-past one.*

How are minutes before the hour expressed?

Menos is used to express minutes between the half-hour and the next hour.

    Son las dos menos cuarto.   *It is a quarter to two.*

Cuarto is used for a quarter of an hour and **media** for the half-hour.

When would **de la noche** versus **por la noche** be used?

When the hour is specified, the period of the day is indicated by **de**; when no definite hour is given, **por** is used.

    Vuelven a las diez de la noche.   *They are coming back at ten at night.*

    Vuelven por la noche.   *They are coming back at night.*

REMEMBER!

- The definite article is used with titles, except in direct address (*Section 36*).

    Buenos días, Sr. Pérez.   *Good morning, Mr. Pérez.*
    ¿Cómo está la Sra. Pérez?   *How is Mrs. Pérez?*

- Whereas English uses a noun as an adjective (*a gold watch*), Spanish must use **de** + noun (*un reloj de oro*) (*Section 35*).

- **Saber** means *to know, to have intellectual knowledge of*; **conocer** means *to know, to be familiar* or *acquainted with* (*Section 30*).

- Direct objects that are persons are preceded by the preposition **a**, except after the verb **tener** (*Section 26*).

Vemos esas tiendas todos los días.	*We see those stores every day.*
Vemos a Laura todos los días.	*We see Laura every day.*
Pobre Alfonso no tiene amigos.	*Poor Alfonso has no friends.*

● **Éste, -a, -os, -as** often translate *the latter*; **aquél, -la, -los, -las** often translate *the former*.

Allí van Juan y Gonzalo; aquél es mi hermano y éste es mi amigo.	*There go Juan and Gonzalo; the former is my brother and the latter is my friend.*

● Numbers from 16–29 can be expressed as one word (**veintiocho**) or as three (**diez y seis**); from 31 on, units are added solely with **y** (*Section 23*).

● Spanish does not use a present progressive to refer to future action, but rather **ir a** + infinitive or occasionally the simple present.

Voy a escribir la carta mañana.	*I'm going to write the letter tomorrow.*
Escribo la carta mañana.	*I'm writing the letter tomorrow.*

● **Volver** means *to return, to go back*; **devolver** means *to return, to give back*.

Voy a volver a la biblioteca para devolver el libro.	*I'm going to return to the library to return the book.*

● Conjunction **y**, *and*, becomes **e** before **i** or **hi**; **o**, *or*, becomes **u** before **o** or **ho**.

Padres e hijos.	*Parents and children.*
Uno u otro.	*One or the other.*

● **Uno** (**veintiuno, treinta y uno**, etc.) becomes **un** before masculine nouns.

Hay veintiún alumnos en la clase.	*There are twenty-one students in the class.*

A • Transformation Drill   Present → Present Progressive

MODEL   Escribo la composición en casa.
STUDENT   **Estoy escribiendo** la composición en casa.

1. ¿Qué me dices?
2. Carlota me da los nombres.
3. Los muchachos ya traen los refrescos.
4. Acabo esa composición en mi cuarto.

5. ¿Miras el periódico de hoy?
6. Pienso mucho en aquella noche.
7. Empezamos a hablar español un poco.
8. Tú me criticas.
9. Comen los platos retesabrosos que hay en la mesa.
10. No hacemos nada con estos trastes usados.

B • Complete the sentences with the correct form of an appropriate verb from the following list. In some cases there may be more than one suitable verb.

hacer	poner	traer	salir	saber
conocer	cerrar	costar	defender	entender
querer	perder	pensar	empezar	volver
encontrar	poder	oír	decir	ver

1. Miguel y Mónica _____ al alcalde.
2. Yo no _____ mi tarea en clase nunca.
3. ¿_____ venir Ud. a la venta hoy?
4. Mi compadre _____ muchas cosas a mi casa hoy.
5. Uds. la _____ bien, pero no la comprenden.
6. ¿Quién _____ la lección de hoy?
7. Vamos a _____ la verdad.
8. Tere y Margarita _____ la causa.
9. ¿A qué hora _____ el concierto?
10. Esa bicicleta _____mucho dinero.

C • Complete the sentences with **ser** or **estar**.

1. No puedo ir ahora; no _____ lista.
2. Esos _____ los hijos del gobernador.
3. Mis amigos ya _____ en la discoteca.
4. La mesa que _____ en el pasillo, ¿_____ del rector?
5. Eugenio y yo _____ terminando nuestra discusión.
6. Tú _____ muy listo, pero también _____ un sinvergüenza.
7. Tenemos que _____ allí a las tres. ¿Qué hora _____ ahora?
8. Este premio _____ para la orquesta infantil.
9. Nosotros _____ amigos de sus padres.
10. Ignacio y Alfonso _____ componiendo una sinfonía.

D • Query   Patterned Response   DO → DP

MODEL   ¿Ya tienes una bicicleta nueva?
STUDENT   Sí, ya **la** tengo.

1. ¿Gonzalo trae mucha comida sabrosa?
2. ¿Dices la verdad siempre?
3. ¿Podemos recitar un poema en clase?
4. ¿Sabes la Sinfonía India de memoria?
5. ¿Estás escondiendo tus pensamientos?

Change the direct object pronoun into *any appropriate noun.*

MODEL   ¿Lo escribe Laura?
STUDENT   Sí, Laura escribe **su nombre** (**el poema**, **ese libro**, **un verso**, etc.)

6. ¿Lo traen todos los días?
7. ¿La defienden?
8. ¿Los haces por la mañana?
9. ¿Las miran tus padres?
10. Estás entendiéndolos bien, ¿no es verdad?

E • Query   Free Response

Answer the questions in Spanish.

1. ¿Estás empezando a escribir mejor el español?
2. ¿Cuándo está Ud. de mal humor?
3. ¿Qué piensas hacer esta noche?
4. ¿Prefiere Ud. comida americana o comida mexicana?
5. ¿Dónde pones tu tarea cuando llegas a clase?
6. ¿Sales de tu casa temprano por la mañana todos los días?
7. ¿Piensas mucho en el porvenir?
8. ¿Qué hace Ud. todo el día?
9. ¿Conoce Ud. al alcalde de la ciudad donde vive?
10. ¿Puedes recitar un verso de José Martí?

F • Translation Drill

Translate into Spanish.

1. Those bicycles are new but this one is old.
2. What does that matter! I only want to use it for a few weeks.
3. But where am I going to put this contraption?
4. Now I know! There is a hallway at home where I already have my motorcycle.
5. My mother is going to tell me that I'm a pest.
6. She always criticizes me when I do these things.
7. At least I'm trying to be smart: it is a small bicycle.
8. By the way, do you have a room in your house for motorcycles?
9. One moment! Why don't you wait for me?
10. I cannot understand these friends that hear, but don't listen.

G • Guided Composition

Imagine that you are a public figure and that you are being criticized. You are defending yourself by debating the criticisms. Write a brief paragraph expressing your defense.

Office building,
Bogotá, Colombia

Lección nueve

IRONÍAS DEL TRABAJO

CARLITOS	Por fin es viernes. ¡Gracias a Dios! Aquí trabajamos como burros.	**por fin** *finally, at last* **viernes** *Friday*
CRISTINA	Carlitos, ven aquí. Revisa estas facturas. Lee estas cartas.	**revisar** *to go over* **facturas** *invoices* **leer** *to read* **cartas** *letters*
CARLITOS	¡Qué! Ya estoy cansado. Harto. Solamente nos falta una hora más en esta cueva.	**cansado** *tired* **harto** *fed up* **faltar** *to lack, need* **más** *more* **cueva** *cave*
CRISTINA	Carlitos, no seas así. Te queda tiempo para hacer un trabajo ligero como éste.	**quedar** *to have left (over)* **ligero** *light; quick*
CARLITOS	Bah. Déjalo para el lunes. ¡Juanita! Ven conmigo al cine. ¿Te gustan las películas de	**dejar** *to leave* **lunes** *Monday* **conmigo** *with me* **cine** *movie house* **gustar** *to like; to appeal to* **películas** *movies, films*
	Cantinflas? Al salir de aquí te llevo al Caballo Bayo para cenar y tomar unas copas.	**al salir** *upon leaving, when we get out* **llevar** *to take* **cenar** *to have supper* **copas** *drinks*
JUANITA	Majo, no me hagas reír con tus donjuanerías. Para mí, tú no eres más que un bufón.	**reír (i)** *to laugh* **no... más que** *nothing more than* **bufón** *clown*
CARLITOS	¿Qué te pasa, mujer?	
LUIS	¡Así! ¡Dale duro! Lo merece.	**¡Dale duro!** *"Let him have it!"* **merecer** *to deserve*
ERNESTO	¡Pssst! ¿Sabes quién viene? El jefe de todos los jefes y el mandamás de todos los mandamases.	**jefe** *boss* **mandamás** *chief; big shot*
LUIS	¡No me digas! ¿Don Santiago?	**¡No me digas!** *You don't say!*
CARLITOS	¡El viejo en persona! A nosotros no nos preocupa. Aquí todos trabajamos como fanáticos.	**el viejo** *the old guy* **preocupar** *to bother*

Sin duda viene para felicitarnos.

(*Entran don Santiago y don Agapito.*)

DON AGAPITO	¿Dónde está Carlitos Cebollero, alias "el Majo" o "el Bufón"?
CARLITOS	A sus órdenes, don Santiago. Mande Ud.
D. SANTIAGO	Venga Ud. conmigo. Suba Ud. Allí, al escritorio. Sí, hombre. Haga el favor de complacerme.
D. AGAPITO	Estimados compañeros. Préstenme Uds. atención. Va a hablar nuestro director.
D. SANTIAGO	Gracias a una iniciativa espontánea del señor Cebollero, —una comparación original y cómica entre nuestra compañía y los competidores— ¡parece que vamos a conseguir un contrato de la Central Azucarera Martínez!
TODOS	¡Bravo! ¡Arriba Carlitos Cebollero!
D. SANTIAGO	Tal contrato puede significar un aumento para todos. Pero necesitamos una propuesta formal inmediatamente. ¡Todos a trabajar! Hay que terminar antes de las seis de la mañana. Nos quedan menos de catorce horas. ¡Manos a la obra!

sin duda *without a doubt*
 felicitar *to congratulate*

Cebollero *from* **cebolla,** *onion, i.e., Mr. Onionpeeler*

a sus órdenes *at your service*
subir *to go up, climb*
 escritorio *desk*
complacer *to oblige, please*

estimados *dear, esteemed*
 prestar atención *to pay attention*

parecer *to seem*

Central Azucarera Martínez *Martínez Sugar Mill*

tal *such a* **aumento** *raise*

propuesta *proposal, bid*

antes de *before*

menos (de) *less (than)*
 ¡Manos a la obra! *Everybody to work!* (**manos** *hands*)

NOTES

Tú and Usted Commands

Both familiar (**tú**) and formal (**usted**) commands appear in the dialog above. The workers use the **tú** form among themselves, but between workers and superiors **usted** commands are used. Spanish has many set command and akin phrases for the **usted** relationships.

> **Mande Ud.**   *What can I do for you?* (literally, *Command*.)
>
> **A sus órdenes.**   *At your service.* (Under your orders.)
>
> **Haga el favor de...** (**esperar**, etc.)   *Please (wait).* (*Do the favor of waiting.*)
>
> **Sírvase...** (**entrar**, etc.)   *Please (come in).* (*Help yourself to entering.*)

Don, Majo, Donjuanerías

Don, which is placed before a first name, was formerly used in addressing aristocracy, in a manner equivalent to English *Sir*. Now it is used as a casual title of respect, without regard per se to a person's position in society.
Majo is a term used mainly in Spain to refer to a showoff, a dandy.
Donjuanerías refers to mannerisms or speech reminiscent of the legendary Don Juan, the rogue figure in literature.

Caballo Bayo

Caballo Bayo is an alliterative play on words. Literally, the phrase means *the bay horse*. Apparently Juanita doesn't think it's too savory an establishment!

Cantinflas

Mario Moreno, "Cantinflas," is the foremost film comedian in Mexico. He is also well known in other Hispanic countries.

6 FEBRERO 79

LANGUAGE STRUCTURES

37   Direct commands: **usted, ustedes,**[1] **tú**

A.   FORMAL COMMANDS: **usted, ustedes**

▶   In almost all verbs, the endings for the **usted, ustedes** commands are added to the stem of the first person singular of the present tense. For **-ar** verbs add **-e** (singular) and **-en** (plural). For **-er** and **-ir** verbs add **-a** (singular) and **-an** (plural).

	Infinitive	Stem from first person singular present	Singular ending (Usted)	Singular command	Plural ending (Ustedes)	Plural command
Regular verbs: **-ar, -er, -ir**	hablar	habl	-e	hable Ud.	-en	hablen Uds.
	aprender	aprend	-a	aprenda Ud.	-an	aprendan Uds.
	escribir	escrib	-a	escriba Ud.	-an	escriban Uds.
Class I verbs: **-ar, -er**	cerrar	cierr	-e	cierre Ud.	-en	cierren Uds.
	mostrar	muestr	-e	muestre Ud.	-en	muestren Uds.
	defender	defiend	-a	defienda Ud.	-an	defiendan Uds.
	devolver	devuelv	-a	devuelva Ud.	-an	devuelvan Uds.
Verbs irregular in the first person singular	complacer	complazc[2]	-a	complazca Ud.	-an	complazcan Uds.
	decir	dig	-a	diga Ud.	-an	digan Uds.
	hacer	hag	-a	haga Ud.	-an	hagan Uds.
	salir	salg	-a	salga Ud.	-an	salgan Uds.
	traer	traig	-a	traiga Ud.	-an	traigan Uds.
	tener	teng	-a	tenga Ud.	-an	tengan Uds.
	poner	pong	-a	ponga Ud.	-an	pongan Uds.
	venir	veng	-a	venga Ud.	-an	vengan Uds.
	ver	ve	-a	vea Ud.	-an	vean Uds.

Examples:

1. Presten Uds. atención.   *Pay attention.*
2. Venga Ud. conmigo. Suba Ud. allí.   *Come with me. Climb up there.*

[1] The **vosotros** command forms can be found in section 1 of the Appendix.

[2] **Complacer**, as well as **merecer** and **parecer**, is conjugated like **conocer** and other **-cer** verbs (see section 30).

▶ The following verbs are irregular in the command form. These forms are not based on the first person singular (respectively, **doy, estoy, voy, soy, sé**).

Irregular Commands

Infinitive	Singular Command	Plural Command
dar	dé Ud.	den Uds.
estar	esté Ud.	estén Uds.
ir	vaya Ud.	vayan Uds.
ser	sea Ud.	sean Uds.
saber	sepa Ud.	sepan Uds.

▶ There is no change in formal commands when they are negative.

1. No sea Ud. así.   *Don't be that way.*
2. No vuelva Ud. mañana.   *Don't come back tomorrow.*

B. FAMILIAR COMMANDS: tú

▶ Regular affirmative **tú** commands have the same form as the third person singular of the present indicative tense. Irregularly formed affirmative **tú** commands must be memorized separately. Several of them (**ten, ven, pon, sal**) simply use the stem as it appears in the infinitive.

▶ To form all negative **tú** commands, add **-s** to the **usted** command form.

Regularly formed affirmative **tú** command = third person singular, present	Negative **tú** command: Add **-s** to the **usted** command
habla	no hables
aprende	no aprendas
escribe	no escribas
cierra	no cierres
muestra	no muestres
defiende	no defiendas
vuelve	no vuelvas
conoce	no conozcas
trae	no traigas

ve (from ver)[3]	no veas
da	no des
está[4]	no estés
sabe[4]	no sepas

Irregularly formed affirmative commands

(decir)	di	no digas
(hacer)	haz	no hagas
(salir)	sal	no salgas
(tener)	ten	no tengas
(poner)	pon	no pongas
(venir)	ven	no vengas
(ser)	sé	no seas
(ir)	ve[3]	no vayas

1. Ven aquí. Revisa estas facturas.   *Come here. Go over these invoices.*
2. No me hagas reír. No seas así.   *Don't make me laugh. Don't be that way.*
3. Ten cuidado. ¡Sal de allí!   *Be careful. Come out of there!*
4. No comas más. No cierres la puerta.   *Don't eat any more. Don't close the door.*

▶ The pronouns **usted** and **ustedes** are often used with their command form for courtesy, at least the first time in a conversation. As the conversation progresses they may be used only intermittently. On the other hand, in familiar commands, the pronoun **tú** is omitted, except for emphasis.

> **No hable Ud. / No hables.**
> **No sea Ud. así. / No seas así.**

A · Transformation Drill Present Tense → Ud. Command

MODEL   Mi compañero trabaja mucho.
STUDENT   Compañero, **trabaje Ud.** mucho.

1. Agapito escribe mucho.
2. El profesor borra los versos.
3. El doctor come unas enchiladas.
4. El joven habla español.
5. Gonzalo vuelve por el pasillo.

6. Alfonso charla con Cecilia.
7. El hombre hace el guacamole.
8. El amigo trae una cerveza.
9. Raquel canta una canción.
10. Mónica cierra el libro.

---

[3] Note that **ve** is the affirmative **tú** command for both **ir** and **ver**.
    ¡Ve allí! *Go there!*   **¡Ve esto!** *See this!*
[4] The familiar affirmative command for **estar** is almost always **estate**, a reflexive construction (**está** + reflexive pronoun **te**); for **saber**, it is usually **sábete**.

B • Transformation Drill   Present Tense → tú Command

MODEL   Carlitos deja su trabajo.
STUDENT   Carlitos, **deja tu** trabajo.

1. Rubén habla con su novia.
2. Emiliano mira a su hijo.
3. Carlota escucha a su comadre.
4. Miguel lee su poema.
5. El compadre come sus tamales.
6. El joven escribe su composición.
7. Eugenio recibe su dinero.
8. Álvaro consulta con sus amigos.
9. Santiago revisa sus facturas.
10. Carlitos escucha sus discos.

C • Transformation Drill   Present Tense → tú Command

MODEL   Luis sale pronto.
STUDENT   Luis, **sal** pronto.

1. Susana viene conmigo.
2. Carmen hace la propuesta.
3. Gonzalo pone las revistas en la mesa.
4. Agapito tiene cuidado.
5. Carlitos sale ahora.
6. Emiliano va a la tienda.
7. Miguel dice unas palabras.
8. Rubén es bueno.

D • Transformation Drill   Present Tense → Uds. Command

MODEL   Los señores tienen cuidado.
STUDENT   Señores, **tengan Uds.** cuidado.

1. Los señores miran el contrato.
2. Los señores van con el jefe.
3. Los señores toman unas copitas.
4. Las señoritas leen las cartas.
5. Las señoras están en la biblioteca por la mañana.
6. Las señoritas vuelven a casa.
7. Las señoritas muestran las demandas a Carlos.
8. Las señoritas luchan por la justicia social.
9. Los señores escuchan al poeta chicano.
10. Las señoras traen a sus comadres.

E • Query   Patterned Response   Interrogative → Ud. Command

MODEL   ¿Borro?
STUDENT   **Sí, borre Ud.**

1. ¿Escribo?
2. ¿Espero?
3. ¿Salgo?
4. ¿Vuelvo?
5. ¿Como?
6. ¿Leo?
7. ¿Termino?
8. ¿Trabajo?

Interrogative → Uds. Command

1. ¿Debemos decidir?
2. ¿Necesitamos esperar?
3. ¿Debemos debatir?
4. ¿Hay que trabajar?
5. ¿Hay que ayudar?
6. ¿Hay que luchar?
7. ¿Hay que ir?
8. ¿Hay que devolver el dinero?

Interrogative → tú Command

No pronoun is necessary with **tú** commands.

1. ¿Puedo estudiar?
2. ¿Tengo que comer?
3. ¿Tengo que venir?
4. ¿Debo salir?

5. ¿Necesito trabajar?
6. ¿Tengo que borrar?
7. ¿Tengo que terminar?
8. ¿Necesito escuchar?

F • Transformation Drill   Affirmative tú Command → Negative tú Command

MODEL   Susana, habla así.
STUDENT   Susana, **no hables** así.

1. Susana, canta una bamba.
2. Compadre, haz el plato fundamental.
3. Sinvergüenza, ven aquí.
4. Pancho, pon esto en la mesa.

5. Carlitos, ve a la venta.
6. Vuelve a las tres.
7. Trae unos periódicos.
8. Ayuda a los estudiantes.

G • Transformation Drill   Indicative → Negative tú Command → Affirmative tú Command

MODEL   Rubén borra las palabras.
STUDENT 1 Rubén, **no borres** las palabras.
STUDENT 2 Rubén, **borra** las palabras.

1. Rubén escribe las palabras.
2. La muchacha compra una Coca-Cola.
3. Cecilia tiene cuidado.
4. Mamá sale por la tarde.

5. Marta viene aquí al mediodía.
6. Álvaro pone el premio en la mesa.
7. Alfonso va a la tienda.
8. Carlota hace el trabajo.

38   Placement of object pronouns in commands

▶ With affirmative commands, object pronouns are placed after the verb and are attached to it. In negative commands, object pronouns immediately precede the verb.

Affirmative commands:

1. Hazlo. Hágalo[5] Ud. Háganlo[5] Uds.   *Do it.*
2. Dime qué hacer. Dígame[5] Ud. qué hacer. Díganme[5]   *Tell me what to do.*
   Uds. qué hacer.

Negative commands:

1. No lo pongas ahí. No lo ponga Ud. ahí. No   *Don't put it there.*
   lo pongan Uds. ahí.
2. No la cierres. No la cierre Ud. No la cierren Uds.   *Don't close it.*

---

[5] As with the present participle, when a pronoun is attached to a command, a written accent is often necessary to show that the stress remains on the original syllable (see page 11).

Summary of the Position of Object Pronouns

A.   When you have a conjugated verb, the object pronoun comes *before* it.

   Laura lo compra.   *Laura is buying it.*
   Me buscan.   *They are looking for me.*

B.   When you have an infinitive or a present participle, the object pronoun comes *after* and is *attached* to the infinitive or the present participle.

   Te escribimos una carta para ayudarte.   *We are writing you a letter in order to help you.*

   Pensándolo bien, ya sé qué hacer.   *Thinking it over well, I now know what to do.*

   However, when the infinitive or the present participle completes the meaning of a preceding conjugated verb, the object pronoun may either come *before* the conjugated verb or be *attached* to the infinitive or present participle.

   Me va a dar el dinero.
          or   *He is going to give me the money.*
   Va a darme el dinero.
   Estamos haciéndolo.
          or   *We are doing (making) it.*
   Lo estamos haciendo.

C.   With negative commands the object pronoun comes immediately *before* the verb.

   No lo hagas.   *Don't do it.*
   No le escriba Ud.   *Don't write to him.*

   With affirmative commands, the object pronoun comes *after* and is *attached* to the command.

   Hazlo.   *Do it.*
   Escríbale Ud.   *Write to him.*

A • Transformation Drill   Present Tense → Ud. Command

MODEL   El profesor López me trae la revista.
STUDENT   Profesor López, **tráigame Ud.** la revista.

1. El profesor me escribe en español.
2. El señor me dice que está bien.
3. La señora me trae una cerveza.
4. El joven me hace una propuesta.

Present Tense → tú Command

MODEL   Susana me trae la revista.
STUDENT   Susana, **tráeme** la revista.

5. La joven me revisa las facturas.
6. La señorita me ayuda a estudiar.

7. Carlitos me vende la bicicleta.
8. La muchacha me compra un disco.

B • Transformation Drill Affirmative tú Command → Negative tú Command

MODEL   Hazlo.
STUDENT   **No lo hagas.**

1. Cómpralo.
2. Léelo.
3. Piénsalo más.
4. Dime otra vez.

5. Ponlo allí.
6. Déjalo para mañana.
7. Hazlo para mí.
8. Escúchame.

Affirmative Ud. Command → Negative Ud. Command

1. Tráigalo Ud. aquí.
2. Devuélvalo Ud.
3. Termínela Ud.
4. Convídeme Ud. a un refresco.

5. Espéreme Ud.
6. Cántelas Ud.
7. Prepárelos Ud.
8. Acéptelos Ud.

C • Query Patterned Response

MODEL   ¿Vendo las enchiladas o no, jefe?
STUDENT   **Véndalas Ud. No las venda Ud.**

1. ¿Hago las facturas o no, jefe?
2. ¿Reviso el contrato o no, jefe?
3. ¿Miro la película o no, jefe?
4. ¿Preparo la comida o no, jefe?
5. ¿Escucho el disco o no, jefe?

6. ¿Vendo el loro o no, jefe?
7. ¿Cierro la clínica o no, jefe?
8. ¿Abro la oficina o no, jefe?
9. ¿Ayudo a Carmen o no, jefe?
10. ¿Espero a Luis o no, jefe?

D • Query Patterned Response

MODEL   ¿Te veo mañana o no, Pancho?
STUDENT   **Veme** mañana. **No me veas** mañana.

1. ¿Te espero mañana o no, Rafa?
2. ¿Te hablo mañana o no, Rubén?
3. ¿Te escribo mañana o no, Raquel?
4. ¿Te complazco mañana o no, Alfonso?
5. ¿Te convido mañana o no, Gonzalo?

6. ¿Te digo mañana o no, Carmen?
7. ¿Te ayudo mañana o no, Felipe?
8. ¿Te consulto mañana o no, Diego?
9. ¿Te llevo mañana o no, Eugenio?
10. ¿Te defiendo mañana o no, Cecilia?

13 DE FEBRERO

E • Translation Drill

Translate into Spanish.

1. Look at me! Don't look at me! We are looking at it. We are going to look at it.
2. Write to her! Don't write to her! I am writing to her. I want to write to her.
3. Bring it here! Don't bring it here! They are bringing it here. They can't bring it here.
4. Put them there. Don't put them there. She is putting them there. She intends to put them there.
5. Help me! Don't help me! You help us every day. I am writing in order to help you.

39 Nominalization

▶ Just as adjectives of nationality are used as nouns (see section **5**), so are many other adjectives (examples 1 and 2) and modifiers such as **de** phrases (example 3) or **que** clauses (example 4).

1. el hombre viejo	*the old man*	el viejo	*the old guy (one)*
2. un estudiante alucinado	*a bewitched student*	un alucinado	*a bewitched person (one)*
3. el libro de español y el de portugués		*the Spanish book and the Portuguese one*	
4. los discos que tienes y los que te vendo		*the records that you have and those that I am selling you*	

▶ When noun modifiers function in place of the original noun, they are said to be "nominalized." In such cases the nominalized word agrees in gender and number with the noun understood. English frequently uses the words *one*, *ones* or *that*, *these*, etc. in order to avoid using the noun. Nominalization often occurs in contexts in which the noun is understood because it has been used earlier (examples 1 and 2), but a number of nominalized adjectives referring to persons are so common that they are understood independently of a context (examples 3, 4, and 5).

1. Hay un cine grande allí. ¿Dónde hay uno[6] pequeño?	*There is a large movie house over there. Where is there a small one?*
2. Necesito estos trastes y ésos[7] y aquéllos[7] allá.	*I need these contraptions and those and those over there.*
3. Mira, el viejo en persona.	*Look, the old guy in person.*
4. ¡Huy, es un tonto!	*Wow, he's a dummy!*
5. Hola, guapo. ¿Qué tal? Hola, chica. ¿Qué hay de nuevo?	*Hi, handsome, what's new? Hi, girl. What's new with you?*

[6] **Un** becomes **uno** before a nominalized adjective.

[7] Demonstrative pronouns are simply a special case of nominalization.

A • Transformation Drill   Modified Noun → Nominalized Adjective

MODEL   La tienda grande está aquí.
STUDENT   **La grande** está aquí.

1. La bici nueva está aquí.
2. Este hombre tonto me hace reír.
3. Esos estudiantes quieren justicia social.
4. Esta clase de baile es muy buena.

5. La señorita simpática es alumna.
6. La Calle Veintitrés está cerca.
7. El poeta loco escribe y escribe.
8. Esa clase de matemáticas es muy difícil.

B • Query   Patterned Response

MODEL   ¿Cuál bicicleta necesitas, la grande o la pequeña?
STUDENT   Necesito **la grande.**   or   Necesito **la pequeña**.

1. ¿Cuál muchacha está aquí, la simpática o la antipática?
2. ¿Cuál estudiante está leyendo, el francés o el italiano?
3. ¿Cuál hombre es, el guapo o el feo?

4. ¿Cuál alumna es, la inteligente o la tonta?
5. ¿Cuáles libros son, los buenos o los malos?
6. ¿Cuáles revistas quieres, éstas o ésas?
7. ¿Cuál señor es, ése o aquél?
8. ¿Cuál enchilada comes, ésta o ésa?

C • Transformation Drill   Noun → Nominalized Phrase or Clause

MODEL   Tengo tus facturas y las facturas del jefe.
STUDENT   Tengo tus facturas y **las** del jefe.

1. Busco nuestra propuesta y la propuesta de las autoridades.
2. Este contrato y el contrato de la Azucarera son muy buenos.
3. Mi tío y el tío de Luis están en casa.
4. ¿Vamos a ver esta película o la película de Cantinflas?
5. ¿Estás leyendo este libro o el libro de inglés?
6. Aquella mujer y la mujer que pasa por aquí los lunes son hermanas.
7. Este poema y el poema que voy a recitar son de Martí.
8. Esta compañía y la compañía que está en la Calle Cuarenta no tienen dinero.

40   Pronouns after a preposition

▶ With the exception of **mí** and **ti** the forms of the pronouns used after prepositions are the same as the subject pronouns. Note, however, how they change in meaning.

para	mí	*me*
sin	ti	*you* (familiar)
a	usted	*you* (formal)
de	él, ella	*him, her*
en	nosotros, nosotras	*us*
por	ustedes	*you*
cerca de, etc.	ellos, ellas	*them* (people or things)

1. ¿Dónde está la oficina del rector?	*Where is the president's office?*
Estás en ella.[8]	*You are in it.*
2. ¿Tienes tu libro? No, estoy sin él.	*Do you have your book? No,*
	I'm without it.
3. Me va a dar el anillo a mí.	*He's going to give the ring to me.*
4. ¿Esto es para nosotros? No, es para ellos.	*Is this for us? No, it's for them.*

▶ The first and second persons singular combine with **con** to make the special forms **conmigo** and **contigo**. But: **con Ud., con ella,** etc.

¿Podemos ir contigo? No, vayan con él.   *Can we go with you? No, go with him.*

▶ Here is a list of common prepositions; those in color are new vocabulary.

para[9]	*in order to, for*	antes de	*before*
por	*by, per, for*	después de	*after*
de	*of, from*	cerca de	*close to*
a	*to*	acerca de	*concerning, about*
en	*in*	en vez de	*instead of*
con	*with*	**detrás de**	*behind*
sin	*without*	**encima de**	*on top of*
		debajo de	*beneath*
		lejos de	*far from*

---

[8] Remember that in Spanish all pronouns must agree in gender and number with the nouns they represent.

[9] Recall that the indirect object indicates to or for whom an action is performed and that the indirect object pronoun as well as the indirect object phrase may appear in the same sentence (see section **28**). However, this occurs when **a** and not **para** is the preposition in the indirect object phrase. Compare:

Le abro la puerta a Susana.
Abro la puerta para Susana.   *I open the door for Susana.*

▶ The prepositional phrase **de** plus **él, ella, usted, ellos, ellas,** or **ustedes** may replace the ambiguous possessive adjectives **su** and **sus** for clarification or to express greater emphasis.

Unstressed (occasionally ambiguous)   Stressed (unambiguous)

			él	*his*
			ella	*her*
su iniciativa	*his, her* *your* (sing. and pl.) *their initiative*	**la iniciativa de**	**Ud.**	*your*
			ellos	*their*
			ellas	*their*
			Uds.	*your*

initiative

			él	*his*
			ella	*her*
sus burros	*his, her* *your* (sing. and pl.) *their donkeys*	**los burros de**	**Ud.**	*your*
			ellos	*their*
			ellas	*their*
			Uds.	*your*

donkeys

A • Variable Substitution Drill

MODEL   A mí no me preocupa.
          nos
STUDENT   A **nosotros** no **nos** preocupa.

1. A mí no me preocupa.
     ti
        nos
     él
        te
     Uds.

2. ¿Dónde está Juan? Yo no salgo sin él.
     María?
     el dinero?
     los discos?
     las composiciones?
     la factura?

B • Query   Patterned Response

MODEL   ¿Esto es para Ud. o para ella?
STUDENT 1   **Esto es para mí.**
STUDENT 2   **Esto es para ella.**

1. ¿Esto es para ti o para Juan?
2. ¿Piensas en mí o en él?
3. ¿Voy contigo o con ellos?
4. ¿Le ayudamos a Ud. o a Carmen?
5. ¿Trabajamos cerca de ti o cerca de ellas?
6. ¿Quieres hablar conmigo o con él?
7. ¿Salen sin mí o sin Marta?
8. ¿Llegan después de mí o después de Juan?
9. ¿Luchas con él o con Susana?
10. ¿Trabajan cerca de mí o cerca de ella?

C • Translation Drill

MODEL   Is she your student?
STUDENT   **¿Es su alumna?**
MODEL   Is she a student of yours?
STUDENT   **¿Es una alumna de Ud.?**

1. Is he his student?
   Is he a student of his?
2. Am I your professor?
   Am I a professor of yours?
3. Is it her song?
   Is it a song of hers?
4. Are they their friends?
   Are they friends of theirs?

D • Translation Drill

Translate into Spanish.

1. Come with me. Go without me.
2. She lives close to him. She lives close to it (the store).
3. They are talking about you. They are talking about us.
4. The money is from them. The money is from you.
5. After you. Before him. Close to us. From me.
6. Where's the contract? Don't come without it.
7. Where are the newspapers? Don't study without them.
8. Where are the demands? Don't go without them.

41 Use of **gustar**, **quedar**, and **faltar**

Indirect object pronoun necessary	Verb in third person singular or plural	Indirect object optional
me	gusta(n)	a mí
te		a ti
le	queda(n)	a Juanita
nos		a nosotros
les	falta(n)	a ellos

▶ There is a small class of verbs—including **gustar**, *to be appealing,* *"to like"*; **quedar**, *to have* (a thing) *left, to remain*; and **faltar**, *to be lacking, to be missing, to need*—that always calls for an indirect object pronoun. These constructions are the reverse of English in that the "thing" is the subject of the clause and the person is the indirect object. When *it* or *they* (in the sense of plural things rather than persons) is the subject in these constructions, the "it" or the "they" is not expressed, but rather is implicit in the verb endings (examples 1 and 2). Also, because **gustar**, **quedar**, and **faltar** agree with the thing, not the person, only two forms are regularly used: third person singular and third person plural. However, when followed by an infinitive, these verbs appear in the singular.

1. Me gusta.
2. Ya no les quedan amigos.

3. ¿Qué te falta?

4. A nosotros nos falta una hora más.

5. ¿A ti te gustan las películas de
   Cantinflas?
6. Le queda tiempo a Juan.

7. Me gusta ir al cine y leer.

I like it. ("It appeals to me.")
*They have no friends left. ("There are
no friends left to them.")*
*What do you need? ("What is lacking
to you?")*
*We have one more hour to go. ("One
more hour is lacking to us.")*
*Do you like Cantinflas' films? ("Are
Cantinflas' films pleasing to you?")*
*Juan has time left. ("Time is left to
Juan.")*
I like to go to the movies and read.

▶ In addition to the necessary indirect object pronoun, **gustar**, **quedar**, and **faltar** may also take the indirect object phrase (see section **28**). The position of the indirect object phrase is flexible but it is often expressed first for greater emphasis (examples 4 and 5).

LA CUCARACHA

"La Cucaracha" is a popular Mexican song written about Pancho Villa's large, dilapidated black car, which was referred to as **La Cucaracha**, *The Cockroach.*

La cucaracha, la cucaracha
ya no puede caminar
porque no tiene, porque le falta
marijuana que fumar.

La cucaracha, la cucaracha
ya no puede caminar
porque no tiene, porque le faltan
las dos patitas de atrás

A • Variable Substitution Drill

MODEL   A mí me gusta comer.
         ti
STUDENT A **ti te** gusta comer.

1. A mí me gusta trabajar.	2. Me falta el dinero.	3. ¿Te quedan seis o siete?
ella	queda	¿Me
te	los libros.	¿Les
él	gustan	¿Nos
nos	la película.	¿Le
ellos	falta	¿Te
me	los contratos.	¿Me

B • Replacement Drill

Replace the verb with **faltar** or **gustar**, making the necessary adjustments.

MODEL   ⟶ faltar
         Yo no tengo tiempo.
STUDENT **Me falta** tiempo.

1. ⟶ faltar
   Yo no tengo catorce horas.
   Tú necesitas tiempo.
   Ella quiere muchas cosas.
   Nosotros deseamos trabajo.
   Yo no doy eso.
   ¿Qué busca él?
   ¿Qué dejan ellos?
   ¿Qué esconde Ud.?

2. ⟶ gustar
   Necesito el grande.
   ¿Buscas éste?
   ¿Tomas la cerveza fría?
   Escuchamos la sinfonía.
   Miro la película.
   Escribimos los poemas.
   Queremos estudiar.
   Voy a comer guacamole.

C • Query   Free Response

Answer in Spanish.

1. ¿Te falta tiempo para estudiar?
2. ¿Te gusta la comida mexicana?
3. ¿A Ud. le queda dinero?
4. ¿Te gustan las películas?
5. ¿Qué le falta a Ud.?
6. ¿Qué te gusta?
7. ¿A Ud. le gusta hablar español?
8. ¿Al profesor le falta tiempo para terminar la lección?

D • Translation Drill

Translate into Spanish.

1. I like it. I like them.
2. I lack it. I lack them.
3. I have no time left (use **quedar**). I have six or seven left (use **quedar**).

4. Carlitos likes the movies.
5. We lack the big one, but we have the little one left (use **quedar**).
6. Ernesto likes the song; Ernesto likes the songs.
7. Susana has one contract left; Susana has many contracts left.
8. The group lacks a name; the students lack a class in order to finish.

42 Infinitive after a preposition

Spanish		English
Preposition + infinitive	=	Preposition + *-ing*
antes de comer		*before eating*
después de hacerlo		*after doing it*
al salir de aquí		*upon leaving here*

▶ In Spanish, the infinitive rather than the present participle is regularly used after a preposition. Thus, the Spanish preposition and infinitive corresponds to English preposition and *-ing*. **Al** plus the infinitive is the equivalent to English *on* or *upon* plus the present participle, or *when* plus a verb.

Al llegar, voy a llamarla.   *On arriving, I am going to call her.*
When I arrive, I am going to call her.

A • Variable Substitution Drill

MODEL   Antes de hacerlo, ven conmigo.
               buscarlo
STUDENT   Antes de **buscarlo**, ven conmigo.

1. Antes de escribirlo, ven conmigo.
         buscarlos
   Después de
            devolverla
   Para
            conocerlas
   Antes de
            decidirlo

2. Tenemos que hacerlo en vez de hablar.
            antes de
   decidirlo
            para
   saberlo
            en vez de
   escucharla
            sin

B • Translation Drill

Translate into Spanish.

1. After eating, look for it.
2. Before leaving, go there.
3. When you finish it (Upon finishing it), come here.
4. Without voting, we cannot do it.
5. In order to act, we have to decide.

REVIEW

I   The following questions are related to the dialog. Answer in Spanish.

1. ¿A Carlitos le gusta trabajar mucho?
2. ¿Es Carlitos un Don Juan o un bufón?
3. ¿Quiénes vienen a visitar la oficina?
4. ¿Por qué felicita el jefe a Carlitos?
5. ¿A don Santiago le gustan las iniciativas espontáneas?
6. ¿Quiere el jefe un trabajo ligero?
7. ¿Crees que todos van a conseguir un aumento?
8. ¿Cuánto tiempo les queda para trabajar?

II   Translate the following into Spanish.

1. Who is a donkey? You! At least you work like a donkey.
2. When can I get out of this cave? I'm tired already.
3. What! It's only four o'clock. You have time left to finish the invoices.
4. Please, don't be that way. I have to leave now. I'm going to take my girlfriend to the sale.
5. Are you crazy? Come here. Go over these contracts. The big shots want the proposal today.
6. You know what? Rubén thinks that he is a Don Juan, but for me he's nothing more than a clown.
7. I deserve a raise! When I see (Upon seeing) the boss, I'm going to tell him that I have initiative and I need more money.
8. Do me a favor. Get up on the table. Sing a song. Dance a dance. Make me laugh.

III   Write your own dialog.

At work you have a brilliant idea. You tell it to everybody, but they all make fun of you.

PRONUNCIATION

Spanish **t** and **d**

I The Spanish **t** is pronounced by pressing the tip of the tongue against the back of the upper front teeth rather than against the gum ridge above the teeth as in English. Also, the Spanish **t** is never followed by a puff of air (aspiration) as occurs in English. Pronounce after your instructor.

también	tarea	todo
tampoco	tengo	tomar
tango	terminar	toro
tanto	tiempo	traer
tarde	tienda	trono

También tengo que terminar toda mi tarea a tiempo.

¿Te traigo el tango que tengo en la tienda?

El toro toma toda la tarde para terminar.

II The Spanish **d** has two distinct sounds. At the beginning of an utterance or after a pause and after **l** or **n** it is pronounced /d/ like English *d* but, as in the Spanish **t**, the tip of the tongue touches the upper front teeth rather than the gum ridge above the teeth. Pronounce after your instructor.

donde	después
cuando	domingo
el día	dental
vender	depende

In all positions other than those stated above, the Spanish **d** is pronounced /đ/ like a weak English *th*, as in *father*, *this*. Pronounce after your instructor.

todo	cuidado
vida	estudiamos
verdad	usted
ciudad	pared
enamorado	nada

The pronunciation of **d** depends on what comes before and after, that is, on the phonemic context. On the left the **d**'s are pronounced /d/, and on the right, /đ/. Pronounce after your instructor.

/d/	/đ/
el domingo	ese domingo
el día	¡Qué día!
de José Luis	la novia de José Luis
de Ingeniería	Facultad de Ingeniería

Cognates & Contexts

El Ratón Miguelito

El Pato Donald

Pluto

ERNESTO	Yo soy una persona muy creativa. Sin duda voy a ganar mucho dinero en la industria o en el comercio.

ganar *to earn*

FELIPE	¡Ni pensarlo! A las grandes compañías no les gusta la originalidad. Quieren contratar a esas personas que trabajan como burritos todo el día haciendo trabajos rutinarios.

¡Ni pensarlo! *No way!*

ERNESTO	No seas tan cínico. Ya no vivimos en el siglo diecinueve. Ahora el mundo comercial necesita mentes ágiles, gente con talento, para las computadoras, las ventas, la publicidad...

siglo *century*

mundo *world* **mentes** *minds*

publicidad *advertising*

FELIPE	¡La publicidad! No me hables de publicidad. Allí te dan gato por liebre.

dar gato por liebre *to gyp* ("*to serve cat in place of hare.*")

DIEGO	Mi hermanito tiene su primera cita esta noche.

cita *date*

LUPE	Ay, pobre. ¡Qué iniciación! ¿Tiene miedo?

tener miedo *to be afraid*

DIEGO	¿Miedo? No. ¡Terror! Tiene todo preparado como un maníaco. Va a traer un cordón de zapato adicional... ¡por si las moscas!

cordón de zapato *shoelace*

por si las moscas *just in case* (**moscas** lit. *flies*)

LUPE	¡Ay, pobre! Y, ¿adónde van?
DIEGO	Sin duda a un cabaret elegante.
LUPE	No seas así. Solamente tiene catorce años tu hermanito.
DIEGO	Creo que van a dar un paseo por la plaza y después al festival de dibujos animados para ver al Ratón Miguelito.

dar un paseo *to take a stroll*

dibujos animados *film cartoons* **Ratón Miguelito** *Mickey Mouse*

Soccer match, Buenos Aires, Argentina

Lección diez

AL PARTIDO DE FÚTBOL

partido *game, match*

REFLEXIVES

PAQUITO	¡Gabriel! Despiértate ya. ¿Te das cuenta de la hora?	despertarse (ie) *to wake up (oneself)* darse cuenta (de) *to realize*
GABRIEL	¡No, quiero dormir! No puedo ni abrir los ojos. Paquito... sé un hermano bueno. Déjame dormir media hora más. Es demasiado temprano. No te preocupes, llegamos a tiempo.	dormir (ue) *to sleep* ojos *eyes* dejar *to allow, let* media hora *half an hour* demasiado temprano *too early* preocuparse *to worry* llegar *to arrive* a tiempo *on time*
PAQUITO	¡Gabriel! Tienes que levantarte y vestirte ahora mismo. Lávate la cara con agua helada. Ya son las cinco y media.	levantarse *to get up* vestirse *to get dressed* lavarse *to wash (oneself)* cara *face* agua *water* helada *cold, frozen*
GABRIEL	¡Las cinco y media de la mañana! No te burles de mí. ¡Qué lata son los hermanos menores! Cómo te atreves a molestarme a esta hora obscena? Despiértame más o menos a las ocho.	burlarse (de) *to make fun (of)* ¡Qué lata! *What a pain!* menores *younger* atreverse (a) *to dare (to)* molestar *to bother*
PAQUITO	¡Gabriel! Toma. Ponte los pantalones. No te olvides de que éste es el partido más importante del año. ¡El Real Madrid contra el Botafogo! Tú dices que el uno juega tan bien como el otro pero ahora sí vamos a saber quién es el mejor.	ponerse *to put on* pantalones *pants* olvidarse (de que) *to forget (that)* jugar (ue)[1] *to play* tan bien como *as well as* el mejor *the best (one)*
GABRIEL	Está bien. No te pongas tan agitado.	

[1] **Jugar** changes **u → ue: juego, juegas, juega, jugamos, juegan.**

PAQUITO	Se dice que más de cien mil personas van a intentar presenciar el partido. ¿Puedes creerlo? Acuérdate de Elena y su hermana mayor. ¿Cómo se llama ella? Sonia, ¿verdad? Tenemos que llevarlas también.	**se dice** *it is said, "they" say* **más de** *more than* **intentar** *to try* **presenciar** *to watch* **acordarse (ue) (de)** *to remember* **mayor** *older* **llamarse** *to be named (lit., to name oneself)*
GABRIEL	Sí, ¿qué más da? Las taquillas se abren a la una, ¿verdad? ¡Nos quedan unas siete horas y pico!	**¿qué más da?** *what difference does it make?* **taquillas** *ticket offices* **abrirse** *to open up* **... y pico** *. . . and a little*
PAQUITO	Sí, ¿pero no te das cuenta de que tenemos que llegar lo más pronto posible para hacer cola? Solamente así podemos conseguir las mejores entradas.	**lo más pronto posible** *as soon as possible* **hacer cola** *to get in line* **entradas** *tickets*
GABRIEL	¡Qué fastidio! Creo que no soy tan aficionado como tú. Vamos a malgastar la mayor parte del día haciendo cola.	**¡Qué fastidio!** *What a pain! What a problem!* **malgastar** *to waste* **la mayor parte de** *the greater part of*
PAQUITO	Pero piensa en el ambiente... los expertos discutiendo sutilezas, la gente apostando a su favorito, los vendedores ambulantes ofreciendo banderines y fotos, empanadas, churros y pepitas. ¿Cómo puedes estar tan tranquilo? ¡La antipación es tan emocionante como el espectáculo mismo!	**ambiente** *atmosphere* **discutir** *to discuss* **sutilezas** *subtleties* **apostar (ue) (a)** *to bet (on)* **vendedores** *salesmen* **ofrecer** *to offer* **banderines** *banners* **emocionante** *exciting*

think about

Pelé, world's most famous soccer player

NOTES

Fútbol refers to soccer in the Hispanic world; **fútbol americano** is football as played in the United States.

Real Madrid, Botafogo
El Real Madrid is one of the most popular and most highly regarded professional soccer teams in Spain. El Botafogo occupies a similar status in Brazil.

Empanadas, Churros, Pepitas
Empanadas are turnovers filled with either meat or sweets; **churros** are cruller-type pastries; **pepitas** are pumpkin seeds.

LANGUAGE STRUCTURES

43 Reflexive pronouns and verbs

▶ Reflexive pronouns are identical to direct and indirect object pronouns except in the third person, where **se** is used.

Reflexive Pronouns[2]	
me	*myself; to, for myself*
te	*yourself* (familiar); *to, for yourself* (familiar)
se	*himself, herself, yourself* (formal), *itself, oneself; to, for himself, herself, yourself* (formal), *itself, oneself*
nos	*ourselves; to, for ourselves*
se[3]	*themselves, yourselves; to, for themselves, yourselves*

▶ A verb functions reflexively when it is used with a reflexive pronoun that corresponds to the subject of the sentence. The pronoun **se** affixed to the infinitive is the conventional indication of a reflexive verb: **lavar**, *to wash* (something); **lavarse**, *to wash oneself*.

▶ Reflexive pronouns are used as direct and indirect objects. In addition some intransitive verbs may be made reflexive as well, with a change of meaning.

ir	*to go*	**marchar**	*to march*
irse	*to go away*	**marcharse**	*to go away*

▶ The position of the reflexive pronouns is the same as that of the direct and indirect object pronouns—before a conjugated verb or negative command but attached to a present participle, infinitive, and affirmative command.

Reflexive Pronouns as Direct Object Pronouns

The second version in each example is the reflexive.

1. Despiértalo.
   Despiértate. No te despiertas.

   Wake him up.
   Wake up (yourself). Don't wake (yourself) up.

2. (Yo) lavo los pantalones.
   (Yo) me lavo.

   I am washing the pants.
   I wash (am washing) myself.

3. Ud. tiene que levantarlo (Ud. lo tiene que levantar).
   Ud. tiene que levantarse (Ud. se tiene que levantar).

   You have to lift it (him).
   You have to get up (literally, pick yourself up).

---

[2] **Mismo, -a, -os, -as,** when following a noun also means *-self*: **yo mismo,** *I myself*; **el espectáculo mismo,** *the spectacle itself*. **Mismo** also may be used after an expression to add emphasis: **hoy mismo,** *today (without fail)*; **ahora mismo,** *right now*. In addition **mismo** substitutes for certain verbs that are rarely used reflexively in Spanish:

El poeta mismo está aquí. *The poet himself is here.*
Tú mismo eres un bufón. *You're a clown yourself.*

[3] See the Appendix, section **1**, for the **vosotros** reflexive pronoun.

WORD PLAY

No me vendo ni me doy
Porque de mi dueño soy.

Here is a common engraving found on gifts. What does it mean?

Reflexive Pronouns as Indirect Object Pronouns

The second version is the reflexive.

1. Ponle los[4] pantalones.   *Put on his pants (for him).*
   Ponte los[4] pantalones.   *Put on your pants (for yourself).*
2. (Yo) le lavo la[4] cara.   *I am washing her (his) face.*
   (Yo) me lavo la[4] cara.   *I am washing my face.*
3. Ud. le va a comprar una bicicleta.   *You are going to buy him a bicycle*
                or   *(buy a bicycle for him).*
   Ud. va a comprarle una bicicleta.

   Ud. se va a comprar una bicicleta.   *You are going to buy yourself a bicycle*
                or   *(buy a bicycle for yourself).*
   Ud. va a comprarse una bicicleta.

A • Variable Substitution Drill

MODEL   Tienes que levantarte y vestirte.
                          me
STUDENT   **Tengo** que **levantarme** y **vestirme**.

1. Tienes que levantarte y vestirte.   2. Mañana yo me despierto a las ocho.
                    nos   tú
   Tiene   ella
                          me.   él
   Tienen   Ud.
                    te   nosotros
   Tengo   Uds.
                          nos.   ellos
                    me   ellas

---

[4] The definite article rather than the possessive adjective is used with nouns referring to the body or wearing apparel. See section **46**.

B • Transformation Drill   Direct or Indirect Object Pronoun → Reflexive Pronoun

MODEL   Le lavo la cara.
STUDENT   **Me lavo** la cara.

1. ¿Te escondemos ahora mismo?
2. No quiero vestirla de verde.
3. ¡Ponle los pantalones!
4. No te defendemos siempre.
5. ¡Despiértalo!

6. Levántala.
7. No la ponga Ud. tan agitada.
8. No lo olvides.
9. Prepárale la comida.
10. Susana le canta una canción.

C • Query   Patterned Response

MODEL   ¿Me levanto?
STUDENT   **Sí, Ud. debe levantarse.**

1. ¿Me lavo?
2. ¿Me despierto?
3. ¿Me compro un disco?
4. ¿Me voy por la trade?
5. ¿Me olvido de ese bufón?

6. ¿Me pongo los pantalones?
7. ¿Me tomo una cerveza?
8. ¿Me marcho?
9. ¿Me defiendo?
10. ¿Me escondo?

D • Query   Free Response

Answer in Spanish.

1. ¿Cómo se llama Ud.?
2. ¿Cómo se llama la profesora (el profesor) de español?
3. ¿A qué hora te despiertas?
4. ¿A qué hora te levantas?
5. ¿Te das cuenta de la hora?
6. ¿Te escondes del profesor cuando no tienes la tarea?
7. ¿Te pones agitado cuando tienes que hacer cola?
8. ¿Te amas... o te odias?

E • Translation Drill

Translate into Spanish.

1. Wash him! Wash yourself!
2. Don't bother me! Don't bother (yourself)!
3. Don't worry me! Don't worry (yourself)!
4. Lift it! Get up (Lift yourself up)!
5. Paquito looks at her. Paquito looks at himself.
6. Gabriel loses the tickets. Gabriel gets lost (loses himself).
7. They buy the motorcycle for him. They buy themselves the motorcycle.
8. Don't say those things to me. Don't tell yourself those things.

44   Some special aspects of the reflexive

▶ I. The plural reflexive pronouns (**nos** and **se**) can be used as reciprocal pronouns. Used in this way they are equivalent to *each other* or *one another*.

> **Gabriel y Elena se escriben todos los días.**   *Gabriel and Elena write to each other every day.*
>
> **¡Huy! ¡Nos odiamos!**[5]   *Ugh! We hate one another!*

▶ II. The concept of "becoming" as expressed in English by such verbs as *to get, to become, to change into, to turn into*, etc. is often expressed in Spanish by reflexive constructions.

> **ponerse** + adjective   *to become, to get, to assume a certain physical or emotional state, usually temporary*
>
> > **¡No te pongas agitado!**[6]   *Don't become upset!*
> > **Esto se pone bueno.**   *This is getting good (exciting).*

> **hacerse**   *to become, to effect a change in status as a result of a conscious effort*
>
> > **¿Cómo vas a hacerte rico?**   *How are you going to become rich?*
> > **¿Cuándo se hace ingeniero?**   *When does he become an engineer?*

> **volverse**   *to become, as by sudden change; to turn into as a result of an external cause rather than a voluntary effort*
>
> > **Los niños me vuelven loco.**   *The kids are making me (driving me) crazy.*
> >
> > **Con dos copitas se vuelve un bufón.**   *With two little drinks he turns into a clown.*

▶ Another way to express the equivalent of *to become* is **llegar a ser**, *to become as the culmination of a successful process*

> > **Uno de estos días voy a llegar a ser un poeta famoso.**   *One of these days I'm going to become (come to be) a famous poet.*

---

[5] Two interpretations of the reflexive when used in this way may be possible: **Nos odiamos.** *We hate each other* or *We hate ourselves.* Context makes the meaning clear.

[6] The same meaning conveyed by **ponerse** + adjective can sometimes be conveyed by the reflexive use of the verb formed from the adjective in question. For example, **No te pongas agitado.** *Don't become upset.* (**agitarse**) **No te agites.** *Don't become upset.* **Cada vez que lo veo me pongo enfermo.** *Every time I see him I get sick.* (**enfermarse**) **Cada vez que lo veo me enfermo.** *Every time that I see him I get sick.*

▶ III. Some verbs in Spanish are used almost solely in the reflexive. Of the listing that follows, you have encountered the first group in the dialog of Lección diez; the verbs in color are new vocabulary.

acordarse (ue) (de)	*to remember*
atreverse (a)	*to dare*
burlarse (de)	*to make fun (of)*
darse cuenta (de)	*to realize*
olvidarse (de)[7]	*to forget*
preocuparse	*to worry*
fijarse (en)[7]	*to look (at), to notice*
enorgullecerse (de)[8]	*to pride oneself, to be proud (of)*
jactarse (de)	*to boast, to brag (about)*
quejarse (de)	*to complain (about)*
suicidarse	*to commit suicide*

A • Query   Patterned Response

MODEL   ¿Así que se conocen ustedes dos?
STUDENT   **¡Huy! Claro que nos conocemos.**

1. ¿Así que se conocen ustedes dos?
2. ¿Así que se escriben ustedes dos?
3. ¿Así que se aman ustedes dos?
4. ¿Así que se odian ustedes dos?
5. ¿Así que se ayudan ustedes dos?
6. ¿Así que se necesitan ustedes dos?
7. ¿Así que se hablan ustedes dos?
8. ¿Así que se comprenden ustedes dos?

B • Variable Substitution Drill

MODEL   ¿Por qué se burla Juanito de mí?
        tú
STUDENT   ¿Por qué **te burlas** tú de mí?

1. ¿Por qué se olvida Juanito de mí?
   tú
   él?
   ellos
   te fijas en
   ella
   ellos?

2. Yo no me acuerdo del señor Méndez.
   Él
   te
   quejas de
   él.
   enorgulleces de
   nos

[7] The verbs **olvidar** and **fijar** exist, but with entirely different meanings.
   olvidar   *to leave behind*   **fijar**   *to paste, to fix, to fasten*
[8] Formed from the adjective **orgullo**. Other such verbs formed from adjectives are
   enloquecerse (from **loco**)   *to become crazy*   **enriquecerse** (from **rico**)   *to get rich*

C • Query   Free Response

Answer in Spanish.

1. ¿Se acuerda Ud. de la tarea para mañana?
2. ¿Te gusta burlarte de tus amigos?
3. ¿Vas a llegar a ser ingeniero?
4. ¿Se hablan Ud. y su mejor amigo todos los días?
5. ¿Se fija Ud. mucho en el reloj cuando está en clase?
6. ¿Se pone agitada (agitado) cuando hace cola?
7. ¿Quiere Ud. hacerse rico?
8. ¿Te vuelves loco con todo el trabajo que tienes?
9. ¿Crees que los profesores y los alumnos se conocen bien?
10. ¿Por qué siempre te quejas de todo?

D • Translation Drill

Translate into Spanish.

1. They love each other. We love each other.
2. We hate each other. Do they hate each other?
3. They help one another. Do you help one another?
4. Do you realize that it is good? I am beginning to realize that he is bad.
5. Don't you go (become) crazy here? Do you want to get rich?

45   Reflexives with nonpersonal subjects

▶   I. *Reflexive substitute for the passive.* In the active voice the subject acts upon the object.

> **El hombre abre las taquillas a la una.**   *The man opens the ticket offices at one.*

In the passive voice the subject is acted upon by the verb.

> **Las taquillas se abren a la una.**   *The ticket offices are opened at one.*

In Spanish the passive voice is often expressed by using **se** with the third person singular or plural of the verb to agree with a singular or plural subject. There are other ways to express the passive (see section **83**) but the **se** form is especially used when the agent (who or what performs the action) is not pertinent or specifically identified. Imagine that the subject does the action of the verb to itself.

	Normal English	Literal English
1. Se habla español.	*Spanish is spoken.*	*Spanish speaks itself.*
2. ¿Cuándo se cierran las universidades?	*When are the universities closed?*	*When do the universities close themselves?*
3. Se hace el trabajo.	*The work is done.*	*The work does itself.*

▶ II. **Se** *used as an indefinite subject.* To express the occurrence of an action without any grammatical subject, **se** is used with the third person singular of the verb. This use of **se** corresponds to the English use of *one, they, you, people,* when not referring to a definite person.

▶ When used with a third person singular verb, often **se** may be considered either as an indefinite subject or as a reflexive substitute for the passive (examples 1 and 2).

	They say
1. Se dice que el Botafogo es mejor.	*People say that Botafogo is better (best).*
	It is said
2. Se habla español en Nueva York.	*They speak Spanish*
	People speak Spanish in New York.
	Spanish is spoken
3. Se come bien aquí.	*You (one) eat(s) well here.*

With both the reflexive substitute for the passive and **se** used as an indefinite subject, the sentence usually begins with **se** followed by the verb.

A • Query   Patterned Response

MODEL   ¿Qué hablan en el Canadá? ¿Francés?
STUDENT   **¡Exacto! Se habla francés en el Canadá.**

1. ¿Qué hablan en los Estados Unidos? ¿Español?
2. ¿Qué hacen aquí? ¿Contratos?
3. ¿Qué comen allí? ¿Cerdo?
4. ¿Qué preparan allí? ¿Guacamole?
5. ¿Qué escriben en la clase? ¿Poemas?
6. ¿Qué leen en la biblioteca? ¿Libros?
7. ¿Qué buscan aquí? ¿Un fanático?
8. ¿Qué necesitan en la Central? ¿Un bufón?
9. ¿A quiénes ven allí todos los días? ¿A Susana y a su hermana?
10. ¿A quién felicitan por el trabajo? ¿Al alcalde?

B • Transformation Drill   Active → se Form

MODEL   El hombre no hace el trabajo.
STUDENT   **No se** hace el trabajo.

1. Los muchachos comen bien.
2. El mandamás necesita un burro.
3. Gabriel no hace la propuesta.
4. El vendedor ofrece pepitas y churros.
5. El joven come empanadas.
6. Mil personas presencian el partido.
7. Muchos dicen que es el mejor.
8. Los expertos discuten sutilezas.
9. Carlitos revisa facturas.
10. Marta vende bicicletas viejas.

C • Translation Drill

Translate into Spanish.

1. Spanish is spoken in Mexico. One can speak Spanish here.
2. One says, "thank you." One says, "hello."
3. One learns a lot here. One writes a lot there.
4. The library is opened at 9; it is closed at 6.
5. Newspapers are sold here; old books are bought there.

46 The definite article for possession

▶ Spanish generally uses the definite article rather than the possessive adjective with an object when it is obvious who the possessor is. Nouns referring to clothing or parts of the body generally take the definite article. This also happens occasionally in English: He hit me in *the* eye, not *my* eye. In addition, when reflexive pronouns are used, they clarify who the possessor is and therefore often permit use of the definite article.

1. No puedo ni abrir **los** ojos.   *I can't even open my eyes.*
2. ¿Qué tengo en **la** cara?   *What do I have on my face?*
3. Lávate **la** cara.   *Wash your face.*

But: **Sus** pantalones están en la mesa.   *Your (his) pants are on the table.*
       Tu cara está sucia.   *Your face is dirty.*

A • Query   Patterned Response

MODEL   ¿Me pongo tu sombrero?
STUDENT   **No, yo** me pongo **el** sombrero.

1. ¿Me tomo tu cerveza?
2. ¿Preparo tu comida?
3. ¿Busco tu anillo?
4. ¿Escribo tu tarea?
5. ¿Traigo tus pantalones?
6. ¿Recito tus versos?
7. ¿Acabo tu trabajo?
8. ¿Le doy tu composición a Mónica?

B • Translation Drill

Translate into Spanish.

1. Put on your pants. Don't open your eyes.
2. Close your mouth. Don't put on your pants.
3. Prepare your food. Don't wash your face.

47 Comparisons of inequality

▶ Spanish normally uses **más** (*more, most*) and **menos** (*less* or *fewer, least* or *fewest*) to show a greater or lesser degree or amount of something. The use of **más** and **menos** corresponds both to the English use of *more, most,* and *less, least, fewer, fewest* and to the use of the suffixes *-er, -est* with certain adjectives and adverbs (*older, oldest, later, latest,* etc.). You tell from the context when an adjective has comparative or superlative force; that is, whether **más** means *more* or *most,* and whether **menos** means *less* or *least, fewer* or *fewest.*

Nouns

1. Hay más españoles aquí que mexicanos.
   There are more Spaniards here than Mexicans.
2. Necesitamos tener menos actividades militantes.
   We need to have fewer militant activities.

Verbs

1. Este anillo me gusta más.
   I like this ring more.
2. Sí, lo sé, más o menos.
   Yes, I know (it), more or less.

Adjectives

1. Es el partido más importante del año.
   It is the most important match of the year.
2. Esta clase es menos interesante.
   This class is less interesting.

Adverbs

1. Media hora más tarde, llega Sonia.
   A half hour later, Sonia arrives.
2. ¿Puedes ir más rápidamente, por favor?
   Can you go more quickly, please?

Irregular Comparative of Adjectives and Adverbs: **-or** form

▶ The following four **-or** forms are the only comparatives not formed with **más** or **menos.**

bueno (adj.) bien (adv.)	(el) mejor	*(the) better, best*
malo (adj.) mal (adv.)	(el) peor	*(the) worse, worst*
grande (adj.)	(el) más grande	*(the) larger, largest*
	(el) mayor	*(the) greater, older, greatest, oldest*
pequeño (adj.)	(el) más pequeño	*(the) smaller, smallest*
	(el) menor	*(the) smaller, younger, smallest, youngest*

▶ **Grande** and **pequeño, -a,** have regular forms that refer to physical size; **mayor** and **menor** usually refer to persons and mean *older* and *younger*, respectively. **Mayor** also carries the meaning of *greater*. **La mayor parte de** is the equivalent of *most (of), the greater part of*: **la mayor parte del día,** *most of the day.*

1. ¿Estás bien? Oh, sí, ahora estoy mejor.
   Are you okay? Oh, yes, now I'm better.

2. Carlitos se vuelve peor y peor.
   Carlitos is getting worse and worse.

3. ¿Quién es el mejor?
   Who is the best? or *Who is better?*

4. Hoy es el peor día de mi vida.
   Today is the worst day of my life.

5. Los hermanos menores y las hermanas mayores son una lata.
   Younger brothers and older sisters are a bother.

But

6. Soy más grande que tú pero más pequeño que Elena.
   I'm bigger than you but smaller than Elena.

▶ As a rule of thumb, *than* is translated by **que** before a noun or pronoun (example 1) but when dealing with quantities it is translated by **de** (example 2).

1. Éste está más sucio que el otro.
   This one is dirtier than the other one.

2. Tengo menos de cinco días para terminar.
   I have less than five days to finish.

▶ After a superlative *in* is translated by **de.**

Ésta es la universidad más grande de México.
This is the largest university in Mexico.

▶ When an adverb with **más** or **menos** (or **mejor** or **peor** used as adverbs) is further modified, **lo**[9] precedes it.

Tengo que llegar lo más pronto posible.
I have to arrive as soon as possible.

Hago lo mejor que puedo.
I do the best that I can.

---

[9] This **lo** is the neuter definite article. See section **66** for other examples of usage.

A • Variable Substitution Drill

MODEL   Ella es menor que Sonia.
Ellas
STUDENT   Ellas **son menores** que Sonia.

1. Ella es menor que Sonia.
Nosotros
Nosotras
Él
Tú
Ellos

2. Este anillo es más precioso que el otro.
mejor
profesor
peor
libro
más grande

B • Query   Patterned Response

MODEL   ¿Es grande la tienda?
STUDENT   **Sí, es más grande que la otra.**

1. ¿Es precioso el anillo?
2. ¿Es difícil el poema?
3. ¿Es interesante aquella tradición?
4. ¿Es grave la situación?
5. ¿Es romántica la muchacha?
6. ¿Es guapo el muchacho?
7. ¿Es simpática la señorita?
8. ¿Es aficionado el señor?
9. ¿Es bueno el libro?
10. ¿Es malo el espectáculo?

C • Query   Patterned Response

MODEL   ¿Es fácil la clase?
STUDENT   **Sí, es la más fácil de todas.**

1. ¿Es creativa esa persona?
2. ¿Es romántica la canción?
3. ¿Es seria la chica?
4. ¿Es difícil el trabajo?
5. ¿Es aburrida esa lección?
6. ¿Es trivial el ejemplo?
7. ¿Es bárbaro el deporte?
8. ¿Es admirable el poema?
9. ¿Es antipático el bufón?
10. ¿Es ambigua la situación?

D • Query   Patterned Response

MODEL   ¿Voy rápidamente?
STUDENT   **Por favor, vaya Ud. lo más rápidamente posible.**

1. ¿Salgo pronto?
2. ¿Escribo lentamente?
3. ¿Como rápidamente?
4. ¿Hablo claramente?
5. ¿Vengo pronto?
6. ¿Vengo tarde?
7. ¿Le hablo pronto?
8. ¿Lo hago temprano?
9. ¿Lo como rápidamente?
10. ¿Lo escribo mejor?

E • Query   Patterned Response

MODEL   ¿Estás mejor?
STUDENT   **No, estoy peor.**

1. ¿Estás peor?
2. ¿Eres el mayor?
3. ¿Eres el menor?
4. ¿Estás mejor?

5. ¿Tienes las peores entradas?
6. ¿Vienen las mejores personas?
7. ¿Es Ud. mayor que ella?
8. ¿Es la peor parte del día?

F • Translation Drill

Translate into Spanish.

1. I like this one more. She likes that one less.
2. There are more here; there aren't more there.
3. I'm the oldest; she's the youngest.
4. He's the biggest; you're the smallest.
5. I'm worse today; she's better now.
6. Do it as fast as possible. We do it the best we can.

48   Comparisons of equality

tanto, -a, -os, -as + [noun] + como	*as many (much) . . . as*
tan + adjective or adverb + como	*as . . . as*

▶ The forms **tan(to)... como** are equivalent to the kinds of comparisons expressed with English *as . . . as.*

1. ¿Discos? Tengo tantos como tú.
2. Ella no come tanto como él.
3. Carlos tiene tanto dinero como don Santiago.
4. La anticipación es tan buena como el espectáculo.

Records? I have as many as you.
She doesn't eat as much as he (does).
Carlos has as much money as Don Santiago.
The anticipation is as good as the show.

A • Variable Substitution Drill

MODEL   El poema es tan bueno como la canción.
           Los bailes
STUDENT   **Los bailes son** tan **buenos** como la canción.

1. El poema es tan bueno como la canción.
       malo
   Los bailes
       fáciles
   El discurso
       difícil

2. Carlitos no aprende tanto como yo.
       come
       escribe
       baila
       habla
       charla

3. Tengo tantas revistas como libros.
     periódicos
     discos
     trastes
     facturas
     películas

B • Integration Drill

MODEL Ella escribe bien. Yo escribo bien también.
STUDENT **Yo escribo tan bien como ella.**

1. Ella escribe rápidamente. Yo escribo rápidamente también.
2. Carla está harta. Susana está harta también.
3. Luis revisa mucho. Ernesto revisa mucho también.
4. Marta es aficionada. Susana es aficionada también.
5. Diego sale pronto por la mañana. Elena sale pronto por la mañana también.

C • Integration Drill

MODEL Yo tengo mucho dinero. Tú tienes mucho dinero.
STUDENT **Yo tengo tanto dinero como tú.**

1. Yo tengo dos bicicletas. Tú tienes dos bicicletas.
2. Yo tomo tres cervezas. Mi compadre toma tres cervezas.
3. Yo puedo cantar muchas canciones. Ella puede cantar muchas canciones.
4. Yo tengo cinco contratos. Don Agapito tiene cinco contratos.
5. Yo vendo banderines. El vendedor ambulante vende banderines.

D • Query   Patterned Response

MODEL ¿Tiene Ud. más entradas que yo?
STUDENT **No, tengo tantas entradas como Ud.**

1. ¿Tiene Ud. más tangos que yo?
2. ¿Tiene Ud. más clases que yo?
3. ¿Tiene Ud. más trabajo que yo?
4. ¿Tiene Ud. más tarea que yo?
5. ¿Tiene Ud. más dinero que yo?

MODEL ¿Tengo yo tanto tiempo como Ud.?
STUDENT **No, Ud. tiene menos tiempo que yo.**

6. ¿Tengo yo tanto guacomole como Ud.?
7. ¿Tengo yo tantos libros como Ud.?
8. ¿Tengo tantas firmas como Ud.?
9. ¿Tengo tantos zapatos como Ud.?
10. ¿Tengo tanta gente con talento como Ud.?

E • Query   Patterned Response

MODEL   ¿Tiene Ud. más compadres que comadres?
STUDENT **No, tengo tantas comadres como compadres.**

1. ¿Tiene Ud. más discos que libros?
2. ¿Tiene Ud. más periódicos que revistas?
3. ¿Tiene Ud. más canciones que bailes?
4. ¿Tiene Ud. más libros que películas?
5. ¿Tiene Ud. más novios que amigos?

MODEL   ¿Tiene Ud. tantas mujeres como hombres?
STUDENT **No, tengo más hombres que mujeres.**

6. ¿Tiene Ud. tantos dentistas como ingenieros?
7. ¿Tiene Ud. tantos estudiantes como profesores?
8. ¿Tiene Ud. tantas bicicletas como motocicletas?
9. ¿Tiene Ud. tantos alumnos como alumnas?
10. ¿Tiene Ud. tantas enchiladas como tamales?

F • Query   Free Response

Answer in Spanish.

1. ¿Cuál te gusta más, el fútbol americano o los toros?
2. ¿Es tan bueno (malo) el machismo como el feminismo?
3. ¿Cuál te gusta menos, un bufón o un sinvergüenza?
4. ¿Es mejor un brillante que un ópalo?
5. ¿Es mejor ser un hermano mayor o un hermano menor?
6. ¿Qué es peor? ¿Ser joven pero pobre o ser rico pero viejo?
7. ¿Es tan malo un cínico como un majadero?
8. ¿Es tan bueno ser inteligente como ser guapo(a)?

G • Translation Drill

Translate into Spanish.

1. I have more than you. She has less than I have.[10] He has as many as she has.
2. I know more than you. He knows less than she knows.   We know as much as they know.
3. I have **fewer** signatures than you. You have as many photographs as my brother.
4. I am as rich as you are.   You are richer than she is.
5. I have more than eight rings. Do you have as many as I do?

---

[10] Although repetition of the same verb for a new subject is often necessary in English, it is omitted in
Spanish.
    Yo tengo tantos como él.   *I have as many as he has.*

REVIEW

I The following questions are related to the dialog. Answer in Spanish.

1. ¿Paquito le deja dormir a Gabriel?
2. ¿Es Gabriel mayor o menor que Paquito?
3. ¿Se pone agitado Paquito cuando ve a su hermano tan tranquilo?
4. ¿Les queda mucho tiempo para comprar las entradas?
5. ¿Van otras personas al partido con Gabriel y Paquito?
6. ¿Qué es lo más emocionante del espectáculo?
7. ¿Quién es el más aficionado, Paquito o Gabriel?
8. ¿Se entienden bien los dos hermanos?

II Translate into Spanish.

1. Wake up! Open your eyes! It's a magnificent day. Do you realize what time it is?
2. Oh God! Please, be a good friend. Let me sleep another four or five hours.
3. Are you crazy? Get up! You have to get dressed. Wash your face with ice water.
4. Creep! How dare you bother me at this obscene hour? Wake me up tonight.
5. Tonight! Are you making fun of me? By the way, don't forget Elena and Sonia. You have to pick them up at ten thirty.
6. Wow! They are waiting for us, aren't they? They are going to be furious (*furiosas*).
7. You deserve it. Here you are wasting most of the day. The anticipation is killing me.
8. Now what am I going to do? I can't find my shoes. What time is it? Six o'clock in the morning? Go away!

III Write your own dialog.

Imagine that you want to go to a soccer game, bullfight, or movie, but your brother (sister) is not sure whether he (she) wants to go along. You try to convince him (her).

PRONUNCIATION

Spanish s, c + vowels

In English, *t, s*, and *c* followed by *i* are often pronounced *sh* as in *position, mansion, malicious*. Spanish **s** and **c** are pronounced /s/, not **sh** in these and similar words. Pronounce after your instructor.

ambicioso	nación	inicial	discusión
malicioso	posición	ejercicio	Casio
gracioso	sección	social	usual
gracias	expansión	paciencia	socio
diecisiete	introducción	institucional	hacia

Spanish ti and tu

Students tend to mispronounce Spanish **ti** and **tu**. The **t** is pronounced /t/, never like **ch**. Repeat after your instructor.

conceptual	cuestión	bestial
natural	Portugal	celestial
cultural	indigestión	
intelectual	fortuna	
puntual	impetuoso	

Cognates & Contexts

GLORIA   ¿Qué es mejor? Ser la mayor de la familia o ser la menor?

LUCHO   Pues, yo no sé tu caso. Pero yo soy el menor y mi situación es horrible.

GLORIA   ¿Por qué? Como tú sabes, soy la mayor y siempre siento celos hacia mis hermanitos porque ocupan toda la atención de mis padres. ¡Mis padres ya ni me conocen!

     sentir (ie) celos *to feel jealous*

LUCHO   Pues, para comenzar, tengo que vestirme las camisas de mis hermanos mayores, incluso los calcetines y los zapatos. ¡Hasta la ropa interior!

     camisas *shirts*
     calcetines *socks*
     ropa interior *underwear*

GLORIA   No seas vulgar. Además, exageras. Yo sé que tu mamá te mima como loca. Hasta te prepara flan cada vez que lo deseas.

     mimar *to spoil* **flan** *caramel custard*

LUCHO   ¿Y qué? No me dejan comerlo. Mis hermanos se burlan de mí por ser "el mimado". Me quitan el flan, lo comen... y yo, rabioso.

     rabioso *furious*

GLORIA   Creo que tienes razón. Puede ser mejor ser el mayor.

     tener razón *to be right*

Street in Managua, Nicaragua

Lección once

REUNIÓN DE MINISTROS: ESTADO DE EMERGENCIA

MINISTRO DE OBRAS PÚBLICAS Respetables señores, me duele tener que contarles una noticia grave y lamentable.

respetables *honorable*
doler (ue) *to pain, grieve*
contar (ue) *to tell*

MINISTRO DE TRANSPORTE ¿Qué pasó?

pasar *to take place, happen*

MINISTRO DEL INTERIOR ¿Cuándo pasó?

MINISTRO DE OBRAS PÚBLICAS Esperen, señores. Tal vez algunos de ustedes ya saben los pormenores del asunto. Fue ayer

tal vez *perhaps* **algunos (de)** *some (of)*
pormenores *particulars*
asunto *matter* **ayer** *yesterday*

por la tarde. Es decir, a las quince horas, veintitrés minutos y dieciocho segundos del día viernes, primero de abril de mil novecientos ochenta y cuatro. Hubo un ataque contra nuestro proyecto de investigación extraterrestre.

es decir *that is to say*
segundos *seconds*

hubo *there was* **contra** *against*
extraterrestre *outer space (adj.)*

MINISTRO DE JUSTICIA Gracias, Sr. Ministro. Yo puedo continuar el relato. Así fue, exactamente. De pronto salieron a la carretera unos bandidos o qué sé yo, terroristas de la oposición. Atacaron los camiones de construcción y hasta el automóvil del Jefe de Seguridad Pública que llegó por casualidad en ese momento. Pero no se preocupen. Ya lo arreglamos. Despachamos a esos fulanos y el

relato *story, tale* **de pronto** *suddenly*
carretera *highway* **o qué sé yo** *or whatever*
camiones *trucks*

por casualidad *by chance*

arreglar *to fix; to arrange*
despachar (coll.) *to kill, polish off* **fulanos** (coll.) *guys, so-and-so's*
sufrir daños *to suffer damages*

proyecto no sufrió daños.

MINISTRO DEL INTERIOR ¡Por Dios! ¿Sabe esto nuestro presidente?

MINISTRO DE JUSTICIA Sí, volvimos a la capital anoche y fuimos

anoche *last night*

directamente al palacio presidencial para informarle de la situación.

MINISTRO DE AGRICULTURA ¿Y el Jefe de Seguridad Pública? ¿Está bien?

MINISTRO DE JUSTICIA Sí. Lo tengo encarcelado... digo, protegido por guardias especiales.

encarcelado jailed, locked up **protegido** *protected*

MINISTRO DEL INTERIOR Eso suena raro. ¿Por qué no está aquí en persona, en carne y hueso? Tenemos que asegurarnos que está sano y salvo.

sonar (ue) to sound **raro** *strange*
en carne y hueso "in flesh and blood" **(hueso,** *lit., bone)* **asegurarse** *to make sure*
sano y salvo safe and sound

MINISTRO DE OBRAS PÚBLICAS Óigame, menso, ¿no le informaron que está protegido?

menso dummy

MINISTRO DE JUSTICIA Bueno, señores, voy al grano. Después de consultar con las fuerzas armadas, aquí estoy para informarles que pienso invocar la ley marcial por el bien del pueblo. Tenemos que protegernos de los terroristas. Vamos a montar una guardia en seguida y yo mismo me hago responsable por la seguridad de todos hasta tener la situación bajo control.

ir al grano to get to the point
fuerzas armadas armed forces
ley law
el pueblo the people
montar to mount, set up
en seguida right away
hasta until
bajo under

MINISTRO DEL INTERIOR Yo estoy de acuerdo y sé que mis colegas también. Las ideas de usted fueron siempre una inspiración; creo que su decisión es admirable; Ud. tiene el carácter de...

estar de acuerdo to be in agreement

MINISTRO DE JUSTICIA Siéntese Ud. y cállese, imbécil. Ya me cansé de sus impertinencias. ¿No se dio cuenta? Le vamos a exigir su renuncia. Ud. está en la boca del lobo.

sentarse (ie) to sit down **callarse** *to shut up, be quiet* **cansarse** *to become tired*
renuncia resignation

lobo wolf

Mysterious pre-
Columbian markings,
Plain of Nazca, Peru

NOTES

ministros   cabinet members, equivalent of our *secretaries*
   Ministro de Obras Públicas   *Minister of Public Works*
hubo   *there was, there were.* The preterit form of **hay.**
qué sé yo   *what do I know,* often has the additional implication of *and what
      do I care.*
fulano   *guy, so-and-so,* is a colloquial form used to refer to a person in an
      indefinite way. For further examples see page 229.
en la boca del lobo   literally, *in the wolf's mouth,* means metaphorically, *in
      great danger.*

LANGUAGE STRUCTURES

49   Preterit of regular verbs

Regular Preterit Endings	
-ar *verbs*	**-er** *and* **-ir** *verbs*
-é	-í
-aste	-iste
-ó	-ió
-amos *– same as present*	-imos
-aron[1]	-ieron[1]

[1] The preterit **vosotros** forms can be found in the Appendix, section **1**.

Examples

hablar	**aprender**	**escribir**
hablé	aprendí	escribí
hablaste	aprendiste	escribiste
habló	aprendió	escribió
hablamos	aprendimos	escribimos
hablaron	aprendieron	escribieron

▶ Recall that there is no difference between **-er** and **-ir** verbs except in the present tense. Thus the preterit endings of regular **-er** and **-ir** verbs are identical.

▶ In the *we* form (**nosotros, nosotras**) the preterit of **-ar** and **-ir** verbs is the same as the present. For example, **hablamos** means *we speak* or *we spoke*; **escribimos** means *we write* or *we wrote*. The two meanings are distinguished by context.

▶ Spanish has two past tenses, the preterit and the imperfect (explained in Lección trece). English also provides various ways to express an event in the past. For example, I learn*ed*, I *did* learn, I *was* learning, I *used to* (or *would*) learn.

In Lección trece we will explain more fully how the preterit and the imperfect function to express the past. However, generally (but not always) the preterit corresponds to the English *-ed* form[2] and the *did* form.

1. Lo aprendí.	*I learned it.*
2. Ayer informamos al pueblo.	*Yesterday we informed the people.*
3. No salí de casa hoy.	*I didn't leave the house today.*
4. ¿No te contaron la noticia?	*Didn't they tell you the news?*

A • Substitution Drill

MODEL   El presidente volvió a la capital.
         Los ministros
STUDENT Los ministros **volvieron** a la capital.

1. El presidente volvió a la capital.
   Juan
   Tú
   El jefe y don Miguel
   Yo
   Tú y yo

2. ¿Por quién votaron ellos?
   tú?
   yo?
   él y yo?
   Tere y Rafa?
   nosotras?

---

[2] English has a number of irregular verb forms that correspond to the *-ed* form. These also are generally equivalent to the Spanish preterit. For example, *I wrote it*, **lo escribí**; *she left yesterday*, **ella salió ayer**.

3. ¿Con quién habló tu compadre?
   Pepita?
   él?
   nosotros?
   ellas?
   tú?

4. Los ministros no salieron hasta el viernes.
   Uds.
   Yo
   Diego y Miguel
   La profesora
   La profesora y yo

B • Transformation Drill   Present → Preterit

MODEL   Vuelvo³ a las diez.
STUDENT   **Volví** a las diez.

1. Vuelven a las diez.
2. Lo cierro a la una.
3. ¿Cuándo empiezan?
4. ¿Por qué no me defiendes?
5. No entiendo nada.

6. ¿Cuánto cuesta el libro?
7. ¿Te muestro las fotos?
8. ¿Te cuentan la noticia?
9. ¿Por qué no te acuerdas?
10. ¿Cuándo lo encuentras?

C • Transformation Drill   Present → Preterit

MODEL   ¿A quién ve Ud?
STUDENT   ¿A quién **vio**⁴ Ud?

1. Las tiendas se abren a las nueve.
2. Ya se da cuenta.
3. Nos levantamos a las diez.
4. Te olvidas de una cosa.
5. Nosotros no nos escribimos.
6. ¿Por qué se quejan tanto?

7. ¿Cuándo te despiertas?
8. Nosotros no nos entendemos.
9. ¿Cómo se atreve Ud. a hacer eso?
10. Salgo a las once menos cuarto.
11. ¿Te falta tiempo?
12. ¿Cuándo practicas la canción?

D • Query   Patterned Response

MODEL   ¿Cuándo salieron Uds.?
STUDENT   **Salimos ayer.**

1. ¿Cuándo volvieron Uds.?
2. ¿Cuándo estudiaron Uds.?
3. ¿Cuándo se acordaron Uds.?
4. ¿Cuándo se dieron cuenta Uds.?

5. ¿Cuándo lo recibieron Uds.?
6. ¿Cuándo lo vendieron Uds.?
7. ¿Cuándo la encontraron Uds.?
8. ¿Cuándo la discutieron Uds.?

³ Remember that Class I stem-changing verbs are irregular only in the present tense (see section **31**).
⁴ The first person and the third person singular preterit of **ver** have no accents: **yo vi, Ud. vio**.

E • Query   Patterned Response

MODEL   ¿Quién lo vio?
STUDENT **Yo lo vi.**

1. ¿Quién lo despachó?
2. ¿Quién los vendió?
3. ¿Quién lo compró?
4. ¿Quién se perdió?

5. ¿Quién lo aseguró?
6. ¿Quién lo debatió?
7. ¿Quién se protegió?
8. ¿Quién lo decidió?

F • Query   Patterned Response

MODEL   ¿Lo escribí bien?
STUDENT **Claro que lo escribiste** bien.

1. ¿Lo decidí bien?
2. ¿La entendí bien?
3. ¿Lo resistí bien?
4. ¿Lo pesé bien?

5. ¿Me preparé bien?
6. ¿Me fijé bien?
7. ¿Te informé bien?
8. ¿Te protegí bien?

50   Preterit of **dar**, **ser**, and **ir**

dar[5]	ser, ir[5]
di	fui
diste	fuiste
dio	fue
dimos	fuimos
dieron	fueron

▶ **Dar** is irregular because it takes the endings of **-er, -ir** verbs. **Ser** and **ir** are identical in the preterit but context makes their meaning clear. Remember that **hubo** is the preterit form of **hay**.

1. Ya te di el dinero.
2. Don Santiago fue rector de la universidad.
3. Fuimos directamente a la capital.
4. Hubo una venta allí ayer.

I already gave you the money.
Don Santiago was president of the university.
We went directly to the capital.
There was a sale there yesterday.

---

[5] Just as in the case of **ver** (**vi, vio**), **dar, ser,** and **ir** do not take accents on the first and third persons singular in the preterit.

A • Substitution Drill

MODEL   ¿No fuiste tú a la venta?
          él

STUDENT   ¿No **fue** él a la venta?

1. ¿No fuiste tú a la venta?
   Rosa
   Rosa y Carlos
   ellas
   yo
   Ud.

2. José Martí fue poeta.
   Juana
   Yo
   Tú
   Tú y yo
   Nosotros

3. Mónica le dio el traste viejo.
   Uds.
   Nosotras
   Tú
   Él
   Él y ella

B • Transformation Drill   Present → Preterit

MODEL   No te doy gato por liebre.
STUDENT   No te **di** gato por liebre.

1. Damos la entrada a Gabriel.
2. ¿Quién va?
3. Eso es fácil.
4. ¿Vas a la corrida de toros?
5. ¿Qué es eso? ¡Es queso!

6. Las noticias son magníficas.
7. Vamos a la clase de español.
8. Hay que ir.
9. ¿Me das ese periódico?
10. Hay que vender todo.

C • Translation Drill

Translate into Spanish.

1. Give me the book! I already gave you the book!
2. Go to the library! We went to the library!
3. Didn't you realize the problem? Yes, I did realize the problem!
4. Where did they learn that? I don't know where they learned it.
5. What happened? When did it happen? Where did it happen? How did it happen? Why did it happen?

51   Cardinal numerals above 99

100	ciento = number *one hundred*. But: cien bandidos; cien casas
101	ciento uno = number *one hundred one*. But: ciento un bandidos; ciento una casas
200	doscientos, -as
300	trescientos, -as
400	cuatrocientos, -as
500	quinientos, -as

600	seiscientos, -as
700	setecientos, -as
800	ochocientos, -as
900	novecientos, -as
1.000	mil[6]
1.001	mil uno = number *one thousand one*. But: mil un bandidos; mil una casas
1.200	mil doscientos, -as
2.000	dos mil
21.000	veintiún mil
33.000	treinta y tres mil
100.000	cien mil
101.000	ciento un mil
500.000	quinientos mil
1.000.000	un millón = number *one million*. But: un millón de bandidos; un millón de casas
2.000.000	dos millones

▶ The word for number 100 is **ciento**; **ciento** is also used before numerals smaller than one hundred.

ciento	*one hundred*
ciento diez	*one hundred ten*
ciento once alumnas	*one hundred eleven students*

Before a noun and before the numerals **mil** and **millones**, **ciento** is shortened to **cien.**[7]

cien profesores	*one hundred professors*
cien mil disculpas	*one hundred thousand apologies*
cien millones	*one hundred million*

▶ The word **y** is used only between tens and units, not between hundreds and units or hundreds and tens.

sesenta y seis	*sixty-six*
seiscientos seis	*six hundred six*
doscientos veinte y ocho	*two hundred twenty-eight*

---

[6] Where English uses a comma to punctuate cardinal numerals, Spanish uses a period. The comma is used as a decimal point in Spanish.

[7] It is becoming more common for **cien** to be used as a noun as well as an adjective.

▶ Compounds of 100, such as **doscientos**, agree in gender with the noun they modify.[8]

doscientos automóviles	*two hundred automobiles*
trescientas muchachas	*three hundred girls*
seiscientas tres mujeres	*six hundred three women*

▶ **Un** is omitted before **cien(to)** and **mil** but is used before **millón**. If a noun follows **cientos, miles, millón,** or **millones, de** is used before the noun. As always, when a numeral ends in one and precedes a masculine noun, **uno** shortens to **un**.

cien mesas	*one hundred tables*
mil periódicos	*one thousand newspapers*
un millón de espectadores	*a million spectators*
dos millones de poetas	*two million poets*
ciento un versos	*one hundred one verses*

▶ When a number terminating in one modifies a following number, the masculine **un** (**-ún**) is always used regardless of the gender of the noun modified.

ciento un mil personas	*one hundred one thousand persons*
veintiún mil bandidos	*twenty-one thousand bandits*

▶ When one of the **-cientos** numbers modifies a following thousand, it agrees in gender with the noun it modifies.

quinientas mil horas	*five hundred thousand hours*
quinientos mil discos	*five hundred thousand records*

▶ Numbers in the thousands are never represented as multiples of hundreds.

1.200 **mil doscientos**
2.300 **dos mil trescientos**

A • Replacement Drill

Replace the number with the written word.

MODEL   100 automóviles
STUDENT   **cien** automóviles

1. 111 días	6. 1.000.000 chicanos	11. 121 anillos	16. 2.000.000 causas
2. 2.000 viajes	7. 100.000 competidores	12. 121 bicicletas	17. 1.001 libros
3. 101.000 entradas	8. 101 gobernadores	13. 600 años	18. 1.001 revistas
4. 1976 comparaciones	9. 708 firmas	14. 600 canciones	19. 100 días
5. 1492 compañías	10. 200.000 cervezas	15. 100 mesas	20. 2.000.000 premios

[8] The singular word **ciento** does not have a feminine form:
ciento dos casas   *one hundred two houses*

B • Query   Patterned Response

MODEL   ¿Cuántos son 1.000 y 1.000?
STUDENT   **Mil y mil son dos mil.**

1. ¿Cuántos son 1.000 y 2.000?
2. ¿Cuántos son 1.000.000 y 1.000.000?
3. ¿Cuántos son 500 y 600?
4. ¿Cuántos son 800 y 10?
5. ¿Cuántos son 25.000 y 26.000?

6. ¿Cuántos son 100 y 71?
7. ¿Cuántos son 99 y 1?
8. ¿Cuántos son 199 y 1?
9. ¿Cuántos son 300 y 300?
10. ¿Cuántos son 200.000 y 300.000?

C • Query   Patterned Response

MODEL   ¿Cuántos son 100 menos 100?
STUDENT   **Ciento menos ciento son cero.**

1. ¿Cuántos son 1.000 menos 1.000?
2. ¿Cuántos son 2.000.000 menos 1.000.000?
3. ¿Cuántos son 500.000 menos 400.000?
4. ¿Cuántos son 1.000 menos 1?
5. ¿Cuántos son 50.000 menos 25.000?

6. ¿Cuántos son 887 menos 87?
7. ¿Cuántos son 1.110 menos 9?
8. ¿Cuántos son 1.000.000 menos 300.000?
9. ¿Cuántos son 1.000.000 menos 500.000?
10. ¿Cuántos son 1.002 menos 1?

52   Ordinal numerals

first	primero (the number). But: primer automóvil; primera hora
second	segundo, -a
third	tercero (the number). But: tercer día; tercera canción
fourth	cuarto, -a
fifth	quinto, -a
sixth	sexto, -a
seventh	séptimo, -a
eighth	octavo, -a
ninth	noveno, -a
tenth	décimo, -a

▶ Ordinal numerals agree in gender and number with the nouns they modify.[9] If the nouns are plural, the ordinal numerals will end in **-os, -as.**

el segundo pasillo; la quinta oficina   *the second corridor; the fifth office*
los primeros días; las primeras horas   *the first days; the first hours*

[9] When ordinal numerals (particularly **primero**) are used as adverbs, they end in the masculine singular.
Quiero hablar con ustedes primero.   *I want to talk to you first.*
Primero hagan Uds. las facturas.   *First do the invoices.*

▶ **Primero** and **tercero** are shortened by dropping the final **-o** before a masculine singular noun.

    el tercer estudiante; el primer anillo   *the third student; the first ring*

▶ While ordinal numerals have only one form through *tenth*, beyond *tenth* there is considerable variation with different speakers.[10] A frequent and easily learned procedure is to use the cardinal numerals and place them after the noun.

    Alfonso Trece   *Alfonso the Thirteenth*
    Calle Quince   *Fifteenth Street*

▶ When ordinals numbers are used as nouns (nominalized), they are preceded by a definite article.

    La primera que entró fue Elena.   *The first one who came in was Elena.*
    No fui al primer partido pero   *I didn't go to the first match but I went*
    fui al tercero.   *to the third.*

A • Query   Patterned Response

Answer each question, using the next higher ordinal number.

    MODEL   Perdón, ¿es la octava sinfonía?
    STUDENT   **No, es la novena.**

1. Perdón, ¿es el primer día?
2. Perdón, ¿es el segundo ministro?
3. Perdón, ¿es la séptima mesa?
4. Perdón, ¿es el noveno presidente?
5. Perdón, ¿es el cuarto automóvil?
6. Perdón, ¿es la segunda vez?
7. Perdón, ¿es la quinta firma?
8. Perdón, ¿es el octavo baile?
9. Perdón, ¿es la tercera compañía?
10. Perdón, ¿es el sexto escándalo?

B • Translation Drill

Translate into Spanish.

1. Who did it first?
2. The second (one) arrived yesterday.
3. Where is the third bicycle?
4. Who has the fourth book?
5. What is the fifth lesson?
6. When is the sixth sale?
7. I was the seventh.
8. She was the eighth.
9. They were the ninth.
10. That was the tenth day.

---

[10] For example, *eleventh* may be **onceavo**, **undécimo**, **décimo primero**, or simply, **once**.

53   Days, months, and years

domingo	*Sunday*	enero	*January*
lunes	*Monday*	febrero	*February*
martes	*Tuesday*	marzo	*March*
miércoles	*Wednesday*	abril	*April*
jueves	*Thursday*	mayo	*May*
viernes	*Friday*	junio	*June*
sábado	*Saturday*	julio	*July*
		agosto	*August*
		septiembre	*September*
		octubre	*October*
		noviembre	*November*
		diciembre	*December*

▶ The days of the week and the names of the months are not capitalized in Spanish. The definite article is used with the days of the week except after **ser**. The article can also translate English *on*.

1. Te veo el martes; los veo los martes.[11]
   I'll see you (on) Tuesday; I see them on Tuesdays.
2. Hoy es sábado.
   Today is Saturday.
3. ¿Cuándo salimos? El jueves, o quizá el viernes.
   When do we leave? On Thursday, or perhaps on Friday.
4. Todos los miércoles voy al cine.
   I go to the movies every Wednesday (on Wednesdays).

WORD PLAY

¿Cuántos días en el mes?
Here is a Spanish jingle for remembering the number of days in a month.
Treinta días tiene noviembre,
con abril, junio y septiembre,
veintiocho o veintinueve, uno,
y los demás treinta y uno.   **demás** *rest*

---

[11] Spanish words of more than one syllable that end in unaccented **-es** (and **-is**) have the same form for the singular and the plural.

3 ABRIL 79

Dates

▶ The days of the month are designated by cardinal numerals except for the first: **el dos de mayo, el diez de mayo**; but, **el primero de mayo**. Here are some standard ways to ask the day of the month, with appropriate responses.

¿Cuál es la fecha (de hoy)?
or
¿Qué fecha es (hoy)?
or
¿A cuántos estamos?

(Hoy) es el primero de octubre.
or
Estamos a quince de mayo.

▶ In reading dates as well as in counting, thousands are not represented as multiples of hundreds: *seventeen seventy-six* is **mil setecientos setenta y seis**. Normally the preposition **de** appears twice in a complete date.

July 4, 1776   el 4 de julio de 1776 (mil setecientos setenta y seis)
September 16, 1810   el 16 de septiembre de 1810 (mil ochocientos diez)

Origin of the Days of the Week in Spanish and in English	
lunes, from **luna** *moon*	Monday, from *moon*
martes, from **marte** *Mars*	Tuesday, from *Tīw*, Germanic god of War
miércoles, from **mercurio** *Mercury*	Wednesday, from *Woden*, chief god of Germanic peoples
jueves, from **Júpiter** *Jupiter (Jove)*	Thursday, from *Thor*, Germanic god of the sky
viernes, from **Venus** *Venus*	Friday, from *Frīa*, Germanic goddess of love
sábado, from Hebrew, *sabat* *Sabbath*	Saturday, from *Saturn*
domingo, from Latin, *dominus* *Lord*	Sunday, from *sun*

A • Query Patterned Response

MODEL   ¿A cuántos estamos? ¿A diecisiete de octubre?
STUDENT **Así es. Estamos a** diecisiete de octubre.

1. ¿A cuántos estamos? ¿A quince de mayo?
2. ¿A cuántos estamos? ¿A primero de junio?
3. ¿A cuántos estamos? ¿A diez de enero?
4. ¿A cuántos estamos? ¿A tres de octubre?
5. ¿A cuántos estamos? ¿A siete de septiembre?

Answer the question **¿Qué fecha es?**, using the following month.

MODEL   ¿Qué fecha es? ¿El dos de febrero?
STUDENT **No, hoy es el dos de marzo.**

6. ¿Qué fecha es? ¿El treinta de noviembre?
7. ¿Qué fecha es? ¿El nueve de abril?
8. ¿Qué fecha es? ¿El dos de julio?
9. ¿Qué fecha es? ¿El diecisiete de agosto?
10. ¿Qué fecha es? ¿El veintidós de diciembre?

B • Query Patterned Response

Answer in the negative, responding with a day earlier than the question.

MODEL   ¿Volvió Ud. el dos de agosto?
STUDENT **No, volví el primero de agosto.**

1. ¿Escribió Ud. la carta el tres de junio?
2. ¿Compró Ud. el brillante el diez de mayo?
3. ¿Consultó Ud. con el jefe el miércoles?
4. ¿Esperaste a Rafa el viernes?
5. ¿Ganaste el partido el jueves?
6. ¿Felicitaste a la novia el martes?
7. ¿Hablaste con el bufón el sábado?
8. ¿Llevaste a Mónica el lunes?

54 Negative and indefinite expressions

The two possible word orders in a negative sentence

Negative Word	+	verb
No		
Nadie		
Nada		
Nunca		
Ninguno		
etc.		

No	+	verb	+	negative word other than **no**
				nadie
				nada
				nunca
				ninguno
				etc.

▶ Negative words other than **no** may either precede or follow the verb. If they follow, **no** (or some other negative[12]) must precede the verb.

1. Nada tengo. *or* No tengo nada.   *I have nothing (I don't have anything).*
2. Nadie me conoció. *or* No me   *No one knew me.*
   conoció nadie.
3. Nunca hablamos con él. *or* No   *We never talk to him.*
   hablamos nunca con él.
4. Ninguno aprendió la lección. *or*   *None (of them) learned the lesson.*
   No aprendió ninguno la lección.

Affirmative and negative counterparts

alguien	*someone, somebody, anyone, anybody*	**nadie**	*no one, nobody, not anyone*
alguno, -a -os, as	*some, any, someone,* pl., *some, a few*	**ninguno, -a**[13]	*none, no one; not any (of them)*
algo	*something, anything*	**nada**	*nothing, not anything*
siempre	*always*		
algún día	*someday*	**nunca**	*never, not ever*
alguna vez	*sometime*	**jamás**	*not at any time*
también	*also*	**tampoco**	*neither, not either*
con	*with*	**sin**	*without*
o... o	*either . . . or*	**ni... ni**	*neither . . . nor*

¡Cuidado!

Beware of these common errors.

Incorrect	**Correct**	
No vi a alguno.	No vi a ninguno.	*I didn't see any of them. (I saw none of them.)*
No conozco a alguien.	No conozco a nadie.	*I don't know anyone.*
Ella nunca da algo a alguien.	Ella nunca da nada a nadie.	*She never gives anything to anyone.*

---

[12] The negative that precedes the verb need not be **no**. Thus it is possible to have two negatives other than **no**, one before and the other after the verb: **Aquí nadie dice nada.** *Here no one says anything.* Actually Spanish will accept any number of negatives and still conserve the negative meaning of the sentence. For example, **Aquí nadie nunca dice nada.** *Here no one ever says anything.*

[13] Since **ninguno, -a** means *none*, the plural, **ningunos, ningunas**, rarely appears in current Spanish.

▶   The **alguien-nadie** pair differs from the **alguno-ninguno** pair (when used as pronouns) in that the former refers to persons unknown or not mentioned before while the latter refers to persons within a certain group already held in mind (examples 1 and 2). When **alguien-nadie** or **alguno-ninguno** are the direct objects of the verb, they call for a personal **a** (examples 1 and 3).[14]

In addition, **alguno-ninguno** may be used as adjectives, in which case they drop the final **-o** before masculine singular nouns and are accented on the final syllable (example 4).

1. ¿Viste a alguien? No, no vi a nadie.

   Did you see anyone? No, I didn't see anyone (I saw no one).

2. Tal vez algunos de Uds. ya saben los pormenores del asunto.

   Perhaps some of you already know the particulars of this matter.

3. ¿Despacharon a alguno? No despacharon a ninguno.

   Did they finish off (kill) any of them? They didn't finish off any of them.

4. algún día, ningún hombre, algunos bandidos, ninguna ley

   someday, no (not one) man, some bandits, no (not one) law

Picturesque Indefinites

Fulano, -a
Zutano, -a
Mengano, -a
These indefinites, originally incorporated into Spanish from Arabic, are colloquial. Here are some equivalents in English: *so-and-so, character, guy, fellow, chap, bloke, John Doe, John Q. Public.*

In Spanish, if one such indefinite is expressed, it is always **fulano**; if two are needed it is **fulano** and **zutano** (or perhaps **fulano de tal** and **zutano de cual**); the whole series, **fulano, zutano y mengano**, corresponds to something like *the butcher, the baker, the candlestick maker*; or *Tom, Dick, and Harry.*

[14] Recall that a personal **a** is necessary only to introduce a direct object that is a person. **Alguno-ninguno** do not necessarily refer to persons. When they don't, they will not be introduced by a personal **a**. For example, **¿Ves las bicicletas? No, no veo ninguna.** *Do you see the bicycles? No, I don't see any (of them).*

A • Replacement Drill   No → Other Negative Word

MODEL   No conoce a Paco.   /Nadie/
STUDENT **Nadie** conoce a Paco.

1. No sabe dónde está.   /Ninguna/
2. No voy a ir.   /Nunca/
3. No estoy cansada.   /Nunca/
4. No está protegido.   /Nadie/

5. No me gusta ir de compras.   /Nunca/
6. No les escribió.   /Jamás/
7. No aprendí el poema.   /Nunca/
8. No compró la foto.   /Nadie/

B • Transformation Drill   Negative Word → No... Negative Word

MODEL   Nadie lo tiene.
STUDENT **No** lo tiene **nadie.**

1. Ninguno quiere ir.
2. Nada tengo.
3. Nadie puede entrar.
4. Ni Paco ni Diego está en casa.
5. ¿Tampoco lo compraste?

6. Nunca fui a la Avenida de las Américas.
7. Jamás hablo con él.
8. Nadie fue a la venta.
9. Nunca volvieron a la oficina.
10. Ninguno sabe hacerlo.

C • Query   Patterned Response

MODEL   ¿Hay alguien aquí?
STUDENT **No, no hay nadie aquí.**

1. ¿Hay algo en la tienda?
2. ¿Siempre estás tan cansado?
3. ¿Necesitas a alguno de ellos?
4. ¿Son ellos o bandidos o terroristas?
5. ¿Quieres ir algún día?

6. ¿Puedes ir alguna vez?
7. ¿Puede ir alguien a la capital?
8. ¿Puede escribir algo?
9. ¿Viste a alguien ayer?
10. ¿Le diste algo al profesor?

D • Transformation Drill   Negative → Affirmative

MODEL   No vimos a nadie ayer.
STUDENT **Vimos a alguien** ayer.

1. Nadie habla ahora.
2. El jefe no sabe nada.
3. No piensa ir sin María.
4. No hay nada en la oficina.
5. El ministro no conoce a nadie.

6. Nadie dice nada.
7. Nadie nunca dice nada.
8. Tampoco vi a nadie.
9. Ella jamás da nada a nadie.
10. Él nunca dice nada tampoco.

E • Translation Drill

Translate into Spanish.

1. I saw someone. We saw no one.
2. I need one of them. They don't need any of them.
3. Nobody believes you. I never believe you either.
4. I never give anything to anyone.
5. Nobody ever says anything.
6. He doesn't know Susan. He doesn't know anyone.

REVIEW

I   The following questions are related to the dialog. Answer in Spanish.

1. ¿Contra qué fue el ataque?
2. ¿Qué pasó en la carretera?
3. ¿Quién llegó a la obra por casualidad?
4. ¿Dónde está el Jefe de Seguridad Pública ahora?
5. ¿Qué va a hacer el Ministro de Justicia?
6. ¿Quién se hace responsable por la seguridad de todos?
7. ¿Está de acuerdo el Ministro del Interior?
8. ¿Qué le dice al Ministro del Interior el Ministro de Justicia?

II   Translate the following into Spanish.

1. Friends! I have to tell you something very grave and important. I don't think that you are going to like it.
2. What is it? Is it something very bad? What happened? When did it happen?
3. Sit down, please. Listen to me. I don't know how it happened or when it happened.
4. The situation is that yesterday, Friday, April 1, 1984, there was an attack at six-thirty in the morning.
5. What! This is a scandal! I can't believe it. Where is our president?
6. Yesterday at noon he went to Macondo, in Colombia. By the way, he took along 6,000,000 dollars.
7. That is a lot of money, isn't it? Maybe we should tell him that he can return. We need that money for [the] public education.
8. Are you crazy? The opposition is already in the presidential palace. We have ten minutes (in order) to write our resignations.

III   Write your own dialog.

You are a reporter at a cabinet meeting. The ministers are discussing the state of education in the nation. What do they say?

PRONUNCIATION

Spanish n and ñ

Spanish **n** is not unlike English *n*, but English has no **ñ**. The sound of **ñ** is similar to **ni** and **ny** in English words such as *onion, canyon.* Repeat after your instructor.

sin	ganso	cañón
son	pongo	año
ven	ancho	mañana
lana	infiel	bañar
ando	suena	sueña

Spanish s and z Between Vowels

In Spanish there is never a *z* sound between vowels, even when the spelling is **z**.[15] Repeat after your instructor.

casar (*to marry*)	vez (*time*)	Isabel
cazar (*to hunt*)	ves (*you see*)	Venezuela
roza (*a clearing*)	zeta (letter **z**)	César Chávez
rosa (*rose*)	seta (*mushroom*)	Brasil
		Jesús

---

[15] In Castile the letter **z** is pronounced *th* as in *thin*.

Cognates & Contexts

Election rally, Mexico City

ARTURO Yo creo que los Estados Unidos es una nación muy
corrupta. Mira el caso "Watergate". Los ministros, la
agencia de investigación, hasta el presidente, culpables — **culpables** *guilty*
de crímenes contra el pueblo.

GLORIA Eso de "crímenes" es un poco fuerte, ¿no? Además, — **fuerte** *strong*
aquí no es nada diferente. Para ser jefe de estado en
este país uno tiene que pertenecer a una de las cuatro- — **pertenecer** *to belong*
cientas familias selectas. El presidente Fulano de Tal
termina su período presidencial y empieza el de
Zutano de Cual, su hermano o su amigo.

ARTURO Bueno, tienes razón. Anoche vi una película donde unos
astronautas establecieron una sociedad utópica en la
luna.

GLORIA ¡Qué ridículo!

ARTURO ¡Te hablo en serio! Nombraron jefe al más sabio. Tú — **en serio** *seriously* **más**
sabes, el antiguo concepto del filósofo rey. **sabio** (*the*) *wisest*
rey *king*

233

GLORIA   Y alguna compañía de Hollywood te regaló esa fantasía. Allí en los Estados Unidos corrupto. ¿Cuánto pagaste por la entrada? ¿Diez pesos?

ARTURO   No te burles de mí, Gloria. Además, arreglaron perfectamente la cuestión del sexo. Ni familia, ni padres, ni madres. Nada de eso. A las nueve de la noche sonaron una campana y después hubo una lotería para determinar la compañera para la noche.

GLORIA   Eso sí te gustó ¿verdad?

ARTURO   Bueno, tiene algunos atractivos.

GLORIA   ¡Bah! ¿A ti qué te importa la luna? La luna está hecha de queso verde. Tú tienes que pasar tus exámenes de derecho para formar parte de nuestra sociedad corrupta. Y después, a casarte con alguna muchacha atractiva y/o rica para establecer una familia.

regalar *to give as a gift*

peso *monetary unit in many Spanish American countries*

campana *bell*

atractivos *attractions, good points*

exámenes de derecho *law exams*

casarse *to get married*

Statue of Don Quijote and Sancho Panza, Madrid

Lección doce

Lectura y estudio

EUFEMISMOS, DICHOS Y PROVERBIOS

dichos *sayings*

Toda lengua se sirve de elementos pintorescos para darle variedad e interés, y el español es especialmente rico en este aspecto. Los diálogos entre Sancho Panza y don Quijote son ejemplos magníficos.

lengua *tongue; language*
  servirse (**i**) *to make use of*

Los eufemismos (palabras o frases que se usan para enmascarar temas desagradables, inmorales o socialmente inaceptables) son graciosos y frecuentes en español. Para referirse a la muerte hay el sobrio "pasó a mejor vida", parecido al inglés, pero también oímos "estiró la pata", "hincó el pico", "colgó el

enmascarar *to mask*
  desagradables *unpleasant*
graciosos *clever*

muerte *death*

estirar *to stretch out*   **pata** *leg (of an animal)*   **hincar** *to sink in*   **pico** *beak*   **colgar** *to hang up*   **caminar** *to walk*

teléfono", entre otras expresiones. Si caminamos, tomamos "el coche de San Fernando (un rato a pie y el otro andando)"; al tonto "le falta un domingo"; y los que cohabitan sin matrimonio "están casados detrás de la iglesia".

coche *car*   **rato** *while*   **a pie** *on foot*
andar *to walk*

casados *married*

iglesia *church*

Muy frecuentemente una observación o una

Hincó el pico.

Estiró la pata.

Colgó el teléfono.

conversación está puntualizada por un refrán; a
veces viene de la literatura; otras veces es un dicho
popular; otras, un juego de palabras.

puntualizada *punctuated* **refrán**
proverb

> ANA   Nuestro mundo va de Guatemala a
> guatepeor.[1]
>
> PAQUITA   Sí, con los impuestos nos tienen entre la
> espada y la pared.
>
> ANA   Tienes razón. Poderoso caballero es don
> Dinero.[2]

impuestos *taxes*

espada *sword*   **pared** *wall*

poderoso *powerful*   **caballero**
knight

   El juego verbal que existe entre los participantes de
una conversación puede dejar fuera al novato, ya que
muchas veces sólo se da la introducción de un dicho
conocido y el auditorio está obligado a completarlo
mentalmente para entender el sentido del comentario.

dejar fuera *to leave out*   **novato**
amateur

el sentido *the meaning*

---

[1] A play on words: **mala... peor. Guatepeor** has no real meaning in Spanish.
[2] Taken from *Libro de buen amor*, written by the Arcipreste de Hita in 1343. Note the chivalric references
in this maxim and the one above.

LUIS   ¿Sabes que Pancho se casó?

ELENA   ¡No me digas! ¿Con quién? ¿Cuándo?

LUIS   Con Isabel, el martes pasado.

ELENA   ¿Con ésa? Bien dicen "Trece y martes..."[3]

LUIS   Ay, no seas así. Fue una boda muy bonita.

ELENA   Ni modo. Hay que llamar al pan, pan y al vino, vino.[4] Aunque la mona se vista de seda...[5] En fin, veremos.

Ni modo. *It makes no difference.*
pan *bread*
vino *wine*   **mona** *monkey*
seda *silk*   **veremos** *we'll see*

Muchos refranes son consejos morales, otros ofrecen astutas observaciones sobre la condición y el carácter humano y otros simplemente son referencias a lo cotidiano, dándole una orientación nueva, alegre o irónica. Bajo cualquier interpretación, el uso extendido de estas expresiones representa un elemento muy característico del habla española al igual que un reflejo de su cultura.

¿Puede Ud. crear una situación apropiada para cada uno de los refranes siguientes?

consejos *advice*

lo cotidiano *everyday life*

alegre *happy*   **bajo cualquier** *under any*

el habla *speech, language*

al igual que *as well as*   **reflejo** *reflection*

siguientes *following*

Más enseña la necesidad que la universidad.
En boca cerrada no entran moscas.
Más sabe el diablo por viejo que por diablo.
Ojos que no ven, corazón que no siente.[6]
Dios da almendras al que no tiene dientes.
Cada loco con su tema.
El hábito no hace al monje.[7]
Quien con perro se acuesta, con pulgas se levanta.
Hoy casado, mañana cansado.
Cuando el río suena, agua lleva.[8]

diablo *devil*

corazón *heart*   **sentir (ie)** *to feel*

almendras *almonds*   **dientes** *teeth*
tema *theme*

monje *monk*

perro *dog*   **acostarse (ue)** *to lie down, go to bed*   **pulgas** *fleas*

río *river*   **sonar (ue)** *to make noise*

---

[3] ... ni te cases ni te embarques." Tuesday the thirteenth is considered bad luck in some Hispanic countries.
[4] A saying equivalent to the English "Call a spade a spade."
[5] ... mona se queda." "Even if the monkey dresses in silk, she's still a monkey."
[6] "Out of sight, out of mind."
[7] "You can't tell a book by its cover."
[8] "Where there's smoke, there's fire."

VOCABULARY STUDY

The following words have additional meanings or forms besides those already given in the dialogs.

mandar   to command; *to send*
helado   cold; frozen; *ice cream*
peso   monetary unit; *weight* (remember **pesar?**)
el pueblo   the people[9]; *village*

llevar   to take
  llevarse   *to take along; to buy*
      Me lo llevo.   *I'll take (buy) it.*
prestar atención   to pay attention
  prestar   *to lend*
      ¿Me prestas siete dólares?   *Will you lend me seven dollars?*
parecer   to seem
  parecerse a   *to look like*
      Juan se parece a su padre.   *Juan looks like his father.*
quedar   to have (something) left
  quedarse   *to remain, stay*
      Yo me quedo en casa.   *I'll stay home.*
  quedarse con   *to keep*
      ¿Te quedas con el abrigo?   *Are you keeping the coat?*
demasiado   too; *too much*
      Comes demasiado.   *You eat too much.*
derecho   law (profession); *straight; right* (direction)
      Tienes que ir derecho.   *You have to go straight.*
      Éste es el lado derecho.   *This is the right side.*
a la derecha   *to the right*
      A la derecha hay una tienda.   *To the right there is a store.*
leyes   *laws*
      Aprendemos acerca de las leyes en la   *We learn about the laws in*
      Escuela de Derecho.   *law school.*

These verbs take a preposition before an object.

acordarse (de)   *to remember*
      ¿Te acuerdas de esa canción?   *Do you remember that song?*
apostar (a)   *to bet (on, that)*
      Apuesto a que Juanito va a ganar.   *I bet that Juanito is going to win.*

---

[9] The people in the sense of *nation*; **gente** means people as a group.

atreverse (a) *to dare*

No se atreve a hacerlo.   *He doesn't dare to do it.*

burlarse (de) *to make fun (of)*

Mi hermano siempre se burla de mí.   *My brother always makes fun of me.*

darse cuenta (de) *to realize*

Él no se da cuenta de que estoy aquí.   *He doesn't realize I'm here.*

fijarse (en) *to take a close look (at)*

Él nunca se fija en ella.   *He never takes a close look at her.*

olvidarse (de) *to forget*

No te olvides de los tamales.   *Don't forget the tamales.*

preocuparse (por) *to worry (about)*

Susana siempre se preocupa por su trabajo.   *Susana always worries about her work.*

quejarse (de) *to complain (about)*

Nunca me quejo de la comida aquí.   *I never complain about the food here.*

Remember the various ways to express *to become* (*Section 44*).

ponerse + adjective.

To assume a certain physical or emotional state, usually temporary.

hacerse   To effect a change in status, usually through conscious effort.

volverse   To turn into as a result of an external cause.

Me volví loca.   *I became crazy.*

Volver with an indirect object pronoun can also be used with the same meaning.

Esos muchachos me vuelven loca.   *Those kids drive me (get me) crazy.*

llegar a ser   emphasis on outcome of a successful process, "to come to be"

The English expression *What a . . .!* is translated into Spanish simply by **¡Qué...!** without an indefinite article. Thus, **qué** can be followed by an adjective or adverb as well as a noun in Spanish.

¡Qué hombre!	*What a man!*
¡Qué día!	*What a day!*
¡Qué emocionante!	*How exciting!*
¡Qué bien!	*Great!*

Many words in English that begin with *s-* + consonant, begin with **es-** + consonant in Spanish. What do the following words mean?

especialista	escena	escorpión
escrúpulo	esfera	estatua
estúpido	espíritu	espina
esquiar	estación	estadística

There is no double **m** in Spanish; note **inmediatamente**. What is the English for the following words?

inmaduro	inmensamente	inmigración
inminente	inmodesto	inmoral
inmortal	inmóvil	inmunización

What is the difference between **acerca de** and **cerca de**?

El libro es acerca del profesor.

El libro está cerca del profesor.

The English word *time* covers a variety of meanings that are expressed in many ways in Spanish.

¿Qué hora es?	*What time is it?*
No tengo tiempo.	*I don't have time.* (length or period of time in general)
Esta vez llego temprano.	*This time I'll arrive early.* (time in a series)
Pasamos un buen rato.	*We had (spent) a good time.* (a short while)

¡Cuidado!

el camión
la mano
emocionante = *exciting* (not *emotional*)
   emocional, conmovedor = *emotional*
mayor = *older* (not *mayor, city official*)
   alcalde, alcaldesa = *mayor*

A • Substitution Drill

Rewrite the sentences, using antonyms of the underlined words or expressions.

1. Me acuerdo de su nombre.
2. ¿A qué hora te duermes los sábados?
3. Ésta es mi hermana mayor.
4. Ignacio llegó antes de las siete.
5. ¿Quieres dar un paseo con tus hijos?
6. Estos anillos son iguales, pero me gustan mucho.
7. Siempre te callas a tiempo.
8. Tere tiene razón también. (¡cuidado!)

B • Complete each sentence with a suitable word or phrase from the list. The words are to be used in the form in which they appear.

pantalones	burlarse	dibujos animados
tienes razón	conmigo	camisa
ridículos	bufón	

1. Pancho, si quieres venir _____, tienes que vestirte mejor.
2. Esos _____ que llevas puestos son _____.
3. La _____ tampoco es atractiva.
4. Mis amigos van a decirme que eres un _____ de los _____ _____.
5. Sí, Miguel, _____ _____; todos van a _____ de mí.

solamente	atractivo	gusta
sentarte	¿qué más da?	Sin duda
sientes celos	complacer	modelo

6. Pero, ¿_____ _____ _____? Me _____ estar así.
7. Yo no quiero vestirme bien _____ para _____ a otros.
8. Tú _____ _____ porque no puedes _____ en el suelo como yo.
9. Tu abrigo lujoso es muy _____ pero no es práctico.
10. _____ _____ costó mucho dinero y el _____ es muy original.

preocuparte	ponerme	Ahora mismo
me doy cuenta de	dar un paseo	tengo miedo
Manos a la obra	felicito	escandalosa

11. Pero siempre tienes que _____.
12. Yo no _____ _____ de nada.
13. Te _____, Pancho, _____ _____ _____ _____ que tú eres quien tiene razón.
14. _____ _____ voy a _____ una camisa _____ y unos pantalones viejos.
15. ¡_____ _____ _____ _____, Miguel! Luego vamos a _____ _____

    _____por las mejores calles de la capital.

C • Complete the sentences with **hacerse, ponerse, volver(se), llegar a ser.**

1. Algún día va a _____ una persona muy importante.
2. Mamá siempre _____ nerviosa antes de una fiesta.
3. Mis padres _____ locos con esta música moderna.
4. Yo nunca _____ cansado cuando juego al fútbol.
5. Después de muchos años, Rosa Amador _____ presidente ayer.
6. Uds. nos _____ cínicos con tantos conceptos fantásticos.
7. Miguel y Mónica _____ novios en junio.
8. Creo que ese joven va a _____ un profesor excelente.

D • Many new time expressions have appeared in the three previous lessons. Match the sentences on the left with a suitable expression on the right (there may be more than one possible completion).

1. La propuesta es muy urgente. Termínala _____.	temprano
2. Aunque trabajamos mucho, siempre tenemos tiempo para comer _____.	nunca
	jamás
3. _____ levantarte, tienes que lavarte la cara.	inmediatamente
4. Felipe siempre llega a sus clases _____.	a tiempo
5. Cuando estoy durmiendo, _____ suena una campana y me despierta.	lo más pronto posible
	media hora
6. Nosotros no nos quejamos _____ de aquella compañía.	por fin
7. _____ voy a llegar a ser una persona respetable.	de pronto
8. ¡_____ compraste la moto! ¿Puedo verla esta tarde?	antes de
9. Tienes razón, terminaron la reunión en _____.	después de
10. Tenemos que hablar con el jefe _____ irnos hoy.	algún día
	alguna vez
	al mediodía
	ahora mismo

Rompecabezas

Sam enñase al dadsinece euq al siuniverdad

GRAMMAR: SELF-TESTING

Cover the right side of the page and try to answer the questions in the left margin.

VERBS

In a direct command, what is the **Ud.** form ending for **-ar** verbs? For **-er**, **-ir** verbs?

In a direct command, what is the **Uds.** form ending for **-ar** verbs? For **-er**, **-ir** verbs?

What are the **Ud.** direct command forms for **dar**, **estar**, and **ir**? What are the **Uds.** direct command forms for **ser** and **saber**?

Do these forms change if they are affirmative or negative?

How is the **tú** form affirmative command regularly formed?

I DIRECT COMMANDS: usted, ustedes, tú (*Section 37*)

Ud., Uds. To the stem of the first person singular of **-ar** verbs add -e (Ud.)
-en (Uds.)

-er, -ir verbs add -a (Ud.)
-an (Uds.)

habl-o	hable Ud.	*Exceptions:*	
aprend-o	aprendan Uds.	dar	(dé, den)
muestr-o	muestre Ud.	estar	(esté, estén)
teng-o	tengan Uds.	ir	(vaya, vayan)
conozc-o	conozca Ud.	ser	(sea, sean)
		saber	(sepa, sepan)

There are no changes in these forms, whether affirmative or negative.

Sean simpáticos.
No sean así.

Tú Affirmative: Use the same form as the third person singular of the present indicative.

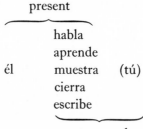

<table>
<tr><td>*Exceptions:*</td><td>decir</td><td>di</td><td>poner</td><td>pon</td></tr>
<tr><td></td><td>hacer</td><td>haz</td><td>venir</td><td>ven</td></tr>
<tr><td></td><td>salir</td><td>sal</td><td>ser</td><td>sé</td></tr>
<tr><td></td><td>tener</td><td>ten</td><td>ir</td><td>ve (also for</td></tr>
<tr><td></td><td></td><td></td><td></td><td>regular verb **ver**)</td></tr>
</table>

There are some exceptions; what is the **tú** affirmative command form for **decir? Hacer? Salir? Poner? Ir? Tener? Venir? Ser?**

Negative: Add **-s** to the **Ud**. command form.

no hable-s
no escriba-s
no diga-s
no sea-s   (tú)

How are negative commands formed for **tú?**

If the subject pronoun is used with commands (rarely in the case of **tú**), it usually follows the verb.

II PRETERIT (*Sections 49, 50*)

The preterit is one of two simple past tenses in the indicative in Spanish.

Formation. Regular verbs:

	-ar verbs	-er, -ir verbs
stem of the infinitive +	-é	-í
	-aste	-iste
	-ó	-ió
	-amos	-imos
	-aron	-ieron

How is the preterit formed for **-ar** verbs? For **-er, -ir** verbs?

The **nosotros** form of **-ar** and **-ir** verbs is the same in the preterit and in the present. The two tenses are distinguished by context.

Irregular verbs (*Section 50*):

dar	ser, ir
di	fui
diste	fuiste
dio	fue
dimos	fuimos
dieron	fueron

What is the preterit conjugation of the irregular verb **dar?** Of **ser?** Of **ir?**

III REFLEXIVES (*Sections 43, 44, 45*)

Verbs used reflexively in Spanish indicate
a) that the action of the verb is being done by the subject to itself (**lavarse, vestirse**);
b) that the verb is often reciprocal, when used in the plural.
   Se ven.   *They see one another.*

When verbs are used reflexively in Spanish, what do they indicate?

PRONOUNS

Sometimes a verb will change in meaning when used
reflexively:

| ir | *to go* |
| irse | *to leave* |

A reflexive verb is accompanied by a reflexive pronoun (**me,
te, se, nos, se**) that agrees with the subject.

Some verbs in Spanish are used almost solely in the reflexive.

acordarse	quejarse
atreverse	suicidarse
darse cuenta	enorgullecerse, etc.

A reflexive construction can also be used to substitute for the
passive voice when the agent is not identified or important.

se + third person singular or plural of verb (to agree
with a singular or plural subject).

Las tiendas se abren a las dos.   *The stores are
opened at two.*
Se habla inglés.   *English is spoken.*

Se is used with the third person singular of the verb to express
the occurrence of an action without any grammatical subject.

Se come bien aquí.   *One eats well here.*
No se habla así en casa.   *You don't speak like that at
home.*

I REFLEXIVE PRONOUNS   (*Section 43*)

me	Reflexive pronouns are the same as direct and
te	indirect object pronouns except in the third
se	person, where **se** is used both in the singular
nos	and in the plural.
se	

II POSITION OF OBJECT AND REFLEXIVE PRONOUNS
(*Sections 38, 43*)
Direct and indirect object pronouns and reflexive pronouns
all have the same placement in relation to the verb:

verb and when are they attached to it?
And reflexive pronouns?

a) immediately before a conjugated verb (between a negative word and the verb in a negative sentence) and a negative command.

¿Conoces a Paquito? **Lo** vi en el cine ayer.
No **le** di las entradas.
El **se** levantó temprano hoy.
No **lo** despiertes todavía.

b) after and attached to an infinitive,
No voy a verlo.
a present participle,
Estoy dándole un consejo.
an affirmative command.
Levántese temprano.

Where both a conjugated verb and an infinitive appear in a verbal construction, pronouns may either precede the conjugated verb or be attached to the infinitive.

Vamos a vernos mañana.   *We are going to see*
Nos vamos a ver mañana.   *each other tomorrow.*

What pronouns are used as objects of a preposition?

III   PRONOUNS AS OBJECTS OF A PREPOSITION
(*Section 40*)

a	mí
sin	ti
para	Ud., él, ella
de	nosotros, -as
en	Uds., ellos, ellas
por, etc.	

With the exception of **mí** and **ti**, pronouns used after prepositions have the same form as subject pronouns.

Exceptions: conmigo, contigo, consigo
but: con Ud., con él, etc.

How is *with me* expressed in Spanish?

COMPARISONS: ADJ. & ADV.
(*Sections 47, 48*)

How are comparisons of inequality expressed in Spanish?

Más and **menos** are used with adjectives and adverbs (as well as nouns and verbs) to express comparisons of inequality. *Than* is usually translated by **que**, except in dealing with quantities, when **de** is used.

Yo tengo más camisas que tú.   *I have more shirts than you.*
Tú tienes menos de cinco camisas.   *You have less than five shirts.*
Susana es más bonita que su hermana.   *Susana is prettier than her sister.*

What are the irregular comparatives for **bueno/bien, malo/mal, grande** and **pequeño**?

Irregular comparatives:

bueno (adjective) ⎫
bien (adverb)   ⎬ mejor

Este libro es bueno pero ése es mejor.

This book is good but that one is better.

malo (adjective) ⎫
mal (adverb)   ⎬ peor

Mi hermana habla mal pero mi hermanito habla peor.

My sister speaks badly but my little brother speaks worse.

grande   mayor (*greater, older*)

Susana es mayor que yo.

Susana is older than I.

más grande   (*larger, bigger*)

¿Quién es más grande, Carlitos o Ernesto?

Who is bigger, Carlitos or Ernesto?

pequeño   menor (*younger, little*)

Éste es mi hermano menor.

This is my little brother.

más pequeño (*smaller—size*)

Mi casa es más pequeña que la tuya.

My house is smaller than yours.

What is the formula used in Spanish when comparing nouns equally?
When comparing verbs?

Tanto (-a, -os, -as)... como is used with nouns to compare them equally.

Lucho tiene tantos enemigos como amigos.

Lucho has as many enemies as friends.

Tanto como is used to compare verbs equally.

Nadie sabe tanto como ella.

No one knows as much as she does.

When comparing adjectives and adverbs?

Tan... como is used with adjectives and adverbs to compare them equally.

La película es tan emocionante como el libro.

The movie is as exciting as the book.

CARDINAL AND ORDINAL NUMERALS
(*Sections 51, 52*)

Is **y** placed between hundreds and units or hundreds and tens?

I   CARDINAL NUMERALS

Y is used only between tens and units, not between hundreds and units or hundreds and tens.

novecientos cuarenta y cuatro

nine hundred forty-four

Is **un** used before
cardinal numerals
cien, mil, or **millón**?

Un is omitted before **cien(to)** and **mil** but is used before
millón. **De** is used before a noun following **cientos, miles,**
and **millón(es)**.

Hay miles de personas.   *There are thousands of persons.*
Before a noun, **mil,** or **millones, ciento** is shortened to **cien.**

When is **ciento**
shortened to **cien**?
How do compounds of
hundreds agree with the
noun modified?

Compounds of hundreds agree in gender as well as number
with the noun modified; **ciento(s)** does not.

II ORDINAL NUMERALS

What are the ordinal
numerals in Spanish for
first through *tenth*?

primero	*first*	sexto	*sixth*
segundo	*second*	séptimo	*seventh*
tercero	*third*	octavo	*eighth*
cuarto	*fourth*	noveno	*ninth*
quinto	*fifth*	décimo	*tenth*

Ordinal numerals are rarely used above **décimo** in Spanish;
cardinal numbers are used instead.

What is normally used
instead of ordinal
numerals above *tenth*?
How do ordinal
numerals agree with the
nouns they modify?

Alfonso Doce   *Alfonso the Twelfth*
All ordinal numerals agree in gender and number with the
nouns they modify.

Éstas son las primeras propuestas.   *These are the first
proposals.*

REMEMBER!

- **Gustar, quedar,** and **faltar** always call for an indirect object. They are
  normally used in the third person singular or plural, depending on the
  number of the thing or things in the subject, which usually follows the
  verb (*Section 41*).

Nos gusta la película.	*We like the movie.*
Me quedan siete fotos.	*I have seven photos left.*
Le falta uno para terminar.	*He lacks one to finish.*

- A verb that is the object of a preposition always appears in the infinitive
  in Spanish (*Section 42*).

  Después de comer, dormí dos horas.   *After eating, I slept two hours.*

- Noun modifiers (adjectives, **de** phrases, **que** clauses) can be nominalized and function in place of the original noun. *One* and *ones* used in these constructions in English are omitted in Spanish (*Section 39*).

El viejo viene todos los días.	*The old one (man) comes every day.*
La clase de español es después de la de matemáticas.	*The Spanish class is after math (class).*
Me gustan estos discos y los que vienen después.	*I like these records and the ones that come after (next).*

- The preterit of **hay** is **hubo** (*there was, there were*).

- Spanish generally uses the definite article rather than the possessive adjective with parts of the body and articles of clothing when it is obvious who the possessor is (*Section 46*).

  Yo me lavo las manos.   *I wash my hands.*

- The masculine definite article (**el, los**) is used with the days of the week except after **ser** and translates *on* (*Section 53*).

  el lunes   *on Monday*   los lunes   *on Mondays*

- Days of the week and the months are not capitalized in Spanish (*Section 53*).

- In counting or in reading dates, thousands are never represented as multiples of hundreds in Spanish (*Section 53*).

  1400   mil cuatrocientos   *fourteen hundred*

- A negative word (**no, nadie, nunca, nada, ninguno**, etc.) must precede the verb in negative sentences. Remember that Spanish takes double or even triple negatives (*Section 54*).

  No veo a nadie nunca.   *I don't ever see anyone.*

- When **alguien** and **nadie** are direct objects of a verb, they are preceded by the personal **a** (*Section 54*).

No veo a nadie.	*I don't see anyone.*
¿Tú le diste un libro a alguien?	*Did you give a book to someone?*

A • Transformation Drill   Present Indicative → Command

Use either the familiar command or the formal command, depending on the context.

MODEL   Don Agapito pide un aumento para los trabajadores.
STUDENT **Don Agapito, pida Ud.** un aumento para los trabajadores.

1. Juan no abre la oficina.
2. Diego discute la propuesta con don Santiago.
3. Uds. prestan atención a las palabras de los compañeros.
4. El Sr. González comprende que no se puede trabajar sin dinero.
5. Uds. son listos y escuchan con cuidado.
6. Susana y Laura deciden su posición.
7. Alfonso no tiene miedo de nadie.
8. Tú dices la verdad.
9. Elena llega a una decisión.
10. Sí, reciben el aumento que merecen hoy mismo.

B • Transformation Drill   Present Indicative → Preterit

MODEL   Hoy vamos al cine.
STUDENT Hoy **fuimos** al cine.

1. Hoy pasa algo extraordinario.
2. Juanita me recoge a las ocho y media.
3. Vamos a visitar el palacio presidencial.
4. De pronto escucho en la radio que hay un atentado contra el presidente.
5. El Ministro de Seguridad Pública cuenta que los bandidos atacan por todas partes.
6. El pueblo recibe las noticias con terror.
7. Yo me preocupo mucho por la situación también.
8. Juanita me mira y regresamos a casa lo más pronto posible.
9. ¿Tú te das cuenta de qué informan?
10. Solamente es una publicidad para una película nueva.

C • Query   Free Response

Treat exercise B as a narrative and answer the following questions in Spanish.

1. ¿Cuántas personas fueron a visitar el palacio?
2. ¿Pasó algo emocionante?
3. ¿Quién habló en la radio?
4. ¿Qué hubo?
5. ¿El pueblo recibió las noticias tranquilamente?
6. ¿Discutieron Juanita y su amiga qué hacer?
7. ¿Llegaron al palacio las dos amigas o regresaron a casa?
8. ¿Se dio Ud. cuenta de que no ocurrió el atentado?

D • Substitution Drill

Rewrite the following sentences, inserting the pronouns.

1. le   Yo doy una entrada.
   Queremos dar una entrada.
   Den una entrada.
   No des una entrada.

2. me   Yo llamo Gonzalo.
   Gonzalo llama.
   ¿Nunca piensas llamar?
   ¡Llama lo más pronto posible!

E • Query   Free Response

Answer in Spanish.

1. ¿Cómo se llama tu mejor amigo? ¿Cómo llamas a tu novio (novia)?
2. ¿Te lavas la cara por la mañana? ¿Lavas los calcetines de tu padre?
3. ¿Se abren las tiendas a las nueve y media? ¿Abres la puerta cuando llega alguien?
4. ¿Cuándo hay que ponerse un abrigo? ¿Dónde pones tus libros al llegar a casa?
5. ¿Por qué te despiertas temprano los lunes? ¿Quién te despierta?

F • Translation Drill

1. Although Diego is stronger than Elena, she is as quick as he is.
2. When you went to the soccer game, did you have any money left?
3. We don't ever see anyone.
4. They congratulated each other.
5. After returning home, I washed my face.
6. You have as many photos as I do, but Arturo's (ones) are more interesting.
7. We don't like to go to the store with them.
8. Don't give them the contract, give them the proposal.
9. There were two hundred women at the sale on Tuesday.
10. The first days after the concert, thousands of letters arrived.

G • Guided Composition

Choose one of the following proverbs and create a situation it would illustrate.

Más enseña la necesidad que la universidad.
Ojos que no ven, corazón que no siente.
Cada loco con su tema.

to here 17 Abril

Mayan ruins at Tikal, Guatemala

Lección trece

EXPLORACIONES ENTRE LAS RUINAS MAYAS

IRIS   ¡Papi! Cuéntanos otra vez cómo descubriste el lugar del famoso templo de los mayas.

descubrir *to discover*

lugar *place; location*

TOMASITO   Sí, el templo que ningún hombre vio antes que tú.

PAPÁ   Bueno, si insisten. Hace mucho tiempo que les conté esa historia, ¿verdad?

TOMASITO   Sí, pero nos gusta mucho oírla. ¿Tú eras estudiante?

PAPÁ   Sí, en aquel entonces yo estaba estudiando antropología. Tenía muchas ganas de ser explorador. Conocí a un joven en la capital. Su familia tenía una hacienda en Tabasco.

en aquel entonces *back then, at that time*
tener ganas de *to be anxious to, want to*

IRIS   ¿El joven se llamaba don Ignacio?

PAPÁ   Bueno, en esos días lo llamábamos Nachito, el sabelotodo. Me contó que de vez en cuando algún indio llegaba a su hacienda con artefactos indígenas para vender.

sabelotodo *know-it-all*
de vez en cuando *once in a while*

indígenas *native, Indian*

IRIS   ¿Así que fueron a Tabasco?

así que *so*

PAPÁ   Sí, fuimos allí y ganamos la confianza del cacique de uno de los pueblos. Él nos llevó a las ruinas de la antigua ciudad maya.

confianza *confidence*

cacique *chieftain*

antigua *ancient*   **ciudad** *city*

TOMASITO   ¿Así fue? ¿Tan fácil? ¡Eso no tiene chiste!

no tener chiste (coll.) *not to be any fun* (**chiste** *joke*)

PAPÁ   Sólo fue el comienzo. El Instituto de Antropología e Historia nos dio dinero para las ex-

comienzo *beginning*

	cavaciones. Nos tomó tres años no más para excavar una fachada del templo mayor.	**no más** *only*
		fachada *façade* **mayor** *main; greater*
IRIS	¡Tres años! ¡Qué trabajo!	
PAPÁ	Un día increíble logramos encontrar la entrada. Hacía un calor atroz. Por casualidad me respaldé	**lograr** *to manage, attain* **entrada** *entrance*
		calor *heat* **atroz** *atrocious* **respaldarse** *to lean*
	sobre una piedra curiosa, rectangular, que abrió la entrada secreta. Cautelosamente entramos en el templo.	**piedra** *rock*
		cautelosamente *cautiously*
IRIS	¡Ay! ¿Tenías miedo, papi?	
PAPÁ	Un poco. Pero más bien estaba asombrado.	**más bien** *rather* **asombrado** *amazed, astonished*
	Hacía un fresco eterno en las entrañas del	**hacer fresco** *to be cool* **entrañas** *middle, midst, innards*
	templo. El pasillo tenía una forma curiosamente gótica.	**forma** *shape*
TOMASITO	¿Entonces qué pasó?	
PAPÁ	De pronto encontramos la tumba del rey maya. A su alrededor había serpientes emplumados de	**tumba** *tomb*
		a su alrededor *around it, surrounding it* **había** *there were* **serpientes emplumados** *plumed serpents*
	obsidiano, changos de jade. También un collar de oro y una máscara funeraria encrustada con joyas. Todos los artículos necesarios para pasar al reino de los muertos.	**changos** *monkeys* **collar** *necklace*
		mascara funeraria *funeral mask*
		joyas *jewels*
		reino *kingdom* **los muertos** *the dead*

NOTES

había   *there was, there were.* Imperfect form of **hay**.

tú form   The children in this dialog use the familiar (**tú**) form with their father, who, of course, responds with the familiar. Reciprocal use of **tú** is becoming more widespread in Hispanic families, although it is by no means universal. Usually it correlates with higher socioeconomic levels, urban rather than rural life, and increased education on the part of the parents.

los mayas   advanced pre-Columbian civilization that inhabited southern Mexico and parts of Central America.

Tabasco   Tabasco is a state in southern Mexico where important Mayan archeological sites, such as Palenque, have been discovered.

cacique   The traditional meaning (as used here) is *Indian chieftain*; it has also come to mean political boss.

papi   endearment of **papá**.

chango   Used in Mexico to mean monkey; the more common Spanish word is **mono**.

Museum of Anthropology, Mexico City

LANGUAGE STRUCTURES

55 Imperfect

Regular Imperfect Endings	
-ar *Verbs*	**-er** *and* **-ir** *Verbs*
-aba	-ía
-abas	-ías
-aba	-ía
-ábamos	-íamos
-aban	-ían

Examples

hablar	**aprender**	**escribir**
hablaba	aprendía	escribía
hablabas	aprendías	escribías
hablaba	aprendía	escribía
hablábamos	aprendíamos	escribíamos
hablaban[1]	aprendían[1]	escribían[1]

▶ The imperfect tense *describes* an action or condition in the past without any regard to its termination. English *used to* or *would* (as a synonym of *used to*) are among the equivalents of the imperfect, as is, generally, *was (were) . . . -ing*.

1. En esos días lo llamábamos Nachito, el sabelotodo.
   In those days we used to call him Nachito, the know-it-all.
2. De vez en cuando un indio llegaba a la hacienda.
   Once in a while an Indian would arrive at the ranch (estate).
3. ¿Tenías miedo, papi?
   Were you afraid, daddy?
4. Yo estudiaba cuando entró Iris.
   I was studying when Iris entered.

Imperfect of **ser**, **ir**, **ver**		
ser	**ir**	**ver**
era	iba	veía
eras	ibas	veías
era	iba	veía
éramos	íbamos	veíamos
eran	iban	veían

[1] For the **vosotros** forms, see the Appendix, section **1**.

▶ **Ser**, **ir**, and **ver** are the only verbs that are irregular in the imperfect tense. Only the imperfect of **ser** is used to express time of day in the past.

1. ¿Tú eras un estudiante entonces?	*You were a student then?*
2. ¿Ibas a ir? Sí, iba a ir.	*Were you going to go? Yes, I was going to go.*
3. En aquel entonces íbamos mucho a la hacienda.	*In those days we used to go to the ranch a lot.*
4. Sí, ella lo veía de vez en cuando.	*Yes, she would see him once in a while.*
5. Eran las cinco de la tarde.	*It was five in the afternoon.*
6. ¿Qué hora era? Era la una de la mañana.	*What time was it? It was one in the morning.*

A • Variable Substitution Drill

MODEL	¿Tú eras un estudiante entonces?
	¿Él
STUDENT	¿Él **era** un estudiante entonces?

1. ¿Tú eras un estudiante entonces?
   éramos
   ¿Iris
   eran
   ¿Papá y yo
   ¿Ud.

2. De vez en cuando un indio llegaba.
   llegabas.
   alguien
   llegábamos.
   Papá e Iris
   ellos

3. Ellos tenían una azucarera en Tabasco.
   Yo
   tenías
   Ud.
   teníamos
   Ellas

4. Yo iba a ir.
   Papi
   ibas
   Papi y ella
   iban
   Ud.

B • Transformation Drill   Present → Imperfect

MODEL	Todos los días la veo en el pasillo.
STUDENT	Todos los días la **veía** en el pasillo.

1. Todos los días la veo en el pasillo.
   Ella siempre compra una Coca-Cola.
   Cuando me ve, me da una sonrisa.
   Quiero hablarle pero no puedo.
   Las palabras no me salen.
   Soy un pobre alucinado.

2. La situación es ambigua.
   El rector acepta muchas de nuestras demandas.
   Por ejemplo, van a abrir la biblioteca.
   El rector es buena gente.
   Pero la autoridad municipal no ayuda.
   Hay que votar.

C • Query   Patterned Response

MODEL   ¿Quiénes la veían de vez en cuando? ¿Iris y tú?
STUDENT   **Sí, de vez en cuando Iris y yo la veíamos.**

1. ¿Quién iba a Tabasco de vez en cuando? ¿Nachito?
2. ¿Quiénes llegaban a la hacienda en esos días? ¿Unos indígenas?
3. ¿Quién tenía miedo en aquel entonces? ¿Tú?
4. ¿Quiénes tenían ganas de ser exploradores en esos días? ¿Los antropólogos?
5. ¿Quiénes querían ser antropólogos en aquel entonces? ¿Tú y Diego?
6. ¿Quién se daba cuenta de la hora todos los días? ¿Tu papá?
7. ¿Quién se ponía agitado de vez en cuando? ¿Don Santiago?
8. ¿Quién se olvidaba de la tarea siempre? ¿Juanito Cebollero?

D • Query   Patterned Response

Answer using a suitable time expression from the previous exercise (**de vez en cuando,** etc.).

MODEL   ¿Cuándo eras estudiante?
STUDENT   **Era estudiante en aquel entonces.**

1. ¿Cuándo estudiabas inglés?
2. ¿Cuándo ibas al Caballo Bayo?
3. ¿Cuándo querían ser Uds. exploradores?
4. ¿Cuándo la querías?
5. ¿Cuándo contaba Papi esa historia?
6. ¿Cuándo hacía frío?
7. ¿Cuándo tenía miedo Iris de Tomás?
8. ¿Cuándo se despertaban Uds. a las ocho?

E • Query   Patterned Response

MODEL   ¿Qué hacía Ud. cuando iba al fútbol?   (mirar el partido)
STUDENT   **Cuando iba al fútbol miraba el partido.**

1. ¿Qué hacía Ud. cuando iba a Tabasco?   (explorar las ruinas)
2. ¿Qué hacía Ud. cuando era estudiante?   (estudiar como un loco)
3. ¿Qué hacía Ud. cuando llegaba a clase temprano?   (escribir la tarea)
4. ¿Qué hacía Ud. cuando su novia quería ir al cine?   (llevarla)
5. ¿Qué hacían Uds. cuando vivían en México?   (trabajar en las excavaciones)
6. ¿Qué hacían Uds. cuando visitaban Texas?   (comer chile con carne)
7. ¿Qué hacía yo cuando estaba en la universidad?   (estudiar español e inglés)
8. ¿Qué hacías tú cuando trabajabas en el Instituto?   (revisar los artefactos)

56 Imperfect versus preterit

▶ The preterit and the imperfect tenses represent two different ways of looking at events in the past.

▶ The imperfect is *descriptive;* it is used to describe past actions or conditions without any indication of an end. The imperfect *ignores* the end, the outcome.

▶ In contrast, the preterit tense reports a completed action or condition, whatever its duration. This can be indicated by a specific time reference.

    1. Salió de su casa a las tres de la tarde.   *He left home at three in the afternoon.*
    2. Estudió por dos horas.   *He studied for two hours.*
    3. ¿Fuiste a España el año pasado?   *Did you go to Spain last year?*

▶ It is the very nature of certain verbs to express brief or sudden action. These verbs normally are used in the preterit.

    Ella se sentó.   *She sat down.*
    Decidí aceptar la propuesta.   *I decided to accept the proposal.*

▶ The imperfect tense always translates English *used to* (or *would* when used as a synonym of *used to*) because in these expressions of habitual action the outcome or end is disregarded by the speaker.

    Yo iba mucho al dentista.   *I used to go to the dentist a lot.*
    Mi familia vivía en Tabasco.   *My family used to live in Tabasco.*

The imperfect tense generally translates English *was* (*were*), either alone or with the *-ing* form.

    Cuando éramos estudiantes, estudiábamos   *When we were students we*
    en la biblioteca.   *used to study in the library.*
    ¿Qué hacías cuando te informaron?   *What were you doing when they informed you?*

▶ The English *-ed* form (or equivalent forms such as *left, wrote, went, gave, bought, sold,* etc.) is less generalizable. Whether the imperfect or the preterit is used depends precisely on the emphasis: description versus sudden or completed action.

Description (no outcome or end)		*Completed Action (focus on outcome or end)*	
Le escribía todos los días.	*I wrote to him every day.*	Le escribí ayer.	*I wrote to him yesterday.*
Te necesitaba pero no estabas.	*I needed you but you weren't in.*	Te necesité el lunes.	*I needed you on Monday.*

▶ Often both the preterit and the imperfect appear in the same expression, complementing each other.

    activity in progress   *sudden action*
    ¿Qué hacías cuando entraron?   *What were you doing when they came in?*

    condition   *completed action*
    Yo estaba cansado cuando volví a casa.   *I was tired when I returned home.*

▶ Certain adverbial expressions indicate continuance and call for the imperfect; others pinpoint time and call for the preterit. The following two lists are useful cues for the imperfect or the preterit. Those expressions in color are new vocabulary.

Usually Take the Imperfect		*Usually Take the Preterit*	
siempre	*always*	ayer	*yesterday*
en aquel entonces	*at that time*	**anoche**	*last night*
de vez en cuando	*once in a while*	**anteayer**	*the day before*
en esos días	*in those days*		*yesterday*
todos los días	*every day*	**el otro día**	*the other day*
(lunes, años, etc.)	*(Monday, year, etc.)*	**la semana pasada**	*last week*
a veces	*sometimes*	**el año** (viernes, etc.)	*last year (Friday,*
frecuentemente	*frequently*	**pasado**	*etc.)*
con frecuencia	*frequently*		
a menudo	*often*		
muchas veces	*many times, often*		
cada día (año, mes,	*each day (year,*		
jueves, etc.)	*month, Thursday, etc.)*		

Speaker's Choice

Occasionally, two seemingly contradictory time expressions may be used in the same sentence.

La semana pasada iba a mi clase de baile todos los días.
Last week I would go to my dance class every day. (emphasis on going to dance class each day)

La semana pasada fuiste a tu clase de baile todos los días.
Last week you went to your dance class every day. (emphasis on the week as a completed unit)

A • Transformation Drill   Preterit → Imperfect or Imperfect → Preterit

Change the following sentences to the imperfect or to the preterit according to the words or phrases that are substituted.

MODEL   En mil novecientos cuarenta y ocho (1948) estudié antropología.
En aquel entonces
STUDENT   En aquel entonces **estudiaba** antropología.

1. Ayer escribí una carta a mi novia.
   Todos los días

2. Siempre pasaba por aquí.
   Anoche

3. Yo nunca vi a ese hombre.
   Todos los días yo

4. Muchas veces yo iba al cine.
   Después de media hora

5. La semana pasada comí enchiladas suizas.
   En aquel entonces

6. De vez en cuando llegaba algún explorador.
   Anteayer

7. El otro día vimos a Tomasito y a Iris.
   A menudo

8. Todos los jueves iba al dentista.
   Ayer

9. El año pasado ganó el Botafogo.
   Todos los años

10. A veces me hablaba de su trabajo en la oficina.
    Anoche

B • Transformation Drill   Infinitive → Preterit or Imperfect

Repeat each sentence, changing the underlined verbs to the appropriate past tense, either preterit or imperfect.

MODEL   Tomás pensar que ser una persona muy creativa.
STUDENT   Tomás **pensaba** que **era** una persona muy creativa.

1. Tomás pensar que ser una persona muy creativa.
   Él creer que ir a ganar mucho dinero en el comercio.
   Un día él ir a un lugar muy interesante.
   Tomás informar al mandamás que él querer un trabajo magnífico.
   Pero, ¡qué lástima! No haber trabajos en el banco para personas con los talentos de Tomás.

2. Anoche haber una venta en la tienda de discos.
   La venta ser para ayudar a la orquesta infantil.
   La venta empezar a las ocho en punto.
   Toda la gente del barrio llegar para cenar y comprar los artículos.
   A las once terminarse la venta y todos volver a casa.

3. El otro día Arturo ir al cine.
   Arturo ver una película donde, en el año 2050, los astronautas establecer una sociedad utópica en la luna.
   Los astronautas pensar que el hombre y la mujer ser iguales.
   Ellos votar como jefe a la persona más sabia de todas.
   Ella llamarse María Elena.

C • Free Response

Write original sentences in Spanish, using either the preterit or the imperfect with the following expressions.

MODEL   a veces
STUDENT   A veces **íbamos a la capital para escuchar una sinfonía.**

1. el otro día
2. un domingo
3. a menudo
4. todos los días
5. anteayer

6. luego
7. muchas veces
8. ayer
9. la semana pasada
10. de vez en cuando

D • Translation Drill

Translate into Spanish.

1. I write to her every day. I used to write to her every day. I wrote to her last week.
2. Today she's going to the dentist. Yesterday she went to the dentist. She would go to the dentist on Mondays.
3. The boss informed me that he was not going to the office.
4. What happened? Iris sang a beautiful song.
5. Why were they living in Tabasco? They were excavating a temple.

57 Past progressive

▶ The past progressive expresses continuous action in the past just as the present progressive expresses action in progress in the present (see section **32**). Either the preterit or the imperfect of **estar** may be used as the auxiliary verb preceding the present participle. The preterit of **estar** is irregular.

Imperfect of **estar**	Preterit of **estar**	Present Participle
estaba	estuve	
estabas	estuviste	hablando
estaba	estuvo	aprendiendo
estábamos	estuvimos	escribiendo
estaban	estuvieron[2]	

▶ With the preterit of **estar** the progressive expresses action that ended in the past. Once again, the focus is on the outcome or end. With the imperfect the progressive expresses continuous action in the past with no reference to its termination.

1. En aquel entonces yo estaba estudiando antropología.

At that time I was studying anthropology.

[2] For the **vosotros** form, see the Appendix, section **1**.

2. Yo estuve estudiando antropología,
   pero me cansé.

*I was studying anthropology but I got
tired.*

3. ¿Qué estuviste haciendo anoche?

What were you doing last night?

4. Estaba hablando con Rosa acerca de
   Tabasco.

I was talking to Rosa about Tabasco.

A • Transformation Drill   Present Progressive → Imperfect Progressive

MODEL   Estoy buscando a Marta.

STUDENT   **Estaba** buscando a Marta.

1. ¿Qué estás haciendo?
2. ¿Qué estás escribiendo?
3. ¿Qué estás comiendo?
4. ¿Qué estás cantando?
5. Carlitos no está trabajando.

6. Estamos excavando como locos.
7. Estamos trabajando como burros.
8. Ya me estoy dando cuenta.
9. Quizás se está acordando.
10. Está burlándose de nosotros.

B • Transformation Drill   Imperfect → Imperfect Progressive

MODEL   Vendía joyas en la venta.

STUDENT   **Estaba vendiendo** joyas en la venta.

1. Vendía libros en la venta.
2. Compraba discos para la tienda.
3. Escribía poemas para su novia.
4. Jugábamos fútbol cuando ocurrió.
5. Discutíamos cuando nos informó.
6. Estudiaba cuando me contó la noticia.

Preterit → Preterit Progressive

7. Escribí la propuesta.
8. Revisé las facturas.
9. Hablé con la central azucarera sobre el contrato.
10. Consulté con los otros ministros.
11. Ayer trabajamos como burros.
12. Anoche comimos en la venta.

58   Expressions with **tener**

▶   Spanish has a number of expressions that use **tener** + noun where English uses *to
be* + adjective. The adjective **mucho, -a** is used to modify these nouns, not the adverb
muy. These expressions always have living beings as their subjects, never things.
Here are the most common expressions.

Masculine Nouns

	frío.		*cold.*
	calor.		*hot.*
Iris tiene (mucho)	sueño.	Iris is (very)	*sleepy.*
	miedo.		*afraid.*
	cuidado.		*careful.*

Feminine Nouns

	paciencia.		*patient.*
	hambre.		*hungry.*
	sed.	Iris is (very)	*thirsty.*
Iris tiene (mucha)	suerte.		*lucky.*
	razón.		*right.*
	prisa.	Iris is in a great hurry.	

Iris tiene (muchas) ganas de + infinitive   *Iris is (very) anxious to . . .*

¿Qué edad tiene Iris?

or   *How old is Iris?*

¿Cuántos años tiene Iris?

While **tener suerte** = *to be lucky,* **no tener suerte** = *to be unlucky.*

Nacho no tiene suerte.   *Nacho is unlucky (not lucky, has no luck).*

To be wrong may be expressed by **no tener razón** or by **estar equivocado (-a, -os, -as).**

Iris y Tomás no tienen razón.

or   *Iris and Tomás are wrong.*

Iris y Tomás están equivocados.

▶ Because **tener** + noun only refers to living beings, *hot* and *cold* are expressed differently, according to context.

La cerveza está muy fría.	*The beer is very cold.* (thing)
La muchacha tiene mucho frío.	*The girl is very cold.* (person)
El café está muy caliente.[3]	*The coffee is very hot.* (thing)
Los exploradores tienen mucho calor.	*The explorers are very hot.* (persons)

Additional examples:

1. Tenía muchas ganas de ser explorador.   *I was very anxious to become an explorer.*
2. Tomás tiene diez años.   *Tomás is ten years old.*
3. Tenga Ud. paciencia, por favor.   *Please be patient.*

[3] Adjective form of *hot* (temperature, not spice).

to here 24 de abril 79

Children's Rhyme

> Los pollitos dicen
> pío, pío, pío[4]
> cuando tienen hambre
> cuando tienen frío.

A • Query   Patterned Response

MODEL   (**tener**)   ¿Quién tiene prisa? ¿Marta?
STUDENT   **Así es, Marta tiene mucha prisa.**

MODEL   (**ser** or **estar**)   ¿Qué está fría? ¿La cerveza?
STUDENT   **Así es, la cerveza está muy fría.**

1. ¿Quién tiene paciencia? ¿El profesor?
2. ¿Quién está cansado? ¿Carlitos?
3. ¿Quién tiene suerte? ¿Tere?
4. ¿Quién es lista? ¿Mónica?
5. ¿Qué está frío? ¿El café?
6. ¿Quién tiene ganas de comer? ¿Álvaro?
7. ¿Qué están calientes? ¿Los churros?
8. ¿Quién tiene calor? ¿El jefe?
9. ¿Quién está aburrido? ¿Rafa?
10. ¿Quién es vivo? ¿Diego?

B • Query   Patterned Response

MODEL   ¿Tienes frío o tienes calor?
STUDENT   **¡Te digo que tengo frío!** *or* **¡Te digo que tengo calor!**

1. ¿Tienes suerte o no tienes suerte?
2. ¿Tienes paciencia o tienes prisa?
3. ¿Tiene Ud. razón o no tiene Ud. razón?
4. ¿Tienes razón o estás equivocado?
5. ¿Tiene Ud. sueño o tiene sed?
6. ¿Tienes ganas o estás cansada?
7. ¿Tienen hambre o tienen sed?
8. ¿Tiene veinte años o tiene veinticinco años?
9. ¿Tiene Ud. sed o tiene hambre?
10. ¿Tiene paciencia o está aburrido?

C • Query   Free Response

Answer in Spanish.

1. ¿Cuántos años tienes?
2. ¿Tenía Ud. mucha hambre ayer por la tarde?
3. ¿Tienen Uds. frío ahora?
4. ¿Tenían Uds. miedo del profesor (de la profesora) el primer día de clases?
5. ¿Tienen miedo de la profesora (del profesor) ahora?
6. ¿Tienen ganas de trabajar?
7. ¿Tengo razón si digo que Los Ángeles es la capital de California?
8. ¿Tiene mucha paciencia el profesor (la profesora)?
9. ¿Tiene Ud. sed?
10. ¿Tiene Ud. noventa y nueve años?

[4] **Pío** is the Spanish onomatopoeia that would correspond to "*peep*" or "*cheep*".

59 Expressions with **hacer**

Idioms to Express the Weather

▶ **Hacer** is used idiomatically in order to describe the temperature or the weather. When used in this way, **hacer** is impersonal (the English equivalent takes *it* as a subject). Just as in the idioms with **tener**, where English uses *to be*, Spanish uses **hacer** + noun. Thus, adjectives such as **mucho** (not **muy**), **bueno, malo**, etc., are used to modify the nouns.

¿Qué tiempo hace (hacía)?	*What is (was) the weather like? How is (was) the weather?*
Hace (hacía) buen tiempo.	*It is (was) nice weather.*
Hace (hacía) mal tiempo.	*It is (was) bad weather.*
Hace (hacía) calor (frío, fresco, viento, sol[5]).	*It is (was) hot (cold, cool, windy, sunny).*

1. Hacía un calor atroz en Tabasco. *It was frightfully* (lit., *atrociously*) *hot in Tabasco.*

2. Hacía un fresco eterno en el templo. *It was eternally cool in the temple.*
3. Hacía mucho calor; hacía mucho viento. *It was very hot; it was very windy.*
4. Hace mucho frío en Nueva York. *It is very cold in New York.*

¡Cuidado!

Not all expressions concerning the weather must use the **hacer** idiom. Here is a list of expressions using either **ser** or **estar**.

Es un buen día. Es un mal día.	*It's a nice day. It's a bad day.*
Es un día muy agradable.	*It is a very pleasant day.*
Está nublado; está muy nublado.	*It is cloudy; it is very cloudy.*
Está despejado; está muy despejado.	*It's clear; it's very clear (the day).*

A • Query   Free Response

Answer in Spanish.

1. ¿Hace frío hoy?
2. ¿Qué tiempo hace?
3. ¿Qué tiempo hace en el verano?[6]
4. ¿Qué tiempo hace en el invierno?[6]
5. ¿Qué tiempo hace en la primavera?[6]
6. ¿Qué tiempo hace en el otoño?[6]
7. ¿En qué meses hace calor aquí?
8. ¿Dónde hace más viento, aquí o en la luna?

[5] One can also say, **Hay sol.** *It is sunny.* (*There is sun.*)
[6] **Verano, invierno, primavera, otoño** = *summer, winter, spring, fall.*

B • Completion Drill

Complete with the appropriate present tense form of **ser**, **estar**, **tener**, or **hacer**.

1. ¿Qué tiempo _____ hoy?
2. _____ un día muy agradable, ¿verdad?
3. _____ sol y no _____ mucho viento.
4. Ella _____ mucha hambre.
5. Cuando _____ mucho sol, yo no _____ frío.
6. La Coca-Cola no _____ muy fría.
7. ¿_____ sueño Eugenia o solamente _____ cansada?
8. Iris, ¿cuántos años _____ tú?
9. ¿_____ caliente el café?
10. A veces _____ mucho viento en el otoño.
11. ¿_____ razón el profesor o _____ equivocado?
12. Hoy _____ buen tiempo: _____ un buen día para tener una venta.
13. Hoy _____ mal tiempo, _____ nublado.
14. Yo no _____ paciencia porque _____ mucha prisa.
15. Nosotros _____ muchas ganas de explorar las ruinas.

C • Translation

Translate into Spanish.

1. Be patient! Be good! Be careful! Be here at five!
2. I'm in a hurry. I'm sleepy. I'm tired. I'm bored.
3. She is very clever. She is very afraid. She is very ill.
4. It's cold today. I'm cold. The enchiladas are cold.
5. It's hot today. We're hot. The churros are hot.

Hacer in Expressions of Time

▶ **Hacer** is used idiomatically with the present, imperfect, and preterit tenses in order to express time.

▶ The formula **hace** + *the present tense of the verb* indicates an action or condition that began in the past and continues into the present (the verb in English is in the present perfect).

Hace + period of time + **que** + present tense of verb

Hace   mucho tiempo   que   espero aquí.

I have been waiting here for a long time. (literally, *It makes a long time that I wait here.*)

Hace   tres días   que   estoy en Tabasco.

I have been in Tabasco for three days.

In questions, the period of time usually comes first, followed by **hace**.

> **¿Cuánto tiempo hace que hablas español?**
> *How long have you been speaking Spanish?*

▶ The formula **hacía** + *the imperfect tense of the verb* indicates an action or condition that began in the past, continued for a period of time, and ended (or was interrupted) in the past (the verb in English is in the pluperfect).

> **Hacía** + period of time + **que** + imperfect tense of verb
> **Hacía   mucho tiempo   que   esperaba allí.**
> *I had been waiting there for a long time.* (literally, *It made a long time that I was waiting there.*)
> **Hacía   tres días   que   estaba en Tabasco.**
> *I had been in Tabasco for three days.*

▶ The formula **hace** + *preterit tense of the verb* indicates an action or condition that took place a period of time *ago* (the verb in English is in the past).

> **Hace** + period of time + **que** + preterit tense of verb[7]
> **Hace   mucho tiempo   que   esperé allí.**
> *I waited there a long time ago.*
> **Hace   tres días   que   estuve en Tabasco.**
> *I was in Tabasco three days ago.*

A • Transformation Drill

MODEL	Él escribe un poema. (hace una hora)
STUDENT	**Hace una hora que él escribe un poema.**

1. Arturo estudia antropología. (hace un año)
2. Nacho excava el templo mayor. (hace tres años)
3. Estoy en Tabasco. (hace un día)
4. Miramos el partido de fútbol. (hace media hora)
5. Vivíamos en Barcelona. (hacía seis meses)
6. Trabajábamos como fanáticos. (hacía dos días)
7. Gabriel estudiaba en una universidad latinoamericana. (hacía tres meses)
8. Queríamos ir al norte. (hacía una semana)
9. Lo compré. (hace media hora)
10. Lo vendí. (hace unos días)
11. Fui a Valencia. (hace mucho tiempo)
12. Salieron para San Juan. (hace tres horas)

---

[7] An alternate word order is frequently used.
> Preterit tense of verb + **hace** + period of time (the **que** is dropped).
> **Esperé allí   hace   mucho tiempo.**   *I waited there a long time ago.*
This alternate word order is rarely used with the other formulas.

B • Query   Patterned Response

MODEL   ¿Cuánto tiempo hace que estás enamorada de Diego?   (una semana)
STUDENT   **Hace una semana que estoy enamorada de Diego.**

1. ¿Cuánto tiempo hace que estudias español e inglés?   (muchos años)
2. ¿Cuánto tiempo hace que tienes miedo del rector?   (algunos meses)
3. ¿Cuánto tiempo hace que esperas a tu novio (novia)?   (hora y media)
4. ¿Cuántos años hace que eres aficionada al fútbol?   (años y años)
5. ¿Cuántos días hace que tienes ese disco?   (cuatro días)
6. ¿Cuánto tiempo hacía que estaba Ud. en Madrid?   (diez años)
7. ¿Cuánto tiempo hacía que vivía Ud. en Nuevo México?   (mucho tiempo)
8. ¿Cuánto tiempo hacía que trabajaba Ud. allí?   (unos años)
9. ¿Cuánto tiempo hace que recogieron Uds. esas entradas?   (un día)
10. ¿Cuánto tiempo hace que arreglaron Uds. la bicicleta?   (muy poco)
11. ¿Cuánto tiempo hace que fueron a la capital?   (mucho)
12. ¿Cuánto tiempo hace que discutieron eso con José?   (algún tiempo)

C • Query   Free Response

Answer the following with the **hace** + period-of-time formula.

1. ¿Cuánto tiempo hace que estudias español?
2. ¿Cuánto tiempo hace que es Ud. estudiante?
3. ¿Cuánto tiempo hace que compraste el libro?
4. ¿Cuánto tiempo hace que comes tamales?
5. ¿Cuánto tiempo hace que fuiste al cine?
6. ¿Cuándo perdió Ud. el anillo?
7. ¿Cuándo fuiste al concurso?
8. ¿Cuándo escribió Ud. a su compadre?
9. ¿Cuándo terminaste el trabajo?
10. ¿Cuándo te diste cuenta de la situación?

D • Translation

Translate into Spanish.

1. I bought it a long time ago. We sold it an hour ago.
2. How long have you been waiting here?
3. We've been waiting here for three hours.
4. How long had you been waiting here when they informed you?
5. We had been waiting here for half an hour when they informed us.

60   Summary of shortened forms of adjectives

▶ Most of the limited number of adjectives that undergo shortening are summarized in the following chart.

| Before a Singular Noun | | Elsewhere (after a noun; in the plural; when used as a noun) |
Masculine	Feminine	
buen	buena	bueno, -a, -os, -as
mal	mala	malo, -a, -os, -as

algún	alguna	alguno, -a, -os, -as
ningún	ninguna	ninguno, -a
un	una	uno, -a, -os, -as
primer	primera	primero, -a, -os, -as
tercer	tercera	tercero, -as, -os, -as
	gran	grande, -s

▶ With the exception of **grande**, shortened forms of the adjectives are found only in the masculine singular when the adjective precedes the noun. **Gran** is used before the masculine and feminine singular with the meaning *great*.

▶ Recall also that **ciento** is shortened to **cien** in many circumstances and that multiples of **uno** (**veintiuno**, **treinta y uno**, etc.) are also shortened when used as adjectives (see section **51**).

1. Fue un gran jefe; fue una gran jefa.[8]   *He was a great boss; she was a great boss.*

2. Ningún hombre vio ese templo antes que tú.   *No man saw that temple before you.*

3. El primer día de las excavaciones descubrió la puerta; el tercero la abrió.   *The first day of the excavations he discovered the door; the third (day) he opened it.*

But:

1. Eran grandes caciques; son unas mujeres grandes.[8]   *They were great chieftains; they are large women.*

2. Algunos de los hombres estuvieron aquí.   *Some of the men were here.*

3. Los primeros en llegar fueron los indios.   *The first to arrive were the Indians.*

A • Variable Substitution Drill

MODEL   Creo que es una buena persona.
                              hombre.
STUDENT   Creo que es **un buen** hombre.

1. Creo que es una buena persona.
                  día.
          gran
              jefe.
      unos
          jefa.

2. ¿Dónde está el primer libro?
                              libros?
                              factura?
                              facturas?
                              hombre?
                              indio?

---

[8] Recall that, normally, descriptive adjectives are placed after the noun and limiting adjectives are placed before the noun (see section **18**). However, the adjectives **grande**, **bueno**, and **malo** have different meanings, depending on whether they come before or after the noun. For example, **Es un gran hombre** means *He is a great man*, whereas **Es un hombre grande** means *He is a big man*. For a fuller discussion of the special cases of adjective position, see section **76**.

B • Translation

Translate into Spanish.

1. One explorer. One of those explorers.
2. A good newspaper. One of these newspapers.
3. Are you acquainted with (do you know) the first poem? No, but I'm acquainted with the third one.
4. Some man, some person, a good man, a good woman.
5. He's a bad engineer; she's a great teacher.

REVIEW

I The following questions are related to the dialog. Answer in Spanish.

1. ¿Hacía mucho tiempo que el papá de Iris y Tomasito les contaba su historia del templo de los mayas?
2. ¿Dónde descubrieron el famoso templo de los mayas?
3. ¿Cómo llamaban a don Ignacio cuando él era estudiante?
4. ¿Quién les dio dinero a los exploradores y antropólogos para hacer excavaciones?
5. ¿Cuánto tiempo les tomó para excavar una fachada del templo mayor?
6. ¿Qué cosas había alrededor del rey maya?
7. ¿Para qué eran todos esos artículos?
8. ¿Tenía miedo el papá?

II Translation. Translate into Spanish.

1. Tell me where the famous temple of the Mayas is and how you discovered it.
2. It is far away in Tabasco. In order to get (arrive) there you have to be an explorer.
3. And you say you found a tomb in the temple? I thought there were no tombs in Mayan temples.
4. You are right. We used to think that way. But now we know that some of the temples were also tombs.
5. Incredible! Were you very afraid when you first entered the temple?
6. A little. But I was also very astonished. I was anxious to find the tomb.
7. It was very cool in the temple. The corridors had a Gothic form.
8. Then suddenly we found the tomb of the king. Around him were all the articles that he needed in the kingdom of the dead.

III Guided Composition

Imagine that you are living in the future. You have unearthed the ruins of a twentieth-century city. Describe what you have found.

Cognates & Contexts

Sculpture of a Chac Mool, Mayan ruins at Chichén Itzá

Cuando los conquistadores españoles llegaron al Nuevo Mundo, encontraron tres grandes civilizaciones pre-colombinas: los aztecas, los mayas y los incas.

Los aztecas y los mayas vivían en Norteamérica, los aztecas en el centro de México, y los mayas en el sur de México, en Guatemala y en Honduras. Los incas vivían en el territorio que ahora es Ecuador, Perú, Bolivia y Chile.

Las tres civilizaciones son conocidas por sus enormes ciudades y otras grandes obras públicas de construcción. Por ejemplo, cuando Hernán Cortés entró a Tenochtitlán (ahora la ciudad de México), juzgó a la capital de los aztecas como una ciudad más grande y hermosa que Sevilla. Algunas de las antiguas ciudades mayas eran Palenque (donde se descubrió una tumba dentro del templo mayor), Chichén Itzá y Uxmal. La capital de los incas era el Cuzco. A unos ochenta kilómetros (cincuenta millas) del Cuzco, en 1911,

sur *south*

son conocidas por *are known for*

juzgar *to judge*
hermosa *beautiful*

el Dr. Hiram Bingham descubrió Machu Picchu. Machu
Picchu quiere decir "la ciudad perdida de los incas".   **perdida** *lost*
Ningún español llegó a conocerla.

Los incas eran magníficos ingenieros; construyeron   **construyeron** (from **construir**)
      they constructed
carreteras que cruzaban los Andes y puentes de suspensión   **cruzar** *to cross* **puentes** *bridges*
como el puente de San Luis Rey que duró de 1350 hasta   **durar** *to last*
1890.

Por su parte, los aztecas y los mayas inventaron calendarios
de gran precisión. También cultivaron muchos productos
que llegaron a ser importantes para el occidente, como maíz,   **occidente** *the West*
tomates, papas, chocolate y vainilla.   **papas** *potatoes*

Hernán Cortés (1485–1547) was the leader of the Spanish group that first
made contact with the Aztec empire. He sub-
sequently conquered that empire and colonized
what is now Mexico.

Lección catorce

PRESENCIANDO UN DRAMA DE LOPE DE VEGA

drama *play* (theat.)

JULIO   Te llamé ayer por la noche pero no estabas. ¿Te dieron el mensaje?

mensaje *message*

LUISA   Sí, me lo dieron, pero no lo recibí hasta hoy.

JULIO   Ya me lo imaginaba. Hace unas horas que supe que ustedes fueron al teatro.

imaginarse *to imagine*

LUISA   Estábamos en la Plaza Mayor tomando unas horchatas cuando conocimos a un estudiante que se llama Rogelio Zamora. Él nos dijo que iban a presentar *Fuenteovejuna* de Lope de Vega.

horchata *a type of beverage*

presentar *to produce, present*
obra *work*

JULIO   Creo que conozco esa obra.

LUISA   ¿Te traigo el programa?

JULIO   Sí, tráemelo.

LUISA   Aquí está. Es un drama excelente, muy serio y movido. Lo mejor es cuando el pueblo se rebela en contra del aristócrata malvado. Una mujer valiente, Laurencia, los incita a la rebelión.

movido *fast-moving* **lo mejor** *the best part or thing*
malvado *malicious, fiendish*

valiente *courageous, brave*

JULIO   Ya recuerdo. Este aristócrata, el comendador...

rapta y viola a Laurencia en su noche de bodas.

recordar (ue) *to remember*
comendador *commander (of military order)*
raptar *to kidnap* **violar** *to rape*

LUISA   Así es. El descarado tenía la actitud de "lo mío

descarado *scoundrel, rogue*
lo mío *what is mine*

es mío, y lo tuyo es mío también." Pero después de soltar a Laurencia, el pueblo lo castiga con la muerte. Luego entra el rey, y sus soldados torturan a los ciudadanos de Fuenteovejuna. Quieren saber quién mató al comendador. Pero todos responden,

—Fue Fuenteovejuna.

Es decir, todo el pueblo mató al infame.

JULIO   Esa obra de Lope es extraordinaria. Conozco otras obras suyas que son similares. El pueblo, muchas veces con la ayuda del rey, triunfa contra la aristocracia. Generalmente Lope escribía para el pueblo. Durante su vida su teatro fue muy popular.

LUISA   ¡Y todavía es popular! ¡Dios mío! ¡Qué impresión me hizo ese momento glorioso cuando los ciudadanos de Fuenteovejuna, avergonzados por las reclamaciones de Laurencia, deciden destruir al tirano que los gobierna!

lo tuyo *what is yours*

soltar (ue) *to release*
castigar *to punish*
soldados *soldiers*

ciudadanos *citizens*

responder *to answer*

infame *villainous scoundrel*

suyas *of his (hers, yours)*
triunfar *to win, triumph*

durante *during*

avergonzados *shamed, ashamed*
reclamaciones *protests; accusations; complaints*
destruir *to destroy*

to here
1 mayo 1979

NOTES

Plaza Mayor   A square in the center of Madrid, enclosed by the arcades of old buildings. Whereas in times past these arcades served as bleachers for bullfights and theatrical productions, they now house a variety of outdoor cafés.

horchata   a sweet, milky beverage made of almonds that is very popular in the hot summer months.

Lope de Vega (1562–1635)   One of the best-known and most prolific playwrights of the Spanish Golden Age (sixteenth and seventeenth centuries).

Fuenteovejuna   The title of one of Lope's best-known plays. It is the name of the village where the action takes place, and it becomes one of the main characters. The name is a composite of **fuente** (*fountain*) and **ovejuna** (*pertaining to sheep*). In the play, **ovejuna** is used ironically by Laurencia against the village's (initially) inactive citizens.

comendador   During the period in which the play is set, it was not uncommon for a high official in a religious/military order to rule over an area or village in the name of the monarch. This official was known as the **comendador**.

LANGUAGE STRUCTURES

61 Additional verbs irregular in the preterit

The Unstressed -e, -o Endings

andar *to walk*[1]	**tener**[2] (compare with **estar**, section **57**)		
and**uve**	t**uve**		
and**uv**iste	t**uv**iste		
and**uvo**	t**uvo**		
and**uv**imos	t**uv**imos		
and**uv**ieron	t**uv**ieron		
poder	**poner**[2]	**saber**	**-u-** stem
p**ude**	p**use**	s**upe**	
p**ud**iste	p**us**iste	s**up**iste	
p**udo**	p**uso**	s**upo**	
p**ud**imos	p**us**imos	s**up**imos	
p**ud**ieron	p**us**ieron	s**up**ieron	
querer	**hacer**[2]	**venir**[2]	**-i-** stem
qu**ise**	h**ice**	v**ine**	
qu**is**iste	h**ic**iste	v**in**iste	
qu**iso**	h**izo**	v**ino**	
qu**is**imos	h**ic**imos	v**in**imos	
qu**is**ieron	h**ic**ieron	v**in**ieron	
traer[2]	**decir**	**producir**[3] *to produce*	**-j-** stem
tra**je**	di**je**	produ**je**	
tra**j**iste	di**j**iste	produ**j**iste	
tra**jo**	di**jo**	produ**jo**	
tra**j**imos	di**j**imos	produ**j**imos	
tra**j**eron	di**j**eron	produ**j**eron	

[1] **Andar** has the additional meanings of *to go, wander; to travel; to work, function.*
For example:

| **Anduvieron por aquí y por allá.** | *They wandered around here and there.* |
| **¿Anda tu automóvil?** | *Is your car working (running)?* |

[2] Derivatives of these verbs are identical except for the prefix. For example: **detener** (*to detain*), **detuve**; **retener** (*to retain*), **retuve**; **componer** (*to fix or to compose*), **compuse**; **deshacer** (*to undo*), **deshice**; **prevenir** (*to warn*), **previne**; **extraer** (*to extract*), **extraje**, etc.

[3] All verbs that end in **-ducir** are irregular in the same way. For example: **traducir** (*to translate*), **traduje, tradujiste, tradujo, tradujimos, tradujeron.** Other such verbs are **conducir** (*to guide; to drive*), **reducir** (*to reduce*).

▶ Both the stems and the endings of the above verbs are irregular. Note that the **-e** and **-o** endings (first person and third person singular, respectively) are not stressed as in the preterit of regular verbs. **Traer**, **decir**, and **-ducir** verbs (the **-j-** stem verbs) use **-eron** instead of **-ieron** in the third person plural. The third person singular of **hacer** is **hizo**.

Verbs That Change i → y in the Preterit				
caer(se)[4] *to fall*	**creer**	**leer**	**oír**	**destruir**
caí	creí	leí	oí	destruí
caíste	creíste	leíste	oíste	destruíste
cayó	creyó	leyó	oyó	destruyó
caímos	creímos	leímos	oímos	destruímos
cayeron	creyeron	leyeron	oyeron	destruyeron

▶ The same verbs that change **i → y** in forming the present participle (see section **32**) change **i → y** in the third person singular and plural in the preterit, except **traer** and its derivatives (**-j-** stems).

A • Variable Substitution Drill

MODEL   Hace unas horas que yo supe que fueron al teatro.
                    tú
STUDENT   Hace unas horas que tú **supiste** que fueron al teatro.

1. Hace unas horas que yo supe que fueron al teatro.
        tú
        él
          supe
        Uds.
          supimos
2. Él dijo que iban a presentar *Fuenteovejuna*.
   Julia y Luisa
     dije
   Julio y yo
     dijiste
   Ud.
3. Ayer por la noche nosotros anduvimos por la Plaza Mayor.
          anduviste
       tú y Paco
         anduve
         anduvimos
      Julia y Luis

[4] The present tense of **caer(se)** is conjugated like **traer**: **caigo, caes, cae, caemos, caen**.

4. Rogelio leyó muchas obras de Lope de Vega.
         leí
Rogelio y él
         leíste
Ud.
         leímos

5. Yo lo hice para ti.
         hicimos
Luisa
Tere y Julio
         hice
Papi

B • Query   Patterned Response

MODEL   ¿Quién tradujo *Fuenteovejuna* al inglés? ¿Ella?
STUDENT   **Sí, ella tradujo *Fuenteovejuna* al inglés.**

1. ¿Quién tradujo *Fuenteovejuna* al inglés? ¿Tú?
                                     ¿Julio?
                                     ¿Ud.?
                                     ¿Luisa?
                                     ¿Él?
                                     ¿Ellas?

MODEL   El rector no quiso hacerlo, ¿y ustedes?
STUDENT   **No, nosotros no quisimos hacerlo tampoco.**

2. El rector no quiso hacerlo, ¿y el presidente?
                              ¿y tú?
                              ¿y ellas?
                              ¿y el pueblo?
                              ¿y los señores Zamora?
                              ¿y él?

MODEL   ¿Quiénes trajeron el programa? ¿Uds.?
STUDENT   **Sí, nosotros trajimos el programa.**

3. ¿Quiénes trajeron el programa? ¿Ellos?
                                  ¿Tú y Luis?
                                  ¿Julia y Luisa?
                                  ¿Rogelio y ella?
                                  ¿Ignacio y Ud.?
                                  ¿Uds.?

MODEL   ¿Oíste tú la noticia?
STUDENT   **Sí, yo la oí pero no la creí.**

4. ¿Oyó él la noticia?
    Tere y él
    Uds.
    papá
    Ud. y el jefe
    tú

C • Transformation Drill   Present → Preterit

MODEL   Te llamo cuando llego a casa.
STUDENT   Te **llamé** cuando **llegué** a casa.

1. Leen a Lope en clase.
2. ¿No me das el mensaje?
3. Estamos en la Plaza Mayor.
4. El descarado tiene una actitud infame.
5. ¿Te traigo el programa?

6. No vienen porque no pueden.
7. ¿Te dicen cuándo van allí?
8. ¿Sabes qué pasa en la universidad?
9. Allí no hay nadie.
10. ¿Quién dice eso?

D • Transformation Drill   Imperfect → Preterit

(Note the differences in meaning conveyed by the preterit as compared to the imperfect.)

MODEL   Los dos iban al dentista.
STUDENT   Los dos **fueron** al dentista.

1. Todos respondían: —Fuenteovejuna.
2. Los soldados torturaban a los ciudadanos.
3. ¿Cuándo venían por aquí?
4. ¿Cuándo traían sus bicicletas a la universidad?

5. ¿Cuándo hacían la tarea?
6. Julio y Luisa andaban por la Plaza Mayor.
7. ¿Quién creía el niño?
8. Había que decidir.
9. No se daban cuenta de lo mejor.
10. ¿Quién decía esas donjuanerías?

62 Verbs with special meanings in the preterit

▶ Recall that the imperfect tense describes while the preterit reports or narrates a completed action. This narrative function alters the meaning of certain verbs when used in the preterit from the one conveyed in the imperfect.

Verb	Meaning in the Preterit	Meaning in the Imperfect
conocer	*to meet, to be introduced to someone*	*to be acquainted with*
saber	*to find out, learn (of)*	*to know*
poder	*to manage to do something; to succeed*	*to be able to do something but with no reference to trying*
no poder	*to try to do something but to fail*	*not to be able to do something but with no reference to trying*
querer	*to try in the sense of wanting to, but to fail*	*to want*
no querer	*to refuse in the sense of not wanting to do something and in fact not doing it*	*not to want*

Examples

1. Julio habló con Luisa porque la conocía.

   Julio spoke with Luisa because he knew (was acquainted with) her.

   Julio conoció a Luisa anoche.

   Julio met Luisa last night.

2. ¿Cuándo supieron la verdad?

   When did they learn (of) the truth?

   Ya la sabían.

   They already knew it.

3. El Botafogo pudo ganar el partido.

   Botafogo managed to win the game.

   El Botafogo podía ganar el partido; ¡qué lástima que no jugaron!

   Botafogo could win the game; what a pity they didn't play!

4. El Botafogo no pudo ganar el partido.

   Botafogo could not (failed to) win the game.

   El Botafogo no podía ganar contra nosotros; ¡qué lástima que no jugamos!

   Botafogo couldn't win against us; what a pity we didn't play!

5. Quise darle el mensaje.

   I tried (wanted to but failed) to give him the message.

   ¿Por qué no quisiste darle el mensaje?

   Why did you refuse to (not want to and in fact didn't) give him the message?

   (No) quería darle el mensaje.

   I wanted (did not want) to give him the message. (No indication of whether or not I did give him the message.)

What are the meanings of the following pairs of sentences?

Julio pudo conseguir trabajo, porque quiso.

Julio podía conseguir trabajo, pero no quiso.

Papá no quiso salir.

Papá no quería salir.

A • Query Patterned Response

MODEL   ¿Cuándo quiso Ud. presentar la obra?
STUDENT 1 **Ayer quise presentarla.**
STUDENT 2 **Hacía mucho tiempo que quería presentarla.**

1. ¿Cuándo pudo Ud. discutir la propuesta?
2. ¿Cuándo quiso Ud. llamar a Juan?
3. ¿Cuándo supo Ud. la noticia?
4. ¿Cuándo tuvo Ud. que hacer la tarea?
5. ¿Cuándo pudo Ud. devolver el libro?
6. ¿Cuándo quiso Ud. cantar la canción?
7. ¿Cuándo tuvo Ud. esa idea?
8. ¿Cuándo pudo Ud. conseguir el dinero?

B • Query Free Response

Answer in Spanish.

1. ¿Cuándo supo Ud. que *Fuenteovejuna* era un famoso drama español?
2. ¿Sabía Ud. que *Fuenteovejuna* era un famoso drama español?
3. ¿Cuándo conoció a su profesor (profesora) de español?
4. ¿Conocía Ud. a su profesor (profesora) de español el año pasado?
5. ¿Por qué no quisiste hacer la tarea anoche?
6. ¿Querías hacer la tarea anoche?
7. ¿Pudiste comprar las cosas que necesitabas?
8. ¿Por qué no podías verme en la biblioteca?
9. ¿Hubo una reunión de tu comité ayer?
10. ¿Había mucha gente en el cine el otro día?

C • Translation Drill

Translate into Spanish. Do not translate the cues in parentheses.

1. Did he manage to win? I was able to (could) win.
2. I already knew her in Colombia. We met them in Bolivia.
3. When did you learn of it? Oh, I already knew it!
4. I tried to go but I couldn't (I failed to).
5. He refused to write it.

63 Combinations of two object pronouns

▶ When two object pronouns are combined, their relative position is the following:

| Reflexive | Indirect object | Direct object |
| pronoun | pronoun | pronoun |

The indirect object pronoun precedes the direct object pronoun when both are used as objects of the same verb. A reflexive pronoun precedes any other object pronoun.[5] It is very rare for more than two object pronouns to appear in combination.

[5] Examples of the combination of a reflexive pronoun + indirect object pronoun will not be encountered until Lección veintitrés (section **104**).

> ### Special Case: Indirect and Direct Object Pronouns Beginning with l-
>
> | | |
> |---|---|
> | se (= le, les) | lo |
> | | la |
> | | los |
> | | las |

Examples

Reflexive + Direct Object Pronouns

1. Póntelos.[6]	*Put them on.*
2. Voy a comprármela.[6]	*I'm going to buy it for myself.*
3. Ella se lo puso.	*She put it on.*
4. Mis manos están sucias; estoy lavándomelas.[6]	*My hands are dirty; I'm washing them.*

Indirect + Direct Object Pronouns

5. Dáselo.[6]	*Give it to him (her).*
6. Voy a comprártelo.[6]	*I'm going to buy it for you.*
7. No se lo dieron.	*They didn't give it to her (him, you).*
8. Estamos lavándotelas.[6]	*We are washing them for you.*

▶ The position of combinations of two object pronouns remains the same with respect to the verb: they precede conjugated verbs and negative commands; they are attached to affirmative commands, present participles, and infinitives.

Oral Practice

Repeat the following aloud. Make sure that you understand the meaning of each sentence.

1. Julio y Tomás se pusieron los calcetines. Julio y Tomás se los pusieron. Julio y Tomás no pudieron ponérselos. Julio y Tomás estuvieron poniéndoselos. Julio y Tomás, pónganselos, por favor. Julio y Tomás, no se los pongan, por favor.

2. Luisa le da el mensaje a papá. Luisa se lo da. Luisa va a dárselo. Luisa está dándoselo. Luisa, dáselo. Luisa, no se lo des.

3. ¿Te lavaste la cara? ¿Quieres lavártela? ¿Estás lavándotela? ¡Lávatela! ¡No te la laves!

4. La Srta. Azuela me vende el libro. La Srta. Azuela me lo vende. Va a vendérmelo. Está vendiéndomelo. Srta. Azuela, véndamelo Ud. Srta. Azuela, no me lo venda Ud.

---

[6] Infinitives, affirmative commands, and present participles take a written accent mark when two pronouns are added to them, as the stressed syllable of the verb is not changed by adding pronouns.

A • Replacement Drill   Direct Object → Direct Object Pronoun

MODEL   ¿Le dieron el mensaje?
STUDENT   **¿Se lo** dieron?

1. ¿Te dieron el mensaje?
2. ¿Le trajiste las horchatas?
3. ¿Te doy el libro?
4. ¿Les vendo el traste?
5. ¿Te conté la historia?

6. ¿Te presté la bici?
7. ¿Le escribo una carta?
8. ¿Se lavó las manos?
9. ¿Se puso la camisa?
10. ¿Te compraste esa motocicleta?

B • Replacement Drill   Direct Object → Direct Object Pronoun

MODEL   Voy a contarle la historia.
STUDENT   Voy a **contársela.** or **Se la** voy a contar.

1. Voy a escribirle una carta.
2. Voy a ofrecerle el trabajo.
3. Tengo que traerle el dinero.
4. Quiso contarle la noticia otra vez.
5. No pudo ponerse los pantalones.

6. Estábamos comprándole el automóvil.
7. Estaban vendiéndonos artefactos.
8. Estuve prestándole la tarea.
9. Estaba poniéndose los calcetines.
10. Estaba escribiéndome un mensaje.

C • Replacement Drill   Direct Object → Direct Object Pronoun

MODEL   Deme Ud. el libro. No me dé Ud. el libro.
STUDENT   **Démelo** Ud. No me **lo** dé Ud.

1. Tráigame Ud. el periódico. No me traiga Ud. el periódico.
2. Véndame Ud. esa mesa. No me venda Ud. esa mesa.
3. Escríbame Ud. un artículo. No me escriba Ud. un artículo.
4. Póngase Ud. la camisa. No se ponga Ud. la camisa.
5. Dése Ud. otra oportunidad. No se dé Ud. otra oportunidad.
6. Escríbeme una carta. No me escribas una carta.
7. Dale el dinero. No le des el dinero.
8. Cómprate las enchiladas. No te compres las enchiladas.
9. Lávate la cara. No te laves la cara.
10. Ponte los pantalones. No te pongas los pantalones.

D • Query   Patterned Response

MODEL   ¿Te lavaste las manos?
STUDENT   **Claro que me las lavé.**
MODEL   ¿Cuándo te las lavaste?
STUDENT   **Me las lavé anoche.**

1. ¿Te lavaste la cara?
   ¿Cuándo te la lavaste?

2. ¿Te hiciste el vestido?
   ¿Cuándo te lo hiciste?

3. ¿Se compró Ud. un automóvil nuevo?
   ¿Cuándo se lo compró Ud.?
4. ¿Se puso Ud. la camisa?
   ¿Cuándo se la puso Ud.?
5. ¿Se lavó Ud. las manos?
   ¿Cuándo se las lavó Ud.?

E • Query Patterned Response

MODEL   ¿Le diste las facturas?
STUDENT **Sí, se las di.**
MODEL   ¿Cuándo se las diste?
STUDENT **Se las di ayer.**

1. ¿Le ofreciste el trabajo?
   ¿Cuándo se lo ofreciste?
2. ¿Le presentaste el contrato?
   ¿Cuándo se lo presentaste?
3. ¿Le prestaste el dinero?
   ¿Cuándo se lo prestaste?

4. ¿Le escribió Ud. la carta?
   ¿Cuándo se la escribió Ud.?
5. ¿Le contó Ud. la historia?
   ¿Cuándo se la contó Ud.?

F • Patterned Response Drill

MODEL   Voy a darte la revista.
STUDENT **Por favor, no me la des.**
MODEL   ¿Por qué no?
STUDENT **Está bien. Dámela.**

1. Voy a escribirte la carta.
   ¿Por qué no?
2. Voy a traerte el café.
   ¿Por qué no?
3. Voy a venderte el programa.
   ¿Por qué no?

4. Voy a componerte el automóvil.
   ¿Por qué no?
5. Voy a comprarte una horchata.
   ¿Por qué no?

G • Translation

Translate into Spanish.

1. Buy it for me! Don't buy it for me! Buy it for yourself! Don't buy it for yourself!
2. Are you washing your face? Yes, I am washing it. Are you washing her face? Yes, I am washing it.
3. We are giving them to him. We want to give them to him. Give them to him! Don't give them to him!
4. He is putting it on. He is going to put it on. Put it on! Don't put it on!

64 Possessive adjectives that do not precede the noun

Possessives That Precede Nouns		Possessives That Follow Nouns	Alternate Form with **de**	
mi, -s	*my*	mío, -a, -os, -as		*of mine*
tu, -s	*your* (familiar)	tuyo, -a, -os, -as		*of yours* (familiar)
su, -s	*your* (formal)	suyo, -a, -os, -as	de usted	*of yours* (formal)
	his, her		de él	*of his*
	its		de ella	*of hers*
nuestro, -s	*our*	nuestro, -a, -os, -as		*of ours*
nuestra, -s				
su, -s	*your* (plural)	suyo, -a, -os, -as	de ustedes	*of yours* (plural)
	their		de ellos	*of theirs*
			de ellas	

▶ You have already learned the short forms of possessive adjectives, which always precede the noun. The long forms always follow the noun. Just as with the short forms, the long-form possessive adjectives agree with the thing possessed and *not* with the possessor. The alternate forms with **de** are sometimes needed where the **suyo** forms would be ambiguous. **De** forms can also be used instead of **su, -s** (see section **40**).

▶ The **mi, tu, su**, etc., possessives are equivalent to the English *my, your, his*, etc., whereas the **mío, tuyo, suyo**, etc., possessives usually translate *of mine, of yours, of his*, etc. In addition, the long forms are commonly used in direct address, particularly in speeches or letters (example 4), and in certain set phrases (example 5). The long forms are also required after the verb **ser** (example 6).

1. Pancho es un amigo mío.   *Pancho is a friend of mine.*
2. Julio y un hermano suyo.   *Julio and a brother of his.*
3. Julio y una hermana de ellos.   *Julio and a sister of theirs.*
4. Estimados compañeros nuestros. *Esteemed colleagues (of ours).*
5. ¡Dios mío!   *My God! Heavens!*
6. Ese traste no es suyo.   *That contraption is not theirs.*

▶ The Spanish usage of these possessive adjectives does not always conform to English. The essential difference between the short forms and the long forms in Spanish is one of emphasis. **Mi, tu, su**, etc., simply indicate possession, whereas **mío, tuyo, suyo**, etc., single out the noun(s) from among many as being the one (or ones) possessed.[7]

---

[7] In spoken Spanish, as in English, the short forms may be used emphatically simply by means of intonation.

Mi ejemplo es mejor.   *My example is better.*
     or
Este ejemplo **mío** es mejor.   *This example of mine is better.*

▶ Although the noun may be preceded by a definite article when using the long-form possessive adjectives, it is more commonly preceded by an indefinite article or a demonstrative adjective.

Contrast the following.

1. ¿Es ésta tu camisa?   *Is this one your shirt?*
(emphasis on *this one*)

   ¿Es tuya esta camisa?   *Is this shirt yours?*
(emphasis on *yours*)

2. Mi idea fue aceptada.   *My idea was accepted.*
(indicates the idea is mine, but the emphasis is on its acceptance)

   Una idea mía fue aceptada.   *An idea of mine was accepted.*
(emphasis on the idea being *mine*, as opposed to anyone else's)

A • Variable Substitution Drill

MODEL   Ese drama no es mío.
            bicicletas
STUDENT **Esas** bicicletas no **son mías.**

1. Ese programa no es mío.
             suyo.
  Esos
    cerveza
           son
           tuyas.

2. El amigo nuestro es de California.
         compañeras
             tuya
       abrigo
            míos
            suyo

3. ¿Es tuya la camisa?
         calcetines?
  suyos
         bicicletas?
  mía
        mensaje?

4. Él dice que esta obra no es suya.
  Yo
  Nosotros
  Tú
  Ellos
  Ella

B • Transformation Drill Short Form Possessives → Long Form Possessives

MODEL   Nuestro libro ya está aquí.
STUDENT **El libro nuestro** ya está aquí.

1. Tu amigo es un bufón.
2. Mi obra es excelente.
3. Su café está frío.
4. Nuestras cervezas están calientes.
5. Nuestra opinión es admirable.
6. Tu profesor no viene los jueves.
7. Su novia es una militante.
8. Mi bicicleta cuesta muchos billetes.
9. Nuestro rey permaneció en la capital.
10. Su hermana no puede decidir.

C • Transformation Drill   Exchange Pattern: de Phrase → suyo, -a, -os, -as

MODEL   ¿Llega ahora un amigo de ella?
STUDENT   ¿Llega ahora un amigo **suyo**?

1. ¿Es de ella ese brillante?
2. ¿Dónde están los libros de Uds.?
3. La orquesta de ellos es muy buena.
4. La obra de ella es muy seria.
5. Los amigos de Uds. van a la protesta.

6. Mónica va allí con dos hermanas de ella.
7. Este poema es de Ud.
8. ¿Va con un amigo de Ud.?
9. Paquito trabajaba con un hermano de él.
10. ¿Son de Uds. estas camisas?

D • Translation Drill

Translate into Spanish.

1. This friend of ours, those books of mine, that play of his.
2. Is it yours? No, it is hers.
3. Julio and two brothers of his. Luisa and a sister of hers.
4. You and a friend of yours. My teacher and some students of hers.
5. My God! My esteemed friend.

65   Possessive pronouns

el	mío tuyo suyo nuestro suyo[8]	el de usted, ustedes, él, ellos, etc.	la	mía tuya suya nuestra suya[8]	la de usted, ustedes, él, ellos, etc.
los	míos tuyos suyos nuestros suyos[8]	los de usted, ustedes, él, ellos, etc.	las	mías tuyas suyas nuestras suyas[8]	las de usted, ustedes, él, ellos, etc.

▶ The long-form possessive adjectives as well as the forms with **de** are nominalized in the same way as other adjectives (see section **39**).

1. Aquí está tu libro. ¿Dónde está el mío?   *Here's your book. Where is mine?*
2. ¿Tiene Ud. el suyo?   *Do you have yours?*
3. Mi profesor no es como el de ellos.   *My teacher is not like theirs.*

[8] For the possessive pronouns that correspond to the **vosotros** form, see the Appendix, section **1**.

A • Substitution Drill

MODEL Aquí están mis entradas, ¿dónde están las suyas?
libros
STUDENT Aquí están mis libros, ¿dónde están **los suyos**?

1. Aquí están mis libros, ¿dónde están los suyos?
    camisas
    cerveza
    anillo
    mensajes
    hermanas
2. Nuestra bicicleta está aquí pero no sabemos dónde está la de ustedes.
    automóvil
    profesora
    padre
    amigos
    dibujo

B • Query Patterned Response

MODEL ¿Es suya esta Coca-Cola?
STUDENT **No, aquí tengo la mía.**

1. ¿Son suyas estos discos?
2. ¿Son suyos estos poemas?
3. ¿Este contrato es el de Ud.?
4. ¿Esta entrada es la de Ud.?
5. ¿Es suya esta máscara?
6. ¿Es tuyo este collar?
7. ¿Son tuyas estas joyas?
8. ¿Son tuyos estos banderines?
9. ¿Estas máquinas son las tuyas?
10. ¿Este ejercicio es el de Ud.?

C • Query Patterned Response

MODEL ¿Dónde están nuestros programas?
STUDENT **Los suyos están perdidos.**

1. ¿Dónde están nuestros abrigos?
2. ¿Dónde está nuestra ropa interior?
3. ¿Dónde está nuestro billete?
4. ¿Dónde están nuestras tareas?
5. ¿Dónde están nuestras revistas?
6. ¿Dónde están nuestros periódicos?
7. ¿Dónde están nuestros hijos?
8. ¿Dónde está nuestra bicicleta?
9. ¿Dónde está nuestro flan?
10. ¿Dónde está nuestra máquina?

D • Translation

Translate into Spanish.

1. Here's my chocolate, where's hers?
2. Mine arrived yesterday. When does yours arrive?
3. His is excellent. Yours is horrible.
4. My teacher is not like theirs.
5. Are we going in your car or mine?

66 Nominalization with the neuter article **lo**

lo bueno	*the good*	
lo malo	*the bad*	
lo mejor	*the best*	
lo peor	*the worst*	*part, thing, aspect,* etc.
lo poco	*the little*	
lo imposible	*the impossible*	
lo increíble	*the incredible*	

lo mío	*my matter, problem, affair,* etc.; *what is mine*
lo tuyo	*your matter, problem,* etc.; *what is yours*
lo suyo (lo de él, lo de ella, etc.)	*his (her,* etc.) *matter, problem,* etc.; *what is his (hers,* etc.)

lo de ayer	*yesterday's goings-on, yesterday's events,* etc.
lo del presidente	*the president's doings, the president's matter,* etc.
lo de Rogelio	*that Rogelio business, that Rogelio thing,* etc.

lo que	*what, that which*

▶ The definite articles **el, la, los, las,** which indicate number and gender, are used to nominalize adjectives that refer to known nouns. The neuter article **lo** is used to nominalize adjectives that do not refer to known nouns or to clearly defined antecedents. **Lo** is placed before the masculine singular form (examples 1, 2, 3, and 4). Placing **lo** (rather than **el, la, los, las**) before the adjective tells the listener to treat the adjective as a noun and to make its meaning cover as broad an area as the context will permit. The English equivalent of this usage usually involves one of numerous cover words such as *thing, part, aspect, matter, problem, business, affair, stuff, events, goings-on,* etc.

Since **de** phrases and **que** clauses are used to modify nouns, they also may be nominalized in the same fashion (examples 5, 6, and 7).

1. Lo mejor es cuando el pueblo se rebela.   *The best part is when the people rebel.*

2. Lo mío es mío y lo tuyo es mío también.   *What is mine is mine, and what is yours is mine too.*

3. Lo poco que hicimos no es importante.   *The little that we did is unimportant.*

4. No puedo hacer lo imposible.   *I cannot do the impossible.*

5. Lo de ayer fue horrible.   *Yesterday's events were horrible.*

6. Lo de Rogelio fue peor.   *That Rogelio business was worse.*

7. Lo que dices es increíble.   *What you are saying is incredible.*

El Que versus Lo Que

Because **lo** is neuter, **lo que** cannot refer to anything already concretely mentioned. Note the difference between the following.

Con mi dinero y el que tú tienes, podemos comprar un automóvil.
With my money and what you have, we can buy a car. (what = money)

Con lo que tú tienes y mi dinero, podemos comprar un automóvil.
With what you have and my money, we can buy a car. (what is something not previously referred to, unidentified assets)

A • Query   Patterned Response

MODEL   ¿Qué como?
STUDENT **Come lo que tienes.**

1. ¿Qué traigo?
2. ¿Qué vendo?
3. ¿Qué preparo?
4. ¿Qué me pongo?

5. ¿Qué te presto?
6. ¿Qué te doy?
7. ¿Qué tomo?
8. ¿Qué apuesto?

B • Query   Patterned Response

MODEL   Lo que dijo Luis fue importante, ¿no?
STUDENT **Sí, lo de Luis fue importante.**

1. Lo que pasó anoche fue malo, ¿no?
2. Lo que dijo el jefe fue inteligente, ¿no?
3. Lo que busca Carlitos es muy romántico, ¿no?
4. Lo que hizo la clase fue interesante, ¿no?
5. Lo que dice Rogelio está bien, ¿no?
6. Lo que contaron el otro día fue increíble, ¿no?
7. Lo que dijo Diego fue trivial, ¿no?
8. Lo que escribió Martí fue admirable, ¿no?

C • Query   Patterned Response

MODEL   ¿Cuál fue la parte mejor de la obra? ¿Lo de la rebelión?
STUDENT **¡Por supuesto! Lo mejor de la obra fue lo de la rebelión.**

1. ¿Cuál fue el momento importante de la protesta? ¿Lo del rector?
2. ¿Cuál fue la parte admirable del poema? ¿Lo del amor?
3. ¿Cuál fue el momento dramático de la obra? ¿Lo del rey?
4. ¿Cuál fue la parte difícil de la tarea? ¿Lo de la matemática?
5. ¿Cuál fue la parte interesante del concurso? ¿Lo de los muchachos?
6. ¿Cuál fue el momento horrible del día? ¿Lo del Sr. Zamora?
7. ¿Cuál fue la parte bella de la sinfonía? ¿Lo de los ritmos indios?
8. ¿Cuál fue el momento romántico de la canción? ¿Lo de la sonrisita?

REVIEW

I The following questions are related to the dialog. Answer in Spanish.

1. ¿Dónde estaba Luisa cuando Julio llamó por la noche?
2. ¿Qué estaban haciendo en la Plaza Mayor cuando conocieron a Rogelio Zamora?
3. ¿Qué dijo Rogelio?
4. Según Luisa, ¿qué fue lo mejor de *Fuenteovejuna*?
5. ¿Cuál era la actitud del comendador descarado?
6. ¿Cómo castigaron al comendador?
7. ¿Qué hizo el rey a los ciudadanos de Fuenteovejuna?
8. ¿Para quién escribía Lope de Vega, para el pueblo o para los aristócratas?

II Translation. Translate into Spanish.

1. I called you last night in order to tell you that I was going to the theater.
2. Did you receive the message? I imagine that you didn't receive it yesterday.
3. What (that which) happened was that we met a student called Rogelio.
4. He took us to see an excellent play, *Fuenteovejuna*, by Lope de Vega.
5. Do you think you are familiar with (know) that play? Didn't I bring the program to you?
6. Yes, you brought it to me. That play is about a brave (courageous) woman who inspires a rebellion, right?
7. Exactly. The aristocrat is a scoundrel who has the attitude (of) "Whatever is mine is mine, and whatever is yours is mine too."
8. Now I know one of the reasons why Lope was so popular. He wrote for the people, not the aristocrats.

III Guided Composition

Do you think that theater is still popular? Why or why not? What other art forms are popular? What are they like? Why do people enjoy them?

Royal Theater, Madrid

Cognates & Contexts*

Here is a famous moment in Lope de Vega's *Fuenteovejuna* in Spanish, together with an English translation. Read the Spanish version, using the translation as a support. The Spanish uses the **vosotros** form. **Vosotros = Uds.** in this text; **os = los, las**, or **les**, depending on context; words such as **sois, nacisteis, pensáis**, correspond to **son, nacieron, piensan**, in this text.

ESTEBAN.   ¡Santo cielo!
¿No es mi hija?
¡Hija mia!
LAURENCIA.   No me nombres
tu hija.
ESTEBAN.   ¿Por qué, mis ojos?
¿Por qué?
LAURENCIA.   Por muchas razones,
y sean las principales,
porque dejas que me roben
tiranos sin que me vengues
traidores sin que me cobres.
La oveja al lobo dejáis,
como cobardes pastores.

ESTEBAN.   My heavens!
Can this be my daughter?
My daughter!
LAURENCIA.   Do not call me
Your daughter.
ESTEBAN.   Why, light of my eyes?
Why?
LAURENCIA.   For many reasons,
The principal ones being
Because you let me be taken away
By tyrants without avenging me,
By traitors without rescuing me.
You abandoned the sheep to the wolf
Like cowardly shepherds.

*In contrast to other "Cognates & Contexts," the unfamiliar vocabulary included here is not part of the active vocabulary in subsequent lessons.

Production of Lope de Vega's *Fuenteovejuna,* by INTAR, New York City, 1973

¿Qué dagas no vi en mi pecho?
¡Qué desatinos enormes,
qué palabras, qué amenazas,
y qué delitos atroces,
por rendir mi castidad
a sus apetitos torpes!
Mis cabellos, ¿no lo dicen?
¿No se ven aquí los golpes,
de la sangre y las señales?
¿Vosotros sois hombres nobles?
¿Vosotros padres y deudos?
¿Vosotros, que no se os rompen
las entrañas de dolor,
de verme en tantos dolores?
Ovejas sois, bien lo dice
de Fuenteovejuna el nombre.

What daggers did I not see in my breast?
What monstrous depravation,
What words, what threats,
And what frightful iniquities,
To bend my chastity
To their sordid craving!
My hair, does it not tell the story?
Do you not see the blows,
The blood and the bruises?
You are noble men?
You are parents and friends?
You, whose entrails
Do not burst with grief
Upon seeing me in such despair?
You are indeed sheep;
Fuenteovejuna is well named.

¡Dadme unas armas a mí!
Liebres cobardes nacisteis;
bárbaros sois, no españoles.
Gallinas, ¡vuestras mujeres
sufrís que otros hombres gocen!
Poneos ruecas en la cinta;
¿para qué os ceñís estoques?
¡Vive Dios, que he de trazar
que solas mujeres cobren
la honra de estos tiranos,
la sangre de estos traidores,
y que os han de tirar piedras,
hilanderas, maricones,
amujerados, cobardes,
y que mañana os adornen
nuestras tocas y basquiñas,
solimanes y colores!
ESTEBAN.   Yo, hija, no soy de aquellos
que permiten que los nombres
con esos títulos viles.
Iré solo, si se pone
todo el mundo contra mí.
JUAN ROJO.   Y yo por más que me asombre
la grandeza del contrario.
REGIDOR.   ¡Muramos todos!
MENGO.   ¡Los Reyes[9] nuestros señores
vivan!
TODOS.   ¡Vivan muchos años!
MENGO.   ¡Mueran tiranos traidores!
TODOS.   ¡Tiranos traidores mueran!

Give your weapons to me!
You were born timid rabbits;
You are barbarians, not Spaniards.
Hens! You suffer your women
to the pleasures of other men!
Put spindles in your belts;
Why wear those swords?
As God is my witness, I shall prove
That women alone can wrest
Their honor from these tyrants,
The blood from these traitors,
And that they will cast stones at you,
You spinning-wheel gossips, sissies,
Effeminate boys, cowards,
And tomorrow may they dress you
In our petticoats and bonnets,
Paint your faces and rouge your lips!
ESTEBAN.   My child, I am not of those
Who permit themselves to be named
In such vile terms.
I shall go alone, should the whole world
Turn against me.
JUAN ROJO.   So will I!
Though frightened by the greatness of our foe.
ALDERMAN.   Let us all die!
MENGO.   Long live the Monarchs,
our rightful masters!
ALL.   Long live!
MENGO.   Death to the traitor-tyrants!
ALL.   Death to the traitor-tyrants!

---

[9] **Reyes**, like **padres**, uses the masculine plural to include both genders. Here **Reyes** refers to the Catholic Monarchs, Ferdinand and Isabel (**los Reyes Católicos**), who ruled Spain jointly during the period in which this play is set, the late fifteenth century.

Bilingual education class, New York City

Lección quince

LA EDUCACIÓN BILINGÜE

SRA. RAMÍREZ Me pareció que Ud. decidió no darles una educación bilingüe a sus hijos. No lo niegue Ud. Ud. me dijo, "Es mejor que ellos aprendan inglés inmediatamente porque es la lengua oficial de los Estados Unidos."

negar (ie) *to deny* subj.

lengua *language, tongue*

SRA. RIVERA Tiene Ud. razón. Así lo preferí. Pero en la escuela me refirieron al Dr. López, el director del programa. Él me explicó varias cosas acerca de la educación bilingüe. Por ejemplo, no es cuestión de aprender inglés en vez de español. Los niños aprenden las dos lenguas a la vez. Además... y esto es lo más importante... no creo que sea bueno que mis hijos pierdan su cultura hispana.

preferir (ie, i) *to prefer*

escuela *school* **referir (ie, i)** *to refer*
explicar *to explain* **varias** *several*

a la vez *at the same time, at once*

SRA. RAMÍREZ Ya entiendo. Por eso la llaman educación bilingüe-bicultural, ¿verdad? Dicen que el bilingüismo los ayuda a mantener las nociones básicas de las dos culturas.

mantener *to maintain*

SRA. RIVERA Precisamente. Y un ejemplo perfecto es el Dr. López mismo. Habla tanto el español como el inglés a la perfección. Pero no sólo eso. Tiene un profundo entendimiento de los dos modos de pensar: el norteamericano y el hispano.

SRA. RAMÍREZ Sin embargo, dudo que todo funcione tan fácilmente. Espero que todo resulte como Ud. desea, pero... puede ser que haya clases especiales para todos los hispanos. Yo no quiero que mis hijos estén segregados de los chiquillos norteamericanos con el pretexto de la educación bilingüe.

SRA. RIVERA Para decirle la verdad, yo sentí ese temor también. Y así se lo indiqué al Dr. López. Pero él me aseguró que no es lo que sucede. Muchos padres norteamericanos están pidiendo que sus hijos estudien y aprendan español también.

SRA. RAMÍREZ ¡No me diga! ¿Es cierto?

SRA. RIVERA Sí, es verdad. Yo estaba un poco asombrada, pero es lógico. Aquí estamos viviendo todos juntos dentro de esta gran ciudad. ¡Es necesario que nos entendamos mejor!

a la perfección *perfectly*

profundo *deep, profound*
modos *ways*

dudar *to doubt* funcionar *to function, work*
resultar *to work out, result*

puede ser que *perhaps*

chiquillos *youngsters, small children*

temor *fear*

indicar *to indicate*

asegurar *to assure* suceder *to happen*

¿Es cierto? *Is that right (true)?*

juntos *together* dentro (de) *inside (of)*

NOTES

Bilingual-Bicultural Education

Bilingual education in the United States implies instruction in English and in a second language, which is usually the native tongue of the child receiving the instruction. Since language and culture are intimately related, bilingual education is at the same time bicultural: the child learns the mores, values, history, traditions, etc., of both cultures.

-illo, **-illa**, **-illos**, **-illas** are diminutives in Spanish, referring more to emotion than to size.

LANGUAGE STRUCTURES

67   Stem-changing verbs, Class II and Class III

	Class II		Class III
Present Indicative	**sentir**	**dormir**	**pedir**
	siento	duermo	pido
	sientes	duermes	pides
	siente	duerme	pide
	sentimos	dormimos	pedimos
	sienten[1]	duermen[1]	piden[1]
Preterit	sentí	dormí	pedí
	sentiste	dormiste	pediste
	sintió	durmió	pidió
	sentimos	dormimos	pedimos
	sintieron[1]	durmieron[1]	pidieron[1]
Present Participle	sintiendo	durmiendo	pidiendo

▶ In the present tense of certain **-ir** verbs (Class II), the last vowel of the stem, *when stressed*, changes from **e** → **ie** or from **o** → **ue**. This is the same change that we have encountered in Class I verbs, which end in **-ar** and **-er** (see section **31**). In addition, Class II verbs change **e** → **i** or **o** → **u** in the third person singular and plural of the preterit and in the present participle. Class II verbs are indicated thus: **sentir** (**ie, i**), **dormir** (**ue, u**).

▶ Class III verbs, which also end in **-ir**, change **e** → **i** in the present tense, when stressed. In addition, Class III verbs, just like **-e-** stem Class II verbs, change **e** → **i** in the third person singular and plural of the preterit and in the present participle. Class III verbs are indicated thus: **pedir** (**i, i**).

---

[1] For the **vosotros** form, see the Appendix, section **1**.

▶ Here are a number of important Class II and Class III stem-changing verbs. The verbs in color are new vocabulary.

Class II

preferir (ie, i) *to prefer*
referir (ie, i) *to refer*
sentir (ie, i) *to feel, to regret*
  sentirse (ie, i) *to feel*
divertirse (ie, i) *to have a good time, amuse oneself*
convertir (ie, i) *to convert, turn into*

dormir (ue, u) *to sleep*
  dormirse *to go to sleep*
morir(se) (ue, u) *to die*

Class III

seguir (i, i)[2] *to continue; to keep on, go on; to follow*
conseguir (i, i)[2] *to get; to manage; to accomplish*
reír (i, i)[3] *to laugh*
  reírse de[3] *to laugh at*
vestir (i, i) *to dress*
despedirse (i, i) *to take (one's) leave*
  despedirse de *to take leave of*
pedir (i, i) *to ask, ask for, request*
servir (i, i) *to serve*
repetir (i, i) *to repeat*

Pedir versus Preguntar

Preguntar means *to ask a question, inquire, inquire about.* **Pedir** means *to ask to be given something, make a request of someone.* Complete the sentence with the appropriate form of **pedir** or **preguntar**.

¿Le puedo _____ algo, profesor?   ¿Te puedo _____ diez pesos, papá?

---

[2] Verbs that end in **-guir**, such as **conseguir (i, i)** and **seguir (i, i)**, change **gu** to **g** before **a** and **o**. Thus, for example, the present indicative of **seguir** is **sigo, sigues, sigue, seguimos, siguen**.

[3] **Reír (i, i)** has written accents in the present indicative: **río, ríes, ríe, reímos, ríen**. The present participle of **reír** is **riendo** and the preterit is **reí, reíste, rio, reímos, rieron**.

A • Variable Substitution Drill

MODEL La Sra. Ramírez prefiere la educación bilingüe.
Los Sres. Ramírez

STUDENT Los Sres. Ramírez **prefieren** la educación bilingüe.

1. Los Sres. Ramírez prefieren la educación bilingüe.
   Yo
   Tú y yo
                        preferiste
   El Sr. Ramírez
   Nosotros

2. ¿Por qué se durmió Tomasito en clase?
   tú
   ellas
   dormimos
   Ud.
   el Dr. López

3. Yo sentí mucho lo de ayer.
   sentimos
   Ud.
   sentiste
   Ella
   Uds.

B • Query Patterned Response

MODEL ¡Nosotros nos morimos de hambre! ¿Y tú?

STUDENT **Sí, yo me muero de hambre también.**

1. ¡Yo me muero de hambre! ¿Y Mónica?
   ¿Y él?
   ¿Y tú y Miguel?
   ¿Y Ud.?
   ¿Y Uds.?

MODEL Tú repetiste los versos perfectamente, ¿y Cecilia y yo?

STUDENT **Sí, ustedes repitieron los versos perfectamente.**

2. Ustedes repitieron los versos perfectamente, ¿y nosotras?
   ¿y ellas?
   ¿y el poeta?
   ¿y José Martí?
   ¿y yo?

MODEL Iris consiguió el dinero para el cine, ¿y Juan?

STUDENT **No, él no lo consiguió.**

3. Juan no consiguió el dinero para el cine, ¿y tú?
   ¿y Ud?
   ¿y ella?
   ¿y los Sres. Rivera?
   ¿y los chiquillos?

C • Transformation Drill   Present → Preterit

MODEL   Gabriel prefiere dárselo al profesor.
STUDENT Gabriel **prefirió** dárselo al profesor.

1. Carlitos se ríe como loco.
2. Con esa gente me convierto en un fanático.
3. ¡Ya comienzas a darte cuenta!
4. Laura se viste en media hora.

5. Ella defiende a su familia.
6. Me piden el automóvil.
7. ¿Cuándo vuelves al Perú?
8. ¿Cuándo consigue Ud. el dinero?

D • Transformation Drill   Preterit → Present

MODEL   ¿Te refirieron al Dr. López?
STUDENT **¿Te refieren** al Dr. López?

1. ¿Por qué me pidió Ud. los libros?
2. Iris se rió de Pancho.
3. ¡Con esa película no se divirtieron!
4. Miguel se durmió en el teatro.

5. Los soldados se murieron.
6. ¿Cuándo te contó esa historia?
7. ¿Cómo consiguió Laura el tiempo?
8. Ella se sintió mejor.

68   Regular forms of the present subjunctive

Regular Present Subjunctive Endings	
-ar *verbs*	**-er** *and* **-ir** *verbs*
-e	-a
-es	-as
-e	-a
-emos	-amos
-en[4]	-an[4]

Examples

hablar	**aprender**	**escribir**
hable	aprenda	escriba
hables	aprendas	escribas
hable	aprenda	escriba
hablemos	aprendamos	escribamos
hablen	aprendan	escriban

▶ The subjunctive endings are roughly the *reverse* of those in the indicative. The endings of **-ar** verbs begin with **-e**, while those of **-er** and **-ir** verbs begin with **-a**. The endings are added to the stem of the first person singular, which is the same as the stem of the infinitive for all regular verbs.

[4] For the **vosotros** present subjunctive forms, see the Appendix, section **1**.

You have already been exposed to the subjunctive forms in the third person because the **usted**, **ustedes** commands are identical to these forms. The negative familiar command also uses the subjunctive form (see section **37**).

▶ There is no one English equivalent for the Spanish subjunctive. Some of the possible translations are shown in the following examples.

1. Es mejor que ellos aprendan español. *It is better for them to learn Spanish (it is better that they [should] learn Spanish).*

2. Dudo que todo funcione fácilmente. *I doubt that everything will work out easily.*

3. Muchos padres están pidiendo que sus hijos estudien español. *Many parents are requesting that their children study Spanish.*

4. Esperamos que tú lo vendas.[5] *We hope that you will sell it (we hope that you are selling it).*

A • Substitution Drill

MODEL   Quieren que yo hable inglés y español.
              tú
STUDENT   Quieren que tú **hables** inglés y español.

1. Quieren que yo hable español e inglés.
   tú
   la Sra. Ramírez
   los Sres. Ramírez
   ellos
   Ud.

2. Es mejor que tú no lo escribas ahora.
   ella
   él
   él y ella
   él y yo
   nosotros

3. Espero que Juan lo venda.
   tú
   Juan y tú
   nosotros
   ellas
   la Sra. Rivera

4. Dudamos que Carlitos se levante a tiempo.
   Mónica y Carmen
   tú
   Uds.
   Ud.
   él

B • Query   Patterned Response

MODEL   ¿Canto?
STUDENT   **Sí, deseo que cantes.**

1. ¿Bailo?
2. ¿Estudio?
3. ¿Como?
4. ¿Voto?
5. ¿Abro?
6. ¿Lo escribo?
7. ¿Lo termino?
8. ¿La miro?
9. ¿Las escucho?
10. ¿Los ayudo?
11. ¿La aprendo?
12. ¿Los cierro?

[5] Object pronouns always precede verbs used in the subjunctive, in contrast to their position with affirmative commands: **¡Hágalo!** *Do it!* **Quiero que lo hagas.** *I want you to do it.*

C • Query   Patterned Response

MODEL   ¿Quiere Ud. escribirlo?
STUDENT   **No, prefiero que Ud. lo escriba.**

1. ¿Quiere Ud. comerlo?
2. ¿Quiere Ud. abrirlas?
3. ¿Quiere Ud. terminarlas?
4. ¿Quiere Ud. devolverlo?
5. ¿Quiere Ud. mirarlo?

6. ¿Quiere Ud. llevarlos?
7. ¿Quiere Ud. escribirla?
8. ¿Quiere Ud. arreglarlo?
9. ¿Quiere Ud. ganarlos?
10. ¿Quiere Ud. verlo?

D • Query   Patterned Response

MODEL   Don Ernesto, hágalo ahora.
STUDENT   **No, quiero que Ud. lo haga ahora.**

1. Doña Elena, baile un tango.
2. Sr. Rivera, revise las facturas.
3. Srta. Azuela, escriba sus nombres.
4. Dr. López, ayude al rector.

5. Señores, acepten las propuestas.
6. Compañeros, cómprenlas aquí.
7. Pepita, tráelos mañana.
8. Álvaro, véndeselo.

69   Irregular forms of the present subjunctive

I   Subjunctives formed from the irregular first person singular of the present indicative

Infinitive	Stem (from first person singular of the present)	Subjunctive Endings
conocer[6]	conozc-	
parecer[7]	parezc-	
producir[8]	produzc-	-a
tener[9]	teng-	-as
venir	veng-	-a
poner[10]	pong-	-amos
salir	salg-	-an
traer	traig-	
hacer[11]	hag-	
decir	dig-	
oír	oig-	
ver	ve-	

[6] The stem of complacer is formed similarly: **complacer, complazc-**.
[7] Most other **-ecer** verbs have the same feature: **merecer, merezc-; agradecer, agradezc-; ofrecer, ofrezc-**.
[8] All other **-ducir** verbs form the stem similarly, for example, **traducir, traduzc-; conducir, conduzc-; reducir, reduzc-**.
[9] Similarly, all other **-tener** verbs: **detener, retener**, etc.
[10] Similarly, all other **-poner** verbs: **componer, suponer**, etc.
[11] Similarly, **deshacer**.

▶ In these verbs the present subjunctive is based on the stem of the first person singular of the present indicative, which is not the same as the stem of the infinitive. The endings are regular.

II   Subjunctives of stem-changing verbs

Class I stem-changing verbs

-ar verbs		-er verbs	
pensar	**encontrar**	**entender**	**poder**
piense	encuentre	entienda	pueda
pienses	encuentres	entiendas	puedas
piense	encuentre	entienda	pueda
pensemos	encontremos	entendamos	podamos
piensen	encuentren	entiendan	puedan

▶ Class I verbs have the same stem changes in the present subjunctive as in the present indicative. The endings are regular.

Class II stem-changing verbs		Class III stem-changing verbs
sentir	**dormir**	**pedir**
sienta	duerma	pida
sientas	duermas	pidas
sienta	duerma	pida
sintamos	durmamos	pidamos
sientan	duerman	pidan

▶ Class II and Class III stem-changing verbs (which always end in **-ir**) have the same stem changes in the present subjunctive that they have in the present indicative throughout the singular and in the third person plural. In addition, Class II verbs change $e \rightarrow i$ or $o \rightarrow u$ in the first person plural; Class III verbs change $e \rightarrow i$ in this form also.

III   Irregular subjunctives not formed from the first person singular present indicative

dar	**estar**	**haber**	**ir**	**ser**	**saber**
dé	esté	haya	vaya	sea	sepa
des	estés	hayas	vayas	seas	sepas
dé	esté	haya	vaya	sea	sepa
demos	estemos	hayamos	vayamos	seamos	sepamos
den	estén	hayan	vayan	sean	sepan

▶ These verbs do not form the present subjunctive from the first person singular of the present indicative. Note the accents on **dé** and **esté, estés, estén**.

▶ **Haya,** *there is, there are, there be,* is the present subjunctive form for **hay**.
    Dudo que haya otra solución.   *I doubt that there is another solution.*
    Preferimos que haya más tiempo.   *We prefer that there be more time.*

A • Substitution Drill

MODEL   Es importante que yo venga a las seis.
              probable   tú
STUDENT   Es probable que tú **vengas** a las seis.

1. Es importante que yo venga a las seis.

probable	tú
necesario	él
posible	nosotros
imposible	ellos
asombroso	tú y yo

2. Espero que ella sepa hacerlo.

Espera	tú
Quieres	ellos
Quieren	Ud.
Duda	Uds.
Dudan	nosotros

3. Me alegro que Tere sea así.

Nos	Pancho y Tere
Te	nosotras
Se	Ud.
Nos	Uds.
Te	ella

4. Estoy asombrado que tú hagas eso.

Estamos	Uds.
Están	Carlos
Estoy	ellas
Estás	yo
Está	él y ella

5. Papá exige que nosotros durmamos más.

Nosotros	tú
Ud.	él
Yo	Tomasito
Su mamá	Tomasito e Iris
Tú	nosotros

6. Es importante que tú lo consigas.

probable	yo
posible	ella
increíble	él y yo
Conviene	ellas
Puede ser	nosotros

B • Transformation Drill   Present Indicative → Formal Command → Present Subjunctive

MODEL   (El Sr. Cebollero no viene aquí.)
STUDENT 1 **Sr. Cebollero, venga Ud. aquí.**
STUDENT 2 **Sr. Cebollero, prefiero que Ud. venga aquí.**

1. (El Sr. Cebollero no produce resultados.)
2. (El Dr. López no trae los libros.)
3. (Don Agapito no está listo.)
4. (El Sr. Ramírez no tiene cuidado.)
5. (Don Ernesto no va a la oficina.)
6. (Diego y Laura no se lo dan.)
7. (Rafa y Juana no lo ponen allí.)
8. (Felipe y Cecilia no la ven.)
9. (Los Sres. Azuela no lo dicen.)
10. (Los Sres. Zamora no las traen.)

C • Query   Patterned Response

MODEL   ¿Lo hacemos?
STUDENT   **Sí, quiero que lo hagan.**

1. ¿Lo traemos?
2. ¿Nos dormimos?
3. ¿La seguimos?

4. ¿Nos vamos?
5. ¿Lo producimos?
6. ¿Nos divertimos?

7. ¿Le decimos?
8. ¿Nos despedimos?
9. ¿Lo conseguimos?

to here   22 mAYo 79   to here   2 OCT 79

70 General view of the subjunctive

The Subjunctive in English

▶ The subjunctive is more widely used in English than is often realized. The reason why it is difficult to detect is because its forms differ from the indicative only in the third person singular and in certain irregular verbs. In addition English often uses the auxiliaries *may*, *might*, or *should* instead of a subjunctive form. Here are its common uses.

I Indirect or implied command
It appears regularly after certain verbs of wanting, suggesting, requesting, commanding, and telling (to do or not do something).

1. It is important that you *be* here on time (rather than, you *are* here on time).
2. The boss insisted that she *do* the work (rather than, she *does* the work).
3. She should demand that he *leave* at once (rather than, he *leaves* at once).

II Emotion
1. I wish I *were* on my vacation (rather than, I *am* on my vacation, or I *was* on my vacation).
2. (I hope that . . .) God *be* praised (rather than, God *is* praised).

III Unreality (*in a grammatical sense*[12])
Doubt, uncertainty
1. It is possible that they *may* come (rather than, they *are* coming).
2. It is incredible that you *should* do such a thing (rather than, you *are doing* such a thing).

Indefinite future
3. Come what *may* (rather than, come what *will*).
4. We are telling you this so that you *may* be prepared (rather than, *are* prepared).

Conditions contrary to fact
5. If I *were* rich (but I'm not) I would go to Acapulco (rather than, I *am* rich).

---

[12] By "unreality in a grammatical sense" we mean expressions that deny or cast doubt on something, that refer to an uncertain future or that grammatically express a condition contrary to fact. Do not confuse this type of unreality with the matter of the speaker being right or wrong. For example, if we say, "We are certain that they are coming," but it's untrue, the sentence is still in the indicative. However, "It is possible that they may come" is in the subjunctive because it casts doubt.

The Subjunctive in Spanish

▶ These concepts—indirect or implied command, emotion, unreality—are precisely the concepts of the subjunctive in Spanish as well.

I Indirect or Implied Command

When someone is addressed directly and given an order, we have a direct command. (The subjunctive endings are used for the **Ud., Uds.** commands and for the negative **tú** command.)

Hazlo. No lo hagas.	*Do it! Don't do it!*
Dígamelo Ud. No me lo diga Ud.	*Tell it to me. Don't tell it to me.*

When an order is not given directly but is incorporated into a request or an expression of a person's will, we have an indirect or implied command. The actions commanded are found in subordinate clauses. A subordinate clause has its own subject and verb that fit into and become part of a larger structure. The force of the command, no matter how weak or strong, causes the verb in the subordinate clause to be formed in the subjunctive.

Te mando que lo hagas.[13]	*I order you to do it.*
Es necesario que ellos aprendan el inglés y el español.	*It is necessary that they learn English and Spanish.*
Preferimos que Ud. lo traiga mañana.	*We prefer that you bring it tomorrow.*

In the preceding sentences, the force of command in **mando**, **es necesario**, and **preferimos** causes the verbs in the subordinate clauses (**hacer, aprender, traer**) to be in the subjunctive.

II Emotion

When the main clause expresses emotions such as hope, fear, pleasure, surprise, pity, regret, sorrow, etc., the depth of the emotion that is expressed causes the verb in the subordinate clause to be formed in the subjunctive.

Es lástima que no sepas hablar dos lenguas.	*It's a shame that you don't know how to speak two languages.*
Estamos asombrados que el Dr. López no esté aquí.	*We are surprised that Dr. Lopez is not here.*
Espero que podamos vender estos trastes.	*I hope that we will be able to sell these contraptions.*

In these sentences, the depth of emotion in **es lástima, estamos asombrados**, and **espero** causes the verbs in the subordinate clauses (**saber, estar, poder**) to be in the subjunctive.

---

[13] The indirect object pronoun in the main clause is often the antecedent of the subject in the subordinate clause. This is a common construction in Spanish.

III   Unreality (*in a grammatical sense*)

The subjunctive reflects that which is doubtful, uncertain, indefinite, unfulfilled, or denied in the main clause. The sense of unreality will cause the verb in the subordinate clause to be formed in the subjunctive.

Dudo que todo funcione fácilmente.	*I doubt that everything will work easily.*
No creo que mis hijos pierdan su cultura hispana.	*I don't believe that my children will lose their Hispanic culture.*
Puede ser que pongan a todos los hispanos en clases especiales.	*It might be that they will place all the Hispanic students in special classes.*
No es verdad que Ernesto estudie.	*It is not so that Ernesto studies.*
Negamos que el error sea importante.	*We deny that the error is important.*

In these sentences, the sense of unreality in **dudo, no creo, puede ser, no es verdad,** and **negamos** causes the verbs in the subordinate clauses (**funcionar, perder, poner, estudiar, ser**) to be in the subjunctive.

71   Indicative versus subjunctive in noun clauses

▶ As we stated earlier, subordinate clauses have a subject and verb separate from the main clause. One type of subordinate clause, the noun clause, occupies the same place that might be occupied by a noun or pronoun. For example, "I insist on it" may be expanded

SUBJ. VERB

to "I insist that you be here on time." The segment, "that you be here on time" is a noun clause and the object of the main verb, *insist* .

▶ In Spanish, the verb in the noun clause may be formed in the indicative or in the subjunctive. Whether the subordinate verb will be in the subjunctive or the indicative depends on the nature of the main verb or on the nature of an impersonal expression using **ser** (+ predicate adjective). If the main verb is used to express

      I   Indirect or Implied Command
     II   Emotion
   III   Unreality

the force of any one of those concepts will cause the subordinate verb to be formed in the subjunctive. If none of those concepts is expressed in the main verb or the impersonal expression, then the subordinate verb will be in the indicative.

	Noun Clause in the Subjunctive		*Noun Clause in the Indicative*
Indirect Command	1. Preferimos que Álvaro venga mañana. *We prefer that Álvaro come tomorrow.*	Fact	1. Sabemos que Álvaro viene mañana. *We know that Álvaro is coming tomorrow.*
	2. Es necesario que lo traigas. *It is necessary that you bring it (for you to bring it).*		2. Es evidente que lo traes. *It is evident that you are bringing it (that you have it with you).*
Emotion	3. Sienten que Miguel no esté. *They regret that Miguel is not here.*	Fact	3. Saben que Miguel no está. *They know that Miguel is not here.*
	4. Es lástima que viva lejos. *It's a shame that he lives far away.*		4. Es verdad que vive lejos. *It is true that he lives far away.*
Unreality	5. No creo que todo vaya muy bien. *I don't believe everything is going well.*	Fact	5. Creo que todo va muy bien. *I believe that everything is going well.*
	6. Puede ser que salgan pronto. *It may be that they are leaving soon.*		6. Es que salen pronto. *The fact is that they are leaving soon.*

Subjunctive Versus Indicative
Matched Pairs

Why does one sentence take the indicative and the other take the subjunctive? The pictures provide the clues!

1. Papá insiste que Paco estudie mucho.

   Father insists that Paco study a lot.

1. Papá insiste que Paco estudia mucho.

   Father insists that Paco studies a lot.

2. No creemos que la eduación bilingüe sea lo mejor para nuestros hijos.

We don't think that bilingual education is the best thing for our children.

2. Creemos que la educación bilingüe es lo mejor para nuestros hijos.

We think that bilingual education is the best thing for our children.

▶ As stated earlier, the Spanish subjunctive has various translations in English. The possibilities include the present; the future; an auxiliary verb such as *may*, *might*, or *should*; the infinitive; and the *-ing* form.

Quieren que estemos a las tres.   *They want (for) us to be there at three.*
  They want that we be there at three.

Dudo que venga.   *I doubt that he is coming.*
  I doubt that he will come.

No me gusta que trabajes tanto.   *I don't like your working so much.*
  I don't like it that you work so much.

¡Cuidado!

Many constructions that take the infinitive in English take a noun clause in Spanish. Be careful of literal translations from English to Spanish!

	Unacceptable	**Correct**
We want you to come with us.	Queremos usted venir con nosotros.	Queremos que usted venga con nosotros.
We know him to be a good person.	Lo sabemos ser una buena persona.	Sabemos que es una buena persona.
Dad says to Carlos to go to the store.	Papá le dice a Carlos ir a la tienda.	Papá le dice a Carlos que vaya a la tienda.

▶ In order to have a noun clause in the subjunctive in Spanish, it usually is necessary that there be a change of subject. If there is no change of subject the verb will generally take the infinitive.[14]

1.	Tú quieres que esperemos.	*You want us to wait* *(that we wait).*	(change of subject: you → we)
	Tú quieres esperar.	*You want to wait.*	(no change of subject)
2.	Queremos que Ud. lo haga.	*We want you to do it.*	(change of subject: we → you)
	Queremos hacerlo.	*We want to do it.*	(no change of subject)

A • Transformation Drill   Infinitive → Subordinate Clause in Subjunctive

MODEL   Prefiero hacerlo.   (que tú)
STUDENT   Prefiero **que tú lo hagas.**

1. Prefiero hacerlo.   (que él)
2. Dudamos poder ir.   (que tú)
3. Es necesario esperar.   (que ellos)
4. Siento no tenerlos.   (que Ud.)
5. Esperan volver algún día.   (que yo)
6. Niego estar allí. (que el Sr. López)
7. Es importante estudiar mucho.   (que nosotros)
8. Me gusta cantar guantanameras.   (que tú)
9. Tienen miedo de ir.   (que Ud.)
10. Es importante hacerlo bien.   (que ellas)

B • Variable Substitution Drill

IP   SUBJECT

MODEL   Te dice que no seas así.
              Nos
STUDENT   Nos dice que no **seamos** así.

1. Nos dice que no seamos así.
   Me
              seas
   Le
              seamos
   Les

2. Me piden que vaya a Bolivia.
   Le
              vayas
   Nos
              vayan
   Me

3. ¿Me exiges que lo haga ahora?
   ¿Nos
              hagas
   ¿Me
              hagan
   ¿Le

4. Le escribe que venga el martes.
              vengas
   Les
              vengamos
   Me
              vengan

---

[14] There are some exceptions to this rule, but they are rare:
     Dudo que pueda ir.   *I doubt I can go.*   **Espero que pueda verla.**   *I hope that I may see her.*
Even the exceptions can generally take the infinitive: **Dudo poder ir. Espero poder verla.**

C • Replacement Drill

Change each of the subordinate clauses to the subjunctive or the indicative, as required by the main clause.

MODEL   Es evidente que Mónica es bonita.
No es verdad
STUDENT   No es verdad que Mónica **sea** bonita.
MODEL   Es verdad
STUDENT   Es verdad que Mónica **es** bonita.

1. Es evidente que Mónica es bonita.
Es claro
Es imposible
Dudo
Puede ser
Es cierto

2. Me gusta que tú estés aprendiendo eso.
No me gusta
Espero
Sé
Prefiero
Es importante

3. Tenemos miedo que Juan pierda su cultura.
Es lástima
Es evidente
Me doy cuenta de
Es verdad
Creo

4. Creen que el Dr. López tiene razón.
No creen
Saben
Es probable
Dudan
Esperan

D • Query   Free Response

Answer in Spanish.

1. ¿Insiste tu profesor que llegues a clase a tiempo?
2. ¿Es necesario que estudiemos mucho para aprender el español?
3. ¿Desea Ud. que sus hijos aprendan el español y el inglés?
4. ¿Es importante que haya clases de español todos los días?
5. ¿Prefiere Ud. que le traigan cerveza con la comida o agua?
6. ¿Tiene Ud. miedo que la clase de español sea demasiado difícil?
7. ¿Le gusta a Ud. que sus clases sean muy fáciles?
8. ¿Quiere Ud. que el profesor siempre (nunca) le dé tarea?
9. ¿Es lástima que no tengas mucho dinero?
10. ¿Es posible que vayas a la luna uno de estos días?

E • Translation Drill

Translate into Spanish.

1. Do it! I want you to do it! Bring it! We hope that you will bring it.
2. They prefer to write it. They prefer that you write it.
3. It's important to study. It's important that we study.
4. I know he's here. I believe he's here. I doubt he's here. I'm afraid he's here.
5. She tells her brother to be home at six. She says that her brother is home at six.

72 Verbs with changes in spelling in the preterit and in the present subjunctive

▶ A general spelling rule in Spanish is that

c, to maintain a hard sound, changes to **qu** before **e** or **i**

g, to maintain a hard sound, changes to **gu** before **e** or **i**

z changes to **c** before **e** or **i**

This spelling rule affects the first person singular preterit of all **-car, -gar,** and **-zar** verbs.

buscar	**llegar**	**empezar**
busqué	llegué	empecé
buscaste	llegaste	empezaste
buscó	llegó	empezó
buscamos	llegamos	empezamos
buscaron	llegaron	empezaron

Similarly, all forms of the present subjunctive reflect the spelling change.

buscar	**llegar**	**empezar**
busque	llegue	empiece
busques	llegues	empieces
busque	llegue	empiece
busquemos	lleguemos	empecemos
busquen	lleguen	empiecen

▶ These same rules affect nouns. For example:

el lápiz	*the pencil*	los lápices	*the pencils*
la luz	*the light*	las luces	*the lights*
la cruz	*the cross*	las cruces	*the crosses*
el chico, la chica	*the boy, the girl,* *the youngster*	el chiquillo, la chiquilla	*the youngster* (more affectionate than **el chico, la chica**)
amigo	*friend*	amiguito	*dear friend*

Oral Practice

Read out loud.

Command (*subjunctive form*)	Indicative
1. Búsquelo.	1. Ya lo busqué.
2. Llegue pronto.	2. Ya llegué.
3. Empiece ahora.	3. Ya empecé.
4. Niéguelo.	4. Ya lo negué.

5. Explíquela.
6. Indíquenoslo.
7. Juegue conmigo.
8. Practíquelo más.

5. Ya la expliqué.
6. Ya se lo indiqué.
7. No, ya jugué.
8. ¡Pero ya practiqué!

A • Substitution Drill

MODEL   ¿Quieres que yo lo busque?
                    él
STUDENT ¿Quieres que él lo **busque**?

1. ¿Quieres que yo lo busque?
        él
        ellos
        nosotros
        ella
        yo

2. Yo indiqué que eso no estaba bien.
        Tú
        Él
        Ella
        Nosotros
        Yo

3. El Dr. López manda que tú empieces.
        ella
        nosotros
        yo
        Ud.
        Uds.

4. Carlos empezó la composición.
        Yo
        Tú
        Ella
        Ellos
        Nosotros

5. Es que Carlos llegó anoche.
        yo
        Rogelio
        tú
        ellos
        Ud.

6. Es importante que nosotros juguemos con él.
        tú
        yo
        tú y yo
        él y ella
        él y yo

B • Query   Patterned Response

MODEL   ¿Explicó Ud. la lección?
STUDENT **Sí, lo expliqué ayer.**

1. ¿Jugó Ud. el partido?
2. ¿Empezó Ud. la tarea?
3. ¿Buscó Ud. los lápices?
4. ¿Explicó Ud. su situación?
5. ¿Indicó Ud. su decisión?
6. ¿Practicaste las canciones?
7. ¿Empezaste a comer?
8. ¿Explicaste las nociones básicas?

C • Query   Patterned Response

MODEL   ¿Quieres buscarlo?
STUDENT **No, es mejor que tú lo busques.**

1. ¿Quieres buscarlo?
2. ¿Quieres empezarlo?
3. ¿Quieres indicarlo?
4. ¿Quieres jugarlo?
5. ¿Quieres practicarla?
6. ¿Quieres explicarlo?

D • Transformation Drill   Familiar Command → Formal Command

MODEL   Practícalo.
STUDENT   **Practíquelo Ud.**

1. Empiézalos.
2. Indícamelos.
3. Juégala.

4. Niégalo.
5. Explícamela.
6. Búscalas.

REVIEW

I The following questions are related to the dialog. Answer in Spanish.

1. ¿Prefiere la Sra. Ramírez que sus hijos sólo estudien el inglés o que estudien tanto el inglés como el español?
2. ¿Por qué llaman al programa, "educación bilingüe-bicultural"?
3. ¿Quién hablaba inglés y español a la perfección?
4. ¿Tiene miedo la Sra. Ramírez de que pongan a sus hijos en clases segregadas?
5. ¿Por qué muchos padres norteamericanos piden que sus hijos estudien y aprendan el español?
6. ¿Podía entender el Dr. López los modos de pensar norteamericanos tan bien como los modos de pensar hispanos?
7. ¿Por qué es necesario que los norteamericanos y los hispanos se entiendan mejor?
8. ¿Por qué es necesario que todos nos entendamos mejor?

II Translation. Translate into Spanish.

1. Don't deny it! You think that bilingual education is a pretext to segregate Hispanic youngsters.
2. You are right. I used to think that way. But yesterday I met Dr. López; she is the director of the program.
3. She does not believe that it is good for our children to lose[15] their Hispanic culture.
4. Yes, but it is better that they learn English immediately because it is the official language here.
5. No, it is necessary that there be English as well as Spanish in this city.
6. It is important that Americans and Hispanos understand each other better!
7. I hope that you are right. Nevertheless, I doubt that everything will work out (function) so easily.
8. Don't worry. With bilingual-bicultural education, our children are going to understand Hispanic as well as American ways of thinking.

---

[15] Either an infinitive or a second noun clause in the subjunctive may be used for *to lose*.

III Guided Composition

Why are you studying Spanish? Do you think learning another language is useful? Can bilingual-bicultural education be successful?

Cognates & Contexts

La educación bilingüe en los Estados Unidos

¿Qué es la educación bilingüe? La contestación a esta pregunta es un poco difícil porque hoy día en realidad hay por lo menos tres versiones de educación bilingüe en los Estados Unidos. El hecho es que en 1974 la Corte Suprema exigió la educación bilingüe para enseñar a aquellos niños que no conocían el inglés. Por lo tanto la educación bilingüe pasó a ser un derecho civil para diversas minorías lingüísticas como los hispanos, los chinos, los indios norteamericanos y otros grupos. Sin embargo, la Corte Suprema no especificó el tipo de educación bilingüe.

contestación *answer*

hoy día *nowadays*

hecho *fact*

enseñar *to teach*

Una versión de la educación bilingüe es enseñar a los estudiantes minoritarios en la lengua nativa hasta cierto punto. Cuando ya saben inglés, no reciben más instrucción en su lengua nativa. La mayor parte de los educadores piensan que esta versión es inferior porque el resultado es que los niños pierden el conocimiento de su lengua original. Sin embargo, a muchos administradores les gusta porque cuesta poco.

Otra versión es no suprimir la lengua nativa. En este programa los estudiantes aprenden durante toda su carrera estudiantil tanto en la lengua nativa como en el inglés. Así logran dominar dos lenguas en vez de una. Claro que este tipo de programa cuesta más que el primero.

suprimir *to eliminate*

carrera *career*

El programa más costoso y más idealista es la versión recíproca. Aquí tanto los estudiantes monolingües de habla inglesa como los estudiantes minoritarios reciben instrucción bilingüe. El resultado de este programa es que todos los estudiantes aprenden dos lenguas y llegan a entender las dos culturas que se asocian con esas lenguas.

de habla inglesa *English-speaking*

29 mayo 79

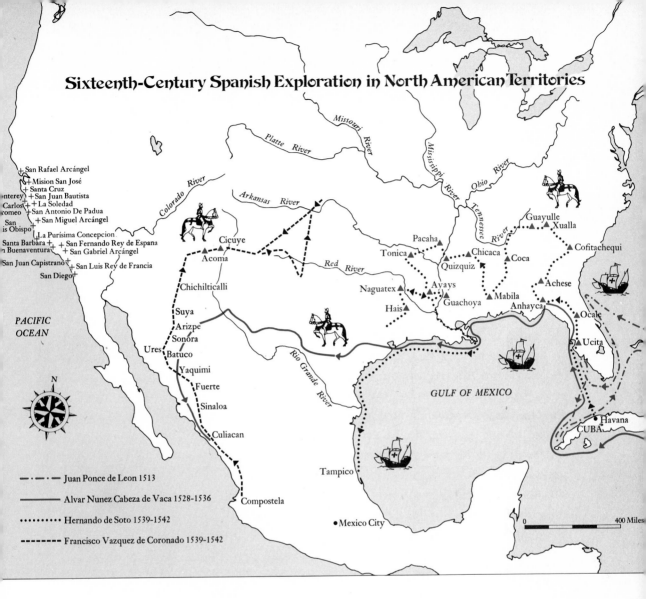

Sixteenth-Century Spanish Exploration in North American Territories

San Rafael Arcángel
Mision San José
Santa Cruz
San Juan Bautista
La Soledad
San Antonio De Padua
San Miguel Arcángel
La Purísima Concepcion
San Fernando Rey de Espana
San Gabriel Arcángel
San Luis Rey de Francia
San Juan Capistrano
San Diego

Monterey
Carlos
romeo
San
is Obispo
Santa Barbara
n Buenaventura

PACIFIC
OCEAN

Colorado River
Platte River
Missouri River
Mississippi River
Ohio River
Tennessee River
Arkansas River
Red River
Rio Grande River

Cicuye
Acoma
Chichilticalli
Suya
Arizpe
Sonora
Batuco
Yaquimi
Fuerte
Sinaloa
Culiacan
Ures

Pacaha
Tonica
Quizquiz
Chicaca
Coca
Naguatex
Avays
Hais
Guachoya
Mabila
Anhayca
Guayulle
Xualla
Cofitachequi
Achese
Ocale
Ucita

GULF OF MEXICO

Havana
CUBA

Tampico

●Mexico City

Compostela

–·–· Juan Ponce de Leon 1513
––––– Alvar Nunez Cabeza de Vaca 1528-1536
········· Hernando de Soto 1539-1542
– – – – Francisco Vazquez de Coronado 1539-1542

0   400 Miles

Lección dieciséis

Lectura y estudio

EL MUNDO HISPANO EN LOS ESTADOS UNIDOS

La idea del crisol de razas tuvo mucha popularidad en los Estados Unidos a principios de siglo. Se consideraba a este país como un gran calderón que aceptaba todas las razas, todos los credos y todas las nacionalidades para crear un producto que tenía el mérito de ser, sobre todo, americano.

Hoy día esta idea se está rechazando más y más. La sociedad americana sigue compuesta de una gran variedad de culturas y procedencias nacionales, pero cada una mantiene ciertas características que resisten la amalgamación. Según este modo de pensar, la riqueza cultural de los Estados Unidos reside precisamente en las diferencias y no en el anonimato de la colectividad.

La tradición hispana ha dejado una gran huella en este país. Los españoles cruzaron el continente americano siglos antes de la declaración de independencia estadounidense y casi un siglo antes de la llegada del Mayflower. En 1512 Juan Ponce de León atravesó el estrecho al norte de Cuba y llegó a una tierra que llamó La Florida. Según la leyenda, descubrió la Fuente de la Juventud en lo que hoy es San Agustín. Álvar Núñez Cabeza de Vaca partió de

crisol de razas *melting pot*

a principios de *at the beginning of*

calderón *cauldron*

rechazar *to reject*

procedencia *origin*

según *according to*

riqueza *wealth*

ha dejado *has left* **huella** *imprint, mark*

estadounidense *United States* (adj.), *American*

atravesar *to cross* **estrecho** *strait*

partir *to leave*

La Florida con un séquito de hombres y viajó hasta la parte occidental del continente. Este viaje tuvo lugar entre 1528 y 1536. Muchos frailes españoles, acompañando a exploradores como Cabeza de Vaca o a los conquistadores de México, establecieron numerosas misiones en el suroeste del país, algunas de las cuales siguen en existencia.

Pero esas raíces hispanas se han extendido, especialmente durante este siglo cuando la mobilidad social, la facilidad de transporte y las dificultades políticas han dado impulso a la inmigración. Muchos mexicanos cruzaron las fronteras de los estados del suroeste, uniéndose a otros cuyos antepasados se quedaron en esos estados cuando se declararon independientes de México. Así nació el chicano (palabra quizás derivada de *mexicano*), de tradición indio-mexicana.

El Caribe también contribuye a la cultura hispana en los Estados Unidos. Hay una numerosa población puertorriqueña, sobre todo en los barrios de Nueva York. Más recientemente, muchos cubanos y dominicanos se han establecido en el este del país.

Hay una reducida población vasca que vive

séquito *retinue*

frailes *priests, friars*

de las cuales *of which*

raíces *roots* **se han extendido** *have extended themselves*

han dado impulso *have stimulated*

fronteras *borders*

cuyos *whose* **antepasados** *ancestors*

nacer *to be born*

población *population*

barrios *neighborhoods*

se han establecido *have established themselves* **el este** *the east*
vasca *Basque*

mayormente en los estados de Nevada, Montana, Wyoming y los Dakotas. Algunos siguen la ocupación tradicional de sus antepasados españoles: pastores de ovejas.

Otros países de la América Central y del Sur también tienen su representación en los Estados Unidos. Basta dar un paseo por las grandes ciudades del país para encontrar un restaurante argentino o colombiano, testimonio de una presencia hispana en el interior.

El aporte de todas estas nacionalidades a la cultura americana es muy grande: la música del Caribe influye en muchos ritmos contemporáneos, las literaturas chicana y boricua están encontrando amplia lectura, el fenómeno de la educación bilingüe se debe en gran medida a la insistencia por parte de padres hispanos en conservar su lengua y su cultura para sus hijos, y muchos de los mayores deleites gastronómicos a través del país son de procedencia hispana.

El mundo hispano en los Estados Unidos es de una enorme variedad. Representa, a la vez, diferentes influencias que han contribuido a dar a sus componentes una personalidad única.

mayormente *principally*

pastores de ovejas *shepherds*

basta *it suffices*

testimonio *evidence*

aporte *contribution*

influir *to influence*
amplia *wide, wide-spread*

medida *measure*

deleites *delights*
a través de *throughout*

Coffee shop and bakery, Miami, Florida

VOCABULARY STUDY

The following words have additional meanings or forms besides those already given in the dialogs.

antiguo   ancient; *former* (when it precedes the noun. See section **76**).

    El Sr. Pérez es mi antiguo profesor.   *Mr. Pérez is my former professor.*

asegurar   to assure; *to insure*

el centro   the center; *downtown*

    ¿Vienes al centro conmigo?   *Are you coming downtown with me?*

entenderse   to understand one another; *to come to an agreement; to get along*

    Los dos chiquillos se entienden bien.   *The two youngsters get along well.*

    Los ministros se entiendieron con el presidente sobre la propuesta.   *The ministers came to an agreement with the president about the proposal.*

descubrir   to discover; *to uncover; to disclose*

    Me descubrió el secreto.   *He disclosed the secret to me.*

lograr   to manage (+ infinitive); *to attain, achieve*

    Logramos lo que queríamos.   *We achieved what we wanted.*

oficial   official; *officer*

perdido   lost

  pérdida   *loss*

presentar   to produce; to present; *to introduce*

recordar (ue)   to remember; *to remind, call to mind*

servir (i, i)   to serve

  servir para   *to be good for*

    Ese traste no sirve para nada.   *That contraption isn't good for anything.*

tener paciencia   to be patient

  paciente   *patient* (adjective and noun)

modo   way

  moda   *fashion*

The following verbs take a preposition before an object.

despedirse (de)   *to take leave (of), say goodbye (to someone)*

tener cuidado (con)   *to be careful (with)*

tener ganas (de)   *to be anxious (+ infinitive)*

insistir (en)   *to insist (on)*

responder   *to answer*

  responder a   *to respond to, answer*

    ¡Responde a la pregunta!   *Respond to (answer) the question!*

The endings **-dor** and **-tor** often indicate the person engaged in the action expressed by the verb they derive from. What are the meanings of the following nouns?

conquistador	bailador	ganador	conductor
explorador	descubridor	conocedor	traductor
jugador	gobernador	director	productor

¡Cuidado!

> **el año pasado** (not **el año último**)   *last year*
> **suceder**   *to happen* (not *to succeed*)
> *la* **labor**   another exception to the **-or** masculine ending
> **cada día**   *each day*
> **todos los días**   *every day*

A • Substitution Drill

Rewrite the sentences, using a synonym of the underlined word or expression.

1. El español es un <u>idioma</u> fácil.
2. Nachito es un <u>chiquillo</u> atroz.
3. Iris y yo nos vemos <u>con frecuencia</u>.
4. Esas dos personas no pueden <u>comprenderse</u>.
5. Nunca sé qué <u>responder</u> en esas situaciones.

Now give the antonym for the underlined word or expression.

6. En esta casa siempre hace <u>frío</u>.
7. Quiero <u>olvidar</u> su nombre pero no puedo.
8. ¿Quieres <u>deshacer</u> esa labor?
9. ¿Por qué te <u>caíste</u> tanto?
10. Hace un día muy <u>hermoso</u>.

B • Complete each sentence with a suitable word or phrase from the list. The words are to be used in the form in which they appear.

el año pasado	juntas
En aquel entonces	por casualidad
Durante	a menudo
El otro día	antigua
sabelotodo	Resulta

1. _____ _____ _____ me encontré _____ _____ con Rosario, una _____ compañera de clase.
2. _____ siete años estuvimos _____ en una escuela de San Francisco.

3. _____ _____ _____ la llamábamos la _____.
4. Hacía muchos años que no nos veíamos aunque hasta _____ _____ _____ nos escribíamos _____ _____.
5. _____ que perdí su dirección y no pude seguir la correspondencia.

<table>
<tr><td>descarada</td><td>tenía ganas de</td></tr>
<tr><td>nos divertimos</td><td>suya</td></tr>
<tr><td>recordó</td><td>asombradas</td></tr>
<tr><td>castigó</td><td>recordar</td></tr>
<tr><td>Anteayer</td><td>chistes</td></tr>
</table>

6. ¡Imagínate cómo estábamos _____ de vernos de nuevo!
7. Yo _____ _____ _____ pasar un rato con ella y _____ los viejos tiempos.
8. _____ vino a casa y _____ _____ muchísimo.
9. Me _____ la vez que nuestro profesor me _____ porque Rosario me contaba _____ y yo reía.
10. ¡Esa _____ nunca admitió que la culpa era _____.

<table>
<tr><td>lenguas</td><td>es cuestión de</td></tr>
<tr><td>De vez en cuando</td><td>agradables</td></tr>
<tr><td>logré</td><td>a la perfección</td></tr>
<tr><td>gran</td><td>ciudad</td></tr>
<tr><td>Puede ser que</td><td>verano</td></tr>
</table>

11. _____ _____ _____ _____ ella me ayudaba con la tarea.
12. Ella hablaba dos _____ extranjeras, el francés y el italiano, _____ _____ _____.
13. Pero eso _____ _____ _____ talento y yo nunca _____ ser una _____ estudiante de lenguas.
14. _____ _____ _____ Rosario venga a vivir a esta _____ el _____ que viene.
15. ¡Entonces sí que vamos a pasar momentos _____!

C • Query   Free Response

Treat exercise B as a narrative and answer the following questions in Spanish.

1. ¿Con quién se encuentra la persona que narra?
2. ¿De dónde se conocen las dos muchachas?
3. ¿Se veían a menudo? ¿Por qué?
4. ¿Qué hicieron las dos compañeras en casa?
5. ¿Por qué no castigó el profesor a Rosario?
6. ¿Por qué ayudaba Rosario con la tarea?
7. ¿Cuándo puede ser que Rosario venga a vivir a esta ciudad?
8. ¿Cómo sabemos que la persona que cuenta el relato es mujer?

D • In the previous three lessons you learned many expressions using **tener** + noun. Complete the following sentences in any way that makes sense in Spanish.

1. ¡Ten cuidado con _____!
2. Cuando tengo hambre _____.
3. Hoy tengo ganas de _____.
4. Hay que tener paciencia para _____.
5. Siempre tengo prisa cuando _____.
6. Nunca tengo suerte _____.

Complete the following sentences with an expression using **tener**.

7. Los niños no quieren comer; no _____.
8. Marta no quiere salir esta noche porque _____.
9. Si tú _____, puedes tomar un refresco.
10. Me pongo el abrigo porque _____.
11. Ellos no _____; la respuesta es incorrecta.
12. El bandido no _____ de la policía.

E • You also learned many ways to express weather conditions. Match the sentences on the left with appropriate expressions on the right.

1. Cuando hay nubes en el cielo _____.   está nublado
2. Cuando no hay nubes en el cielo _____.   hace fresco
3. Siempre estoy constipado cuando _____.   hace buen tiempo
4. Me gusta jugar al fútbol cuando _____.   hace viento
5. No podemos jugar bien al tenis cuando _____. hay sol
6. Hace mucho calor cuando _____.   está despejado

Rompecabezas

Se portetanim uqe danapren NIEB le tisubjunvo.

ES IMPORTANTE
QUÉ APRENDEN BIEN EL SUBJUNTIVO,

GRAMMAR: SELF-TESTING

Cover the right side of the page and try to answer the questions in the left margin.

VERBS

What are the two simple past tenses in the indicative?

What are the imperfect tense endings for **-ar** verbs? For **-er**, **-ir** verbs?

I Simple Past Tenses: Indicative

Spanish has two simple past tenses, the imperfect and the preterit.

IMPERFECT   (*Section 55*)

	-ar verbs		**-er/-ir** verbs
	-aba		-ía
	-abas		-ías
habl- +	-aba	aprend- +	-ía
	-ábamos	escrib- +	-íamos
	-aban		-ían

There are only three verbs that are irregular in the imperfect indicative.

What is the imperfect indicative conjugation of **ver**? Of **ser**? Of **ir**? Are there any other verbs that are irregular in the imperfect indicative?

ver	**ser**	**ir**
veía	era	iba
veías	eras	ibas
veía	era	iba
veíamos	éramos	íbamos
veían	eran	iban

PRETERIT   (*Section 49*)

What are the preterit endings for regular verbs?

The preterit endings for regular verbs are

	-ar verbs		**-er/-ir** verbs
	-é		-í
	-aste		-iste
habl- +	-ó	aprend- +	-ió
	-amos	escrib- +	-imos
	-aron		-ieron

You have already learned the preterit conjugation for irregular verbs **dar**, **ser**, and **ir** (see section **50**).

Other verbs that are irregular in the preterit:

In what way are first and third person singular

Unstressed **-e/-o** endings (*Section 61*): first person singular endings sometimes irregular in the preterit? Are other endings irregular?

ends in unstressed **-e**; third person singular ends in unstressed **-o**; other endings are the same as those of regular **-er/-ir** verbs.

Conjugate **andar, tener,** and **estar** in the preterit. What vowel is characteristic of their stems?

-u- *stem*

andar	anduve, anduvo
tener	tuve, tuvo
estar	estuve, estuvo
poder	pude, pudo
poner	puse, puso
saber	supe, supo

Conjugate **querer** and **hacer** in the preterit. What stem vowel do we observe in them?

-i- *stem*

querer	quise, quiso
hacer	hice, hizo
venir	vine, vino

stem irregularities are maintained throughout the conjugation

What is the preterit conjugation of the verbs **traer** and **decir**?

-j- *stem* (the third person plural ending is **-eron**)

traer	trajeron
decir	dijeron (also **-i-** stem)
producir	produjeron

What are the preterit tense irregularities for **leer, oír,** and **caer**?

Change **i** → **y** in the endings of the third person singular and plural (*Section 61*):

leer	leyó	leyeron
caer(se)	cayó	cayeron
creer	creyó	creyeron
oír	oyó	oyeron
destruir	destruyó	destruyeron

(and other **-uir** verbs)

How are Class II and Class III stem-changing verbs irregular in the preterit?

Class II, III (**-ir** verbs) stem changes:

Class II **e** → **i**, **o** → **u** in the third person singular and plural

sentir	sintió	sintieron
dormir	durmió	durmieron

Class III **e** → **i** in the third person singular and plural

pedir	pidió	pidieron

PRETERIT VERSUS IMPERFECT (*Section 56*)

What are the differences in usage between the preterit and the imperfect?

The imperfect is *descriptive*; it describes past actions or conditions without any indication of termination or outcome.

Susana era mi mejor amiga.	*Susan was my best friend.*
Todos los días iba el cine.	*Every day I went to the movies.*
Rogelio estaba triste.	*Rogelio was sad.*

The preterit reports a sudden or completed action or condition, whatever its duration.

Mi hermano se cayó.	*My brother fell down.*
Ayer estudié por tres horas.	*Yesterday I studied for three hours.*

Which simple past tense is used to tell time in the past?

The imperfect of **ser** is used in telling time in the past.

Eran las seis. *It was six o'clock.*

Both tenses may be used together to express a situation in progress when another suddenly took place or was completed.

Estudiaba cuando llamaste. *I was studying when you called.*

What is the change in emphasis between the following sentences?
a. Ayer Marta estaba enferma.
b. Ayer Marta estuvo enferma.

Sometimes either the preterit or the imperfect may be used, depending on the intention of the speaker (see section **56**).

Ayer Marta estaba enferma.	The emphasis is on describing a condition.
Ayer Marta estuvo enferma.	The emphasis is on limiting the condition to a time frame: **ayer**.

How are the preterit and the imperfect expressed in the progressive?

Both the preterit and the imperfect can be expressed in the progressive form by using the auxiliary verb **estar**.

Estuve estudiando por tres horas.	*I was studying for three hours.* (The studying was completed at the end of three hours.)
Estábamos esperando tu llegada.	*We were awaiting your arrival.* (No indication of termination or outcome.)

The verb **hacer** is used in combination with the present, preterit, and imperfect to convey certain time relationships (*Section 59*).

What are the following two idioms used for?

a. **Hace** + time expression + **que** + present tense

b. **Hacía** + time expression + **que** + imperfect tense

Hace + time   expression + **que** + (present)   expresses   an action that began in the past and continues into the present.

Hace tres horas que estudio.   *I have been studying for three hours.*

Hacía + time   expression + **que** + (imperfect)   expresses   an action that took place for a period of time in the past.

Hacía tres horas que estudiaba cuando llamaste.   *I had been studying for three hours when you called.*

How is the idea of *ago* expressed in Spanish?

Hace + time expression + **que** + preterit tense expresses an action that was completed a period of time ago.

Hace dos horas que llamaste.   *You called two hours ago.*

II   Present Subjunctive

CONJUGATION OF REGULAR VERBS   (*Section 68*)

	-ar verbs		**-er/-ir** verbs
	-e		-a
	-es		-as
habl- +	-e	aprend- +	-a
	-emos	escrib- +	-amos
	-en		-an

What are the present subjunctive endings for **-ar** verbs? For **-er/-ir** verbs?

CONJUGATION OF IRREGULAR VERBS   (*Section 69*)

Because the present subjunctive stem is taken from the first person singular of the present indicative, there are some irregularities.

a. Subjunctives taken from verbs that are irregular in the first person singular form of the present indicative.

What are the irregularities of **conocer**, **salir**, and **oír** in the present subjunctive?

conocer	conozco	conozca, etc.
tener	tengo	tenga
poner	pongo	ponga
salir	salgo	salga
traer	traigo	traiga
hacer	hago	haga
decir	digo	diga
oír	oigo	oiga

<table>
<tr><td>

What is the present
subjunctive of **dar**?
Of **estar**? Of **haber**?
Of **ir**? Of **ser**? Of
saber?

</td></tr>
</table>

b. Irregular subjunctives not formed from the first person
singular of the present indicative.

dar	estar	haber	ir	ser	saber
dé	esté	haya	vaya	sea	sepa
des	estés	hayas	vayas	seas	sepas
dé	esté	haya	vaya	sea	sepa
demos	estemos	hayamos	vayamos	seamos	sepamos
den	estén	hayan	vayan	sean	sepan

USES OF THE SUBJUNCTIVE   (*Section 70*)

The subjunctive is used in subordinate clauses after expressions of

When is the subjunctive
used in subordinate
clauses?

    a. indirect or implied command.

    b. emotion.

    c. unreality (doubt, uncertainty, indefinite future, conditions
           contrary to fact).

Noun clauses are one type of subordinate clause.

When will the verb in a
noun clause be expressed
in the subjunctive?

The use of the subjunctive in a noun clause depends on the
nature of the main clause (*Section 71*). If the main clause
expresses an indirect command, emotion, or unreality, the verb
in the noun clause will be expressed in the subjunctive.

Queremos que vengas con nosotros.   *We want you to*
come with us.

Es lástima que no tengamos más   *It is a shame that*
tiempo.   *we don't have more*
time.

Puede ser que salgan temprano.   *It is possible that*
they will leave
early.

When will the verb in the
noun clause be in the
indicative?

If the main clause doesn't express any of the above concepts
the indicative will be used in the subordinate noun clause.

Yo sé que estás cansado.   *I know you are tired.*

How will the second
verb appear if there
is no change of subject
between the main and
the subordinate clause?

Also, for a subjunctive to be used, it is generally necessary
that there be a change of subject between the main clause and
the noun clause. If there is no change of subject, the second
verb will generally appear in the infinitive form, thus elimi-
nating the noun clause.

Tú quieres que lo hagamos.   *You want us to do it.*

Tú quieres hacerlo.   *You want to do it.*

What are the stem
changes in Class I
verbs?
What are the stem
changes in Class II
verbs?

III Summary of Stem-Changing Verbs

Class I (**-ar, -er** verbs) (*Section 31*)

e → ie, o → ue, in the present indicative and subjunctive
when stressed: **pensar, volver**

Class II (**-ir** verbs) (*Section 67*)

e → ie, o → ue, in the present indicative and subjunctive
when stressed; in addition **e → i, o → u**, in the third person
singular and plural of the preterit, the first person plural of
the present subjunctive, and in the present participle.

	Present Indicative	Preterit	Present Subjunctive	Present Participle
	siento	sentí	sienta	sintiendo
	sientes	sentiste	sientas	
sentir	siente	sintió	sienta	
	sentimos	sentimos	sintamos	
	sienten	sintieron	sientan	

What are the stem
changes in Class III
verbs?

Class III (**-ir** verbs) (*Section 67*)

e → i in the present indicative when stressed; **e → i** in the
third person singular and plural of the preterit, in the present
participle, and throughout the present subjunctive.

	Present Indicative	Preterit	Present Subjunctive	Present Participle
	pido	pedí	pida	pidiendo
	pides	pediste	pidas	
pedir	pide	pidió	pida	
	pedimos	pedimos	pidamos	
	piden	pidieron	pidan	

IV Expressions with estar, tener, and hacer
(*Sections 34, 58, 59*)

For what purpose is
estar + adjective
used in Spanish?
What is the difference
between expressions
using **tener** + noun
and expressions using
hacer + noun?

estar + adjective = *to be* + adjective. Used to express a
condition or state of the subject.

tener + noun = *to be* + adjective. Used to describe a
subject that is a living being.

hacer + noun = *to be* + adjective. Used to describe the
temperature or weather.

María está cansada.   *María is tired.*
María tiene mucho calor.   *María is very hot.*
Hoy hace mucho calor.   *It is very hot today.*

ADJECTIVES

What are examples of adjectives that drop the final **-o** before masculine singular nouns?

I Shortened Adjectives (*Section 60*)

Some adjectives drop the final **-o** before masculine singular nouns: **bueno**, **malo**, **primero**, **tercero**, **alguno**, **ninguno**, **uno**.

> **Es el primer día del mes.**   *It is the first day of the month.*
>
> **No hay ningún concierto hoy.**   *There isn't any concert today.*

What is the meaning of **grande**? Do **grande** and **gran** precede or follow the noun they modify?

Grande, when it follows a noun, means *big*. When it precedes a noun, whether masculine or feminine, it is shortened to **gran** and means *great*. In both cases the plural is **grandes**.

> **José Martí fue un gran poeta.**   *José Martí was a great poet.*
>
> **Tenemos grandes mujeres en nuestra historia.**   *We have great women in our history.*

What are the long-form possessive adjectives?

II Long-Form Possessive Adjectives
(*Section 64*)

Long-form possessive adjectives	Alternate form with **de**	
mío, -a, -os, -as		*of mine*
tuyo, -a, -os, -as		*of yours* (familiar)
suyo, -a, -os, -as	de usted	*of yours* (formal)
	de él	*of his*
	de ella	*of hers*
nuestro, -a, -os, -as		*of ours*
suyo, -a, -os, -as	de ustedes	*of yours* (plural)
	de ellos	*of theirs*
	de ellas	*of theirs*

Where are long-form possessive adjectives placed, before or after the noun?

Long-form possessive adjectives follow the noun they modify and agree with it.

> **Juanita y unas amigas suyas vinieron ayer.**   *Juanita and some friends of hers came yesterday.*

When is the alternate form **de** + pronoun used?

The alternate form using **de** + pronoun may be used to clarify the **suyo** forms.

> **¿Son amigos suyos?**
> or   *Are they friends of hers?*
> **¿Son amigos de ella?**

PRONOUNS

From what form of possessive adjectives are possessive pronouns taken?

I Possessive Pronouns (*Section 65*)

The long-form possessive adjectives are nominalized to form possessive pronouns.

No sé dónde está tu libro; éste es el (libro) mío.
I don't know where your book is; this one is mine.

The **de** + pronoun forms can also be nominalized in this way.

Mi hermano y el de usted son buenos amigos.
My brother and yours are good friends.

II Combination of Two Object Pronouns
(*Section 63*)

When two object pronouns go with the same verb, how are they combined?

The indirect object pronoun will always precede the direct object pronoun when both are used as objects of the same verb.

Me los diste ayer.
You gave them to me yesterday.

Queremos decírtelo ahora.
We want to tell it to you now.

Reflexive pronouns precede any other object pronoun.

Tu cara está sucia; lávatela.
Your face is dirty; wash it.

What is the position of a reflexive pronoun when combined with another object pronoun? How are two object pronouns beginning with **l-** combined?

When there is a combination of two object pronouns beginning with **l-**, the indirect object pronoun, whether singular or plural, always becomes **se**.

Paquito no entiende bien la lección; estamos explicándosela.
Paquito doesn't understand the lesson well; we are explaining it to him.

REMEMBER!

- Two object pronouns (or a reflexive and an object pronoun) used as objects of the same verb cannot be separated. Both must either precede a conjugated verb or follow an infinitive, a present participle, or an affirmative command (*Section 63*).

- Affirmative commands and present participles regularly take a written accent when an object pronoun is attached to them; infinitives, affirmative commands, and present participles always take a written accent when two pronouns are attached.

cómelo	escribírselo
viéndote	dándoselo
	cuéntamelo

- The neuter article **lo** is used to nominalize adjectives that refer to unidentified nouns or broad concepts that cannot be given a gender (*Section 66*).

Lo malo es que termino muy tarde.   *The bad part is that I finish very late.*

Lo poco que sabía ya lo olvidé.   *The little I knew I already forgot.*

De and **que** phrases can also be nominalized in the same neutral way.

Lo de Sonia es un escándalo.   *The Sonia business is a scandal.*

Lo que me dijiste es mentira.   *What you told me is a lie.*

- Verbs will generally maintain the consonant sounds of the infinitive when they are conjugated. Therefore, certain consonants will change to conform to the infinitive sound in the following way (*Section 72*):

c → qu before **e** or **i**	buscar	busqué
g → gu before **e** or **i**	llegar	llegué
gu → g before **o** or **a** in **-guir** verbs		
	seguir	sigo, siga
z → c before **e** or **i**	empezar	empecé
(**z** is never followed by **e** or **i** except in proper names)		
c → z before **a, o,** or **u**	convencer	convenzo

These rules also affect nouns.

lápiz	lápices	chico	chiquillo	amigo	amiguito

A • Transformation Drill   Imperfect → Preterit

MODEL   Todos los días teníamos la oportunidad de ver una obra.
Ayer
STUDENT   Ayer **tuvimos** la oportunidad de ver una obra.

1. Todos los días íbamos a la Plaza Mayor.
   Ayer

2. De vez en cuando nuestros hijos querían ir al teatro.
   Anoche
3. Cada viernes me pedían dinero para comprar un libro de Lope de Vega.
   El viernes pasado
4. Yo siempre podía conseguir entradas para ver *Fuenteovejuna.*
   Anteayer
5. Con frecuencia Luisa venía conmigo porque conocía a los actores.
   El otro día
6. A menudo tú me decías cómo terminaba la obra.
   Ayer por la noche
7. De vez en cuando Julio se dormía.
   Anoche a las diez
8. Muchas veces mis padres leían la obra antes de verla.
   La semana pasada

B • Query   Free Response

Answer in the imperfect.

1. ¿Dónde vivías cuando eras pequeño (pequeña)?
2. ¿Qué hacía tu familia durante el verano?
3. ¿Se burlaban de ti a menudo en la escuela?
4. ¿Sabías algo de español antes de asistir a esta clase?

Answer in the preterit.

5. ¿Qué hiciste la semana pasada?
6. ¿A qué hora te acostaste anoche?
7. ¿Cómo viniste a la universidad esta mañana?
8. ¿Dónde estuviste el verano pasado?

C • Translation Drill

Use expressions with **tener, hacer,** and **estar.**

1. Today it is very cold here. We are very cold.
2. You are wrong. The classroom is open.
3. Tomás is lucky; it's nice weather.
4. The children have been hungry for three days.
5. We were here three days ago.

D • Transformation Drill   Present Indicative → Present Subjunctive

MODEL   Yo sé que tienes mucho dinero.
         Dudo
STUDENT Dudo que **tengas** mucho dinero.

1. Yo sé que trabajas mucho.   2. Es evidente que piensan como tú.
   Dudo   Es posible

3. Creen que hacemos la tarea.
   Insisten en
4. Es verdad que no sabemos hacerlo.
   Es lástima
5. Es cierto que van al concierto.
   Es importante
6. Es claro que decimos la verdad.
   Se alegran de
7. Nos damos cuenta de que vienes con nosotros.
   Queremos
8. Sabes que vuelvo temprano.
   Puede ser
9. Creo que eres el mejor de todos.
   Espero
10. Es evidente que estás triste.
    Sienten

E • Translation Drill

Translate into Spanish.

1. You want us to bring it. You want to bring it.
2. I hope they will hear me. I know they will hear me.
3. Put the plate on the table (Uds.)! I insist that you put the plate on the table.
4. We are sure they are here. We doubt they are here.
5. It's a shame that you have to leave. We are sorry that you have to go to school.

F • Query   Patterned Response

MODEL   ¿Dónde están las revistas de Miguel?
STUDENT   **No sé dónde están las suyas** (or **las de él**).

1. ¿Dónde está mi abrigo?
2. ¿Dónde está tu bicicleta?
3. ¿Dónde está el programa de los invitados?
4. ¿Dónde están nuestros billetes?
5. ¿Dónde están los mensajes del director?
6. ¿Dónde está mi camisa?
7. ¿Dónde están tus calcetines?
8. ¿Dónde está su anillo?
9. ¿Dónde está nuestro contrato?
10. ¿Dónde están los ejercicios de ustedes?

G • Replacement Drill

Drop the direct and indirect object nouns, and add the appropriate pronouns for them where necessary, making any required changes.

MODEL   Uds. le dieron el disco a Ignacio.
STUDENT   Uds. **se lo** dieron.

1. Ud. me dio la respuesta.
2. Yo te voy a escribir un poema.
3. Luisa les está explicando las preguntas.
4. Los Sres. Rivera nos quieren dar sus entradas.
5. Tomás y Felipe no se lavaron las manos.
6. Cuéntales el chiste a tus hermanos.
7. ¿Me pueden Uds. hacer un collar de plata?
8. No me prepares los tamales todavía.
9. ¿Te van a presentar un anillo?
10. No le entendemos las palabras.

H • Guided Composition

Imagine that you are taking a trip through the United States. Describe the varied cultural contributions (Hispanic and/or other) that you observe during your travels.

Ruins of Machu Picchu, Peru

Lección diecisiete

VIAJE EN AUTOMÓVIL A LA AMÉRICA DEL SUR

ISABEL	Dicen que tú y Laura son las primeras mujeres que viajaron a Latinoamérica en automóvil.	
DIANA	Creo que sí. ¡Fue un viaje increíble!	**Creo que sí.** *I think so.*
ISABEL	¿Echaste de menos a tus amigos?	**echar de menos** *to miss*
DIANA	Un poco. Pero fue una gran oportunidad para nosotras.	
ISABEL	¿Por qué hicieron el viaje?	**hacer un viaje** *to take a trip*
DIANA	Acabábamos de graduarnos. Puro estudio durante cuatro años. ¡Una vida cansadísima! Mi padre quería que yo continuara los estudios. Pero antes yo pensaba vivir un poco.	**acabar de** *to have just*
ISABEL	Sin duda el viaje les costó muchísimo.	
DIANA	No, una agencia de turismo, la que organiza viajes a Latinoamérica, hacía una promoción. Necesitaban dos individuos que pudieran viajar en automóvil a la América del Sur.	**agencia de turismo** *travel agency* **promoción** *publicity campaign*
ISABEL	Me imagino que no pensaban en mujeres.	
DIANA	Precisamente. Pero los convencimos que éramos las personas que buscaban. ¡Dos mujeres por Latinoamérica! ¡Qué novedad!	**novedad** *novelty*
ISABEL	¿Y tuviste problemas con los hombres? Les gusta perseguir a las gringas, ¿no?	**perseguir (i)** *to chase*

DIANA	Yo creo que exageran algo. Nuestro problema mayor fue el automóvil. En Guatemala nos estancamos. Puro lodo en el camino.
ISABEL	¿Qué hicieron?
DIANA	Aparecieron unos campesinos. Vieron que necesitábamos a alguien que nos ayudara. Sin más, trajeron unas sogas, con las cuales nos sacaron el automóvil del fango.
ISABEL	Cuéntame algunos detalles acerca de tus andanzas.
DIANA	No sé dónde comenzar. La catedral de sal cerca de Bogotá, el lago Titicaca, Buenos Aires con sus espléndidas avenidas anchas, la playa de Ipanema... todo fue una maravilla.
ISABEL	¿Y visitaste Machu Picchu?
DIANA	¡Oh, Machu Picchu! La ciudad perdida de los Incas. Eso fue lo que más me impresionó. Estábamos como en otro mundo. Laura y yo pasamos la noche entre las ruinas en sacos de dormir.

estancarse *to get stuck*
lodo *mud* **camino** *road*

aparecer *to appear*
campesinos *farmers*

sogas *ropes*

fango *mud*

detalles *details*

andanzas *wanderings*

comenzar (**ie**) *to begin*
sal *salt*
lago *lake*

anchas *wide* **playa** *beach*

maravilla *marvel*

impresionar *to impress*

pasar la noche *to spend the night* **sacos de dormir** *sleeping bags*

Avenida 9 de Julio,
Buenos Aires

NOTES

gringo, gringa	This word is derived from **griego**, *Greek*. Originally used to express unintelligibility (in Latin and Spanish, equivalent of *It's Greek to me.*), it has now come to mean foreigner. Since Americans are the most common foreigners in Mexico, by extension, **gringo** is most frequently associated with Americans.
la catedral de sal, Zipaquirá	An enormous underground cathedral located 500 feet below the surface in the salt mines of Zipaquirá, close to Bogotá, Colombia. It has room for 15,000 people.
lago Titicaca	The world's highest lake navigable to large vessels, located in the Andes between Perú and Bolivia.
la playa de Ipanema	a well-known and popular beach in the environs of Río de Janeiro, Brazil.
Machu Picchu	An important archeological site, the ruins of an ancient Incan city, located in the Andes Mountains of south central Perú. In Quechua the name means *the lost city of the Incas.*

LANGUAGE STRUCTURES

73 Imperfect subjunctive

	Infinitive	Third Person Plural Preterit	Imperfect Subjunctive Endings[1]	Imperfect Subjunctive
Regular Verbs	hablar	habla ~~ron~~		hablara, hablaras, hablara, habláramos, hablaran
	aprender	aprendie ~~ron~~		aprendiera, aprendieras, etc.
	escribir	escribie ~~ron~~		escribiera, escribieras, etc.
Class I Verbs (regular in preterit)	pensar	pensa ~~ron~~	-ra	pensara, pensaras, etc.
	volver	volvie ~~ron~~		volviera, volvieras, etc.
	entender	entendie ~~ron~~		entendiera, entendieras, etc.
	encontrar	encontra ~~ron~~	-ras	encontrara, encontraras, etc.
Class II and III Verbs	sentir	sintie ~~ron~~	-ra	sintiera, sintieras, etc.
	dormir	durmie ~~ron~~		durmiera, durmieras, etc.
	pedir	pidie ~~ron~~	-'ramos	pidiera, pidieras, etc.
Verbs Irregular in the Preterit	andar	anduvie ~~ron~~		anduviera, anduvieras, etc.
	caer(se)	caye ~~ron~~	-ran[2]	cayera, cayeras, etc.
	creer	creye ~~ron~~		creyera, creyeras, etc.
	dar	die ~~ron~~		diera, dieras, etc.
	decir	dije ~~ron~~		dijera, dijeras, etc.
	estar	estuvie ~~ron~~		estuviera, estuvieras, etc.
	hacer[3]	hicie ~~ron~~		hiciera, hicieras, etc.
	ir	fue ~~ron~~		fuera, fueras, etc.
	leer	leye ~~ron~~		leyera, leyeras, etc.
	oír	oye ~~ron~~		oyera, oyeras, etc.
	poder	pudie ~~ron~~		pudiera, pudieras, etc.
	poner[3]	pusie ~~ron~~		pusiera, pusieras, etc.
	producir[4]	produje ~~ron~~		produjera, produjeras, etc.
	querer	quisie ~~ron~~		quisiera, quisieras, etc.
	saber	supie ~~ron~~		supiera, supieras, etc.
	ser	fue ~~ron~~		fuera, fueras, etc.
	tener[3]	tuvie ~~ron~~		tuviera, tuvieras, etc.
	venir[3]	vinie ~~ron~~		viniera, vinieras, etc.
	ver	vie ~~ron~~		viera, vieras, etc.

[1] Another form of the imperfect subjunctive exists in Spanish: instead of **-ra, -ras, -ra, -'ramos, -ran,** the endings, **-se, -ses, -se, -'semos, -sen** are used. Examples: **hablase, hablases, hablase, hablásemos, hablasen.** The **-se** forms are not as common as the **-ra** ones in the spoken language, but they are frequently found in written Spanish. There is no difference in meaning between the two forms.

[2] For the **vosotros** imperfect subjunctive forms, see the Appendix, section **1.**

[3] Derivatives of these verbs are identical except for the prefix: **detener detuviera, detuvieras,** etc.; **componer compusiera, compusieras,** etc.; **deshacer deshiciera, deshicieras,** etc.; **prevenir previniera, previnieras,** etc.

[4] Recall that all verbs that end in **-ducir** are irregular in the preterit in the same way (see section **61,** footnote 3). For example, **traducir: tradujeron → tradujera, tradujeras,** etc.

▶ The imperfect subjunctive is *always* formed from the third person plural of the preterit by dropping **-ron** and adding **-ra, -ras, -ra, -'ramos, -ran**. The first person plural form has a written accent mark.

▶ Class I stem-changing verbs are regular in the imperfect subjunctive. Class II and Class III stem-changing verbs change **e** to **i** or **o** to **u** in the third person singular and plural of the preterit, and this change occurs throughout the imperfect subjunctive.

▶ **Ser** and **ir** share the same forms in the preterit and therefore the same forms in the imperfect subjunctive as well.

▶ The imperfect subjunctive is used under the same conditions as the present subjunctive, except that the point of view is in the past. If the main verb is in the past, the subordinate verb will be in the past.

Present	1. *Esperamos* que ella *sepa* hacerlo.	*We hope that she knows how to do it.*
Past	*Esperábamos* que ella *supiera* hacerlo.	*We hoped that she knew how to do it.*
Present	2. *Necesitan* dos individuos que *puedan* viajar en automóvil.	*They need two individuals who can travel by car.*
Past	*Necesitaban* dos individuos que *pudieran* viajar en automóvil.	*They needed two individuals who could travel by car.*
Present	3. *Quiero* que *vengas* conmigo.	*I want you to come with me.*
Past	*Quería* que *vinieras* conmigo.	*I wanted you to come with me.*

A • Substitution Drill

MODEL Querían que tú viajaras a Puerto Rico.
            él
STUDENT Querían que él **viajara** a Puerto Rico.

1. Querían que tú viajaras a Puerto Rico.
    tú y yo
    ella
    Uds.
    el señor López
    tú y Diana

2. Él sentía que ellas se cayeran.
    yo
    Miguel y yo
    Ud.
    Pancho
    tú

3. Era lástima que Juan no fuera con ellas.
    tú y Juan
    tú
    tu mamá
    ellos
    nosotros

4. Yo dudaba que ellos trajeran la cerveza.
    tú
    Rafa
    Uds.
    Rafa y Tere
    mi hermano

B • Transformation Drill   Present Indicative and Present Subjunctive → Past Indicative and Imperfect Subjunctive

MODEL   Es lástima que Pancho no esté en clase.
Era

STUDENT   Era lástima que Pancho no **estuviera** en clase.

1. Necesitamos a alguien que lo sepa hacer.
Necesitábamos

2. Buscan un libro que sea interesante.
Buscaban

3. No hay nadie que estudie como Diana.
había

4. No hay nada que le guste a Diego.
había

5. Prefiere un novio que tenga dinero.
Prefirió

6. Exige que Marta lo haga.
Exigió

7. No creen que sea necesario.
creían

8. Laura tiene miedo que el automóvil no funcione.
tenía

9. La profesora prefiere que estudies en casa.
prefería

10. Niegan que los hombres sean machos.
Negaron

C • Transformation Drill   Past Indicative and Imperfect Subjunctive → Present Indicative and Present Subjunctive

MODEL   Era importante que Paco estudiara todo el día.
Es

STUDENT   Es importante que Paco **estudie** todo el día.

1. Era necesario que José trabajara toda la noche.
Es   "   "   " TRABAJE " ' "

2. Mis padres me pidieron que lo hiciera lo más pronto posible.
piden   HAGA

3. Dudábamos que los muchachos vinieran a la venta.
Dudamos   VENGAN

4. Le preocupaba a Alfonso que su novia no aprendiera español.
preocupa   APRENDA

5. Él sentía mucho que nosotros no lo creyéramos.
siente   CREAMOS

6. No había ninguna muchacha que supiera francés.
hay   SEPA

7. Querían una casa que no fuera muy vieja.
Quieren

8. No conocíamos a nadie que tuviera un automóvil.
conocemos   Tengan

9. ¿No vio Ud. a nadie que pudiera ayudarnos?
ve   Ponga

10. Buscaban un profesor que hablara portugués.
Buscan   HABLE

D • Transformation Drill

MODEL El jefe llegó tarde.
Fue necesario que
STUDENT Fue necesario que el jefe **llegara** tarde.

1. El jefe llegó tarde.
Dudábamos que *el jefe llegara tarde*
Preferían que *el jefe llegara tarde*
Negaron que *el " " "*
Esperaban que *" " "*
Creían que (¡Cuidado!) *el jefe llegó tarde*

2. Vendimos todas nuestras revistas.
Fue una lástima que *vendiéramos todas*
Fue imposible que *"* *nuestras*
Era necesario que *"* *revistas*
Era mejor que *vendiéramos*
Era cierto que *"*

E • Query   Patterned Response

MODEL ¿Qué les era imposible? ¿Hacerlo?
STUDENT **Era imposible que ellos lo hicieran.**

MODEL ¿Qué nos pidió ella? ¿Volver?
STUDENT **Sí, nos pidió que volviéramos.**

1. ¿Qué fue necesario? ¿Terminarlas?
¿Qué era mejor? ¿Irse?
¿Qué fue lástima? ¿Dormirse?
¿Qué era importante? ¿Verlo?

2. ¿Qué nos exigió ella? ¿Comer?
¿Qué me exigió él? ¿Estudiar?
¿Qué te mandó el jefe? ¿Escribir?
¿Qué le pidió la Sra.? ¿Esperar?

74 Relative pronouns used to introduce adjective clauses

▶ An adjective clause is a subordinate clause that modifies a noun or a pronoun. An adjective clause may be introduced by one of the following relative pronouns.

que	*that, which, who, whom*
quien, quienes	*who, whom*
el que (la que, los que, las que)	*that, which, who, whom, the one(s) who,*
el cual (la cual, los cuales, las cuales)	*the one(s) which*
lo que	*what, that which, which*
lo cual	

▶ I **que**   *that, which, who, whom*
Que is the relative pronoun that is most frequently used. When introducing a clause, **que** may be the subject (example 1); the object of the verb, referring to persons or things (examples 2 and 3); or the object of a preposition, referring to things only (example 4).

1. la mujer que me llamó   *the woman who called me*
2. los hombres que conocimos   *the men (that) we met*

3. el automóvil que tienes   *the automobile (that) you have*
4. el viaje de que hablábamos   *the trip (that) we were talking about*

▶ II   **quien, quienes**   *who, whom*

Quien, quienes refers only to persons and is most frequently used after a preposition. **Quien** (with the meaning of *who*) occasionally is used to introduce an adjective clause that is set off from the main clause by commas (example 3).

1. ¿Ves a los campesinos con quienes habla Diana?   *Do you see the farmers with whom Diana is talking?*
2. Yo soy la persona a quien se lo dio.   *I'm the person he gave it to (to whom he gave it).*
3. Dos individuos, quienes eran de la agencia, nos convencieron de hacer el viaje.   *Two individuals, who were from the agency, convinced us to take the trip.*

▶ III   **el cual (la cual, los cuales, las cuales), el que (la que, los que, las que)**
that, which, who, whom, the one(s) who, the one(s) which

The longer forms of the relative pronouns—**el cual**, etc., and **el que**, etc.—are used after prepositions other than **a, con, de,** and **en** (example 1). Often, however, these long relatives are used instead of **que** after the short prepositions as well (example 2). They are also used to make clear which one of two or more possible antecedents the clause modifies (examples 3, 4). The long relative pronouns must agree with their antecedents.

1. Bogotá, cerca de la cual (de la que) vimos la catedral de sal,...   *Bogotá, close to which we saw the salt cathedral, . . .*
2. Trajeron unas sogas con las cuales nos sacaron el automóvil.   *They brought some ropes with which they got our car out.*
3. El novio de Diana, el cual (el que) viajó a Latinoamérica...   *Diana's boyfriend, who traveled to Latin America . . . .*
4. Mi amiga, la que (la cual) estuvo aquí ayer, es cubana.   *My friend, the one who was here yesterday, is Cuban.*

▶ IV   **lo cual, lo que**   *what, that which, which*

The neuter forms **lo cual** and **lo que** sum up a preceding statement or idea in as broad a manner as the context will permit (see section **66**). However, **lo cual** is used only to introduce an adjective clause that is set off from the main clause by commas.

Eso fue lo que más me impresionó.   *That is what impressed me the most.*
Me dijo la verdad, lo cual me pareció muy comendable.   *He told me the truth, which seemed very commendable to me.*

¡Cuidado!

Although English often omits relative pronouns, Spanish does not.

1. The book I read	El libro *que* leí...
2. The trip we took	El viaje *que* hicimos...
3. The house she lives in	La casa en *que* vive...

A • Integration Drill

Combine the following pairs of sentences into one sentence, using **que**.

MODEL   Laura es la mujer. Viajó a Latinoamérica en automóvil.

STUDENT   Laura es la mujer **que** viajó a Latinoamérica en automóvil.

1. Ésa es la agencia. Organiza viajes a Buenos Aires.
2. Ahí va la estudiante. Echó de menos a sus amigos.
3. Éste es el hombre. Persigue a las gringas, ¿no?
4. Ya llegó el automóvil. Va a la playa de Ipanema.
5. Mira la ciudad. Se llama Machu Picchu.
6. ¿Dónde está el poeta boricua? Va a recitar unos poemas.
7. Diego es el español. Tiene una novia norteamericana.
8. Aquí está el profesor. Escribió un libro importante.

B • Integration Drill

Combine the following pairs of sentences into one sentence, using **quien**.

MODEL   Ése es el aficionado. Compré un billete para él.

STUDENT   Ése es el aficionado **para quien** compré un billete.

1. Ésa es la muchacha. Te hablé de ella ayer.
2. Ésas son las compañeras de clase. Hacía la tarea con ellas.
3. Ésa es la profesora. Compré un libro para ella.
4. Ése es el primo. Le di una entrada a él.
5. Ése es el estudiante. Estudiábamos con él.

C • Integration Drill

Combine the following pairs of sentences into one sentence, using **a quien** or **a quienes**.

MODEL   Aquí está el campesino. Le pedí un favor.

STUDENT   Aquí está el campesino **a quien** le pedí un favor.

1. Aquí están los indios. Les ofrecieron dinero.
2. Aquí está el bufón. Le exigí una disculpa.
3. Aquí está el viejo. Le vendí un lápiz.
4. Aquí están los jefes. Les pedimos un aumento.
5. Aquí están los hombres. Les dieron trabajo.

D • Integration Drill

Combine the following pairs of sentences into one sentence, using **el cual** (**la cual, los cuales**, **las cuales**), as in the model.

MODEL   Trabajamos cerca de la catedral. Es muy hermosa.
STUDENT **La catedral cerca de la cual trabajamos** es muy hermosa.

1. Laura me escribió acerca de la playa de Ipanema. Es espléndida.
2. Viven cerca de unos campesinos. Son muy simpáticos.
3. Diana nos hablaba acerca de la agencia de turismo. Organiza viajes a Latinoamérica.
4. Dormimos entre las ruinas de Machu Picchu. Eran increíbles.
5. Trabajamos cerca del palacio. Es muy conocido.

E • Integration Drill

Combine the following pairs of sentences into one sentence, using **que**.

MODEL   Éstas son las sogas. Las voy a traer.
STUDENT Éstas son las sogas **que** voy a traer.

1. Éste es el palacio. Lo acaban de abrir.
2. Éstas son las ruinas. Las acaban de descubrir.
3. Ésa es la playa. La echamos de menos.
4. Ésa es la propuesta. La tienen que leer.
5. Ésas son las facturas. Las deben revisar.

F • Translation Drill

Translate into Spanish.

1. Where is the book we need? We are the persons who can help you.
2. Diana is the student who traveled to Latin America.
3. There are the tickets with which I entered the theater.
4. There are my friends with whom I saw the play.
5. What they say is not true.
6. The problem about which you spoke is very interesting.
7. Those who arrived first, won.
8. The palace, which you saw this morning, is very old.

75 Indicative versus subjunctive in adjective clauses

▶ In Spanish the verb in the adjective clause may be formed in the indicative or in the subjunctive. The concept of reality or unreality, in the grammatical sense, governs the choice of an indicative versus subjunctive verb in the adjective clause.

When the subordinate clause refers back to someone or something (a noun or pronoun) viewed as undetermined or nonexistent (unreal), the subjunctive is used. When the subordinate clause refers back to someone or something viewed as predetermined (real), the indicative is used.

Adjective Clause in the Subjunctive

1. Necesitaban dos individuos que pudieran viajar a la América del Sur. *They needed two individuals who could travel to South America.* (The individuals are not yet determined.)

2. No hay nadie que sea tan inteligente como él. *There is no one (no other person) who is as intelligent as he is.*[5] (The person is nonexistent—**nadie**.)

3. Voy a comprar los que tenga. *I'm going to buy whatever (objects) he has.* (The objects in question are undetermined.)

4. ¿Había una tienda de discos que estuviera en la Avenida de las Américas? *Was there a (any) record shop that was on the Avenue of the Americas?* (The existence of the record shop is undetermined.)

Adjective Clause in the Indicative

1. Conocían a dos individuos que podían viajar a la América del Sur. *They knew two individuals who could travel to South America.* (The individuals have already been determined.)

2. Hay muchas personas que son tan inteligentes como él. *There are many persons who are as intelligent as he is.* (There are *many persons* in existence.)

3. Voy a comprar los que tiene. *I'm going to buy the ones that he has.* (The objects already have been determined.)

4. Había una tienda de discos que estaba en la Avenida de las Américas. *There was a record shop that was on the Avenue of the Americas.* (The existence of the record shop already has been determined.)

Subjunctive Versus Indicative
Matched Pairs

These pairs of sentences are exactly the same except that in the first case the subordinate verb is in the indicative, and in the second case it is in the subjunctive. The meanings of each matched pair are quite different, however. When you translate into English, it is often useful to show that the noun or pronoun that governs the adjective clause is undetermined by using *whatever* or *any* to modify it instead of *the*. Study the translations.

1. Compra el libro que quieres.   *Buy the book that you wish.*
   Compra el libro que quieras.   *Buy whatever book you wish.*

---

[5] Whereas English may or may not repeat the verb in a comparative sentence, Spanish does not.

2. Haz lo que te dice.
   Haz lo que te diga.

3. Vamos a dar este premio al estudiante que sabe el español.

   Vamos a dar este premio al estudiante que sepa el español.

4. Buscamos a[6] la muchacha que quiere hacer el viaje.
   Buscamos[6] una muchacha que quiera hacer el viaje.

Do what he is telling you.
Do whatever he tells you.
We are going to give this prize to the student who knows Spanish. (We already know who the student is.)
We are going to give this prize to the student who knows Spanish. (But we don't know who that student is.)
We are looking for the girl who wants to take the trip.
We are looking for a girl who wants to take the trip.

A • Transformation Drill   Indicative → Subjunctive

MODEL   Conocemos a dos individuos que pueden viajar a la América del Sur.
         Buscamos dos individuos

STUDENT   Buscamos dos individuos que **puedan** viajar a la América del Sur.

1. Hay un profesor aquí que habla inglés y español.
   ¿Hay

2. Tenemos un rector que es buena gente.
   Queremos

3. Conozco a alguien[7] que sabe tanto como él.
   No conozco a nadie[7]

4. Vamos a comprar los que producen más.
                    unos que

5. Quiero conocer a la chica que escribe poemas de amor.
                    una chica

6. Hay una casa cerca de la playa que puedo comprar.
   No hay casa

7. Busco a la muchacha que estudia en la facultad de medicina.
                    una muchacha

8. Tengo alguien que escribe propuestas.
   ¿Tienes alguien

9. Quiero conocer al chicano que es bilingüe.
                    un

10. Hay alguien aquí que vende trastes.
    No hay nadie

---

[6] Recall that the personal **a** is used when the direct object is a definite person, except when following the verb **tener** (see section **26**).

[7] The personal **a** is used with **alguien** and **nadie** (see section **54**).

B • Transformation Drill   Present → Past

MODEL   Deseamos una casa que esté cerca de la playa.
          Deseábamos
STUDENT   Deseábamos una casa que **estuviera** cerca de la playa.

1. Busco a alquien que no sea tan imbécil.
   Buscaba
2. No hay ingeniero que sepa eso.
      había
3. Quiero encontrar una revista que sea bilingüe.
   Quería
4. ¡No hay nadie que sepa excavar ruinas como yo!
      había
5. Buscamos un teatro que presente un drama de Lope.
   Buscábamos
6. ¿Necesitas una motocicleta que sea nueva?
   ¿Necesitabas
7. Prefieren una cerveza que esté bien fría.
   Preferían
8. Deseo una novia que crea en la justicia social.
   Deseaba

C • Query   Patterned Response

MODEL   Había unas bibliotecas que estaban cerradas, ¿verdad?
STUDENT   **No, no había ninguna biblioteca que estuviera cerrada.**

1. Había una chica que era bilingüe, ¿verdad?
2. Había un joven que tenía una hacienda, ¿verdad?
3. Había unos indios que vendían artefactos, ¿verdad?
4. Había unos campesinos que tenían sogas, ¿verdad?
5. Conocías a una familia que vivía en Tabasco, ¿verdad?
6. Conocías a una muchacha que estudiaba el inglés, ¿verdad?
7. Conocías una tienda que vendía música latinoamericana, ¿verdad?
8. Tenías una motocicleta que no funcionaba, ¿verdad?

D • Query   Free Response

Answer in Spanish.

1. ¿Busca Ud. a alguien que pueda explicar la gramática?
2. ¿Ayer buscaba Ud. a alguien que fuera bilingüe?
3. ¿Necesita Ud. una persona que escriba español?
4. ¿Anoche necesitaba Ud. una persona que le explicara el subjuntivo?
5. ¿Conoces a alguien que sepa el inglés y el español?
6. ¿Ayer había alguien que pudiera ir al cine contigo?
7. ¿Es cierto que buscas una novia (un novio) que sea aficionada(-o) al fútbol?
8. ¿Es cierto que buscabas un individuo que supiera dos lenguas?

E • Translation Drill

Translate into Spanish.

1. We know someone who is bilingual. We are looking for someone who is bilingual.
2. They have a student who is from Buenos Aires. They need a student who is from Buenos Aires.
3. There is a record store that is around here. Is there a record store that is around here?
4. Do whatever you have to do. Do what you have to do.
5. There is a student here who knows you. There are no students here who know you.

76   Special cases of adjective position

▶   Normally descriptive adjectives are placed after the noun and limiting adjectives are placed before the noun (see section **18**).

▶   I.   Descriptive adjectives that precede the noun
Sometimes descriptive adjectives are placed before the noun. Usually this occurs for the purpose of enhancement, that is, to suggest a good quality or bad quality or to reinforce an inherent characteristic that we already associate with the noun in question. When a normally descriptive adjective comes before the noun it is not being used to single out or differentiate the noun in question, as would be the case were the adjective placed after the noun. Thus, when the adjective comes before the noun, it informs relatively little about the noun itself, but it often tells us a great deal about the speaker's feelings.

1. Es un buen muchacho.	*He's a nice guy.* (The adjective is used to enhance qualities normally associated with **muchacho**.)
Es un muchacho bueno.	*He is a* good *boy (guy).* (The adjective is used to emphasize this individual or single him out in contrast to others.)
2. ¡Maldito día!	*Damned day!* (The adjective informs us about the speaker's feelings toward the day.)
¡Día maldito!	Damned *day!* (The day itself is singled out as "damned" in contrast to other days.)
3. la blanca nieve	*the white snow* (The adjective reinforces a quality already associated with snow.)
la nieve sucia; la nieve firme	*the dirty snow; the firm snow* (The adjective distinguishes these varieties of snow from others.)

► II.   Adjectives that change their meaning when they precede or follow the noun
A number of adjectives can be regarded as either limiting *or* descriptive. They change
their meanings according to their position.

Adjective Used as Limiter	*Noun*	
gran	hombre	*great man*
el antiguo	presidente	*the former president*
puro	estudio	*strictly study; nothing but study*
un nuevo	automóvil	*a new car* (another one, new to owner)
mi viejo	amigo	*my old* (*long-standing*) *friend*
la pobre	muchacha	*the poor* (*unfortunate*) *girl*

Noun	*Adjective Used as Describer*	
hombre	grande	*big* (*corpulent*) *man*
el palacio	antiguo	*the ancient palace*
leche	pura	*pure milk*
un automóvil	nuevo	*a brand-new car*
mi amigo	viejo	*my elderly friend*
la muchacha	pobre	*poor* (*indigent*) *girl*

A • Vocabulary Drill

Read the first sentence, then complete the second segment by modifying the noun with
an adjective from the preceding list.

> MODEL   La leche es blanca y rica. Es _____.
> STUDENT   **Es lecha pura.**

1. El hombre es inmenso, enorme. Es un _____.
2. La mujer no tiene dinero. Es una _____.
3. El templo es de los mayas. Es un _____.
4. Fue mi novia el año pasado. Es mi _____.
5. Llegaron los automóviles de este año. Son los _____.
6. Aquí vendemos cerveza solamente. Aquí vendemos _____.
7. El muchacho perdió a su novia y está triste. Es un _____.
8. El profesor es excelente. Es un _____.

B • Translation Drill

Translate into Spanish.

1. The former law, the ancient law
2. Pure (nothing but) milk; pure (clean) water
3. My long-standing friend; my elderly friend
4. A new magazine; a brand-new book
5. A great opportunity; a large car

77 Absolute superlative

▶ In order to indicate a high degree of quality without intending any element of comparison, Spanish either uses **muy** before the adjective or adverb or attaches the suffix **-ísimo** (**-a**, **-os**, **-as**) to them. **Muchísimo** (not **muy mucho**) is used for *very much* (*many*).

The suffix **-ísimo** is attached directly to those words ending in a consonant; words ending in a vowel drop the vowel before adding the suffix.

▶ The following orthographic changes occur when **-ísimo** is added to a word (see section **72** for similar examples).

$$\left.\begin{array}{l} c \rightarrow qu \\ g \rightarrow gu \\ z \rightarrow c \end{array}\right\} + \text{ísimo}$$

1. Estoy muy impresionada. *or* Estoy impresionadísima.
    I am very impressed.
2. El viaje costó muchísimo; el viaje costó poquísimo.
    The trip cost a lot; the trip cost very little.
3. ¡Un día larguísimo!
    A very long day!
4. Hablan rapidísimo.
    They speak very quickly.

A • Query   Patterned Response

MODEL   ¿Es guapo su novio?
STUDENT   **Sí, es muy guapo; es guapísimo.**

1. ¿Es viejo tu automóvil?
2. ¿Es cansada tu vida?
3. ¿Es grande el lago Titicaca?
4. ¿Es ancha la avenida?
5. ¿Es difícil la lección?
6. ¿Es simpática la profesora?
7. ¿Es largo el viaje?
8. ¿Es inteligente el estudiante?
9. ¿Es aburrida la canción?
10. ¿Es feo el rector?

78 Some idiomatic uses of acabar, echar, pensar, and querer

▶ **Acabar**   The basic meaning of **acabar** is *to finish, end*. **Acabar de** means *to have just*.

Acabo de entrar; acabo de acabarlo (*or* acabo de terminarlo).	*I have just entered; I have just finished it.*
Acabábamos de graduarnos.	*We had just graduated.*

▶ **Echar**   The basic meaning of **echar** is *to throw*. For example, **Echa tus cosas en el automóvil;** *Throw (Put) your things in the car.* Two idioms formed from **echar** are

echar de menos   *to miss*
echar a perder   *to spoil, ruin*

¿Echaste de menos a tus amigos?	*Did you miss your friends?*
Echas a perder todas tus oportunidades.	*You waste all your opportunities.*

▶ **Pensar**   The basic meaning of **pensar** is *to think*. The following are special meanings formed from **pensar**.

pensar + infinitive   *to intend to, plan to*

Yo pensaba vivir un poco antes.	*I intended to live a little first.*
Pensábamos viajar a la América del Sur.	*We intended to travel to South America.*

pensar de   *to think of, have an opinion of*

¿Qué piensas de mí?	*What do you think of me?*
	What is your opinion of me?

pensar en   *to think about, occupy one's thoughts with*

Siempre estás pensando en hombres.	*You are always thinking about men.*
Todo el día pienso en ti.	*I think about you all day.*

▶ **Querer**   The basic meanings of **querer** are *to want, to love*. **Querer decir** (a single idiomatic unit), like **significar**, is *to mean, signify*. Although **querer decir** is synonymous with **significar**, only **querer decir** can have a personal subject.

¿Qué quiere decir (significa) esto?	*What does this mean?*
¿Qué quieres decir con eso? Quiero decir que no puedes salir esta noche.	*What do you mean by that? I mean that you can't go out tonight.*

A • Query   Free Response

Answer in Spanish.

1. ¿En qué piensas todo el día?
2. ¿Qué piensas del profesor (de la profesora)?
3. ¿Qué piensa el profesor (la profesora) de ti?
4. ¿Echa Ud. de menos a su familia?
5. ¿Echas a perder tu vida?
6. ¿Piensas viajar a Latinoamérica?
7. ¿Acaba Ud. de volver de Buenos Aires?
8. ¿Qué quiere decir tu novio (novia) cuando dice que ya no quiere verte?

B • Translation Drill

Translate into Spanish.

1. What does this mean? What do they mean by this?
2. I missed you. She spoiled the food.
3. We're always thinking about her. What do you think of me?
4. I have just returned. He had just started it.
5. We intend to be there. We intended to see you.

REVIEW

I The following questions are related to the dialog. Answer in Spanish.

1. ¿Cómo era la vida de Diana en la universidad?
2. ¿Quién necesitaba dos individuos que pudieran viajar en automóvil a la América del Sur?
3. ¿Por qué la agencia de turismo mandó a dos mujeres en automóvil por Latinoamérica?
4. ¿Echó de menos Diana a sus amigos?
5. ¿Tuvieron Isabel y Diana algunos problemas en el camino?
6. ¿Quiénes ayudaron a las mujeres a sacar su automóvil del fango?
7. ¿Qué le impresionó más a Diana?
8. ¿Dónde pasaron la noche en sacos de dormir?

II Translation. Translate into Spanish.

1. I think we are the first American women who went to South America by car.
2. Why did you do such a thing? Without a doubt it was a very tiring trip.
3. Oh, no! You can't believe the magnificent things we saw. For example, the Ipanema beach.

4. But didn't you have a lot of problems with the men? Two women alone! What a novelty!

5. Our greatest problem was with the tourist agency. They didn't think women could make that trip.

6. Also, in Guatemala we needed someone to get us out of the mud.

7. I[8] want to travel to Latin America also. But my father told me to work for a year first.

8. When you have the opportunity, visit the ruins of Machu Picchu. They impressed me very much.

III Write your own dialog.

Imagine that you have a problem on the road in a Hispanic country. What would you say to someone coming to help you?

---

[8] The subject pronoun **yo** would be included to contrast this *I* from the one in sentence 1.

Cognates & Contexts

Newspaper kiosk,
Santiago, Chile

EN EL PERIÓDICO

Joven 29 años, buen sueldo y muy responsable, busca una dama a quien interese casarse y establecer una familia. Apartado Postal 810

sueldo *salary*
dama *lady*

apartado postal *post office box*

Señor maduro y tolerante, bien establecido en la sociedad, busca una señorita que quiera compartir días (y noches) durante las vacaciones en villa espléndida en Acapulco. Ofrezco atractivos. Apartado Postal 33

Buscamos obreros que sean robustos y aventureros para completar la carretera trans-amazónica. Preséntense al Hotel Matto Grosso, Calle Bolívar 10, de 9 a 12.

Se solicitan secretarias bilingües
que (hablen) y (escriban) inglés a la
perfección. Inútil presentarse sin
estos requisitos. Nueva Orleans
No. 883-A

inútil *useless*
requisitos *requirements*

Joven mujer de 23 años, recién
divorciada, con hijo precioso de 18
meses, desea conocer un joven que
(tenga) ideas progresivas acerca del
papel de la mujer. Apartado Postal 39

papel *role*

¿Busca Ud. el consorte de sus sueños?
Nosotros lo podemos realizar, *científicamente*, con nuestra COMPUTA-
DORA SOCIAL. Llene Ud. el
cuestionario, indicando sus intereses
y aptitudes y le garantizamos equiparar
su *perfil social* con el de otros (de sexo
opuesto) de índole similar. ¡No hay
caso, por difícil que sea, que no
(podamos) complacer! Contacte: Eros
Visión. Tel. 37-70-40.

sueños *dreams*

equiparar *to match*
perfil *profile*
índole *nature, type*

Necesitamos vendedores que estén
en contacto con farmacias y doc-
tores. Automóvil y gastos pagados.
Apartado Postal 65

gastos *expenses*

Se solicitan camareros que (sepan)
trabajar y con cartas de recomendación. Indispensable buena presentación y personalidad agradable.
El Cordero de Oro, José Antonio,
1145

presentación *appearance*

el Cordero de Oro *the Golden
Lamb*

Subway entrance, Puerta del Sol, Madrid

Lección dieciocho

ESTUDIANDO EN EL
MUSEO DEL PRADO

JOSÉ LUIS   ¿Ya han llegado todos? *have*

MARISOL   Temo que Pilar se haya retrasado un poco.

       Tú sabes como es el tránsito de Madrid.

JOSÉ LUIS   Bueno, vamos a repasar nuestros apuntes.

JUAN IGNACIO   ¡Qué horrible va a ser este examen! Sin duda el profesor Monocromios quiere que memoricemos todas las pinturas del museo.

MARISOL   Eso es imposible. Se dice que hay más de tres mil cuadros en el Prado.

JUAN IGNACIO   A propósito, ¿por quién fue pintado el cuadro *Las Meninas*?

JOSÉ LUIS   Tú sí que estás despistado. Ese cuadro fue pintado por el mejor de todos, El Greco.

MARISOL   ¡Imbéciles! Fue pintado por Velázquez.

JOSÉ LUIS   Ah sí, tienes razón. *I have* He tenido un pequeño lapso de memoria.

MARISOL   Ojalá que hayan estudiado mejor a los pintores medievales y renacentistas.

JUAN IGNACIO   Mira, aquí viene Pilar.

---

temer *to fear* **retrasarse** *to be delayed, late; to fall behind*
tránsito *traffic*

repasar *to review*
apuntes *notes*

pinturas *paintings*

cuadros *paintings, pictures*

pintar *to paint*

estar despistado (coll.) *to be on the wrong track, lost*

pintores *painters*

renacentistas *renaissance* (adj.)

PILAR Perdonen que haya tardado tanto tiempo. El maldito metro se paró en La Puerta del Sol por veinte minutos. ¿Han visto ya la exhibición de *Los caprichos* de Goya? Dicen que son los favoritos del profe.

JUAN IGNACIO ¡No hemos visto nada! Hace más de media hora que te esperamos. Vamos allá.

GUARDIA Jóvenes. Ha habido un accidente. Estos salones están cerrados. Están reparando la electricidad.

JOSÉ LUIS Pero esto es absurdo; tenemos un examen mañana. Insisto en que nos permita entrar.

GUARDIA Entren si así lo desean.

JOSÉ LUIS ¡Entremos, pues!

GUARDIA Sólo que no hay luz. Ahora sí, mañana se abre a las nueve en punto. Regresen entonces.

JUAN IGNACIO ¡Esto es el colmo! Sé que nada sé. A mí me van a dar calabazas en este maldito examen. Es un día tan lindo. No nos quedemos aquí. Mejor vamos a remar en el estanque del Retiro.

---

tardar *to take (time); to be long*
maldito *damned, accursed*
metro *subway* **parar(se)** *to stop*
caprichos *whims, fancies*

salones *rooms*
reparar *to repair*

ahora sí *however, now*
regresar *to return*
¡Esto es el colmo! *This is the limit! This is the last straw!*
dar calabazas *to fail (someone)*
quedarse *to stay*
remar *to row, go rowing*
estanque *pond, reservoir*

NOTES

El Museo del Prado   Built in 1787, the Prado houses one of the finest collections of paintings in the world.

El Greco (1540–1614)   Born Domenicos Theotocopulos in Crete, he settled in Toledo, Spain in 1577. His much admired style of painting is recognizable through his dramatic use of color and his elongated figures.

Diego Velázquez (1599–1660)   Well-known court painter of Felipe IV of Spain. One of his most famous paintings is *Las Meninas* (The Maids of Honor), a masterpiece of perspective and interplay of light and dark areas.

Francisco de Goya (1746–1828)   Court painter, portraitist, tapestry cartoonist. His works often reflect the bitterness he felt toward the society surrounding him. This is especially evident in his collection of etchings *Los caprichos*, where he uses allegorical caricatures to depict decadent Spain and humanity.

La Puerta del Sol   Busy square in the old part of Madrid from which road distances throughout Spain are measured.

El Retiro   Large park located in the center of Madrid.

ojalá   An impersonal expression of hope or desire, from the Arabic equivalent of *Allah be willing*.

profe   The abbreviation of **profesor**, used frequently among students in discussing their instructors.

Diego Velázquez, *Las Meninas,* 1656. Museo del Prado, Madrid

Francisco Goya, *The Sleep of Reason Produces Monsters,* Plate 43 of *Los caprichos,* first edition 1799. Pomona College Collection (gift of Norton Simon)

El Greco, *St. Paul, c.* 1605–10. The St. Louis Art Museum

LANGUAGE STRUCTURES

79 Formation of the past participle

▶ Past participles are regularly formed by adding **-ado** to the stem of **-ar** verbs and **-ido** to the stem of **-er** and **-ir** verbs.

hablar	habl**ado**	*spoken*
aprender	aprend**ido**	*learned*
vivir	viv**ido**	*lived*

If the stem ends in **-a**, **-e**, or **-o**, a written accent is required as follows.

caer	caído	*fallen*
creer	creído	*believed*
leer	leído	*read*
oír	oído	*heard*

▶ These are the verbs that you have encountered so far that have irregular past participles.

abrir	abierto	*opened*
escribir	escrito	*written*
morir	muerto	*died*
volver[1]	vuelto	*returned*
poner[2]	puesto	*placed*
ver	visto	*seen*
cubrir[3]	cubierto	*covered*
romper	roto	*broken*
decir	dicho	*said*
hacer[4]	hecho	*done*
ir	ido	*gone*
despertar	*DESPIERTO*	*wakened*

▶ The compound, or perfect, infinitive consists of **haber** plus a past participle.

haber hablado	*to have spoken*
haber dicho	*to have said*
haber escrito	*to have written*

---

[1] All derivatives of **volver** form their past participles in the same way—**devolver: devuelto**.

[2] All derivatives of **poner** form their past participles in the same way—**componer: compuesto; suponer: supuesto.**

[3] All derivatives of **cubrir** form their past participles in the same way—**descubrir: descubierto.**

[4] All derivatives of **hacer** form their past participles in the same way—**deshacer: deshecho.**

When pronouns are used in connection with this construction, they are appended to the infinitive.

    Después de haberme⁵ levantado, fui al partido.   *After having gotten up, I went to the game.*

    Además de habernos⁵ dicho una mentira, se burló de nosotros.   *Besides having told us a lie, he made fun of us.*

▶ The compound, or perfect, present participle consists of **habiendo** plus a past participle. An alternate way to express the idea of this construction is **después de** + infinitive.

    habiendo hablado (después de hablar)   *having spoken (after speaking)*
    habiendo dicho (después de decir)   *having said (after saying)*
    habiendo escrito (después de escribir)   *having written (after writing)*

When pronouns are used in connection with this construction, they are attached to the present participle.

    Habiéndolo dicho, me acordé que era un secreto.   *Having said it, I remembered that it was a secret.*

80 The present perfect indicative

▶ The auxiliary verb **haber** is used with the past participle to form perfect tenses both in the indicative and in the subjunctive. The present indicative of **haber** plus a past participle forms the present perfect indicative.

he		*I have*	
has	hablado	*you have*	*spoken*
ha	aprendido	*you have; he, she has*	*learned*
hemos	escrito	*we have*	*written*
han⁶		*you, they have*	

▶ Remember that there are two verbs in Spanish that express *to have* (**haber, tener**), whereas English has only one. The verb **haber** is always used as the auxiliary to form the perfect tenses.

    He tenido que esperar antes.   *I have had to wait before.*

---

⁵ Recall that a verb following a preposition will appear in the infinitive in Spanish, whereas a present participle is used in English (see section **42**).

⁶ For the **vosotros** form of all perfect (compound) tenses, see the Appendix, section **1**.

▶ The Spanish **ha habido** means *there has (have) been*. Here is a summary of impersonal *to be* expressions encountered so far.

hay	*there is, there are*
va a haber	*there will be*
hubo	*there was (there were)*
había	*there was (there were)*
dudo que haya	*I doubt that there is*
quería (esperaba, etc.) que hubiera	*I wanted (I hoped, etc.) that there would be*
ha habido	*there has been (there have been)*

Ha habido muchos problemas en esta clase.	*There have been a lot of problems in this class.*
Ha habido un golpe de estado en Chile.	*There has been a* coup d'etat *in Chile.*
Insistimos en que hubiera más libertad en la universidad.	*We insisted that there be more freedom in the university.*

▶ The past participle, when used to form perfect tenses, always ends in **-o**. The conjugated form of **haber** and the past participle are not separated in Spanish in contrast with English, which often divides the construction. Thus, negative particles and object or reflexive pronouns come before the conjugated form of the auxiliary verb **haber**.

No le hemos dado nada a él.	*We have not given anything to him.*
¿Han ido ellos al Prado?	*Have they gone to the Prado?*

A • Substitution Drill

MODEL ¿Ya han llegado todos?
ella?
STUDENT ¿Ya **ha** llegado ella?

1. ¿Han llegado todos a tiempo?
   José Luis
   Marisol y Pilar
   yo
   él y ella
   mi madre y yo

2. Pilar ha tenido un lapso de memoria.
   Yo
   Tú y yo
   Tú y él
   Sonia y José
   Nosotros

3. Nosotros ya hemos visto los cuadros.
   Ud.
   Uds.
   Él
   Ella y yo
   Tú

4. ¿Has traído tú los apuntes?
   él
   nosotros
   Uds.
   Juan Ignacio
   ellas

B • Transformation Drill   Present → Present Perfect

MODEL   Así que tenemos un examen.
STUDENT   Así que **hemos tenido** un examen.

1. Preparo bien mis apuntes.
2. Eso es imposible.
3. Estamos en el Museo del Prado.
4. Hay un problema en el museo.
5. Tengo que trabajar como un loco.
6. José Luis viaja en el metro.
7. ¿Estás en el Retiro?
8. Siempre me levanto a las ocho.
9. ¿Se da cuenta del problema?
10. Echamos de menos al profesor Monocromios.

C • Transformation Drill

MODEL   Hemos escuchado al rector y podemos discutir las propuestas.
STUDENT 1   **Habiéndolo escuchado**, podemos discutir las propuestas.
STUDENT 2   **Después de haberlo escuchado**, podemos discutir las propuestas.

1. Hemos visto a las muchachas y queremos invitarlas.
2. He repasado la lección y sé las respuestas.
3. Has aceptado el trabajo y tienes que hacerlo bien.
4. Han devuelto los zapatos y reciben el dinero.
5. Ha oído la canción y la sabe de memoria.
6. Hemos conocido a los actores y los llevamos a comer.
7. He revisado las facturas y se las presenté al jefe.
8. Han conseguido las entradas y decidieron ir al partido.
9. Has terminado la exploración y quieres volver.
10. Hemos recibido el premio y vamos a ir a París.

D • Query   Patterned Response

MODEL   ¿Ya visitaste el museo?
STUDENT   **Sí, ya lo he visitado.**

1. ¿Ya comiste las enchiladas?
2. ¿Ya vendiste el cuadro?
3. ¿Ya repasaste los apuntes?
4. ¿Ya pintaste la casa?
5. ¿Ya viste *Los caprichos*?
6. ¿Ya trajo Ud. los libros?
7. ¿Ya devolvió Ud. el anillo?
8. ¿Ya hizo Ud. la tarea?
9. ¿Ya rompió Ud. el traste?
10. ¿Ya escribió Ud. los versos?

E • Query   Free Response

Answer in Spanish, using the present perfect tense.

1. ¿Has tenido problemas con tu novio (novia)?
2. ¿Ha visitado Ud. España o Latinoamérica?
3. ¿Ha leído Ud. alguna obra de Lope de Vega?
4. ¿Has sido un buen estudiante?
5. ¿Has estado enfermo?
6. ¿Has escrito tu tarea?

7. ¿Ha visto Ud. algún cuadro de El Greco?[7]
8. ¿Te han dado calabazas en algún examen?
9. ¿Se ha levantado Ud. temprano en estos días?
10. ¿Se ha dado Ud. cuenta de que el español es una lengua fácil de aprender?

F • Variable Pattern Drill

Practice orally the patterns in the following chart.

Juan y Pilar				el museo.
	quieren piensan tienen que pueden van a		visitar	
	han	querido pensado tenido que podido ido a		
	están		visitando	
	han	estado		
	quieren piensan tienen que pueden van a	estar		
	tienen que pueden	haber	visitado	

G • Translation Drill

Translate into Spanish.

1. I have been here. I have been good. I have been afraid.
2. I have had a lot of work. I have had to work a lot.

---

[7] When a definite article is part of a proper name, it does not contract.

    Este cuadro es de El Greco.   *This painting is by El Greco.*
    Voy a El Salvador.   *I'm going to El Salvador.*

3. There has been no time. There have been two accidents today.
4. Juan has been doing it. Pilar has intended to visit her.
5. We have wanted to go to Mexico. We have been able to sell the house.

81   The present perfect subjunctive

▶ The present perfect subjunctive tense is formed by the present subjunctive of the auxiliary verb **haber** plus the past participle.

haya	
hayas	hablado
haya	aprendido
hayamos	escrito
hayan	

▶ The present perfect subjunctive is used in the same situations as the present subjunctive. It follows the concepts, respectively, of indirect command, emotion, or grammatical unreality.

Prefieren a alquien que   *They prefer somebody who has learned the lesson.*

Esperan que ella   haya aprendido la lección.   *They hope that she has learned the lesson.*

No creen que yo   *They don't think that I have learned the lesson.*

▶ The Spanish present perfect subjunctive translates English *has* or *have* with the past participle, whereas the present subjunctive corresponds to the English present and future (see section **68**). Compare the following matched pairs.

1. Es posible que esté aquí.   *It is possible that he is here.*

                                  or

                        It is possible that he will be here.

   Es posible que haya estado aquí.   *It is possible that he has been here.*

2. Espero que Sonia entienda bien su   *I hope that Sonia is understanding her
   lección.   lesson well.*

                                  or

                        *I hope that Sonia will understand her
                        lesson well.*

   Espero que Sonia haya entendido   *I hope that Sonia has understood her
   bien su lección.   lesson well.*

¡Cuidado!

The present perfect subjunctive follows only present tense verbs in the main clause, not verbs in the past tense. Compare the following.

Es lástima que Cecilia esté enferma.   *It's a shame that Cecilia is sick.*
Es lástima que Cecilia haya estado   *It's a shame that Cecilia has*
enferma.   *been sick.*
Fue lástima (era lástima) que Cecilia   *It was a shame that Cecilia was*
estuviera enferma.   *sick.*

A • Substitution Drill

MODEL   Temo que Pilar se haya retrasado.
             ellos
STUDENT   Temo que ellos se **hayan** retrasado.

1. Temen que yo me haya retrasado.
    tú
    tú y yo
    Ud.
    Ud. y yo
    Juan y Pilar

2. Ojalá que ella haya preparado sus apuntes.
    ellas
    Marisol
    tú y ella
    Uds.
    nosotras

B • Transformation Drill   Present Subjunctive → Present Perfect Subjunctive

MODEL   Es posible que Juan Ignacio llegue antes.
STUDENT   Es posible que Juan Ignacio **haya llegado** antes.

1. Tenemos miedo que ellos no vuelvan.
2. No creo que Marisol rompa la bicicleta.
3. Ojalá que Uds. vean *Los caprichos* de Goya.
4. Es lástima que todavía no lo hagas.
5. Me asombra que Sonia diga eso.
6. Puede ser que Pilar vaya a Puerto Rico.
7. No es verdad que él trabaje como un burro.
8. Niego que Mónica escriba tales cosas.
9. Esperamos que te guste la obra.
10. Es necesario que lo memorices bien.

C • Replacement Drill

MODEL   Creemos que ha llegado.   (No creemos)
STUDENT   **No creemos que haya llegado.**

1. Conocen a alguien que ha pintado cuadros.   (Buscan a alguien)
2. Sabemos que Isabel ha estado en el museo.   (Dudamos)

3. Es cierto que Diana ha tenido miedo de los exámenes.   (No es cierto)
4. Esperan a las dos mujeres que han viajado a Latinoamérica.   (Necesitan dos mujeres)
5. Es verdad que Laura ha sido una estudiante excelente.   (Puede ser)
6. Hay alguien aquí que ha escrito facturas.   (No hay nadie aquí)
7. Tenemos un estudiante que ha estudiado en Costa Rica.   (Preferimos un estudiante)
8. Sé que tú no has preparado tus lecciones.   (Estoy asombrado)

D • Variable Pattern Drill

Practice orally the patterns in the following chart.

No creo que Juan y Pilar ... el Retiro.

quieran piensen tengan que puedan vayan a		visitar
hayan	querido pensado tenido que podido ido a	
estén		
hayan	estado	
quieran piensen tengan que puedan vayan a	estar	visitando
tengan que puedan	haber	visitado

E • Translation Drill

Translate into Spanish.

1. I don't believe you have been here. I doubt that you have been very intelligent in this matter.
2. It's a shame that you have been so sleepy. It's not true that we have been afraid.

3. We deny that Marisol has had to be there. We don't believe that Marisol has had her exam yet.
4. We are surprised that she has had to do it. They hope that he has done the work.
5. We need someone who has memorized the poem. We are looking for a person who has traveled to Nicaragua.
6. There has been an accident. We hope that there has not been an accident.

82 Past participles used as adjectives

▶ Past participles may be used as adjectives and as such they agree with the noun they modify.

La carta abierta	*The opened letter*
Las lecciones aprendidas	*The learned lessons*
Estos salones están cerrados.	*These rooms are closed.*
El estudiante está cansado.	*The student is tired.*

▶ Like any other adjective, past participles may be nominalized.

Los muertos ya no tienen secretos.	*The dead don't have secrets any longer.*
Lo escrito en ese documento no importa.	*What is written in that document doesn't matter.*

¡Cuidado!

When the past participle is part of a perfect tense, it always ends in **-o**; when it is used as an adjective it agrees with the noun it modifies.

Hemos cerrad*o* las ventanas.	*We have closed the windows.*
Las ventanas están cerrad*as*.	*The windows are closed.*
Los poemas han sid*o* escrit*os* por Martí.	*The poems have been written by Martí.*

Fill in the blanks with the proper endings.

Estamos cansad _____ porque hemos trabajad _____ mucho.

Ha habid _____ una reunión en la oficina del rector.

La carta está escrit _____ en español.

Los salones han estad _____ cerrad _____ por varios días.

Los cuadros han sid _____ pintado _____ por Goya.

A • Query   Patterned Response

MODEL   ¿Ha abierto Ud. las ventanas?
STUDENT **Sí, están abiertas.**

1. ¿Ha cerrado Ud. los libros?
2. ¿Ha terminado Ud. la tarea?
3. ¿Ha pintado Ud. los cuadros?
4. ¿Ha escrito Ud. la lección?
5. ¿Ha aprendido Ud. la canción?

6. ¿Has vendido las revistas?
7. ¿Has hecho la comida?
8. ¿Has puesto las cosas allí?
9. ¿Has lavado el automóvil?
10. ¿Has abierto la puerta?

B • Translation Drill

Translate into Spanish.

1. Is the letter written? Yes, we have written it.
2. Is the door closed? Yes, she has closed it.
3. Are the books opened? Yes, the students have opened them.
4. Is the automobile painted? Yes, I have painted it.
5. Is the work done? Yes, I have done it.

83 A summary of Spanish equivalents of the passive voice

▶ In the English passive voice, the subject of the sentence receives the action of the verb. There are four equivalents of the English passive construction in Spanish.

a. When an action is performed by an agent, Spanish uses **ser** and the past participle (which agrees with the subject). The agent is introduced by **por**. This same construction may be used even when an agent is implied but not expressed directly.

Las puertas fueron cerradas por Marisol.	*The doors were closed by*
or	*Marisol.*
Las puertas fueron cerradas.	*The doors were closed.*

b. When the agent is not expressed (or implied) and the subject is a thing, the reflexive substitute for the passive is regularly used (see section **45**).

Se cerró la puerta.	*The door was closed.*
Las tiendas se abren a las diez.	*The stores are opened at ten* (*The stores open at ten*).

c. Alternately, an impersonal (no subject noun or pronoun) third person plural active construction may be used.

Cerraron la puerta.	*They closed the door.*	(*They* refers to no one in
Abren las tiendas.	*They open the stores.*	particular.)

d. When a condition resulting from a prior action is referred to, **estar** plus a past participle is used. In this construction the past participle agrees with the subject.

Las puertas estaban cerradas.   *The doors were closed.*

Susana lleva el loro a
la casa de su amiga.

El loro es llevado por Susana
a la casa de su amiga.

Summary

Both action and agent (expressed or implied)	La carta fue escrita (por Pilar).
Action but no agent expressed	Se escribió la carta. or Escribieron la carta.
Neither action nor agent expressed; result of an action	La carta estaba escrita en español.

► While it is theoretically possible to express an English passive construction in various ways in Spanish, usually, depending on the construction, there would be only one or two Spanish analogues that would sound satisfactory.

1. Fue pintado por Velázquez.

   It was painted by Velázquez. (Since there is an agent, **ser** plus a past participle is called for.)

2. Se habla español.

   Spanish is spoken. (The reflexive is used because the agent is "everybody" in the context alluded to, but no one in particular.)

3. Se dice (*or* Dicen) que el Real Madrid va a ganar.

   It is said (or *They say*) *that the Real Madrid is going to win.* (There is no interest in specifying the agent.)

4. Estas tiendas han estado abiertas desde las ocho.

These stores have been open since eight o'clock. (Describes a state that results from prior actions that are not expressed.)

A • Substitution Drill

MODEL   El libro fue escrito por Cervantes.
          libros
STUDENT   **Los** libros **fueron escritos** por Cervantes.

1. La tarea fue hecha por Laura.
   cuadros
   guacamole
   facturas
   anillos
   propuesta

2. La puerta fue abierta por el antropólogo.
   templo
   oficina
   bibliotecas
   agencia
   libros

B • Transformation Drill   Active Voice → Passive Voice

MODEL   Roberto cerró la ventana.
STUDENT   **La ventana fue cerrada por Roberto.**

1. Nacho vendió el automóvil.
2. Marisol trajo los apuntes.
3. El profesor preparó el examen.
4. Carlos buscó los billetes.

5. Ellos han comprado las cervezas.
6. El poeta ha escrito los versos.
7. El guardia ha cerrado la agencia.
8. Laura ha abierto la oficina.

C • Query   Patterned Response

MODEL   ¿Abren las tiendas a las diez?
STUDENT   **Sí, se abren las tiendas a las diez.**

1. ¿Venden revistas aquí?
2. ¿Reparan automóviles?
3. ¿Mandan los periódicos?
4. ¿Celebran una boda?

5. ¿Aceptan la propuesta?
6. ¿Establecen la verdad?
7. ¿Sirven platos típicos?
8. ¿Comienzan una investigación?

D • Query   Patterned Response

MODEL   ¿Van a escribir la composición?
STUDENT   **La composición ya está escrita.**

1. ¿Van a acabar la tarea?
2. ¿Van a arreglar la máquina?
3. ¿Van a hacer las facturas?
4. ¿Van a poner la bicicleta en su lugar?
5. ¿Van a traducir ese poema?

6. ¿Van a construir el museo?
7. ¿Van a comenzar la obra?
8. ¿Van a informar al ministro?
9. ¿Van a vender los trastes viejos?
10. ¿Van a devolver los libros?

E • Translation Drill

Translate into Spanish. There may be more than one satisfactory translation.

1. He painted it. It was painted by him.
2. She said it. It is said that these are the best.
3. We speak Spanish. Spanish is spoken.
4. When I arrived it was closed.
5. Who wrote that? That was written by Cervantes.

84 Equivalent of *let's*: first person plural commands

▶ The first person plural of the present subjunctive is used to express *let's* (*let us*) plus a verb. (**Vamos** and its reflexive, **vámonos**, used affirmatively, are exceptions, since the indicative is used.) As with other commands, object pronouns precede when the verb is negative and follow when it is affirmative. However, when the reflexive pronoun **nos** follows the verb, the final **-s** is dropped from the verb.

1. ¡Entremos, pues!	*Well, let's go in!*
2. Vamos allá.	*Let's go there.*
3. Vámonos.	*Let's go. Let's get going.*
4. Levantémonos más temprano.	*Let's get up earlier.*
5. No nos levantemos todavía.	*Let's not get up yet.*

▶ **Vamos a** + infinitive is another way of expressing *let's*, though only in the affirmative.[8] The subjunctive **vayamos** must be used in the negative for *let's not go*. (While **vamos a repasar nuestros apuntes** may mean, depending on context, *let's review our notes* or *we are going to review our notes*, **no vamos a repasar nuestros apuntes** can only mean, *we aren't going to review our notes*.)

1. Vamos a remar en el estanque.	*Let's row in the pond.*
	or
	We are going to row in the pond.
2. Vamos a preparar bien para el examen.	*Let's prepare well for the exam.*
	or
	We are going to prepare well for the exam.
3. No nos vayamos todavía.	*Let's not go yet.*
4. No nos vamos todavía.	*We are not going yet.*

For *let's see*, **a ver** is often used without **vamos**.

> (**Vamos**) **A ver qué pasa.**   *Let's see what happens.*

---

[8] Although **vamos a** + infinitive and the command form can be used interchangeably, the command form is slightly more emphatic.

A • Transformation Drill   Affirmative Command → Negative Command

MODEL   Vámonos.
STUDENT   **No nos vayamos.**

1. Hagamos el trabajo ahora.
2. Busquemos a Berta.
3. Preparémoslos bien.
4. Sentémonos.
5. Levantémonos.

6. Escribamos.
7. Entremos, pues.
8. Leámoslo.
9. Bailemos y cantemos. (Use **ni** in the negative.)
10. Pronunciémoslas.

B • Transformation Drill   Negative Command → Affirmative Command

MODEL   No la llamemos hoy.
STUDENT   **Llamémosla** hoy.

1. No pongamos ese disco ahora.
2. No pintemos el cuarto hoy.
3. No trabajemos todo el día.
4. No esperemos a los otros.
5. No bailemos el último tango.

6. No continuemos los estudios.
7. ¡No lo ayudemos!
8. No las hagamos.
9. No nos quedemos aquí.
10. No nos vayamos al partido.

C • Query   Patterned Response

MODEL   ¿Leemos la carta?
STUDENT   **Sí, leámosla. No, no la leamos.**

1. ¿Buscamos la clase?
2. ¿Revisamos las facturas?
3. ¿Tomamos unas cervezas?
4. ¿Hacemos el trabajo?
5. ¿Miramos la película?

6. ¿Escribimos la tarea?
7. ¿Componemos el automóvil?
8. ¿Cantamos la canción?
9. ¿Memorizamos los apuntes?
10. ¿Practicamos el español?

D • Patterned Response

MODEL   ¿Escribimos la carta?
STUDENT 1   **Sí, vamos a escribirla hoy.**
STUDENT 2   **Sí, escribámosla hoy mismo.**

1. ¿Repasamos los apuntes?
2. ¿Vendemos estos trastes viejos?
3. ¿Discutimos el proyecto con el ingeniero?
4. ¿Hacemos un plato mexicano?
5. ¿Compramos entradas para el concierto?

6. ¿Pintamos la mesa?
7. ¿Regresamos a la ciudad?
8. ¿Nos reunimos con los estudiantes?
9. ¿Nos ayudamos con la lección?
10. ¿Nos encontramos en el café?

E • Translation Drill

Translate into Spanish. There may be more than one translation.

1. Let's go there. Let's not go there.
2. Let's wash it. Let's not wash it. Let's wash ourselves. Let's not wash ourselves.
3. Let's buy the magazine. Let's not sell the tickets.
4. Let's stay here. Let's not stay here.
5. Let's sit down. Let's go away.

REVIEW

I The following questions are related to the dialog. Answer in Spanish.

1. ¿Por qué han visitado el museo los estudiantes?
2. ¿Qué quiere hacer José Luis mientras todos esperan a Pilar?
3. ¿Por qué tiene miedo Juan Ignacio que le van a dar calabazas en el examen?
4. ¿Dónde se paró el metro de Pilar?
5. A propósito, ¿por quién fueron pintados *Los caprichos*?
6. ¿Cuántos cuadros se dice que hay en el Prado?
7. ¿Por qué no pueden ver los cuadros de Goya?
8. ¿Qué quiere hacer Juan Ignacio en vez de quedarse en el museo?

II Translation. Translate into Spanish.

1. Has everybody prepared the homework? I am sure that the professor has prepared an exam for us.
2. I don't think that she has done that. She likes to give us a week to prepare ourselves.
3. I don't know. She is worried that we have not memorized enough paintings.
4. By the way, what paintings were painted by El Greco?
5. El Greco? I'm not sure, but *Las Meninas* was painted by Velázquez.
6. Look! Here she comes. I hope that I don't flunk this damn exam.
7. Hello, Professor. All of us have had a very difficult week. We have had to work a lot.
8. I know it. And today is such a pretty day. Let's not stay here. Let's go to the museum to see the Goya exhibition.

III   Write your own dialog.

Imagine that you are late for a play. Your friends are angry with you but forgive you when you invite them to have dinner with you at a good restaurant.

Cognates & Contexts

¿ Desea Ud. ser artista ?

¡ Aprenda a dibujar en su casa por correo !

¡ Gane dinero fabuloso !

¡ No importa su edad !

¿Sabe Ud. cuánto dinero ganan los artistas? Hace unos meses que una sola pintura de Picasso se vendió en... ¡ 3.000.000 de pesos !

El Instituto de Arte Patraña ha preparado un curso fabuloso y completo que le enseña todo lo que necesita para ser un artista.

Publicidad

Las agencias y el comercio necesitan cada vez más dibujantes para la preparación de anuncios, catálogos y materiales gráficos en general. Este curso ofrece magníficas oportunidades para personas de ambición y talento.

Instálese por su Cuenta

Haga como muchos de nuestros alumnos que se han instalado por su cuenta y ahora ganan mucho dinero creando historietas y colaborando desde su casa con diarios y revistas de todo el mundo.

por correo *by mail*

edad *age*

comercio *business, commerce*

dibujantes *illustrators, designers*
anuncios *ads, announcements*

instalarse *to get installed, set up*
por su cuenta *on their own*
historietas *comic strips*

diarios *daily newspapers*

Nuestra Garantía

Nosotros le garantizamos que todos los dibujos sin excepción son evaluados por el ilustre y famoso director del Instituto, Pancho Patraña. Él mismo evalúa todas las asignaciones de sus aprendices y les da valiosas observaciones y sugerencias.

asignaciones *assignments*

valiosas *valuable*

sugerencias *suggestions*

Si desea más información, escriba a:
Instituto de Arte Patraña
Calle Miró No. 13-Bis
Villaviciosa del Mar, Andurria
Nombre_____Edad_____
Dirección _____
Ciudad o Pueblo _____
Provincia, Departamento o Estado

departamento *Spanish equivalent to district or county*

Meeting of the United Farm Workers, California

Lección diecinueve

EL PRIMER ENCUENTRO CON LA RAZA

– ud form – Tu = perdona m

n becomes m

encuentro *meeting, encounter*

SANDRA	Perdone, señor, ¿podría decirme qué se está celebrando aquí?
SR. CARVAJAL	¡Cómo no, señorita! Durante los próximos días tendremos el Congreso de La Raza aquí en el Centro de Convenciones. ¿Le gustaría asistir?
SANDRA	Francamente, no sé qué es La Raza.
SR. CARVAJAL	¡Ah, señorita! Se ve que Ud. no es de por aquí. Si fuera de esta parte de los Estados Unidos, sabría mucho de nuestra gente. Ése es el propósito del Congreso: familiarizarlos con la realidad chicana.
SANDRA	Eso sería útil. Seguramente hay muchas otras personas como yo que no saben muy bien qué representa La Raza. Me gustaría platicar más con Uds. Me llamo Sandra.
SR. CARVAJAL	Mi nombre es Juan Carvajal. Mi hija Elenita vendrá pronto. Si desea, espérela Ud. y ella la llevará por toda la exposición.
SANDRA	Mil gracias, Sr. Carvajal. Estaré allí enfrente mirando los carteles.
SR. CARVAJAL	Elenita, quiero que acompañes a esta señorita a ver las exhibiciones. Luego deberían ir a ver la obra del Teatro Campesino. No sé si ella

celebrarse *to take place; to be celebrated*
¡Cómo no! *Of course!*
próximos *next*
asistir *to attend*

assist = ayudar

Past perfect
ser

propósito *purpose*

útil *useful*

platicar *(Mex.) to chat*

enfrente (de) *in front (of); across (from)*
carteles *posters*

acompañar *to accompany*
exhibiciones *exhibits*

entenderá todas las expresiones nuestras pero tú podrás ayudarla.

SANDRA   Son ustedes muy amables. Mi tío me dijo que aprendería mucho en California. Parece que hoy mismo comenzaré.   **amables** *kind, nice* **tío** *uncle*

ELENITA   Ándale pues. Si quieres ver el Teatro, tendremos que ir al auditorio y está lejos.   **ándale pues** (coll.) *get going then* **lejos** *far*

SANDRA   ¿Qué hacen todas esas personas?

ELENITA   Estarán esperando a César Chávez. Viene para hablarnos de La Causa.

SANDRA   Quisiera saber más sobre el significado de estas palabras: La Raza, La Causa, el Teatro Campesino... ¿Es cierto que Uds. no quieren ser norteamericanos sino que han escogido una nacionalidad aparte?   **significado** *meaning* **sino** *but rather* **escoger** *to choose* **aparte** *aside, separate*

ELENITA   Nosotros los chicanos queremos participar en todos los derechos y las responsabilidades del ciudadano americano, porque lo somos también. Sin embargo, no es necesario cambiar nuestra propia cultura de tradición mexicana e india. Estamos orgullosos de nuestras raíces.   **derechos** *rights* **cambiar** *to change* **estar orgulloso** *to be proud* **raíces** (sing., **raíz**) *roots*

SANDRA   Veo que estoy recibiendo toda una educación hoy.

ELENITA   Sí, pero démonos prisa. La función comienza en quince minutos y allí aprenderás más acerca de lo nuestro.   **darse prisa** *to hurry* **función** *show*

NOTES

La Raza   Refers to the Chicano people. It is a term that emphasizes ethnic pride and the shedding of traditional false prejudices and stereotypes concerning Mexican-Americans.

el Teatro Campesino   El Teatro Campesino, established by Luis Valdez, is closely linked to the United Farm Workers. It is a politically-oriented form of bilingual theater that attempts to raise the consciousness of Chicano farm workers and simulate the conflicts that they might encounter in pursuing their employment and social goals.

La Causa   Refers to the Chicano social, political, and economic movement and its attendant goals.

César Chávez—United Farm Workers   César Chávez is one of the best-known leaders of the Chicano movement. He was the key figure in establishing the United Farm Workers, which for the first time organized the migrant farm workers in California and other states. This union not only seeks to better the migrant workers' wages and employment conditions but also aspires to reawaken in them a positive sense of identity that is the essential precondition for social advancement.

LANGUAGE STRUCTURES

85 The future and conditional tenses of regular verbs

Infinitive	Future Endings	Conditional Endings
hablar	-é	-ía
	-ás	-ías
aprender	-á	-ía
escribir	-emos	-íamos
	-án[1]	-ían[1]

▶ The formation, irregularities, and uses of the future and conditional tenses are closely parallel. For all Spanish verbs (**-ar, -er, -ir**) there is only one set of endings in the

[1] For the **vosotros** forms of the future and conditional, see the Appendix, section **1**.

future and one in the conditional. These endings are attached to the infinitive of regular verbs. The future endings, except for the accents, are the same as the present indicative endings of the irregular verb **haber** (see section **80**). The conditional endings are the same as the imperfect indicative endings for **-er** and **-ir** verbs.

1. Estaré allí al mediodía.   *I will be there at noon.*
2. Elenita regresará pronto.   *Elenita will return soon.*
3. Me gustaría platicar con Uds.   *I would like to talk with you.*
4. Eso sería útil.   *That would be useful.*

▶ The future tense, much as the **ir a** + infinitive construction that you have already learned (see section **9**), generally indicates actions yet to take place. Although these two constructions can be used interchangeably, as with English, the Spanish future tense indicates stronger commitment or determination.

▶ The equivalent of the Spanish future tense is indicated in English by the auxiliary verbs *shall* and *will*; the equivalent of **ir a** + infinitive is *to be going* + infinitive.

Mañana te voy a hablar.   *Tomorrow I am going to speak to you.*
Mañana te hablaré.   *Tomorrow I will (shall) speak to you.*

" " HABLO — PRESENT ⊂ FUTURE MEANING.

▶ The conditional is to the past what the future is to the present. It is used to convey future meaning with regard to a point of reference in the past. Contrast the following:

1. Te aseguro que llegarán mañana.   *I assure you they will arrive tomorrow.*

   Te aseguré la semana pasada que llegarían.   *I assured you last week they would[2] arrive.*

2. Yo sé que Elenita regresará pronto.   *I know that Elenita will return soon.*

   Yo sabía que Elenita regresaría pronto.   *I knew that Elenita would return soon.*

Conditional uses imperf. endings of verb haber
✓ había
✓ habías
✓ había
✓ habíamos
✓ habían

[2] Although the conditional is usually translated as *would*, the meaning of the sentence must be interpreted from context, as *would* can also translate the imperfect expressing a habitual action.

Cuando vivía en Madrid iba al teatro todas las noches.   *When I lived in Madrid I would go to the theater every night.*

▶ Recall that progressive forms of tenses are made with a conjugated form of **estar** + present participle. The future progressive and the conditional progressive express continuous action within their respective time frames, just like the present progressive (see section **32**) and the past progressive (see section **57**).

Estarán trabajando aquí mañana.	*They will be working here tomorrow.*
Yo sabía que tú estarías mirando los carteles.	*I knew you would be looking at the the posters.*

progressive not used as much in Spanish as in English.

A • Substitution Drill

MODEL   Yo aprenderé muchas cosas sobre La Raza.
             Tú

STUDENT Tú **aprenderás** muchas cosas sobre La Raza.

1. Tú aprenderás muchas cosas sobre La Raza.
   Ella
   Juan y yo
   Los americanos
   Ud.
   Tú y él

2. El Sr. Carvajal me estará llevando allí.
   Elenita
   Tú
   Mi tío
   Uds.
   Ellas

B • Substitution Drill

MODEL   Mi tío me dijo que él llegaría hoy.
                    Juanita

STUDENT Mi tío me dijo que Juanita **llegaría** hoy.

1. Mi tío me dijo que Juanita llegaría hoy.
        nosotros
        tú
        ellas
        la carta
        Uds.

2. Yo sabía que tú estarías mirando la función.
        nosotras
        todas las personas
        la Sra. López
        tú
        tú y yo

C • Transformation Drill   ir a + Infinitive → Future

MODEL   Voy a volver temprano.
STUDENT **Volveré** temprano.

1. Van a volver temprano.
2. Voy a abrir la tienda los lunes.
3. Vamos a convidar a los estudiantes.
4. Vas a perder las fotos.
5. ¿Me van a contar la noticia?

Future → ir a + Infinitive

6. Estaré listo.
7. El profesor leerá con cuidado.
8. Nos despediremos de ellos.
9. No comprenderemos la obra.
10. Repasarás los apuntes antes del examen.

notes

D • Transformation Drill   Present/Future → Past/Conditional

| MODEL | Dice que llegará a las ocho.   (Dijo) |
| STUDENT | **Dijo** que **llegaría** a las ocho. |

1. Escribe que visitará Machu Picchu.   (Escribió)
2. Sabes que insistirán en pagar.   (Sabías)
3. Aseguro que los tamales serán buenos.   (Aseguré)
4. Nos acordamos que el director nos dará un aumento.   (Nos acordamos)
5. ¿Comprendes que ellos no pagarán?   (¿Comprendiste)
6. ¿Crees que pedirán tu dirección?   (¿Creías)
7. Decide que la obra empezará hoy.   (Decidió)
8. Veo que necesitarás más dinero.   (Vi)
9. Pensamos que se retrasarán los camiones.   (Pensábamos)
10. Es cierto que no seguiremos sus sugerencias.   (Era cierto)

suggestions

E • Transformation Drill   Future or Conditional → Future Progressive or Conditional Progressive

| MODEL | Hablaré con ella. |
| STUDENT | **Estaré hablando** con ella. |

| MODEL | Dijo que él lo miraría. |
| STUDENT | Dijo que él lo **estaría mirando**. |

1. Estudiaré en la biblioteca mañana.
2. Mi hermano me acompañará.
3. Yo no comería a estas horas.
4. ¿Perderíamos mucho tiempo?
5. ¿Es verdad que pintaremos carteles para el Teatro?
6. Yo sabía que platicaría con ella.
7. ¿Crees que se celebrará el Congreso aquí?
8. Juan dijo que miraría el cuadro.
9. Visitaremos muchos lugares en Caracas.
10. Ella aprendería esto perfectamente.

F • Query   Patterned Response

MODEL   ¿Te levantaste tarde ayer?
STUDENT **Sí, pero mañana me levantaré temprano.**

1. ¿Volvieron ellos tarde ayer?
2. ¿Comiste tarde ayer?
3. ¿Regresó Elenita tarde ayer?
4. ¿Acabaste tarde ayer?
5. ¿Se despertaron Uds. tarde ayer?

6. ¿Tu papá llegó tarde ayer?
7. ¿Terminaron ellas la tarea tarde ayer?
8. ¿Se despertó Ud. tarde ayer?
9. ¿Se levantó Sandra tarde ayer?
10. ¿Fueron Uds. al trabajo tarde ayer?

G • Query   Patterned Response

MODEL   ¿Van Uds. a ver la exposición?
STUDENT **¡Quién sabe si la veremos!**

1. ¿Van a castigar a los bandidos?
2. ¿Vas a discutir la propuesta con el jefe?
3. ¿Va Ud. a devolverle el anillo?
4. ¿Van ellos a traer la comida?
5. ¿Vamos a lograr nuestros deseos?

6. ¿Vas a esperar al Sr. Carvajal?
7. ¿Vamos a mirar los carteles?
8. ¿Va Ud. a ver la obra del Teatro Campesino?
9. ¿Voy a entender las palabras?
10. ¿Vamos a bailar un tango?

H • Query   Patterned Response

MODEL   ¿Empezó ella el trabajo el jueves?
STUDENT **No, pero dijo que lo empezaría el lunes.**

1. ¿Lo trajeron el jueves?
2. ¿Lo compraron el jueves?
3. ¿Acompañaste a Juan el jueves?
4. ¿Habló César Chávez el jueves?
5. ¿Escogiste un anillo el jueves?

6. ¿Charló contigo el jueves?
7. ¿Cambiaron Uds. el dinero el jueves?
8. ¿Fuiste a la función con Elenita el jueves?
9. ¿Consiguió Ignacio el dinero el jueves?
10. ¿Recibieron ellos la carta el jueves?

I • Query   Patterned Response

MODEL   ¿Compraste el cartel?
STUDENT **¡Qué! Yo no compraría eso.**

1. ¿Aprendieron Uds. el poema?
2. ¿Miraron ellos la obra?
3. ¿Preparaste la comida?
4. ¿Compró Ud. esos trastes?
5. ¿Aceptaron Uds. la demanda?

6. ¿Contaste el chiste?
7. ¿Construyeron ellos la carretera?
8. ¿Ofreciste mil dólares por el cuadro?
9. ¿Tomaron Uds. una horchata?
10. ¿Reparó Ud. el automóvil?

J • Query   Free Response

Answer in Spanish.

1. ¿Les gustaría a Uds. ver una obra del Teatro Campesino?
2. ¿Te volverás loco (loca) si no llama tu novia (novio) pronto?
3. ¿Cuánto dinero me prestarías? ¿O no me prestarías nada?
4. ¿Adónde irán Uds. después de la clase?
5. ¿Qué compraría Ud. con cien dólares (pesos)?
6. ¿Dónde pasará Ud. sus vacaciones?
7. ¿Qué preferirías ser, rico o pobre?
8. ¿A quién visitarás pronto?
9. ¿Asistirías a un concierto de música clásica?
10. ¿Estarás cambiando tus ideas en el futuro?

quepo 1st pers. sing.

86   Verbs with irregular stems in the future and conditional

▶ The following verbs do not use the infinitive as the stem for the future and conditional tenses but rather undergo certain changes in the stem that remain throughout the conjugation. The verbs in bold type are new vocabulary.

Infinitive	Irregular Future and Conditional Stem		Future Endings	Conditional Endings
caber[3] *to fit* INTO	cabr-	⎫	-é	-ía
haber	habr-	drop **-e-**		
poder	podr-	in infinitive	-ás	-ías
querer	querr-	ending		
saber	sabr-	⎭	-á	-ía
poner[4]	pondr-	⎫	-emos	-íamos
salir	saldr-	drop vowel		
tener[4]	tendr-	in infinitive		
valer[5] *to be worth*; *to cost*	valdr-	ending;	-án	-ían
venir[4]	vendr-	insert **-d-** ⎭		
decir[4]	dir-	⎫ irregular stem		
hacer[4]	har-	⎭		

[3] **Caber** is irregular in both the present and the preterit. Present: **quepo, cabes, cabe, cabemos, caben.** Preterit: **cupe, cupiste, cupo, cupimos, cupieron.**

[4] Derivatives of these verbs undergo the same changes: **prevenir, prevendré; deshacer, desharías; componer, compondrá; retener, retendríamos; predecir, predirán.**

[5] The present indicative of **valer** is irregular in the first person singular: **valgo, vales, vale, valemos, valen.**

TO BE WORTH   PREDICT

A • Substitution Drill

MODEL   Yo pondré las revistas en la mesa.
         Nosotros
STUDENT Nosotros **pondremos** las revistas en la mesa.

MODEL   Dijo que tú vendrías antes de las diez.
              yo
STUDENT Dijo que yo **vendría** antes de las diez.

1. Sabíamos que ellos dirían eso.
       tú
       el Sr. Carvajal
       las señoras
       el director
       Ud.

2. Nosotros pondremos las revistas en la mesa.
       Tú
       Los niños
       El jefe
       Elenita y yo
       Uds.

3. ¿Qué podrán hacer esos tontos allí?
       mi comadre
       tú
       yo
       él y sus hijos
       la gente

4. ¿Protestar? ¡Claro que ellos lo harían!
       ¿Luchar?   yo
       ¿Hacer un viaje?   nosotros
       ¿Resistir?   La Raza
       ¿Divertirse?   los chiquillos
       ¿Meter la pata?   tú

B • Transformation Drill   Present → Future

MODEL   Tenemos la respuesta
STUDENT **Tendremos** la respuesta.

1. Tengo la respuesta.
2. Salimos a las once todos los días.
3. Ud. se pone furioso con esos jóvenes.
4. Ellos saben la verdad.
5. ¿Quieres venir conmigo al museo?
6. Las entradas valen mucho dinero.
7. Nunca vengo temprano a clase.
8. ¿Cuándo haces la tarea?
9. Hay un congreso aquí.
10. ¿Qué te dicen tus padres?

C • Transformation Drill   Imperfect of ir a + Infinitive → Conditional

MODEL   Dijeron que iba a caber aquí.
STUDENT Dijeron que **cabría** aquí.

1. Creían que íbamos a tener suerte.
2. El profesor pensaba que no iban a saber la tarea.
3. Insistían que iba a haber una protesta hoy.
4. Sabían que íbamos a decir una mentira.
5. Le aseguré que iba a poner las facturas en la oficina.
6. No sabíamos que iba a valer tanto.
7. Estábamos seguros que Uds. iban a salir temprano.
8. No dudé que Ud. iba a poder ganarlo.

D • Query   Free Response

Answer in Spanish.

1. ¿Podrás visitar otro país este año?
2. ¿Tendrás buenas noticias hoy?
3. ¿Qué harás durante las próximas vacaciones?
4. ¿Dará Ud. un paseo esta tarde?
5. ¿Saldrá Ud. con su novio (novia) hoy?
6. ¿Por qué pedirías un aumento a tu jefe?
7. ¿Qué deberían hacer las autoridades aquí?
8. ¿Qué dirían sus amigos de esta universidad?
9. ¿Quién de tu familia tendría ganas de ir a un concierto?
10. ¿Ahora dirías que el español es fácil?

E • Translation Drill

Translate into Spanish.

1. Will they have the plates on the table? Yes, I already told you they would have them there!
2. Will he give them the news? Of course! He assured us he would tell it to them right away.
3. Will we be able to go? No, you would come back too late.
4. Will I arrive on time? No, but I informed them that you would attend another show.
5. Will they tell jokes? By the way, would they also sing guajiras?

87 Future and conditional for probability or conjecture

▶ The future tense can be used to express probability or conjecture about a present action or condition (examples 1, 2, and 3). The conditional tense can often be used to express probability or conjecture about a past action or condition (examples 4 and 5). In order to express the equivalent, English needs to use expressions such as *I wonder, probably, do you suppose, can . . . be, must,* etc. **Probablemente**, **tal vez**, or other expressions of probability are not normally included in Spanish constructions of this type.

1. ¿Qué hacen esas personas? Estarán esperando al Sr. Chávez.
   What are those people doing? They must be waiting for Mr. Chávez.

2. Hablarán de tonterías, como siempre.
   They are probably talking about nonsense, as usual.

3. ¿Qué hora será? Serán las once ya.
   What time do you suppose it is? It must be eleven already.

4. ¿Dónde estaría Manuel cuando intenté llamarlo? Estaría en el Congreso.
   I wonder where Manuel was when I tried to call him. He was probably at the convention.

when there is an interrogative word the
intonation falls at end of sentence.

5. Serían las ocho cuando llegaste, pero no miré el reloj.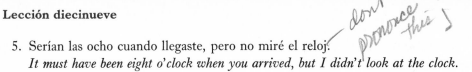
   It must have been eight o'clock when you arrived, but I didn't look at the clock.

Están saliendo del teatro ahora.

Estarán saliendo del teatro ahora.

A • Transformation Drill

MODEL	Probablemente los bandidos se esconden de nosotros.
STUDENT	**Los bandidos se esconderán** de nosotros.

MODEL	Tal vez estuvo aquí ayer.
STUDENT	**Estaría** aquí ayer.

1. Probablemente viene ahora.
2. Tal vez te cansaste de hacer tantos viajes.
3. Probablemente eligen un nuevo alcalde durante esta sesión.
4. Probablemente comenzaron ya la obra.
5. Tal vez sale sin dinero.
6. Probablemente prefirieron regresar más temprano.
7. Tal vez terminó las facturas ayer.
8. Probablemente bailó hasta la medianoche y por eso tiene sueño.

B • Query   Patterned Response

MODEL	¿Dónde está Mónica? ¿En casa?
STUDENT	**Sí, como de costumbre, estará en casa.**

1. ¿Dónde está tu hermana? ¿En la biblioteca?
2. ¿Qué escuchan los chiquillos? ¿Su programa favorito?
3. ¿De qué hablan los ministros? ¿De política?
4. ¿Cuándo van a México? ¿Durante el verano?
5. ¿Dónde celebran el Congreso? ¿En el centro de convenciones?
6. ¿Cuándo escribe ella la composición? ¿Después de la clase?
7. ¿En quién piensa Ignacio? ¿En su novia?
8. ¿Qué traen Uds. a la venta? ¿Trastes viejos?

C • Query   Patterned Response

MODEL   ¿Quiénes dejaron abierta la puerta? ¿Los niños?
STUDENT   **Pues sí... los niños dejarían abierta la puerta.**

1. ¿Quién dejó abierta la puerta? ¿Tu hermanito?
2. ¿Por qué no nos visitaron ayer? ¿Estaban enfermos?
3. ¿Qué sirvieron? ¿Una comida para reyes?
4. ¿Cuántas personas asistieron a la protesta? ¿Más de diez mil?
5. ¿Dónde compró Tere ese disco? ¿En la Avenida de las Américas?
6. ¿Qué leyeron en clase ayer? ¿*Fuenteovejuna*?
7. ¿Cómo encontraron las ruinas? ¿Por casualidad?
8. ¿Cuándo enseñaba esa clase? ¿El año pasado?

D • Translation Drill

Translate into Spanish.

1. I wonder what time it is? It must be three o'clock.
2. Who do you suppose was there? It probably was César Chávez.
3. Who can it be? It is probably Mr. Carvajal.
4. I wonder who would say that? It must have been a liar.
5. They probably think we aren't going to come. They must be worried.

88   Clauses with si

▶ Clauses with **si** are another type of subordinate clause, even though they often come at the beginning of a sentence. In English the equivalent structure is the *if* clause. *If* clauses, coupled with a main clause, can express the following.

I A condition that is contrary to fact.

If I were rich, I would buy a car.   (English uses the subjunctive *I were*, not the indicative *I am*.)

II An improbable event in the future.

If they were to come tomorrow, they would do it.   (English uses the subjunctive *they were to come*, not *they come*).

Si vinieran mañana lo harían.

III The prediction of certain circumstances that are expected to take place (or took place).

If it rains, we won't go.
If it rained, they didn't go.   (English uses the indicative *we won't go, they didn't go*.)

Si llueve no iremos.
Si llovió no fueron.

Both English and Spanish call for the subjunctive in cases I, conditions contrary to fact, and II, improbable events in the future, because of the unreality inherent in such expressions. In case III, predictions of what is expected to occur, the indicative is used in both English and Spanish.

▶ To express a condition that is contrary to fact (examples 1 and 2) or an improbable event in the future (example 3), Spanish uses the imperfect subjunctive in the **si** clause. The main clause is usually expressed in the conditional.[6]

1. Si fuera de por aquí, sabría más de nuestra gente.

If you were from around here (which you aren't), *you would know more about our people.*

2. Podríamos visitar al profe, si supiéramos dónde vive.

We could visit the prof if we knew where he lived (but we don't).

3. Si vinieran mañana, lo harían.

If they were to come tomorrow (which isn't likely), *they would do it.*

▶ When the **si** clause does not express a condition contrary to fact but rather presumes that something did in fact happen (examples 1 and 2) or is likely to occur (examples 3 and 4), the indicative is used in Spanish, as in English. The main clause is in the indicative or is a command (example 3).

1. Si perdiste tu anillo en la tienda, ¿por qué no regresaste?

If you lost your ring in the store, why didn't you return?

2. La profesora me castigaba si no corregía todos mis errores.

The professor would (used to) punish me if I didn't correct all my mistakes.

3. Si puedes, escríbeme una carta de Argentina.

If you can, write me a letter from Argentina.

4. Nos llamarán en seguida si hay buenas noticias.

They will call us right away if there is good news.

¡Cuidado!

The future and conditional tenses are never used after **si** when it means *if*. However, **si** can also mean *whether* and when it does, the future and conditional may be used.

No sabemos si discutirán esa propuesta.   *We don't know whether (or not) they will discuss that proposal.*

---

[6] The imperfect subjunctive may also be used in the main clause. However, in this text only the conditional is used.

No sabía si vendrías conmigo.

I didn't know whether (or not) you would come with me.

But:

Si discuten esa propuesta, asistiremos a la reunión.

If they discuss that proposal, we will attend the meeting.

The present subjunctive is rarely used in a **si** clause and no examples of its use are included in this textbook.

A • Variable Substitution Drill

MODEL   Si tú fueras de por aquí, conocerías la carretera.
               él
STUDENT   Si él **fuera** de por aquí, **conocería** la carretera.

1. Si Ud. hablara menos, estudiaría más.
    tú
       habláramos
    yo
    Uds.
            estudiarías.

2. Si él fuera de por aquí, conocería la carretera.
    ella
                    conoceríamos
    Uds.
                    conocerías
    Ud.

B • Replacement Drill

MODEL   Me compraría un automóvil, pero no soy rico.
STUDENT   **Si fuera rico**, me compraría un automóvil.

1. Iría al cine, pero no tengo dinero. *tuviera*
2. Asistiríamos al Congreso, pero no tenemos tiempo.
3. Acompañarían a Sandra, pero no pueden. *pudieran*
4. Llamaría a Elenita, pero no sé su teléfono. *supiera*
5. Visitarían la exposición, pero no saben dónde está. *supieran*
6. Bailaría contigo, pero no conozco esta música. *conociera*
7. Entendería todas las expresiones, pero Elenita no me las explica. *explicara*
8. Veríamos el Teatro Campesino, pero no tenemos entradas. *tuviéramos*

C • Transformation Drill   Present Indicative/Future → Imperfect Subjunctive/Conditional

MODEL   Si tengo tiempo, vendré a verte.
STUDENT   Si **tuviera** tiempo, **vendría** a verte.

1. Si tienen tiempo, vendrán a verme.
2. Si me ayudas, terminaré temprano.

3. Si nos vestimos ahora, estaremos listos.
4. Si te pregunto, ¿me dirás la verdad?
5. Si estudias tus apuntes, no te darán calabazas en el examen.
6. Si no les gusta esa música, nos lo dirán.

Imperfect Subjunctive/Conditional → Present Indicative/Future

MODEL   Si tuviera tiempo, escribiría la carta.
STUDENT   Si **tengo** tiempo, **escribiré** la carta.

7. Si ofrecieran un curso de arte, yo lo tomaría.
8. Si vinieran, la conocerían.
9. Si supieras su nombre, podrías llamarlo.
10. Si me acompañaras, te compraría un helado.
11. Si escogiera ese anillo, mi novia estaría contenta.
12. Si cambiaran la exhibición, vendrían más personas.

D • Query   Patterned Response

MODEL   ¿Escribirías (¿Escribirás) la composición? ¿Tienes tiempo?
STUDENT   **Bueno, si tuviera tiempo, escribiría la composición.**

1. ¿Irás a la convención? ¿Tienes el dinero?
2. ¿Aceptarías la propuesta? ¿Te parece bien?
3. ¿Trabajarías con don Agapito? ¿Es buena gente?
4. ¿Lavarás las camisas? ¿Te queda jabón?
5. ¿Llamarás a Juan Carvajal? ¿Te acuerdas de su número?
6. ¿Vendrán a la reunión? ¿Están en clase?
7. ¿Trabajaría Sandra en Arizona? ¿Conoce a mucha gente allí?
8. ¿Traducirías del inglés al español? ¿Eres bilingüe?
9. ¿Pagarás la factura? ¿Te doy cinco pesos?
10. ¿Pintarías como Picasso? ¿Tienes talento?

E • Query   Free Response

Answer in Spanish.

1. ¿Qué harías si fueras rico?
2. ¿Cuántos exámenes tomarías si pudieras decidirlo?
3. ¿Aprenderías el español si no tuvieras que hacerlo?
4. ¿Te despiertas temprano si no tienes clases?
5. ¿Adónde irá Ud. si le dan vacaciones?
6. ¿Serviría Ud. bien a su país si fuera presidente?
7. ¿Te sentirías mejor si tuvieras un millón de dólares?
8. ¿Qué dirías si insistieran en más tarea?
9. ¿Se preocupará si hay una protesta estudiantil en su universidad?
10. Si encontrara un anillo de oro, ¿lo devolvería?

F • Translation Drill

Translate into Spanish.

1. If she is here, I'll tell her I love her. If she were here, I would tell her I hate her.
2. If they come, they will bring us the automobile. If they were to come, they wouldn't bring anything.
3. If the store is closed, we'll return tomorrow. If the store were closed, we would have more money.
4. Will you go with them if they go to the Retiro? Would you go with them if they went in a car?
5. They didn't know whether you would come. I don't know whether I will go.

89 The conditional and the imperfect subjunctive for softened assertions

▶ As in English, the conditional tense is frequently used in Spanish to soften or tone down an assertion, request, or criticism.

1. Me gustaría[7] mirar los carteles.	*I would like to look at the posters.*
2. ¿Podría salir con Sandra hoy?	*Could I go out with Sandra today?*
3. Deberías escuchar sus palabras.	*You should listen to his words.*

▶ The imperfect subjunctive is also used for this purpose, although rarely with verbs other than **querer**, **poder**, **haber**, and **deber.**

1. Quisiera[7] dos entradas, por favor.	*I would like two tickets, please.*
2. ¿Pudieras verme mañana?	*Could you see me tomorrow?*
3. Debiéramos darnos prisa.	*We should (ought to) hurry.*

A • Transformation Drill   Present → Conditional

MODEL   Me gusta ir al cine contigo.
STUDENT   Me **gustaría** ir al cine contigo.

1. Por favor, señorita, deseo ver otros collares.
2. ¿Puedes decirme dónde trabaja el Sr. Carvajal?
3. No debes exagerar su importancia.
4. Desean responder a su pregunta.
5. Nos gusta jugar al fútbol americano.
6. Yo digo que es así.
7. Agradezco su ayuda.
8. A Susana le gusta escuchar tus discos.

[7] In softened assertions, **gustar** is used exclusively in the conditional, whereas **querer** is used mainly in the imperfect subjunctive.

B • Transformation Drill   Present → Imperfect Subjunctive

MODEL   Quiero darte mi palabra de honor.
STUDENT **Quisiera** darte mi palabra de honor.

1. Debes escribir una carta a tu tío.
2. ¿Puede ser mañana?
3. Debo comprar algo para mi novia.
4. ¿Podemos quedarnos aquí?
5. Debemos traer más dinero para comprar la moto.
6. Quiero despedirme de ellos antes de irme.
7. ¿Podemos ayudarlos con la publicidad?
8. Quieren organizar una exposición de pinturas.

C • Query   Free Response

Answer in Spanish.

1. ¿Te gustaría explorar Machu Picchu?
2. ¿Podrías terminar tu tarea hoy?
3. ¿Quisiera Ud. preparar una comida española?
4. ¿Debería Ud. permanecer en casa hoy?
5. ¿Le gustaría a Ud. ser un chiquillo (una chiquilla) otra vez?
6. ¿Desearía Ud. visitar el Museo del Prado?
7. ¿Pudiera Ud. decirme quién escribió la "Guajira Guantanamera"?
8. ¿Quisieras actuar en una obra de teatro?
9. ¿Desearías pintar como Velázquez?
10. ¿Debiéramos estar orgullosos de nuestras raíces?

D • Translation Drill

Translate into Spanish.

1. Tell me what La Raza is! Could you tell me what La Raza is?
2. Teach me Spanish. Could you teach me Spanish, please?
3. Write a letter to your friend. You should write a letter to your friend.
4. I like going to the theater. I would like to go to the Teatro Campesino.
5. He wants to talk to you. He would like to wait for you.

90 Pero versus sino

▶ Both **pero** and **sino** are equivalent to *but*. However, they cannot be used interchangeably. **Sino** is equivalent to *but rather* or *on the contrary*. **Sino** is used in place of **pero** in an affirmative statement that contradicts a preceding negative statement (examples 1, 2 and 3). **Sino** is also used in sentences in which the idea expressed is *not only . . . but also* (example 4). If two different clauses are joined, **sino que** is used (example 5).

1. No es doctor sino dentista.   *He's not a doctor but (rather) a*
                                           dentist.

2. No estuvo ella allí, sino su hermana.   *She wasn't there, but her sister was.*[8]

3. No estudia arqueología, sino historia. *He doesn't study history, but rather*
                                           archaeology.

4. Me gusta no solamente el teatro de   *I like not only Lope's theater but*
   Lope sino también el de los chicanos.   *also the Chicanos'.*

5. No lloraba sino que reía.   *She wasn't crying but, on the*
                                           contrary, she was laughing.

▶ When the second clause of a negative sentence does not contradict what was stated in the first or when it is the second clause that is negative, **pero** is used.

1. No quiero ir, pero es necesario.   *I don't want to go, but it is necessary.*

2. Nunca preparamos la lección, pero   *We never prepare the lesson, but we*
   practicamos mucho en clase.   *practice a lot in class.*

3. Les gustaría vernos, pero no pueden.   *They would like to see us, but they*
                                           can't.

4. Piensan hacer una exhibición, pero   *They are thinking about doing an*
   primero tienen que pintar muchos   *exhibit, but first they have to paint*
   cuadros.   *many pictures.*

A • Completion Drill

Complete the sentences with **pero**, **sino**, or **sino que**, whichever is appropriate.

1. No es lunes _____ martes.
2. La comida está retesabrosa _____ no tenemos hambre.
3. Juan me prestó el libro _____ no quiso vendérmelo.
4. No aprenden el francés _____ el italiano.
5. Panchito no vino ayer _____ se quedó en casa.
6. La agencia de viajes no está abierta hoy _____ se abre temprano mañana.
7. Luis no escribe una composición _____ versos.
8. Ignacio recibe muchas cartas _____ nunca contesta.
9. El domingo las tiendas no están abiertas _____ están cerradas.
10. Sonia no es estudiante _____ profesora.
11. No quiero que me digas lo que crees, _____ la verdad.
12. Mi hermana no me acompaña _____ voy solo.
13. Aquella muchacha no es mi hermana _____ la hermana de Elenita.
14. Quiero ir _____ no puedo.
15. No son palabras nuevas _____ nuevos significados.

---

[8] Note that in this construction, the verb is not repeated in the second clause in Spanish.

REVIEW

I The following questions are related to the dialog. Answer in Spanish.

1. ¿Qué se está celebrando en el Centro de Convenciones?
2. ¿Cómo sabe el Sr. Carvajal que Sandra no es de por allí?
3. ¿Cuál es el propósito del Congreso?
4. ¿Quién llevará a Sandra por toda la exposición?
5. ¿Qué hace Sandra mientras espera a Elenita?
6. ¿Qué deberían hacer las dos muchachas después de ver las exhibiciones?
7. ¿Sobre qué palabras quisiera Sandra saber más?
8. ¿Qué cree Sandra que han escogido los chicanos?
9. ¿Quiénes son los chicanos?
10. ¿Aprendería Sandra algo sobre La Raza durante su visita al Congreso?

II Translate into Spanish.

1. I would like to go to the Congreso de La Raza. Could you tell me where it is taking place?
2. Of course! I'm not from around here, but I know the city well.
3. If you spend all day there, I will take you afterwards to see the Teatro Campesino.
4. You are very kind. At what time will the show begin?
5. It begins at eight, but it (probably) won't end until midnight.
6. Really? Is it true that it isn't a traditional theater but rather an important part of the Chicano culture?
7. Yes, you would learn a great deal about how the Chicanos have to fight for their rights if you could understand all the expressions.
8. That is the purpose of my presence here. I hope I will be able to visit all the exhibits also. Perhaps I should come again tomorrow.
9. That would be the best. But we'll meet near the posters at 7:30.
10. Then you can decide whether you'll attend the Congreso tomorrow, too.

III Guided Composition

Describe your awareness of Hispanic culture in the United States. Has your awareness grown since you have been studying Spanish? Have you had any personal contact with Hispanic people or culture outside the classroom situation?

Mural on a freeway wall,
San Diego, California

Cognates & Contexts

¿Quiénes son los chicanos?

Los chicanos forman una minoría de aproximadamente siete millones y medio de habitantes, dispersos principalmente en los cinco estados del suroeste: Arizona, California, Colorado, Nuevo México y Texas. Los chicanos constituyen un grupo distinto que ha habitado los Estados Unidos por más de un siglo. Las raíces de esta minoría se extienden a dos grandes y antiguas culturas —la española y la indígena. Por lo tanto, hay que recordar que los antepasados del chicano ya vivían en el suroeste cuando el norteamericano todavía no llegaba a estas tierras.

distinto *distinct*

antepasados *ancestors*

Los problemas padecidos por esta minoría son similares a los que existen en otras áreas urbanas y rurales: la pobreza, el desempleo, la falta de asistencia médica, el analfabetismo, la explotación económica y el poco éxito de los programas de educación.

padecidos *suffered*

analfabetismo *illiteracy*

Se ha creado un estereotipo durante años de lo que es este grupo y se han creado prejuicios contra él, a veces por el color de su piel, por su pobreza, porque habla mal el inglés o porque no lo habla del todo, o porque no está familiarizado con la sociedad norteamericana.

prejuicios *prejudices*

piel *skin*

César Chávez and the United Farm Workers, Delano, California

El cine, la televisión y los anuncios comerciales estereotipan al chicano en dos extremos: uno, lo pinta como el machista, arrogante, con bigote grande y una navaja al cinturón; el otro, lo romantiza como un campesino fuerte de dulce disposición y con mente de niño. La actitud del público en los Estados Unidos es ambivalente; por una parte, afecto hacia esta gente "exótica" y por otra, rechazo por encontrarla "extraña". Estos conceptos causan un sentimiento de humillación y hostilidad en los chicanos.

La situación socio-económica y política del chicano y el hecho de que ha retenido su cultura y lengua tradicionales, han ayudado a la creación de un movimiento de humanismo y unidad comunal que tiene como lema "La Raza". Tal término no se refiere a una distinta raza biológica. Lo que significa es un sentido de comunidad y de identidad. El lema

bigote *mustache* **navaja** *knife*
cinturón *belt*
dulce *sweet; mild*

rechazo *rejection*

lema *motto*

también se emplea por toda Hispanoamérica para referirse a
las características únicas de la mezcla indioespañola. En el   **mezcla** *mixture*
suroeste de los Estados Unidos, sin embargo, se refiere
únicamente a la minoría mexicano-americana e implica el   **implicar** *to imply*
orgullo de ser miembro de este grupo étnico.

A causa de su decisión y su fe en el porvenir, la minoría
chicana va progresando en sus ideales. Por ejemplo, el
movimiento para sindicalizar a los trabajadores agrícolas,   **sindicalizar** *to unionize*
establecido por César Chávez, ha tenido gran éxito. Otras
organizaciones, algunas culturales, como el Teatro Campesino, una forma de teatro político-social, han podido
mostrar al chicano cuáles son sus intereses vitales y cómo
debe realizarlos—mediante la organización política, el
rechazo de estereotipos tradicionales basados en la ignorancia,
y la participación en actividades culturales en las cuales
ponen ánimo y orgullo.

San Sebastián, Spain

Lección veinte

Lectura y estudio

Miami, Florida, 22 de agosto de 1970

Sr. D. Joaquín Aizpúrua, Director
Spanish philospher Univ. Salamanca
Empresas Euzkadi, S.A.
Avenida Miguel de Unamuno, 33
San Sebastián 17, España

empresa *company, firm; enter-prise* **S.A. (Sociedad Anónima)** *Inc.*

Muy señor mío:

Recientemente tuve la oportunidad de comunicarme con Ud. por teléfono sobre el puesto vacante que tiene su empresa para un gerente. Tal como Ud. me indicó en esa ocasión que hiciera, adjunto le envío un resumen de mis datos escolares y profesionales y tres cartas de recomendación.

puesto *position*

gerente *manager*

adjunto *attached, enclosed*

He trabajado como gerente de oficina durante dos años en Miami con una compañía de importación/exportación mientras terminaba mis estudios. Creo que esa experiencia me ha capacitado para el puesto que Ud. ofrece.

capacitar *to qualify*

although Aunque tengo ciudadanía de los EE.UU., pasé mi juventud en Cuba donde cursé estudios en La Habana. Por lo tanto, mi manejo del español no debe presentar ningún impedimento para mi funcionamiento eficaz dentro de su compañía.

ciudadanía *citizenship* **EE.UU. (Estados Unidos)** *U.S.*
cursar estudios *to take courses*

por lo tanto *therefore* **manejo** *handling* (noun)

eficaz *efficient*

Si necesita más informes o documentación, no deje Ud. de comunicármelo para que se lo haga enviar a vuelta de correo.

a vuelta de correo *by return mail*

Esperando su decisión, queda de Ud. muy atentamente

Su seguro servidor,

Rodolfo Rivera

Rodolfo Rivera

Sr. D. Rodolfo Rivera   30 de agosto de 1970
478 North 52nd Street
Miami, Florida 30303

Estimado Sr. Rivera:

Mediante la presente acusamos recibo de su carta   **acusar recibo** *to acknowledge*
del día 22 de agosto.   *receipt*

Sentimos informarle que el puesto de gerente no
sigue vacante. Una señora que lleva ya muchos
años con la empresa fue seleccionada para ocuparlo.

Sin embargo, a partir de principios de enero   **a partir de** *as of* **principios de** *the*
estaremos buscando a alguien para encargarse de   *beginning of*
nuestra División Internacional. Aunque por el mo-   **encargarse de** *to be in charge of*
mento el volumen de productos exportados es bas-
tante reducido, tenemos la intención de incremen-
tarlo. Una persona de su experiencia y con dominio   **dominio** *domination*
de tres idiomas, ya que su resumen indica que tam-
bién maneja el alemán, sería la indicada para ocupar
este puesto de creciente importancia.   **creciente** *increasing, growing*

En caso de que le interesara a Ud. ser considerado
para el puesto que le propongo, sea tan amable de   **proponer** *to propose* **sea tan**
comunicármelo cuanto antes para poder iniciar los   **amable de** *be so kind as to*
trámites necesarios.   **cuanto antes** *as soon as possible*

                                                      trámites *steps, transactions*

Mis saludos al Sr. Richard Henderson con quien
tuve el gusto de hablar recientemente a su respecto   **el gusto** *the pleasure* **a su**
en la conferencia económica celebrada en Caracas.   **respecto** *about you*

           Con toda cordialidad,

           Joaquín Aizpúrua Sánchez
           Joaquín Aizpúrua Sánchez
           Director

NOTES

Business letters in Spanish often adopt formal language making use of polite expressions that have become accepted formulas.

Greetings emphasize respect and admiration for the addressee.

> Estimado Sr. González:
> Muy señor mío:
> Muy distinguida señora:

Closing phrases, as is the case in friendly letters, are usually complete sentences. Especially in Spain, polite formulas reminiscent of by-gone traditions are still employed, although they are often reduced to abbreviations or initials.

> Queda de Ud. S.S.S. (su seguro servidor)
> q.b.s.m. (que besa su mano)
> Queda suyo afmo. (afectísimo)
> S.S.S.q.e.s.m. (su seguro servidor que estrecha su mano)

In Spanish America, this type of closing is rarely used nowadays, having been replaced by phrases such as

> Queda de Ud. muy atentamente...
> Con mis cordiales saludos...

The use of **Sr.D., Sra.Dña. (señor don, señora doña)** is common in addresses in Spain; however, **don** and **doña** are less frequent in Spanish America.

The names Aizpúrua and Euzkadi are typically Basque. San Sebastián is one of the major cities of the Basque region in Spain.

VOCABULARY STUDY

The following words have additional meanings or forms besides those already given in the dialogs.

distinto   distinct; *different*   *distinto a*
 diferente de
    Mi libro es distinto al tuyo.   *My book is different from yours.*

pararse   to stop; *to stand up*

puro   pure; *cigar*
    ¿Quieres fumar un puro?   *Do you want to smoke a cigar?*

diario   newspaper; *daily*; *diary*

    Éste es un trabajo diario.   *This is a daily job.*

    Escribo en mi diario todos los días.   *I write in my diary every day.*

cuadro   painting

  cuadra   (city) block   *also manzana*

función   show; *function, use*

implicar   to imply; *to implicate*

metro   subway; *meter*; *yardstick*

    Voy a medirlo con el metro.   *I'm going to measure it with the yardstick.*

pintura   painting; *paint*

         ¡OJO! = LOOK OUT, FRESH PAINT.

Remember: *a new word.*

memorizar = aprender de memoria

todos = todo el mundo

estar orgulloso   *to be proud*

  tener orgullo   *to have pride*

darse prisa   *to hurry up*   = *give oneself haste.*

  tener prisa   *to be in a hurry*

    Date prisa porque tengo prisa.   *Hurry up because I'm in a hurry.*

dar calabazas   *to fail*, literally, *to give pumpkins* (i.e., big zeros)

tener buen carácter   *to have a good disposition*

¡Cuidado!

bigote = *mustache* (not *biggot*)

individuo = *individual* (*person*)

  individual = *individual* (*separate*)

carácter = *disposition*   *plural* **los caractéres**

  personaje = *character* (*in a play, book*)

mente = *mind*

  menta = *mint*

propósito = *purpose*

  proposición = *proposition*

buen provecho = good appetite.

The following verbs have additional meanings when they occur with certain prepositions or in certain set phrases.

> **acabar**   *to finish*
> **acabar de** + infinitive   *to have just* + past participle
>> Acabo de acabar.   *I have just finished.*
>
> **echar**   *to throw*
> **echar de menos**   *to miss*
>> ¿Echas de menos a tu familia?   *Do you miss your family?*
>
> **echar a perder**   *to spoil, ruin*
> **pensar**   *to think*
> **pensar** + infinitive   *to intend to, plan to*
>> Pienso escribirle mañana.   *I plan to write to him tomorrow.*
>
> **pensar de**   *to think of, have an opinion of*
> **pensar en**   *to think about, occupy one's thoughts with*
> **querer**   *to want; to love*
> **querer decir**   *to mean, signify*
>> ¿Esto quiere decir que ya no   *Does this mean that you don't*
>> me quieres?   *love me any more?*

Many verbs ending in **-ar** in Spanish have cognates in English ending in **-ate**. What do the following verbs mean?

colaborar	evaluar	exagerar
implicar	participar	celebrar
cultivar	explicar	indicar
negar	segregar	terminar

A • Substitution Drill

Rewrite the sentences, using a synonym for the underlined word or phrase.

1. Ayer hubo una exposición de pinturas de El Greco en nuestro pueblo.
2. No tengas miedo. Esos elefantes no te harán nada.
3. Cuando íbamos por el camino, nos estancamos en el lodo.
4. Me gustaría platicar con Ud. sobre ese asunto.
5. La exhibición de dibujos de Goya fue un éxito.
6. Mediante la influencia de su padre pudo conseguir el trabajo.
7. Quiero encontrar una casa semejante a la tuya porque me gusta mucho.
8. No creo que puedan arreglar mi automóvil hoy.

Use an antonym for the underlined word or expression.

9. La vida rural presenta muchos problemas.

10. Tu libro es distinto al mío, pero tenemos asignaciones diferentes.
11. Todos esos apuntes que tomas en clase son inútiles para el examen.
12. ¿Cuándo vas a comenzar los estudios de ingeniería?
13. Sandra siempre sale por esa puerta, pero nunca la cierra.
14. La pobreza de una persona no se refiere solamente a dinero.

B • Complete each sentence with a suitable word or phrase from the list. The words are to be used in the form in which they appear.

camino	pobreza
analfabetismo	vida
individuo	pensar en
sentido	prejuicios
propias	rechazo

1. El _____ es uno de los peores problemas que confronta al hombre moderno.
2. Para el _____ que no sabe leer ni escribir, la _____ no presenta grandes esperanzas.
3. No puede _____ un porvenir ambicioso a causa de estar sumergido en sus _____ dudas.
4. El temor al _____ y a los _____ contribuyen a un _____ de inferioridad.
5. La _____ parece ser el único _____ posible para él.

comienza	mediante
Por lo tanto	sino
distintas	cambian
significado	anhelos
habitantes	valioso
diarias	fomentan

6. En un contexto mayor, el _____ de este mal _____ a ser comprendido.
7. Los _____ de un país se logran _____ los esfuerzos[1] de sus _____.
8. _____, un pueblo educado es el recurso más _____ de una nación.
9. No solamente los conocimientos académicos _____ también las discusiones _____ con personas de _____ opiniones enseñan al estudiante a vivir en un mundo complejo.
10. Las nuevas ideas recibidas en la escuela _____ una perspectiva más amplia y _____ el ritmo de desarrollo del país.

todos	quedarse
Es cierto	crear
próximos	antepasados
por su cuenta	convencer
asista	estar orgullosos
escoger	Por medio de

[1] **Esfuerzos,** *efforts*

Rural School in Bolivia

11. Poco a poco las actitudes se están modificando: los padres ya no obligan a sus hijos a _quedarse_ con ellos y continuar el trabajo de sus _antepasados_.
12. Las autoridades se están dando cuenta de que hay que _crear_ más escuelas y _convencer_ a la población que _asistan_ a ellas.
13. _Por medio de_ la educación pública obligatoria, los jóvenes estarán capacitados para _escoger_ sus carreras.
14. Así podrán _estar orgullosos_ de tener la oportunidad de decidir _por su cuenta_.
15. _Es cierto_ que no todas las dificultades están resueltas, pero se espera que en los _próximos_ años la enseñanza libre estará a la disposición de _todos_.

C • Query Free Response

Treat exercise B as a narrative and answer the following questions in Spanish.

1. ¿Qué es uno de los peores problemas que confronta al hombre moderno?
2. ¿Cómo afecta este problema al individuo?
3. ¿Cómo afecta este problema a un país?
4. ¿Qué aprende el estudiante en la escuela?
5. ¿Qué modificaciones se ven en las actitudes tradicionales?
6. ¿Qué es el deber de las autoridades respecto a la educación?
7. ¿Qué oportunidad tienen los jóvenes por medio de la educación?

Now answer the following questions according to your own opinion.

8. ¿Cree Ud. que una educación académica es útil? ¿Por qué?
9. ¿Cree Ud. que es necesario asistir a la escuela para ser una persona educada?
10. ¿Qué piensa Ud. de las ideas expresadas en la narrativa precedente?

Rompecabezas

¿Se teés nu narg broli o nu broli narged¿

¿Es éste un gran libro o un libro grande?

GRAMMAR: SELF-TESTING

Cover the right side of the page and try to answer the questions in the left margin.

VERBS

From where is the stem for the imperfect subjunctive taken?

What are the imperfect subjunctive endings?

What is the imperfect subjunctive of **ir** and **ser**?

Under what conditions is the imperfect subjunctive used?

I Subjunctive

IMPERFECT (*Section 73*)

The imperfect subjunctive stem is always formed by dropping **-ron** from the third person plural of the preterit. The endings **-ra, -ras, -ra, -'ramos, -ran** are then added to the stem.

Regular Verbs	hablar	hablaron	habla-	
	aprender	aprendieron	aprendie-	
	escribir	escribieron	escribie-	
Class I	pensar	pensaron	pensa-	
	volver	volvieron	volvie-	
Class II Class III	sentir	sintieron	sintie-	-ra
	dormir	durmieron	durmie-	-ras
	pedir	pidieron	pidie-	-ra
Verbs That Are Irregular in the Preterit	andar	anduvieron	anduvie-	-'ramos
	creer	creyeron	creye-	-ran
	decir	dijeron	dije-	
	hacer	hicieron	hicie-	
	ir/ser	fueron	fue-	
	producir	produjeron	produje-	
	querer	quisieron	quisie-	
	saber	supieron	supie-	

The imperfect subjunctive is used under the same conditions as the present subjunctive except that the point of view is in the past: if the main verb is in the past, the subordinate verb is in the past.

| **Quiero que te quedes conmigo.** | *I want you to stay with me.* |
| **Quería que te quedaras conmigo.** | *I wanted you to stay with me.* |

Tememos que lleguen tarde.	*We fear they'll arrive late.*
Temíamos que llegaran tarde.	*We feared they'd arrive late.*

The imperfect subjunctive of **querer**, **poder**, **haber**, and **deber** can be used in a main clause to soften or tone down an assertion, request, or criticism (*Section 89*).

Quisiera quedarme aquí.	*I would like to stay here.*

ADJECTIVE CLAUSES   (*Section 74*)

An adjective clause is a subordinate clause that modifies a noun. When the subordinate clause refers back to someone or something (a noun or pronoun) undetermined or nonexistent (unreal), the subjunctive is used. When it refers to someone or something predetermined (real), the indicative is used (*Section 75*).

Necesito dos individuos que quieran trabajar.	*I need two individuals who want to work.*
Conozco a dos individuos que quieren trabajar.	*I know two individuals who want to work.*
No hay nadie que quiera venir.	*There isn't anyone who wants to come.*
Hay muchas personas que quieren venir.	*There are many people who want to come.*

CLAUSES WITH *SI*   (*Section 87*)

What is a **si** clause? When is a subjunctive used in a **si** clause?

What tense is usually used in the main clause if the **si** clause is in the imperfect subjunctive?

A **si** clause is a type of subordinate clause equivalent to the English *if* clause. To express a condition that is contrary to fact or an event that is not expected to occur in the future, Spanish uses the imperfect subjunctive in the **si** clause because of the unreality inherent in such expressions. In these cases, the main clause (which often follows the **si** clause) is usually expressed in the conditional.

Si fueras rico, tendrías un palacio.	*If you were rich, you would have a palace.*
Si vinieran mañana, lo harían.	*If they were to come tomorrow, they would do it.*

| When is an indicative used in the **si** clause? | If the **si** clause expresses something that has happened or is likely to occur, the indicative is used. The main clause will also be in the indicative. |

Si sabían la respuesta,   *If you knew the answer,*
¿por qué no contestaron?   *why didn't you answer?*
Si tengo tiempo, vendré   *If I have time, I'll come*
a verte mañana.   *to see you tomorrow.*

II Future and Conditional Tenses
(*Sections 85, 86*)

| How is the future tense formed? How is the conditional tense formed? | For regular verbs, the future and conditional endings are attached to the infinitive. In each tense, the endings are the same for **-ar**, **-er**, and **-ir** verbs. |

	Future	*Conditional*
	-é	-ía
hablar	-ás	-ías
aprender +	-á	-ía
escribir	-emos	-íamos
	-án	-ían

| What type of irregularity occurs in the future and conditional? Are these irregularities the same in both tenses? | Irregularities in both of these tenses occur only in the stem. The same stem irregularity of a verb occurs in both the future and the conditional. |

| What are the stems for **poder**, **querer**, and **saber** in the future? | caber ⎫ drop **-e-** in ⎫ cabr-
 haber ⎪ infinitive ⎪ habr-
 poder ⎬ ending ⎬ podr-
 querer ⎪   ⎪ querr-
 saber ⎭   ⎭ sabr- |

| What are the stems for **poner**, **tener**, and **venir** in the conditional? | poner ⎫ drop vowel in ⎫ pondr-
 salir ⎪ infinitive ⎪ saldr-
 tener ⎬ ending; insert ⎬ tendr-
 valer ⎪ **-d-** ⎪ valdr-
 venir ⎭   ⎭ vendr- |

| For **hacer** and **decir** in the future? | decir   dir-
 hacer   har- |

	-é	-ía
	-ás	-ías
+	-á or	-ía
	-emos	-íamos
	-án	-ían

What does the future tense express?	The future tense is used a. to express future occurrences. b. to express probability or conjecture about a present situation or occurrence (expressions such as **probablemente** are not normally included).

	¿Marta no está aquí? Estará en su casa.	*Marta isn't here? She's probably at home.*

When is the conditional tense used?	The conditional tense is used a. to convey future meaning with regard to a point of reference in the past.

	Te dije ayer que vendría hoy.	*I told you yesterday I would come today.*

b. to express probability or conjecture about a past situation or occurrence.

	Sería la una cuando llegué, pero no estoy segura.	*It must have been one when I arrived, but I'm not sure.*

c. to soften or tone down an assertion, request, or criticism (*Section 89*).

	Me gustaría ir contigo.	*I would like to go with you.*

III   Past Participles and Perfect Tenses
(*Sections 79, 80, 81*)

How are past participles regularly formed?	Past participles are regularly formed by adding **-ado** to the stem of **-ar** verbs (**habl-ado**) and **-ido** to the stem of **-er** and **-ir** verbs (**aprend-ido, viv-ido**).

What are the irregular past participles for escribir, volver, poner, ver, decir, and hacer?	Some verbs have irregular past participles.

abrir	abierto	cubrir	cubierto
escribir	escrito	romper	roto
morir	muerto	decir	dicho
volver	vuelto	hacer	hecho
poner	puesto	ir	ido
ver	visto		

How are the perfect tenses formed?	The perfect tenses are formed by conjugating **haber** (in the present for the present perfect, future for the future perfect, etc.) and adding a past participle, which in this construction always ends in **-o**.

How is the present perfect indicative formed?	The present indicative of **haber** + a past participle forms the present perfect indicative.

he			*I have*	
has	hablado		*you have*	*spoken*
ha	+	aprendido	*you have*; *he, she has*	*learned*
hemos		escrito	*we have*	*written*
han			*you, they have*	

How is the present perfect subjunctive formed?	The present subjunctive of **haber** + a past participle forms the present perfect subjunctive.

haya		
hayas	hablado	
haya	+	aprendido
hayamos	escrito	
hayan		

When is a present perfect subjunctive used in the subordinate clause?	When the verb in the main clause is in the present or future, the subordinate clause uses the present perfect subjunctive if the action in it occurred prior to the time indicated in the main clause.

| **Espero que hayas hablado con él.** | *I hope you have spoken (spoke) with him.* |
| **Consultarán con alguien que haya estado allí.** | *They will consult with someone who has been there.* |

IV Passive Voice (*Section 83*)

There are four equivalents to the English passive voice in Spanish.

When is the **ser** + past participle construction used to express the passive voice?	a. **ser** + past participle (which agrees with the subject): used when the action received by the subject is performed by an expressed or implied agent.

| **La casa fue construida (por Miguel) en 1970.** | *The house was built (by Miguel) in 1970.* |

When is the reflexive substitute for the passive used?	b. reflexive substitute for the passive: used when the agent is neither expressed nor implied and the subject is a thing.

| **Se construyó la casa en 1970.** | *The house was built in 1970.* |

When is a third person active construction used to express the passive?

c. third person plural active construction used impersonally (no subject noun or pronoun):
   used when the agent is neither expressed nor implied.

   Construyeron la casa en 1970.   *They built the house in 1970.*

When is **estar** + past participle used to express a passive construction?

d. **estar** + past participle (which agrees with the subject):
   used to refer to a condition resulting from a prior action.

   La casa ya estaba construida en 1971.   *The house was already built in 1971.*

V   First Person Plural Commands   (*Section 84*)

First person plural commands (equivalent to *let's* + verb) have the same verb form as the first person plural of the present subjunctive.

How is *let's* expressed?

   Llamemos a Sonia.   *Let's call Sonia.*

Vamos a + infinitive is another way of expressing *let's*, although just in the affirmative.

   Vamos a comer ahora.   *Let's eat now.*

What is the affirmative first person plural command for **ir** and **irse**? The negative?

Vamos and its reflexive, **vámonos**, used affirmatively, are exceptions, as the indicative is used. The subjunctive **vayamos** must be used in the negative for *let's not go.*

PRONOUNS

Relative Pronouns   (*Section 74*)

The following relative pronouns are used to introduce adjective clauses.

How is the relative pronoun **que** used?

a. **que** (*that, which, who, whom*):
   used as the subject or object of the verb in a clause (referring to persons or things), or the object of a preposition (referring only to things).

   la mujer que estuvo aquí   *the woman who was here*

   los hombres que conocimos   *the men that we met*

   la clase de que hablamos   *the class of which we spoke (we spoke about)*

How is the relative pronoun **quien** most frequently used?	b. **quien, quienes** (*who, whom*): refers only to persons and is most frequently used after a preposition.

¿Conoces a los muchachos con quienes vine?   *Do you know the boys with whom I came?*

How are **el cual, el que** and their variants used?	c. **el cual, el que** (*that, which, who, whom, the one(s) who, the one(s) which*) and their variants: used primarily to clarify the identity of the antecedent, they may appear in place of **que** or **quien**.

Mi hermana, la que vino conmigo, tiene diez años.   *My sister, the one who came with me, is ten years old.*

Esos artefactos, los cuales descubrieron ayer, son muy valiosos.   *Those artifacts, which were discovered yesterday, are very valuable.*

El lápiz con el cual escribo mejor está perdido.   *The pencil with which I write best is lost.*

How are **lo cual** and **lo que** used?	d. **lo cual, lo que** (*what, that which, which*): used to sum up a preceding statement or idea in as broad a manner as the context will permit.

Eso era lo que yo quería.   *That's what I wanted.*

Quieren que tomemos tres exámenes hoy, lo cual me parece absurdo.   *They want us to take three exams today, which seems absurd to me.*

in some countries dar & tomar are reversed when applied to exams.

ADJECTIVES

Special Cases of Adjective Position   (*Section 76*)

How are descriptive adjectives used when they precede the noun?	a. Descriptive adjectives may precede the noun for enhancement or to reinforce an inherent characteristic that we normally associate with the noun:

Es un hermoso día.   *It's a beautiful day.*
el brillante sol   *the brilliant sun*

cada has only one form
verde has 2

b. Adjectives that change their meaning when they precede or follow the noun:

How do the following adjectives change their meaning when they precede or follow the noun: **gran** (**grande**), **antiguo, puro, nuevo, pobre, viejo?**

1. un gran jugador	*a great player*
un jugador grande	*a big player*
2. el antiguo templo	*the former temple*
el templo antiguo	*the ancient temple*
3. puro estudio	*strictly study, nothing but study*
leche pura	*pure milk*
4. un nuevo automóvil	*a new (another) car*
un automóvil nuevo	*a new (vs. old) car*
5. la pobre mujer	*the poor (unfortunate) woman*
la mujer pobre	*the poor (vs. rich) woman*
6. mi viejo amigo	*my old (long-standing) friend*
mi amigo viejo	*my elderly friend*

REMEMBER!

● In softened assertions, **gustar** is used exclusively in the conditional, whereas **querer** is used mainly in the imperfect subjunctive (*Section 89*).

● The first person plural form of the imperfect subjunctive always has a written accent on the second-from-last syllable (*Section 73*).

> **habláramos**
> **fuéramos**, etc.

● The future and conditional can only be used in **si** clauses when **si** means *whether* (*Section 87*).

No sé si vendremos.	*I don't know whether (or not) we will come.*
No sabíamos si irían contigo.	*We didn't know whether (or not) they would go with you.*

● The present subjunctive is not used in a **si** clause in modern Spanish (*Section 87*).

● Both **haber** and **tener** mean *to have* in Spanish. **Haber** is used almost exclusively as an auxiliary for the perfect tenses or as an impersonal expression (**hay, hubo,** etc.). **Tener,** not **haber,** is used to indicate *to have, possess* (*Section 79*).

- Since the conjugated forms of **haber** are considered part of the verb in the perfect tenses, negative particles and object or reflexive pronouns come before the conjugated form of **haber** (*Section 79*).

  No he visto a Marta. *I haven't seen Marta.*
  Lo ha terminado. *She has finished it.*

- When a reflexive verb is used affirmatively in a first person plural command, the final **-s** is dropped from the verb before adding the reflexive pronoun **-nos** (*Section 84*).

  Levantémonos.

- **Muy** before an adjective or adverb, or the suffix **-ísimo,** is used to indicate an absolute superlative, with no comparison intended (*Section 77*).

  Es un hombre muy rico./Es un hombre *He is a very rich man.*
  riquísimo.

  muchísimo (not **muy mucho**) = *very much*

- Past participles may be used as adjectives; when they are, they agree with the noun they modify (*Section 82*).

  Estos salones están cerrados. *These rooms are closed.*

  As with other adjectives, past participles can be nominalized.

  Los muertos ya no tienen *The dead no longer have secrets.*
  secretos.

A • Substitution Drill

MODEL Conozco a alguien que sabe inglés.
   Busco
STUDENT Busco a alguien que **sepa** inglés.

1. Conozco a alguien que puede ayudarte.
   Busco
2. Hay una muchacha que estudia en Madrid.
   ¿Hay
3. Conseguimos entradas que sólo cuestan dos pesos.
   Preferimos
4. Quiero hablar con el chiquillo que estudia música.
       un chiquillo
5. Hay alguien que baila a la perfección.
   No hay nadie

6. ¿Quieres encontrar a la muchacha que escribe poemas?
   una muchacha
7. Eso quiere decir que estás terminado.
   Eso no quiere decir
8. ¿Tienes el libro que trata de la civilización maya?
   algún libro
9. Necesitamos al individuo que revisa las facturas.
   un individuo
10. Hay una bicicleta que me gusta.
    No hay ninguna

B • Transformation Drill   Present Indicative/Present Subjunctive→ Imperfect Indicative/Imperfect Subjunctive

MODEL   Quiero que lo hagas hoy.
STUDENT   **Quería** que lo **hicieras** hoy.

1. Es importante que vayas al Congreso.
2. Dudo que ellos te digan la verdad.
3. Necesitan a alguien que sepa cantar en inglés.
4. ¿Quieres que yo vuelva contigo?
5. No hay nadie que entienda esa obra.
6. Espero que me creas.
7. ¿No crees que el Sr. Carvajal piense como tú?
8. La agencia busca dos personas que comprendan el francés.

C • Completion Drill

Complete the sentences in Spanish.

1. Si yo pudiera hablar bien el español, _____.
2. Si llegas a tiempo, _____.
3. Si pudiéramos hacer un viaje, _____.
4. Si pensaras en el porvenir, _____.
5. Si regresan temprano, _____.
6. Yo estaría orgulloso(a) de ti si _____.
7. Mis amigas se quedarán aquí si _____.
8. ¿Asistirías a clase si _____?
9. Él tardará si _____.
10. Yo enseñaría el italiano si _____.

D • Translation Drill

Translate into Spanish.

1. I think they will be proud. I thought they would be proud. I don't know whether they will be proud.
2. They will return tomorrow. They would like to return tomorrow.
3. You are (probably) tired. You were (probably) tired.
4. We know they will come. We knew they would come. We doubted they would come.
5. Sandra will look for something for you. She said she would look for something that would please you.

E • Query   Patterned Response

Answer, using the present perfect indicative.

MODEL   ¿Vas a la biblioteca ahora?
STUDENT   **No, ya he ido.**

1. ¿Terminas a las cinco hoy?
2. ¿Salen los periódicos más tarde?
3. ¿Vuelven tus padres mañana?
4. ¿Hacemos la tarea juntos?
5. ¿Pongo los platos en la mesa?

Now answer, using the present perfect subjunctive.

MODEL   ¿Vieron ellos los carteles?
STUDENT   **No, qué lástima que no hayan visto los carteles.**

6. ¿Fuiste al teatro ayer?
7. ¿Escribieron tus tíos antes de venir?
8. ¿Abrieron la tienda temprano esta mañana?
9. ¿Le dijo Susana la verdad al jefe?
10. ¿Hice bien las facturas?

F • Translation Drill

Translate into Spanish. There may be more than one satisfactory translation.

1. She broke the plate. The plate was broken by her.
2. The children were lost. They looked for the children.
3. Spanish is spoken here. They speak Spanish in Spain.
4. The store is open. It was opened by Elenita.
5. The temple was built by the Mayas. It was built before the twelfth century.

G • Query   Patterned Response

MODEL   ¿Entramos?
STUDENT 1   **Sí, entremos ahora.**
STUDENT 2   **No, no entremos todavía.**

1. ¿Comemos?
2. ¿Repasamos los apuntes?
3. ¿Decidimos la cuestión?
4. ¿Lo buscamos?
5. ¿Devolvemos el libro?
6. ¿Nos despedimos?
7. ¿Nos levantamos?
8. ¿Nos vamos? (¡Cuidado!)

H • Translation Drill

Translate into Spanish, using a relative pronoun.

1. Here are the girls who went to Bogotá.
2. This is my former teacher for whom I brought the book.
3. My brother, the one you know, leaves for Mexico tomorrow.
4. That is what surprised me.
5. He wants to leave, which is a shame.

University of Salamanca, Spain

I · Guided Composition

Write a formal letter to a fictitious Hispanic university, requesting admittance into their summer program. Include your reasons for wanting to participate in it.

Lección veintiuno

CLASE DE HISTORIA

PABLO	¿Te gustó la conferencia de historia de hoy, Ricardo?	**conferencia** *lecture*
RICARDO	Sí, mucho. El profesor Ortiz recrea los sucesos como si hubiera vivido en aquella época.	**recrear** *to recreate* **sucesos** *events* **época** *era, period*
CARMEN	A mí me pareció muy interesante cuando habló del Libertador. Después de que había hecho tanto por conseguir una América unida, su propio pueblo lo rechazó.	**tanto** *so much* **rechazar** *to reject*
ARMANDO	¡Bah! Yo no estoy de acuerdo con todo eso. Ese Libertador habrá vivido por lo menos trescientos años para hacer todo lo que dijo el profe.	
RICARDO	Jorge Washington hizo tanto o más por los Estados Unidos aunque tú no lo quieras creer. ¿Vivió trescientos años también?	
CARMEN	Y antes de que sigas criticando, piensa en los grandes historiadores que se pasan la vida verificando datos.	**historiador** *historian* **verificar** *to verify* **datos** *facts*
ARMANDO	Eres demasiado crédula. ¿Tú crees que haya sido posible que Washington durmiera en todas esas camas? No habría hecho otra cosa que dor-	**camas** *beds*

mir si hubiera estado en tantos lugares. Todo eso me parece muy sospechoso.

PABLO Y tú eres demasiado cínico. Lo que esos hombres hacían fue anotado por contemporáneos suyos en documentos y cartas.

CARMEN Exactamente. Por eso podemos verificar que Simón Bolívar fue un gran patriota. Sacrificó toda su vida para establecer la independencia de los países suramericanos. Creó la República de Gran Colombia y junto con San Martín...

ARMANDO ¡Nada! La historia es un pretexto para que los maestros de historia tengan empleo.

RICARDO No seas tan irrespetuoso. Tal vez cuando seas mayor habrás comprendido la importancia que esos hombres tienen para nosotros.

ARMANDO Por lo pronto, allí los dejo con la discusión. Tengo algunas cosas que hacer para mañana.

PABLO ¿Adónde vas?

ARMANDO Voy a recrearme en esa mitología por unas horas; permítanme recordarles que mañana tenemos un examen de historia.

sospechoso *suspicious*

anotar *to write down*

por eso *that's why*

¡Nada! (coll.) *Forget it!*

maestros *teachers*
empleo *job, work*
irrespetuoso *disrespectful*
ser mayor *to be older; to be an adult*

por lo pronto *for now, for the time being*

recrearse *to amuse oneself*

433

José de San Martín

NOTES

Simón Bolívar (1783–1830) General and statesman, also known as **El Libertador**. Having led Venezuela and Nueva Granada (now Colombia) to independence from Spanish domination, he created the Republic of Gran Colombia in 1821, which included the territory of those two countries and Ecuador. He tried to make a federation of all the South American states. Accused of aspiring to become dictator of the federation, he abdicated all power and died shortly thereafter.

José de San Martín (1778–1850) Argentine general and statesman. He liberated Chile and Peru from Spanish domination and instituted many social and economic reforms, the most notable being the abolition of slavery in those countries.

Gran Colombia The name given to the republic formed in 1819 that comprised the territories of Venezuela, Colombia, and Ecuador. It was dissolved in 1830, giving rise to three independent republics—Venezuela, Nueva Granada, and Ecuador.

LANGUAGE STRUCTURES

91 Conjunctions used to introduce adverbial clauses

▶ Adverbial clauses are subordinate clauses that modify a verb. They are introduced by conjunctions, some of which are derived from prepositions.[1]

[1] In turn, some prepositions are derived from adverbs. For example:
Yo entraré antes.   **Yo entraré antes de comer.**   **Yo entré antes de que Juan volviera.**

Preposition	Conjunction
después de estudiar	**después de que** tú estudies *futuro*
antes de ir	**antes de que** Carmen vaya *subj.*
hasta terminar	**hasta que** terminemos *futuro*
para entender	**para que** entiendan *futuro*
sin verificar	**sin que** verifiquen *futuro*
desde ir a la conferencia	**desde que** fui a la conferencia *past*

▶ As in the case of adverbs, adverbial conjunctions express the circumstances under which the action of the verb takes place: when, where, how, why, under what conditions, etc. Here are some common adverbial conjunctions.

when	antes (de) que	*before*
	cuando (cuandoquiera que)	*when (whenever)*
	tan pronto como	*as soon as*
	después (de) que	*after*
	hasta que	*until*
	mientras	*while*

Fue muy interesante cuando habló del Libertador. — *It was very interesting when he spoke of the* Libertador.

Nos quedamos hasta que llegaron los invitados. — *We stayed until the guests arrived.*

— pret. pret. ind.

how	como (comoquiera que)	*as, how (however), the way*
	como si	*as if*
	según	*as, according to what*

Escriben como hablan. — *They write as (the way) they speak.*

Explícamelo según lo entiendes. — *Explain it to me as you understand it.*

where	donde (dondequiera que)	*where (wherever)*

Te llevaré adonde comimos ayer. — *I'll take you where we ate yesterday.*

Ella encontrará amigos dondequiera que vaya. *subj.* — *She'll find friends wherever she goes.*

why	de modo (manera) que	*so that, so, and therefore*
	puesto que	*since*
	para que	*so that, for*

Carmen habla despacio de modo que podemos entenderla. — *Carmen speaks slowly so (and therefore) we can understand her.*

Es un pretexto para que tengan empleo. — *It's an excuse so that they'll have a job (for them to have a job).*

can be ind. or subj.

	aunque	*although, even though*
under what	a menos que	*unless*
conditions	con tal que	*provided that*
	sin que	*without*

Iremos aunque llueve.   *We will go, although it's raining.*
Quiero ir con tal que tú me   *I want to go provided that you*
acompañes.   *accompany me.*

A • Transformation Drill   Preposition→Conjunction

MODEL   Nos quedamos hasta llegar Juan.
           llegó
STUDENT   Nos quedamos hasta **que** llegó Juan.

1. Es un pretexto para tener empleo.
              ellos tengan
2. Estoy muy interesada desde asistir a esa conferencia.
              asistí
3. No se vayan antes de anotar los datos.
              yo anote
4. No puedes ser rico sin hacer un esfuerzo.
              hagas
5. El chiquillo insistió hasta conseguir lo que quería.
              consiguió
6. Llámame para ir al cine.
              vayamos
7. Comprenderás mejor después de ser mayor.
              seas
8. Siempre discuten desde hacerse novios.
              se hicieron

B • Translation Drill

Translate into Spanish. (The last sentence in each series will take a subjunctive in the adverbial clause.)

1. I will leave before. I will leave before eating. I left before they ate.
2. Who came in after? Who came after the party? Who will come in after Miguel has his party?
3. He went without me. He went without calling. He went without her calling him.
4. Can you stay until tomorrow? Can you stay until finishing? Can you stay until they finish?
5. She works for (*para*) Mr. Ortiz. She works in order to earn money. She works in order that her children can go to the university.

92   Indicative versus subjunctive in adverbial clauses

▶ Like noun and adjective clauses, Spanish adverbial clauses may be formed in either the indicative or the subjunctive. The concept of unreality embodied in an indefinite future or an uncertain or negative outcome governs the use of the subjunctive in the adverbial clause. If the subordinate verb indicates something as fact, the indicative is used.

▶ Some conjunctions will take either the indicative or the subjunctive, depending on their context.

	Conjunction	*Indicative*	*Subjunctive*
subordinate clause in the indicative or the subjunctive	cuando hasta que tan pronto como mientras (que) después (de) que	the action of the adverbial clause has taken place, is in progress, or happens regularly	the action of the adverbial clause has yet to take place
	como (comoquiera que) según donde (dondequiera que) aunque *although* de modo que — *so that* de manera que — *so that*	the adverbial clause refers to a factual situation or true outcome	the adverbial clause refers to an unknown situation or outcome

Compare the following.

Adverbial Clause in the Indicative

1. Ella viene cuando puede.
   She comes when she can.
   (Established pattern)
2. Escribí tan pronto como llegué.
   I wrote as soon as I arrived.
   (Established fact)

Adverbial Clause in the Subjunctive

Ven cuando puedas.
Come when(ever) you can.
(Indefinite future)
Escribiré tan pronto como llegue.
I'll write as soon as I arrive.
(By virtue of the arrival being in the future, it is indefinite, uncertain.)

present subj.

3. Deja la factura donde te dijo el jefe.

Deja la factura dondequiera que te diga el jefe.

Leave the bill where the boss told you to.

(The boss has established a location where the bill is to be left.)

Leave the bill wherever the boss tells you to.

(The boss has not yet indicated where, so the future is undetermined.)

Indicative Versus Subjunctive
Matched Pair

Susana escribe rápidamente de manera que termina a las cinco todos los días.

Susana escribe rápidamente de manera que termine a las cinco.

▶ Some conjunctions, because of the meaning they convey, will always be followed by the subjunctive, even when the main and subordinate verbs are in the past. These conjunctions are

subordinate clause always takes subjunctive	antes (de) que para que con tal que a menos que sin que como si

before

antes (de) que   always makes the subordinate verb future and therefore indefinite from the time reference of the main verb, even in a past framework.

Le habló antes de que se fuera.   *He spoke to her before she left.*

so that

para que   always expresses a purpose but never its fulfillment.

Te doy dinero para que compres un vestido.

I am giving you money so that you can buy a dress.

con tal que   expresses a condition, but not that it has been met.

provided that

Puedes ir con tal que regreses temprano.   *You may go provided that you return early.*

unless

a menos que   presents an alternative, but does not indicate its acceptance.

Ven conmigo a menos que prefieras ir con Pablo.   *Come with me unless you prefer to go with Pablo.*

without

sin que   always expresses a negative result.

Armando se fue sin que pudiéramos convencerlo.   *Armando left without our being able to convince him.*

as if

como si (always followed by an imperfect or pluperfect subjunctive)   implies unreality by its very nature.

Habla como si fuera imbécil.   *He talks as if he were an imbecile.*

▶   Some adverbial conjunctions are always followed by the indicative, since they indicate facts.

subordinate clause always takes the indicative	puesto que	*since*
	ya que	*since, now that*
	ahora que	*now that*
	porque	*because*

Nunca tengo hambre puesto que como todo el día.   *I'm never hungry since I eat all day.*

No puedes hacer un viaje, ahora que no tienes más dinero.   *You can't take a trip now that you don't have any more money.*

A • Variable Pattern Drill

Practice orally the patterns in the following charts.

1.
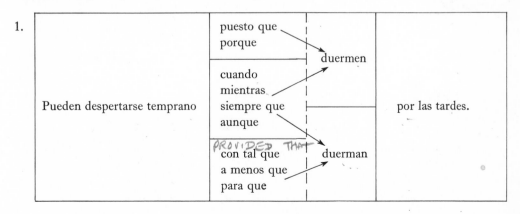

in the past tense a fact.

2.

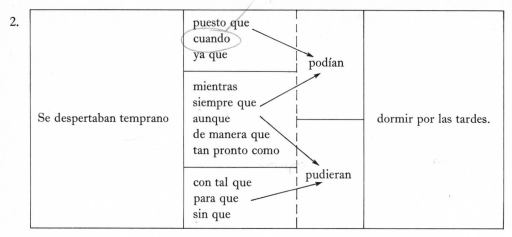

	puesto que		
Se despertaban temprano	cuando	podían	dormir por las tardes.
	ya que		
	mientras		
	siempre que		
	aunque		
	de manera que		
	tan pronto como	pudieran	
	con tal que		
	para que		
	sin que		

B • Replacement Drill Preterit/Past→Future/Present Subjunctive

MODEL   Te escribí cuando llegué.
            escribiré
STUDENT   Te escribiré cuando **llegue**.

1. Hablé con el jefe cuando terminó.
   Hablaré   *termine*
2. Anoté los datos tan pronto como pude.
   Anotaré   *pueda*
3. ¿Pudiste estudiar mientras comías?
   ¿Podrás   *comas*
4. ¿Nos llamaste después de que llegaste?
   llamarás   *llegues*

5. No dormí aunque hacía fresco.
      dormiré   *haga fresco.*
6. Respondiste según recordabas la lección.
   Responderás   *recuerdes*
7. Trataron de hacerlo como pudieron.
   Tratarán   *puedan.*
8. Nos sentamos donde nos dijo el maestro.
      sentaremos   *diga*

C • Replacement Drill Present Indicative/Present Subjunctive→ Past/Imperfect Subjunctive

The adverbial conjunctions used in this drill always take the subjunctive.

MODEL   Te doy el libro para que sigas la lección.
            di
STUDENT   Te di el libro para que **siguieras** la lección.

1. Se lo digo antes que se vaya.
      dije   *fueran*
2. Siempre voy con tal que tenga automóvil.
            iba   *tuviera*
3. No te creemos a menos que verifiques los datos.
      creíamos   *verificaras*

4. No quiero hacerlo sin que Ud. esté de acuerdo.
   quise   *estuviera*
5. Hablo con tu padre para que puedas ir a la fiesta.
   Hablé   *pudieras*
6. No debes hacerlo a menos que te lo exija el jefe.
   debiste   *exigiera*
7. Siempre repasamos los apuntes antes que comience la clase.
   repasábamos   *comenzara*
8. ¿Sales de casa sin que nadie te oiga?
   ¿Saliste   *oyera*

D • Integration Drill

Combine the following pairs of sentences, using a suitable adverbial conjunction. There may be more than one possible answer.

MODEL   Te contaré un chiste. Estamos juntos.
STUDENT   Te contaré un chiste **cuando estemos** juntos.

1. Yo le daré su mensaje. Llega el jefe. *cuando llegue*
2. Busca una pelota. Juegan al fútbol. *para que jueguen*
3. Simón Bolívar fue rechazado por su pueblo. Sacrificó toda su vida. *aunque sacrificó*
4. El Sr. Ortiz recrea los sucesos. Parecen actuales. *como si pareciera*
5. Mañana iremos de compras. Las tiendas cierran temprano hoy. *porque*
6. Me das la respuesta. Te hago la pregunta.
7. Tengo que encontrar el collar. Puedo ponérmelo con el vestido nuevo. *para que pueda*
8. Nos quedamos allí. Llegó ayuda. *hasta que llegó*

E • Completion Drill

Complete the sentences in Spanish.

1. Quiero que me digas tu nombre antes que _____.
2. Parece que van a dar un paseo aunque _____.
3. Podremos terminar ahora mismo a menos que _____.
4. Es muy fácil puesto que _____.
5. Tienes que escuchar para que _____.
6. No quiero irme sin que _____.
7. Rubén siempre come mientras _____.
8. Armando habla como si _____.
9. Ricardo viajaba dondequiera que _____.
10. Practicábamos mucho el español de modo que _____.

F • Translation Drill

Translate into Spanish.

1. We will finish before they start. They finished before we started.
2. You left after they came. You said you would leave after they came.

3. Call me before they decide. Call me after they decide. Call me as soon as they decide. Call me even though they decide.
4. Let's go where you said. Let's go wherever you want.
5. Do it any way I tell you. Do it wherever I tell you. Do it whenever I tell you. Don't do it until I tell you.
6. I will bring them provided that she pay me. I will bring them so that she will pay me. I won't bring them unless she pays me.

93   Additional perfect tenses

PLUSCUAMPERFECTO

Pluperfect Indicative		Pluperfect Subjunctive	
había *(past perfect)*		hubiera	
habías	hablado	hubieras	hablado
había +	aprendido	hubiera +	aprendido
habíamos	escrito	hubiéramos	escrito
habían		hubieran	

▶ The pluperfect indicative is formed by the imperfect indicative of the auxiliary verb **haber** + past participle. The Spanish pluperfect indicative translates English *had* + past participle and expresses an action completed prior to another implied or expressed past action.[2]

> **Su pueblo lo rechazó después de que había hecho tanto.**
> *His people rejected him after he had done so much.*
> **No fui porque ya había visto la película.**
> *I didn't go because I had already seen the film.*

▶ The pluperfect subjunctive is formed by the imperfect subjunctive of the auxiliary verb **haber** + past participle. Subordinate clauses requiring a past subjunctive use the pluperfect subjunctive if the action of the subordinate verb is prior to the time indicated by the main verb (examples 1 and 2). The pluperfect subjunctive may also express a hypothetical or unfulfilled past occurrence (examples 3 and 4).

1. Buscaban a alguien que ya hubiera visitado la América del Sur.
   They were looking for someone who had already visited South America.
2. Temían que nos hubiéramos ido.
   They feared we had left.
3. Dudo que hubieras podido entenderlo.
   I doubt you would have been able to understand him.
4. Si hubiera estado allí, habría bailado durante horas.
   If I had been there, I would have danced for hours.

---

[2] There is a preterit perfect tense in Spanish (**hube, hubiste, hubo, hubimos, hubieron** + past participle). However, it is rarely used; instead, the simple preterit is generally used. The preterit perfect tense will not appear in this text.

Future Perfect		Conditional Perfect	
habré		habría	
habrás	hablado	habrías	hablado
habrá +	aprendido	habría +	aprendido
habremos	escrito	habríamos	escrito
habrán		habrían	

▶ The future perfect is formed by the future of **haber** + past participle and translates English *will have* + past participle. It expresses an occurrence that will have been completed by some time in the future (examples 1 and 2). It may also express probability or conjecture in the present about a completed action (examples 3 and 4).

1. Para mañana habré leído todo el libro. — *By tomorrow I will have read the whole book.*
2. Para la semana que viene, habrán terminado la casa. — *By next week they will have finished the house.*
3. Habrán venido (Probablemente vinieron) ayer. — *They probably came yesterday.*
4. ¿Habrán estado allí? — *Might they have been there?*

▶ The conditional perfect is formed by the conditional of **haber** + past participle and translates English *would have* + past participle. It may also express probability or conjecture in the past about a completed action (example 4).

1. Yo habría hecho el trabajo pero Juanito me llamó. — *I would have done the work but Juanito called me.*
2. Sé que tú no habrías hecho eso. — *I know you wouldn't have done that.*
3. Creíamos que habrían terminado. — *We thought they would have finished.*
4. Gonzalo habría encontrado otra solución. — *Gonzalo must have found another solution.*

Han dicho que he dicho un dicho;
Tal dicho no lo he dicho yo.
Porque si yo hubiera dicho el dicho,
Bien dicho habría estado dicho el dicho
Por haberlo dicho yo.

A • Substitution Drill

or por

MODEL   Nosotros habíamos esperado durante horas.
        Carmen
STUDENT   Carmen **había** esperado durante horas.

1. Carmen había esperado durante horas.
   Tú
   Ricardo y yo
   Pablo y Armando
   Yo
   Uds.

2. Para mañana tú habrás terminado, ¿verdad?
   él
   Pablo y Elenita
   el Sr. Ortiz
   nosotros   *habremos*
   tú y Miguel

3. Uds. no habrían hecho otra cosa que dormir si hubieran estado allí.
   Nosotras   *hubiéramos*
   Yo
   Tú   *hubieras*
   Ud.
   Ellos

B • Query   Patterned Response

MODEL   ¿Por qué no dejaste los periódicos entonces?
STUDENT   **Porque ya los había dejado.**

1. ¿Por qué no abrieron la tienda entonces?
2. ¿Por qué no buscaron Uds. el anillo allí entonces?
3. ¿Por qué no comiste los churros entonces?
4. ¿Por qué no escribieron las respuestas entonces?
5. ¿Por qué no podían escoger los premios entonces?
6. ¿Por qué no hacían la tarea de historia entonces?
7. ¿Por qué no te vendían el artefacto maya entonces?
8. ¿Por qué no pagó Ud. la factura entonces?

C • Replacement Drill   Present Indicative/Present Perfect Subjunctive → Past/Pluperfect Subjunctive

MODEL   Buscan a alguien que haya conocido al bandido.
        Buscaban
STUDENT   Buscaban a alguien que **hubiera** conocido al bandido.

1. Buscan voluntarios que hayan trabajado allí antes.
   Buscaban   *hubieran*
2. Tememos que se hayan perdido.
   Temíamos   *hubiera*
3. Dudo que esa máquina haya funcionado.
   Dudaba   *hubiera*

4. ¿No conoces a nadie que haya hablado con él?
   conocías   *hubiera*

5. ¿Hay alguien aquí que haya estudiado la propuesta?
   ¿Hubo   *hubieran*

6. Vamos a invitar a los que hayan ganado más premios.
   Íbamos   *hubieran*

7. Susana está comiendo todo sin que le hayas dicho nada.
   comió   *hubieras*

8. Prefiero que lo hayas abierto antes.
   Preferí   *hubieras*

D • Query   Patterned Response

MODEL   Has terminado el libro, ¿verdad?
STUDENT **No, pero lo habré terminado para el miércoles.**

1. Has acabado las facturas, ¿verdad?
2. Ya tradujiste el libro, ¿verdad?
3. Hoy ofrecieron una solución, ¿verdad?
4. Le has devuelto el anillo, ¿verdad?
5. El lunes empezaron las clases, ¿verdad?
6. Ya han elegido un presidente, ¿verdad?
7. Regresó tu jefe, ¿verdad?
8. Ya aprendieron Uds. esos datos, ¿verdad?

E • Transformation Drill   Imperfect Subjunctive/Conditional→ Pluperfect Subjunctive/Conditional Perfect

MODEL   Si tuviera dinero, compraría una casa.
STUDENT Si **hubiera tenido** dinero, **habría comprado** una casa.

1. Si yo supiera la respuesta, contestaría.
2. Si tuviéramos tiempo, iríamos al museo contigo.
3. Si estudiaras más, no te darían calabazas.
4. Si Uds. se levantaran más temprano, podrían jugar.
5. Si Rosa practicara todos los días, recitaría el poema de memoria.
6. Si ellos entendieran el español, nos divertiríamos más.
7. Si yo te dijera un secreto, ¿me escucharías?
8. Si me dieran un aumento, estaría muy contento.

habríamos ido
dado
habrían podido

F • Query   Free Response

Answer in Spanish.

1. ¿Te habías dado cuenta de que el español sería tan fácil?
2. ¿Cuándo habrás terminado tus estudios universitarios?
3. ¿Qué habrías hecho si te hubiera llamado el presidente de los Estados Unidos anoche?
4. ¿Por qué había decidido Ud. tomar una lengua extranjera?
5. ¿Habría contestado estas preguntas si no lo hubiera pedido su profesor?
6. ¿Habrías levantado la mano si yo no te hubiera seleccionado antes?
7. ¿Te habían dicho algo sobre esta clase antes de tomarla?
8. ¿Para cuándo habrá ganado Ud. su primer millón de dólares?

G • Translation Drill

Translate into Spanish

1. I think that they would have written. I doubt that they would have answered.
2. Have you finished already? No, but I will have finished within an hour.
3. We were looking for someone who had read the book. We found someone who had known the writer.
4. When might the letter have arrived? They hadn't received it the last time I called.
5. Since he received the message yesterday, he will have fixed it already. If not, we would have known it.

94   Sequence of tenses

▶ When a subjunctive is called for in a subordinate clause in Spanish, a certain sequence of tenses is followed, depending on the time relationship between the main verb and the subordinate verb. The way Spanish sequences its tenses is very much the same as in English. The examples that follow in this section demonstrate the parallelism between English and Spanish.

Main Verb (Indicative, command, conditional)	*Subordinate Verb* (Subjunctive)
Future Future perfect[3] Command	Present Present Perfect
Present Present Perfect	
Imperfect Pluperfect Preterit Conditional Conditional Perfect	Imperfect Pluperfect

[3] When the future perfect expresses probability or conjecture about a completed action, it is usually followed by an imperfect or a present perfect subjunctive.

Carmen se habrá ido antes de que su padre pudiera darle (haya podido darle) el mensaje.

Carmen must have left before her father could give her the message.

▶ When the main verb is in the future, future perfect, or command form, the subordinate verb normally appears in the present or present perfect subjunctive, depending on the time relationship between the two verbs.

1. Buscaré a alguien que pueda ayudarte.   *I will look for someone who can help you.*

2. Me habré ido cuando llegues.   *I will have left when you arrive.*
3. Dígale que abra la puerta.   *Tell her to open the door.*
4. Te daré el libro cuando lo haya terminado.   *I'll give you the book when I've finished it.*
5. Agradécele que te haya invitado.   *Thank him for having invited you.*

▶ When the main verb is in the present or the present perfect indicative, the subordinate verb may be in the present, present perfect, imperfect or pluperfect subjunctive, depending on the time relationship between the two verbs.

Dudo que $\begin{cases} \textbf{hagas} \\ \textbf{hayas hecho} \\ \textbf{hicieras} \\ \textbf{hubieras hecho} \end{cases}$ **eso.**   *I doubt you* $\begin{cases} \textit{do (will do)} \\ \textit{have done} \\ \textit{did} \\ \textit{would have done} \end{cases}$ *that.*

Nunca hemos empezado antes que $\begin{cases} \textbf{llegue} \\ \textbf{haya llegado} \\ \textbf{llegara} \\ \textbf{hubiera llegado} \end{cases}$ **el maestro.**

We have never begun before the teacher $\begin{cases} \textit{arrives.} \\ \textit{has arrived.} \\ \textit{arrived.} \\ \textit{had arrived.} \end{cases}$

▶ When the main verb is in the preterit, imperfect, conditional, or one of their compound (perfect) counterparts, the subordinate verb is regularly expressed in the imperfect or pluperfect subjunctive.

1. No hubo nadie que supiera su nombre.   *There wasn't anyone who knew his name.*

2. Temía que te cayeras (hubieras caído).   *I was afraid you might fall (have fallen).*

3. ¿Harías eso si pudieras?   *Would you do that if you could?*
4. Te habría explicado la situación si hubieras hablado con él.   *He would have explained the situation to you if you had spoken with him.*

5. Se había levantado sin que nadie lo despertara (hubiera despertado).   *He had gotten up without anyone awakening (having awakened) him.*

A • Replacement Drill   Present Indicative→Present Subjunctive → Present Perfect Subjunctive

Note the difference in meaning between the two subordinate clauses.

MODEL   Yo sé que vienen.
          dudo
STUDENT 1 Yo dudo que **vengan**.
STUDENT 2 Yo dudo que **hayan venido**.

1. Es seguro que regresan hoy.
   Es posible *que hayan*
2. Creo que puede encontrar el lugar.
   ¿No crees
3. Es evidente que Pilar se retrasa.
   Puede ser
4. Sabemos que es sospechoso.
   Tememos

5. ¿Es cierto que consigues el empleo?
   Espero
6. Es verdad que nos roban el dinero.
   Es increíble
7. Creo que estamos de acuerdo.
   No creo
8. ¿Es cierto que no encuentras el collar?
   Sienten

B • Query   Patterned Response

MODEL   ¿Le has dado el regalo?
STUDENT   **No, pero estará contento cuando se ~~la~~ dé.**   *lo*

1. ¿Le has dicho las noticias?
2. ¿Les has hecho el guacamole?   *se lo haga*
3. ¿Le has traducido la lectura?   *se la traduzca*
4. ¿Te han ofrecido el contrato?   *me lo ofrezca*

5. ¿Has conseguido su dirección?   *estaré cuando la consiga*
6. ¿Le has enseñado el premio a Susana?   *se lo ense*
7. ¿Han recibido Uds. la respuesta?   *la recibamos*
8. ¿Han llegado tus tíos?   *lleguen.*

C • Patterned Response Drill

yet, still   *invoices*

MODEL   Ya comencé la labor.
STUDENT   **¡Eres imposible! Te dije que no la comenzaras todavía.**

1. Ya empecé a hacer el café.   *empezaras*
2. Ya compré el anillo.   *no lo compraras*
3. Ya abrieron el regalo.   *no lo abrieras*
4. Ya sirvió Pablo los refrescos.   *no los sirvieras*

5. Ya recogimos los periódicos.   *no los recogieran*
6. Ya revisé las facturas.   *no las revisaras*
7. Ya preparó Elenita la comida.   *no la prepararas*
8. Ya le llevamos los carteles al señor.   *no se los llevaran*

D • Patterned Response Drill

MODEL   Como no llegué temprano, no pude ver al jefe.
STUDENT   **Si hubieras llegado temprano, ¿lo habrías visto?**

1. Como no llevábamos dinero, no pudimos comprar la bicicleta.
2. Puesto que no estudié, no pude contestar la pregunta.
3. Como no vino César Chávez, no pudimos platicar con él.
4. Puesto que no estaba don Santiago, no pudimos discutir la propuesta.
5. Puesto que no comprendimos la lección, no pudimos hacer la tarea.
6. Como no me levanté temprano, no pude ir.

habría ido,

7. Como Armando no nos escuchaba, no insistimos en nuestras ideas.
8. Puesto que los jugadores no merecían el premio, no se lo dimos a nadie.

E • Completion Drill

Complete the sentences in Spanish.

1. Te daré mis apuntes cuando _____.
2. Habré hablado con él antes que _____.
3. Dígale Ud. que _____.
4. Es posible que _____.
5. Hemos venido para que _____.
6. Buscábamos una máquina que _____.
7. Yo temía que _____.
8. Me había dibujado sin que _____.
9. Si fueras inteligente _____.
10. Yo te habría dado dinero para que _____.
11. Iríamos al concierto juntos si _____.
12. No creo que _____.
13. Fui a la venta después que _____.
14. No había nadie que _____.

F • Translation Drill

Translate into Spanish.

1. I hope you will study the proposal. I hope you studied the proposal.
2. It's a shame that he isn't here. It's a shame that he wasn't here.
3. I doubt that you wrote. I doubted that you would have written.
4. Will you have given him an answer before he leaves? Would you have given him an answer before he left?
5. Do you know anyone who has lived in Colombia? Have you spoken with anyone who has visited the museum?
6. They would go if they were able. They would have gone if they had been able.

95 Progressives formed with **seguir, continuar, venir, ir,** etc.

▶ You have already learned that **estar** is used with a present participle to indicate the progressive form of a verb tense (see section **32**). While **estar** is most frequently used, other verbs that indicate continuance or motion can also be used as auxiliaries in this construction. Some of the verbs used in this way are **continuar, seguir, venir, ir,** and **andar.**

1. ¿Por qué sigues criticando?
2. En el metro iba pensando en muchas cosas.
3. Continuamos estudiando derecho.
4. Sonia siempre viene cantando a casa.
5. Los chiquillos andan buscando algo que hacer.

Why do you keep on criticizing?
In the subway I was going along thinking about many things.
We continue (are still) studying law.
Sonia always comes home singing.
The children are wandering (going) around looking for something to do.

A • Replacement Drill

MODEL   Estoy esperando los resultados.   (seguir)
STUDENT **Sigo** esperando los resultados.

1. Estoy componiendo una sinfonía.   (seguir)
2. Los estudiantes están defendiendo la causa.   (andar)   *ellos andan - - -*
3. Ya estoy comprendiendo la lección.   (ir)
4. Ese profesor está dando calabazas a todo el mundo.   (andar)
5. Siempre estamos malgastando el tiempo.   (venir)
6. Los bandidos estaban atacando la capital.   (seguir)
7. En el centro, ¿estabas mirando las tiendas?   (ir)
8. No creo que estén trabajando.   (continuar)   *continúan*

B • Translation Drill

Translate into Spanish.

1. He's criticizing everybody. He goes around criticizing everybody. He comes around criticizing everybody.
2. You're always talking. You keep on talking. You continue talking all the time.
3. What are you writing? Are you still writing it? Why do you go around writing silly poems?
4. Sonia is worrying me. Why does she keep on living in the past? She can't continue thinking like this.

96   **Por** versus **para**

▶ **Por** and **para** cannot be used interchangeably, although often they are both translated as *for* in English.

▶ **Para** is used to indicate a deadline, a goal, a purpose, or a destination or recipient. It can also express a comparison.

1. Tienen que hacerlo para mañana.   *They have to do it by tomorrow.*
                                        (deadline)

2. Estudia para (ser) médico.   *He studies to be a doctor.*
                                        (the goal of the studies)

3. Estudiamos para aprender.   *We study (in order) to learn.*
                                        (purpose; goal)

4. Esta taza es para té.   *This cup is for tea.*
                                        (purpose)

5. Vamos para el estanque.   *Let's head for the pond.*
                                        (destination)

6. El libro es para Manuel.   *The book is for Manuel.*
                                        (recipient)

7. Para su edad, ella habla muy bien.   *For her age, she speaks very well.*
                                        (comparison)

▶ **Por** indicates a time span or a location. It also indicates substitution, exchange, cause, or motive. In addition, **por** is used to express the agent or means by which something is done as well as to express a mistaken identity.

1. Anoche estudié por dos horas.

   (PASEAR)

2. ¿Nos paseamos por el parque?

Last night I studied for two hours.
(time span)

Shall we take a walk through (around, by, near) the park?
(location)

3. Cuando mi hermanita no puede levantar algo, yo lo hago por ella.

When my little sister can't lift something, I do it for her.
(substitution)

4. Te doy cinco pesos por ese anillo.

I'll give you five pesos for that ring.
(exchange)

5. Paso por Ricardo a las cinco.

I'll come by for Ricardo at five.
(cause: Ricardo is the cause of my coming by)

6. Luchan por sus ideas.

or en

7. Ayer llegué (por) avión.

They fight for (on account of) their ideas.
(motive)

Yesterday I arrived by plane.
(agent)

8. Te tomé por tu hermano.

I took you for your brother.
(mistaken identity)

Matched Pairs

Por	**Para**
1. Trabajo por mi padre.	Trabajo para mi padre.
I work for my father (in his place).	*I work for my father (he is the recipient of my labor).*
(substitution)	(recipient)
2. Vamos por la carretera.	Vamos para la carretera.
We are going along the highway.	*We are going toward the highway.*
(location)	(destination)
3. Hacen el trabajo por la mañana.	Hacen el trabajo para mañana.
They do the work during the morning.	*They do the work for (by) tomorrow.*
(time span) *or porque*	(deadline)
4. Estudia por ser científico.	Estudia para ser científico.
He studies because he is a scientist.	*He studies in order to become a scientist.*
(cause)	(purpose, goal)

5. La Sra. *de* Ortiz me dio dinero por los tamales.
Mrs. Ortiz gave me money for (in exchange for) the tamales.
(exchange)

6. Este poema es por mi novio.
This poem is by my fiancé.
(agent)

7. Lo tomé por un español.
I took him for a Spaniard.
(mistaken identity)

La Sra. Ortiz me dio dinero para los tamales.
Mrs. Ortiz gave me money for (to buy) the tamales.
(purpose)

Este poema es para mi novio.
This poem is for my fiancé.
(recipient)

Habla bien el español para un americano.
He speaks Spanish well for an American.
(comparison)

intend of

Escribo la carta por ti.

intended for

Hay una carta para ti.

▶ **Por** is used in many set phrases. The phrases in bold type are new vocabulary.

por ejemplo	*for example*
por ahora	*for the time being, for now*
por lo pronto	
por Dios	*for heaven's sake, my God*
por el estilo	*like that, accordingly, along those lines*
por eso	*for that reason, that's why, therefore*
por favor	*please*
por fin	*finally*
por lo menos	*at least*
por lo visto	*apparently*
¿por qué?	*why?*
porque	*because*
por cierto	*as a matter of fact*
por ciento	*percent*

A • Translation Drill

Translate into Spanish, using **para**.

1. I'll finish by Monday.
2. The bicycle is for Tomás.
3. Let's go toward the lake.
4. We eat in order to live.

5. The night is for sleeping.
6. She is studying to be a teacher.
7. Is there a letter for me?

8. For a professor, she is very young.
9. You have to come to hear the record.
10. We work for Don Santiago.

B • Translation Drill

Translate into Spanish, using **por**.

1. I can't close the door; please do it for me.
2. For that reason, I can't come.
3. Yesterday we talked for an hour.
4. He gave me two dollars for the book.
5. The house was constructed by a friend.
6. I asked for (about) you at the party.
7. I want to go along Fifth Avenue.
8. I always take her for a Spaniard.
9. He studies a lot on account of (for) his father.
10. Ten percent of the students don't study.

C • Completion Drill

Complete the sentences with **por** or **para**.

1. Tengo que acabar _PARA_ la semana que viene.
2. Tenemos que salir _PARA_ el cine ahora mismo.
3. Quiero terminar temprano _PARA_ regresar a casa.
4. Como eres mi novia, escribí unos versos _PARA_ ti.
5. Puesto que Diego no puede ir, yo iré _POR_ él.
6. Se dice que estudiamos _PARA_ aprender.
7. Yo estuve en el centro _POR_ seis horas ayer.
8. Esto es una máquina _PARA_ refrescos.
9. Vamos a hacer un viaje _POR_ la América del Sur.
10. Llegó rápidamente porque vino _POR_ avión.
11. La tomé _POR_ Luisa, pero luego me di cuenta que era Mónica.
12. _POR_ ahora, me parece bien que sigas estudiando.

D • Translation Drill

Translate into Spanish.

1. We are going to (heading for) the pond. We are going through the city.
2. She works for Mr. Gutiérrez (he is her employer). She fights for her ideas.
3. I will study for two hours. I'm studying for the history exam.
4. You took her for a Chicana? He is very nice for a teacher.
5. Why are they coming? In order to go with us.

REVIEW

I The following questions are related to the dialog. Answer in Spanish.

1. ¿De qué trata la clase de historia?
2. ¿Por qué le gusta la clase a Ricardo?
3. ¿Están de acuerdo los tres compañeros sobre el valor de la historia?

4. ¿Qué piensa Armando de la historia en general?

5. ¿Cómo defiende Carmen la autenticidad de la historia? ¿Y Pablo?

6. ¿Había Ud. oído hablar antes de Simón Bolívar? ¿Y San Martín?

7. ¿Qué fue la república de Gran Colombia?

8. ¿Por qué deja Armando la discusión?

9. ¿Cree Ud. que Armando habrá cambiado cuando sea mayor?

10. Si usted hubiera asistido a la discusión, ¿qué posición habría tomado?

II Translation. Translate into Spanish.

1. I keep on thinking about the lecture by Prof. Ortiz. If I had lived in that period, I would have fought with Bolívar.

2. Bah! I had heard that story before. As a matter of fact, Pablo and I were discussing it the other day before you came.

3. Bolívar must have been like ten men in order to do all that the books say.

4. It's not possible that he could have traveled through all South America; it's certain he didn't go by plane.

5. You are ridiculous! I don't think that George Washington crossed the Delaware in a submarine (*submarino*) either.

6. But apparently he arrived at the other side, or our history would have been different.

7. You talk as if you knew it all. The facts keep changing through the years without our being able to verify them.

8. That's why what you call history, I call mythology. In a thousand years, when historians talk about us, there will be exaggerations also.

9. You're a cynic. Perhaps by then people will have understood the importance of learning historical facts.

10. For the time being, allow me to remind you that we have to know all about Bolívar for a history exam tomorrow, even if you think it's only mythology.

III Guided Composition

Do you think history is a science or an art? Do historians distort the past with their own ideas and experiences? Would you be able to write an objective account of a contemporary event?

Cognates & Contexts

La Batalla de Araure,
by Tito Salas, 1955

Colonización e independencia de Hispanoamérica

Para fines del siglo XVI, la mayor parte de lo que hoy se conoce como Hispanoamérica había sido explorado y conquistado por los españoles. Nombres como Cristóbal Colón (descubridor de América), Núñez de Balboa (descubridor del Océano Pacífico), Hernando de Magallanes (un portugués al servicio de España que circumnavegó el mundo, descubriendo Tierra del Fuego, el punto sur del continente suramericano), Hernán Cortés (conquistador de México), Francisco Pizarro (conquistador del Perú), y muchos otros grandes exploradores que habían ayudado en esta empresa, ya quedaban grabados en la historia. Ahora empieza la época de colonización.

Las colonias españolas estaban bajo el poder absoluto del monarca que las administraba mediante el Consejo de Indias, creado en 1524. Este Consejo estaba encargado de dirigir los territorios en todos sus aspectos: legislativo, jurídico,

para fines de *towards (by) the end of*

no, he died in the Phillipines

empresa *undertaking*

western hemisphere

mediante *by means of*

phrase anglo slant of author.

455

administrativo, económico y hasta religioso. También estaba encargado de una tarea cronista que nos ha proporcionado un diario muy detallado de las actividades de los españoles al igual que de las culturas y tradiciones encontradas por ellos en las tierras conquistadas.

proporcionar *to provide*

El Consejo enviaba sus dictámenes desde España. Más tarde, gran parte de sus poderes se trasladaron a los virreyes que gobernaban las colonias en nombre del rey. El Virreinato de Nueva España (México) se creó en 1535; luego se crearon otros virreinatos en el Perú y a fines del siglo XVIII, en Nueva Granada y en Buenos Aires.

dictámenes *edicts*
trasladar *to transfer*

Las consecuencias de este sistema fueron opresión política, desigualdad social y explotación ecónomica. Ya en el siglo XVIII, siguiendo el modelo de las colonias norteamericanas, habían estallado algunos levantamientos aislados en las colonias españolas. La Guerra de Independencia propiamente dicha, comenzó en 1810 con dos centros principales: uno al norte dirigido por Simón Bolívar, y otro al sur, mandado por José de San Martín. Ambos líderes lucharon con tropas mal preparadas y a veces desunidas, pero lograron imponer un fin común: la independencia.

estallar *to break out; to explode*

imponer *to impose*   **fin** *goal; end*

Bolívar y San Martín se reunieron por primera vez en Guayaquil, Colombia en 1822. Aunque no sabemos el contenido de las discusiones sostenidas, la diferencia de personalidad entre los dos generales impidió que se desarrollara una fuerte amistad entre ellos. Sin embargo, sí hay evidencia de gran respeto y admiración profesional.

impedir *to prevent*

Tras largos años de lucha intensa, la independencia de las repúblicas suramericanas se fue haciendo realidad, completándose en 1828 con la independencia del Uruguay.

tras *following, after*

Los dos grandes impulsores de esta realidad, Bolívar y San Martín, murieron en desgracia: Bolívar en 1830, San Martín en 1850, desterrado en Francia. Como sucede tantas veces en la historia, sus contemporáneos los rechazaron. La perspectiva de los años ha sido necesaria para darles la importancia que en verdad merecen, junto con otros grandes patriotas, en el esquema de la independencia de Hispanoamérica.

impulsor *catalyst*

desterrar *to exile*

Luquillo Beach, Puerto Rico

Lección veintidós

TO P. 472

CASI A LUQUILLO

Rosario = rosary a woman's name in Spanish, not in Italian

ROSARIO	¿Por qué no vamos a Luquillo? Pepe tiene un auto...
VICTORIA	¿Quién quiere llamarlo? *— ello?*
CECILIA	Que lo haga Rosario. Ella es la más diplomática. *LET R. DO IT* Quizás pueda convencerlo.
ROSARIO	¡Qué cobardía! ¿Cuál es su número de teléfono?
VICTORIA	Déjame buscarlo. Lo apunté el otro día [por si las moscas] *JUST IN CASE* cuando hablábamos de ir a la playa. Aquí está. Es el 760-3790.
ROSARIO	Hola. ¿Puedo hablar con Pepe, por favor?
TOÑÍN	¿De parte de quién?
ROSARIO	De parte de Rosario Negrón.
TOÑÍN	Ah, hola, Rosario. Habla Toñín. Pepe no se encuentra aquí en este momento. ¿Quieres que le deje un recado? *= mensaje*
ROSARIO	¡Toñín! ¡Cuánto me alegro de oír tu voz! ¿Cuándo llegaste del Norte? *from*
TOÑÍN	Ayer por la tarde. Vengo a pasar las vacaciones de Navidad.
ROSARIO	Llamaba a Pepe para ver si podíamos ir juntos a Luquillo a pasar el día. ¿Te vienes con nosotros?
TOÑÍN	Es que...

convencer *to convince*
cobardía *cowardice*
apuntar *to write down*

recado *message*
alegrarse *to be (become) happy* **voz** *voice*

Navidad *Christmas*

venirse *to come along*

458

ROSARIO Nada. No te preocupes, vienen Cecilia y Victoria también y entre todas llevaremos comida. Ya sé que con Uds. dos el hambre es la que manda.

TOÑÍN No es eso. Es que...

ROSARIO ¿Qué te pasa? ¿Perdiste el gusto por el agua del Caribe en tus andanzas norteñas?

TOÑÍN ¡Eso nunca! Ya sabes que los peces y yo, cuando podemos nadar, no tenemos por qué ir en barco.

ROSARIO Entonces todo está resuelto. ¿Qué te parece el martes que viene? Pepe puede recogernos a todas en mi casa a las ocho. Luego al regreso tal vez pasemos por el Yunque.

TOÑÍN Rosario, ¿quieres escucharme un momento? Ojalá estuviera Pepe pero se fue a Luquillo esta mañana y no regresa hasta el miércoles.

ROSARIO ¡Cómo! ¿Sin avisarme? ¡Qué caradura! Ojalá pesque un resfriado o una insolación... Bueno, Toñín, que lo pases bien. Hasta la próxima.

TOÑÍN ¿Rosario? No cuelgues todavía. ¡Rosario! ¿Rosario?

gusto *taste*

norteñas *northern*

peces *fish*

nadar *to swim*

barco *boat*

resuelto *settled*

avisar *to advise, let know*
  caradura *scoundrel*
pescar *to fish, catch*
  resfriado *cold* **insolación** *sunstroke*
pasarlo bien *to have a good time*
colgar(ue) *to hang up*

NOTES

Names

Pepe is the nickname for **José**; **Toñín** is a nickname for **Antonio**. Because of the strong Catholic tradition among Spanish-speaking people, religious given names are quite common: Rosario, Concepción, Inmaculada, Jesús, etc.

Places

Luquillo   One of the most popular beaches on the northern coast of Puerto Rico.

El Yunque   A mountain in the shape of an anvil (**yunque**) located to the southeast of San Juan in Puerto Rico. It is surrounded by a tropical rain forest.

el Norte   People in Puerto Rico often refer to the United States as "el Norte."

How to Get There

en barco, en avión, en tren   *by boat, plane, train*
    but **a pie, a caballo**   *on foot, on horseback*

Telephone Etiquette

Ways of answering the phone vary widely in the Spanish-speaking world. In Spain, you would hear **Diga** or **Dígame**. In Mexico, **Bueno** is most commonly heard. In Puerto Rico **Aló** or **Hola** is frequent.

¿De parte de quién? *Who's calling?*

LANGUAGE STRUCTURES

used ē present + past subj

97   The subjunctive with **ojalá, tal vez, quizás, acaso**

▶   **Ojalá** is always followed by the subjunctive. When it is followed by a present subjunctive, it expresses hope, wish, or expectation regarding a future event. When it is followed by an imperfect subjunctive, it expresses regret, or vain wishes, often equivalent to English *would that* or *if only*.

Ojalá Pedro tenga un jonrón.   Ojalá Pedro estuviera aquí.

Oral Drill.   Repeat the following sentences, noting the difference in meaning.

1. Ojalá podamos convencer a Pepe. Ojalá pudiéramos convencer a Pepe.
2. Ojalá estén en casa. Ojalá estuvieran en casa.
3. Ojalá encuentren Uds. una solución. Ojalá encontraran Uds. una solución.
4. Ojalá ganen el partido. Ojalá ganaran el partido.
5. Ojalá nos den algo de comer. Ojalá nos dieran algo de comer.

▶ **Tal vez**, **quizás**, and **acaso**, which mean *perhaps* and therefore express doubt, are usually followed by the subjunctive.

1. Tal vez pasemos por el Yunque.	*Perhaps we will go by el Yunque.*
2. Quizás pesque un resfriado.	*Perhaps he will catch a cold.*
3. Acaso lleguen mañana.	*Perhaps they will arrive tomorrow.*
4. Quizás hubiera sido diferente.	*Perhaps it might have been different.*

▶ Since all these expressions are used without a subject in Spanish, the verb in the subjunctive will appear in the main clause.

▶ When **tal vez, quizás,** or **acaso** come after the verb or when they are simply added to a sentence to seek confirmation of a statement given as fact, the verb will appear in the indicative.

1. Hoy vendrá más temprano, tal vez.	*Today he will come earlier, perhaps.*
2. Quizás tienen hambre.	*Perhaps they're hungry.*
3. Acaso querían más café, ¿no te parece?	*Perhaps they wanted more coffee, don't you think?*

Quizás podamos ir juntos.   Tal vez no hay sitio para mi perro.[1]

[1] **Perro**, *dog.*

A • Replacement Drill   Indicative→Subjunctive

MODEL   Fuimos al museo hoy.   (Ojalá)
STUDENT **Ojalá fuéramos** al museo hoy.

1. Contesta Pepe.   (Ojalá)   *conteste*
2. Termino antes de las cinco.   (Tal vez) *termine*
3. Escriben en inglés. (Acaso)
4. Volvemos con Rosario.   (Quizás)
5. Tendremos mejor suerte mañana.   (Ojalá)

6. Han visto la película.   (Quizás)
7. Encontrarás una solución. (Tal vez)
8. Puedo enviártelo por correo.   (Acaso)
9. Yo habría hecho otra cosa.   (Quizás)
10. Estaban juntos.   (Ojalá)

B • Replacement Drill

Restate the sentences, using **Supongo que** or **Es posible que**, depending on the context.

MODEL   Estabas cansado, tal vez.
STUDENT **Supongo que** estabas cansado.
MODEL   Acaso estén ocupados.
STUDENT **Es posible que** estén ocupados.

1. Tal vez entienden el español.
2. Quizás encuentres trabajo allí.
3. Acaso estén esperando a Toñín.
4. Fue la semana pasada, quizás.

5. Tal vez ya no te quiere.
6. Quizás tomen un refresco con nosotros.
7. Acaso Victoria trae la comida.
8. Nos llamarán antes de venir, tal vez.

C • Query   Free Response

Answer in Spanish using **ojalá**, **tal vez**, **acaso**, or **quizás**.

1. ¿A qué hora te levantarás mañana?
2. ¿Podrás ir a la playa este verano?
3. ¿Cuándo irás a ver a tu familia?
4. ¿Hizo sol ayer en Puerto Rico?
5. ¿Qué vas a hacer esta noche?
6. ¿Tendrás tiempo para ver a tus amigos esta semana?

7. ¿Dónde estaba tu novio(a) ayer?
8. ¿Entienden tus amigos realmente cómo eres?
9. ¿Crees que te van a dar calabazas en esta clase?
10. ¿Habrá paz en el mundo algún día?

98   Use of the infinitive in place of a clause

▶ After the verbs **dejar**, **permitir**, **mandar**, and **hacer**, an infinitive rather than a clause is often used, especially if the object of the verb is a pronoun.[2] This use of the infinitive takes place even when there is a change in subject.

---

[2] **Hacer** and **dejar** usually take a direct object pronoun; **permitir** and **mandar** usually take an indirect object pronoun. Recall that the subject of the subordinate clause often appears as an indirect object pronoun in the main clause (see section **70**, footnote 13): **¿Me dejas que mire la televisión?** *Will you let me watch television?* **Mándales que lo devuelvan.** *Order them to return it.*

1. Le mandé escribir un poema.	*I ordered him to write a poem.*
2. Permítanme recordarles algo.	*Allow me to remind you of something.*
3. Déjame buscarlo.	*Let me look for it.*
4. Me hizo esperar dos horas.	*He made me wait two hours.*

A • Transformation Drill   Subjuntive Clause→Infinitive

MODEL   Deja que yo lo busque.
STUDENT **Déjame buscarlo.**

1. Dejen que ellos lo digan.   *Déjenles decirlo*
2. Permite que yo hable primero.
3. Mándeles que lo escriban.   *mándeles escribirlo.*
4. El profesor hace que escriban una composición.   *les hace escribirla*
5. Dejaré que ellas jueguen contigo.
6. La maestra les permitió que se fueran temprano.
7. El jefe siempre mandaba que trabajáramos hasta las seis.
8. ¿Dejarías que yo saliera con Pepe?

B • Query   Patterned Response

MODEL   ¿Me permites que cierre la tienda?
STUDENT **Por supuesto que te permito cerrar la tienda.**

1. ¿Permite Ud. que tomen el examen mañana?
2. ¿Me deja que compre el libro?
3. ¿Les mando que lleguen temprano?
4. ¿Hago que ella repita la respuesta?
5. ¿Me dejas que yo escoja el regalo?
6. ¿Hacen que tú cierres la puerta?
7. ¿Permiten ellos que traduzcamos la obra al inglés?
8. ¿Mandan que aceptes la propuesta?
9. ¿Hace el jefe que revisen Uds. las facturas?
10. ¿Te permiten que devuelvas el libro tarde?

C • Translation Drill

Express the following sentences in two ways, using a clause and then an infinitive.

MODEL   Let them do it.
STUDENT 1 **Deja que ellos lo hagan.**
STUDENT 2 **Déjalos hacerlo.**

1. Permit me to help you.
2. The professor made them repeat each word.
3. Order them to bring it.
4. The boss is going to let us eat here.
5. We must allow them to discuss the proposal.

99   Indirect commands

▶ Indirect commands are expressed in Spanish by using the present subjunctive of the verb preceded by **que**. These expressions are translated in English with *let* or *have*, not in the sense of *permit* or *cause* but with the force of a command.

Que se vaya.	*Have (Let) him leave.*
Que trabajen los otros.	*Let the others work.*

▶ Object pronouns precede the verb in indirect commands, whether affirmative or negative. The subject, when expressed, usually follows the verb.

Que lo haga Rosario.	*Let Rosario do it.*
¡Que no los vuelva a ver aquí!	*Don't ever let me see you here again.*

A • Query   Patterned Response

MODEL   ¿Lo hago yo o Rosario?
STUDENT **Que lo haga Rosario.**

1. ¿Lo hacemos nosotros o los otros?
2. ¿Lo escribes tú o el director?
3. ¿Apunto el teléfono yo o Cecilia?
4. ¿Comemos nosotros o los chiquillos?
5. ¿Te vienes tú conmigo o se viene Toñín?
6. ¿Me llevas tú o mi hermano?
7. ¿Cuelga primero Ud. o ella?
8. ¿Quiénes empiezan primero, Uds. o los invitados?
9. ¿La espero yo o la espera él?
10. ¿Los ayudo yo o la maestra?

B • Transformation Drill   Direct Command → Indirect Command

MODEL   ¡Repásenlo Uds.!
STUDENT **No, que lo repase otro.**

1. ¡Dime la noticia!
2. ¡Cuéntemelo Ud.!
3. ¡Cántalo!
4. ¡Decidamos la cuestión!
5. ¡Prepáralo!
6. ¡Tradúzcanlo Uds.!
7. ¡Destruye la información!
8. ¡Defiéndeme!
9. ¡Ponte esa camisa!
10. ¡Inténtenlo Uds.!

C • Translation Drill

1. I want Elena to prepare it. Have Elena prepare it.
2. We hope they will come. Have them come.
3. Do you doubt the children will call? Don't let the children call.
4. Tell them to bring the newspaper. Have them bring it.
5. I don't think she can explain it to them. Let her explain it to them.

100 Exclamations ¡**qué**! and ¡**cuánto**!

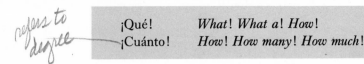

¡Qué!	What! What a! How!
¡Cuánto!	How! How many! How much!

▶ ¡**Qué**! used before a noun means *What a*! or *What*! If the noun is followed by an adjective, **tan** or **más** is generally inserted between the noun and the adjective (examples 3 and 4).

    1. ¡Qué trabajo!   *What a job*!
    2. ¡Qué cobardía!   *What cowardice*!
    3. ¡Qué mujer más simpática!   *What a pleasant woman*!
    4. ¡Qué sucesos tan importantes! *What important events*!

▶ ¡**Qué**! before an adjective or adverb means *How*!

    1. ¡Qué simpática es!   *How pleasant she is*!
    2. ¡Qué bien hablas español!   *How well you speak Spanish*!

▶ ¡**Cuánto**! before a verb functions as an adverb and means *How*! ¡**Cuánto (-a, -os, -as)**! means *How many*! or *How much*! when it precedes a noun; in this case it functions as an adjective and thus agrees in gender and number with the noun it modifies.

    1. ¡Cuánto me alegro!   *How happy I am*!
    2. ¡Cuánta comida han preparado las   *How much food the girls have prepared*!
        muchachas!
    3. ¡Es lástima cuánto dinero gasta   *It's a shame how much money Toñín*
        Toñín!   *spends*!

▶ As with interrogatives, all exclamatory words are accented in Spanish.

A • Transformation Drill

Change the sentence to an exclamation using ¡**Qué**! and including **más** or **tan**, if necessary.

    MODEL   Pintó un cuadro magnífico.
    STUDENT **¡Qué cuadro tan magnífico pintó!**

  1. Visitamos una playa muy hermosa.   6. Habla muy rápido.
  2. Pesqué un resfriado.   7. El lugar está lejos.
  3. Tenemos hambre.   8. Lo pasé bien en el Norte.
  4. Nadas muy bien.   9. Se fueron temprano.
  5. Vimos una obra muy buena.   10. Pasé un día inolvidable.

B • Transformation Drill

Change the sentence to an exclamation using **¡Cuánto!** or its variants.

MODEL   Me divertí en la fiesta.
STUDENT **¡Cuánto me divertí en la fiesta!**

1. Te echo de menos.
2. Hay peces en el estanque.
3. Tienes muchos trastes viejos.
4. Aposté dinero.
5. Victoria exagera mucho.

6. Nadamos en aquel lago.
7. La profesora nos hizo preguntas ayer.
8. Me impresionas.
9. Nos gustó la película.
10. Devolví los libros a la biblioteca.

C • Query   Patterned Response

MODEL   ¿Hizo un día agradable ayer?
STUDENT **Sí, ¡qué día tan agradable hizo ayer!**

MODEL   ¿Te alegras de verme?
STUDENT **Sí, ¡cuánto me alegro de verte!**

1. ¿Compraste un perro grande?
2. ¿Te preocupas por él?
3. ¿Tienes un buen maestro?
4. ¿Lo necesitas?
5. ¿Piensas en Pepe?

6. ¿Viste un drama interesante?
7. ¿Nos retrasamos hoy?
8. ¿Vendo camisas elegantes?
9. ¿Tengo buenas ideas?
10. ¿Trataste de llamarme ayer?

D • Translation Drill

Translate into Spanish.

1. What a beautiful day! What lies!
2. How well she sings! How much they travel!
3. How they worry about me! What a problem!
4. How angry she was! How I think about him!
5. How many times I told you not to go! How disobedient you are!

101   ¿Qué? versus ¿Cuál(-es)?

▶ I. **¿Qué?** and **¿cuál(es)?** as interrogative pronouns.

Both **¿qué?** and **¿cuál(-es)?** are used as interrogative pronouns. **¿Qué?** *what?* is used when identification or definition is sought. **¿Cuál(-es)?** *what?* or *which (one-s)?* refers to a selection or choice from a set.

1. ¿Qué escogiste?   *What did you choose?*
2. ¿Con qué hiciste los tamales? *With what did you make the tamales?*

3. Tengo dos discos. ¿Cuál quieres?   *I have two records. Which one do
                                        you want?*

4. ¿Cuáles de las playas conoces?   *Which of the beaches do you know?*

Compare the following:

1. ¿Qué te gusta?   ¿Cuál te gusta más?
   What do you like?   *Which do you like better?*

2. ¿Qué hicieron ayer?   Hicieron dos ejercicios. ¿Cuál hicieron
   *What did they do   primero?
   yesterday?*   *They did two exercises. Which one did they
                                do first?*

3. ¿De qué está hecho?   ¿Cuáles de estos libros prefieres?
   What is it made of?   *Which of these books do you prefer?*

¿Qué es un astronauta?

¿Cuál es un astronauta?

Since English *what?* can translate either **¿qué?** or **¿cuál?**, the difference must be taken from context.

1. ¿Cuál es la fecha de hoy?   ¿Qué es la fecha de tu nacimiento?
   What is today's date?   *What is your date of birth?*
   (from the set of possible dates)   (identification)

2. ¿Cuál es la capital de Venezuela?   ¿Qué es Venezuela? ¿Una república?
   What is the capital of Venezuela? *What is Venezuela, a republic?*
   (from the set of possible cities)   (definition)

▶ II. **¿Qué?** and **¿cuál(-es)?** as interrogative adjectives.

Both **¿qué?**, *what?* and **¿cuál(-es)?**, *which* are used as interrogative adjectives with the same differences as when they are interrogative pronouns: **¿Qué?** asks for identification, **¿cuál?** asks for selection or choice.

1. ¿Qué libro lees?   *What book are you reading?*
2. ¿A qué playa quieres ir?   *What beach do you want to go to?*

3. ¿Cuál libro lees? *Which book are you reading?*

4. ¿A cuál playa quieres ir? *Which beach do you want to go to?*

A • Completion Drill

Complete the following sentences with **¿qué?** or **¿cuál(-es)?**. In some cases either may be possible, depending on your interpretation of the context.

1. ¿___qué___ es una insolación? *sunstroke*
2. ¿___cuál___ es tu programa de televisión favorito?
3. ¿___qué___ son las características de una tragedia?
4. ¿___qué___ son espectros?
5. ¿___cuáles___ prefieres, tamales o enchiladas?
6. ¿___cuál___ de estas facturas es mía?
7. ¿___cuáles___ de estos cuadros fueron pintados por El Greco?
8. Tengo muchos vestidos. ¿___cuál___ me pongo para ir al teatro?
9. ¿___qué___ piensas hacer hoy?
10. ¿___qué___ compraste en la venta?
11. ¿___qué___ hicieron en clase ayer?
12. ¿Con ___qué___ construyeron el palacio?
13. ¿___qué___ hay en el periódico de hoy?
14. ¿___cuáles___ libros vas a comprar?
15. ¿___cuál___ automóvil tiene Toñín?
16. ¿___qué___ es la explicación de esto?
17. ¿___cuáles___ son sus defectos?
18. ¿De ___qué___ me hablas?
19. ¿___cuáles___ son los ingredientes?
20. ¿En ___cuál___ libro leíste eso?

B • Translation Drill

Translate into Spanish.

1. What do you prefer? Which do you prefer?
2. What day is it today? What is the first day of the week?
3. What is the question? What is a question?
4. What is this, a message? Which messages are mine?
5. Which of the students arrived late? What students didn't come?
6. What is this? Which is better?

102 El and un with feminine nouns

▶ When a feminine singular noun begins with stressed **a** or **ha**, the article preceding it is in the masculine in order to avoid fusing a feminine article with such words.

Some examples are

el agua	*the water*	un águila	*an eagle*
el hambre	*the hunger*	un hada	*a fairy*
el hacha	*the ax*	un aula	*a classroom*
el alma	*the soul*	un ala	*a wing*
el álgebra	*(the) algebra*	un arma	*a weapon*

▶ If the noun is in the plural or is preceded by an adjective, the article is in the feminine.

¡Cuidado!

Why don't these words have a masculine definite article?

la arena
la abuela
la amiga
la hamaca
la hacienda

A • Substitution Drill

MODEL El agua está clara.
          aguas
STUDENT **Las** aguas **están claras**.

1. Las hachas están en el garage.
   hacha
2. El águila es un pájaro majestuoso.
   águilas
3. Tengo un arma antigua.
   antiguas.
4. El hada del cuento no existe.
   existen.
5. ¿Te gusta el hacha que compré?
   hachas

6. El aula está cerrada.
   cerradas.
7. El álgebra es difícil.
   nueva álgebra
8. Tiene un alma de oro.
   Tienen
9. Mi loro tiene un ala rota.
   Estos
10. El hambre viene de no comer.
    enorme hambre

B • Translation Drill

Translate into Spanish.

1. The water is cold here. The waters of the North are colder.
2. Where is the classroom? Where are the other classrooms?
3. He has a weapon! Where are our weapons?
4. I am so hungry that my soul hurts me.
5. Have you seen the wing of an eagle? They are tremendous.

REVIEW

I The following questions are related to the dialog. Answer in Spanish.

1. ¿Qué están planeando las muchachas?
2. ¿Por qué dejan que Rosario llame a Pepe?
3. ¿Quién contesta el teléfono?
4. ¿Por qué regresó Toñín del Norte?
5. ¿Qué le propone Rosario a Toñín?
6. ¿Qué van a contribuir las muchachas?
7. ¿Por qué no pueden ir todos a Luquillo?
8. ¿Cómo reacciona Rosario?
9. ¿Le parece a Ud. que en realidad Rosario sea tan diplomática? ¿Por qué?
10. ¿Cree Ud. que Toñín quería proponer otra cosa? ¿Qué le hace pensar eso?

II Translation. Translate into Spanish.

1. Girls! I have an idea; let me tell you what it is. Why don't we all go to the beach?
2. What an excellent idea! But none of us has a car. How will we go?
3. I already thought about that! Let's call Pepe. Perhaps he can take us. But which one of us dares to call him?
4. Let Victoria do it; she knows him best. What is his phone number?
5. Hello. Is Pepe at home? It's (from) Victoria Gutiérrez. Please have him call me when he returns.
6. What a scoundrel! How many times have I called him and Toñín always answers and says he's not there!
7. He wants to make me think he has twenty girlfriends. I hope he loses his voice!
8. Don't worry, Victoria. We can go to another place. During Christmas there are too many people at the beach and the water is cold.
9. I am very hungry. Let's go to El Cid. The food is excellent. I never know what to ask for there.
10. Then everything is settled. We'll have a good time and perhaps we'll meet someone who has a car.

III Write your own dialog.

You and two friends are planning an outing. Discuss where to go, how to get there, and what to take along.

Cognates & Contexts

Festival of San Juan Bautista, Puerto Rico

En San Juan, la capital de Puerto Rico, se celebra con mucha alegría el 24 de junio, día de San Juan Bautista. Desde la catedral, que se encuentra en la parte antigua de la ciudad, hay una procesión que desfila por las estrechas calles de la capital. El Santo Patrón de la villa merece ser visto por todos los habitantes. Hay misas especiales en las iglesias de toda la ciudad.

desfilar *to parade*
estrechas *narrow*

misas *masses*
iglesias *churches*

El día de San Juan es celebrado en el mundo católico con un rito especial: recordando el bautismo efectuado por San Juan, el pueblo va al agua —un lago, un río, el mar, etc.—

río *river*

a bañarse. En algunas partes del mundo, este acto marca la apertura oficial de la estación veraniega, negándose muchos a ir a nadar antes del "Día de San Juan". Su coincidencia casi exacta con el solsticio de verano justifica la creencia.

San Juan, Puerto Rico, disfruta de una posición geográfica especialmente favorecida para la participación en el rito balneario. Situada en la costa norte de la isla, hay muchas playas fácilmente acequibles para los sanjuaneros. Desde Dorado hasta Luquillo, todo San Juan se va a nadar antes de la medianoche, incluso el alcalde de la capital. Familias enteras se reúnen y festejan la ocasión con grandes comidas al aire libre y bailes sobre las arenas tropicales, los cuales a veces duran hasta el amanecer del otro día.

Aunque hay muchas fiestas religiosas que se celebran en San Juan durante el año, los sanjuaneros ponen especial atención y regocijo en la observación del día de su Santo Patrón: San Juan.

bañarse *to bathe*

apertura *opening* **estación** *season*

favorecida *favorable*

balneario *bathing* (adj.)

acequibles *accessible*

enteras *whole*

al aire libre *in the open air*
arenas *sands*
amanecer *sunrise*

regocijo *joy*

Lighting of the torch, Pan-American Games, Mexico City

Lección veintitrés

DESFILE EN LOS JUEGOS PANAMERICANOS

CAROLINA ¡Por fin llegaste, Patricia! El desfile va a comenzar de un momento a otro y tú tienes que llevar la bandera.

de un momento a otro *any minute now*
bandera *flag*

PATRICIA ¿Yo? ¿Por qué? No me gusta estar en evidencia así.

estar en evidencia *to stand out, be apparent*

CAROLINA Eres una atleta y como tal tienes que estar delante del público. ¿Qué son estos nervios a última hora?

tal *such*
a última hora *at the last minute*

BEATRIZ Carolina, si quieres, yo llevo la bandera.

CAROLINA No, tiene que ser el atleta más joven del equipo. Además, mira como está tu uniforme.

equipo *team*

BEATRIZ Sí, ya sé que está arrugado. Se me hizo tarde en el Centro de Deportes y no pude plancharlo.

arrugado *wrinkled*
planchar *to iron*

JORGE ¿De quién es este sombrero que está en el suelo?

EMILIO Será mío, puesto que acabo de descubrir que no llevo ninguno puesto.

puesto que *since*

CAROLINA Eso no tiene gran importancia. Pero no descubras mañana que no llevas puesto el traje de baño.

traje de baño *bathing suit*

OLGA Ya empezó la música. Creo que llega el momento que hemos estado esperando. ¿Dónde me pongo?

VICENTE Patricia va primero con la bandera, seguida de los tres entrenadores. Luego sigue el equipo en filas de cuatro por orden de tamaño, como hicimos en el ensayo ayer.

entrenadores *coaches*
filas *rows* **tamaño** *size*
ensayo *rehearsal*

MARIO ¿Hay alguien cuyo tamaño haya cambiado desde ayer, compatriotas? La cena de anoche...

compatriotas *countrymen*

ESPERANZA ¡Cállate, ogro! Sólo para ti nunca hay suficiente.

VICENTE Terminado el desfile, quiero que vayan todos inmediatamente a los autobuses. Nada de chá- chara con los otros equipos porque mañana empezamos a las seis y media.

cháchara *chitchat, chatter*

ENRIQUE Como yo tengo el tobillo torcido y no voy a desfilar, ¿puedo sentarme a la salida del estadio?

tobillo *ankle* **torcido** *twisted*
salida *exit*

VICENTE Sí, y te recogemos después, pero no te pierdas. Tienes que cubrirte de gloria deportiva, no femenina.

recoger *to pick up*

ENRIQUE No se preocupe, mi general, seré un modeol de buen comportamiento.

comportamiento *behavior*

VICENTE ¡Payaso! Bueno, los demás. ¿Listos? ¡Adelante! Sonríe, Patricia.

payaso *clown*
sonreír (i,i) *to smile*

Pan-American Games, Mexico City

NOTES

Juegos Panamericanos

The Pan-American Games. These sports events are held every four years and are often referred to as the "Olympics of the Western Hemisphere." The atmosphere of the dialog reflects the giddiness and last minute "crises" that invariably arise just prior to the parade of nations that officially opens the games.

Addressing Authority

As with old English usage *milord*, Spanish uses **mi** when addressing persons in positions of authority, especially in the military: **mi jefe, mi coronel, mi general**. In this dialog, Enrique is being facetious.

LANGUAGE STRUCTURES

103 Additional progressives

▶ All verb tenses can be expressed in the progressive form in Spanish to indicate or emphasize an action in progress. When a perfect tense is put into the progressive, **estar** becomes a past participle (examples 3 through 8).

	Non-progressive Form	*Progressive Form*
1. Present Subjunctive	Espero que duerman. *I hope they sleep.*	Espero que estén durmiendo. *I hope they are sleeping.*
2. Imperfect Subjunctive	Buscaban a alguien que trabajara en el proyecto. *They were looking for someone to work on the project.*	Buscaban a alguien que estuviera trabajando en el proyecto. *They were looking for someone who was working on the project.*
3. Present Perfect Indicative	Ha llegado el momento que hemos esperado. *The moment we have waited for has arrived.*	Ha llegado el momento que hemos estado esperando. *The moment we have been waiting for has arrived.*
4. Pluperfect Indicative	Habían viajado por todo México. *They had traveled through all of Mexico.*	Habían estado viajando por todo México. *They had been traveling through all of Mexico.*
5. Future Perfect	Se habrán entrenado durante meses. *They must have trained for months.*	Habrán estado entrenándose durante meses. *They must have been training for months.*
6. Conditional Perfect	Tú habrías comido hasta mañana. *You would have eaten until tomorrow.*	Tú habrías estado comiendo hasta mañana. *You would have been eating until tomorrow.*
7. Present Perfect Subjunctive	¿Crees que nos hayan esperado? *Do you think they waited for us?*	¿Crees que nos hayan estado esperando? *Do you think they have been waiting for us?*
8. Pluperfect Subjunctive	¡Ojalá hubiéramos escuchado! *I wish we had listened!*	¡Ojalá hubiéramos estado escuchando! *I wish we had been listening!*

Now that you have learned all the tenses in Spanish, try your hand at this.

Sinfonía: Conjugación del verbo "amar" (adapted)

Pedro Antonio de Alarcón[1]

CORO DE ADOLESCENTES	Yo amo, tú amas, aquél ama; nosotros amamos, ¡todos aman!	
CORO DE NIÑAS (*a media voz*)	Yo amaré, tú amarás, aquélla amará; ¡nosotras amaremos!, ¡todas amarán!	**a media voz** *in a whisper*
UNA FEA Y UNA MONJA (*a dúo*)	¡Nosotras hubiéramos, habríamos y hubiésemos amado!	**monja** *nun*
UNA COQUETA	¡Ama tú! ¡Ame usted! ¡Amen ustedes!	
UN ROMÁNTICO	¡Yo amaba!	
UN ANCIANO (*indiferentemente*)	Yo amé.	
UNA BAILARINA (*trenzando delante de un banquero*)	Yo amara, amaría... y amase.	**trenzando** *prancing*
DOS ESPOSOS (*al final de la luna de miel*)	Nosotros habíamos amado.	**luna de miel** *honeymoon*
UNA MUJER HERMOSÍSIMA (*al tiempo de morir*)	¿Habré yo amado?	
UN SINVERGÜENZA	Es imposible que yo ame, aunque me amen.	
EL MISMO SINVERGÜENZA (*de rodillas ante una sinvergüenza*)	¡Mujer amada, sea usted amable, y permítame ser su amante!	**rodillas** *knees*
UN TONTO	¡Yo soy amado!	
UN RICO	¡Yo seré amado!	
UN POBRE	¡Yo sería amado!	
UN SOLTERÓN (*al hacer testamento*)	¿Habré yo sido amado?	**solterón** *old bachelor*
UNA LECTORA DE NOVELAS SENTIMENTALES	¡Si yo fuera amada de este modo!	
EL AUTOR (*pensativo*)	¡Amar! ¡Ser amado!	

A • Transformation Drill   Non-Progressive → Progressive

MODEL   Dudo que me espere a la salida.
STUDENT Dudo que me **esté esperando** a la salida.

1. ¿Te has entrenado con el equipo?
2. Tal vez hayan charlado con los otros.
3. ¿Habías comprado algunos discos ese día?
4. ¿Qué has hecho?
5. Vicente se habría quejado de tu uniforme.
6. Era posible que nos hubiera llamado por teléfono.
7. Los muchachos habrán desfilado por más de dos horas.
8. ¡Ojalá Jorge me mire!
9. Quizás diga la verdad.
10. ¿Cuánto habías apostado?

---

[1] Well-known Spanish novelist and playwright (1833–1891), best known in the United States for his novel **El sombrero de tres picos**, *The Three-Cornered Hat*.

B • Query Patterned Response

Answer in the affirmative, using a progressive.

MODEL   ¿Has desfilado con el equipo?
STUDENT **Sí, he estado desfilando con el equipo.**

1. ¿Has pensado en lo que te dije?
2. ¿Habría trabajado contigo?
3. ¿Es posible que ataquen ahora?
4. ¿Discutirán la propuesta mañana?
5. ¿Habías escuchado la discusión?

6. ¿Esperabas que te miraran?
7. ¿Habrán revisado las facturas anoche?
8. ¿Trabajarían en otras cosas?
9. ¿Le ha dolido mucho el tobillo?
10. ¿Pensabas que hubieran hecho un viaje?

C • Translation Drill

Translate into Spanish.

1. We have eaten everything. We have been eating everything.
2. I doubt that they have discussed the proposal. They doubt that you have been discussing the proposal.
3. I would have read the note if I had known. She would have been doing the work if she had been there.
4. They had been sleeping but when I arrived they already had gotten up.
5. Look how tired they are. They must (probably) have been working all day.

104   Se + indirect object pronouns for unplanned occurrences

▶ **Se** + verb, in a fashion similar to the reflexive substitute for the passive (see section **45**), may be used to suggest something happening of itself. In this type of expression (just as with **gustar**, **quedar**, and **faltar**), the thing is the subject and the verb is used only in the third person singular or plural. The equivalent English expression often uses *get*.

Se rompió la mesa.	*The table broke ("broke itself").*
Se perdió el dinero.	*The money got lost ("lost itself").*

▶ **Se** may be followed by an indirect object pronoun to express the person affected by the unexpected occurrence. The preposition *on* is the common English equivalent.

1. Se hizo tarde. *It got late.*
   Se me hizo tarde. *It got late on me.*
2. Se rompió el plato. *The plate broke.*
   Se te rompió el plato. *The plate broke on you. (You broke the plate.)*

3. Se cayeron los discos.   *The records dropped (fell).*
Se le cayeron los discos a Ernesto.   *The records dropped on Ernesto. (Ernesto dropped the records.)*

4. Se quedaron los libros en casa.   *The books were left at home.*
Se les quedaron los libros en casa.   *They left the books at home.*

Se cayó el florero.

Se me cayó el florero.

▶ The **se** construction expressing sudden or unforeseen occurrences is also used with some verbs involving thought processes, such as **ocurrir** and **olvidar**.

Se nos ocurrió una idea.   *An idea occurred to us. (We had an idea.)*
¿Se te olvidó su nombre?   *Did you forget her name?*

A • Query   Patterned Response

MODEL   ¿Qué se le cayó a Ud.?   (los periódicos)
STUDENT   **Se me cayeron los periódicos.**

1. ¿Qué se te cayó?   (el sombrero)
2. ¿Qué se le olvidó al profe?   (las composiciones)
3. ¿Qué se les quedó a los atletas?   (la bandera)
4. ¿Qué se nos ocurrió?   (una idea mejor)
5. ¿Qué se le rompió a Ud.?   (el uniforme)
6. ¿Qué se te olvidó?   (su dirección)
7. ¿Qué se le quedó en casa a Olga?   (el número de teléfono)
8. ¿Qué se me quedó en el estadio?   (el traje de baño)
9. ¿Qué se les ocurre a Uds.?   (ir a verla)
10. ¿Qué se nos rompió?   (el automóvil)

B • Transformation Drill

MODEL   Acabé el café.
STUDENT   **Se me acabó el café.**

1. Acabaron las tortillas.
2. Terminé las pepitas.
3. Rompiste la máquina.
4. Olvidaron los boletos.
5. Paré el automóvil.

6. Rompimos el vaso.
7. ¿Cerraste los ojos?
8. Perdió el reloj.
9. Ud. olvidó el ensayo.
10. Voy a apagar la televisión.

C • Query Free Response

Answer, using **se** and an indirect object pronoun.

1. ¿Qué se te quedó en casa ayer?
2. ¿Se le cayó a Ud. algo esta semana?
3. ¿Qué se le ocurre a Ud. ahora?
4. ¿Se le ocurre algo bueno al maestro?
5. ¿Has roto algo recientemente?
6. ¿Olvidaste algo hoy?
7. ¿Perdiste el número?
8. ¿Se te paró el reloj?

105   The absolute use of the past participle

▶ Recall that a past participle can be used as an adjective, in which case it agrees in gender and number with the noun it modifies (see section **82**). The past participle of many verbs can be used with an accompanying noun or pronoun in a detached clause. The English translation varies with context.

a. When the clause expresses a time relationship, the past participle agrees with the noun that accompanies it within the detached clause. This construction is equivalent to **después de** + infinitive or **habiendo** + past participle.

1. Terminado (Después de terminar) el desfile, vayan al autobús.

   After (Once) the parade is over, go to the bus.

2. Tomadas (Habiendo tomado) las aspirinas, me sentí mejor.

   Having taken the aspirins, I felt better.

3. Escrita (Habiendo escrito) la composición, se la entregué a la maestra.

   After writing the composition, I handed it in to the teacher.

b. When the clause expresses circumstances, means, or manner, the past participle agrees with a noun in the main clause (for example, subject, direct object, etc.). This construction is equivalent to **ser** or **estar** + past participle used as a predicate adjective.

1. Invitados a la misma fiesta, fuimos juntos.

   Having been invited to the same party, we went together.

2. Ayudada por el profe, pasó el examen.

   Assisted by the teacher, she passed the exam.

A • Substitution Drill

MODEL   Terminado el desfile, vayan al autobús.
             la obra
STUDENT **Terminada** la obra, vayan al autobús.

1. Acabada las clase, hablamos con el Sr. Gutiérrez.
      las reuniones

2. Traducido el libro, nos pagaron.
        los poemas
3. Escritas las preguntas, la maestra esperó.
        los apuntes
4. Escogido el regalo, Olga fue a pagar.
        la camisa
5. Escrito el libro en italiano, no pude leerlo.
        la obra
6. Ensayado el desfile, fuimos a comer.
        las canciones
7. Decidida la cuestión, anunciaron el resultado.
        las elecciones
8. Devuelto el dinero, regresó a casa.
        los libros
9. Vendidos los periódicos, cerraron la tienda.
        las bicicletas
10. Ganado el partido, regresamos al Centro.
        los premios

B • Substitution Drill

MODEL   Presentadas por los niños, las canciones fueron un éxito.
                    el baile
STUDENT **Presentado** por los niños, el baile **fue** un éxito.

1. Obligada a defender a su novio, Laura se puso furiosa.
              Laura y Adela
2. Rota por Cebollero, el jefe tuvo que arreglar la máquina.
          los trabajadores
3. Anunciado en todos los periódicos, el alcalde dio comienzo al desfile.
                        las conferencias.
4. Establecida por los españoles, Buenos Aires llegó a ser un centro importante de comercio.
                las repúblicas suramericanas
5. Estudiadas por las autoridades, nuestras propuestas fueron aceptadas.
                demanda
6. Pintados en el siglo diecisiete, los cuadros de El Greco produjeron gran impresión.
              las pinturas
7. Comenzados con un desfile, los Juegos Panamericanos duraron una semana.
              el Congreso
8. Vendido en mil pesos, el anillo hoy vale más de diez mil.
          la joya
9. Conocida por todo el mundo hispano, Delmira Agustini fue una gran artista.
              Lope de Vega
10. Informado del ataque, el presidente salió de la capital.
          los ministros

C • Integration Drill

Combine the two sentences.

MODEL   Estábamos cansados de tanto trabajo. Fuimos a la playa.
STUDENT   **Cansados de tanto trabajo, fuimos a la playa.**

1. Estuve sentada allí por una hora y media. Por fin me trajeron la comida.
2. Estaban obligados a estudiar. Fueron a la biblioteca.
3. Estaba abierta desde las 9:00. La tienda no se cerró hasta las 6:00.
4. Estabas decidida a ir a Valencia. Tomaste el primer avión posible.
5. Fue escrita por Lope de Vega. La obra es excelente.
6. Fue rota por Adela. La moto fue compuesta por Sergio.
7. Fueron ayudados por sus compañeros. Los chiquillos pudieron hacer el examen.
8. Fueron ofrecidos por la universidad. Los diplomas fueron entregados por el rector.

D • Integration Drill

Combine the two sentences, using a past participle.

MODEL   Memorizó los versos. Los recitó en clase.
STUDENT   **Memorizados** los versos, los recitó en clase.

1. Recitó el poema. Lo aplaudieron.
2. Terminó el cuadro. Lo expuso en el salón.
3. Regalé la moto. Esperé su reacción.
4. Revisaste las facturas. ¿Las mandaste?
5. Recogimos los periódicos. Regresamos a casa.
6. Ud. deshizo el collar. ¿Lo arregló Ud.?
7. Vimos la película. No nos gustó.
8. Repasó los apuntes. Fue a casa.

E • Query   Patterned Response

MODEL   ¿Cuándo regresó Vicente del estadio? ¿Después de terminar el desfile?
STUDENT   **Sí, terminado** el desfile, Vicente regresó del estadio.

1. ¿Cuándo hicieron la declaración? ¿Después de encontrar una solución?
2. ¿Cuándo hablaste con el presidente? ¿Después de verificar los hechos?
3. ¿Cuándo podemos irnos? ¿Después de revisar los contratos?
4. ¿Cuándo avisaron al jefe? ¿Después de hacer la investigación?
5. ¿Cuándo colgaste el teléfono? ¿Después de confirmar los datos?
6. ¿Cuándo fuiste a la venta? ¿Después de dejar tu automóvil?
7. ¿Cuándo fuimos a la Plaza Mayor? ¿Después de visitar el Museo del Prado?
8. ¿Cuándo se dieron cuenta que faltaba el café? ¿Después de servir la comida?
9. ¿Cuándo ganaste el premio? ¿Después de jugar el partido?
10. ¿Cuándo debo escribir la composición? ¿Después de leer el libro?

F • Translation Drill

Translate into Spanish, using a past participle.

1. The attack forgotten, we visited the palace.
2. After fixing the machine, he will give us a bill.
3. Having accepted our proposals, the authorities spoke to us.
4. Convinced by his speech, the two sisters went to the meeting.
5. Having lost the match, the players were furious.
6. Having won the war, the people decided to elect Bolívar.

106   ¿De quién? versus cuyo

▶ **¿De quién(-es)?** *whose? of whom?* is an interrogative expression and is usually followed by a form of the verb **ser**.

¿De quién es este sombrero?   *Whose hat is this?*

¿De quiénes son los libros?   *Whose are the books?*

▶ **Cuyo(-a, -os, -as)**, *whose*, is a relative adjective that connects two clauses. It can refer to persons or things and agrees in gender and number with the noun it modifies.

**¿Hay alguien cuyo tamaño haya   *Is there anyone whose size has changed?*
cambiado?**

**Beatriz, cuyas hermanas ya   *Beatriz, whose sisters you already know,*
conoces, llega mañana.**   *arrives tomorrow.*

A • Integration Drill

Combine the following sentences, using **cuyo (-a, -os, -as)**.

MODEL   Elena llega el lunes. Su madre vino ayer.
STUDENT   **Elena, cuya madre vino ayer, llega el lunes.**

1. José Martí fue cubano. Sus poemas son conocidos.
2. El equipo es muy bueno. Sus entrenadores están desfilando ahora.
3. Enrique habla italiano. Su familia vive en Roma.
4. Los Sres. Carvajal siempre llegan tarde. Su casa está al lado.
5. Mario y Vicente nunca comen suficiente. Su apetito es enorme.
6. Patricia es mi compañera. Su hermano es mi novio.
7. Los atletas llegaron hoy. Sus uniformes están arrugados.
8. Hoy empieza la conferencia. Su tema es el teatro chicano.
9. Voy a Puerto Rico. Sus playas son muy hermosas.
10. Le van a dar calabazas a Carolina. Sus composiciones son muy malas.

B • Patterned Response Drill

MODEL   Estos apuntes son de Rosario y Rubén.

STUDENT   **¿De quiénes dices que son estos apuntes?**

1. Este traste es de Uds.
2. Los cuadros en este salón son de Goya.
3. Los boletos son de mis tíos.
4. Los versos que recité son de Alfonsina Storni.
5. Esa bicicleta es mía y de mi hermana.
6. Aquel sombrero es de Enrique.
7. La casa amarilla y la blanca son del Sr. Salcedo.
8. Estas composiciones son de mis compañeros de español.

C • Translation Drill

Translate into Spanish.

1. Whose uniforms are these? The athlete whose uniform you have is seated there.
2. Whose flag is this? There is a country whose flag I don't know (I'm not familiar with).
3. Whose (plural) is this money? Whose (singular) are these records?
4. Whose name is this? That place, the name of which I can't remember, is very famous.

107   Summary of the uses of **de**

▶ The preposition **de** covers a wide variety of meanings, many of which have already been dealt with in preceding sections. **De** is used to convey

a. possession, belonging, composition, origin: *'s, of, from, to, in* (sections **16** and **34**)

Yo tengo el libro de Juan.	*I have John's book.*
la llave de la casa	*the key to the house*
el más joven de la clase	*the youngest in the class*
la casa de madera	*the wooden house*
Pepe es de Puerto Rico.	*Pepe is from Puerto Rico.*

b. comparison of quantities: *than* (section **47**)

Hay más de veinte equipos.	*There are more than twenty teams.*

c. time expressions (section **24**)

Llegué a las diez de la noche.	*I arrived at 10 P.M.*
Trabajan de noche.	*They work by night.*

d. compound nouns (section **35**)

English uses a noun as an adjective; Spanish uses an adjectival phrase introduced by **de**.

la casa de campo   *the country house*
un billete de diez pesos   *a ten-peso bill*

e. adverbial expressions telling how, in what manner, circumstances, etc.

Trabajan de mala gana.   *They work unwillingly.*

f. occupation, capacity: usually translating *as a*

Vicente trabaja de entrenador.   *Vicente works as a coach.*

De + infinitive is used to modify an adjective.

Esos versos son difíciles de recitar.   *Those verses are difficult to recite.*
Este examen parece imposible de terminar.   *This exam seems impossible to finish.*

▶ **De** is used instead of **por** to mean *by* after a past participle when physical location is expressed. **Por** indicates a more active relationship.

Patricia irá seguida de los entrenadores.   *Patricia will be followed by the coaches.*
El discurso fue seguido por aplausos.   *The speech was followed by applause.*

▶ **De** is sometimes used instead of **con**, *with*, or **en**, *in*. **De** is used when appearance or condition is affected; the **de** phrase is viewed as integrated with the word it modifies. **Con** and **en** refer to the means; the intention is to separate and single out each of the components.

1. La persona de la bandera es Patricia.
   The person with the flag is Patricia.
   (The flag and the person are viewed as a single unit.)

   La persona con la bandera es Patricia.
   The person carrying the flag is Patricia.
   (The flag and the person are viewed as separate units.)

2. Tienes que cubrirte de gloria.
   You have to cover yourself with glory.
   (refers to moral or psychological condition)

   Él se cubre la cabeza con un sombrero.
   He covers his head with a hat.
   (expresses the means)

3. Nuestro equipo está vestido de verde.
   Our team is dressed in green.
   (a characteristic appearance of the team)

   Ella se viste en su uniforme.
   She dresses in her uniform.
   (expresses the means)

▶ **De** is also used in certain set phrases.

de acuerdo	*in agreement*
de nada	*you're welcome (for nothing)*
de todos modos	*anyway, in any case*
de manera (modo) que	*so, so that, in order that*
de un momento a otro	*any minute (moment) now*

A • Completion Drill

Complete the sentences with **de, por, con, en,** or **que**. There may be more than one correct completion, depending on your interpretation of the context.

1. Jorge tiene más _____ dos trajes de baño.
2. Olga se viste _____ su uniforme.
3. ¿Tú conoces a la hermana _____ Vicente?
4. El libro fue escrito _____ Cervantes.
5. Yo tengo más amigos _____ enemigos.
6. Ella cerró la puerta _____ la llave.
7. Los tamales están hechos _____ maíz.
8. ¿Quién trabaja aquí _____ noche?
9. ¿Quieres un plato _____ aceitunas?
10. Las tierras están cultivadas _____ tabaco.

B • Translation Drill

Translate into Spanish.

1. This is Carolina's mother. She is from San Juan.
2. I am going to cover myself with athletic glory.
3. Your book is difficult to translate but I intend to finish (have the intention of finishing) it.
4. The coaches will be followed by rows of four athletes.
5. Today you are in a very good mood. Thank you. You're welcome.

108   En versus a

▶ In addition to their other meanings, **en** and **a** can both mean *at*. **En** is used to express a location within specific dimensions. **A** is used when a point in time or space is conveyed. **A** is also used to translate *at* when "motion toward" is expressed.

1. ¿Qué vas a hacer en casa?	*What are you going to do at home?*
2. Adela me espera en el Centro de Deportes.	*Adela is waiting for me at the Sports Center.*
3. Enrique vive a diez kilómetros de aquí.	*Enrique lives (at a distance of) ten kilometers from here.*
4. Mañana empezamos a las seis y media.	*Tomorrow we start at 6:30.*
5. Patricia me buscó a la salida.	*Patricia was looking for me at the exit.*
6. Vamos a sentarnos a la mesa.	*Let's be seated at the table.*

A • Completion Drill

Complete the sentences with **en** or **a**.

1. Te espero _____ la salida.
2. Dicen que vienen _____ las ocho.
3. ¿Están protestando _____ tu universidad?
4. Vi a tus primos _____ el museo.
5. Llegamos _____ Bogotá el lunes.
6. ¿Sabes quién llamó _____ la puerta?
7. Beatriz vive _____ cincuenta kilómetros de Madrid.
8. Nos encontramos _____ el cine.
9. ¿Qué decidieron _____ la reunión?
10. La familia se sentó _____ la mesa.
11. _____ la entrada del palacio hay cien guardias.
12. Esta noche voy a quedarme _____ casa.

B • Translation Drill

Translate into Spanish.

1. Please leave it at the door. I am at home.
2. Patricia was at the stadium at eight-thirty.
3. Mario lives (at a distance of) five kilometers from here. He lives at the university this year.
4. We arrived at the museum. No one was waiting for us at the entrance.
5. What is happening at the meeting? Will they finish at noon?

REVIEW

I The following questions are related to the dialog. Answer in Spanish.

1. ¿Cuándo va a comenzar el desfile?
2. ¿Qué tiene que hacer Patricia?
3. ¿Qué le pasa al uniforme de Beatriz? ¿Por qué no lo planchó?
4. ¿Por qué cree Emilio que el sombrero es de él?
5. ¿Cómo va a desfilar el equipo?
6. ¿Por qué no va a desfilar Enrique?
7. Terminado el desfile, ¿qué tienen que hacer los atletas? ¿Por qué?
8. ¿Qué le parece a Ud. este grupo de atletas?
9. ¿Qué ambiente hay antes del desfile de equipos?
10. ¿Ha participado Ud. o le gustaría participar en juegos deportivos?

II Translation. Translate into Spanish.

1. What have you been doing with your uniform? Why is your uniform wrinkled?
2. It got late on me at the Sports Center, and I also forgot to bring the flag.
3. What! These nerves at the last minute only bring us problems.
4. Jorge, you have to go back to the Center. Then I want you to come back right away.
5. Olga, you will be first in the parade, followed by the coaches.
6. But I'm not the youngest athlete of the team. Beatriz, whose birthday is two months after mine, should go before me.
7. Whose bathing suit is this? Tomorrow it might occur to someone that he can't swim without it.
8. I think I have a twisted ankle. Can I wait for you at the exit?
9. Yes, but after the parade is over, don't get lost.
10. Tomorrow we start at 6:00 A.M. and I want all of you to be ready.

III Guided Composition

Imagine that you are about to participate in a major event in your life. Describe your feelings and your thoughts.

Cognates & Contexts

Synchronized swimming, Pan-American Games, Mexico City

Los Juegos Panamericanos, al igual que los Juegos Olímpicos, fueron creados para fomentar la buena voluntad y el
entendimiento entre naciones. Los patrocinadores piensan   **patrocinadores** *sponsors*
que esto se puede lograr mejor mediante los deportes que
por cualquier otro medio.   **medio** *means*

Los primeros Juegos Panamericanos debieron haberse
llevado a cabo en 1942, pero a causa de la segunda guerra   **llevarse a cabo** *to take place*
mundial se suspendieron hasta 1951. En febrero y marzo
de ese año tuvieron lugar los primeros Juegos en Buenos

Aires, Argentina, ante un público de más de 100.000 espectadores. La entrada al estadio deportivo de un atleta griego llevando una antorcha iluminada en el Monte Olimpo, Grecia, varios meses antes, causó gran emoción en el público. El equipo argentino repitió el juramento olímpico en nombre de todos los competidores y el entonces presidente de Argentina, Juan Perón, declaró abiertos los Primeros Juegos Panamericanos.

juramento *oath*

Desde entonces, los Juegos se celebran cada cuatro años en un país distinto del hemisferio occidental, desde Canadá hasta la Argentina. De ahí que sean conocidos como "los Juegos Olímpicos del Hemisferio Occidental". En efecto, sirven de preludio a las competiciones olímpicas, ya que su celebración en el año precedente a las Olimpiadas permite ver a muchos de los atletas que se reunirán próximamente en el foro mundial.

Los deportes que se practican son los siguientes:

Baloncesto (masculino y femenino)
Béisbol
Natación (masculina y femenina)
Natación sincronizada
Campo y pista
Equitación
Esgrima (femenina y masculina)
Fútbol
Gimnasia (masculina y femenina)
Ciclismo
Tenis
Tiro
Pentatlón moderno
Judo
Boxeo
Polo acuático
Lucha
Vóleibol (masculino y femenino)
Levantamiento de peso
Navegación de yate
Remo

baloncesto *basketball*

campo y pista *track and field*
equitación *equestrian events*
esgrima *fencing*

tiro *shooting*

lucha *wrestling*

levantamiento de peso *weight
  lifting*

remo *rowing*

Como verán, con la excepción de béisbol (deporte neta-
mente occidental, aunque empieza a tener auge en el Japón   **auge** *popularity*
y algunos países de Europa), natación sincronizada, y tenis,
todos son deportes celebrados también en los Juegos Olímpicos. Hasta el presente, nunca se han incluido deportes
invernales.

Se espera que el propósito ideado por los iniciadores de
los Juegos Panamericanos se lleve a cabo durante todas las
competencias venideras con el apoyo incondicional de las   **apoyo** *support*
naciones participadoras.

Lección veinticuatro

Lectura y estudio

CARTA ABIERTA

Estimados estudiantes y lectores:

Con esta lección llegamos al final de nuestro estudio de la lengua española. En las lecciones anteriores hemos intentado darles unas nociones básicas de la estructura y de la gramática del español al igual que algún conocimiento de la cultura y el carácter hispánicos. Ahora sería conveniente revisar las aplicaciones prácticas que este estudio puede representar para ustedes.

Una lengua es, ante todo, un medio de comunicación. La comunicación nos permite entendernos mejor, aprender sobre aspectos de la vida anteriormente desconocidos, indicar nuestros anhelos y sentimientos. De nada sirve emitir sonidos si no son comprendidos por los que nos rodean.

Teniendo esto en cuenta, el conocimiento de un idioma extranjero rebasa los límites impuestos por el estudio metódico dentro de un ambiente escolar.

lectores *readers*

anteriores *preceding*

anhelos *desires*
sentimientos *feelings*
rodear *to surround*
tener en cuenta *to bear in mind*
rebasar *to surpass* **impuestos**
  imposed

El poder expresarse en otra lengua abre la puerta a toda una gama de nuevas experiencias ajenas a las de nuestra propia cultura. También incrementa nuestra aceptación entre otras gentes.

toda una gama *a whole gamut*
ajenas a *different from*
incrementar *to increase*

Esto no ocurre solamente en países extranjeros. En los Estados Unidos, el porcentaje de hispanoparlantes es asombroso. Sus costumbres reflejadas en el teatro, en la literatura, en sus canciones, siempre se pueden apreciar mejor en su lengua original. Por otra parte, también ellos tienen necesidad de servicios médicos, sociales y políticos. El niño chicano que va al médico, ¿no se sentirá mucho más confiado con un médico que pueda hablarle en la lengua que oye en su hogar? Le será mucho más agradable a la ama de casa regresar a una tienda donde los dependientes hablen su idioma que a una donde tenga que esforzarse para ser entendida. El más pequeño esfuerzo por parte de Uds. de comunicarse

porcentaje *percentage*

hogar *home*

ama de casa *housewife*

esforzarse *to make an effort*

con una persona de habla española en español le
será ampliamente recompensado.   **recompensado** *rewarded*

Es cierto que el español hablado en los Estados
Unidos se ha adaptado en algunos casos a vocablos
y usos del inglés para facilitar su comprensión: se
oye *factoría* en vez de *fábrica* para decir "factory",
parquear en vez de *estacionar* para "to park", *troca*
en vez de *camión* para "truck", *nursa* en vez de *enfermera* para "nurse", *bifstek* en vez de *filete* para
"steak", etc. Pero la lengua básica sigue siendo la
misma y estas variaciones no impiden su comprensión.

Esperamos que, armados con los conocimientos
adquiridos mediante este libro y otros externos a él,
puedan Uds. disfrutar más del mundo que los rodea   **disfrutar** *to enjoy*
y encontrar aplicaciones para el empleo del español
que no se habían imaginado al iniciar su estudio.

¡Buena suerte!

Los autores

Mary D. Kelly

Nancy Sebastiani

Francisco Jiménez

VOCABULARY STUDY

The following words have additional meanings or forms besides those already given in
the dialogs.

favorecida   favorable; *lucky*

Siempre ha sido favorecida en asuntos   *She has always been lucky in matters*
del amor.   *of love.*

apuntar   to write down; *to aim*

No le apuntes el revólver.   *Don't aim the revolver at him.*

avisar   to advise, let know; *to warn*

No me avisaron a tiempo.   *They didn't warn me in time.*

marcar   to mark; *to dial* (a phone number)

¿Qué número marcó Ud.?   *What number did you dial?*

entrenador   coach; *trainer*

amanecer   sunrise; *to awaken* (at the beginning of the day)
   Amaneció cansada.   *She woke up tired.*
conferencia   lecture; *conference*
balneario   bathing (*adj.*); *beach resort, spa*
   ¿Has ido a ese balneario?   *Have you been to that beach resort?*
estación   season; *station*
ensayo   rehearsal; *essay*
   Manuel escribió un ensayo muy bueno.   *Manuel wrote a very good essay.*

All of the following express the variety of meanings of *since*: **ya que** and **puesto que** are conjunctions, **desde** is a preposition.

Ya que estás aquí, quiero hablarte.	*Since you are here, I want to talk with you.*
Puesto que lo conoces, puedes presentarme.	*Since you know him, you can introduce me.*
No la he visto desde el lunes.	*I haven't seen her since Monday.*

But what else does **desde** mean?

¡Cuidado!

> **fila** = *row*
> **lima** = *file, rasp*
> **fichero** = *file, catalog*
> **sucesos** = *events*
> **éxitos** = *successes*
> **salidas** = exits
> **datos** = *facts, data*
> **fechas** = *dates* (calendar)
> **dátiles** = *dates* (fruit)
> **alma** = *soul*
> **limosna** = *alms*
> **arma** = *arm* (weapon)
> **brazo** = *arm* (physical limb)

Remember:
tener un resfriado = **estar constipado**
los demás = **los otros**
   Vendiste tres bicicletas; ¿qué vas a hacer con las demás (las otras)?
   You sold three bicycles. What are you going to do with the rest?

What is the plural of **voz**? The singular of **peces**?

A • Substitution Drill

Rewrite the sentences, using a synonym for the underlined word or phrase.

1. ¿Quieres anotar mi número de teléfono?
2. ¡Ese Armando es un bufón!
3. Pepe no está. ¿Puedo darle un mensaje?
4. El pobre Sr. Velázquez tiene un resfriado.
5. Carmen tiene un trabajo muy bueno; gana mucho dinero.
6. El mandamás en la clase es el profesor.
7. ¿Dónde está la sala de clase número 17?
8. Ya que perdí mi sombrero, no puedo desfilar.
9. Tal vez tengamos tiempo para ir al museo.
10. Los hechos en la capital son horribles.

Use an antonym for the underlined word or phrase.

11. Yo siempre estudio de día.
12. Esa Patricia es muy respetuosa en clase.
13. Siempre que voy a casa de Vicente, lo paso mal.
14. ¿Me esperas a la entrada?
15. Los datos confirman la valentía de aquel hombre.

B • Complete each sentence with a suitable word or phrase from the list. The words are to be used in the form in which they appear.

tamaño	al aire libre
recrearon	desfilaron
por lo visto	procesión
payasos	suficiente
acaso	

1. El otro día fuimos todos a ver un circo _____ _____ _____.
2. El _____ de la arena era mucho más grande de lo que yo me esperaba; _____ cabían 2.500 personas en las gradas.[1]
3. Lo primero que ocurrió fue que _____ todos los participantes.
4. El grupo más numeroso era el de los _____ y los niños se _____ al verlos pasar.
5. Luego yo me di cuenta que muchos de los que estaban en la _____ hacían varias cosas; _____ _____ _____ no había _____ personal.

entrenando	fila
regocijo	sospechoso
sucesos	apuntando
perro	apertura
ensayo	banderas
crédula	lugar

6. Durante el _____ esa tarde, cuando los acróbatas se estaban _____, dos se cayeron y tuvieron que ir al hospital.

[1] **Gradas,** *grandstands.*

7. Pero en el momento de la _____ esa noche, todo el mundo estaba alegre, con _____ y música y _____.

8. Nosotros estábamos sentados en un _____ muy bueno en la cuarta _____ y podíamos ver los _____ en la arena muy bien.

9. Cuando salió el mago, todos aplaudieron mucho, pero yo me puse _____ en seguida.

10. Rosario, que es más _____, casi se puso a llorar cuando vio que el mago estaba _____ una pistola a un _____. Claro, el perro se convirtió en ocho perritos.

salida	equipo
voz	avisaba
los demás	sonreír
hambre	resueltos
lo habíamos pasado muy bien	fuera mayor
de un momento a otro	comportamiento

11. Durante el intermedio[2], Paco y yo tuvimos _____ y fuimos a buscar comida; _____ _____ esperaron sentados.

12. La segunda parte iba a comenzar _____ _____ _____ _____ _____, según _____ una _____ en el micrófono cuando volvimos.

13. El último acto fue un _____ de gitanos que parecían _____ a morir ahí mismo. Ellos sí me impresionaron.

14. A la _____ todos comentamos que _____ _____ _____ _____ _____.

15. Pero tuve que _____ cuando Rosario dijo que cuando _____ _____ su _____ iba a ser más serio en el circo. Rosario tiene 27 años.

C • Query   Free Response

Treat exercise B as a narrative and answer the following questions in Spanish.

1. ¿Adónde fueron todos el otro día?
2. ¿Qué le asombró al narrador cuando llegó a la arena?

[2] **Intermedio,** *intermission.*

3. ¿Cuál era el grupo más numeroso en el desfile? ¿Quiénes se divirtieron más al verlos pasar?
4. ¿Qué había pasado durante el ensayo esa tarde?
5. ¿Dónde estaban sentados? ¿Era un buen lugar? ¿Por qué?
6. ¿Qué pasó cuando salió el mago?
7. ¿Adónde fuimos Paco y yo durante el intermedio?
8. ¿Qué era el último acto?
9. ¿Lo pasaron bien los amigos de la narración?
10. ¿Qué comentario hizo Rosario a la salida?

D • In past lessons, you have learned many expressions using **por**. Complete the sentences on the left with a phrase from the right column. In some cases there may be more than one appropriate completion.

1. Yo no sé _____ dices eso.
2. Quería hablar contigo antes del programa; _____ llegué temprano.
3. No lo ha terminado, pero ha trabajado suficiente _____.
4. No quiere decirme su nombre _____ dice que voy a reírme de él.
5. No debió hacer eso; _____, yo le avisé que acabaría mal.
6. Ayer apunté su dirección, _____, pero ahora no lo puedo encontrar
7. _____ no pudiste hablar con ella; me lo dice tu cara triste.
8. Puedes hacer eso después; _____ termina lo que empezaste la semana pasada.
9. Llegaste tarde, _____ perdiste el acto de los payasos.
10. El cincuenta _____ de los alumnos ya saben el español.

a. por ahora
b. por eso
c. por cierto
d. por ciento
e. por lo pronto
f. por lo visto
g. porque
h. por si las moscas
i. por lo tanto
j. por qué

E • Complete each sentence with the most suitable word or phrase in parentheses.

1. A Juan le gusta nadar y jugar al fútbol. Es una persona (deportiva, crédula, irrespetuosa).
2. Tú me haces reír mucho. Eres un (águila, tobillo, payaso).
3. Ya empezó la música. El equipo va a (planchar, desfilar, bañarse).
4. Simón Bolívar luchó por la independencia de Venezuela, Colombia y Ecuador. (Por ahora, por lo pronto, por eso) es conocido como El Libertador.
5. Durante las próximas vacaciones pensamos hacer un viaje por (cama, barco, pez).
6. Sus actividades en la universidad me parecen muy (acequibles, arrugadas, sospechosas).
7. Mañana irán a Luquillo al (amanecer, recado, alma).
8. Ellos quieren hablar con el maestro pero yo no (soy mayor, estoy de acuerdo, me recreo).

Rompecabezas

Sol resauto sel andese étoxi ne sus diostues.

GRAMMAR: SELF-TESTING

Cover the right side of the page and try to answer the questions in the left margin.

VERBS

What are adverbial clauses?

What do the conjunctions introducing adverbial clauses express?

What governs the use of the subjunctive in an adverbial clause?

When is the indicative used in an adverbial clause?

What are some adverbial conjunctions that may take either the subjunctive or the indicative?

I Subjunctive

ADVERBIAL CLAUSES (*Sections 91, 92*)

Adverbial clauses are subordinate clauses that modify a verb.

They are introduced by conjunctions that express the circumstances under which the action of the verb takes place: when, where, how, why, under what conditions, etc.

The concept of unreality embodied in an indefinite future, an uncertain or negative result, or an unknown effect governs the use of the subjunctive in an adverbial clause.

If the subordinate verb indicates something established as fact, the indicative is used.

The adverbial conjunctions below can be followed by either the subjunctive or the indicative, depending on context.

siempre que	*whenever*
cuando	*when*
hasta que	*until*
tan pronto como	*as soon as*
mientras (que)	*while*
después (de) que	*after*
como	*as, how, however*
según	*as, according to what, in whatever way*
donde	*where*
aunque	*although, even though*
de modo (manera) que	*so that, so, and therefore*

Indicative	Subjunctive
1. Lo hizo cuando llegó.	Lo hará cuando llegue.
He did it when he arrived.	*He'll do it when he arrives.*
2. Iré aunque llueve.	Iré aunque llueva.
I'll go even though it's raining.	*I'll go although it may rain.*

3. Repite según lo oyes.   Repite según lo oigas.
   Repeat as you hear it.   *Repeat in whatever way you hear it.*

Which adverbial conjunctions are always followed by the subjunctive?

Because of the meaning they convey, the adverbial conjunctions below always cause the verb following them to be in the subjunctive.

antes (de) que	*before*
para que	*so that, for*
a menos que	*unless*
sin que	*without*
como si	*as if*

(always followed by the imperfect or pluperfect subjunctive)

Which adverbial conjunctions are always followed by the indicative?

Some adverbial conjunctions indicate facts and thus are always followed by the indicative.

puesto que	*since*
ya que	*since, now that*
ahora que	*now that*
porque	*because*

SEQUENCE OF TENSES   (*Section 94*)

If the main verb is in the future, future perfect, or command form and the subordinate verb must be in the subjunctive, which tenses may be used?

When a subjunctive is called for in the subordinate clause and the verb in the main clause is in the future, future perfect, or command form, the subordinate verb normally appears in the present or present perfect subjunctive, depending on the time relationship between the two verbs.

1. Será imposible que la acompañe.   *It will be impossible for me to accompany you.*

2. Ya habré terminado cuando me llames.   *I will already have finished when you call me.*

3. Dígale que repita la pregunta.   *Tell him to repeat the question.*

If the main verb is in the present or present perfect, which subjunctives may be used in the subordinate clause and what do they convey?

When the verb in the main clause is in the present or present perfect indicative, the subjunctive in the subordinate clause will be in the present to express present or future action; it will be in the present perfect, or sometimes the imperfect or pluperfect subjunctive, to express past action.

1. Espero que lo hagas.
                hayas hecho.
                hicieras.
                hubieras hecho.
   I hope that you do (will do) it.
                have done
                did
                would have done

2. Siempre se han ido antes de que llames.
                                    hayas llamado.
                                    llamaras.
                                    hubieras llamado.
   They have always left before you call.
                                    have called.
                                    called.
                                    had called.

When the main verb is in the preterit, imperfect, conditional, or one of their perfect counterparts and a subjunctive is called for, the subordinate verb must be expressed in the imperfect or pluperfect subjunctive.

<table>
<tr><td>1. Era posible que llegaran temprano.</td><td>*It was possible they arrived early.*</td></tr>
<tr><td>2. No hubo nadie que nos llevara.</td><td>*There wasn't anyone who would take us.*</td></tr>
<tr><td>3. Iría contigo si me invitaras.</td><td>*I would go with you if you invited me.*</td></tr>
<tr><td>4. Habían preparado la comida antes de que llegaras.</td><td>*They had prepared the food before you arrived.*</td></tr>
<tr><td>5. Temía que hubieras visto la película.</td><td>*I was afraid you had seen the movie.*</td></tr>
</table>

MAIN CLAUSE SUBJUNCTIVES (*Section 97*)

Ojalá, an impersonal expression, is always followed by a subjunctive. If it is followed by a present subjunctive, **ojalá** conveys wishing or hoping; if it is followed by a past subjunctive, **ojalá** conveys regret over an unfulfilled wish or expectation (*would that, if only*).

Ojalá vengan.   *I hope they come.*
Ojalá vinieran.   *Would that (If only) they had come.*

Margin notes:

When the main verb is in the preterit, imperfect, conditional, or one of their perfect counterparts, which subjunctives may be used in the subordinate clause?

Can **ojalá** be followed by a verb in the indicative? What is conveyed by **ojalá** + present subjunctive? **Ojalá** + past subjunctive?

When do **tal vez**, **quizás**, and **acaso** take a subjunctive, and when an indicative?

Tal vez, quizás, and **acaso** all mean *maybe* or *perhaps*. They take either a subjunctive or an indicative, depending on the degree of doubt or conviction of the speaker.

> **Tal vez escriban hoy.** *Perhaps they will write today.*
>
> **Quizás tiene más dinero que tú.** *Maybe he has more money than you do.* (Appearances indicate he does.)

INFINITIVE IN PLACE OF A CLAUSE (*Section 98*)

When is an infinitive used rather than a clause?

After the verbs **dejar**, **permitir**, **hacer**, and **mandar**, an infinitive rather than a clause is often used, especially if the object of the verb is a pronoun (**hacer** and **dejar** usually take a direct object pronoun; **permitir** and **mandar** usually take an indirect object pronoun).

> **Déjalos venir.** *Let them come.*
>
> **Permítanme hablar.** *Permit me to speak.*

INDIRECT COMMANDS (*Section 99*)

How are indirect commands expressed in Spanish?

Indirect commands are expressed in Spanish by using the present subjunctive of the verb, preceded by **que**.

What is the position of object pronouns in relation to the verb? And the subject?

Object pronouns precede the verb; the subject, when expressed, follows it.

> **Que lo hagan los alumnos.** *Have (Let) the students do it.*

II Additional Perfect Tenses (*Section 93*)

How is the pluperfect indicative formed?

Pluperfect indicative: imperfect indicative of **haber** + a past participle
(*had* + past participle)

> **Todavía no lo había hecho.** *He still hadn't done it.*

How is the pluperfect subjunctive formed? How is it used?

Pluperfect subjunctive: imperfect subjunctive of **haber** + a past participle
(*had* + past participle or *would have* + past participle)

It is used when the action of the subordinate verb takes place prior to the time indicated by the main verb. It may also express a hypothetical or unfulfilled past occurrence.

Dudaba que lo hubieras hecho.	*I doubted that you had done it.*
No creo que hubiera regresado.	*I don't think that he would have returned.*

How is the future perfect formed?
What does it express?

Future perfect: future of **haber** + past participle (*will have* + past participle)

It expresses an occurrence that will have been completed by some time in the future. It also expresses conjecture or probability about an action completed by the present time.

Lo habrán terminado para mañana.	*They will have finished it by tomorrow.*
¿Dónde lo habré puesto?	*Where did I put it? (Where could I have put it?)*

How is the conditional perfect formed? What does it express?

Conditional perfect: conditional of **haber** + past participle (*would have* + past participle)

It may express probability or conjecture about a completed action in the past.

Él no habría dicho eso.	*He wouldn't have said that.*
¿Qué habrían hecho?	*What do you suppose they would have done?*

III Additional Progressive Tenses (*Section 103*)

Which verb tenses can be expressed in the progressive in Spanish? What do they indicate?

All verb tenses can be expressed in the progressive form in Spanish to indicate or emphasize an action in progress.

Estaré esperando tu carta.	*I'll be waiting for your letter.*

What happens to **estar** when a perfect tense is formed in the progressive?

When a perfect tense is formed in the progressive, **estar** becomes a past participle.

Habían estado hablando con tu padre.	*They had been speaking with your father.*

PRONOUNS

Why is an indirect object pronoun sometimes included when **se** is used to indicate something happening of itself?

SE + INDIRECT OBJECT PRONOUNS FOR UNPLANNED OCCURRENCES (*Section 104*)

Se + verb may be used to suggest something happening of itself. In this construction, an indirect object pronoun following **se** indicates the person affected by the action. Verbs involving thought processes (**ocurrir, olvidar,** etc.) are sometimes used in this construction to indicate sudden or unforeseen occurrences.

Se me quedaron los discos en casa. — *I left the records at home.*

No se nos ocurrió eso. — *That didn't occur to us.*

PREPOSITIONS

Can **por** and **para** be used interchangeably? How is **para** used?

POR VERSUS *PARA* (*Section 96*)

Por and **para** cannot be used interchangeably. **Para** is used to indicate a deadline, a goal, a destination or recipient, a purpose. It can also express a comparison.

1. Tengo que terminar para mañana. — *I have to finish by tomorrow.*
2. Vamos para el estanque. — *Let's head for the pond.*
3. Me doy prisa para llegar a tiempo. — *I am hurrying in order to arrive on time.*

How is **por** used?

Por indicates time span or location; it also indicates substitution, exchange, cause or motive. **Por** is also used to express the agent or means by which something is done as well as to express a mistaken identity.

1. Te doy cien dólares por la moto. — *I'll give you a hundred dollars for the motorcycle.*
2. ¿Quieres pasear por la ciudad? — *Do you want to walk around the city?*
3. Envié la carta por avión. — *I sent the letter by air mail.*

In what ways is **de** used?

USES OF *DE* (*Section* 107)

De covers a wide variety of meanings.

a. possession, belonging, composition, origin
   El libro de Juan — *John's book*
b. comparison of quantities
   más de seis — *more than six*

c. time expressions

las tres de la tarde   *three in the afternoon*

d. compound nouns

sala de clase   *classroom*

e. adverbial expressions

de mal humor   *in a bad mood*

f. occupation, capacity

Trabaja de abogado.   *He works as a lawyer.*

De + infinitive is used to modify an adjective.

No es fácil de leer.   *It isn't easy to read.*

When is de used instead of por?

De is used instead of **por** to mean *by* after a past participle when physical location is indicated.

Ella va acompañada de sus   *She is accompanied by her*
padres.   *parents.*

When is de used instead of con or en?

De is used instead of **con**, *with*, or **en**, *in*, when appearance or condition is affected. **Con** and **en** refer to the means.

El hombre del sombrero   *The man in the black hat is*
negro es mi hermano.   *my brother.*
El templo está cubierto   *The temple is covered with*
de oro.   *gold.*

REMEMBER!

- **En** is used for *at* to express location within specific dimensions; **a** is used when a point in time or space is conveyed or when "motion toward" is expressed (*Section 108*).

- To express a question with *whose?* Spanish uses **¿de quién(-es)?** usually followed by a form of the verb **ser. Cuyo(-a, -os, -as)** is a relative adjective that also means *whose* and can refer to persons or things (*Section 106*).

- The past participle of many verbs can be used with an accompanying noun or pronoun in a detached clause to express time relationship, circumstance, or manner (*Section 105*).

Terminada la clase, vayan a   *Once the class is over, go home.*
sus casas.

Ayudado por sus compañeros,   *Helped by his classmates, he was*
pudo terminar la composición.   *able to finish the composition.*

- In addition to **estar**, progressives may also be formed with the auxiliary verbs **continuar**, **seguir**, **venir**, **ir**, **andar**, etc. The meaning will vary to include that' of the auxiliary verb (*Section 95*).

- **¡Qué!** used before a noun means *What a!* or *What!* If the noun is followed by an adjective, **tan** or **más** is generally inserted between the noun and the adjective. **¡Qué!** before an adjective or adverb means *How!* (*Section 100*).

¡Qué trabajo tan duro!	*What hard work!*
¡Qué bien escribes!	*How well you write!*

- **¡Cuánto!** used before a verb functions as an adverb and means *How!* **¡Cuánto (-a, -os, -as)!** means *How many!* or *How much!* when it precedes a noun and agrees with it in gender and number (*Section 100*).

- Both **¿qué?** *what?* and **¿cuál(-es)?** *what? which (one-s)?* are used as interrogative pronouns. **¿Qué?** is used when identification or definition is sought. **¿Cuál(es)?** refers to a selection or choice from a set. **¿Qué?** *what?* and **¿cuál(es)?** *which?* are used as interrogative adjectives with the same differences as when they are interrogative pronouns: identification versus selection or choice (*Section 101*).

1. ¿Qué es la cobardía?	*What is cowardice?*
2. ¿Cuál es el día del examen?	*Which is the day of the exam?*
3. ¿Qué diccionario usas?	*What dictionary do you use?*

- When a feminine singular noun begins with stressed **a** or **ha**, the article preceding it will be in the masculine (*Section 102*).

el agua	un hambre
el aula	un hacha

A • Replacement Drill

MODEL   Te llamé en cuanto se fue.
              antes de que
STUDENT   Te llamé antes de que se **fuera**.

1. Me lo dijo para que supiera todo.
   puesto que
2. Le daré el recado cuando llegue.
   di
3. No lo hagas sin que él lo mande.
   sólo porque
4. Rosario viene siempre que quiere.
   Rosario, ven

5. No le dije nada mientras lo leía.
   para que
6. Avísale ahora que tienes teléfono.
   tan pronto como
7. No me habla aunque me conoce.
   te hablara
8. Me quedaré hasta que cierren la tienda.
   ya que

B • Replacement Drill   Main Clause→ojalá, tal vez, quizás, acaso

MODEL   Espero que podamos verlo.
Tal vez
STUDENT **Tal vez** podamos verlo.

1. Es posible que ya hayan visto la obra.
Tal vez
2. Dudo que nos entrenemos mañana.
Quizás

3. Me alegro que lo pasen bien.
Ojalá
4. No creo que estés de acuerdo conmigo.
Acaso

Main Clause → dejar, permitir, hacer, mandar + Infinitive

MODEL   Quiero que ellos hagan la tarea ahora.
Mándeles
STUDENT Mándeles **hacer** la tarea ahora.

5. Quiero que Uds. recuerden el suceso.
Permítanme
6. Pídales que apunten los datos.
Déjelos

7. Dile que repita el recado.
Hazla
8. Insisto que planches tu uniforme.
Te mando

C • Patterned Response Drill

MODEL   Escríbeles a tus tíos.   (Ricardo)
STUDENT **No tengo tiempo. Que les escriba Ricardo.**

1. Apunta lo que te voy a decir. (otro)
2. Llámame más tarde. (tu hermano)
3. Dinos las respuestas. (la maestra)
4. Jueguen conmigo. (Susana)

5. Espérame a la salida. (Olga y Mario)
6. ¿Me planchas los pantalones? (tu mamá)
7. Explíqueme la lección. (un compañero)
8. Hazme unos calcetines. (Patricia)

D • Transformation Drill   Simple Tense→Corresponding Perfect Tense

MODEL   Mañana haré la tarea.
STUDENT Mañana **habré hecho** la tarea.

1. Terminaremos la lección para el lunes.
2. ¿Trabajarías más horas si pudieras?
3. Buscábamos un disco nuevo en la tienda.
4. Esperábamos que lo pasaras bien.
5. ¿Venderá las bicicletas?

6. Emilio y Juan siempre comían primero.
7. ¿Qué harías si tuvieras mil dólares?
8. He viajado mucho, pero no esperaba ver eso.
9. ¿Te gustaría venir con nosotros?
10. ¡Ojalá fuera posible!

E • Translation Drill

Translate into Spanish.

1. I hope they will be here. I hope they have been here. Would that they had been here.
2. She will visit you when she comes. You visited her when she came?

3. I wouldn't have written the letter if I had known the news. Maybe she hasn't received it.
4. You will have finished the assignment before I have begun it.
5. They hadn't found anyone who could read Italian. Then permit me to read it. No, let Carlos read it.

F • Transformation Drill   Non-Progressive → Progressive

MODEL   Mañana pensaré en ti.
STUDENT   Mañana **estaré pensando** en ti.

1. Discutirán la cuestión hasta tarde.
2. Habían bailado durante horas.
3. Habrán escrito en inglés.
4. Es posible que hayan comido.
5. Tal vez hubieran repetido el ejercicio.
6. ¿Me habrías dicho más mentiras?
7. Hablas como si me echaras de menos.
8. No creo que trabajen mucho.

G • Completion Drill

Complete the sentences with **por** or **para**.

1. Tengo una llave _____ abrir la puerta.
2. Isabel cambió su automóvil _____ mi motocicleta.
3. Como mi hermano no podía traer los periódicos, yo los traje _____ él.
4. Mañana _____ la tarde mis padres salen _____ la Argentina.
5. Estos poemas fueron escritos _____ Gabriela Mistral.
6. Juanito practica mucho _____ llegar a ser un atleta famoso.
7. Hacen el desfile _____ la noche.
8. Yo lo tomé _____ un cubano.
9. Terminaré las facturas _____ mañana.
10. Tienes que venir _____ trabajar conmigo.

H • Translation Drill

1. The team with the white uniforms is from Colombia. My brother's girlfriend is with them.
2. I'll look for you at the stadium. Will you be at the entrance?
3. You keep on using these words. Once you've finished your composition, I want to go over them.
4. What a beautiful day! Do you know what bus we have to take to go to the lake? The water must be perfect today.
5. Which of these two readings do you prefer? I don't know what to tell you.

I • Guided Composition

In what way do you feel that studying a foreign language permits you to understand language in general and its relation to reality, thought, and culture?

Appendix

1

VOSOTROS

Preparativos entre amigos

(*Alicia y Mariana son dos hermanas gemelas que están pasando*   **gemelas** *twins*
un año estudiando en Madrid.)

ALICIA   ¡Hola, Gustavo y Adolfo! ¿Cómo estáis?

GUSTAVO   ¿Qué tal, Alicia? Venimos a ver si queréis
acompañarnos a la verbena de la Paloma esta
noche.

ALICIA   Justamente os iba a llamar por teléfono esta
tarde. Nuestros padres llegan el viernes que
viene de Chicago y queremos llevarlos a Segovia
el domingo. ¿Os gustaría venir?

ADOLFO   No cabemos todos en vuestro coche, pero
podríamos encontrarnos allí.

MARIANA   Hola. Os oí hablando desde la cocina. Pasaos
por aquí a eso de las ocho y media el domingo
y así desayunamos todos juntos antes de irnos.

ADOLFO   No os preocupéis con eso. Tendréis suficiente   **dar la lata** (coll.) *to bother,*
que hacer sin que estemos dándoos la lata.   *disturb*

ALICIA ¡No seáis tontos! Donde comen cuatro, comen seis.

GUSTAVO De acuerdo. Estaremos aquí. Estaréis contentas de poder demostrar a vuestros padres que habéis podido defenderos solas en un país extranjero.

MARIANA Bueno, creo que ya se han resignado a nuestras aventuras. Pero al principio creían que los españoles iban a comerse vivas a sus hijitas.

GUSTAVO Sí, pero sois dos y eso sería un banquete demasiado enorme. ¡No somos tan tremendos!

ALICIA No, hemos podido convencer a la familia que todos os portáis muy bien con nosotras.

ADOLFO ¡Viva! Y puesto que somos tan gentiles, haced lo mismo y veníos con nosotros esta noche. Os recogemos a las nueve.

puesto que *since*

ALICIA ¿Qué te parece, Mariana? ¿Los acompañamos?

MARIANA Sí, no tienen mal aspecto estos chicos; creo que podemos arriesgarnos.

arriesgarse *to take a chance, risk*

GUSTAVO ¡Guasonas! Hala, hasta las nueve y no pidáis demasiado de comer —¡somos pobres!

NOTES

la verbena de la Paloma   **La Virgen de la Paloma** is a patron saint of Madrid. Every year a festival is held in her honor, beginning August 15. Along with special masses, processions, and bullfights, there is a **verbena**, or open-air fair, set up in the older part of the city. People of all ages enjoy dancing, eating the variety of food sold at booths, and riding on amusement-park attractions.

Segovia   A city north of Madrid, well known for its Roman aqueduct.

Vocabulary Meanings

guasón, guasona   A Spanish colloquialism referring to a joker or kidder.

hala   An expression used in Spain much as *OK* is used in the United States.

Mealtimes in Spain

Meals are eaten much later in Spain than in the United States. Lunch is between 2:00 and 4:00 P.M. Supper never begins before 9:30.

LANGUAGE STRUCTURES

▶   The language structures in this lesson will deal solely with aspects of **vosotros (-as)**, a second person form used in Spain as the plural counterpart of the familiar form **tú**. Other parts of the Spanish-speaking world use the **ustedes** form as the plural of both the **tú** and the **usted** forms.

Spain

Singular	*Plural*
¿Eres americano?	¿Sois americanos?
¿Es Ud. español?	¿Son Uds. españoles?

Spanish America

¿Hablas francés?	¿Hablan Uds. francés?
Ud. habla muy bien.	Uds. hablan muy bien.

I. Verbs

A. Regular verbs: **vosotros, -as** endings

	-ar	-er	-ir
Indicative			
Present	habl -áis	aprend -éis	escrib -ís
Imperfect	habl -abais	aprend -íais	escrib -íais
Preterit	habl -asteis	aprend -isteis	escrib -isteis
Future	hablar -éis	aprender -éis	escribir -éis
Conditional	hablar -íais	aprender -íais	escribir -íais
Subjunctive			
Present	habl -éis	aprend -áis	escrib -áis
Imperfect	habla -rais	aprendie -rais	escribie -rais

Transformation Drill   Uds. → vosotros / vosotras

MODEL   Uds. hablan español muy bien.
STUDENT   **Vosotras habláis** español muy bien.

1. ¿Qué aprendieron Uds. ayer?
2. Ojalá revisen Uds. la factura pronto.
3. Uds. volverán mañana.
4. Uds. preferirían otra película, ¿verdad?
5. Uds. estaban haciendo la tarea.
6. Era probable que Uds. no comprendieran sus palabras.
7. ¿Cuándo traducen Uds. el libro?
8. ¿Merecían Uds. otra oportunidad?

B. Perfect tenses

▶ As they are for all other persons, the perfect tenses for **vosotros (-as)** are formed with **haber** + past participle. **Haber** takes regular **-er** verb endings for **vosotros (-as)**. Stem irregularities for **haber** in the **vosotros** form are the same as those found in other persons, except in the present indicative.

Indicative		*Conditional*	*Subjunctive*	
Present	habéis	habríais	*Present*	hayáis
Imperfect	habíais		*Imperfect*	hubierais
Preterit	hubisteis			
Future	habréis			

Habréis visitado el Prado en Madrid, ¿no?
You probably visited the Prado in Madrid, right?
Si hubierais hablado con él, habríais aprendido mucho.
If you had spoken with him, you would have learned a lot.

Query   Patterned Response

> MODEL   ¿Hemos terminado?
> STUDENT   Sí, **habéis terminado.**

1. ¿Habíamos trabajado juntos?
2. ¿Habríamos llegado antes?
3. ¿Es posible que lo hayamos visto?
4. ¿Hemos vuelto a lo mismo?
5. ¿Querías que te hubiéramos llamado?
6. ¿Lo habremos aprendido para mañana?

C. Command forms

▶ To form the affirmative **vosotros (-as)** command, the final **r** of the infinitive of the verb is changed to **d**. Negative commands have the same form as the present subjunctive.

¡Hablad más despacio!	*Speak more slowly!*
Insistid en su renuncia.	*Insist on his resignation.*
¡No comáis eso!	*Don't eat that!*

Object and reflexive pronouns follow and are attached to affirmative commands; they precede the verb in negative commands.

Preparadlo hoy.	*Prepare it today.*
No les digáis nada.	*Don't tell them anything.*

Query   Patterned Response

Answer in the affirmative.

> MODEL   ¿Lo hacemos?
> STUDENT   **Sí, hacedlo ahora mismo.**

1. ¿Escribimos la carta?
2. ¿Las escondemos?
3. ¿Se los damos?
4. ¿Te ayudamos?

Now answer in the negative.

> MODEL   ¿Lo aceptamos?
> STUDENT   **No, no lo aceptéis todavía.**

5. ¿Leemos la composición?
6. ¿Las devolvemos?
7. ¿Compramos esas bicicletas?
8. ¿Lo decidimos?

D. Irregular verbs

▶ Class I stem-changing verbs. As in the **nosotros (-as)** form, there is no stem change in Class I verbs in the **vosotros (-as)** form.

> **¿Queréis acompañarnos esta noche?** *Do you want to accompany us tonight?*
> **Espero que encontréis la salida.** *I hope you find the exit.*

▶ Class II and Class III stem-changing verbs have the same stem changes in the **vosotros (-as)** form as in the **nosotros (-as)** form.

> **No pidáis demasiado de comer.** *Don't ask for too much to eat.*
> **Sentía que no durmierais bien.** *I was sorry you didn't sleep well.*

▶ Other verbs that are irregular in the stem follow the same pattern for **vosotros (-as)** as for **nosotros (-as)**.

> **Dijisteis la verdad.** *You told the truth.*
> **Ojalá estuvierais aquí.** *I wish you were here.*
> **¿Supisteis la respuesta?** *Did you find out the answer?*
> **Tendréis mucho éxito.** *You will be very successful.*
> **No creo que conozcáis al ministro.** *I don't think you know the secretary.*
> **Siempre veíais la diferencia.** *You would always see the difference.*

▶ Additional irregular verbs:

> **ser: sois, erais, fuisteis,** seréis, seríais, **seáis,** fuerais
> **dar:** dais, dabais, **disteis,** daréis, daríais, **deis,** dierais
> **ir: vais, ibais, fuisteis,** iréis, iríais, **vayáis,** fuerais

Transformation Drill   nosotros → vosotros

MODEL   Siempre defendemos la causa estudiantil.
STUDENT   Siempre **defendéis** la causa estudiantil.

1. Podemos escribirle en español.
2. No recordamos dónde vive.
3. ¿Tenemos mucho que hacer?
4. Pusimos las revistas detrás del sofá.
5. Quisiéramos saber más sobre eso.
6. Trajimos los discos para la fiesta.
7. No pidamos lo imposible.
8. Somos sus mejores amigos.
9. Seamos inteligentes.
10. Quieren que vayamos temprano.

II. Possessive adjectives

	Singular	*Plural*
Masculine	vuestro	vuestros
Feminine	vuestra	vuestras

▶ Possessive adjectives can either precede or follow the noun modified. In the case of **vuestro** and its variants (as with **nuestro**), there is no change in form if the adjective precedes or follows the noun. In either position, the adjective agrees in gender and number with the thing possessed.

vuestra casa; las hermanas vuestras   *your house; your sisters*
vuestro plato; los libros vuestros   *your plate; your books*

Completion Drill

Complete each sentence, using **vuestro, vuestra, vuestros,** or **vuestras.**

MODEL   Me gustan _____ camisas.
STUDENT   Me gustan **vuestras** camisas.

1. ¿Quiénes son _____ líderes?
2. Ya pasasteis _____ exámenes de derecho.
3. _____ poema es muy hermoso.
4. No sabemos dónde está _____ billete.
5. ¿Cuándo llegan _____ tías?
6. Van a instalarse en _____ oficina.
7. Los amigos _____ piensan quedarse.
8. ¿Dónde están las facturas _____?
9. La venta _____ comienza antes que la nuestra.
10. El número del contrato _____ está anotado.

III. Pronouns

▶ Unlike the second person plural pronoun **ustedes, vosotros (-as)** is not usually included in a sentence as a subject pronoun.

¿Saben Uds. su nombre? ¿Sabéis su nombre?   *Do you know her name?*

▶ Like **nosotros, vosotros** has a feminine form.

Ellas juegan bien, pero vosotras ganáis más partidos.
They play well, but you win more games.

▶ Both **vosotros** and **vosotras** are used as objects of prepositions.

Queremos ir con vosotros.	*We want to go with you.*
Este libro es de vosotras.	*This book is yours.*

▶ The direct and indirect object pronouns and the reflexive pronoun for the **vosotros** form are the same:

Os recogemos a las nueve.	*We will pick you up at 9:00.*
¿Os gustaría venir (a vosotras)?	*Would you like to come?*
Todos os portáis muy bien.	*All of you behave very well.*
Voy a dároslo a ti y a Pepe.	*I'm going to give it to you and Pepe.*

When a reflexive pronoun is attached to an affirmative **vosotros** command, the final **d** of the command is dropped in all forms except **idos** (from **irse**).

Pasaos por aquí a las ocho.	*Stop by here at 8:00.*
Veníos¹ con nosotros.	*Come with us.*

But: **No os preocupéis.** *Don't worry.*

When **os** is attached to an infinitive or a present participle, the verb form undergoes no change.

¿Habéis podido defenderos?	*Have you been able to protect yourselves?*
Siempre estamos dándoos la lata.	*We are always bothering you.*

▶ The possessive pronouns for the **vosotros** form are derived from the possessive adjectives.

No me gusta el plan de ellos, pero sí me gusta el vuestro.
I don't like their plan, but I do like yours.

Query Patterned Response

MODEL	¿A quién ves?
STUDENT	**Os veo a ti y a Alicia.**
MODEL	¿A quién das el libro?
STUDENT	**Os doy el libro a vosotras.**

1. ¿A quién buscas?
2. ¿A quién mostraste las fotos?
3. ¿A quién vas a invitar?

4. ¿A quién diste el dinero?
5. ¿A quién piensas ayudar?
6. ¿A quién cuentas el relato?

¹ To maintain the original stress of the command form, a written accent is sometimes necessary when the pronoun is attached.

Query Free Response

MODEL ¿Quieres sus entradas?
STUDENT **No, quiero las vuestras.**

1. ¿Buscas su número de teléfono?
2. ¿Quieres sus resultados?
3. ¿Sabes su dirección?
4. ¿Prefieres sus ideas?
5. ¿Entendiste sus expresiones?
6. ¿Atacas su posición?

Translation Drill

Translate into Spanish. you → **vosotros, -as; os**

1. Did he give it to you? Did he see you?
2. Is she bothering you? Is she going to meet you there?
3. I want them to discuss it with you.
4. Prepare the lesson! Prepare yourselves!
5. Sit down! Don't sit down!

REVIEW

Translate into Spanish, using forms of **vosotros.**

1. Hello. How are you? I didn't expect to see you here.
2. We wanted to invite you to the movies. Would you like to come?
3. Do we all fit in your car? Your sister is coming too, isn't she?
4. Don't worry. We have a surprise for you.
5. OK, but come by here early and we'll eat together.
6. Will you have enough for three more people? As you know, we like to eat.
7. We'll give you what we have. But don't ask for an enormous banquet.
8. Agreed, since you are so kind. Make the main dish and we'll bring the refreshments. See you at six.

2

Regular Verbs

INFINITIVE	**hablar** *to speak*	**aprender** *to learn*	**recibir** *to receive*
PRESENT PARTICIPLE	hablando	aprendiendo	recibiendo
PAST PARTICIPLE	hablado	aprendido	recibido

The Simple Tenses

Indicative Mood

PRESENT	hablo	aprendo	recibo
	hablas	aprendes	recibes
	habla	aprende	recibe
	hablamos	aprendemos	recibimos
	(habláis)[1]	(aprendéis)[1]	(recibís)[1]
	hablan	aprenden	reciben
IMPERFECT	hablaba	aprendía	recibía
	hablabas	aprendías	recibías
	hablaba	aprendía	recibía
	hablábamos	aprendíamos	recibíamos
	(hablabais)	(aprendíais)	(recibíais)
	hablaban	aprendían	recibían
PRETERIT	hablé	aprendí	recibí
	hablaste	aprendiste	recibiste
	habló	aprendió	recibió
	hablamos	aprendimos	recibimos
	(hablasteis)	(aprendisteis)	(recibisteis)
	hablaron	aprendieron	recibieron

[1] Forms in parentheses correspond to the **vosotros, vosotras** form.

FUTURE	hablaré	aprenderé	recibiré
	hablarás	aprenderás	recibirás
	hablará	aprenderá	recibirá
	hablaremos	aprenderemos	recibiremos
	(hablaréis)	(aprenderéis)	(recibiréis)
	hablarán	aprenderán	recibirán
CONDITIONAL	hablaría	aprendería	recibiría
	hablarías	aprenderías	recibirías
	hablaría	aprendería	recibiría
	hablaríamos	aprenderíamos	recibiríamos
	(hablaríais)	(aprenderíais)	(recibiríais)
	hablarían	aprenderían	recibirían

Subjunctive Mood

PRESENT	hable	aprenda	reciba
	hables	aprendas	recibas
	hable	aprenda	reciba
	hablemos	aprendamos	recibamos
	(habléis)	(aprendáis)	(recibáis)
	hablen	aprendan	reciban
IMPERFECT (**-ra** form)	hablara	aprendiera	recibiera
	hablaras	aprendieras	recibieras
	hablara	aprendiera	recibiera
	habláramos	aprendiéramos	recibiéramos
	(hablarais)	(aprendierais)	(recibierais)
	hablaran	aprendieran	recibieran
IMPERFECT (**-se** form)	hablase	aprendiese	recibiese
	hablases	aprendieses	recibieses
	hablase	aprendiese	recibiese
	hablásemos	aprendiésemos	recibiésemos
	(hablaseis)	(aprendieseis)	(recibieseis)
	hablasen	aprendiesen	recibiesen

Imperative[2]

habla (tú)	aprende (tú)	recibe (tú)
hablad (vosotros)	aprended (vosotros)	recibid (vosotros)

[2] For the negative **tú** and **vosotros** command forms, and for both affirmative and negative **usted, ustedes,** and **nosotros** command forms, the corresponding subjunctive forms are used.

The Compound Tenses

| PERFECT INFINITIVE | haber hablado (aprendido, recibido), *to have spoken* (*learned, received*) |
| PERFECT PARTICIPLE | habiendo hablado (aprendido, recibido), *having spoken* (*learned, received*) |

Indicative Mood

PRESENT PERFECT

he
has
ha
hemos
(habéis)
han
} hablado aprendido recibido

PLUPERFECT

había
habías
había
habíamos
(habíais)
habían
} hablado aprendido recibido

PRETERIT PERFECT

hube
hubiste
hubo
hubimos
(hubisteis)
hubieron
} hablado aprendido recibido

FUTURE PERFECT

habré
habrás
habrá
habremos
(habréis)
habrán
} hablado aprendido recibido

CONDITIONAL PERFECT

habría
habrías
habría
habríamos
(habríais)
habrían
} hablado aprendido recibido

Subjunctive Mood

PRESENT PERFECT

haya
hayas
haya
hayamos
(hayáis)
hayan
} hablado aprendido recibido

PLUPERFECT (-ra and -se forms)

hubiera, hubiese
hubieras, hubieses
hubiera, hubiese
hubiéramos, hubiésemos
(hubierais, hubieseis)
hubieran, hubiesen
} hablado aprendido recibido

3

Irregular Verbs

Stem-Changing Verbs

Class I (-ar, -er)

cerrar *to close*

PRESENT INDICATIVE   **cierro, cierras, cierra,** cerramos, (cerráis), **cierran**
PRESENT SUBJUNCTIVE   **cierre, cierres, cierre,** cerremos, (cerréis), **cierren**
COMMAND (**tú**)   **cierra, no cierres**

Like **cerrar**: atravesar, *to cross*; comenzar, *to begin*; despertar(se), *to awaken, wake up*; negar, to *deny*; pensar, *to think*; recomendar, *to recommend*; sentar(se), *to sit down.*

perder *to lose*

PRESENT INDICATIVE   **pierdo, pierdes, pierde,** perdemos, (perdéis), **pierden**
PRESENT SUBJUNCTIVE   **pierda, pierdas, pierda,** perdamos, (perdáis), **pierdan**
COMMAND (**tú**)   **pierde, no pierdas**

Like **perder**: defender, *to defend*; entender, *to understand.*

encontrar *to find*

PRESENT INDICATIVE   **encuentro, encuentras, encuentra,** encontramos, (encontráis), **encuentran**
PRESENT SUBJUNCTIVE   **encuentre, encuentres, encuentre,** encontremos, (encontréis), **encuentren**
COMMAND (**tú**)   **encuentra, no encuentres**

Like **encontrar**: acordarse, *to remember*; acostarse, *to go to bed*; almorzar, *to have lunch*; colgar, *to hang*; contar, *to count, to narrate*; costar, *to cost*; demostrar, *to demonstrate*; mostrar, *to show*; probarse, *to try on*; recordar, *to remember*; rogar, *to beg, ask*; sonar, *to sound, ring*; volar, *to fly.*

volver *to return*

PRESENT INDICATIVE   **vuelvo, vuelves, vuelve,** volvemos, (volvéis), **vuelven**
PRESENT SUBJUNCTIVE   **vuelva, vuelvas, vuelva,** volvamos, (volváis), **vuelvan**
COMMAND (**tú**)   **vuelve, no vuelvas**

Like **volver**: devolver, *to return (something)*; doler, *to ache*; envolver, *to wrap up*; llover, *to rain*; mover, *to move.* Also: jugar, *to play (a game).*

Class II (**-ir**)

sentir   *to feel*

PRESENT PARTICIPLE	**sintiendo**
PRESENT INDICATIVE	**siento, sientes, siente,** sentimos, (sentís), **sienten**
PRESENT SUBJUNCTIVE	**sienta, sientas, sienta, sintamos,** (sintáis), **sientan**
COMMAND (**tú**)	**siente, no sientas**
PRETERIT	sentí, sentiste, **sintió,** sentimos, (sentisteis), **sintieron**
IMPERFECT SUBJUNCTIVE	**sintiera,** etc. **sintiese,** etc.

Like **sentir:** advertir, *to warn*; convertir, *to convert*; divertir(se), *to amuse* (*oneself*); preferir, *to prefer*; referir, *to refer.*

dormir   *to sleep*

PRESENT PARTICIPLE	**durmiendo**
PRESENT INDICATIVE	**duermo, duermes, duerme,** dormimos, (dormís), **duermen**
PRESENT SUBJUNCTIVE	**duerma, duermas, duerma, durmamos,** (durmáis), **duerman**
COMMAND (**tú**)	**duerme, no duermas**
PRETERIT	dormí, dormiste, **durmió,** dormimos, (dormisteis), **durmieron**
IMPERFECT SUBJUNCTIVE	**durmiera,** etc. **durmiese,** etc.

Like **dormir:** morir, *to die.*

Class III (**-ir**)

pedir   *to ask*

PRESENT PARTICIPLE	**pidiendo**
PRESENT INDICATIVE	**pido, pides, pide,** pedimos, (pedís), **piden**
PRESENT SUBJUNCTIVE	**pida, pidas, pida, pidamos,** (pidáis), **pidan**
COMMAND (**tú**)	**pide, no pidas**
PRETERIT	pedí, pediste, **pidió,** pedimos, (pedisteis), **pidieron**
IMPERFECT SUBJUNCTIVE	**pidiera,** etc. **pidiese,** etc.

Like **pedir:** conseguir, *to get*; despedirse, *to take leave*; repetir, *to repeat*; seguir, *to follow*; servir, *to serve*; vestir, *to dress.*

Other Irregular Verbs

Of the verbs that follow, only the tenses having one or more irregular forms are listed. Irregular forms are printed in bold type. Present subjunctive forms like **caiga, diga, haga, incluya, oiga, ponga, salga, tenga, traiga, vea,** and **venga** are not listed because their formation is in accordance with the rules given. For the same reason, imperfect subjunctive forms such as **cayera, diera, dijera, estuviera, fuera, hiciera, hubiera, incluyera, produjera, pudiera, pusiera, quisiera, supiera, trajera, tuviera,** and **viniera** are not given.

andar   *to walk, go*

PRETERIT	**anduve, anduviste, anduvo, anduvimos, (anduvisteis), anduvieron**

caber   *to fit*

PRESENT INDICATIVE	**quepo,** cabes, cabe, cabemos, (cabéis), caben
FUTURE	**cabré, cabrás,** etc. CONDITIONAL **cabría, cabrías,** etc.
PRETERIT	**cupe, cupiste, cupo, cupimos, (cupisteis), cupieron**

caer   *to fall*

PARTICIPLES	**cayendo, caído**
PRESENT INDICATIVE	**caigo,** caes, cae, caemos, (caéis), caen
PRETERIT	caí, **caíste, cayó, caímos (caísteis), cayeron**

conocer   *to know, be acquainted with*

PRESENT INDICATIVE	**conozco,** conoces, conoce, conocemos, (conocéis), conocen

conseguir   *to get*

PRESENT INDICATIVE	**consigo, consigues, consigue,** conseguimos, (conseguís), **consiguen**
PRESENT SUBJUNCTIVE	**consiga, consigas, consiga, consigamos, (consigáis), consigan**

Like **conseguir:** seguir, *to follow.*

creer   *to believe*

PARTICIPLES	**creyendo, creído**
PRETERIT	creí, **creíste, creyó, creímos, (creísteis), creyeron**

Like **creer:** leer, *to read.*

dar   *to give*

PRESENT INDICATIVE	**doy,** das, da, damos, (dais), dan
PRESENT SUBJUNCTIVE	**dé, des, dé, demos, (deis), den**
PRETERIT	**di, diste, dio, dimos, (disteis), dieron**

decir   *to say, tell*

PARTICIPLES   **diciendo, dicho**
PRESENT INDICATIVE   **digo, dices, dice,** decimos, (decís), **dicen**
PRETERIT   **dije, dijiste, dijo, dijimos, (dijisteis), dijeron**
FUTURE   **diré, dirás,** etc.   CONDITIONAL   **diría, dirías,** etc.
COMMAND **(tú)**   **di, no digas**

estar   *to be*

PRESENT INDICATIVE   **estoy, estás, está,** estamos, (estáis), **están**
PRESENT SUBJUNCTIVE   **esté, estés, esté,** estemos, (estéis), **estén**
PRETERIT   **estuve, estuviste, estuvo, estuvimos, (estuvisteis), estuvieron**

haber   *to have*

PRESENT INDICATIVE   **he, has, ha, hemos,** (habéis), **han**
PRESENT SUBJUNCTIVE   **haya, hayas, haya, hayamos, (hayáis), hayan**
PRETERIT   **hube, hubiste, hubo, hubimos, (hubisteis), hubieron**
FUTURE   **habré, habrás,** etc.   CONDITIONAL   **habría, habrías,** etc.

hacer   *to do, make*

PAST PARTICIPLE   **hecho**
PRESENT INDICATIVE   **hago,** haces, hace, hacemos, (hacéis), hacen
PRETERIT   **hice, hiciste, hizo, hicimos, (hicisteis), hicieron**
FUTURE   **haré, harás,** etc.   CONDITIONAL   **haría, harías,** etc.
COMMAND **(tú)**   **haz, no hagas**

incluir   *to include*

PRESENT PARTICIPLE   **incluyendo**
PRESENT INDICATIVE   **incluyo, incluyes, incluye,** incluimos, (incluís), **incluyen**
PRETERIT   incluí, incluiste, **incluyó,** incluimos, (incluisteis), **incluyeron**

Like **incluir**: construir, *to construct*; contribuir, *to contribute*; distribuir, *to distribute*; huir, *to flee*; sustituir, *to substitute*.

ir   *to go*

PRESENT PARTICIPLE   **yendo**
PRESENT INDICATIVE   **voy, vas, va, vamos, (vais), van**
PRESENT SUBJUNCTIVE   **vaya, vayas, vaya, vayamos, (vayáis), vayan**
IMPERFECT INDICATIVE   **iba, ibas, iba, íbamos, (ibais), iban**
PRETERIT   **fui, fuiste, fue, fuimos, (fuisteis), fueron**
COMMAND **(tú)**   **ve, no vayas**

oír *to hear*

PARTICIPLES	**oyendo, oído**
PRESENT INDICATIVE	**oigo, oyes, oye,** oímos, (oís), **oyen**
PRETERIT	oí, **oíste, oyó, oímos,** (oísteis), **oyeron**

poder *to be able*

PRESENT PARTICIPLE	**pudiendo**
PRESENT INDICATIVE	**puedo, puedes, puede,** podemos, (podéis), **pueden**
PRETERIT	**pude, pudiste, pudo, pudimos,** (pudisteis), **pudieron**
FUTURE	**podré, podrás,** etc. CONDITIONAL **podría, podrías,** etc.

poner *to put, place*

PAST PARTICIPLE	**puesto**
PRESENT INDICATIVE	**pongo,** pones, pone, ponemos, (ponéis), ponen
PRETERIT	**puse, pusiste, puso, pusimos,** (pusisteis), **pusieron**
FUTURE	**pondré, pondrás,** etc. CONDITIONAL **pondría, pondrías,** etc.
COMMAND (**tú**)	**pon, no pongas**

producir *to produce*

PRESENT INDICATIVE	**produzco,** produces, produce, producimos, (producís), producen
PRETERIT	**produje, produjiste, produjo, produjimos, (produjisteis), produjeron**

Like **producir**: traducir, *to translate*.

querer *to want; to love*

PRESENT INDICATIVE	**quiero, quieres, quiere,** queremos, (queréis), **quieren**
PRETERIT	**quise, quisiste, quiso, quisimos,** (quisisteis), **quisieron**
FUTURE	**querré, querrás,** etc. CONDITIONAL **querría, querrías,** etc.

saber *to know*

PRESENT INDICATIVE	**sé,** sabes, sabe, sabemos, (sabéis), saben
PRESENT SUBJUNCTIVE	**sepa, sepas, sepa, sepamos,** (sepáis), **sepan**
PRETERIT	**supe, supiste, supo, supimos,** (supisteis), **supieron**
FUTURE	**sabré, sabrás,** etc. CONDITIONAL **sabría, sabrías,** etc.

salir *to leave, go out*

PRESENT INDICATIVE	**salgo,** sales, sale, salimos, (salís), salen
FUTURE	**saldré, saldrás,** etc. CONDITIONAL **saldría, saldrías,** etc.
COMMAND (**tú**)	**sal, no salgas**

ser   *to be*

PRESENT INDICATIVE	**soy, eres, es, somos, (sois), son**
PRESENT SUBJUNCTIVE	**sea, seas, sea, seamos, (seáis), sean**
IMPERFECT INDICATIVE	**era, eras, era, éramos, (erais), eran**
PRETERIT	**fui, fuiste, fue, fuimos, (fuisteis), fueron**
COMMAND **(tú)**	**sé, no seas**

tener   *to have*

PRESENT INDICATIVE	**tengo, tienes, tiene,** tenemos, (tenéis), **tienen**
PRETERIT	**tuve, tuviste, tuvo, tuvimos, (tuvisteis), tuvieron**
FUTURE	**tendré, tendrás,** etc. CONDITIONAL **tendría, tendrías,** etc.

traer   *to bring*

PARTICIPLES	**trayendo, traído**
PRESENT INDICATIVE	**traigo,** traes, trae, traemos, (traéis), traen
PRETERIT	**traje, trajiste, trajo, trajimos, (trajisteis), trajeron**

valer   *to be worth*

PRESENT INDICATIVE	**valgo,** vales, vale, valemos, (valéis), valen
FUTURE	**valdré, valdrás,** etc. CONDITIONAL **valdría, valdrías,** etc.

venir   *to come*

PRESENT PARTICIPLE	**viniendo**
PRESENT INDICATIVE	**vengo, vienes, viene,** venimos, (venís), **vienen**
PRETERIT	**vine, viniste, vino, vinimos, (vinisteis), vinieron**
FUTURE	**vendré, vendrás,** etc. CONDITIONAL **vendría, vendrías,** etc.
COMMAND **(tú)**	**ven, no vengas**

ver   *to see*

PAST PARTICIPLE	**visto**
PRESENT INDICATIVE	**veo,** ves, ve, vemos, (veis), ven
IMPERFECT INDICATIVE	**veía, veías, veía, veíamos, (veíais), veían**

4

Additional Spanish Vocabulary Common to the United States

a todo dar   wonderful, super
¡águila!   watch out!
la alcapurria   typical Puerto Rican dish made of ground plantain mixed with pork, fish, or crab, rolled in a batter
andar juntos   to go steady
apantallar   to show off

el bochinche   gossip
la bodega   grocery store (*standard Spanish*, wine cellar)

café con llantas   coffee with doughnuts
califa(s)   (*slang*) California
el caló   (*Chicano*) slang, jargon
codo   *adj.* stingy (*standard Spanish*, **el codo**, elbow)
el comivete   fast-food stand
¡con safos!   the same to you! the same goes for you!
el coquito   a Puerto Rican drink made from coconut milk, cream, and rum
el corre-corre   confused situation where everyone is running around chaotically
el cuate, la cuatacha   buddy, close friend

la chamba   job, employment
chévere   OK, wonderful, great
el chicle   pest, tag-along (*standard Spanish*, chewing gum)

dejar plantado   to "stand (someone) up," fail to keep a date or appointment

¡epa! ¡épale!   careful! hey!
el escuincle   child
el estofón   bookworm, person who studies hard

flonquear   to flunk

la guagua   bus

el jíbaro   a rural Puerto Rican; a country person

la lana   (*slang*) money

la marqueta   market
mata: la mera mata   the genuine article, "the real McCoy"
la música ranchera   country music in the Mexican or Chicano style

la onda   what is trendy or stylish; **estar en la onda**   to be "with it"
¡órale!   hurry up!

la pachanga   party, festivity
padre   *adj.* (*slang*) terrific, "far out," "groovy"
el (la) pana   buddy, close friend
los pininos   baby's first steps when just beginning to walk
por la buena   willingly
por la mala   by force, against one's will

el rajón   coward
el runrún   gossip

ten con ten   fence sitting, not taking one side or the other
testear   to test (in school)
la trabajanta   babysitter

el vato   (*slang*) guy, dude
el vejigante   masked carnival character who goes about scaring children

Vocabularies

The vocabularies included here are to be used as guides, not as a substitute for a dictionary. The meanings given reflect usage in the text and not necessarily the most common equivalents in either language. In general, the following terms have been omitted: words appearing only in pronunciation drills; Spanish adverbs ending in **-mente** when the corresponding adjective is listed; words used only in examples or Notes; most proper names; and most conjugated verb forms.

Spanish stem-changing verbs are indicated by (**ie**), (**ue**), (**ie, i**), (**ue, u**), or (**i, i**) following the infinitive. Adjectives ending in **-o, -a** are given in the masculine form only. In the English-Spanish Vocabulary, the gender of Spanish nouns is indicated by the definite article except when masculine nouns end in **-o** and feminine nouns end in **-a**.

Abbreviations

adj	adjective	*n*	noun
adv	adverb	*obj*	object
coll	colloquial	*pl*	plural
conj	conjunction	*p p*	past participle
contr	contraction	*pr*	pronoun
d o p	direct object pronoun	*prep*	preposition
f	feminine	*pres part*	present participle
fam	familiar	*refl*	reflexive
inf	infinitive	*s*	singular
indef	indefinite	*sl*	slang
i o p	indirect object pronoun	*subj*	subjunctive
m	masculine	*v*	verb
Mex	Mexican		

Spanish-English Vocabulary

A

a to; at; from; **— menos
que** unless; **— menudo**
often; **— partir de** as of

abajo down

abierto *pp of* **abrir** *and adj*
opened, open

el **abrazo** hug

el **abrigo** overcoat

abril April

abrir to open; **—se** to
open up

absoluto absolute

la **abuela** grandmother

el **abuelo** grandfather; *pl*
grandparents

aburrido bored; boring

acabar to finish, end; **—
con** to finish with, put an
end to; **— de** to have just

acaso perhaps, maybe

el **accidente** accident

la **acción** action

la **aceituna** olive

aceptar to accept

acequible accessible

acerca de about,
concerning

acompañar to accompany

aconsejar to advise

acordarse (ue) (de + *obj)*
to remember

acostarse (ue) to lie down,
go to bed

acostumbrarse (a) to get
used to

la **actividad** activity

el **acto** act

actual *adj* present, present-
day

actuar to act

acuático aquatic

el **acuerdo** agreement; **De
—** Agreed, OK; **estar de
—** to be in agreement,
agree

acusar to accuse; **— recibo**
to acknowledge receipt

¡Adelante! Forward!

además moreover, besides;
— de in addition to

adiós goodbye

adjunto attached, enclosed

¡adónde? where? (with
verbs of motion)

adquirir (ie) to acquire

el **adulto (la adulta)** adult

aéreo *adj* air; **correo —**
air mail

el **aeropuerto** airport

afeitarse to shave (oneself)

el **aficionado (la aficionada)**
fan; **— a** fond of

afortunadamente
fortunately

la **agencia** agency; **— de
turismo** travel agency

agitado excited, upset

agosto August

agradable pleasant

agradecer to thank for, be
grateful for; to appreciate

agrícola (*m and f*) agricul-
tural

el **agua** (*f*) water

el **águila** (*f*) eagle

el **aguinaldo** Christmas
bonus

ahí there (near the person
spoken to)

ahora now; **— mismo**
right now; **— sí** however,
now . . . ; **por —** for now,
for the time being

el **aire** air; **al — libre** in
the open air

aislado isolated

ajeno (a) different from

al *contr of* **a**+**el** to the;
— + *inf* on, upon + *pres
part*

el **ala** (*f*) wing

el **alcalde (la alcaldesa)** mayor

la **aldea** village

alegrarse (de) to be
(become) happy

alegre happy

alemán (alemana) *n and adj*
German

el **álgebra** (*f*) algebra

algo something, anything;
somewhat (+ *adj or adv*)

alguien someone, somebody, anyone, anybody

algún, alguno some, any;
someone; *pl* some, a few

el **alma** (*f*) soul

la **almendra** almond

el **alojamiento** lodging

alrededor (de) around; **a
su —** surrounding it
(him, her)

alto tall, high

el **alucinado** bewitched
creature

el **alumno (la alumna)**
student

allá there; **— tú** that's up
to you; **el más —** the
other world

allí there

el **ama** (*f*); **ama de casa**
housewife

amable kind, nice; **ser tan
— de** to be so kind as to

el **amanecer** sunrise; *v* to
awaken (at the beginning of
the day)

amarillo yellow

la **ambición** ambition

el **ambiente** atmosphere

ambiguo ambiguous

ambos both

americano American

amical *adj* friendly

el **amigo (la amiga)** friend

la **amistad** friendship

el **amor** love

ampliamente fully, widely

amplio wide, widespread

el **analfabetismo** illiteracy
ancho wide, broad
las **andanzas** wanderings
andar to walk, go, amble;
to travel; to work, function
el **anhelo** wish, desire
el **anillo** ring
el **animal** animal
¡Ánimo! Cheer up!
anoche last night
el **anonimato** anonymity
anotar to write down
anteayer day before
yesterday
el **antepasado** ancestor
anterior preceding, former
antes before, formerly;
— de before; **cuanto —**
as soon as possible
la **anticipación** anticipation
anticuado old-fashioned,
antiquated
antiguo ancient; former
antipático unpleasant
el **antojo** whim, gadget
la **antorcha** torch
la **antropología** anthropology
el **anuncio** ad, announcement
el **año** year; **el — pasado**
last year; **llevar muchos
—s** to have spent many
years; **tener ... —s** to be
. . . years old; **todos los
—s** every year
aparecer to appear
apartado: — postal post
office box
aparte aside, separate
apasionadamente passion-
ately
el **apellido** surname
apenas hardly
la **apertura** opening
aplaudir to applaud
la **aplicación** application
aplicado diligent
el **aporte** contribution
apostar (ue) (a) to bet (on,
that)
el **apoyo** support

apreciar to appreciate
aprender (a) to learn (to)
el **aprendiz** apprentice
apropriado appropriate
aproximadamente
approximately
apuntar to write down; to
aim
los **apuntes** notes
aquel (aquella) *adj* that
(over there)
aquél (aquélla) *pr* that
(one)
aquello *neuter pr* that
aquellos (aquellas) *adj*
those (over there)
aquéllos (aquéllas) *pr*
those (ones)
aquí here; **por —** around
here
el **árbol** tree
la **arena** sand
el **aristócrata** aristocrat
el **arma** (*f*) weapon
armado armed; **fuerzas
armadas** armed forces
el **artefacto** artifact
el **artículo** article
el (la) **artista** artist
artístico artistic
arreglar to fix; to arrange
arriba up (with)
arrugado wrinkled
asegurar to assure; to
insure; **—se** to make sure
así that way, so, thus; **así,
así** so-so; **— es** that's
right; **— que** so
asimétrico asymmetrical,
out of balance
asistir (a) to attend
asombrado amazed,
surprised, astonished
asombroso amazing,
surprising, astonishing
el **aspecto** aspect
el **astronauta** astronaut
astuto astute, clever
el **asunto** matter
atacar to attack

el **ataque** attack
la **atención** attention; **prestar
—** to pay attention
el (la) **atleta** athlete
los **atractivos** attractions, good
points; *adj* attractive
atravesar (ie) to cross
atreverse (a) to dare (to)
atroz atrocious
aturdido bewildered
el **auditorio** auditorium
el **auge** popularity
el **aula** (*f*) classroom
el **aumento** raise, increase
aún even, still
aunque although, even
though
auténtico authentic
el **autobús** bus
el **automóvil** car, automobile
el **autor (la autora)** author
la **autoridad** authority,
authorities
avanzado advanced
la **avenida** avenue
el **aventurero** adventurer
avergonzado ashamed,
embarrassed; shamed
el **avión** airplane
avisar to advise, let know;
to warn
ayer yesterday
la **ayuda** aid, help
ayudar to help
azul blue

B

bailar to dance
el **baile** dance
bajar to go down; **— de**
to get off
bajo under, below
el **balneario** swimming
resort; *adj* bathing
el **baloncesto** basketball
la **bamba** Mexican dance
la **bandera** flag
el **banderín** banner
el **bandido** bandit
bañarse to bathe

el **baño**   bath; **traje de —** bathing suit
bárbaro   barbaric
el **barco**   boat
el **barrio**   neighborhood
bastante   *adj and pr* enough; quite a bit; *adv* quite, rather
bastar   to be enough, be sufficient
el **bautismo**   baptism
la **bebida**   beverage
bello   beautiful
el **beso**   kiss
la **biblioteca**   library
la **bicicleta**   bicycle
el **bien**   the good, welfare; *adv* well, fine; **más —**   rather; **pasarlo —**   to have a good time; **¡Qué —!**   Great! **tan — como**   as well as
el **bigote**   mustache
bilingüe   bilingual
el **bilingüismo**   bilingualism
el **billete**   bill, bank note; *pl* (*sl*) folding money
blanco   white
la **blusa**   blouse
la **boca**   mouth
la **boda**   wedding; **noche de —s**   wedding night
bonito   pretty
el (la) **boricua**   Puerto Rican
borrar   to erase
el **boxeo**   boxing
el **brazo**   arm
breve   brief, short
el **brillante**   diamond; *adj* brilliant
el **bruto (la bruta)**   brute, ignoramus
buen, bueno *adj*   good, kind; **Buenos días**   Good morning; **bueno** *adv*   well, OK, all right
el **bufón**   clown
burlarse (de)   to make fun (of), ridicule
el **burro**   donkey
buscar   to look for, seek

C

el **caballero**   gentleman; knight
el **caballo**   horse
caber   to fit
la **cabeza**   head
el **cacique**   chieftain
cada   each, every
caer   to fall; **—se**   to fall down
el **café**   coffee; café
el **calcetín**   sock
el **calderón**   cauldron
el **calendario**   calendar
caliente   hot (temperature)
el **calor**   heat; **tener —**   to be hot
callarse   to shut up, be quiet
la **calle**   street
la **cama**   bed
la **camarera**   waitress
el **camarero**   waiter
el **camarón**   shrimp
cambiar   to change; to exchange
el **cambio**   change; **en —**   on the other hand
el **camello**   camel
caminar   to walk
el **camino**   road, path
el **camión**   truck
la **camisa**   shirt
la **campana**   bell
el **campesino (la campesina)**   farmer, peasant
el **campo**   field; countryside; **— y pista**   track and field (athletic events)
la **canción**   song
cansado   tired
cansarse   to become tired
cantar   to sing
la **cantidad**   quantity; **en —es**   a lot
capacitar   to qualify
la **capital**   capital
la **cara**   face
el **carácter**   character

la **característica**   characteristic
característico   characteristic
el (la) **caradura**   scoundrel, brazen person
el **carbón**   charcoal; coal
cariñoso   affectionate
la **carne**   meat; **en — y hueso**   in flesh and blood
la **carrera**   career; race
la **carretera**   highway
la **carta**   letter
el **cartel**   poster
la **casa**   house; **ama de —**   housewife; **en —**   at home
casado   married
casarse (con)   to get married (to)
casi   almost
el **caso**   case; **en la mayoría de los —s**   in a majority of cases
castigar   to punish
el **castigo**   punishment
la **casualidad**   chance, coincidence; **por —**   by chance
el **catálogo**   catalog
la **catedral**   cathedral
católico   Catholic
catorce   fourteen
la **causa**   cause; **a — de**   because of
cautelosamente   cautiously
la **cebolla**   onion
celebrar   to celebrate; **—se**   to take place; to be celebrated
los **celos**   jealousy; **sentir (ie) —**   to feel jealous
la **cena**   dinner, supper
cenar   to have supper
el **centavo**   cent
el **centro**   center; downtown
cerca   near, nearby; **— de**   near, close to
cerrar (ie)   to close
la **cerveza**   beer
el **ciclismo**   cycling
el **cielo**   sky; heaven

cien, ciento one (a) hundred; **por ciento** percent

científicamente scientifically

cierto true; **por —** as a matter of fact

cinco five

cincuenta fifty

el **cine** movies; movie house

cínico cynical

el **cinturón** belt

circumnavegar to circumnavigate

la **cita** date, appointment

la **ciudad** city

la **ciudadanía** citizenship

el **ciudadano (**la **ciudadana)** citizen

la **civilización** civilization

claro clear; **¡Claro! ¡Claro que sí!** Of course!

la **clase** class(room); kind, type; **— media** middle class; **en —** in class; **toda — de** all kinds of

el **clima** climate

la **clínica** clinic

la **cobardía** cowardice

la **cocina** kitchen; (type of) cooking

el **coche** car

el **código** code

cohabitar to live together

la **coincidencia** coincidence

la **cola** tail (of an animal); **hacer —** to get in line

colaborar to collaborate

el **colega** colleague

colgar (ue) to hang (up)

el **colmo** limit; culmination; **¡Esto es el —!** This is the last straw!

la **colonización** colonization

el **collar** necklace

el **comedor** dining room

el **comendador** commander (of a military order)

comenzar (ie) to begin

comer to eat

el **comercio** commerce, business

cómico funny, comic

la **comida** food; meal

el **comienzo** beginning

el **comité** committee

como *adv* like, as, such as; *conj* since; **— si** as if; **tan bien —** as well as

¿cómo? (cómo!) how? (how!); **¡Cómo no!** Of course!

el **compadre (**la **comadre)** very close friend (among adults)

el **compañero (**la **compañera)** buddy, companion, mate

la **compañía** company

la **comparación** comparison

compartir to share

el **(**la**) compatriota** compatriot

la **competencia** competition; competence

el **competidor (**la **competidora)** competitor

complacer to please, oblige, satisfy

completamente completely

completar to complete

el **componente** part (of a whole)

componer to compose; to fix, repair

el **comportamiento** behavior

la **composición** composition

la **compra** purchase; **ir de —s** to go shopping

comprar to buy

comprender to understand

el **compromiso** engagement; commitment

la **computadora** computer

común common, usual; ordinary

la **comunicación** communication

con with; **— cuidado**

carefully; **— frecuencia** frequently; **— tal (de) que** provided that

conceder to grant

el **concepto** concept

el **concierto** concert

el **concurso** contest, competition

la **condición** condition

conducir to drive; to guide

la **conferencia** lecture; conference

confiado confident

la **confianza** confidence

confiar (en) to confide (in); to trust

el **congreso** convention; congress

conmigo with me

conocer to meet, get acquainted with; to know, be acquainted with

el **conquistador** conquistador, conqueror

conseguir (i, i) to get, avail oneself of

el **consejo** advice

conservar to conserve; to preserve

el **conservatorio** conservatory

constituir to constitute

la **construcción** construction

construir to construct, build

consultar to consult

contar (ue) to tell, relate; to count

contemporáneo contemporary

contento happy, pleased, glad

la **contestación** answer

contestar to answer

contigo with you (*fam*)

el **continente** continent

continuar to continue

contra against

el **contrato** contract

contribuir to contribute

convencer to convince

la **convención** convention
conveniente convenient
la **conversación** conversation
convertir (ie, i) to convert;
to turn into
convidar (a) to invite (to)
la **copa** goblet; drink; **tomar una —** to have a drink
el **corazón** heart
la **corbata** tie
el **cordero** lamb
la **cordialidad** cordiality, hospitality
el **cordón** string, cord; **— de zapato** shoelace
el **correo** mail; **a vuelta de —** by return mail; **por —** by mail
correr to run
la **corrida (de toros)** bullfight
corrupto corrupt
la **cosa** thing
la **costa** coast
costar (ue) to cost; to require (an effort, money, etc.)
costoso costly
la **costumbre** custom
lo **cotidiano** everyday life
crear to create
creativo creative
crecer to grow
creciente increasing, growing
el **crecimiento** growth
el **credo** creed
crédulo credulous, gullible
la **creencia** belief
creer to think; to believe; **Creo que sí.** I think so.
la **crianza** upbringing
el **crimen** crime
el **crisol: — de razas** melting pot
criticar to criticize
el (la) **cronista** newscaster, chronicler
la **cruz** cross
cruzar to cross
el **cuaderno** notebook
la **cuadra** (city) block

el **cuadro** painting, picture
el (la) **cual,** los (las) **cuales** that, which, who, whom; **lo cual** which **¿cuál? (¿cuáles?)** which one(s)? what?
la **cualidad** quality
cualquier (cualquiera) any
cuando when, whenever; **de vez en —** once in a while
¿cuándo? when?
cuanto: — antes as soon as possible
¿cuánto? (¿cuántos?) how much? (how many?); **¿A cuántos estamos?** What day is it? **¡Cuánto +** *verb!* How . . . !
cuarenta forty
el **cuarto** room; quarter
cuatro four
cubano Cuban
cubierto (de) covered (with)
la **cuenta** bill, check; **darse — de** to realize; **tener en —** to bear in mind
el **cuento** story
cuerdo sane
el **cuestionario** questionnaire
la **cueva** cave
el **cuidado** care; **¡Cuidado!** Careful! Beware! **tener —** to be careful
culpable guilty
cultivar to cultivate
el **culto** cult, form of worship; *adj* well-mannered, well-educated
la **cultura** culture
el **cumpleaños** birthday
curiosamente curiously
curioso curious
el **curso** course
cuyo whose

CH

la **cháchara** chit-chat, chatter
la **chamaca** (*Mex*) girl

el **chamaco** (*Mex*) boy
charlar to chat
el **chauvinista** chauvinist
la **chica** girl
chicano Chicano, Mexican-American
el **chico** boy
el **chile** chili, hot green pepper
chileno Chilean
el **chiquillo (la chiquilla)** youngster, small child
el **chiste** joke; **no tener —** not to be any fun, not to be funny
el **churro** crullerlike pastry

D

la **dama** lady
el **daño** harm; **sufrir —s** to suffer damages
dar to give; **— calabazas** to fail (someone); **— gato por liebre** to gyp; **—lugar a** to give rise to; **— un paseo** to take a stroll; **— vergüenza** to be embarrassing; **—se cuenta (de)** to realize; **—se prisa** to hurry; **¡Dale duro!** Let him have it! **¿Qué más da?** What difference does it make?
el **dátil** date (fruit)
el **dato** fact
de of; from; about; by; in (after a superlative); than (before numerals); **De nada** You're welcome; **— noche** nocturnal, by night; **— pronto** suddenly
debajo de beneath
debatir to debate, discuss
deber must, ought to, should; to owe; **debido a** due to
débil weak
decidir to decide
décimo tenth

decir (i,i) to tell, say; **es —** that is to say; **querer —** to mean, signify; **¡No me digas!** You don't say!
se dice it is said, they say
la **decisión** decision
la **declaración** statement; declaration
dedicar to dedicate, devote
defender (ie) to defend
dejar to leave (behind); to allow, let
del *contr of* **de** + **el** of the
el **deleite** delight
la **demanda** demand
demás *adj and pr* (the) rest, others
demasiado too; too much; *pl* too many
democráticamente democratically
el (la) **dentista** dentist
dentro (de) inside (of); within
el **departamento** Spanish equivalent to district or county; department
depender (de) to depend (on)
el (la) **dependiente** salesperson, clerk
el **deporte** sport
depravado depraved
la **derecha** right; **a la —** to (on) the right
el **derecho** right; privilege; law; **exámenes de —** law exams; *adj* straight
desagradable unpleasant
desayunar to have breakfast
descansar to rest
el **descarado** scoundrel, rogue
el **desconocido (la desconocida)** stranger
descubrir to discover; to disclose, uncover
el **descuido** neglect; oversight
desde since; from
desear to wish, want

el **desempleo** unemployment
desfilar to parade
el **desfile** parade
la **desgracia** misfortune; **en — ** in disfavor; **por —** unfortunately
deshacer to undo
el **desierto** desert
la **desilusión** disappointment
desobediente disobedient
despacio slowly
despachar (*coll*) to kill, polish off
despedirse (i,i) to take leave (of); to say goodbye
despejado clear (weather)
despertarse (ie) to wake up (oneself)
despistado: estar — (*coll*) to be on the wrong track, lost
después later; then, afterwards; **— de** after
desterrar to exile
destruir to destroy
el **detalle** detail
detener to stop, detain
determinar to determine, decide
detrás de behind
devolver (ue) to return, give back
el **día** day; **algún —** someday; **Buenos —s** Good morning; **de —** by day; **Día de Reyes** Epiphany; **hoy —** nowadays; **todo el —** all day; **todos los —s** everyday
el **diablo** devil
el **diálogo** dialog
el **diario** newspaper; diary; *adj* daily
el (la) **dibujante** illustrator
dibujar to draw
el **dibujo** drawing; **— animado** film cartoon
el **diccionario** dictionary
diciembre December
el **dictado** dictation
el **dictamen** judgment,

opinion; suggestion
el **dicho** saying
el **diente** tooth
diez ten
diferente different
difícil difficult
la **dificultad** difficulty
el **dinero** money
Dios God
el **diplomático (la diplomática)** diplomat; *adj* diplomatic
la **dirección** address; direction
la **disciplina** discipline
el **disco** record
la **discoteca** record library; discothèque
la **disculpa** apology
la **discusión** discussion; argument
discutir to discuss, argue
disfrutar (de) to enjoy
disperso dispersed
la **disposición** disposition; **a su —** at your service
distinto different; distinct
el **distrito** district
diverso diverse, varied
divertirse (ie,i) to have a good time, amuse oneself
doce twelve
el **doctor (la doctora)** doctor
el **documento** document
el **dólar** dollar
doler (ue) to ache, pain; to grieve
doméstico domestic
domingo Sunday; **los —s** on Sundays
dominicano Dominican
el **dominio** domination
don (doña) title of respect used before a first name
donde where, wherever
¿dónde? where? **¿(en) — más?** where else?
dormir (ue, u) to sleep; **—se** to go to sleep, fall asleep
dos two; **los (las) —** both

doscientos two hundred
el **drama** drama, play
la **duda** doubt; **sin —** without a doubt
 dudar to doubt
 dudoso doubtful
el **dueño (**la **dueña)** owner, master (mistress)
 dulce sweet
 durante during; for
 durar to last
 duro hard

E

 e and (used for **y** before the sound /i/)
 EE.UU. (Estados Unidos) U.S.
 echar to throw out; **— a perder** to spoil, ruin; **— de menos** to miss
la **edad** age
el **edificio** building
la **educación** education; upbringing
el **educador** educator
 eficaz efficient
 egoísta selfish
el **ejemplo** example; **por —** for example
 el the (*m s*); **— de** that (the one) of (with, in); **— que** the one that
 él he, him (*after prep*); **de — ** of his, his
la **electricidad** electricity
el **elemento** element
 ella she, her (*after prep*); **de—** of hers, hers
 ellos (ellas) they, them (*after prep*); **de — ** of theirs, theirs
la **emancipación** emancipation
el **embajador (**la **embajadora)** ambassador
 embarazada pregnant
 embargo: sin — nevertheless, however
 emitir to emit

 emocionante exciting
 empezar (ie) (a + ** *inf* **) to begin (**+** *inf*)
el **empleado (**la **empleada)** employee
el **empleo** job, work
la **empresa** undertaking; company, firm, enterprise
el **empujón** shove
 en in, on, at; **— casa** at home; **en fin** in short; **— punto** on the dot, sharp; **— seguida** right away; **— serio** seriously
 enamorado in love
 enamorarse (de) to fall in love (with)
 encarcelado jailed, locked up
 encargarse de to be in charge of; to take care of
 encerrar to imprison; to enclose; to include
 encima de on top of
 encontrar (ue) to find; to meet, encounter; **— se con** to meet, come across
 encrustado encrusted
el **encuentro** meeting, encounter
el **enemigo** enemy
 enero January
el **enfermero (**la **enfermera)** nurse
el **enfermo (**la **enferma)** patient; sick person; *adj* sick, ill
 enfrente (de) in front (of); across (from)
 enigmático enigmatic
 enloquecerse to become crazy
 enmascarar to mask
 enorgullecerse (de) to pride oneself, be (become) proud (of)
 enorme enormous
 enriquecerse to become rich
el **ensayo** rehearsal; essay

 enseñar to show; to teach; **— a (+** *inf*) to show or teach how to
 entender (ie) to understand
el **entendimiento** understanding
 entero entire; whole
 entonces then; **en aquel — ** back then, at that time
la **entrada** admission ticket; entrance
la **entraña** innard; middle, midst
 entrar (en) to enter, come in, go in
 entre between, among; **— familia** among family
er **entrenador** coach; trainer
 entrenarse to train
el **entusiasmo** enthusiasm
la **época** era, period
 equiparar to equip
el **equipo** team
la **equitación** horsemanship; equestrian events
 equivocado wrong, mistaken
la **escena** scene
la **esclavitud** slavery
 escoger to choose
 escolar school (*adj*)
 esconder to hide
 escribir to write
el **escritorio** desk
 escuchar to listen (to)
la **escuela** school
 ese (esa) *adj* that
 ése (ésa) *pr* that (one)
 esforzarse (ue) to make an effort
la **esgrima** fencing
 eso *neuter pr* that; **¡Eso que importa!** What does that matter! **¡Eso sí!** That's for sure! **por — ** that's why, because of that; therefore
 esos (esas) *adj* those
 ésos (ésas) *pr* those

la **espada** sword

español (española)
Spanish; *n* Spaniard; *m*
Spanish (language)

especial (*m and f*) special

especializarse to
specialize

especialmente especially

especificar to specify

específico specific

el **espectáculo** spectacle,
show

el **espectador** (la **espectadora**)
spectator

el **espectro** ghost, spook

esperar to wait (for); to
expect; to hope; **— que sí**
to hope so

el **espíritu** spirit

espléndido splendid

espontáneo spontaneous

la **esposa** wife

el **esposo** husband; *pl* husband and wife

el **esquema** sketch; scheme

la **esquina** corner

establecer to establish; to
settle

la **estación** season; station

estacionar to park

el **estadio** stadium

el **estado** state; **— de ánimo**
state of mind, mood; **jefe
de —** chief of state; **los
Estados Unidos** the
United States

estadounidense United
States (*adj*), American

estallar to break out; to
explode

estancarse to get stuck

el **estanque** pond, reservoir

estar to be; **¿A cuántos
estamos?** What is the
date? **— constipado** to
have a cold; **— en evidencia** to stand out, be
apparent; **— listo** to be
ready; **— vivo** to be alive

este (esta) *adj* this

éste (ésta) *pr* this (one)

el **este** east

el **estereotipo** stereotype

el **estilo** style, fashion; **por el
—** like that, along those
lines; accordingly

estimado dear, esteemed

estimar to esteem

estirar to stretch (out)

esto *neuter pr* this

el **estómago** stomach

estos (estas) *adj* these

éstos (éstas) *pr* these

el **estrecho** strait; *adj*
narrow; tight

la **estructura** structure

el (la) **estudiante** student

estudiantil student (*adj*)

estudiar to study; **— para**
to study to be

el **estudio** study; **cursar —s**
to take courses

estupendo wonderful, great

eterno eternal

el **eufemismo** euphemism

evaluar to evaluate

evitar to avoid

exactamente exactly

exagerar to exaggerate

el **examen** examination, test

la **excavación** excavation

excavar to excavate

excelente (*m and f*)
excellent

la **excepción** exception; **sin
—** without exception

exclusivamente exclusively

la **exhibición** exhibition,
exhibit

exhibir to exhibit, display

exigir to demand, require

la **existencia** existence

existir to exist

el **éxito** success

el **experto** (la **experta**) expert

la **explicación** explanation

explicar to explain

la **exploración** exploration

el **explorador** (la **exploradora**)
explorer

la **exposición** display, exhibit

expresar to express

la **expresión** expression

expresivo expressive

extenderse (ie) to extend,
spread out; to continue

externo external

extraer to extract

el **extranjero** (la **extranjera**)
foreigner; *adj* foreign

extraño strange, unusual

extraordinario extra-
ordinary

extra-terrestre outer-space
(*adj*)

F

la **fábrica** factory

fácil easy

la **facilidad** ease; facility

la **factura** invoice, bill

la **facultad** school or division
within a university

la **fachada** façade

la **falta** lack

faltar to be lacking; to be
missing; to need

la **familia** family; **entre —**
among family

familiar family (*adj*)

familiarizar to familiarize

famoso famous

el **fanático** fan; fanatic; *adj*
fanatical

el **fango** mud

la **fantasía** fantasy, illusion

la **farmacia** drugstore,
pharmacy

el **fastidio: ¡Qué —!** What
a problem! How annoying!

el **favor** favor; **por —** please

favorecido favorable; lucky

favorito favorite

febrero February

la **fecha** date

felicitar to congratulate

femenino feminine

el **feminismo** feminism

el **fenómeno** phenomenon

feo ugly

la **feria** fair

festejar to celebrate

el **festival** festival

el **fichero** file, catalog

la **fiesta** party; holiday, festival

fijar to paste; to fix, fasten; **—se (en)** to take a close look (at); to notice

la **fila** row

el **filete** steak

el **filósofo (la filósofa)** philosopher

el **fin** end; goal; **en —** in short; **por —** finally; **para fines de** toward (by) the end of

el **final** end, finale; **al —** at the end

finalmente finally

fino fine; keen; thin

la **firma** signature; firm, company

flamenco Andalusian gypsy music, song, and dance

el **flan** caramel cream custard

la **flexibilidad** flexibility

la **flor** flower

fomentar to spread (good will, hope, etc.)

la **forma** shape, form **— parte de** to be a part of

el **foro** forum

la **fotografía (la foto)** photograph; photography

el **fraile** friar, priest

francamente frankly

francés (francesa) French; *m* Frenchman; French (language); *f* French woman

la **frase** phrase

la **frecuencia** frequency; **con —** frequently

frecuente frequent

frecuentemente frequently

fresco cool; **hacer —** to be cool (weather)

frío cold; **hacer —** to be cold (weather); **tener —** to be (feel) cold

la **frontera** border

la **fruta** fruit

el **fuego** fire

la **fuente** fountain; source

fuera (de) outside (of)

fuerte strong

la **fuerza** strength; **—s armadas** armed forces

el **fulano** (*coll*) guy, so-and-so

la **función** show; function, use

el **funcionamiento** functioning

funcionar to function, work

funerario funeral (*adj*), funereal

furioso furious

el **fútbol** soccer; **— americano** football

el **futuro** future

G

la **gama** gamut

la **gana** desire; **tener —s de** to be anxious to, want to

ganar to win; to earn; to gain

garantizar to guarantee

gastar to spend; to waste

el **gasto** expense

el **gato** cat

generalmente generally

la **gente** people

la **geografía** geography

geográfico geographical

el **gerente** manager

la **gimnasia** gymnastics

el **gimnasio** gymnasium

el **gitano (la gitana)** gypsy

glorioso glorious

el **gobernador (la gobernadora)** governor

gobernar to govern

el **gobierno** government

gordo fat

gótico Gothic

grabar to engrave

gracias thanks, thank you; **dar las —** to thank; **— a** thanks to

gracioso clever; cute

la **grada** grandstand

la **gramática** grammar

gran, grande big, large; great

el **granito** pimple

el **grano** grain; pimple; **ir al —** to get to the point

grave grave, serious

el **gringo (la gringa)** nickname given to foreigners, especially Americans

el **grupo** group

el **guacamole** salad or dip made from avocados

el **guajiro (la guajira)** (*Cuba*) farmer, peasant

guapo good-looking

el **guardia** guard

guatemalteco Guatemalan

la **guerra** war

el (la) **guía** guide

la **guitarra** guitar

gustar to like; to appeal to, be appealing

el **gusto** pleasure; taste; **Mucho —** Glad to meet you

H

haber to have (auxiliary)

había there was (were)

habido (*pp* of **haber**): **ha habido** there has (have) been

el **habitante** inhabitant

el **hábito** habit

el **habla** speech, language; **de — inglesa** English-speaking

hablar to talk, speak

habrá there will be

hacer to do; to make; **— buen tiempo** to be nice weather; **— cola** to stand in line; — **sol** to be sunny; — **una pregunta** to ask a question; — **un viaje** to take a trip; — **viento** to be windy; **—se** to become

hacia toward(s)

la **hacienda** farm, estate

el **hacha** *f* ax

el **hada** *f* fairy

el **hambre** *f* hunger; **tener —** to be hungry

harto fed up

hasta until, to, up to, as far as; *adv* even; — **que** *conj* until

hay there is (are); — **que** one has to, it is necessary to; **¿Qué —?** What's up?

el **hecho** fact; *pl* events

el **helado** ice cream; *adj* cold, frozen

el **hemisferio** hemisphere

la **hermana** sister

el **hermano** brother

hermoso beautiful

el **héroe** hero

el **hielo** ice

la **hija** daughter

el **hijo** son; *pl* sons, son(s) and daughter(s), children

hincar to sink in

el (la) **hipócrita** hypocrite

hispano Hispanic

la **historia** history; story

el **historiador** historian

histórico historic, historical

la **historieta** comic strip

el **hogar** home

la **hoja** leaf

¡Hola! Hello! Hi!

el **hombre** man

hondureño Honduran

el **honor** honor; **código de —** honor code

la **hora** hour; time; **¿A qué —?** At what time? **a última —** at the last minute; **media —** half an hour;

la **horchata** type of beverage

la **hostilidad** hostility

hoy today; — **día** nowadays; — **mismo** today (emphatic)

hubo there was (were)

la **huella** imprint, mark; fingerprint

el **hueso** bone; **en carne y —** in flesh and blood

humano human; **ser —** human being

humilde humble

la **humillación** humiliation

el **humor** mood; **de mal —** in a bad mood; **sentido del —** sense of humor

¡Huy! Wow!

I

la **idea** idea

idear to think up

la **identidad** identity

el **idioma** language; — **extranjero** foreign language

la **iglesia** church

igual equal; the same; **al — que** as well as

iluminado illuminated

la **imagen** image

imaginarse to imagine

la **impaciencia** impatience

el **impedimento** impediment

impedir to prevent

el **imperio** empire

la **impertinencia** impertinence

implicar to imply; to implicate

imponer to impose

importante important

importar to matter; to import; **¡Eso qué importa!** What does that matter!

imposible impossible

impresionante impressive

impresionar to impress

el **impuesto** tax

impulsar to give impetus, stimulate

inaceptable unacceptable

incitar (a) to incite (to)

incluir to include

incondicional unconditional

increíble incredible

incrementar to increase

indefinidamente indefinitely

la **independencia** independence

indicar to indicate

el (la) **indígena** native; Indian

el **indio** (la **india**) Indian

el **individuo** individual

la **índole** nature, type

la **industria** industry

la **industrialización** industrialization

inequívoco unequivocable

el **infame** villainous scoundrel

la **infancia** infancy

infantil childish

inferior (*m and f*) inferior

influir (en) to influence, have an influence (on)

informar to inform

el **informe** report

el **ingeniero** (la **ingeniera**) engineer

Inglaterra England

inglés (inglesa) English; *m* Englishman; English (language); *f* Englishwoman; **de habla inglesa** English-speaking

inhumano inhuman

la **iniciación** beginning; initiation

el **iniciador** (la **iniciadora**) initiator, instigator; founder

iniciar to initiate, begin

la **iniciativa** initiative

la **injusticia** injustice

inmediatamente immediately

la **inmigración** immigration

la **inmoralidad** immorality

la **inocencia** innocence

la **inquietud** anxiety, fear
insincero insincere
la **insistencia** insistence
insistir (en) to insist on
la **insolación** sunstroke
la **inspiración** inspiration
instalarse to get installed, set up
la **instrucción** instruction; schooling
inteligente smart, intelligent
la **intención** intention
intenso intense
intentar to try
el **interés** interest
el **intermedio** intermission
internacional international
la **interpretación** interpretation
inútil useless
inventar to invent
invernal winter (*adj*)
la **investigación** investigation
el **invierno** winter
invitar to invite
invocar to invoke
ir to go; **— a** + *inf* to be going to + *inf*; **— al grano** to get to the point; **— se** to go away, leave
la **ironía** irony
irónico ironic
irrespetuoso disrespectful
la **isla** island
italiano Italian
la **izquierda** left; **a la —** to (on) the left

J

el **jabón** soap
jactarse (de) to boast (of), brag (about)
jamás never, (not) ever, not at any time
japonés (japonesa) Japanese; *m* Japanese language
el **jefe** boss; **— de estado** chief of state

el (la) **joven** young man (woman); *adj* young
la **joya** jewel; *pl* jewelry
el **juego** game; **— de palabras** play on words
el **jueves** Thursday
jugar (ue) to play; **— a** to play at (being)
el **juguete** toy
julio July
junio June
juntos together
el **juramento** oath
la **justicia** justice
justificar to justify
la **juventud** youth
juzgar to judge

K

el **kilo** kilogram
el **kilómetro** kilometer

L

la the (*f s*); *d o p* her, it, you
el **lado** side; **al — de** beside
el **lago** lake
el **lápiz** pencil
largo long
las the (*f pl*); *d o p* them, you
la **lástima** pity; **¡Qué —!** What a shame!
latinoamericano Latin American
lavar to wash; **—se** to wash oneself
le *i o p* (to, for) him, her, it, you
la **lección** lesson
el **lector (la lectora)** reader
la **lectura** reading
leer to read
lejos far; **de —** from afar, at a distance; **— de** far from
el **lema** motto
la **lengua** language; tongue
lento slow

les *i o p* (to, for) them, you
levantar to lift; **—se** to get up; to stand up
la **ley** law
la **leyenda** legend
la **libertad** liberty
libre free
la **librería** bookstore
el **libro** book
el **líder** leader
la **liebre** hare; **dar gato por —** to gyp ("to serve cat in place of hare")
ligero quick, swift; light
la **lima** file, rasp
la **limosna** alm
lindo lovely, pretty
lingüístico linguistic; *f* linguistics
lírico lyrical
listo ready; **estar —** to be ready; **ser —** to be clever
la **literatura** literature
lo *d o p* him, it, you; **— cual** which; **— más pronto posible** as soon as possible; **— mío** what is mine; **— mismo** the same (thing); **— que** what
el **lobo** wolf
loco crazy
el **lodo** mud
lógico logical
lograr to manage, attain, achieve, bring about
el **lomo (de cerdo)** (pork) loin
el **loro** parrot
los the (*m pl*); *d o p* them, you
la **lotería** lottery
la **lucha** struggle; wrestling
luchar to fight
luego then
el **lugar** place, location; **dar — a** to give rise to
la **luna** moon
el **lunes** Monday
la **luz** light

LL

llamar to call; **—se** to be called, named

a **llave** key

llegar to arrive; **— a tiempo** to arrive on (in) time

llevar to take (along); **— a cabo** to carry out (a mission, etc.); **— muchos años** to have spent many years; **— puesto** to wear, have on; **— se** to take along, to buy

llorar to cry

llover (ue) to rain

M

la **madera** wood

la **madre** mother

maduro mature; ripe

el **maestro (la maestra)** teacher

magnífico wonderful, magnificent

el **maíz** corn

el **majadero** pest

el **majo** showoff, dude (*coll*)

mal, malo bad, naughty; ill; **de mal humor** in a bad mood; **mal** *adv* badly, poorly

maldito damned, accursed

malgastar to waste

malvado malicious, fiendish

la **mamá** mom, mother

el **mandamás** chief, big shot

mandar to send; to command

el **manejo** handling

la **manera** manner, way

la **mano** hand; **¡Manos a la obra!** Let's get to work!

mantener to maintain

la **mañana** morning; **de la —** A. M.; **por la —** in the morning; *adv* tomorrow

la **máquina** machine

el **mar** sea

la **maravilla** marvel, wonder

maravilloso wonderful, marvellous

marcar to dial (a phone number)

marchar to march; to walk; **—se** to go away, leave

el **martes** Tuesday

marzo March

más more, any more; plus; **¿dónde —?** where else? **— bien** rather; **— de** more than; **— o menos** more or less; **no —** (*Mex*) only; **no — que** nothing more than; **¿Qué — da?** What difference does it make?; **sin —** without further ado

la **máscara** mask

matar to kill

la **matemática** mathematics

el **matrimonio** marriage; married couple

el **maya** Maya, Mayan

mayo May

mayor older, oldest; greater, greatest; main; **la — parte de** the greater part of; **persona —** adult; **ser —** to be older; to be an adult

la **mayoría** majority

mayormente principally

me me, myself

la **medianoche** midnight

mediante by means of

la **medicina** medicine

el **médico (la médica)** doctor; *adj* medical

la **medida** measure

el **medio** means; middle; environment; *adj* half, a half; **media hora** half an hour; **clase media** middle class

el **mediodía** noon

mejor better, best; **lo —** the best part (thing)

la **memoria** memory; **saber**

de — to know by heart

memorizar to memorize

menor smaller, smallest, younger, youngest

menos less, least; fewer; minus; **a — que** unless; **echar de —** to miss; **más o —** more or less; **— de** less than; **por lo —** at least

el **mensaje** message

el **menso** dummy

la **mente** mind

el **mentiroso (la mentirosa)** liar

menudo: a — often

el **mercado** market

merecer to deserve

el **mérito** merit

el **mes** month

la **mesa** table

meter to put (in); **— la pata** to goof, "stick your foot in"

metódico methodical

el **metro** subway; meter; yardstick

la **mezcla** mixture

mi, mis my

mí *obj of prep* me, myself

el **miedo** fear; **tener —** to be afraid

mientras (que) while; whereas

el **miércoles** Wednesday

mil a (one) thousand

militante militant

el **millón** million

mimado spoiled

mimar to spoil

mimo pampering

el **ministro** minister; cabinet member

la **minoría** minority

el **minuto** minute

mío(s), mía(s) *adj* my, (of) mine; **el mío (la mía, los míos, las mías)** *pr* mine; **lo mío** what is mine

mirar to look (at)

la **misa**   mass (church)
la **misión**   mission
mismo   same; -self; **ahora
— **   right now; **hoy —**   today (emphatic)
misterioso   mysterious
la **mitología**   mythology
la **mobilidad**   mobility
la **moda**   fashion, style
los **modales**   manners
el **modelo**   model
el **modismo**   idiom
el **modo**   way, manner; **de
todos —s**   anyway, in any
case; **de — que**   so that;
— de pensar   way of
thinking
molestar   to bother
el **momento**   moment; **de
un — a otro**   any minute
now
el (la) **monarca**   monarch
el **monje**   monk
el **mono**   monkey
montar   to mount; to set up
la **moral**   morale; *adj* moral
la **moralidad**   morality
morir (ue, u)   to die
la **mosca**   fly; **¡por si las
moscas!**   Just in case!
mostrar (ue)   to show
la **motocicleta (moto)**
motorcycle
movido   fast-moving
el **movimiento**   movement
la **muchacha**   girl
el **muchacho**   boy; *pl* children, boys, boy(s) and girl(s)
mucho *adj*   much, a lot of;
very; *pl* many; *adv* very
much, a lot; **muchas veces**
many times, often
la **muerte**   death
el **muerto (la muerta)**   dead
person, corpse; *adj* dead
la **mujer**   woman; wife
el **mundo**   world; **todo el —**
everybody
el **museo**   museum
la **música**   music
muy   very

N

nacer   to be born
la **nación**   nation
la **nacionalidad**   nationality
nada   nothing, not anything;
de —   you're welcome
nadar   to swim
nadie   no one, nobody, not
anyone
la **naranja**   orange
la **nariz**   nose
la **natación**   swimming
nativo   native
naturalmente   naturally
la **navaja**   knife; blade
la **navegación**   navigation
la **Navidad**   Christmas
necesario   necessary
la **necesidad**   necessity
necesitar   to need
negar (ie)   to deny
el **negocio**   business
negro   black
el **nervio**   nerve
nervioso   nervous
ni   nor; not even; **—... —**
neither . . . nor; **¡Ni
pensarlo!**   No way!
ningún, ninguno   none, not
any, no
la **niña**   girl
el **niño**   boy; *pl* children,
kids
no   no, not; **—... más que**
nothing more than; **¡No me
digas!**   You don't say!
la **noción**   idea, notion
la **noche**   night, evening; **de
la —**   P.M.; **esta —**
tonight; **Nochebuena**
Christmas Eve; **pasar la —**
to spend the night; **por la
—**   in the evening
nombrar   to name
el **nombre**   name; **— de pila**
first name
el **norte**   north
norteamericano   North
American, American
norteño   northern
nos   us, ourselves

nosotros (nosotras)   we,
us (*after prep*)
las **noticias**   news
la **novedad**   novelty
noventa   ninety
la **novia**   financée, girlfriend;
bride
noviembre   November
el **novio**   fiancé, boyfriend;
groom
la **nube**   cloud
nublado   cloudy
nuestro(s), nuestra(s) *adj*
our, of ours; **el nuestro
(la nuestra, los nuestros,
las nuestras)** *pr* ours;
lo nuestro   what is ours
nueve   nine
nuevo   new; **¿Qué hay de
—?**   What's new?
el **número**   number
numeroso   numerous
nunca   never, not ever

O

o   or, either
obedecer   to obey
el **objeto**   object
obligado (a)   obliged (to)
la **obra**   work; play (theater)
¡Manos a la —!   Let's get
to work!
el **obrero (la obrera)**   worker
la **observación**   observation
obtener   to get, obtain
la **ocasión**   occasion
occidental   western
el **occidente**   west
octavo   eighth
octubre   October
la **ocupación**   occupation
ocupar   to occupy
ocurrir   to occur, happen
ochenta   eighty
ocho   eight
odiar   to hate
el **oficial**   officer; official
la **oficina**   office
ofrecer   to offer
oír   to hear

ojalá (que) would that, I hope that

el **ojo** eye

olvidar to forget, leave behind; **—se (de)** to forget (about)

once eleven

la **oportunidad** opportunity

la **oposición** opposition

oponerse (a) to oppose

la **orden** order; **a sus órdenes** at your service

la **organizacion** organization

organizar to organize

orgulloso proud

el **origen** origin

la **originalidad** originality

el **oro** gold

la **orquesta** orchestra

os you, yourselves (*fam pl*)

oscuro dark

el **otoño** autumn, fall

otro other, another; **otra vez** again; **otra cosa** anything (something) else

P

la **paciencia** patience; **tener —** to be patient

el **(la) paciente** patient

padecer to suffer

el **padre** father; priest; *pl* parents; **por parte de —** on the father's side

pagar to pay

la **página** page

el **país** country; nation

la **palabra** word; **juego de —s** play on words, word play

el **palacio** palace

pálido pale

la **palma** palm tree

el **pan** bread

los **pantalones** pants

la **papa** potato

el **papá** father, dad

el **papel** paper; role

el **par** pair; couple

para for, in order to, to; by; **— fines de** towards (by)

the end of; **— que** *conj* so that, in order that

parar(se) to stop, halt; **—se** to stand up

parecer to seem, appear; **— se a** to look like, resemble

la **pared** wall

el (la) **pariente** relative

el **parque** park

la **parte** part, portion; **de — de** from; **en todas —s de** everywhere in; **formar — de** to be a part of

la **participación** participation

participar to participate

el **partido** game, match

partir to leave; **a — de** as of

la **pasada** passing through

el **pasado** past; *adj* past, last; **el año —** last year

pasar to pass, get by; to take place, happen; to spend (time); **—lo bien** to have a good time; **¿Qué pasa?** What's the matter?

el **paseo** walk, stroll; ride; **dar un —** to take a walk

el **pasillo** hallway

el **pastor** (la **pastora**) shepherd

la **pata** leg (of an animal); **meter la —** to goof

el (la) **patriota** patriot

el **patrocinador** (la **patrocinadora**) sponsor

el **payaso** clown

la **paz** peace

pedir (i, i) to ask for, request

la **película** movie, film

peligroso dangerous

el **pelo** hair

el **pensamiento** thought

pensar (ie) to think; to plan, intend (to do something); **— de** to think of, have an opinion of; **— en** to think about, occupy one's thoughts with; **¡Ni pen-**

sarlo! No way!

peor worse, worst

pequeño little, small

perder (ie) to lose; **echar a —** to spoil, ruin; **— el tiempo** to waste one's time; **—se** to get lost

la **pérdida** loss

perdido lost

el **perdón** pardon; **¡Perdón!** Excuse me!

la **perfección** perfection; **a la —** perfectly

el **perfil** profile

el **periódico** newspaper

permanecer to remain

pero but

el **perro** dog

perseguir (i, i) to chase

la **persona** person; **— mayor** adult

perspicaz observant, clever

pertencer to belong

pesar to weigh

pescar to fish

el **peso** monetary unit in many Spanish American countries; weight; **levantamiento de —** weightlifting

el **pez** (*pl* **peces**) fish

el **pico** beak; **... y —** ... and a little

el **pie** foot; **a —** on foot

la **piedra** rock

la **piel** skin

pintar to paint

el **pintor** (la **pintora**) painter

pintoresco picturesque

la **pintura** painting; paint

la **pistola** pistol

la **pizarra** blackboard

planchar to iron

platicar (*Mex*) to chat

el **plato** dish; plate

la **playa** beach

la **plaza** plaza, square; bullring

la **población** population

pobre poor; unfortunate

la **pobreza** poverty

poco little (amount); *pl*
few; **— a —** little by little
poder (ue) to be able, can;
puede ser (que) it may
be (that)
poderoso powerful
el **poema** poem
el **poeta (la poetisa)** poet
poner to put, place; **—se**
to put on; to become
la **popularidad** popularity
por for; by; per; on account
of, because of; along;
through; in exchange for; **—**
ahora for the time being;
— aquí around here; **—**
casualidad by chance; **—**
ciento percent; **— cierto**
as a matter of fact;
— correo by mail; **—**
ejemplo for example;
— el estilo like that,
along those lines; **— eso**
for that reason; therefore;
—favor please; **—fin** at
last, finally; **— lo menos**
at least; **— lo pronto** for
the time being, for now;
—lo tanto therefore; **—lo**
visto apparently; **¡Por si**
las moscas! Just in case!
— su cuenta on one's
own
el **porcentaje** percentage
los **pormenores** particulars
porque because
¿por qué? why?
portugués (portuguesa)
n and adj Portuguese
el **porvenir** future
posiblemente possibly
la **posición** position
postal: apartado — post
office box
practicar to practice
el **precio** price
precioso beautiful, precious
precisamente precisely
preciso necessary; precise
predecir (i, i) to predict

preferir (ie, i) to prefer
la **pregunta** question; **hacer**
una — to ask a question
preguntar to ask (a question)
el **prejuicio** prejudice
el **preludio** prelude
el **premio** prize
la **preocupación** worry
preocupar to bother; **—se**
(por) to worry (about)
preparar to prepare
la **presencia** presence
presenciar to watch; to
witness
la **presentación** presentation;
appearance; introduction
presentar to produce, present; to introduce
el **presidente** president
prestar to lend; **—atención**
to pay attention
el **pretexto** pretext, excuse,
pretense
prevenir to warn
la **primavera** spring
primer, primero first
el **primo (la prima)** cousin
el **principio** the beginning;
a —s de at the beginning
of
la **prisa: darse —** to hurry;
tener — to be in a hurry
privilegiado privileged
el **problema** problem
la **procedencia** origin
la **procesión** procession
el **proceso** process; lawsuit
producir to produce
el **producto** product
el **profe** prof
la **profesión** profession
el **profesor (la profesora)**
professor
el **profesorado** faculty
profundo deep, profound
el **programa** program
el **progreso** progress
prohibir to prohibit,
forbid

la **promoción** publicity, pro-
motion
pronto soon; quickly; **de —**
suddenly; **lo más —**
posible as soon as
possible; **por lo —** for
now, for the time being;
tan — como as soon as
propiamente properly
propio own
proporcionar to provide
el **propósito** purpose; **a —**
by the way
la **propuesta** proposal, bid
proteger to protect
la **protesta** protest
el **proverbio** proverb
la **provincia** province
próximo next, coming
el **proyecto** project
la **publicidad** advertising
el **público** public; audience;
en — publicly
el **pueblo** people; village,
town
el **puente** bridge
la **puerta** door
puertorriqueño Puerto
Rican
pues well...; **¡Pues sí!**
Sure!
el **puesto** position; **llevar —**
to wear, to have on; **— que**
since
la **pulga** flea
el **punto** point; period; **en —**
sharp, on the dot (time)
puntualizado punctuated
el **puro** cigar; *adj* pure

Q

que that, which, who,
whom; than; **el (la, los,**
las) — the one(s) who,
which; **hay — + *inf*** it is
necessary + *inf*; **lo —**
what, that which; **tener —**
to have to
¿qué? what? which? **¿Eso**
qué importa? What does

that matter? **o — sé yo** or
whatever; **¿Qué hay de
nuevo?** What's new?
¿Qué más da? What difference does it make?
¡qué! What (a) . . . !, How
. . . ! **¡Qué bien!** Great!
¡Qué fastidio! What a
problem! **¡Qué lata!**
What a pain! **¡Qué rico!**
Great! How delicious!
quedar to have left (over);
to remain; **— tiempo** to
have time left; **—se** to
stay, remain; **—se con** to
keep
quejarse (de) to complain
(about)
querer (ie) to want; to love;
— decir to mean, to
signify
querido dear
el **queso** cheese
quien, quienes who,
whom; the one(s) who
¿quién? ¿quiénes? who?,
whom? **¿de —?** whose?
quince fifteen
quinientos (quinientas)
five hundred
quinto fifth
quitar to take away; **—se**
to take off
quizá(s) perhaps, maybe

R

rabioso furious
la **raíz** root
el **rancho** ranch
rápidamente quickly,
rapidly
rápido fast
raptar to kidnap
raro strange
el **rato** while, short time;
hace un — a while ago
el **ratón** mouse
la **raza** race
la **razón** reason; **tener —** to
be right

la **realidad** reality; **en —**
actually, in reality
realmente really, actually
rebasar to surpass
rebelarse to rebel
la **rebelión** rebellion
el **recado** message
recibir to receive
el **recibo** receipt; **acusar —**
to acknowledge receipt
recientemente recently
recíproco reciprocal
recitar to recite
la **reclamación** protest,
complaint; accusation
recoger to pick up
recompensar to reward
reconocer to recognize
recordar (ue) to remember; to remind, call to mind
recrear to recreate; **—se**
to enjoy oneself
el **rector** president (of a
university)
rechazar to reject
el **rechazo** rejection
reducir to reduce
la **referencia** reference
referirse (ie, i) (a) to
refer (to)
reflejar to reflect
el **reflejo** reflection
el **refrán** proverb
el **refresco** soft drink; *pl*
refreshments
regalar to give (as a gift)
el **regalo** gift
el **regocijo** joy
regresar to return
regular so-so
la **reina** queen
el **reino** kingdom
reír (i, i) to laugh
relativo relative, as compared to
el **relato** story, tale
religioso religious
el **reloj** watch
remar to row, go rowing
el **remo** rowing; oar

renacentista (*m and f*)
renaissance (*adj*)
la **renuncia** resignation
reparar to repair
repasar to review
repetir (i, i) to repeat
la **representación** represen-
tation, portrayal
el **requisito** requirement
el **resfriado** cold
la **residencia** residence
residir to reside
resistir to withstand; to
resist
resolver (ue) to solve,
resolve
respaldarse to lean against
respetable honorable
el **respeto** respect
responder to answer
la **responsabilidad** responsi-
bility
responsable responsible
restaurado restored
el **restaurante** restaurant
resuelto settled, resolved
el **resultado** result
resultar to work out; to
result, turn out, be
el **resumen** résumé
retener to retain
retesabroso superdelicious
retrasar to delay; **—se**
to be delayed, be late; to
fall behind
la **reunión** meeting
la **reverencia** bow, curtsy
revisar to go over; to
revise
la **revista** magazine
el **rey** king
rico rich; tasty; **¡Qué —!**
Great! How delicious!
ridículo ridiculous
el **río** river
la **riqueza** wealth
la **risa** laugh; laughter
el **ritmo** rhythm
el **rito** rite
robusto robust

rodear to surround
rojo red
romántico romantic
el **rompecabezas** puzzle
la **ropa** clothing; **— interior** underwear
el **ruido** noise
la **ruina** ruin
rutinario routine

S

S.A. (Sociedad Anónima) Inc.
el **sábado** Saturday
el **sabelotodo** know-it-all
saber to know, know how; **— de memoria** to know by heart
sabio wise
sabroso tasty, delicious
el **saco** bag, sack; **— de dormir** sleeping bag
sacrificar to sacrifice
la **sal** salt
la **salida** exit; departure
salir (de) to leave, go (come) out (of)
el **salón** room, living room
salvo safe; **sano y —** safe and sound
sano healthy
el **santo (la santa)** saint
se *i o p* him, her, it, you, them; *refl pr* himself, herself, itself, yourself, themselves, yourselves; *reciprocal pr* each other, one another; *indef subject* one, people, you, etc.
seco dry
secreto secret
la **sed** thirst; **tener —** to be thirsty
segregado segregated
seguida: en — right away
seguir (i, i) to continue, go on; to follow
según according to
segundo second
seguramente surely,

certainly
la **seguridad** security
seis six
seiscientos six hundred
la **semana** week; **fin de —** weekend; **la — pasada** last week; **la — que viene** next week
semejante similar
sencillamente simply
sencillo simple, easy
la **sensibilidad** sensibility, sensitivity
sentar(se) (ie) to sit down
el **sentimiento** feeling, sentiment
sentir (ie, i) to feel; to regret, be sorry; **—se** to feel; **— celos** to feel jealous;
el **señor** (*abbr* Sr.) gentleman, man; sir; Mr.; *pl* Mr. and Mrs., ladies and gentlemen; gentlemen
la **señora** (*abbr* Sra.) lady; wife; ma'am, Mrs.
la **señorita** (*abbr* Srta.) young lady; miss
septiembre September
séptimo seventh
el **séquito** retinue
ser to be; *m* being; **— humano** human being
serio serious; **en —** seriously
la **serpiente** serpent, snake
servir (i, i) to serve; **— para** to be good for; **—se de** to use, make use of
sesenta sixty
setecientos seven hundred
setenta seventy
el **sexo** sex
sexto sixth
la **sexualidad** sexuality
si if; **como —** as if
sí yes; **¿Ah, —?** Really? **Creo que —** I think so; **¡Pues sí!** Sure!
siempre always

siete seven
el **siglo** century
el **significado** meaning
significar to signify, mean
siguiente following, next
la **sílaba** syllable
la **silla** chair
simpático nice, pleasant
simplemente simply
sin without; **— embargo** however; **— más** without further ado; **— que** without
sinceramente sincerely
sincero sincere
sindicalizar to unionize, syndicate
la **sinfonía** symphony
sino but, but rather
el (la) **sinvergüenza** creep, scoundrel
el **sistema** system
el **sitio** place, site
la **situación** situation
sobre on; over; about; **— todo** above all, especially
sobrio sober
la **sociedad** society
la **soga** rope
el **sol** sun
solamente only
el **soldado** soldier
solicitar to solicit
sólido solid
solo alone; single
sólo only, just
el **solsticio** solstice
soltar (ue) to release
sonar (ue) to sound; to ring (a telephone)
el **sonido** noise
sonreír (i, i) to smile
la **sonrisa** smile
soñar to dream
la **sopa** soup
sorprender to surprise
la **sorpresa** surprise
sospechoso suspicious
su, sus his, her, its, your

(*formal*), their
subir   to go up, climb
suceder   to happen
el **suceso**   event
sucio   dirty
el **sueldo**   salary
el **suelo**   ground; floor
el **sueño**   dream; sleep;
   tener —   to be sleepy
la **suerte**   luck; **tener —**   to
   be lucky
suficiente   sufficient,
   enough
sufrir   to suffer; **— daños**
   to suffer damages
la **sugerencia**   suggestion
suicidarse   to commit
   suicide
suizo   Swiss
suponer   to suppose
suprimir   to eliminate
supuesto: por —   of course
el **sur**   south; **la América del
   Sur**   South America
el **suroeste**   southwest
la **sutileza**   subtlety
suyo(s), suya(s) *adj*   his, of
   his, her, of hers, your, of
   yours (*formal*), their, of
   theirs; **el suyo (la suya,
   los suyos, las suyas)** *pr*
   his, hers, yours, theirs

T

tal   such (a); **con — que**
   provided that; **— vez**
   perhaps
el **talento**   talent
el **tamaño**   size
también   also, too
tampoco   neither, not either
tan   so; such; **—... como**
   as . . . as
tanto   so much, as much; *pl*
   so many, as many; **por lo
   —**   therefore; **— como**   as
   much as; as well as
la **taquilla**   ticket office
tardar   to take (time); to be
   long

la **tarde**   afternoon; **de la —**
   P.M.; **por la —**   in the
   afternoon; *adv.*   late
la **tarea**   homework
te   you, yourself (*fam s*)
el **té**   tea
el **teatro**   theater
el **teléfono**   telephone
el **tema**   subject, theme
temer   to fear
el **temor**   fear
el **templo**   temple
temprano   early
tener   to have, possess; **no
   — chiste**   not to be any
   fun; **— ... años**   to be . . .
   years old; **— calor**   to be
   hot; **— cuidado**   to be
   careful; **— en cuenta**   to
   bear in mind; **—frío**   to be
   cold; **— ganas de**   to be
   anxious (to); **— hambre**
   to be hungry; **— lugar**   to
   take place; **— miedo**   to
   be afraid; **— paciencia**
   to be patient; **— prisa**   to
   be in a hurry; **—que**   to
   have to; **— razón**   to be
   right; **— sed**   to be
   thirsty; **— suerte**   to be
   lucky
el **tenis**   tennis
el **tercer, tercero**   third
terminar   to finish
el **territorio**   territory
el **terrorista**   terrorist
el **tesoro**   treasure
el **testimonio**   testimony
ti   *obj of prep*   you, yourself
la **tía**   aunt
el **tiempo**   time; weather;
   al mismo —   at the same
   time; **a —**   on time, in
   time; **en poco —**   in a
   short time; **hacer buen —**
   to be nice weather;
   mucho —   a long time;
   ¿(por) cuánto —?   how
   long?; **—s antiguos**
   ancient times

la **tienda**   store
la **tierra**   land, earth
la **timidez**   shyness
el **tío**   uncle; (*coll*) guy
el **tipo**   type, kind
tirar   to knock over; to throw
el **tiro**   shooting; shot
el **título**   title
el **tobillo**   ankle
tocar   to touch; to play (a
   musical instrument)
todavía   still, yet; **— no**
   not yet
todo   all, whole; every; **— el
   día**   all day; **—s los días**
   every day; *pr* everything;
   sobre —   especially, above
   all; *pl pr* everyone, all of
   them
tomar   to take; to have
   (drink)
el **tomate**   tomato
el **tono**   tone
la **tontería**   foolishness
tonto   silly, stupid
torcido   twisted
el **torero**   bullfighter
el **toro**   bull; **corrida de —s**
   bullfight
torpe   clumsy
torturar   torture
totalmente   totally
trabajar   to work
el **trabajo**   work, job
la **tradición**   tradition
tradicional   traditional
traducir   to translate
traer   to bring
el **traje**   suit; **— de baño**
   bathing suit
el **trámite**   step, transaction
tranquilo   calm, quiet,
   tranquil
el **tránsito**   traffic
el **transporte**   transportation
tras   after, following
trasladar   to transfer, move
el **traste**   contraption, gadget
tratar (de)   to try; **— de**
   to be about, deal with

través: a — de throughout; across, through
trece thirteen
treinta thirty
tremendo tremendous
el **tren** train
tres three
trescientos three hundred
triste sad
la **tristeza** sadness
triunfar to win, triumph
tu, tus your
tú you (*fam*)
la **tumba** grave, tomb
el (la) **turista** tourist
tuyo(s), tuya(s) *adj* your, of yours; **el tuyo (la tuya, los tuyos, las tuyas)** *pr* yours; **lo tuyo** what is yours

U

u or (used for **o** before the sound /o/)
último last, latest; **a última hora** at the last minute
un, uno, una a, an, one
único only; unique
la **unidad** unity
unido united; **los Estados Unidos** the United States
el **uniforme** uniform
unirse (a) to join
la **universidad** university
unos, unas some, a few, several; about (quantity)
urbano urban
usado used
usar to use
el **uso** use, purpose
usted, ustedes (*abbr* **Ud., Uds.**) you (*formal*)
útil useful
utópico utopian
la **uva** grape

V

las **vacaciones** vacation
vacante vacant, empty

la **vacilación** vacillation, hesitancy
la **vainilla** vanilla
la **vajilla** (set of) dishes
valer to be worth; to cost
valiente courageous, brave
valioso valuable
¡Vamos! Come on!
variar to vary
la **variedad** variety
varios several
vasco Basque
el **vaso** glass
el **vecindario** neighborhood
el **vecino** (la **vecina**) neighbor
veinte twenty
vencer to win, triumph; to overcome
el **vendedor** (la **vendedora**) vendor, salesperson
vender to sell
venidero upcoming
venir (i) to come; **—se** to come along
la **venta** sale
la **ventaja** advantage
ver to see
veraniego summery
el **verano** summer
veras: de — real, true; really, truly
la **verdad** truth; **¿verdad?** right? true? **de —** true, real
verde green
la **vergüenza** shame; **dar —** to embarrass
verificar to verify
el **verso** verse; poem
el **vestido** dress
vestir to dress; **—se** to get dressed
la **vez** (*pl* **veces**) time (in a series); **a la —** at the same time, at once; **alguna —** sometime; **a veces** at times, sometimes; **de una —** once and for all; **de — en cuando** once in

a while; **en — de** instead of; **muchas veces** many times, often; **otra —** again; **tal —** perhaps
viajar to travel
el **viaje** trip; **hacer un —** to take a trip
vicioso depraved, perverted
la **vida** life
viejo old; *n* old person
el **viento** wind; **hacer —** to be windy
viernes Friday
el **villancico** Christmas carol
el **vino** wine
violar to rape
vivir to live
vivo alive; clever, bright, lively
el **vocabulario** vocabulary
el **vólibol** volleyball
el **volumen** volume
la **voluntad** will, effort
volver (ue) to return; **— a** + *inf* (verb) again; **—se** to become, turn into
vosotros you, yourselves (*fam*)
votar to vote
la **voz** voice
la **vuelta** turn; return; **a — de correo** by return mail
vuestro(s), vuestra(s) *adj* your, of yours; **el vuestro los vuestros, las vuestras)** *pr* yours; **lo vuestro** what is yours

Y

y and; **— pico** and a little
ya already; now; **— que** since, as
el **yate** yacht
la **yerba** grass
yo I

Z

la **zapatería** shoestore
el **zapato** shoe; **cordón de—** shoelace

English-Spanish Vocabulary

A

a, an un, una
able: be — poder (ue)
about sobre, acerca de; de; **at —** a eso de
accept aceptar
accompany acompañar
according to según
act actuar; portarse
ad anuncio
adult persona mayor, adulto
advantage ventaja
afraid: be — (of) tener miedo (de)
after después (de)
afternoon la tarde; **in the —** por la tarde; de la tarde (when the hour is given)
afterwards después
again otra vez, de nuevo; volver a + *inf*
against contra
age la edad
agency: tourist — agencia de turismo
ago hace + *time expression* + que + *verb in preterit*
airplane el avión
alive vivo
all todo(-a); **— right** bien
allow dejar, permitir
almost casi
alone solo
already ya
also también
although aunque
always siempre
A.M. de la mañana
ambiguous ambiguo
America América; **Spanish —** Hispanoamérica
among entre
ancestor antepasado
ancient antiguo
and y; e
angry furioso
ankle tobillo

another otro(-a)
answer la contestación; *v* contestar, responder
anticipation la anticipación
anxious: be — to tener ganas (de)
any algún, alguno; (*after negative*) ningún, ninguno
anyone alguien; alguno; (*after negative*) nadie
anything algo; (*after negative*) nada
apology disculpa
apparently aparentemente, por lo visto
April abril
aristocrat el (la) aristócrata
arm brazo
around alrededor (de)
arrive llegar; **to have just —** acabar de llegar
article artículo
as como; **as . . . as** tan... como; **— if** como si
ask (*inquire*) preguntar; **— (for)** pedir (i, i)
assignment asignatura
astonished asombrado
at a; en; **— home** en casa; **— noon** al mediodía
athlete el (la) atleta
attack el ataque; *v* atacar
attend asistir (a)
attitude la actitud
August agosto
aunt tía
authorities la autoridad
avenue avenida
awaken despertar(se) (ie)
away: go — irse; **right —** en seguida

B

bad mal, malo
be estar, ser; tener; hacer; **— able** poder (ue); **—**

called llamarse; **— cold** (*a living being*) tener frío, (*weather*)hacer frío; **— sunny** hacer sol; **— . . . years old** tener... años
beach playa
beautiful hermoso, bello, lindo, bonito; precioso
because porque; **— of** a causa de
become ponerse; volverse (ue), hacerse; llegar a ser
bed cama; **go to —** acostarse (ue)
beer cerveza
before antes (de)
begin empezar (ie), comenzar (ie)
behind detrás de
believe creer
beneath debajo de
best mejor; **the — thing** lo mejor
bet apostar (ue)
better mejor
bicycle bicicleta, bici
big grande; **— shot** el mandamás
bilingual bilingüe
bill cuenta; el billete
birthday el cumpleaños
black negro
boast jactarse (de)
book libro
bookstore librería
bored aburrido
born: be — nacer
boss el jefe (la jefa); el mandamás (*sl*)
both ambos
bother molestar; preocupar
boy muchacho, niño, chico, chamaco, chiquillo
boyfriend novio
brave valiente
bravery valentía
break romper

bring traer
brother hermano
bull toro
bus el autobús
but pero; **— rather** sino
buy comprar
by por; **— plane** en avión;
   — the way a propósito

C

call llamar; **be called**
   llamarse
can poder (ue); (*know how*)
   saber
car el coche, el automóvil
careful! ¡cuidado! **be —**
   tener cuidado
carry llevar
cause causa
cave cueva
celebrate celebrar
century siglo
certain seguro
change cambiar
chat charlar, platicar
chauvinist el (la) chauvinista
cheer animar; **Cheer up!**
   ¡Anímate!
cheese queso
children niños, chamacos,
   chiquillos; hijos
choose escoger
Christmas la navidad
church iglesia
citizen ciudadano(-a)
city la ciudad
class la clase; **in —** en clase
classroom el aula (*f*), sala de
   clase
clean limpio
clever listo, perspicaz
climb subir
clinic clínica
close cerca; *v* cerrar (ie)
clown el bufón, payaso
clumsy torpe
coach el entrenador
cold frío; **be —** (*a living
   being*) tener frío, (*weather*)
   hacer frío; **to have a —**

estar constipado, tener un
   resfriado
come venir; **— back** volver,
   regresar; **— by** pasar por
committee el comité
company compañía, empresa,
   firma
complain (about) quejarse
   (de)
compose componer
composition la composición
concert concierto
confide (in) confiar (en)
congratulate felicitar
construct construir
contest concurso
continue continuar, seguir
contract contrato
contraption el traste
convince convencer
cool: be — hacer fresco
cost valer, costar (ue)
country (*nation*) el país;
   (*landscape*) campo
course curso; **Of —!** ¡Claro!,
   ¡Por supuesto!, ¡Cómo no!
cousin primo(-a)
cover cubrir
covered (with) cubierto (de)
cowardice cobardía
crazy loco; **become —**
   enloquecerse, volverse loco
creep majadero, el (la)
   sinvergüenza
criticize criticar
Cuban cubano
culture cultura
cynic cínico

D

damned maldito
dance el baile; *v* bailar
dare atreverse
date cita; fecha
daughter hija
day el día; **all —** todo el día;
   every — todos los días
dead muerto; **the —** los
   muertos
deal: a great — mucho

dear querido
December diciembre
decide decidir
decision la decisión
demand demanda
democratically democráticamente
dentist el (la) dentista
deny negar (ie)
deserve merecer
desk escritorio
destroy destruir
detail el detalle
diamond el brillante, el
   diamante
die morir (ue, u)
different distinto, diferente
difficult difícil
diligent aplicado
dinner cena, comida
dirty sucio
discover descubrir
discuss discutir
dish plato
disobedient desobediente
disrespectful irrespetuoso
do hacer
dollar el dólar
donkey burro
door puerta
doubt duda; **without a —**
   sin duda; *v* dudar
downtown centro
dream sueño; *v* soñar (ue)
dress vestido; **to get —ed**
   vestirse (i, i)
drink tomar, beber
dry seco
during durante

E

each cada
eagle el águila (*f*)
early temprano; **too —**
   demasiado temprano
earn ganar
earth tierra
easily fácilmente
easy fácil
eat comer

education la educación

effort esfuerzo

eight ocho

eighth octavo

either o; (*after negative*) tampoco

elderly viejo, anciano

elect elegir (i, i)

eleven once

engagement compromiso; *adj* de compromiso

engineer ingeniero

English inglés

enjoy disfrutar (de); — **oneself** divertirse (ie, i)

enter entrar (en)

entrance entrada

era época

erase borrar

esteemed estimado

even aun; hasta; — **though** aunque

evening la noche; **in the —** por la noche

event suceso, hecho

everybody todos, todo el mundo

everything todo

exactly exactamente

exaggeration la exageración

exam el examen, prueba

example ejemplo; **for —** por ejemplo

excavate excavar

excellent excelente

exciting emocionante

exhibit la exhibición, la exposición

exhibition la exhibición

exit salida

explain explicar

explorer el explorador (la exploradora)

expression la expresión

eye ojo

F

face cara

fact hecho; *pl* datos, hechos; **as a matter of —** por cierto

faculty profesorado

fall caer(se)

family familia

famous famoso

far lejos

fast rápido

father el padre, el papá, el papi

fear temor; *v* temer

February febrero

feel sentir (ie, i); — **well (bad)** sentirse bien (mal)

few pocos; **a —** unos, unas (pocos, -as)

fifteen quince

fifth quinto

fight luchar

finally por fin

find encontrar (ue)

finish terminar, acabar

first primer, primero; **at —** al principio

fit caber

five cinco

fix arreglar, componer

flag bandera

floor suelo; piso

follow seguir (i, i)

food comida

for por, para

foreign extranjero

forget olvidar(se) (de que)

form forma

former antiguo

four cuatro

fourth cuarto

free libre; gratis

Friday viernes

friend amigo, amiga

from de, desde

front: in — of enfrente de

frozen helado

fun: to make — (of) burlarse (de)

function funcionar, andar

future el porvenir, futuro

G

game partido

generally generalmente

get conseguir (i, i); — **out**

salir (de); — **up** levantarse

gift regalo

girl muchacha, chica, niña

girlfriend novia

give dar; regalar; **to — back** devolver (ue)

glory gloria

go ir (a); — **away** irse, marcharse; **let's —** vamos, vámonos

god el dios

good buen, bueno; **—-looking** guapo, hermoso; **Good morning** Buenos días

goodbye adiós

Gothic gótico

grandparents abuelos

grass yerba

great gran (before a singular noun)

greatest mayor; mejor

green verde

group grupo

grow crecer

guilty culpable

gypsy gitano, gitana

H

half medio; — **an hour** media hora

hallway pasillo

hand la mano

handsome guapo

hang (up) colgar (ue)

happen pasar, ocurrir, suceder

happy contento, feliz; **become —** alegrarse

hate odiar

have tener; (*auxiliary*) haber; (*indirect command*) que + *pres subjunctive*; — **just** acabar de; — **left** quedar; — **to** tener que

he él

healthy sano

hear oír

hello hola

help ayudar

her *adj* su, sus; *d o p* la; *i o p* le, se; *obj of prep* ella

here aquí; **around —** por aquí

hers suyo (-a, -os, -as), de ella

hide esconder

highway carretera

him *d o p* lo; *i o p* le, se; *obj of prep* él

his su, sus, de él

Hispanic hispano

historian el historiador

historical histórico

history historia

home el hogar, casa; **at —** en casa

homework tarea

hope esperar; (*impersonal*) ojalá (que)

hot caliente; **be —** (*weather*) hacer calor; (*a living being*) tener calor

hour hora; **half an —** media hora

house casa

how? ¿cómo? **how . . .!** ¡ qué...! ¡ cuánto...!

however sin embargo

hundred cien, ciento

hungry: be — tener hambre (*f*)

hurry darse prisa; **be in a —** tener prisa

husband esposo, marido

I

I yo

ice hielo

if si; **as —** como si

imagine imaginar(se)

immediately inmediatamente

immorality inmoralidad

importance importancia

important importante

impress impresionar

in en; **— order that** para que; **— order to** para

include incluir

incredible increíble

indefinitely indefinidamente

inform informar

inhabitant el (la) habitante

initiative iniciativa

inside dentro

inspire inspirar

instead (of) en vez de

intelligent inteligente

intend pensar (ie) + *inf*

interesting interesante

introduce presentar

invite convidar (a), invitar

invoice factura

iron planchar

it *d o p* lo, la; *i o p* le, se; *obj of prep* él, ella

J

January enero

jealous: be — sentir (ie, i) celos

jewel joya

job empleo, trabajo

joke el chiste

July julio

June junio

just: have — acabar de

justice justicia

K

keep quedarse con

kid niño(-a), chamaco(-a), chiquillo(-a)

kill matar

kilometer kilómetro

king el rey

kingdom reino

know (*facts*) saber; (*be acquainted with*) conocer

L

lack faltar

lady dama, señora

lake lago

language el idioma, lengua; **foreign —** idioma extranjero

large grande

last último; pasado; *v* durar

late tarde; **too —** demasiado tarde

later después; más tarde

laugh reír

law la ley

leader el líder

learn aprender (a)

least menos; **at —** por lo menos

leave irse, salir, partir; **— behind** dejar

lecture conferencia

lend prestar

less menos

lesson la lección

let dejar, permitir

letter carta

liar mentiroso

library biblioteca

lie mentira

life vida

lift levantar

like como; *v* gustar

listen (to) escuchar

little pequeño; poco; **a —** un poco; **— by —** poco a poco

live vivir

lively vivo

lock up encerrar (ie)

long largo; **— -standing** viejo (before a noun)

look (at) mirar, fijarse (en); **— for** buscar; **— like** parecer(se) (a)

lose perder (ie)

lot: a — mucho

love el amor; *v* querer (ie, i)

lucky afortunado; **be —** tener suerte, ser afortunado

M

machine máquina

magazine revista

magnificent magnífico

mail correo; **by return —** a vuelta de correo

make hacer

man el hombre; **young —** el joven

manage (+*inf*) lograr

manager el gerente

many muchos; **as — . . . as** tantos(-as)... como; **how —?** ¿cuántos(-as)? **so —** tantos(-as)

March marzo

marry casarse

mathematics matemáticas

matter asunto; *v* importar; **What does that —!** ¡Eso qué importa!

May mayo

maybe quizá(s), tal vez, acaso

me me; *obj of prep* mí; **with — ** conmigo

meal comida

mean querer decir

meaning significado

means medios; **by — of** mediante, por medio de

meet conocer

meeting la reunión

memorize aprender de memoria, memorizar

message el mensaje, recado

midnight la medianoche

milk la leche

mine mío(-a, -os, -as)

minus menos

minute minuto; **at the last — ** a última hora

miss señorita, Srta.; *v* echar de menos

moment momento

Monday lunes

money dinero

month el mes; **last — ** el mes pasado

**mood: be in a good (bad) — ** estar de buen (mal) humor

morality la moralidad

more más

moreover además

morning mañana; **Good — ** Buenos días; **in the — ** por la mañana, de la mañana (when the hour is given)

most *adv* más; **— of** la mayor parte de

mother la madre, mamá

motorcycle motocicleta, la moto

mouth boca

movie película; **— house** el cine

Mr. señor, Sr.; **— and Mrs.** los señores, los Sres.

much mucho; **as — (as)**

tanto(a) (como); **how —?** ¿cuánto? **very — ** mucho, muchísimo

mud lodo, fango

museum museo

music música

my mi, mis

mythology mitología

N

name el nombre; **first — ** nombre de pila; **sur—** apellido

near cerca (de)

necessary necesario

need necesitar, faltar

neighborhood barrio, vecindario

neither tampoco; **— . . . nor** ni... ni

nerves nervios

never nunca, jamás

nevertheless sin embargo

new nuevo; *pl* noticias

newspaper periódico

next próximo, siguiente; **— week (month)** la semana (el mes) que viene

nice amable, simpático

night la noche; **at — ** por la noche; **Good — ** Buenas noches; **last — ** anoche

nine nueve

ninth noveno

no no; ningún, ninguno; **— one** nadie

nobody nadie

none ningún, ninguno

noon el mediodía; **at — ** al mediodía

nor ni

north el norte

not no

notes los apuntes

nothing nada; **be — more than** no ser más que; **— special** nada de particular

notice fijarse (en), ver; darse cuenta (de que)

novelty la novedad

November noviembre

now ahora; **right — ** ahora mismo

nowadays hoy día

number número

O

obscene obsceno

**o'clock: at one (three) — ** a la una (las tres)

October octubre

of de, a

offer ofrecer

office oficina

often a menudo, frecuentemente, con frecuencia

old viejo; **be . . . years — ** tener... años; **how — is . . .?** ¿cuántos años tiene...?

older mayor

on en, sobre

once una vez; **— and for all** de una vez

one un, uno; **no — ** nadie; **— must (do)** hay que; **— o'clock** la una

only sólo

open abierto; *v* abrir

opportunity la oportunidad

or o; u

orchestra orquesta

order la orden; **in — to** para; *v* mandar, ordenar

other otro

ought to deber

our, ours nuestro(-a, -os, -as)

over sobre; encima de

owe deber

P

paint pintura; *v* pintar

painter el pintor

painting pintura, cuadro

palace palacio

pale pálido

pants los pantalones

paper el papel

parade el desfile

parents los padres

park el parque

parrot loro

part la parte

party fiesta
past pasado
patient paciente; **be —** tener paciencia
pay pagar
people la gente; pueblo
percent por ciento
perhaps tal vez, acaso, quizá(s); puede ser que
period época; punto
person la persona (*m and f*)
pest majadero
phone teléfono
photograph fotografía, la foto
pick up recoger; pasar por
place el lugar; **take —** tener lugar
plane el avión; **by —** en avión
play el drama, obra; *v* jugar (ue); (*an instrument*) tocar
please por favor; *v* gustar
P.M. de la tarde (noche)
poem el poema, verso
pond el estanque
poor pobre
pork cerdo; **— loin** lomo de cerdo
position puesto
possible posible; **as soon as —** cuanto antes, lo más pronto posible
poster el cartel
poverty pobreza
practice practicar
prefer preferir (ie, i)
prepare preparar
presence presencia
president el presidente; (*of a university*) el rector
pretext pretexto
pretty bonito, hermoso, lindo
prevent impedir (i, i)
prize premio
probably probablemente
problem el problema
professor el profesor, la profesora
proposal propuesta
propose proponer
protest protestar

proud orgulloso; **to be —** estar orgulloso; **to become — (of)** enorgullecerse (de)
provided that con tal que
public público
punishment castigo
purchase compra
purpose propósito
put poner; **— on** ponerse

Q

quantity la cantidad
quarter cuarto
question pregunta; **ask a —** hacer una pregunta
quick ligero, rápido

R

rain lluvia; *v* llover (ue)
raise aumento
read leer
reader el lector, la lectora
reading lectura
ready listo
realize darse cuenta (de)
really? ¿ah, sí? ¿verdad?
reason la razón; **for that —** por eso
rebellion la rebelión
receive recibir
record disco
refreshments refrescos
reject rechazar
remain permanecer, quedar(se)
remember acordarse (ue) (de); recordar (ue)
remind recordar (ue)
repair componer, arreglar
repeat repetir (i, i)
require exigir
resignation renuncia
respectful respetuoso
return regresar, volver (ue); (*something*) devolver (ue)
review repasar
rich rico; **become —** enriquecerse
ridiculous ridículo
right derecho; **be —** tener razón; **right?** ¿verdad?
— away en seguida; **— now**

ahora mismo
ring anillo
river río
road camino
role el papel
room cuarto
root la raíz
row fila
ruins ruinas

S

sad triste
salary sueldo
sale venta
same igual; mismo
Saturday sabado; **on —** el sábado; **on —s** los sábados
say decir (i, i)
scandal escándalo
school escuela
scoundrel malvado, sinvergüenza
second segundo
see ver; mirar
seem parecer
segregate segregar
selfish egoísta (*m and f*)
sell vender
send mandar, enviar
sentence la frase, la oración
September septiembre
serve servir (i, i)
settle arreglar
seven siete
seventh séptimo
several varios
shame vergüenza, lástima, **What a —!** ¡Qué lástima!
share compartir
sharp (*time*) en punto
she ella
shirt camisa
shoe zapato
should deber
shove el empujón
show la función; *v* mostrar (ue); enseñar
shyness la timidez
sick enfermo; **be —** estar malo, estar enfermo; **get —** enfermarse

side lado

signature firma

silly tonto

similar semejante, similar

since desde; puesto que, ya que

sing cantar

sister hermana

sit (down) sentarse (ie)

situation la situación

six seis

sixth sexto

size tamaño

slavery la esclavitud

sleep dormir (ue, u); **go to —** dormirse (ue, u)

sleepy; be — tener sueño

slow lento

slowly despacio

small pequeño

smart inteligente, listo

smile sonrisa; *v* sonreír

so tan; **— many** tantos(-as); **— much** tanto; **— that** para que; de modo (manera) que

soap el jabón

soccer el fútbol

socks los calcetines

soda refresco

soldier soldado

some unos(-as); algunos(-as)

someday algún día

someone alguien

something algo

sometimes a veces, de vez en cuando

somewhat algo

son hijo

song la canción

soon pronto; **as — as possible** lo más pronto posible, cuanto antes

sorry: be — sentir (ie, i)

soul el alma (*f*)

sound sonido; *v* sonar (ue)

soup sopa

Spain España

Spanish el español

speak hablar, charlar, platicar

speech discurso

spend (*time*) pasar; (*money*) gastar

spoil echar a perder

sport el deporte

stadium estadio

stand (up) pararse

start empezar (ie), comenzar (ie)

state estado

stay quedarse

still todavía, aún

stop parar

store tienda

story relato, historia, cuento

strange raro, extraño

street la calle

strong fuerte

student alumno(-a), el (la) estudiante; *adj* estudiantil

study estudiar

subway metro

success éxito

suddenly de pronto

suggestion sugerencia

suit traje; **bathing —** traje de baño

summer verano

sun el sol

Sunday domingo

sure seguro; **Sure!** ¡Claro!

surely seguramente

surprised: be — asombrarse, estar asombrado

surround rodear

swim nadar

T

table mesa

take llevar; tomar; **— along** llevarse; **— a trip** hacer un viaje; **— off** quitarse

talk hablar, platicar

taste gusto; *v* gustar

tasty sabroso

teach enseñar

teacher maestro, maestra, profesor(-a)

team equipo

tell contar (ue); decir (i, i)

temple templo

ten diez

tenth décimo

than que; de

thank agradecer, dar las gracias; **thanks** gracias

that que; *adj* ese, esa; aquel, aquella; *pr* ése, ésa; aquél, aquélla; *neuter pr* eso, aquello

the el, la, los, las

theater teatro

their su, sus

them *d o p* los, las; *i o p* les, se; *obj of prep* ellos, ellas

then entonces; después, luego

there allí, ahí, allá; **— is (are)** hay; **— was (were)** hubo, había

these *adj* estos, estas; *pr* éstos, éstas

they ellos, ellas

thing cosa; **the best —** lo mejor

think pensar; creer; **— about** pensar en; **— of** pensar de

third tercer, tercero

thirsty: be — tener sed

thirty treinta; **. . . thirty** (*hour*) . . . y media

this *adj* este, esta; *pr* éste, ésta; *neuter pr* esto

those *adj* esos, esas; aquellos, aquellas; *pr* ésos, ésas; aquéllos, aquéllas

thought pensamiento

thousand mil

three tres

through por

throw tirar

Thursday jueves

ticket entrada, boleto, el billete

time (*hour*) hora; (*duration*) tiempo; (*sequence*) la vez; **at the same —** a la vez; **at times** a veces; **at what —?** ¿a qué hora? **for the — being** por lo pronto; **have a bad —** pasarlo mal; **have a good —** divertirse (ie, i), pasarlo bien; **have — to** tener tiempo para; **in a short —** en poco

tiempo; **on —** a tiempo
tired cansado; **become —**
  cansarse
to a; para; hacia
today hoy
together juntos
tomb tumba
tomorrow mañana
tonight esta noche
too también; demasiado
toy el juguete
traditional tradicional
traffic tránsito
translate traducir
travel viajar
tree el árbol
tremendous enorme;
  tremendo
trip el viaje
triumph vencer
truck el camión
true cierto, verdad; de verdad;
  be — ser cierto
trust confiar en
try (to) tratar (de), intentar
Tuesday martes
twelve doce
twenty veinte
twisted torcido
two dos

U

uncle tío
under bajo; debajo de
understand comprender,
  entender (ie)
uniform el uniforme
United States los Estados
  Unidos
university la universidad
unless a menos que
until hasta (que)
up: get — levantarse
upon en; al
urban urbano
us *d o p, i o p* nos; *obj of
  prep* nosotros(-as)
use usar
useful útil
useless inútil

V

vacation vacaciones
valuable valioso
verify verificar
very muy; **— much** mucho,
  muchísimo
visit visitar
voice la voz
vote votar

W

wait (for) esperar
wake up despertar(se) (ie)
walk andar, caminar
want querer, desear; **— to**
  tener ganas de
war guerra
wash lavar(se)
waste malgastar
water el agua (*f*)
way manera, modo; camino;
  by the — a propósito;
  that — así; por ahí
we nosotros(-as)
weak débil
wealth riqueza
weapon el arma (*f*)
weather tiempo; **be nice —**
  hacer buen tiempo
wedding boda
Wednesday miércoles
week semana; **last —** la
  semana pasada
weigh pesar
welcome: you're — de nada,
  no hay de qué
well bien; bueno; **as — as**
  tan bien como
what? ¿qué?
when cuando; **when?**
  ¿cuándo?
whenever cuandoquiera
where? ¿dónde? ¿adónde?
  (used with **ir**)
wherever dondequiera
whether si
which que; **which?** ¿qué?
  ¿cuál(-es)?
while mientras
white blanco
who que; quien, quienes;

who? ¿quién? ¿quiénes?
whom quien, quienes
whose cuyo(-a, -os, -as)
why? ¿por qué? **that's —** por
  eso
wife esposa, la mujer
win ganar
wing el ala (*f*)
with con
within dentro de
without sin
withstand resistir
woman la mujer
word palabra; **— of honor**
  palabra de honor
work trabajo, obra; *v*
  trabajar; funcionar
world mundo
worry preocupar(se) (por)
worse peor
Wow! ¡Huy!
wrinkled arrugado
write escribir; **— down**
  anotar, apuntar
writer el escritor, la escritora,
  el autor, la autora
wrong equivocado; **be —**
  estar equivocado, no tener
  razón

Y

year año; **be . . . years old**
  tener... años
yes sí
yesterday ayer
yet todavía
you *subject pr* tú; usted,
  (Ud.); vosotros(-as); ustedes,
  (Uds.); *d o p* te; lo, las;
  os; los, las; *i o p* te; le, se;
  os; les, se; *obj of prep* ti;
  usted; vosotros(-as); ustedes;
  with — contigo, con usted;
  con vosotros(-as); con ustedes
young joven; **— person** el
  (la) joven; **— people** los
  jóvenes
younger menor, más joven
youngster chiquillo(-a)
your tu, tus; su, sus; vuestro
  (-a, -os, -as)

Index

Illustration Credits

Photographs

Illustrations

Illustrations by Bruce Cayard and Vladimir Yevtikhiev.

Illustration p. 493 by Richard Kluger.

Maps by Bill Walker.

A 8
B 9
C 0
D 1
E 2
F 3
G 4
H 5
I 6
J 7